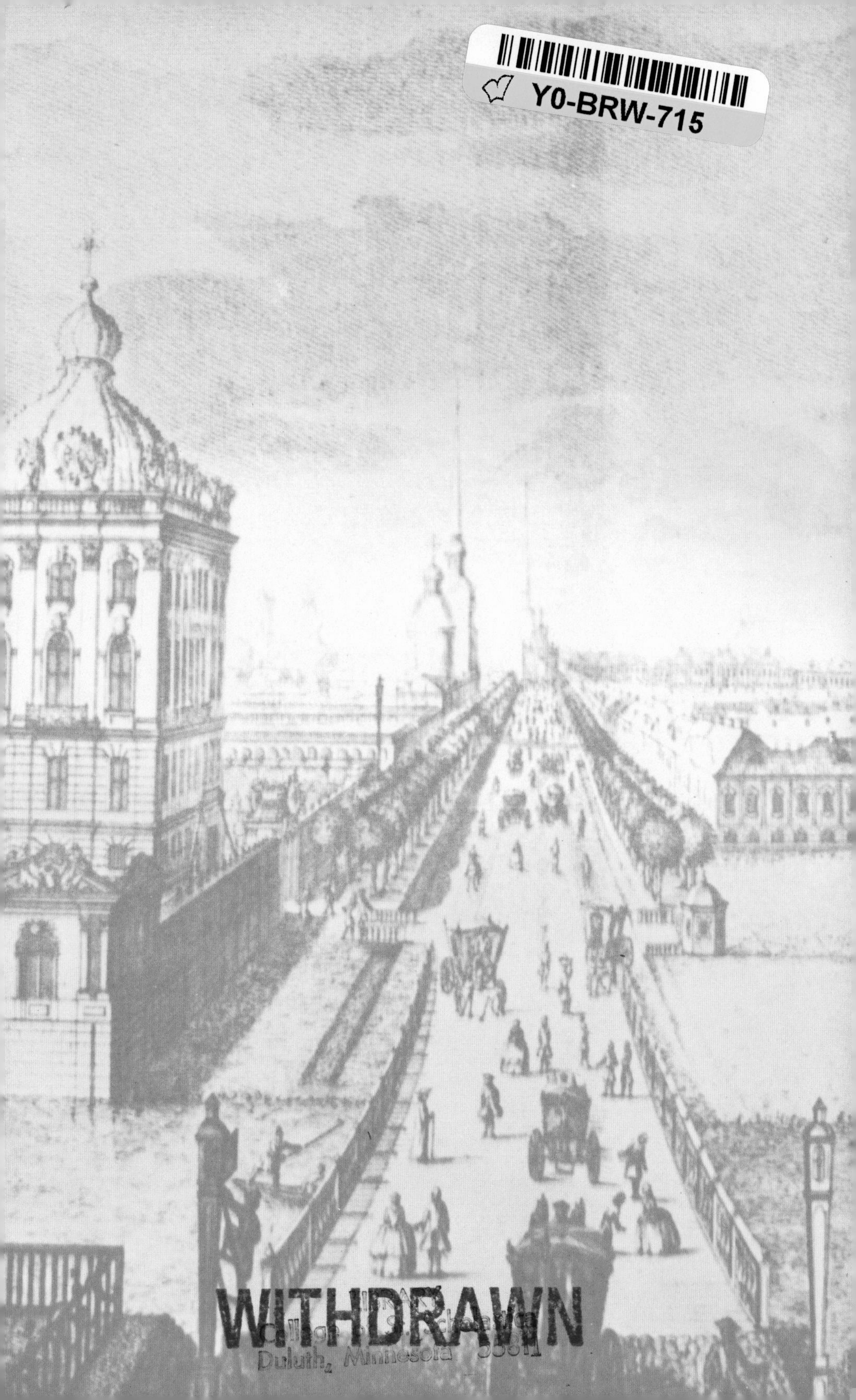

The Nevskiy Prospect was the dominant avenue in St Petersburg by the middle of the eighteenth century. It was laid out between 1712 and 1718 and featured in all subsequent schemes for the architectural embellishment of the capital. This view towards the northwest at mid-century shows the recently completed Anichkov Palace on the left and the spire of the Admiralty in the distance. The vast dimensions of the Prospect, 115 feet at its widest and $2\frac{1}{2}$ miles long when fully developed, are clearly conveyed in this view. From *Plan Stolichnago Goroda Sanktpeterburg* (1753).

STUDIES IN URBAN HISTORY 4

General Editor: H. J. Dyos
Professor of Urban History in the
University of Leicester

Already published in this series:

THE AUTUMN OF CENTRAL PARIS:
The defeat of town planning 1850–1970
by Anthony Sutcliffe

FIT AND PROPER PERSONS:
Ideal and reality in nineteenth-century urban government
by E. P. Hennock

THE PROVINCIAL TOWNS OF GEORGIAN ENGLAND:
A study of the building process 1740–1820
by C. W. Chalklin

St Petersburg

Industrialization and Change

James H. Bater

McGILL-QUEEN'S UNIVERSITY PRESS
MONTREAL
1976

© James H. Bater 1976

First published 1976
by Edward Arnold (Publishers) Ltd.
Published in North America 1976
by McGill-Queen's University Press

ISBN: 0 7735 0266 1
Legal Deposit 2nd Quarter 1976
Bibliothèque nationale du Québec

Text set in 11/12 pt. Monotype Ehrhardt, printed by letterpress, and bound in Great Britain at The Pitman Press, Bath

Foreword

The characteristic setting for modern man is the city and his urban history a necessary dimension in understanding his predicament and potential. Little more than a decade ago that dimension remained obscure and largely unrecognized. Even in Britain, four-fifths of whose population had been officially classified as urban three generations earlier, the study of the urban past attracted little attention. That now appears, looking back, to have been something of a paradox. For if we think, not merely of the agglomeration of numbers, but of the changing attitudes, values, movements, structures and images that this evinced, we become aware of the fact that a whole urban culture had arisen without an historical tradition to explain it. And if we take account of the contemporary urbanisation of the human population as a whole—a global trend which promises to result within another generation in a distribution comparable to that of Britain little more than a century ago, when over half its people had become town-dwellers—the need for an adequate historical framework to elucidate the whole social process becomes adamant. The growth of cities and the phenomenon of an urbanizing world together represent one of the largest historical dimensions of modern times. Urban history constitutes a kind of strategy for encompassing the new knowledge required to represent and explain this experience.

Here is an area of almost limitless possibilities. What those working in it see before them is a field in which they must not only pay attention to particular towns in all their idiosyncratic as well as generic detail—to urban societies fixed more or less in time and space—but must also investigate historical processes and trends that completely transcend the life-cycle and range of experience of any single community when viewed in isolation. The world-wide demographic sweep of urbanization is already overturning our notions of what cities are or might soon

v

come to be. Sociological perceptions of urbanism are forcing us to look deeper for the inherent differences and the necessary connections between urban and agrarian modes of life which our common experience has led us—misled us perhaps—into taking for granted. The political realities of facing urban problems with fewer national characteristics than fundamental human ones are suggesting intercultural comparisons of a type which historians grounded in empirical traditions have generally viewed with alarm. The growth of cities and the rise of industrialized societies have raised searching questions about the extent to which urbanization itself may be regarded as an initiator or a product of economic growth and decline.

The town, which was to historians for so long the unconsidered container of industry and trade and the anonymous masses, is therefore now assuming a new importance in its own right. Historians are addressing it *directly*, partly to understand urban changes better for their own sake but chiefly in order to relate them more coherently to economic, political and cultural developments on an altogether wider plane. Purely 'biographical' studies of individual towns which leave no lasting impression when set in a void offer a basis for making their differences indelible when studied comparatively; investigations of urban life in microscopic detail are being matched by far-reaching research into the fundamental social processes leading towards the urbanization of the whole world. Historians are on common ground here with other disciplines, for towns have always embodied their own history with peculiar tenacity, and this is now causing scholars across a wide front to look at the urban past with growing curiosity. Among them are geographers, economists, sociologists, demographers, archaeologists, civic designers—each of them sharing the problem of interdisciplinary communication. The present mood of urban history is therefore experimental and exploratory. The field is wide open and world-wide, as much concerned with concrete detail where it matters as with imaginative hypotheses wherever they lead, as readily approached by the geographer as by the sociologist or the historian. *Studies in Urban History* is a series designed in this mood.

The present volume exemplifies, quite admirably, the exploratory probing of the urban past now taking place. The author is a geographer whose interest in the spatial implications of that transforming agent of modern times, industrialism, has led him to look not only back in time and outwards from his own academic discipline, but away from the predominantly industrial countries of the West—to one of the trailing rather than the leading edges of the process of modernization. In seizing on St Petersburg, a major growth point in the national economy of Imperial Russia, he has added significantly to our apprehension of its whole economic history. More than that, he has drawn into view the workings of a more pervasive process whereby industrialism extends itself geographically, subsumes new territory, penetrates and adapts the structures of a peasant-based society ill-designed for change.

St Petersburg was from its foundation a vestibule for these intrusions and the sound of whatever took place there has always tended to carry in both directions. It occupied a special place in the moral economy of old Russia; its whole orientation was to the West, and it became a veritable clearing-house for ideas of modernity and social experiment more far-reaching perhaps, even before the Emancipation, than Peter in his wisdom had ever supposed. It is of special value, therefore, to examine this remarkable capital city as searchingly as possible, to recognise it for what it was in addition—the major industrial city, the leading port, the largest concentration of population before the Revolution, the metropolis of a developing economy. Here, in truth, was the central nervous system of the empire but here, too, was the theatre of Russia's future—indeed, of its alternative economic and political futures. If we are to understand how and with what implications industrialism came to old Russia, we must look first at this point of entry. That is what this book enables us to do almost for the first time, for although it has conceivably always been better known and more readily understood in the West than any other Russian city, St Petersburg has remained in many respects a mysterious place, never subject to the kind of analytical scrutiny this book.

Its underlying theme is the interrelation between industrialization and urbanization, a matter more commonly discussed in theoretical than in empirical terms. The main approach here is through location theory, and this imparts the necessary rigour in the study of a place so prone to chance impressions and indelible images. What it issues in is not, however, a purely spatial diagram. On the one hand we can certainly watch the patterns forming, comprehend the logic of the industrial ecology. But if the interpretation of the spatial implications of industrial growth and structural change, thorough as it is, had merely been developed as a formal exercise, what we should have had would have been devoid of any dynamic or even ultimate meaning. Instead we have an altogether more comprehensive picture, not only of the production function of the city in terms of its leading businessmen, its undertakings, and its commercial institutions, but of its demographic and social structure, its greatly varying physical fabric, its municipal functioning and malfunctioning, and something of the value systems and the perceptions of the city that prevailed among its ruling class. The detailed assessment of the impact of industrialism on the deteriorating conditions of life at or near the bottom of the social scale, on the cellared and shiftless condition of the everlasting, swarming peasantry, and on the inexorably rising tide of social problems, including the city's notorious morbidity, is particularly telling. The absence of any very marked flight of those that might have done so to the more controllable environment of the suburbs is equally striking.

Professor Bater has drawn primarily on Russian sources in writing this book but he has kept his eye unfailingly cocked for the measured comparison with the experience of cities in the West. That is of the greatest importance. Such intercultural comparisons will multiply but others drawn against the major cities of Russia before and after the Bolshevik Revolution can now be undertaken. It is not yet easy to see just how far traditional structures persisted into the industrial era nor whether it was in any sense a measure of their failure to accommodate the demands of industrial capitalism that forced it so abruptly to an end. It is as yet difficult to answer with certainty the question whether serfdom itself, or its legacy, constituted a deadweight on the development of urban society in Russia or a kind of release. Certainly this book offers evidence on both sides, but it tends to suggest that whatever the problems imposed in the mass the Russian peasant appears to have been an astonishingly compliant agent within the urban-industrial system, coming and going as its fortunes ebbed and flowed, suffering its privations with almost unbelievable fortitude.

The value of this book lies in its systematic, wide-angled perception of the functional and environmental diversities opened up by each phase of St Petersburg's urban development, and in the whole new perspectives it offers of Russian historical geography as well as economic and urban history. It is above all an invocation to further research. It can but be hoped that we have many more studies of the urbanization of Russia. When they do come the present arduously researched, percipient—dare I say, magisterial?—volume will surely prove to have been their pathfinder.

University of Leicester   H. J. DYOS
January, 1976

Preface

Many volumes have been written about St Petersburg. As an 'artificial' creation, as a planned city, as the centre of administration and, some would argue, of culture as well, and as the largest city in the Russian Empire during the nineteenth century, it is not surprising that it captured the interest of Russians and foreigners alike. Yet for all that has been put on paper, relatively little is known about the industrialization process and the way in which it so very greatly altered the character of the place. What happened in and to St Petersburg during the nineteenth and early twentieth centuries is the basic theme which this book explores. It has been written as a contribution both to our understanding of the development of an important city and, in a smaller way, to Russian urban-historical geography in particular and to urban history in general.

Structure, pattern and process are the common elements in this study and they reflect the perspective of the geographer. Urban history, and urban-historical geography, are still in need of 'a custom of research that would allow a reader to compare the history of one city to the history of any other', and this has not been ignored.[1] Thus, to facilitate comparison, themes common to urban industrialization in general have been singled out for investigation. For this study, cross-sectional analysis has been employed and therefore helps to fill one of the methodological gaps in the literature, that is, the absence of a 'succession of urban environments for any major city'.[2]

The book begins with some questions about the urban industrialization process in St Petersburg. In the second chapter, the city's

---

[1] Sam Bass Warner, Jr, 'If all the World were Philadelphia: a Scaffolding for Urban History—1774–1930', *American Historical Review*, LXXIV (1968), p. 26.
[2] Warner, 'If all the World were Philadelphia'; see also S. G. Checkland, 'The British Industrial City as History: the Glasgow Case', *Urban Studies*, I (1964), pp. 34–7.

history up to mid–nineteenth century is described. The major part of the study is taken up by four cross-sectional chapters. Two cover the urban economy and the city as a place in which to live in the 1860s. These lay the basis for assessing the changes wrought during the years of rapid urban industrialization down to the Great War. A similar set of cross-sections has been created for the city and its economy on the eve of the Great War and it is in these that the analysis of change during the intervening decades is taken up. A final chapter draws out and synthesizes the interrelationships between industrialization and urbanization and puts some of the findings into a broader comparative framework.

This study has evolved from a doctoral dissertation on industrial location in St Petersburg, submitted to the University of London in 1969. In that endeavour I was fortunate indeed in having had the advice and encouragement of Professor W. R. Mead and Dr R. A. French, both of University College, London. What is contained herein represents another stage in my interest in St Petersburg. In attempting to understand something of the city's industrial geography I soon appreciated that the answers often lay outside the rather narrow frame of reference which had been struck. By casting the net much wider in the analysis of the interplay of industrialization and urbanization, I am even more conscious of the need for further exploration of several of the themes. Indeed, some of the conclusions reached should be regarded as tentative. In getting this far I have greatly benefited from the insight and criticism of Professor H. J. Dyos who has read the manuscript probably more times than he cares to think about. Others who have offered much valuable advice on parts or all of the study include Dr Malcolm Falkus of the London School of Economics and Political Science, Dr Olga Crisp of the School of Slavonic and East European Studies, London, Dr Peter Wood of University College, London, and my colleagues at the University of Waterloo, Dr Richard Preston and Dr David Walker. Any errors in fact or interpretation of course remain my responsibility.

The research has been undertaken in a number of libraries. I would like to thank in particular the professional staff of the Slavonic collection at the University of Helsinki library for providing much help during half a dozen sojourns there over the last ten years. I have also benefited from the assistance of staffs of the following institutions: the Library of Congress, Washington; the British Museum, the Victoria and Albert Museum, the School of Slavonic and East European Studies, London;

The National Museum of Finland, Helsinki; and last, but hardly least, the Saltykov-Shchedrin Public Library, Leningrad and the Lenin Library, Moscow. I would like to acknowledge the financial assistance of the Commonwealth Scholarship Committee and the Canada Council during the early years of this project. More recently, the Canada Council and the University of Waterloo Research Grant Committee have helped finance return visits to the Soviet Union, and for their support I am very grateful.

Generous technical support has been provided by the Department of Geography, University of Waterloo and I hereby record my gratitude for all the help I have received. The many figures, maps and plans were drawn and photographed by its staff. For applying design expertise and drawing skills I would like to thank A. Hildebrand, G. Brannon, and N. Adam. D. Wicken did the photographic work not only for the line drawings, but also for many of the plates. During the past three years I have been fortunate in having had the occasional research assistance of the following people: Ms K. Senyshyn, Ms J. Lee, Mr D. Prud'homme and Mr P. Harker; Ms S. Greaves provided some timely help with the index. For typing and retyping the manuscript, I would like to thank Ms S. Cowls and Mrs J. Fraser. The assistance of all these people has helped to make the writing of this book and its preparation for the press less onerous than it might otherwise have been.

Contents

Abbreviations

ISPGOD   Izvestiya S Peterburgskoy Gorodskoy Obshchey Dumy

ISPGD   Izvestiya S Peterburgskoy Gorodskoy Dumy

IMGD   Izvestiya Moskovskoy Gorodskoy Dumy

Och.IL   Ocherki Istorii Leningrada

IRL   Istoriya Rabochikh Leningrada

BPP   British Parliamentary Papers

PRO   Public Record Office, London

Note: The transliteration system used is that suggested by *Soviet Geography: Review and Translation.* Where a different transliteration system has been used by another author, no changes have been made. Unless otherwise indicated, the place of publication of all books cited in the footnotes is St Petersburg/Petrograd/Leningrad.

Illustrations

Plate Acknowledgements

Plates 1, 11, 37, 40, 42, 43, 45 and 46 are reproduced by permission of the National Museum of Finland, Helsinki. The front endpaper and plates 2, 3, 4, 5, 6, 9, 10, 16, 18, 19, 20, 41, 56 and 57 are reproduced by permission of the Trustees of the British Museum, London. Plates 33, 35, 36, 38, 58 and 59 are reproduced by courtesy of the Victoria and Albert Museum, London. Plates 34 and 39 are reproduced by courtesy of the Radio Times Hulton Picture Library, London.

Tables

Note : All tables refer to St Petersburg unless otherwise specified.

Figures

Maps and Plans

To
Linda, Lisa, Steven, Kevin and Ian

I

The City on the Neva

St Petersburg. The name evokes a host of images—'palmyra of the north', canals and rivers 'clad in granite', palaces, the imperial court and sumptuous lifestyles, late-night soirées, the quintessence of Russian urbanity. Intruding perhaps into this kind of scenario are crowds of petty functionaries, soldiers and peasants, scenes of grinding poverty, a senes of despair. St Petersburg embraced all of these images and feelings, and a great deal more besides. As capital of the Russian Empire it fairly hummed with scribbling and paper shuffling; as the principal port the streets were enlivened with the hustle and bustle of commerce. It was also a place of industry; indeed, on the eve of the Great War it ranked as a centre of international, not just national, significance. But of all the images conjured up by the name, that of an industrial centre probably does not figure prominently. Yet, from the mid-nineteenth century on, industrialization and concomitant urbanization colour much of what took place in the city. Labour unrest, political intrigue, massive demonstrations and, ultimately, bloody revolutions were all nurtured by the poverty and despair which were as much a part of industrialization as the factories themselves. In many respects industrialization brought about the metamorphosis of St Petersburg, just as it has of other cities at one time or another. What happened in and to St Petersburg during this tumultuous period is the basic question which this study sets out to answer. The inquiry focuses on industrialization, urbanization, and their interplay—processes and interrelationships as important as they are complex. It is not possible to encompass the whole of the urban industrialization experience in this inquiry; rather, it is the intention to clarify aspects of it. Despite a degree of eclecticism, the themes investigated are common to urban industrialization elsewhere and hence this book offers some grist for the mill of comparative study.

I PLACE AND POSITION

St Petersburg's history is replete with paradoxes. The city arose from the marshy delta of the Neva River in the early 1700s as a direct consequence of Peter I's determination to modernize an Empire that stood very much outside the mainstream of European economic, political, social and intellectual developments. It was to be a planned city, one embodying all that was new in architecture and design. Despite what it stood for in this regard, its very construction was wholly dependent upon the labour of tens of thousands of peasants, dragooned to a remote and inhospitable site at the behest of an absolute autocrat. While the existence of serfdom made the building of the city possible under the most adverse conditions, it was scarcely consonant with the prevailing modes of social organization in those European countries whose technological and military modernity Peter I wished to emulate.[1] St Petersburg acquired many of the trappings of European town planning, but the fabric of civic society was fashioned according to the precepts of serfdom long after its formal abolition in 1861. Although this had many implications, perhaps chief among them was the transient nature of residence in the city for one of its principal groups, the peasantry. As they comprised a larger and larger share of the total population over time, those who had any real attachment to St Petersburg came to be a proportionally smaller part of the whole. A city intended to be a permanent symbol of Russian affinity with Europe was itself anything but permanent in its constituency. As one mid-nineteenth-century commentator accurately observed, it was a place of 'rendezvous'.[2] Thus, a corporate identity was slow to emerge and, with it, an abiding concern for the quality of life of the mass of its inhabitants. When emancipation, industrialization and urbanization brought unprecedented pressures to bear on physical and administrative structures alike, the urban system as a whole reeled in the face of them. What had been initiated as a modern, planned city was by the early

[1] For background on Peter I, see V. Klyuchevsky, *Peter the Great* (London, 1971), translated by L. Archibald.

[2] J. G. Kohl, *Russia* (London, 1842), p. 52. It has been suggested that the absence of common identity among the working classes of nineteenth-century American cities stemmed from a high degree of transience. However, it is probable that in both American and European cities those with vested interests and a sense of corporate identity comprised larger proportions of the populations than was the case in St Petersburg. Stephan Thernstrom, 'Urbanization, Migration, and Social Mobility in Late Nineteenth-Century America', in B. J. Bernstein (ed.), *Towards a New Past: Dissenting Essays in American History* (New York, 1968), pp. 158-75.

1900s decried by Russians and foreigners alike as backward, unplanned and insalubrious.

Had St Petersburg's population been small, the implications of its deserved reputation as the least healthy capital in Europe would have been less serious. However, with almost 300,000 inhabitants in 1800 it already ranked as a large city by European standards.[3] By 1914 its

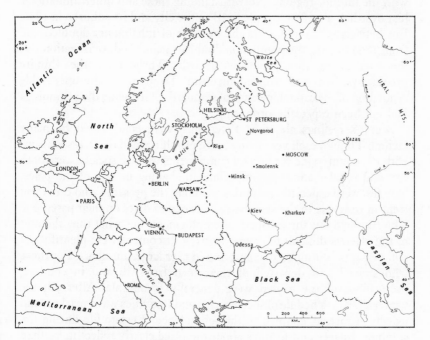

MAP 1. *St Petersburg in the European setting*

population stood at more than two million, a number eclipsed in Europe only by London, Paris, Vienna and Berlin. Within the Russian Empire scarcely 15 per cent of the 160 million people lived in towns. Among them Moscow, Riga, Kiev and Odessa were of considerable size, but only Moscow with just under two million rivalled St Petersburg ⟨*see* map 1⟩.[4] There had been many restraints on urbanization, the most notable of which was the need for peasants to have official permission

[3] G. L. von Attengofer, *Mediko-Topograficheskoye Opisaniye Sanktpeterburga, Glavnago i Stolichnago Goroda Rossiiskoy Imperii* (1820), p. 107.
[4] A. G. Rashin, *Naseleniye Rossii za 100 Let, 1811–1913* (Moscow, 1956), p. 93.

3

to leave the commune. Still, throughout most of the nineteenth century St Petersburg retained pride of place among Russian cities, despite some clear disadvantages. Perched on the edge of the Empire it was remote both from the Russian perspective and the European, its immediate hinterland was desolate and little populated, and it was not until after the middle of the century that it began to be linked by rail with the interior regions. Notwithstanding these and other limitations, just over half a million people lived in the city and its suburbs in 1850. But between 1850 and 1890 the number of inhabitants doubled and from 1890 to 1914 the population doubled again.[5] Industrialization was the catalyst in this phrenetic growth. Throughout the Empire urbanization was gathering momentum. To judge by the unenviable reputation of the capital in terms of standards of hygiene, the beginnings had not been especially promising.

People's feelings about St Petersburg were conditioned by many factors. Though each year many more people resided there, associations with the countryside for several components of civic society were both real and regular and were important in shaping images of the place. The ties were especially plain to see among the peasants who came and went in response to the seasons and the expiry dates on their passports. The city held out the prospect of employment, but what they thought of the place is difficult to gauge; signs of discontent were plentiful yet still peasants continued to come, and in ever larger numbers. For those who arrived and departed of their own free will and in comfort, impressions of the capital were generally favourable. After all, the winter's heavy schedule of social events and festivities was a marked, and usually attractive, contrast to the somnolence of estate life during the summer. Images and feelings about the place clearly reflect more than was ever articulated by members of the upper classes. Like most large industrial centres, the city generated its fair share of criticism as well as commendation simply because it was a large urban-industrial agglomeration. In Russia its image was also coloured by broader philosophical issues. For many people St Petersburg embodied Europe in Russia, much as Peter I had intended, but it was not a welcome intrusion. Its peripheral location symbolized the degree to which it was removed from what was truly Russian.

Moscow, on the other hand, located as it was in central European Russia, was a city whose history was bound up with the fortunes of the Slavs, a city which in real and imagined ways was set apart from

[5] See pp. 67–9, 161–3, 309–11 for sources.

4

St Petersburg. The rectilinearity of the latter's street pattern contrasted sharply with the seeming hotchpotch inherited by Moscow. To the extent that the one's architecture was European, the other's was Russian. St Petersburg served as Russia's administrative heart, Moscow its soul. Indeed, the skyline cluttered with churches, and the constant ringing of bells together registered graphic first impressions of the city in colourful contrast with those of the capital. Moscow was Russian in other ways as well, including the extent to which Russian as a language was used by its inhabitants; in business and in society Russian predominated. But among the social elite in St Petersburg, Russian was seldom in vogue and sophistication was equated with European manners and language, especially French. In the world of business, knowledge of Russian alone was a severe handicap. Foreigners themselves were very much a part of the St Petersburg scene, and during industrialization their influence became all the more pervasive— a development which could be regarded as beneficial or pernicious depending on the viewpoint. All told, in the eyes of the ardent Slavophile there was scarcely anything Russian about the capital, and hence little to redeem it. That St Petersburg and Moscow were both popularly referred to as 'capital' was not unrelated to such feelings and perceptions. By the same token, so-called Westernizers took comfort in St Petersburg's European attributes, however superficial, for they represented a break with the past and thereby held out some hope for transforming a backward, rural country into a modern state.[6]

Images of the capital were created and perpetuated in many ways, including literary ones. The poet Pushkin is renowned for his celebration of the city in poems such as the *Bronze Horseman*. Written in the 1830s, it uses the disastrous flood of 1824 as the central drama for fetching out the feelings of those enthralled with its man-made magnificence:

> A city new, in pomp unmatched,
> Of Northern lands the pride and gem . . .
> I love thee, work of Peter's hand!
> I love thy stern symmetric form;
> The Neva's calm and queenly flow,
> Betwixt her quays of granite stone,
> With iron tracings richly wrought.[7]

---

[6] For elaboration on this general theme, see V. Shelest, *Ideologichna-Borot'ba Mizh Moskvoyu ta Peterburgom—Leningradom i Jiji Vidobrazhennya u Literaturi* (Munich, 1974).

[7] From a translation in G. Dobson, *St Petersburg* (London, 1910), pp. 90, 91.

Such eulogy had not been without precedent, though rarely was it expressed so eloquently. A decade later the short-lived Russian literary genre of physiological introspection added a new dimension to the image of the place. Everyday street life, the poorer parts of town, dingy rooms with squashed cockroaches spattering the walls and drunken, dishevelled lodgers—all became legitimate, albeit somewhat repugnant, subject-matter. In short, the commonplace, not the spectacular, facets of St Petersburg were singled out for commentary.[8] The image of grandeur was clearly being challenged. By the late forties when the rising novelist Dostoevsky began using St Petersburg as a setting, there was each year more and more scope for casting the urban environment in a negative light.[9] Perhaps the best known depiction of the squalor and depravity among the city's poor comes in *Crime and Punishment*. At the time of its publication in 1866, industrialization and its attendant ills had plainly arrived.[10] Dostoevskiy's description of an urban environment was not out of tune with the substance of reports issued by beleaguered sanitary doctors who were charged with the responsibility of keeping the lid on disease and death. Similarly the apprehension over the future which runs throughout A. Biely's *St Petersburg* (1913) was not purely a figment of the imagination.[11] The populace had had a taste of revolution during the abortive uprising of 1905; the reforms which had been introduced whetted appetites for further change; privation was widespread, discontent rife, fears real. Literature could and did mirror reality. It could also propagate images distorted by suspicion. The many foreigners who viewed St Petersburg while in the clutches of Russophobia and later preserved their impressions in print testify to this possibility.[12] Clearly, images were often coloured as much by perceived qualities or deficiencies, personal philosophies and so on as they were by the realities themselves.

2 THE SCOPE OF THE INQUIRY

Despite the possibility of distortion of one kind or another, recorded impressions and images are important in heightening the appreciation

[8] See, for instance, N. Nekrasov (ed.), *Fiziologiya Peterburga* (1845).
[9] For an examination of this theme, see D. Fanger, *Dostoevsky and Romantic Realism: a Study of Dostoevsky in Relation to Balzac, Dickens and Gogol* (Toronto, 1967).
[10] This point will be elaborated in a later chapter, see pp. 201–12.
[11] This was by no means an unusual theme, but we have simply singled out one piece of literature by a noted proponent of the Russian symbolist movement in which it plays a central role.
[12] See Laurence Oliphant, *The Russian Shores of the Black Sea* (2nd edn, Edinburgh, 1853) for some vivid prejudice.

of what St Petersburg was like at various times and they are used here with this purpose in mind. The central concern of the study, however, is not the image of the place and its perceived role, but the reality of urban industrialization. In furthering an understanding of this process, the emphasis is on the discoverable facts, their assessment and analysis, an emphasis which none the less introduces the possibility of yet other kinds of distortion. Before elaborating which aspects of the process we are selecting for examination, and why, it is necessary to set up a general frame of reference for time and place.

While steam power was introduced into St Petersburg in the 1790s, it was not until some time later that there was a widespread shift from hand manufacture to machine production.[13] Inasmuch as concern here is with the ramifications of this change, the late 1860s have been selected as the point in time at which these will first be examined. By then there is no disputing that industrialization was under way.[14] If some of the relationships and repercussions of industrialization and urbanization at this time are established, this provides a benchmark for assessing the tempo and lineaments of change during the years down to 1914. Comparison and analysis of the structure and spatial pattern of the same components of the urban system on the eve of the Great War allow opportunities for insight into the nature of the processes we are dealing with. The times chosen for cross-sectional analysis are propitious for the following reasons. For 1867 and 1913 comprehensive factory statistics are available and these years correspond reasonably well with those for which census materials, city directories and large-scale maps and street plans can be obtained. The late sixties and the half dozen years leading up to the Great War are comparable in that both periods are characterized by economic expansion. When the analysis of industrialization is to rest heavily on employment data, it is clearly essential that the economic climate be broadly similar rather than markedly different. All told, the periods selected constitute as happy a marriage between available sources and comparable years as is feasible. The choice of the War as the point of termination is defensible on many grounds. In the first place, the whole character of industrialization changed, for obvious reasons, and so too did the urban milieu. Russia had been involved in other military conflicts, but none wreaked

---

[13] S. G. Strumilin, *Ocherki Ekonomicheskoy Istorii Rossii i SSSR* (Moscow, 1966), pp. 390–410; V. V. Pokshishevskiy, 'Territorial'noye Formirovaniye Promyshlennogo Kompleksa Peterburga v XVIII–XIX Vekakh', *Voprosy Geografii*, no. 20 (1950), p. 128.
[14] Detailed discussion will be found in chapter 3, pp. 86–91.

the havoc of the Great War; it ended one era and set the stage for the beginning of another. Even the name St Petersburg disappeared after August 1914, having been Russianized to Petrograd in deference to anti-German sentiment; thus it remained until 1924 when, to commemorate the death of V. I. Lenin, the city was renamed Leningrad. While the first century and a half of the city's development rightfully demands some attention, the period of detailed study is that from the 1860s to 1914, a period during which industrialization was the keynote.

What is being referred to when we speak of St Petersburg—the area bounded by the official city border or a larger area which includes functionally related suburbs? The answer requires some qualification. In establishing an areal framework for the study of industrialization, the principal consideration is the inclusion of all factories in the immediate vicinity. Clearly, some establishments would be omitted regardless of where the line is drawn, but the problem in this case is minimal owing to the complete dominance of the capital within its region. The area finally delimited (roughly 11 by 13 kilometres) covers the city proper and the outlying districts or suburbs ⟨*see* end map 70⟩. For 1867, exclusion of important industrial operations was minimal. Most of those omitted were state-owned factories some distance away and they accounted for a small share of the factory work-force.[15] The locational attraction of the capital is underscored by the fact that in 1913 almost 90 per cent of the 218,000 factory workers in the St Petersburg *guberniya* or province were employed by the factories included in the study area. In total, only a handful of plants of any significance are omitted, for the most part the same outlying state-owned plants as in 1867.[16] Discussion of structural shifts in the city's industry and analysis of industrial distributions and change pertain to this particular spatial framework unless otherwise specified. In examining the various attributes of the city and its population during the course of industrialization we are very much dependent upon censuses. The first comprehensive and reliable one, taken in 1869, was restricted to the city proper, the surrounding districts not being brought under the enumerators' purview until 1881.[17] The city itself was very much overbounded and, combined with real restraints on suburbanization, this meant that most of the phenomenal population growth between 1869 and 1910 (the date of the last census) occurred within the official

[15] See chapter 3, pp. 91–2.
[16] See chapter 5, pp. 221–2.
[17] For an assessment of this and other principal sources, see A Note on Sources, pp. 434–50.

borders.[18] The boroughs and wards making up the city area therefore serve as a reasonable basis for assessing what happened to the city during this period ⟨*see* end maps 68 and 69⟩.

Industrialization and urbanization are distinct processes, though as long ago as 1899 Adna Weber demonstrated that they frequently go hand in hand.[19] But what is meant by the terms? In this study both have been used very broadly. Industrialization certainly entails a change in production technology, the rise of the factory system, increased specialization in production and the like. To view the process solely in terms of the growth of factories and factory workers, however, is myopic and misleading. Industrialization demanded regularity of habit among the work-force; it changed the conditions of employment from the close personal relationships, good or bad, in the workshop to the impersonal, bureaucratic ones on the factory floor, thereby creating a void between owner and employee; it required new financial structures; it brought new pressures to the urban land market; it required more transport facilities, if not new modes; it destroyed some handicraft activities and spawned others—in short, the process transformed in both subtle and obvious ways the whole of the urban economy.[20] This study will certainly deal with the scale, structural and spatial components of the workshop-factory continuum, but it must be emphasized that a preoccupation with factory production alone misses both the point and the spirit of industrialization. The process was very much a catalyst and for this reason the focus of attention has been widened to include aspects of the city's commercial, transport and external relations systems. Simply put, our interest is in industrialization as both an example and an agent of modernization.

Urbanization, it will be recognized, implies more than just population growth, particularly when linked with industrialization. Changes in social organization, institutions, behaviour patterns and physical structure are only a few of the possible repercussions.[21] As in the case of

[18] Detailed discussion comes in a later chapter but a comparison of maps 61 and 70 brings out the point.

[19] Adna F. Weber, *The Growth of Cities in the Nineteenth Century* (New York, 1899).

[20] See, for instance, R. E. Turner, 'The Industrial City: Center of Cultural Change', in C. F. Ware (ed.), *The Cultural Approach to History* (New York, 1940), pp. 228–42; S. G. Checkland, 'The British Industrial City as History: the Glasgow Case', *Urban Studies*, I (1964), pp. 34–54; N. J. Smelser, *Social Change in the Industrial Revolution* (Chicago, 1959); Peter G. Goheen, 'Industrialization and the Growth of Cities in Nineteenth Century America', *American Studies*, XIV (1973), pp. 61–2.

[21] For a recent general overview of these and other themes, see Peter G. Goheen, 'Interpreting the American City: some Historical Perspectives', *Geographical Review*, LXIV (July 1974), pp. 362–84.

industrialization, the net has been cast fairly wide in the examination of the urban growth process. We are concerned in the first place with establishing what physical changes occurred in the city. Thus, discussions of the physical fabric, housing stock, municipal services and so on serve to delineate some of the basic characteristics of the habitat at the beginning and near the end of the period. Elaboration of demographic, social class and governmental themes provides a frame of reference for the pulse and pattern of human life within this habitat. In these discussions the underlying objective is to determine what life was like for the masses at the bottom, rather than for the few at the top, of the social-class hierarchy. Though an obvious bias, it is none the less felt to be quite in keeping with the nature of the urban industrialization experience and appropriate to the mood of the times.[22] To round out this side of the discussion, the themes of disease, death and morality are brought into play. A broadening of the terms of reference for the processes under study almost inevitably dictates dealing with aggregates rather than individuals and there is the clear danger of becoming too diffuse. However, if something which approaches the total significance and impact of these processes is thereby conveyed, the risk is worth taking. Whether or not this result is achieved depends very much on the nature of the questions asked and the answers provided.

Three basic questions are raised with regard to industry itself: what changes took place in its structure and growth rates and why; how were these changes reflected spatially; and how might the spatial ramifications be explained? Central to this line of inquiry is the attempt to establish the degree to which the evolving patterns of industrial activity conform to some basic tenets of location theory. For instance, the need for external economies, the impact of rent and land cost, access to transport facilities, labour supply and simple inertia as expressed by distributional stability, have often been cited as reasonable explanations of contemporary location patterns.[23] This may be quite correct, but the influence of these and a host of other factors in an historic and dynamic context is less well known. There is a recognized

[22] For an overview of the period, see Richard Charques, *The Twilight of Imperial Russia* (London, 1965). For something of its flavour, see Peter Kropotkin, *Memoirs of a Revolutionist* (New York, 1962), edited by James A. Rogers.
[23] See, for example, M. J. Wise, 'On the Evolution of the Jewellery and Gun Quarters in Birmingham', *Institute of British Geographers: Transactions and Papers*, 15 (1949), pp. 59–72; P. G. Hall, *The Industries of London since 1861* (London, 1962); Allan R. Pred, *The Spatial Dynamics of US Urban-Industrial Growth, 1800–1914: Interpretive and Theoretical Essays* (Cambridge, Mass., 1966), pp. 196–216.

necessity to evaluate general propositions within the context of the history of the individual city in 'all its uniqueness', but clearly it is not just the significance of industrial location factors which is begged for want of empirical testing.[24]

The analysis of the spatial attributes of industrialization concentrates on the following: the degree of agglomeration or clustering, industrial linkage, stability and rent, transport access, labour supply and zoning. For the most part it will not be feasible to deal exhaustively with individual industries and certainly not individual factories. The locational trends as uncovered through hypothesis testing and how individual industries fit into the overall locational scene are points of interest. The industrial classification used comprises six main groups: metal-working; textiles; food and tobacco; tanning, tallow and wax; chemicals; and paper and printing. Several other industries have been lumped under the general rubric, miscellaneous. In each case there was potential linkage with one or more industries in the six groups.[25] The building, construction and wood-working sphere has been excluded owing to problems created by the pronounced seasonality of the activities.[26] Running through the analysis is the notion that locational decision-making is affected by the scale of operation. Thus, a fivefold factory-size classification based on employment, the most generally available and consistent piece of information about industrial operations, has been created and is used throughout.[27] Two further ideas are bound up with the use of a factory-size class system. In the first place, it is contended that the tendency to minimize 'distance friction' within the city would be greatest for small-scale firms because economies derived from being near to establishments involved in related processes would be of greater importance than in large plants where economies of scale could be substituted. Secondly, increased specialization among the smaller-scale operations in cognate industries is usual during industrialization and over time this might well be expressed spatially through a greater degree of agglomeration or clustering. Both theory and empirical evidence support such a conjecture.[28] The cross-sectional

[24] Oscar Handlin, 'The Modern City as a Field of Historical Study', in Oscar Handlin, John Burchard (eds), *The Historian and the City* (Cambridge, Mass., 1963), p. 26. For related comments, see H. J. Dyos, 'Agenda for Urban Historians', in H. J. Dyos (ed.), *The Study of Urban History* (London, 1968), pp. 14–15.
[25] See A Note on Methods, pp. 425–6.
[26] 'Ischisleniye Naseleniya S. Peterburga 15 Iyulya i 15 Dekabrya 1889 Goda', *Statisticheskiy Yezhegodnik S. Peterburga*, no. 9 (1889), pp. 18–20 gives some idea of the dimension of the problem.
[27] For derivation and discussion, see A Note on Methods, pp. 427–8.

testing of locational hypotheses is intended to provide a basis for drawing some inferences about the industrial location process. To round out the analysis by industrial group, detailed examinations of selected industrial groups as well as of handicraft activities are included. While a fuller statement of specific hypotheses and discussion of analytical methods are deferred to later chapters, it should be noted at this juncture that we are as much interested in the reasons for observed deviations from the conjectured spatial order as in demonstrating its relevance to the St Petersburg situation.

Industrialization changed the face of the city. The precise manner in which this occurred depended upon the spatial mobility of people and things, in other words, upon the technology of transport. Modernization of the transport system is generally acknowledged to be as much a corollary of industrialization as growth in population.[29] Hence, implicit in many of the theoretical propositions and axioms that we will evaluate is the notion that spatial mobility increased. In other cases, the assumption will be explicit in formulating exploratory hypotheses of economic and social change. Inasmuch as the capital was the functional as well as symbolic focal point in the Russian urban-economic system, it is logical to assume that it would lead the way in the adoption of innovations in transport technology. Notwithstanding the propriety of such assumptions, the pervasive significance of what happened in urban transport demands that such assumptions do not supplant the necessary documentation.

The first questions to be asked are simply, what was the structure of the transport system and in what ways did it alter during the years down to the Great War? Having initiated this line of inquiry, a number of other questions come to mind whose answers, in whole or in part, are related to the issue of spatial mobility. An obvious question concerns the journey to work. It has been demonstrated that the inauguration of horse-tram services in North American and European cities after the

[28] See, for instance, P. Sargant Florence, *Investment, Location and Size of Plant* (Cambridge, 1948); S. G. Checkland, *The Rise of Industrial Society in England 1815–1885* (London, 1964); Walter Isard, *Location and Space-Economy* (Cambridge, Mass., 1956); Pred, *Spatial Dynamics*; Hall, *Industries of London*; L. Moses and H. Williamson, 'The Location of Economic Activities in Cities', *American Economic Review*, LVII (1967), pp. 211–22.
[29] G. M. Young, *Victorian England: Portrait of an Age* (2nd edn., New York, 1964); G. A. Nokes, *Locomotion in Victorian London* (London, 1938); G. R. Taylor, 'The Beginnings of Mass Transportation in Urban America, Part I', *Smithsonian Journal of History*, I (summer 1966), pp. 40–48; and 'Part II' (autumn 1966), pp. 35–49; J. R. Kellett, *The Impact of Railways on Victorian Cities* (London, 1969) among the considerable literature on this theme, offer some relevant commentary.

middle of the nineteenth century, together with subsequent technological improvements, particularly electric traction in the 1890s, and their rapid, widespread adoption, certainly improved the mobility of sizable numbers of urban dwellers. Increased mobility as reflected in the lengthening of journeys to work was in turn an important factor in the transformation of the urban fabric.[30] For instance, the extension of electric or steam-railway service beyond the confines of the densely settled city centre made suburbanization a possibility which, where realized, ushered in profound changes to the socioeconomic complexion of the city to say nothing of its morphology.[31] We are thus compelled to ask, what was the nature of the journey to work in St Petersburg? Did it differ according to occupation or socioeconomic status? Did technological innovations bring about changes? If so, how were they manifested? If not, what were the repercussions? To the extent that the movement of goods was facilitated and cheapened, locational decision-making on the part of entrepreneurs was less constrained. If at the same time there was a demonstrable increase in the mobility of the work-force, did this lead to decentralization of industry from the congested inner city? Were trade-offs possible, and if so, how did these affect the pattern of industrial location and in turn the socioeconomic fabric of the city?

The issue of spatial mobility permeates the whole industrial location process, but it affects other components of the urban economy just as much. In retailing, for instance, it might be expected that innovations in transport technology would alter the journey to shop. Presuming the length and propensity increased, we could hypothesize that the mix of retailing activities along the major thoroughfares of the central city would show signs of increased specialization over time. In other words, this would have the effect of intensifying the competition among land-uses so that higher order functions bidding up and absorbing rents displaced lower order retailers unable to pay them. Though the discussion of the commercial sector of the urban economy is primarily concerned with structural attributes, this relationship between movement and pattern merits investigation.

Spatial mobility or the idea of movement constitutes a unifying

---

[30] David Ward, *Cities and Immigrants* (New York, 1971), pp. 105–43; James E. Vance, 'Housing the Worker: the Employment Linkage as a Force in Urban Structure', *Economic Geography*, XLII (October 1966), pp. 294–325.

[31] For instance, Sam B. Warner, Jr, *Streetcar Suburbs: the Process of Growth in Boston, 1870–1900* (Cambridge, Mass., 1962); H. J. Dyos, *Victorian Suburb: a Study of the Growth of Camberwell* (Leicester, 1961).

strand of argument at the intra-urban level and by definition also comes into play when the city's system of external relations is considered. Urban industrialization presumes a widening of linkage systems and changes in the intensity of the flows, following from the garnering of competitive advantage and from improvements in, and articulation of, the transport system at the regional, national and international scales.[32] At best, it is a thorny problem to determine why one city and not others should undergo industrialization. Irrespective of whether the impetus comes from a mercantilist system, which encouraged the accumulation of capital and its investment in means of production instead of leading to conspicuous consumption, or whether it derives from some inherent locational advantage, or simply develops through some chance invention and its application in a propitious economic environment, growth is self-generating and cumulative once it has got under way.[33] What we need to ask of the St Petersburg experience is whether or not urban industrialization had some predictable impact on external relations, that is, whether the linkages were extended, intensified and changed in composition. The composition and pattern of port, railroad and river commodity flows will be examined in this context. We would certainly be justified in postulating that the largest single market could not fail to alter the surrounding rural economy radically, and its agricultural component perhaps most perceptibly. Taking a cue from J. von Thünen's agricultural land-use theory, we can see that during this period the upward pressure on land values within the urban shadow should have generated agricultural activities which were more intensive and more oriented to the city market.[34] One of the most significant external relations is that of rural-urban migration. The question is, to what extent were the patterns and dimensions of migration altered during urban industrialization and why? Knowledge of what was taking place here is an essential prerequisite for the full comprehension of what was happening within the city.

That industrialization produces urban metamorphosis is a general statement with a certain ring of truth. The question is, how did such a

[32] Allan R. Pred, *The External Relations of Cities During 'Industrial Revolution'* (Chicago, 1962).
[33] E. Smolensky and D. Ratajczak, 'The Conception of Cities', *Explorations in Entrepreneurial History*, 2 (1965), pp. 90–131; Pred, *External Relations*; L. Marshall, 'The Emergence of the First Industrial City: Manchester, 1780–1850', in *The Cultural Approach to History*, pp. 140–61.
[34] J. H. von Thünen, *Isolated State* (Oxford, 1966), translated by C. M. Wartenberg.

metamorphosis take place in St Petersburg, and with what consequences? We have noted that recorded perceptions and images help to sharpen the historian's awareness of what the place was like at different times, but we cannot rely on these as our only guides. From other sources we need to ascertain the dimensional and qualitative changes in the built environment. Did urban industrialization prompt intensive or extensive land-use? What was the role of speculative building? Was the stock of buildings qualitatively improved or not? What was the nature of the housing supply? Did it keep abreast of in-migration? If not, how serious was overcrowding and where did it occur? What contribution did municipal services make to the quality of life during these years? These and other queries come to mind with regard to the possible changes in the physical habitat and they provide another theme which will be pursued.

Urban industrialization is usually assumed to bring about a reordering of people and their economic activities. The change is often viewed in the context of the affluent leaving the central city, following the intrusion of commerce and industry, for suburban residential areas. With the advent of fast, cheap public transport the middle classes also depart for the suburbs, leaving the poor to fill, at higher densities, the pockets of housing left intact and to continue their occupation of what had been peripheral slums. Such a sequence is based on notions of the socioeconomic fabric of the city in a preindustrial state and on the course of events in a number of European and North American cities during industrialization.[35] Clearly, it incorporates a large number of assumptions; but the principal one concerns spatial mobility which, as we observed earlier in respect of technological innovations in transport, cannot stand unchallenged. Once we know something about the parameters of spatial mobility, we can begin to put together a picture of the city's social-class fabric. To do this we will need to investigate the rigidity of the class system, or conversely, the extent to which upward mobility through the social-class hierarchy was possible. There is no doubt that by taking a class, ethnic or religious basis for where people lived, we will gain some insight into the reality of the social-class system and the extent to which industrialization introduced some general changes. The questions

---

[35] For instance, Ward, *Cities and Immigrants*, pp. 5, 125–47. For a recent critique of one basic notion, see Peter Burke, 'Some Reflections on the Pre-Industrial City', *Urban History Yearbook 1975* (Leicester, 1975), pp. 6–12.

raised in this context therefore concentrate on the issues of spatial and social mobility.

The demographic, pathological and political environments provide the nexus for the remaining questions to be considered in relation to the urban industrialization of St Petersburg. Cataclysmic events occurred in the city and, without becoming deterministic, we need to ascertain if conditions there were in any sense contributory to the mood and movement which ultimately engulfed society. If they were, then it is necessary to know if the municipal government was willing or able to take up the challenge. The mandate of government was to meet the needs of civic society. But what were the needs? Demographic characteristics, such as population density, give some indication of the quality of life; statistics on disease and death rather coldly insinuate what life was like; others pertaining to public morality add to the picture. The questions asked will not be oriented to the testing of hypotheses and the manipulation of data, as is the case in the analysis of the urban economy, but are intended to extract from statistical and other materials a real and more subtly coloured picture of urban life.

The methodology encompassing these questions is straightforward. An overview of the city's history up to mid-nineteenth century sets the stage for the analysis of industrialization and urbanization. For the 1860s cross-sections or snapshots of the urban economy and of the city as a place in which to live provide benchmarks for assessing the changes wrought during the years down to 1914. A similar set of cross-sections is recreated for the city and its economy on the eve of the Great War. Structure, pattern and process are the common foci in the analysis of intervening changes. In the final chapter the interrelationships between industrialization and urbanization will be drawn out, synthesized and, as far as possible, put into a broader comparative framework.

In asking questions about industrialization and change in St Petersburg one can all too easily give free rein to the imagination. But just as there is sometimes a chasm between image and reality, so there is between what one would like to know and what it is possible to find out from available sources. Having now set the tenor of the inquiry, there remains the search for some answers.

2

The Stamp of Autocracy

His Czarish Majesty . . . having observed that about a German Mile further down, the River *Neva* (Nie) forms several Islands, the conveniency of that situation inspired him with thoughts of building a Town there, in order to get a footing in the Baltick.

Friedrich Christian Weber, 1722[1]

But his lords . . . though they seemingly complement the Czar whenever he talks to them of the beauties and delights of Petersburgh . . . when they get together by themselves, they complain and say that there are tears and water enough at Petersburgh, and they pray God to send them to live again at Mosco.

John Perry, 1716[2]

A less auspicious place for a large number of people to live is difficult to imagine: the delta of the Neva River offered little solid ground; the environs were desolate, the climate dreary; the high latitude was unsettling to those not used to the prolonged darkness of the winter months and the extended daylight of the short summer; and, if that were not enough, whatever man might labour months to build could succumb in a matter of hours to tempestuous autumn flood waters.[3]

---

[1] Friedrich Christian Weber, *The Present State of Russia* (London, 1723), vol. I, p. 298. Republished as number 2 in the series, *Russia through European Eyes*, edited by A. G. Cross (London, 1968).

[2] John Perry, *The State of Russia under the Present Czar* (London, 1716), pp. 261-3. Cited in Peter Putman (ed.), *Seven Britons in Imperial Russia* (Princeton, 1952), p. 62

[3] See K. N. Serbina, 'Istoriko-Geograficheskiy Ocherk Rayona Peterburga do Osnovaniya Goroda', *Och.IL* (1955), vol. I, p. 12 for a general discussion. Details of the flood hazard may be obtained from, *Podrobnoye Istoricheskoye Izvestiye o Vsekh Navodneniyakh Byvshikh v Sanktpeterburge* (1826).

But a city did emerge and endure, and it is the purpose here to say something about the first century and a half of its history. How the city was built, by what means the population sustained itself, how indeed the inhabitants lived from day to day—all these are important questions. In providing some answers the objective will be to present a series of panoramas, painted in fairly broad strokes, against which may be set urban-industrial developments after the middle of the nineteenth century. Our first task is to review some aspects of the physical development of St Petersburg.

I IMPERIAL MUNIFICENCE AND THE GRAND DESIGN

To reckon the costs, human or monetary, involved in the initial stages of building St Petersburg is impossible. The new city was a manifestation of the drive to gain a foothold on the Baltic and to achieve this objective Peter I brought to bear the full authority of an absolute autocracy. From the writings of a Dutch contemporary and Foreign Minister to Russia, Friedrich Christian Weber, some appreciation of what these early days were like may be acquired:

This Resolution was no sooner taken, but Orders were forthwith issued, that next Spring a great number of Men, *Russians*, *Tartars*, *Cosacks*, *Calmucks*, *Finlandish* and *Ingrian* Peasants, should be at the Place to execute the Czar's Design. Accordingly in the beginning of May 1703, many thousands of Workmen, raised from all the Corners of the vast Russian Empire, some of them coming Journies of 200 to 300 German Miles, made a beginning of the Works on the new Fortress. There were neither sufficient Provisions to furnish them with the necessary Tools, as Pick-axes, Spades, Shovels, Wheel-barrows, Planks and the like, they even had not so much as Houses or Huts; notwithstanding which the Work went on with such Expedition, that it was surprizing to see the Fortress raised within less than five Months time, though the Earth which is very scarce thereabouts, was for the greater part carried by the Labourers in the Skirts of their Clothes, and in Bags made of Rags and old Mats, the Use of Wheel-barrows being then unknown to them. It is computed that there perished on this Occasion very nigh one hundred thousand Souls, for in those Places made desolate by the War, no Provisions could be had even for ready Money, and as the usual Supplies carried by the

Lake Ladoga were frequently retarded by contrary Winds, those People often were in the utmost Misery.

At the same time that they were going on with the Fortress, the City also by degrees began to be built, and to this End Numbers of People both of the Nobility and the trading Part of the Nation were ordered to come from Russia to settle at Petersbourg and to build Houses there, all which was executed with such Forwardness, that in a short time the Place swarmed with Inhabitants.[4]

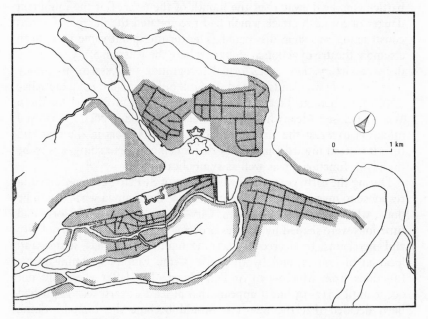

MAP 2. *St Petersburg, 1716*

The fortress was built on what the local Finns called Hare Island in the main channel of the Neva (the Bol'shaya Neva), a spot accessible to the largest vessels then afloat ⟨*see* map 2⟩. The Admiralty shipbuilding complex was soon transferred from Lake Ladoga to a point just across the river. The settlement was equipped with cannon, which gave an

[4] Weber, *The Present State of Russia*, pp. 300–01.

additional measure of protection but was not enough to forestall Swedish harassment. There was clearly much urgency in completing the planned system of fortification. One important link was the bastion on Kotlin Island (started also in 1703 and intended to control the approach to St Petersburg by sea). Despite the difficulties and the cost, the basic components of the system were assembled within five years. Cannon at Kronshtadt, as the naval base on Kotlin Island was called, commanded the narrow channel through the Gulf of Finland passing south of the island and leading to the Neva delta.[5] At St Petersburg, the St Peter and Paul Fortress with cannon ensconced in high stone battlements held sway over the mouth of the river. But the imminent danger of Swedish attack which had precipitated the flurry of fortress construction was soon dissipated. The turning point came in 1709 in a remote theatre of action at Poltava where the Russian army secured a decisive victory. However, formal recognition of Russian hegemony over the newly won lands around the Gulf of Finland did not materialize until 1721 when the Treaty of Nystadt brought the prolonged Northern War to a close.[6] Meanwhile, Peter I was busy making good his avowed intention to wrest the Russian Empire from its roots in the east and turn it instead toward Europe. In this scheme St Petersburg was to be the pivot, functionally as well as symbolically.

During the early years the development of St Petersburg occurred in response to myriad *ukazi* or decrees. These determined what was to be done, where, how, and by whom. City life, as well as urban form and functions were shaped by decrees ordering the presence of the nobility and merchants, by decrees concerning building materials, design and location of houses, and by the shift of the Empire's administrative functions from Moscow to St Petersburg. The latter event did not occur until 1712–13 but it appears that at least as early as 1704 it had been decided that the new city would become the capital.[7] Some appreciation of the impact of these early *ukazi* is gained by noting that in 1710 there was a permanent population of at least 8,000 and that the annual influx of conscripted peasant labourers was usually four to five times this number. There were in addition approximately 16,000

[5] For details, see G. Bogdanov, *Istoricheskoye, Geograficheskoye i Topograficheskoye Opisaniye Peterburga, ot Nachala Zavedeniya Yego s 1703 po 1751 God.* (1779), pp. 515–16.

[6] A. V. Predtechenskiy, 'Osnovaniye Peterburga', in *Peterburg Petrovskogo Vremeni* (1948), p. 36; Bernard Pares, *A History of Russia* (New York, 1964), p. 207.

[7] S. P. Luppov, *Istoriya Stroitel'stva Peterburga v Pervoy Chetverti XVIII Veka* (1957), p. 17, Predtechenskiy, 'Osnovaniye Peterburga', pp. 38–9.

buildings; however, most were small, wooden structures, a logical outcome given the dearth of stone construction material in the vicinity and the urgency in erecting some form of shelter.[8] Wooden structures were tolerated only as a temporary phenomenon for they did not have a place in the emerging conception of what the new capital should, or would, look like. Indeed, in 1714 Peter issued a further *ukaz* to intensify the construction of stone buildings. It was not just those members of the privileged classes living there who were obliged to carry out the order, but all newcomers were required to bring some stone to the city. In issuing this and other decrees, there seem to have been five basic principles guiding the tsar's actions: the streets were to be straight and the buildings of brick or stone; in the overall plan the waterways were to be used to advantage; once determined the plan must be adhered to rigidly; within the city particular groups were to be assigned to specific areas; the management of city affairs would be concentrated in the hands of the resident commercial and industrial elite.[9]

In no sense, however, had the plethora of decrees prevented haphazard construction of inferior buildings and a city planned in accordance with these precepts remained an ideal, although one that was not beyond the reach of an absolute autocracy. An overall perspective—a detailed plan—was needed. Persuaded by Peter I, Jean Leblond became chief architect in 1716 and within six months of assuming the position, Leblond had prepared a much needed general plan, even if a hastily prepared one. At the time the centre of the city was focused, firstly on the port and trading functions of the Strelka (the easternmost tip of Vasil'yevskiy Island); secondly, on the fortress across the Malaya Neva River immediately opposite; and finally, on the Admiralty shipbuilding complex across the broad reach of the Bol'shaya Neva ⟨*see* plate 2⟩. As is clear from map 3, the centre of Vasil'yevskiy Island became the principal element in Leblond's plan, a marked shift from the existing locus of activities. Rectilinearity was emphasized by the regimented street widths and building heights, canals and fountains were to be aesthetic features as well as safeguards against flooding and fires, and separate areas were set aside for specific purposes (manufacturing and handicraft activities, for instance). All told it was an imposing scheme, though an impractical one because of the massive transformation of existing fabric and functional layout of

[8] Luppov, *Istoriya Stroitel'stva Peterburga*, pp. 23, 79; A. Bashutskiy, *Panorama Sanktpeterburga* (1834), p. 95.
[9] Luppov, *Istoriya Stroitel'stva Peterburga*, pp. 23-4.

the city necessary in order to realize it.[10] The project never got off the drawing board, but it embodied many of the basic elements desired by Peter, including the use of Vasil'yevskiy Island as the focal point. If nothing else, Leblond demonstrated the importance of developing the city as an integrated whole and there is no doubt that his scheme had a very considerable influence on Russian city planning during the

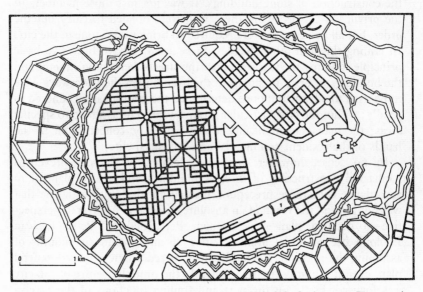

MAP 3. *Leblond's plan for St Petersburg* (1—Admiralty; 2—Fortress)

remainder of the century. Yet while acknowledging the significance of Leblond's plan, we should not lose sight of the fact that he was only one of many skilled architects who had a hand in designing individual buildings and shaping the city. Even before his arrival, some of the best European architectual talents were at work. D. Trezzini was assisting in the construction of the St Peter and Paul Fortress, a project which continued for most of the century. The Summer Palace project in Peterhof, southwest of the city, involved Trezzini, A. Schlüter and others. Beginning in 1710 the Menshikov Palace, a truly magnificent building, took form under the direction of G. Fontana and G. Schädel. The Arsenal, the docks, canals, factories, gardens,

[10] V. Shkvarikov, *Ocherk Istorii Planirovki i Zastroyki Russkikh Gorodov* (Moscow, 1954), p. 71; I. A. Egorov, *The Architectural Planning of St Petersburg* (Athens, Ohio, 1969), translated by Eric Dluhosch, pp. 11–26.

theatres, academies, administrative buildings, a host of other lesser structures and a complement of imposing churches, the most impressive of which was the Orthodox Church of Peter and Paul, whose protestant-like spire soon loomed up behind the fortress walls, all contributed to the emerging image of the city.[11] Leblond, Trezzini, Mattarnovi, Schlüter, Fontana, Schädel, Gerbel, Michetti, Feldten—the names indicated diverse backgrounds though they were at one in bringing European ideas and skills to the construction of St Petersburg.

Peter I did not live long enough to see all these plans realized. None the less, at the time of his death in 1725 the desolate site selected for the new capital barely two decades earlier had undergone a profound change. There were now around 40,000 inhabitants, a population still much augmented by the summer influx of labourers.[12] The tumultuous pace of development meant that a planned environment had not yet been created and from a map dated 1716 we can see something of the emerging, rather irregular street pattern ⟨*see* map 2⟩. The Admiralty on the south shore of the Bol'shaya Neva River was clearly an established node ⟨*see* plate 4⟩. The Winter Palace was just to the east and clustered around both were several imposing princely residences (the occupants frequently having some connection with the Admiralty), and a nondescript workers' settlement. 'From the Post-house down along the River,' as Friedrich Christian Weber saw it,

> stands a long Row of Houses, one of them . . . is the Czar's Winter Habitation and his usual Residence, a Stone Building two Stories high . . .. Round about the Czar live all sorts of People, Russians as well as Germans, but most of the latter . . . have taken up the Streets that lie nearest the Czar's Residence. The High-dutch Lutheran Church . . . a wooden Structure in the Form of a Cross, stands not above three hundred Paces from the Back-side of the Czar's Residence. Further down South-East the said Church . . . are the Habitations of the great Officers of the Admiralty. Five of those Houses are large and built of Stone, the others which are as yet of Wood are likewise to be transformed into Stone Buildings, for which the Materials lie ready. The Back-Street which ends into the large Place . . . is inhabited by Russians and Germans indistinctly, though there are more of the

[11] Construction of the church began in 1712 under Trezzini. Bashutskiy, *Panorama Sanktpeterburga*, p. 95.
[12] For a discussion of several population estimates, see G. E. Kochin, 'Naseleniye Peterburga do 6o-kh Godov XVIII v', *Och.IL* (1955), vol. I, p. 102.

latter, but further to the Left of the said large Place there live none but Russians; the Houses are small and placed at random without any regularity.[13]

Further east, beyond the Fontanka, was the scruffy Moskovskaya *sloboda* or suburb. In it was a large garrison, the Arsenal and a variety of military manufacturers.[14] On the map accompanying Weber's book

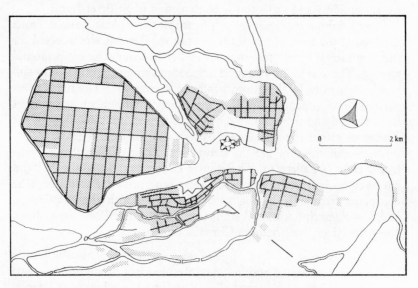

MAP 4. *St Petersburg, 1716* (after Friedrich Christian Weber)

several roads may be seen converging on the Admiralty ⟨*see* map 4⟩. Though their straightness is probably a cartographic embellishment, the orientation did foreshadow what was eventually a key element in the city plan. One road running in an easterly direction went past the Aleksandro-Nevskiy Monastery, founded in 1710, and linked up with the highway to Novgorod. The stretch from the Admiralty to the monastery eventually became the city's principal thoroughfare—the Nevskiy Prospect. On Weber's map, Vasil'yevskiy Island is portrayed in a rather presumptuous manner though it was in keeping with the

---

[13] Weber, *The Present State of Russia*, p. 310.

[14] A major component of the defence industry, the manufacture of gunpowder, was located outside the settlement in Ohkta, where a factory was built in 1715. Bogdanov, *Istoricheskoye Geograficheskoye i Topograficheskoye Opisaniye Peterburga*, p. 132.

spirit of Leblond's plan and Peter's wishes. While a rectilinear street pattern did develop, very little of this 'large and fine Island' was in fact inhabited in 1716 and map 2 gives the more accurate picture of what existed. However, at the time of Peter's death much of what had been built on Vasil'yevskiy Island was distinctive. The Strelka was dominated by the Exchange, customs houses and wharves. Along the Bol'shaya Neva Prince Menshikov's palace and church, the Kunst-kammer and the Twelve Colleges, being built under Trezzini's supervision to house the ministries, added a touch of architectural elegance to an otherwise dreary shoreline.[15] And a good many merchants, Russian and foreign, had built substantial, if wooden homes. All told, the district had an air of prosperity.

Not so Peterburgskiy Island just across the Malaya Neva River. Here the Tartar *sloboda*, the Russian *sloboda*, the markets, fortress and garrisons created a cosmopolitan and commercial atmosphere which by comparison with Vasil'yevskiy Island was rather mean.[16] While architecturally undistinguished, save for the fortress itself, the island at least afforded places of amusement for the rustic folk residing there. Weber noticed that,

> Peasants, Journeymen, and other common People, particularly Boys, meet on Sundays and Holidays and after having fuddled themselves in the neighbouring Cabacks, or Tap-Houses, divide into two Parties, and fight and box for Diversion sake, in the most barbarous Manner, that the Ground lies full of Blood and Hair, and many of them are carried off lame. When they fall on, they make such a dreadful and wild Noise, that they may be heard a Mile off. Those Disorders are connived at by the Government, with this View, that the young People may use themselves to fighting and boxing, and make afterwards the better Soldiers.[17]

By comparing maps 2 and 5, it is at once evident that the few areas affording some protection from flooding, owing to variations in local topography, were not prime areas for development. Yet floods had already taken heavy tolls, notably in 1715. In point of fact, this very

[15] The Twelve Colleges building was planned to accommodate various government bureaucracies. For additional description and details, see Weber, *The Present State of Russia*, pp. 321–6; Bogdanov, *Istoricheskoye Geograficheskoye i Topograficheskoye Opisaniye Peterburga*, pp. 164–6.
[16] Bogdanov, *Istoricheskoye Geograficheskoye i Topograficheskoye Opisaniye Peterburga*, pp. 158–61.
[17] Weber, *The Present State of Russia*, p. 328.

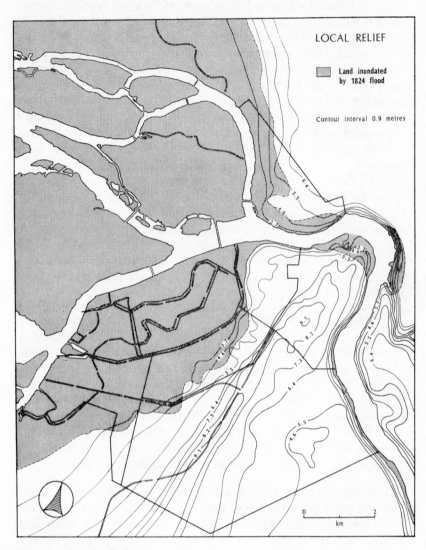

MAP 5. *Local relief*

real danger was subordinated to the concept of a grand design in which Vasil'yevskiy Island was scheduled to be the centre of the city. No effort was spared in support of this basic concept, as Weber makes clear:

> Late Advices from Petersbourg say, that all the Inhabitants in general, who live on the Ingrian Side, in the Sloboda where the Czar's Palace stands, have received Orders to build on the Prince's Island [Vasil'yevskiy Island], and to settle there, which, considering the Expenses they have already been at in building, will be very disagreeable, and a great Hardship to them.[18]

While this particular ambition was frustrated many others were not. Still, what Peter I left as a legacy was more than the material accomplishments embodied in the new capital, whatever its form; rather it was what was represented by it—the absolute authority of the tsar.

Urban growth was clearly forced during Peter's time and following his death a reaction occurred. Many in a position to do so thankfully left the city. Nobles in particular often resumed residence in Moscow and during the brief reign of Peter II it once more became the capital. However, in 1732 Empress Anna redressed this decision, and thereafter concentrated on creating a sumptuous court life in St Petersburg.[19] During these years the growth of the city proceeded with only minimal direction and the south shore of the Bol'shaya Neva was the scene of most development. Indeed, the reconstruction of the Admiralty itself, started in 1727 under the architect I. Korobov, was one of the few notable projects of the time.[20] Despite the earlier decrees to promote construction of stone or brick buildings, the vast majority were wooden. They were therefore susceptible to the ever present risk of fires, the hazard responsible for the decrees in the first place. Fires were a regular occurrence in the city, but in 1736 and 1737 they were of devastating proportion. Most of the structures in the large area between the Neva and Moyka were levelled in these conflagrations.[21] This was not without some benefits, however. The destruction provided a unique opportunity to rebuild an important area of the city according to some desirable standards.

---

[18] Weber, *The Present State of Russia*, pp. 327–8.
[19] *Entsiklopedicheskiy Slovar'* (1900), vol. LVI, p. 295.
[20] Egorov, *The Architectural Planning of St Petersburg*, p. 224.
[21] Bashutskiy, *Panorama Peterburga*, pp. 98–9; Shkvarikov, *Ocherk Istorii Planirovki*, pp. 71–2.

In 1737 a new plan was prepared and a Commission for the Orderly Development of St Petersburg replaced the ineffectual Commission of Building. Five separate administrative units were created in order to facilitate implementation of the plan which focused on rebuilding one of them, the new district of Admiralteyskaya.[22] Within this district the area bounded by the Moyka and the Bol'shaya Neva River was singled out for redevelopment. Noxious industries were prohibited; the few factories still standing after the fires were to be relocated; all new buildings were required to have proper foundations and be made of stone or brick. At the same time Empress Anna banished a large number of courtiers from the palace and by so doing created overnight a demand for private houses. In short, the 'mean' inhabitants were legislated out of a large part of the district, changing in the process both the fabric and functions of the central city.[23]

One of the first tasks of the new Commission involved assembling a topographic inventory of all buildings in the city. From this 1737 map the area devastated by fire shows up clearly as a stippled section near the Admiralty ⟨*see* map 6⟩. With an accurate enumeration and survey in hand, planning proposals were quickly prepared. One of the most significant schemes was the so-called 'three-pronged' street layout in the Admiralteyskaya district, a concept initiated during Peter's era but only little developed. It was significant because of its architectural and planning merits and also because of the timing. Building was to be more extensive here than anywhere else in the city for many years and if not properly coordinated the advantages of beginning from scratch would be lost. The configuration of the three main streets in the plan capitalized not on the Winter Palace as a focal point, but on the newly constructed Admiralty and its gilded spire.[24] From the 1737 map only a trace of the scheme can be seen, but from a segment of the first large-scale map, published in 1753, more of this eventual street pattern is in evidence ⟨*see* maps 6 and 7⟩. The later map shows the relationship between the Great Perspective Road, as the Nevskiy Prospect was then known, Gorokhovaya Street in the centre, the Voznesenskiy Prospect leading off to the southwest, and the Admiralty. The position of the Winter Palace to the east is also clearly presented. St Petersburg at the time was more or less bounded to the south by the

[22] The five districts were: Admiralteyskaya, Vasil'yevskaya, Peterburgskaya, Vyborgskaya and Moskovskaya.
[23] Even the contingent of workers associated with the Admiralty was obliged to relocate. Bashutskiy, *Panorama Peterburga*, p. 99.
[24] The Admiralty project was completed in 1738, but was later damaged by fire.

Fontanka Canal. However, after straightening and redirecting Gorokhovaya Street and Voznesenskiy Prospect, the Commission extended
them beyond the Fontanka and arranged for regimental garrisons to be
located around their termini. This part of the project took decades to
be completed but it is the reason for the grid-iron pattern at the end of
Voznesenskiy, with each street being numbered sequentially as a *rota*

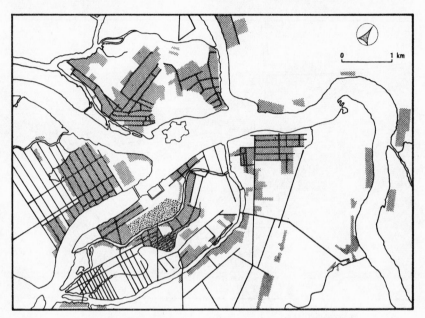

MAP 6. *St Petersburg, 1737*

or company, and the barracks and huge parade ground being placed
at the end of Gorokhovaya. The Aleksandro-Nevskiy Monastery sat at
the end of the Nevskiy Prospect, symbolic of the Church's presence.
With the Izmailovskiy and Semenovskiy regimental guards quartered
at the end of the other two thoroughfares, the autocracy was militarily
secure. Thus, each radial had a symbolic base and a common focal
point. They remained the overriding elements in the city's street
pattern ⟨*see* end maps 70 and 71⟩.[25]

With the plan prepared, there began a period of construction notable
more for the creation of a few outstanding buildings than of whole

[25] For a discussion of this scheme, see Egorov, *The Architectural Planning of St Petersburg*,
pp. 31–6.

city areas. The Winter Palace, gutted in the 1737 fire, the Smol'niy Monastery, the Stroganov Palace, all arose under the unique direction of V. Rastrelli, the Russianized son of a Florentine sculptor brought to the capital during the time of Peter I ⟨*see* plate 10⟩. Outside the city, his talents were applied to the palace of Peterhof, a summer residence begun on a colossal scale by Peter I, and to another imperial residence

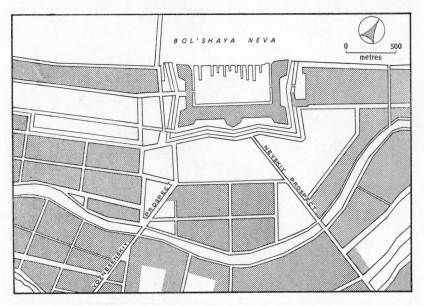

MAP 7. *Part of the central city, 1753*

in Tsarskoye Selo. Ornate, often to the extreme, colourful, owing to the use of painted stuccos in lieu of scarce stone, Rastrelli's work added an entirely new dimension to the growing stock of fine buildings. His coming to the fore was not accidental for he was commissioned by Empress Elizabeth (1741–62).[26] It was under her guidance that the Academy of Arts (1757) came into being, an institution of great importance to St Petersburg's cultural and architectural development.[27] Of course, Rastrelli was not alone in changing the face of the city. M. Zemstov and G. Dmitriyev worked throughout the 1740s on the

[26] A. I. Gegello, V. F. Shilkov, 'Arkhitektura i Planirovka Peterburga do 60-kh Godov XVIII v', *Och.IL* (1955), vol. I, pp. 153–4.
[27] Gegello, Shilkov, 'Arkhitektura i Planirovka Peterburga', pp. 153–5.

Anichkov Palace. This magnificent building and sometime imperial residence, graced the corner of the Nevskiy Prospect and the Fontanka.[28] During the fifties, architect S. Chevakinskiy worked on the Nikol'skiy Church which enhanced the skyline of the western stretch of Sadovaya Street and together with F. Argunov built Count Sheremetev's splendid residence on the Fontanka.[29] By no means did this period witness an exclusive preoccupation with churches, imperial palaces and homes for the nobility, though these represented some of the most outstanding work. Factories, banks and bridges testified to the growing significance of urban economy. The pace of development, however, was soon to be totally overshadowed.

It is said of Catherine II (1762–96) that when she came to St Petersburg it was of wood, when she left it was of stone.[30] The epigram contains more than a germ of truth. It was during the reign of this German born empress that St Petersburg came of age in the sense that it was no longer necessary to oblige the nobility to take up residence there; many now recognized the signs of a maturing civic society for themselves and flocked to the capital to take part in it. The combination of state and private enterprise brought building construction to an unprecedented pitch. By the 1760s the almost overbearing, baroque-like style of Rastrelli was already on the wane and the architects engaged by Catherine—men like J. Vallin de la Mothe, A. Rinaldi, C. Cameron and G. Quarenghi—ensured its demise. The recently created Academy of Arts, which was housed in a building of somewhat severe style designed by Vallin de la Mothe and A. Kokorinov, together with the former's new *Gostinyy Dvor* on the Nevskiy Prospect, in many respects typified the change in architecture.[31] While the volume and quality of building was impressive, it was the overall coordination of it which greatly enhanced the city's image. In this respect the Commission for the Masonry Construction of St Petersburg and Moscow played a central role.

Formed in 1762, the Commission had the heavy responsibility of seeing that planning objectives were realized.[32] Shortly after commencing operations, the Commission held an open competition in which two sets of design specifications for developing the city were

[28] Egorov, *The Architectural Planning of St Petersburg*, p. 224.
[29] *Leningrad, Entsiklopedicheskiy Spravochnik* (1957), p. 176.
[30] Bashutskiy, *Panorama Peterburga*, p. 101.
[31] Vallin de la Mothe was nominated Professor of the Academy of Arts later in the sixties (1767). *Leningrad*, p. 176.
[32] *Leningrad*, p. 177.

invited. The first set entailed proposing a plan based on existing conditions in the city. The second was a competition for a design appropriate to the capital of the Russian Empire, in which existing conditions could be ignored to realize the desired aims—architectural definition of the central area and a harmonious relationship with the suburbs. Out of this competition came many ideas subsequently adopted in the planned development of the city. The principal design problem was that of integrating Vasil'yevskiy and Peterburgskiy Islands with what had been done in the Admiralteyskaya district; development on Peterburgskiy Island was particularly muddled. Under the Commission's direction, the first achievement was to complete the 'three-pronged' ensemble in Admiralteyskaya district by creating an open space in front of the Admiralty and Winter Palace. This entailed demolishing the existing St Isaac's Church. To carry out the entire plan necessitated a continuous line of buildings to the northeast along the Bol'shaya Neva from the Winter Palace, reconstruction of the Admiralty (fortuitously damaged by fire in 1783 but not rebuilt until early in the nineteenth century), the filling-in of the façade along the so-called English Quay to the southwest of the Admiralty and, of course, completion of the embankment of the Bol'shaya Neva in granite. To complement this part of the plan, further development began on the Strelka. The Academy of Arts building was started in 1764 and, following the destruction of the Kunstkammer by fire a few years later, a whole series of new buildings were planned, including the Academy of Science, the University, the Library, the Observatory, an Institute of Geography, as well as the Exchange. Not all these materialized but their number reflected the need to tie together the structures on the Strelka because the waterfront façade had become the element that would give visual unity to the central part of the city. By the end of the century developments on Vasil'yevskiy Island and on the mainland had brought this objective within reach. But what of Peterburgskiy Island? Like Vasil'yevskiy Island, the main streets did not lead off from the emerging focal point of the city plan, and worse, there was not even a coherent pattern. It was proposed that a radial pattern emanating from the St Peter and Paul Fortress be introduced, thus forming a counterpart to the set of radials on the mainland.[33] Despite the visual focus provided by the Fortress the plans came to nought. Still, for the short time that the Commission

[33] See Heinrich von Reimers, *St Petersburg am Ende Seines Ersten Jahrhunderts* (1805), vol. I, pp. 328–40; Egorov, *The Architectural History of St Petersburg*, pp. 54–81.

was directly concerned with proposals for the capital, enormous changes were set in motion and the achievements were on a grand scale.[34] In less than forty years the talents of skilled architects too numerous to detail had transformed the city.[35] Between 1765 and 1795 the number of stone or brick buildings rose from 460 to 1,385, whereas the total number of structures in St Petersburg increased from around 4,090 to 6,900.[36] We can, moreover, gain a different perspective by looking briefly at the city through the eyes of a number of contemporaries.

Clearly, it was not just the buildings, their architecture and layout which influenced perceptions. The rich court life, the ostentation of the nobility, the pervasiveness of the military—indeed, all aspects of city life—helped to shape them and the architectural achievement was sometimes evaluated in minds already predisposed to eulogy or carping comment. However, if there was not always agreement about the merits of what had been done, there was certainly consensus concerning the scale of the endeavours. Late in the century, W. Coxe noted:

> Succeeding sovereigns have continued to embellish Petersburg, but none more than the present empress, who may be called its second founder. Notwithstanding, however, all these improvements, it bears every mark of an infant city, and, is still, 'only an immense outline, which will require future empresses and almost future ages to complete.' The views upon the banks of the Neva exhibit the most grand and lively scenes I ever beheld . . .. On the north side the fortress, the Academy of Sciences, and Academy of Arts, are the most striking objects; on the Admiralty, the mansions of many Russian nobles, and the English line . . .; and the Neva . . . has been lately embanked by a wall, parapet, and pavement of hewn granite; a magnificent and durable monument of imperial munificence.[37]

The view to the south across the broad reach of the Neva offered at least one perspective that was generally approved.

[34] After two decades the Commission's work turned to city planning throughout the Empire.

[35] For discussion, see A. I. Gegello, V. I. Pilyavskiy, 'Arkhitektura Peterburga 60–90 Godov, XVIII v', *Och.IL* (1955), vol. I, pp. 320–60.

[36] Bashutskiy, *Panorama Peterburga*, p. 102. These figures are not directly comparable with the data for the early part of the century during which time many temporary structures were apparently included.

[37] William Coxe, *Travels in Poland, Russia, Sweden, and Denmark* (London, 1802), vol. II, pp. 102, 104. The quotation is from Wraxall's Tour.

The side of the Admiralty . . . occasionally presents . . . a magnificent spectacle, here being the wharf and a dockyard from whence ships of war of sixty to a hundred guns are built, and every launch is a great holiday. The row of houses along the quay, inhabited mostly by English merchants, would not suffer by comparison with any street in the world.[38]

And even those disinclined to see much good in St Petersburg had to acknowledge that the overall scheme was impressive even if its constituent parts did not measure up to preconceived standards. 'Petersburg', wrote one observer of the 1790s, 'is in some respects a finer place than I expected to find it, in others it is not so fine: all the buildings are of coarse brick, and very badly constructed; they are stuccoed, but the white falls off, or grows green and dirty which gives the town the look of a decayed place, rather than of a rising one.'[39] If upon close inspection stucco façades were frequently found to be peeling, walls crooked and columns lopsided, it is not surprising that such observers were unimpressed. The job of erecting buildings on the delta, particularly the more monumental of them, was obviously difficult and it was not helped by the short construction season and the use of hordes of indifferently skilled summer workmen.[40] However, most observers tended to focus on the panorama and not the particular. 'Petersburg,' wrote one French veteran of Catherine II's court, 'some parts of which are singularly magnificent and beautiful, does not badly resemble the sketch of a grand picture, in which are already delineated a face familiar to that of the Apollo Belvidere, and an eye such as would be given to Genius, while the rest is a chaos of unfinished strokes or of dotted lines.'[41] But it was really just the Admiralteyskaya district and the eastern part of Vasil'yevskiy Island, with its rapidly expanding complement of academic and commercial institutions, that created the 'urban' image. Many areas within the city boundaries were decidedly bucolic. For example, Henry Storch late in the century found Peterburgskiy Island heavily wooded, little settled and 'only in part' belonging to the city, while Vyborgskaya 'has the most rural appearance

<hr />

[38] Henry Storch, *The Picture of St Petersburg* (London, 1801), pp. 16, 139. Storch was a tutor in political economy to Alexander I.

[39] *Letters from the Continent describing the Manners and Customs of Germany, Poland, Russia, and Switzerland in the years 1790, 1791 and 1792 to a Friend Residing in England* (London, 1812), p. 114.

[40] For a discussion of the difficulties, see Bashutskiy, *Panorama Peterburga*, pp. 109–13.

[41] Charles F. P. Masson, *Secret Memoirs of the Court of Petersburg* (Philadelphia, 1802), pp. 74–5.

of all . . . it is only occupied by cottages of the peasantry, and its small population is chiefly employed in rural industry.'[42]

After the death of Catherine II, the tempo of building during the brief reign of her son Paul (1796–1801) did not let up, though it was said of him that,

> so far from finishing the most useful of those labours begun by his mother, as the quays, canals, and high roads [he] has built, in his turn, churches and palaces, though there were already more than enough of both in Petersburgh. But the monuments he has erected in greatest number, are houses for military exercise, barracks, guard-houses, and particularly sentry boxes. Happily, however, all these constructions are of wood, and will hardly outlast their founder.[43]

As it turned out, Paul's assassination confounded this prediction. By 1804 the city contained some 7,200 buildings of which only 439 belonged to the state ⟨*see* maps 8 and 9⟩. The Admiralteyskaya district represented the highest property values in the city and the Karetnaya district some of the lowest, despite the fact that it contained half of all state buildings, most of which were inferior wooden barracks, stables and storehouses. By this date there was a marked fall-off in the quality of buildings toward the periphery. And it was toward the edge of the city that the poorer inhabitants had been expelled during the first half of the eighteenth century.

Two basic principles for the planned development of the city emerged during the late eighteenth century. The first was that the city should be made as magnificent as possible and to this end huge squares, monumental buildings and unparalleled vistas were created. The second was that there should be harmonious, continuous façades along the principal streets and to achieve this exacting controls over architectural and planning detail were required. The fulfilment of these aims involved enormous expenditure, more indeed than the state could easily sustain. Thus, a number of projects remained unfinished by the early 1800s for purely financial reasons.[44] The intention to have architecturally harmonious structures along all major

---

[42] Storch, *Picture of St Petersburg*, pp. 54, 57.
[43] Masson, *Secret Memoirs*, p. 78.
[44] For example, construction of Quarenghi's Exchange was beset with financial problems. Egorov, *The Architectural History of St Petersburg*, p. 88.

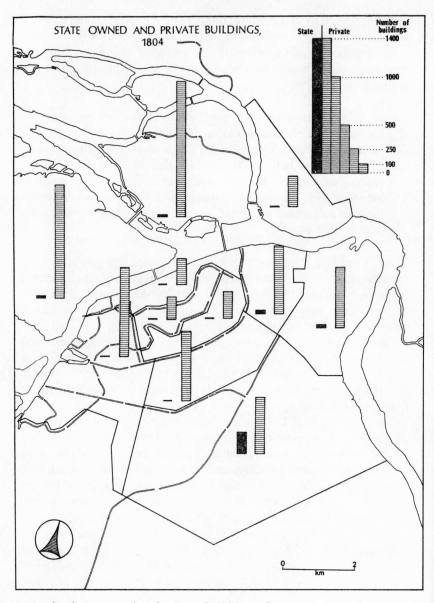

MAP 8. *State-owned and private buildings, 1804*

36

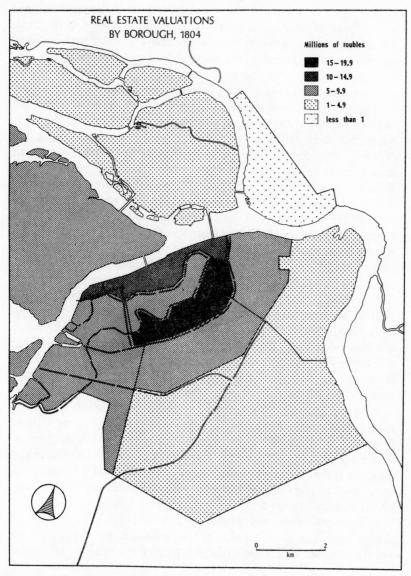

REAL ESTATE VALUATIONS
BY BOROUGH, 1804

Millions of roubles

15 – 19.9
10 – 14.9
5 – 9.9
1 – 4.9
less than 1

0   km   2

MAP 9. *Real-estate valuations by borough, 1804*

37

thoroughfares in the central area also had to be compromised. The upshot was a selective distribution of magnificent buildings, designed in the hope of drawing attention from one open space to the next. During the first quarter of the century many projects were initiated for this purpose; thereafter, the planned development of St Petersburg on a grand scale perceptibly drew to a close.

One of the most immediate tasks was that of rebuilding the Admiralty, a project that had been stalled for more than two decades. Under the supervision of A. Zakharov, it was started in 1806 and in the early 1820s the 'three-pronged' street pattern had a new focus. Along the Nevskiy Prospect, A. Voronikhin's Kazan Cathedral added an appropriately monumental dimension to the city's main street. On the Strelka a new Exchange by T. de Thomon replaced the unfinished building started by Quarenghi twenty years before and the embankment of the waterfront and the addition of two huge granite columns completed the ensemble.[45] The reorganization of the government, the rapid growth in population at the time of the Napoleonic War, and the ensuing need for huge open spaces to demonstrate the military prestige which the war had awakened in Russia, all combined to spur new developments in the city, especially in the Admiralteyskaya district. Thus, in 1816 under the direction of still another coordinating body, the Committee of Construction and Hydraulic Works, the last of the major construction projects was started. Though the Committee was sometimes bypassed when projects captured the interest of the tsar, it was able to coordinate these works to some extent. In conjunction with the reconstruction of the Admiralty building, a sequence of squares was planned. They were to extend from the southwest of the Admiralty through to the northeast in front of the Winter Palace. Beginning in 1819, K. Rossi began reshaping the *Dvortsovaya* or Palace square. The semicircular General Staff building and archway created a quite uniquely shaped 'square' which led into the redesigned open space in front of the Admiralty. The whole ensemble was completed with the Alexander Column providing a splendid focal point.[46] Simultaneously with this project, a new St Isaac's Cathedral on Senate Square, to the other side of the Admiralty, was being built on a scale intended to dominate the complex of squares as well as the

[45] A. I. Gegello, V. I. Pilyavskiy, 'Arkhitektura Peterburga ot Kontsa XVIII v do 1861g.', *Och.IL* (1955), vol. I, pp. 551–4.
[46] See Auguste de Montferrand, *Plans et Détails du Monument Consacré à la Mémoire de l'Empereur Alexandre* (Paris, 1836).

city's skyline.[47] Eventually a series of five squares unified the magnificent and massive projects in the central part of Admiralteyskaya district.

Elsewhere new theatres, palaces, and many institutional buildings were being added to the architectural embellishment of the city. But toward the end of the reign of Nicholas I (1825–55), a change was in evidence. Major projects begun during Alexander's time were duly completed, but the huge architectural setpieces of earlier times were no longer undertaken. With a few notable exceptions the dominant theme was now utilitarian. The exceptions were the Mikhailovskiy and Alexander theatres, both operating by the early 1830s, the new Hermitage designed by N. Efimov and L. Klenze, and A. Staken-schneider's Mariinskiy Palace. The socioeconomic complexion of the city was changing and this was being reflected in what was built, how and by whom.[48] One barometer of the changing social order was the register of real estate owners. Over the preceding decades merchants had steadily augmented their share of holdings. By the early 1830s they had emerged as important property owners and owned a fifth of the 8,000 or so buildings in the city. The relative gain by the merchants occurred largely at the expense of the nobility, bureaucrats and state. Even though we do not have accurate statistics for real estate values by category of owner, the average value of the merchants' property was obviously less than that belonging to the nobility, bureaucrats and state. Still it is noteworthy that, proportionally, the merchants owned more stone or brick buildings than did nobles and bureaucrats.[49]

The nineteenth century was witnessing a change in the balance of wealth between court and commerce and the earlier sensitivity to urban form and function was on the wane. The face of the city reflected these changes. In the early 1840s, official controls over the type of housing built virtually disappeared and, by mid-century, the pace of urban growth started to outstretch the capability of civic authorities to control and supervise it. The coming decades of industrialization and

[47] Designed by A. Montferrand it was not completed for decades. The project was highly controversial and included one abortive start. See Egorov, *The Architectural History of St Petersburg*, pp. 158–62.

[48] Gegello, Pilyavskiy, 'Arkhitektura Peterburga ot Kontsa XVIII v do 1861g.,' pp. 594, 600.

[49] *Statisticheskiya Svedeniya o Sanktpeterburge* (1836), pp. 70–72. One of the reasons for the rapid increase in real-estate ownership by merchants was the fact that the main form of property, serfs, was denied the majority of them. 'Deprived, therefore, of this mode of investment, their chief object is to purchase houses in town, which produce them a high rate of interest for their capitals, and very much enhance the price of house-rent in Petersburg.' Thomas Raikes, *A Visit to St Petersburg in the Winter of 1829–30* (London, 1838), pp. 94–5.

blatant commercialism portended ominous consequences for a city built in accordance with the precepts of grand design and imperial munificence. But before beginning an assessment of what these decades actually meant, we need to consider the development of the urban economy up to mid century and to ask what life in the city was like.

2 THE URBAN ECONOMY

Born in the 'fire of war', industry was carefully nurtured from the beginning in order that the needs of the military might be satisfied. Vast numbers of labourers were conscripted from all corners of Russia, craftsmen and technicians by the hundreds were enticed from Europe and in little more than a decade St Petersburg emerged as one of the major shipbuilding and armament centres in the country.[50] Clearly, the exigencies of war with Sweden dictated that war industries and the industrial and commercial functions necessary to a rapidly growing population be developed swiftly. In large measure such developments occurred because of imperial decrees. Given the conditions of serfdom and an absolute autocracy it was relatively simple to gather workers and soldiers at the site of the new city, but in such a desolate environment feeding them alone was an enormous problem. The horrific losses described by contemporaries like Weber testify to the logistical obstacles in supplying St Petersburg with essential foodstuffs, and thus the state came to be involved not just in the manufacture of munitions and men-of-war, but also in such things as bread, beer and cloth.[51] In many respects Peter I had more success in moulding the urban economy than with the plan and architecture of the city. Although it is not always possible to be precise in describing the industrial and commercial economies toward the end of his reign, there is ample information to convey at least the sense of what had been accomplished.

During the first quarter of the eighteenth century more than 200 manufacturing operations were established in Russia, some of the more important ones being in or around St Petersburg.[52] Reasons for locating industrial concerns outside the city varied, but were usually

[50] During the first quarter of the nineteenth century, for instance, more than 25 per cent of all ships built in Russia came from St Petersburg. A. E. Suknovalov, 'Ekonomicheskaya Zhizn' Peterburga do 60-kh Godov XVIII v', *Och.IL* (1955), vol. I, p. 62.
[51] P. N. Stolpyanskiy, *Zhizn' i Byt Peterburgskoy Fabriki za 1704–1914 gg.* (1925), pp. 12, 27, 66. See also Weber's description quoted above.
[52] Suknovalov, 'Ekonomicheskaya Zhizn' ', p. 53.

based on the availability of raw materials or water power, or on considerations of public safety. Small-scale, state-owned lumbering operations, brickworks and quarries abounded in the region, spreading further and further afield as the escalating demand for building materials exhausted local supplies. Within this fairly sizable group of raw material oriented industries, individual operations engaged a few dozen workers at the most.[53] If we exclude the naval oriented activities at Kronshtadt and the various manufacturers at Narva, more distant still, then by far the largest industrial enterprise was the Sestroretskiy armaments plant. Located some thirty kilometres northwest of the city, it was built between 1721 and 1723 in order to use the water power potential of the Sestra River at a site near the Gulf of Finland. From all other points of view the location was disadvantageous. The fact that several hundred workers were engaged in the manufacture of small arms and miscellaneous metal products points to the overriding need for mechanical power.[54] To the south of the city water power also served to localize industrial operations. Stone-cutting and polishing near Peterhof, the newly created summer residence, and paper production at Krasnoye Selo are illustrations of this. But as a rule such operations were not very large and were usually appended to existing settlements. With slightly more than a hundred workers by the early 1720s, the Okhtenskiy gunpowder plant was the second largest outlying industrial enterprise.[55] Originally gunpowder was to be produced in a factory located just to the north of the St Peter and Paul Fortress on the bank of the Karpovka River but, by 1714 when production began, this part of Peterburgskiy Island was no longer devoid of settlement and the plant therefore constituted a hazard to public safety. Thus, a year later a factory was started on the Okhta River across the Bol'shaya Neva, a good distance beyond the settlement in Okhta itself. From this plant came most of the locally produced powder, while the smaller undertaking in the city concentrated on the development of production technology.[56] Generally speaking, industry outside the city

[53] For example, the Admiralty's sawmilling operation on the Izhora River was one of the notable exceptions; in 1724 it employed 124 workers. Suknovalov, 'Ekonomicheskaya Zhizn'', p. 72.

[54] P. G. Lyubomirov, *Ocherki po Istorii Russkoy Promyshlennosti XVII, XVIII i Nachalo XIX Veka* (Moscow, 1947), p. 332; Suknovalov, 'Ekonomicheskaya Zhizn'', p. 66; L. N. Semenova 'Masterovye i Rabotnye Lyudi v Pervye Desyatiletiya Sushchestvovaniya Peterburga', in S. N. Valk (ed.), *IRL* (1972), vol. I, p. 21.

[55] V. G. Geiman, 'Manufakturnye Predpriyatiya Peterburga', in A. V. Predtechenskiy (ed.), *Peterburg Petrovskogo Vremeni* (1948), p. 62.

[56] Suknovalov, 'Ekonomicheskaya Zhizn'', pp. 68–9; Geiman, 'Manufakturnye Predpriyatiya', pp. 61–2.

was small-scale and reflected the pervasive involvement of the state, while in the city there were many more large-scale establishments and by the early 1720s private enterprise was in evidence.

Industrial employment in St Petersburg fluctuated frequently, both according to season and demand. Its industries were in large measure geared to the needs of war and cyclical patterns of employment were usual. Moreover, huge contingents of men poured in during the summer to work in the building trades and in manufacturing. Hence, it is difficult to be precise in setting a firm figure to industrial employment, but it is probable that from about 1715 to 1725 the number of year-round workers averaged 4,000–5,000. The mainstay of industrial employment was the complex of activities associated with the Admiralty. It reached its peak in 1713 when 10,000 workers were occupied, a third of whom were full-time employees.[57] Thereafter, the work-force dwindled, a change brought about partly by the drain on the Exchequer which the steady pace of development produced, and partly by the shift of shipbuilding from the Baltic to the Black Sea. By the middle of the 1720s the work-force had been reduced by half. St Petersburg remained nevertheless one of the leading shipbuilding centres in Russia, with the Admiralty the dominant element in the city's industrial structure.[58] As a rule, enterprises manufacturing military equipment, arms, powder, uniforms and the like, engaged at most a few hundred persons. More often than not only a few dozen workers were involved. In terms of employment we know that the Arsenal ranked next to the Admiralty. As in shipbuilding, the impetus for development was the imperial *ukaz* and its execution depended upon bringing skilled craftsmen from elsewhere in Russia and from abroad. The first cannon foundry was set up in 1711 and four years later a much expanded Arsenal engaged about 200 craftsmen, three quarters of whom had been conscripted from the Moscow Arsenal that year.[59] By the mid-twenties roughly 150 more workers had been added; however, this was less than a tenth of the number employed by the Admiralty.[60] But irrespective of whether these manufacturing operations were located in the city or outside it, few of them were very large and fewer still bore much resemblance to factories.

In the absence of private initiative, such production as was needed

[57] Semenova, 'Masterovye i Rabotnye Lyudi', p. 15.
[58] For the rapid development of the Admiralty's skilled labour force, see Semenova, 'Masterovye i Rabotnye Lyudi', p. 14–15.
[59] Suknovalov, 'Ekonomicheskaya Zhizn'', p. 65.
[60] Semenova, 'Masterovye i Rabotnye Lyudi', p. 20.

to supplement armaments manufacture and to meet the needs of the population at large was taken up by the state (for example, rope-making, leather-working and the manufacture of woollen uniforms). The growth of the bureaucracy also expanded the demand for paper, printing and minting, and the state itself built plants to meet these demands. In 1719 Peter I created a college or ministry of manufacturers to coordinate production and generally to supervise their operation. But, just as significant, the Ministry expedited the take-over of some state operations and encouraged the development of others by private individuals. In the mid-1720s private enterprise was beginning to develop in manufacturing industry, but the rise of privately owned establishments in such widely assorted industries as leather, rope-making, sugar-refining, and especially fancy textiles like damask (to cater for the court and luxury market emerging in the new capital), often depended not merely on the permission of the state but on some kind of assistance from it.[61] For instance, wages were not the principal force propelling workmen into the city; imperial decrees were. By such means entrepreneurs were guaranteed a labour supply. Notwithstanding this and other inducements, there remained many gaps in the

TABLE 1. *Industrial structure, 1725*

Industrial group		Number of establishments
Textile		7
including:		
fancy textiles	2	
cordage	2	
Food products		7
including:		
milling	3	
Tanning, tallow and soap		4
including:		
tanning	3	
Printing and paper products		5
including:		
printing	3	
Admiralty complex and metal-working		5
Miscellaneous		4
Total		32

Sources: G. Bogdanov, *Istoricheskoye, Geograficheskoye i Topograficheskoye Opisaniye Peterburga, ot Nachala Zavedeniya Yego s 1703 po 1751 God.* (1779), pp. 106–13; P. N. Stolpyanskiy, *Zhizn' i Byt Peterburgskoy Fabriki za 1704–1914 gg.* (1925), pp. 26, 27, 37, 66, 70, 81.

[61] For general discussion, see E. I. Zaozerskaya, *Manufaktura pri Petre I* (Moscow 1947), p. 85; Semenova, 'Masterovye i Rabotnye Lyudi', pp. 28–9.

industrial structure. Although we cannot put employment figures to these establishments (aside from the few already mentioned), nor indeed be absolutely certain that all establishments have been listed, table 1 at least reveals the direction of industrial development to 1725. Additionally, there were something of the order of 1,500 artisans working in the city. However, many were not working for the market at large but for the Admiralty and Arsenal.[62] For the growing numbers at court, local manufacturers supplied little more than fancy textiles and tapestry and their needs had to be met mainly from abroad.

A number of things tended to stimulate commerce in the new capital. If factories and workshops between them could not keep abreast of local requirements, so too local limited agriculture failed to deliver all the foodstuffs required and these had to be shipped from distant places. To accommodate the movement of goods to and from the capital a network of overland routes was established and extensive canal construction started.[63] Although the peripheral location of the capital *vis-à-vis* Russia as a whole was seemingly an advantage for foreign trade, it was reinforced by imperial decrees. As early as 1710 merchants were prohibited from exporting grain through Arkhangel'sk, St Petersburg's northern rival. Thereafter, a flurry of *ukazi* steadily curtailed foreign trade activity at this port, finally reducing it to the export of products from the immediate hinterland.[64] As Arkhangel'sk went down, St Petersburg's position improved and in the process provided a substantial fillip to export oriented industries. Between 1718 and 1726 the total value of exports from Arkhangel'sk slipped from more than 2·3 million roubles to 285,000, whereas exports from the capital rose in value from 268,000 roubles to 2·4 million. Imports virtually ceased to pass through Arkhangel'sk while their value at St Petersburg in the mid twenties was almost three times what it had been at Arkhangel'sk less than a decade before.[65] Thus, in foreign trade the capital soon dominated all other ports and this position was bolstered in succeeding decades.[66]

The needs of commerce were attended to from the beginning. Along with the St Peter and Paul Fortress and port facilities, the construction of a Commodity Exchange and of the *Gostinyy Dvor*, a bazaar-like

[62] Suknovalov, 'Ekonomicheskaya Zhizn' ', p. 79.
[63] The Vyshnevolotskaya Canal, completed in 1709, was the first to link the capital with the Volga River and interior Russia.
[64] I. I. Lyubimenko, 'Torgovlya v Peterburge', *Peterburg Petrovskogo Vremeni*, p. 78.
[65] 'Znacheniye Peterburga vo Vneshney Torgovle Rossii', *ISPGD*, no. 23 (1899), pp. 294–5.
[66] Suknovalov, 'Ekonomicheskaya Zhizn' ', p. 89.

complex of retail and wholesale shops, was begun in 1703.[67] Foreign merchants began to take up residence in the city voluntarily. Russian merchants were not uncommonly dragooned into doing so. Warehouse facilities, wharves and market-places mushroomed. The Commodity Exchange or *Birzha* was rehoused several times before finally getting established on Vasil'yevskiy Island, but by the 1720s its functions had enlarged to provide detailed information on commodity prices throughout the various markets of the Russian interior ⟨*see* plate 8⟩. A ministry or college of commerce was established in 1716—three years ahead of that for manufacturing industry—and within a few years was serving as a regulatory and coordinative body for the city's bustling commercial economy.[68] Though we do not have details of the numbers deriving employment directly or indirectly from commerce, it was probably of the order of 2,000–3,000. Hundreds of *izvoshchiki* or waggoners were also needed to transfer wares arriving via the Bol'shaya Neva River to sea going vessels. Markets sprang up in various parts of the city to retail foodstuffs, clothing and similar day-to-day necessities, while still others were more specialized, dealing in hay, carriages and manufactured goods ⟨*see* plate 7⟩.[69] No matter what their function, all added to the sizable labour force involved in commerce. Russian merchants numbered 122 in 1725, according to one source, but there were in addition the resident foreign merchants, mostly Dutch and English, for whom unfortunately we have no total.[70] At any rate these men comprised the elite of the commercial scene, their activities being focused on the Commodity Exchange and *Gostinyy Dvor*.

The original *Gostinyy Dvor* was located on Peterburgskiy Island but within two decades there was another on Vasil'yevskiy Island and one in the Admiralteyskaya district. In the 1720s the commercial importance of these three areas was in a state of flux. One reason for this situation was the relocation of the port. The first one on Peterburgskiy Island proved inefficient and a new one was constructed along the Malaya Neva River on the eastern tip of Vasil'yevskiy Island. Meanwhile, to accommodate the rising volume of wares passing through the city, wharves were built in several places along the southern shore of the Bol'shaya Neva River. All three areas, therefore, were centres of

[67] Lyubimenko, 'Torgovlya v Peterburge', p. 85.
[68] Lyubimenko, 'Torgovlya v Peterburge', p. 81.
[69] Suknovalov, 'Ekonomicheskaya Zhizn'', pp. 82–3.
[70] Lyubimenko, 'Torgovlya v Peterburge', pp. 82–3. See also Kochin, 'Naseleniye Peterburga', p. 109.

shipping, a function which spawned a host of other commercial activities.

In little more than two decades St Petersburg became not only a major centre of shipbuilding and armaments but the leading port and an important component in the entire Russian commercial system. Its imperial role made a difference, of course, but the complexion of the local economy more and more reflected the processes of industrialization and commercialization that were being forced upon it. The pace of development faltered during the uncertain years following Peter's death; especially hard hit were the war industries where, with few exceptions, employment and production dropped. On the positive side the purposeful enrichment of court life during the reigns of Anna and Elizabeth (1730–61) had their material as well as cultural outcome. Factory production of glass, crystal and porcelain, among other luxury items, was added in response to this reorientation and in the process helped to diversify the capital's industrial structure.[71] Resuscitation of heavy industries had to await the second half of the century when the expansionist policies of Catherine II required it. The earlier growth of light, luxury manufacture for the ordinary market continued undiminished and was increasingly dominated by private capital. At mid century for instance, there were twenty-five privately owned enterprises; in 1797, 110 were operating.[72] While there are no employment data, we can safely assume that most were very small, often nothing much more than workshops. From the bare handful of private entrepreneurial endeavours in the city in 1725 the growth had been significant.

Something of the dimension of industrialization during the course of the eighteenth century is revealed by a list of manufacturing establishments compiled for 1794. Like the earlier data on the industrial structure, those in table 2 cannot be assumed to be especially precise, the main reason in this case being the omission of a number of state operations. While we have tried to account for this, the number of enterprises in each group and indeed the total employment of 6,000–7,000 should be regarded as a rough estimate only. Moreover, many establishments included in the survey were probably workshops. In the absence of any criteria by which to wean out the factories, we have to make do with the general trends conveyed by the data.

[71] Bogdanov, *Istoricheskoye Geograficheskoye i Topograficheskoye Opisaniye Peterburga*, pp. 129–33.
[72] V. M. Paneyakh, 'Masterovye i Rabotnye Lyudi vo Vtoroy Polovine XVIII Veka', *IRL*, p. 51.

In the textile and miscellaneous categories many private firms existed, most of which were geared to the luxury market. Spinning and weaving were decidedly unimportant, as compared with clothing manufacture. Just as the demands of the court precipitated the founding of many new enterprises, so did the administrative functions of the capital. The manufacture of paper and the number of printing firms expanded continuously. Growth was also rapid in the food and tobacco and the tanning, tallow and soap groups. Many of the eighty-five establishments in these categories continued to satisfy external

TABLE 2. *Industrial structure, 1794*

Industrial group		Number of establishments
Textile		55
including:		
clothing	34	
cordage	5	
Food and tobacco products		47
including:		
sugar refining	8	
tobacco	7	
Tanning, tallow and soap		38
including:		
tanning	14	
Printing and paper products		27
including:		
printing	18	
Metal-working		25
Miscellaneous		16
Total		217

Sources: K. K. Zlobin, 'Vedomost' Sostoyashchim v S. Peterburge Fabrikam Manifakturam i Zavodam na Sentyabr' 1794 g.', *Sbornik Russkago Istoricheskago Obshchestva,* I (1867), pp. 352–61 ; V. I. Makarov, 'Ekonomicheskaya Zhizn' Peterburga 60–90kh Godov XVIIIv', *Och.IL* (1955), vol. I, p. 278.

markets, both Russian and foreign, and in so doing maintained the city's importance in break-of-bulk processing. The rise of private enterprise took place in the consumers', rather than producers', goods sector, and for the most part filled long-standing gaps in the industrial structure. State-owned establishments in specialized lines like tapestry and porcelain far from being displaced, continued to receive international recognition. However, most of the production never entered the commercial market but instead embellished the imperial palaces. And in heavy industry the voluminous output from the Admiralty and Arsenal ensured both these organizations prominence in industry as a whole. Shipbuilding had been much developed since the sixties and, including the main Admiralty shipbuilding wharf, nine yards were now operating.[73] Metal-working was not well developed. Output was essentially military in focus or aimed at the luxury market.

Among the very few private ventures was that belonging to a Scotsman, Charles Baird. Established in 1794, it initiated the manufacture of steam engines in Russia.[74] Although this significant event occurred first in the private sector it should be borne in mind that, as in the time of Peter I, these operations came into existence by permission of, and often with assistance from, the state. The adoption of this particular innovation was comparatively late, and despite the fact that state-owned plants soon produced steam engines as well, on the whole the productive system did not stimulate technological change. Three features of Russian industrialization—paternalism, tariff protection and bureaucracy—must be charged with some measure of responsibility for this state of affairs. However, it must be recognized that technological expertise was growing, albeit slowly and with plentiful assistance from foreigners. Seen against the circumstance that, out of the Russian population of thirty-six million, roughly thirty-four million were serfs, in other words, peasants owned by the state, Church or private persons, even limited signs of industrialization take on added meaning. A growing number of the peasants who came and went worked for wages. The laboratories associated with the Admiralty, the Arsenal, the mint and other state enterprises did produce inventions on occasion. Not all were stillborn. Private enterprise was undoubtedly increasing and it accounted for the largest share of the manufacturing establishments set up since mid century.[75]

Although they did not form the largest group, those enterprises serving the local market in the 1790s had to cope with the demands of nearly a quarter of a million inhabitants, a number already greater than Moscow's population, and growing more rapidly.[76] The limited

[73] V. I. Makarov, 'Ekonomicheskaya Zhizn' ', *Och.IL* (1955), vol. I, pp. 255–6. In the Admiralty complex alone more than 120 vessels were built between 1762 and 1800.
[74] *Materialy ob Ekonomicheskom Polozhenii i Professional'noy Organizatsii, Peterburgskikh Rabochikh po Metallu* (1909), p. 2.
[75] Makarov, 'Ekonomicheskaya Zhizn' ', pp. 253, 262–3, 266...
[76] V. V. Pokshishevskiy, 'Territorial'noye Formirovaniye Promyshlennogo Kompleksa Peterburga v XVIII-XIX Vekakh', *Voprosy Geografii*, no. 20 (1950), p. 126. Moscow's population at this time was reckoned to be around 175,000. 'Territoriya i Naseleniye Moskvy', *Istoriya Moskvy* (Moscow, 1954), vol. III, p. 162.

purchasing power of peasants and most military personnel, the two dominant classes, was offset from the standpoint of industry first, by the fact that they still had to be fed, housed and clothed, and second, by the existence of the court, bureaucracy and growing commercial elite as a near insatiable market. The manufacture of luxury wares and general consumers' goods brought into existence not only many of the enterprises enumerated in table 2, but engaged as well several thousand handicraftsmen.[77] As Storch observed at the time:

> That in so large and opulent a city, the residence of a brilliant court, the necessary and useful trades should find employment, may be easily imagined; but perhaps it is not generally known, that, in a city of so modern a date, for the supply of not only the most necessary, but also of the most frivolous demands, for the simplest not more than for the most artificial conveniences, for the most curious as well as the most ordinary luxuries, here are artists and work-shops of all descriptions. Allured by the numerous wants of a great city, and the profusion of a court, many thousands of industrious and ingenious foreigners have been induced to settle here; by the continual influx of whom, and the communication of their talents, this residence is become not only the seat of all ingenious trades, but likewise a source of industry, which flows from hence in beneficial streams through all the adjacent provinces.[78]

Moreover, according to Storch, the earlier heavy reliance on imported luxury wares was a thing of the past:

> Most of the trades that relate to luxuries are here carried on to such an extent, and in so great perfection, as to render it, at least for the residence, unnecessary to import those articles from abroad. The chief of these are works in the nobler metals. Here are forty-four Russian and one hundred and thirty-nine foreign, consequently in all one hundred and eighty-three workers in gold, silver, and trinkets, as masters; and besides them several gilders and silverers;—a monstrous disproportion, when compared with those employed in the useful and indispensable businesses. The pomp of the court, and the luxury of the rich and great, have rendered a taste in works of this kind so common, and carried the

[77] Makarov, 'Ekonomicheskaya Zhizn'', p. 280; G. L. von Attengofer, *Mediko-Topograficheskoye Opisaniye Sanktpeterburga, Glavnago i Stolichnago Goroda Rossiiskoy Imperii* (1820), pp. 263–7.
[78] Storch, *Picture of St Petersburg*, p. 277.

49

art itself to such a pitch, that the most extraordinary objects of it are here to be met with.[79]

Though the case was somewhat overstated, it remains a fact that by the end of the eighteenth century handicraft manufacture had firmly taken root.

St Petersburg was above all else a centre of commerce. Trade more than industry had caused the population to grow, though in this connection we must not lose sight of the court, administrative and military roles fulfilled by the city. After mid-century, foreign trade grew by leaps and bounds, widening the gap between St Petersburg and its closest rival, Riga. Warehouses disgorged each spring enormous volumes of iron, hemp, flax and sailcloth. Loaded on British and Dutch ships for the most part, these and other Russian raw materials fed mouths and factories throughout Europe. According to Storch, this trade kept an average of 770 ships employed each year between 1775 and 1790 and by the latter date a thousand or more were clearing St Petersburg and Kronshtadt together.[80]

Transshipping goods to and from Kronshtadt was only one of the rapidly expanding functions tied in with the boom in trade. Warehouses, intra-urban transport facilities, commercial houses, agents and the like were similarly expected to rise to the occasion.[81] And as more jobs were created in the city, it became in turn a still larger market. The cumulative and circular impact, of course, had wide-ranging ramifications for the system of external relations. As Storch observed,

> The buying up of the foregoing articles, and their conveyance from the midland, and partly from the remotest regions of the empire, form an important branch of the internal commerce. The majority of these products are raised on the fertile shores of the Volga; this invaluable river, which, in its course, connects the most distant provinces, is at the same time the channel of business and industry . . . its course marks the progress of internal culture. But even from a distance of between five and six thousand versts, from the heart of Siberia, rich in metals, St Petersburg receives the stores of its enormous magazines. . . . This astonishing transport becomes still more interesting by the reflection that these products conveyed hither from the neighbourhood of the

[79] Storch, *Picture of St Petersburg*, p. 284.
[80] Storch, *Picture of St Petersburg*, p. 255.
[81] Makarov, 'Ekonomicheskaya Zhizn'', p. 285.

north-eastern ocean, tarry here but a few weeks, in order then to set out on a second, perhaps greater voyage: or after being unshipped in distant countries, return hither under an altered form; and, by a tedious and difficult navigation, come back to their native land. How many scythes of the Siberian boors may have gone this circuit.[82]

Indeed, around 325,000 roubles worth of scythes had been imported annually through St Petersburg between 1780 and 1790, a situation reflecting not inaccurately on the state of metal-working in the Empire. Topping the import ledger were sugar cane, items of silk and wool, and cloth, but predominant among imports were manufactured wares. Over half of all foreign trade was now conducted through St Petersburg, a share four times greater than that of Riga; and if we consider sea trade alone, the capital's share rises to two thirds.[83]

Within the city, the wealth of the merchant class was growing. Some of this wealth derived from foreign trade, but there were even more opportunities to engage in commerce of one kind or another at the local level. Again, Storch conveys the spirit of the time:

Traffic is their darling pursuit: every common Russian, if he can but by any means save up a trifling sum of money, as it is very profitable for him to do, by his frugal and poor way of living, tries to become a merchant. This career he usually begins as a *rasnoschtschik* or seller of things about the streets; the profits arising from this ambulatory trade and his parsimony soon enable him to hire a *lavka* or shop: where, by lending of small sums at large interest, by taking advantage of the course of exchange, and by employing little artifices of trade, he in a short time becomes a pretty substantial man. He now buys and builds houses and shops, which he either lets to others, or furnishes with goods himself, putting in persons to manage them for small wages; begins to launch out into an extensive trade, undertakes podriads, contracts with the crown for deliveries of merchandize, etc. The numerous instances of the rapid success of such people almost exceed description.[84]

The growing commercial success of peasants did not benefit only themselves, for they usually had to pay *obrok*, or quit rent, to their

---

[82] Storch, *Picture of St Petersburg*, pp. 262–3.
[83] Makarov, 'Ekonomicheskaya Zhizn' ', p. 289.
[84] Storch, *Picture of St Petersburg*, pp. 271–2.

owners for the opportunity to take part.[85] Among the dozen or so city markets, wharves and streets themselves, there was ample scope for private enterprise of this kind. Once established, membership in the various guilds (about which there will be more to say later), was essential to further progress. Guild membership in 1790 exceeded 1,650 persons. Despite some changes in the basis for belonging to the merchant guild, the tenfold growth since the 1720s did mirror the advances made in commercial activity. At the end of the century it was legitimate to claim that, 'St Petersburg is the first commercial town of the Russian empire, but it is by no means the principal seat of improving industry.'[86]

From time to time the government gave special recognition to successful industrialists; sometimes state orders and other forms of assistance initiated new industries or maintained existing ones. But these and other measures did not represent an explicit state policy of industrializing the country. Such industrialization as had occurred was not the outcome of government policy so much as the necessary by-product of war. Even had there been such a policy, Russia, with a predominantly agrarian economy and limited borrowing power abroad, could probably not have financed it.[87] From this perspective there was much in common between the range of economic opportunity open to Russia in general in the last half of the eighteenth and first half of the nineteenth centuries.

Tariffs were not unrelated to the progress of industrialization. Under Peter I domestic industry had been afforded some measure of protection. Given the prevailing atmosphere of military conflict such a position makes sense. Thereafter, much more of a free trade spirit obtained and lower tariffs reflected it. It was only from the late 1750s that protectionism gained momentum, once more consonant with the rising incidence of military conflict. Tariffs were revised four times in the latter half of the century and culminated in the very high duties imposed by Paul I in 1797. But by this time it was perfectly clear that the purpose of tariffs had widened to include three functions: 'to increase state revenue, to restore a favourable balance of trade, and to protect Russian industry.'[88] Tariffs could not serve each purpose

---

[85] For a general discussion of *obrok*, see P. I. Lyashchenko, *History of the National Economy of Russia to the 1917 Revolution* (New York, 1949), translated by L. M. Herman, pp. 315–16.

[86] Storch, *Picture of St Petersburg*, p. 273.

[87] William L. Blackwell, *The Beginnings of Russian Industrialization, 1800–1860* (Princeton, 1968), pp. 177–9.

[88] Blackwell, *Beginnings of Russian Industrialization*, p. 170.

equally since external forces often imposed priorities. During the early nineteenth century, the combination of the Continental Blockade and the Napoleonic War promoted rapid expansion of war-serving industries. A prohibitive tariff invoked in 1811 fostered industrialization during these troubled years but, immediately following the cessation of hostilities, the ground rules changed.[89] Alexander I, in keeping with the spirit of the times, introduced a new tariff structure in 1816, one which removed many prohibitions.[90] A further step toward free trade occurred in 1819 with predictable and disastrous consequences for domestic manufacturers. British, and to a lesser extent, Prussian goods poured into the home market, forcing a decline in Russian industrial production and in some instances closure of manufacturing establishments. This progressive debilitation of manufacturing could not be tolerated, politically, militarily or financially. By 1822 a new system of tariffs had been devised and implemented, and for nearly three decades most Russian industries were granted some measure of protection.[91] During the period of Nicholas I and his long-time minister of Finance, Count E. F. Kankrin (1822–44), such progress as occurred did not come from an explicit industrialization policy. Ambivalence, contradiction and compromise were the prevailing features of government decisions in this regard.

Following the raising of tariffs in 1822 (not infrequently for the purpose of increasing revenues rather than manufacturing output), the tempo of industrial growth quickened.[92] The stimulus this time emanated not from the war industries but from cotton textiles. The market for a cheap fabric in rural Russia was huge, even though cotton competed with domestically produced linen and wool. Behind a prohibitive tariff on cloth, but a lower one on yarn, the weaving, dyeing and printing of cotton fabric soared. The rise of the cotton textile industry was significant on two counts—volume of output and production technology. Woollen and linen wares were largely *kustar'* (small-scale rural handicraft) in origin, whereas large-scale factories typically turned out cotton fabric. The rescinding of the ban on exporting cotton textile machinery by Britain in 1842 spurred

[89] M. P. Vyatkin, 'Ekonomicheskaya Zhizn' Peterburga i Period Razlozheniya i Krizisa Krepostnichestva', *Och.IL* (1955), vol. I, p. 449; Blackwell, *Beginnings of Russian Industrialization*, p. 171.

[90] James Mavor, *An Economic History of Russia* (London, 1914), vol. I, p. 557.

[91] M. L. Tengoborskii, *Commentaries on the Productive Forces of Russia* (London, 1856), vol. I, p. 50.

[92] For some specific examples, see Walter M. Pintner, *Russian Economic Policy under Nicholas I* (Ithaca, 1967), pp. 222–32.

53

raw cotton imports and the spinning of cotton yarn in Russia. The industry finally broke free of the dependence on outdated French and Belgian equipment.[93] Large-scale, mechanized factory production had at last arrived in Russia and nowhere else with greater impact than in St Petersburg.

In the adoption of machine-production techniques, St Petersburg was in the forefront. Though it is unlikely that all state-owned factory output has been included in the following figures, they nevertheless bring out the relatively high technical level of industry in and around the capital. In 1852 the value of industrial production reached 31·5 million roubles in the *guberniya* or province. Employment was 21,500. Moscow and Vladimir *gubernii*, the other two principal industrial provinces, had value of output and employment figures of forty-five million and 103,000 and eighteen million roubles and 103,400 workers, respectively.[94] Part of the reason for these quite different relationships hinges on the relative development of factory as opposed to *kustar'* production. However, the fact that St Petersburg *guberniya* led in factory production should not be misconstrued. Russian industry as a whole was backward and thus to be at the forefront did not necessarily imply widespread use of sophisticated technology.[95] In fact, within St Petersburg an environment conducive to the adoption of factory production techniques was only just beginning to emerge.

In 1852, about 19,500 people found employment in the city's factories and the number was expanding fast. That the absolute increase in factory workers from 1800 to 1840 was equalled in the short period from 1846 to 1860 denotes the change of tempo.[96] But, once again, we need to maintain an overall perspective. The population in the area which we have delimited for analysis of urban industrialization exceeded half a million persons in 1852. The number of factory workers, if indeed all were factory workers, was still relatively small.[97] With such information as is available, something can be said about the distribution of workers among the major industrial groups and the way

[93] A. A. Radstig, 'Khlopchato-Bumazhnaya Promyshlennost' Rossii', *Ekonomicheskiy Zhurnal*, no. 3–4 (1891), pp. 12–13.

[94] Although some state enterprises are probably excluded from these figures, the general relationship still holds. P. Kryukov, *Ocherk Manufakturno-Promyshlennykh Sil Yevropeyskoy Rossii* (1853), end-flap table.

[95] Vyatkin, 'Ekonomicheskaya Zhizn'', pp. 459–60; Kryukov, *Ocherk Manufakturno-Promyshlennykh Sil*, pp. 174–8.

[96] A. I. Kopanev, *Naseleniye Peterburga v Pervoy Polovine XIX Veka* (Moscow, 1947), p. 58.

[97] Since individual factory employment is not available, we cannot separate the small-scale, handicraft oriented manufactures from the factories.

TABLE 3. *Industrial structure, 1852*

Industrial group	Number of establishments	Number of workers	Percentage
Metal-working	33	3,897	19·8
Chemical	28	298	1·5
Food and tobacco products	95	3,284	16·7
Tanning, tallow and soap	46	922	4·6
Paper and printing	54	804	2·3
Textile	85	9,537	47·4
Miscellaneous	20	1,129	5·7
Totals	361	19,671	100·0

Sources: P. Kryukov, *Ocherk Manufakturno-Promyshlennykh Sil Yevropeyskoy Rossii* (1853), pp. 174–86; *Materialy ob Ekonomicheskom Polezhenii i Professional'noy Organizatsii, Peterburgskikh Rabochikh po Metallu* (1909), pp. 3–8; 'O Tabachnykh Fabrikakh v S. Peterburge', *Zhurnal Ministerstva Vnutrennikh Del*, no. 11 (1852), p. 266; *Gorodskoy Ukazatel' ili Adresnaya Kniga na 1850* (1849) pp. 487–8. Employment in printing industries was estimated.

can be cleared for interpreting later events in the industrialization process ⟨*see* table 3⟩.

With almost half the industrial work-force at its disposal, textiles dominated the industrial structure and within this group the manufacture of cotton goods was paramount. The rapid growth of Russian cotton textile production is exemplified by the situation in the capital: in 1833 only 224 people were registered as working in cotton textiles; by 1852 more than 5,600 were so occupied.[98] Most of these were now employed in cotton spinning (4,600) which processed the bulk of the 25,465 tons of raw cotton entering St Petersburg customs in 1852.[99] Large-scale spinning factories were the most mechanized and capitalistic enterprises in the industrial structure.[100] Spinning had been vigorously expanded in other parts of the country, particularly in the Moscow and Vladimir *gubernii;* however, the capital possessed the greatest number of spindles and led in output. The manufacture of silk wares, employing around 1,600 and therefore a low second to cotton textiles, was essentially a small-scale operation and in this

[98] 'Mediko-Topograficheskiya Svedeniya o S. Peterburge', *Zhurnal Ministerstva Vnutrennikh Del*, no. 2 (1834), p. 185.
[99] *Gosudarstvennaya Vneshnyaya Torgovlya v Raznykh Yeya Vidakh za 1852 God.* (1854), table XII.
[100] For related discussion, see Reginald E. Zelnik, *Labor and Society in Tsarist Russia, the Factory Workers of St Petersburg, 1855–1870*, (Stanford, 1971), pp. 45–8.

respect an obvious contrast to cotton. Only the St Petersburg Silk Wares Company deviated from this pattern. Located in the suburban district of Shlissel'burg to the southeast of the city, it employed nearly 800 persons. For this company, as well as for the firms producing cotton yarn and cloth, the principal market was the Russian interior.[101]

The metal-working group ranked second in terms of the number of workers. Private enterprise had not yet penetrated this sector on a par with textiles but was making gradual headway. Often this process was aided by the state, lucrative contracts with government departments being a common means of fostering new industries. And while state-owned plants were still the largest enterprises, even in that sector foreign managers and leasing arrangements with private citizens assisted in developing entrepreneurial talents. Though there was still no consistent policy regarding industrialization, encouragement of private enterprise was undertaken in the hope that part of the demand for machinery and metal products might be met domestically.[102] The demand stemmed from the adoption of more modern production technologies and the requirements of an entirely new enterprise— railway construction.[103] Responding to these needs were people like Nobel, Lessner, San-Galli, Carr, and Macpherson, names which were to figure prominently in the industrialization of Russia. But at mid-century the only large-scale privately owned metal-working establish-ment was that belonging to Baird. Within the state sector, metal-working had been much augmented since the 1790s. For instance, the foundry side of the Arsenal's operation was bolstered with a new plant in the Vyborgskaya district. Shipbuilding was vigorously developed at Kolpino to the south of the capital as construction at the Admiralty was phased out after 1844, the building itself being turned over to non-industrial use. Still, the remaining wharves in the city and the new Admiralty operation being developed further along the Bol'shaya River ensured the continuing importance of shipbuilding.[104] Together, state and private enterprises accounted for the bulk of machine-construction and foundry output in Russia. There is no doubt that such

[101] Tengoborskii, *Commentaries*, p. 505; Kryukov, *Ocherk Manufakturno-Promyshlennykh Sil*, pp. 176, 178, 185.
[102] *Materialy ob Ekonomicheskom Polozhenii*, pp. 3, 9.
[103] The first railway linked the capital with the nearby imperial residence at Tsarskoye Selo and was completed in 1837. Construction of the St Petersburg–Moscow line began in the forties. For discussion, see Blackwell, *Beginnings of Russian Industrialization*, pp. 279–302.
[104] Vyatkin, 'Ekonomicheskaya Zhizn'', pp. 463, 468; Pokshishevskiy, 'Territorial'noye Formirovaniye Promyshlennogo Kompleksa', p. 142; T. M. Kitanina, 'Rabochiye Peter-burga v Period Razlozheniya i Krizisa Krepostnichestva (1800–1861 gg.)', *IRL*, pp. 75, 83.

developments down to mid-century were significant.[105] Yet once again we should not overlook the fact that St Petersburg's importance was a relative thing; moreover, its products were customarily of inferior quality and cost more than their closest imported substitutes.

Within the food and tobacco products group, sugar-refining and tobacco led in employment. Over 1,100 workers in more than twenty plants helped process the 28,700 tons of raw cane sugar entering the city in 1852. The St Petersburg refiners had long complained of the growing competition from beet sugar produced in southwestern Russia.[106] But despite the high revenue oriented tariff on imported raw cane and only a minimal levy on domestic product, two thirds of Russian consumption was satisfied by refined cane, and of this the capital's factories had the lion's share of the business.[107] It was an industry, however, which had reached its zenith. The processing of tobacco, on the other hand, was on the threshold of considerable expansion and there were clear signs of a shift away from the small workshop-like operation to large-scale factories. Indeed, five of these already employed more than a hundred workers each.[108]

In the paper and printing group the manufacture of the former stood out in terms of employment, even though there were only two plants.[109] Additional to the long-standing state-owned operation on the Fontanka Canal which produced specialized, high quality papers for government offices, was the Vargunin establishment. This plant, founded in 1839 in Shlissel'burg, was also technically quite advanced. It employed around 300 people, utilized steam power and turned out a high quality, rag-content paper and cardboard.[110]

Of the three remaining groups, only tanning and related manufactures, and carriage production employed numbers of any consequence.

[105] For example, as late as 1854 St Petersburg *guberniya* accounted for more than 60 per cent of total labour force and three quarters of the total value of production in Russia. A. Yeshov, 'O Znachenii Mekhanicheskago Iskusstva i o Sostoyanii Yego v Rossii', *Vestnik Promyshlennosti*, no. 3 (1859), pp. 265–9.
[106] Pinter, *Russian Economic Policy*, pp. 224–5.
[107] The city's factories doubtless processed most of the 28,700 tons of raw sugar cane imported in 1852. *Gosudarstvennaya Vneshnyaya Torgovlya*, table XII.
[108] 'O Tabachnykh Fabrikakh v S. Peterburge', *Zhurnal Ministerstva Vnutrennikh Del*, no. 11 (1852), p. 268.
[109] Only two factories produced paper, three others turned out items made of paper. There were forty eight printing establishments listed in the directory for which employment has been estimated and included in table 3. As they could not be located, the printing industry had to be omitted from map 10. *Gorodskoy Ukazatel' ili Adresnaya Kniga na 1850 g.* (1849), pp. 435–6.
[110] A. Sh., 'O Pischebumazhnom Proizvodstve v Rossii Voobshche i Bumagodelatel'noy Fabrike Brat'yev Varguninykh v Osobennosti', *Zhurnal Manufaktur i Torgovli* no. 1 (1852), pp. 405–9.

In neither case was there yet any sign of modern factory production. Moreover, carriage manufacture in the city was steadily withering in the face of competition from English manufacturers which began late in the eighteenth century. As was so often the case, quality overcame duties and higher prices.[111]

The appearance of factories in St Petersburg often reflected direct government support of one kind or another and we might be excused for assuming that this was regarded as a positive step in modernizing the economy of both the city and the Empire. In fact, the response of Nicholas I, and hence of the government, was frequently negative and on occasion alarmist. Industrialization in itself was not always the main concern but rather, the interplay of industrialization and urbanization. In St Petersburg *guberniya* the labour supply was essentially an urban one. Manufacturing establishments, therefore, were strongly attracted to the city and by 1852 were found throughout the built-up city centre as well as in suburban districts like Shlissel'burg and Vyborg ⟨*see* map 10⟩.

This intrusion of industry and its work-force raised the spectre of European industrial cities with all their attendant horrors.[112] For many people the question of health and sanitation was uppermost; for a larger number still a growing proletariat posed the threat of civil disorder, of which European urban-industrial society provided innumerable relevant examples. In St Petersburg legislation was introduced in 1833 to limit industrial growth within the heavily built-up parts of the city, though only that of a noxious variety.[113] It has been plausibly argued that this set of zoning regulations was nothing more than an attempt to control urban industrialization under the guise of invoking sanitary regulations.[114] The 1833 legislation was certainly not the first of its kind. As early as 1759 certain noxious manufactures had been relegated to outlying, and downstream, locations.[115] Indeed, even

---

[111] K. Nellis, 'Ekipazhnoye Proizvodstvo', *Fabrichno-Zavodskaya Promyshlennost' i Torgovlya Rossii* (1896), pp. 402–6.

[112] Zelnik, *Labor and Society*, pp. 24–9. Industry was far from relegated to the peripheral and suburban regions as map 10 makes clear. The recently completed Obvodnyy Canal (1834) served as a focus for some new industries, especially to the south outside the restricted zone, but there were at least as many to the north of it. Zelnik, quoting contemporary observations and citing other non-cartographic evidence concludes that centrifugal forces were predominant by the late 1830s (pp. 58–61). Such judgements were certainly questionable and were to remain so for decades as we shall later establish. See also Pokshishevskiy, 'Territorial'noye Formirovaniye Promyshlennogo Kompleksa', pp. 143–8.

[113] For details, see 'O Naznachenii Mest Dlya Fabrik i Zavodov v S. Peterburge', *Zhurnal Ministerstva Vnutrennikh Del*, no. 10 (1833), pp. i–xiv.

[114] Zelnik, *Labor and Society*, pp. 22–6, 61–2; Pintner, *Russian Economic Policy*, p. 98.

[115] Makarov, 'Ekonomicheskaya Zhizn' ', p. 273.

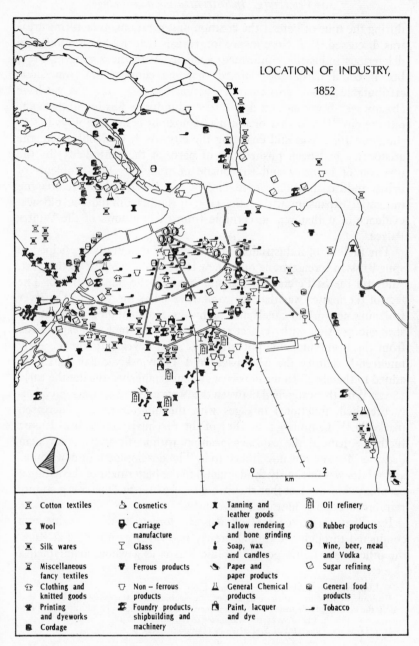

LOCATION OF INDUSTRY,
1852

⟨icon⟩ Cotton textiles	⟨icon⟩ Cosmetics	⟨icon⟩ Tanning and leather goods	⟨icon⟩ Oil refinery
⟨icon⟩ Wool	⟨icon⟩ Carriage manufacture	⟨icon⟩ Tallow rendering and bone grinding	⟨icon⟩ Rubber products
⟨icon⟩ Silk wares	⟨icon⟩ Glass	⟨icon⟩ Soap, wax and candles	⟨icon⟩ Wine, beer, mead and Vodka
⟨icon⟩ Miscellaneous fancy textiles	⟨icon⟩ Ferrous products	⟨icon⟩ Paper and paper products	⟨icon⟩ Sugar refining
⟨icon⟩ Clothing and knitted goods	⟨icon⟩ Non – ferrous products	⟨icon⟩ General Chemical products	⟨icon⟩ General food products
⟨icon⟩ Printing and dyeworks	⟨icon⟩ Foundry products, shipbuilding and machinery	⟨icon⟩ Paint, lacquer and dye	⟨icon⟩ Tobacco
⟨icon⟩ Cordage			

MAP 10. *Location of industry, 1852*

59

during the time of Peter I the creation of separate manufacturing areas was discussed.[116] A close inspection reveals that in 1852 a number of deleterious industries conformed, spatially, with the zoning of 1833; but it could hardly be claimed that the conformation was alone attributable to this particular legislation ⟨*see* map 11⟩. As we have already seen from map 10, non-restricted industry was found throughout the city.[117] Whether or not it was noxious is in some ways beside the point for it was still changing the city. As J. G. Kohl noted, the aristocracy had been pushed out of parts of the central city 'by the invasion of industry and the bustle of trade'.[118] The problems of urban industrialization would clearly not be solved by redirecting industrial expansion within the city; it simply diluted the physical evidence of it that was discernible from the windows of the Winter Palace.

The fuelling of industrialization, literally and figuratively, helped to spur Russian foreign trade on to new levels from one year to the next. And still the St Petersburg customs handled the bulk of traffic. The fact of the matter was that the capital served as the vortex of an ever widening network of canals and highways. Commanding a potentially strategic position with respect to the waterways of European Russia from the beginning, this potential was soon developed. By the early nineteenth century the Mariinskiy and Tikhvinskiy canals had been added to the old Vyshnevolotskaya system established during the early 1700s. With the watershed between the Neva and Volga rivers effectively breached, functional linkages with the interior regions increased markedly.[119] Completion in 1851 of the first major railroad in Russia further enhanced the capital's position within the transport system because Moscow was now linked to it. The development of new routes and modes was obviously fundamental to the betterment of the national economy, but the fact that they were focused on St Petersburg simply reinforced existing locational advantages.

By 1852, 38 per cent of all Russian foreign trade by value was conducted through the capital, nearly five times as much as at Riga, the other main Baltic port.[120] While Russia as a whole maintained a

---

[116] Luppov, *Istoriya Stroitel'stva Peterburga*, pp. 23–4.
[117] While we have no plant-size data, it will be established in the following chapter that among the central city factories were a good many very large ones. For additional information, see A. Grech, *Ves' Peterburg v Karmane* (1851), pp. 233–4, 387–8.
[118] J. G. Kohl, *Panorama of St Petersburg* (London, 1852), p. 13.
[119] Vyatkin, 'Ekonomicheskaya Zhizn'', pp. 497–503 for details.
[120] *Gosudarstvennaya Vneshnyya Torgovlya*, table XII.

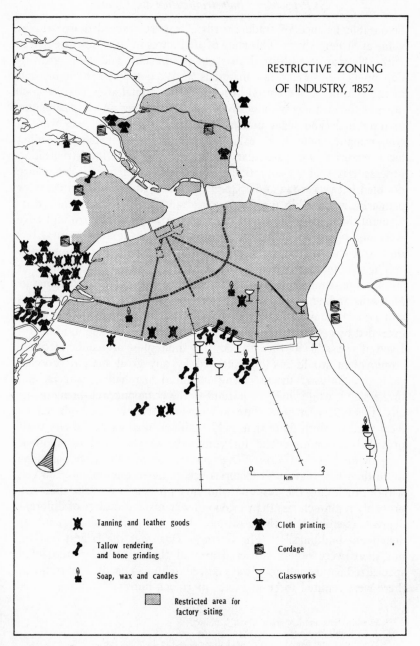

RESTRICTIVE ZONING
OF INDUSTRY, 1852

𝕏	Tanning and leather goods	👕	Cloth printing
🦴	Tallow rendering and bone grinding	⬛	Cordage
🕯	Soap, wax and candles	Y	Glassworks
▨	Restricted area for factory siting		

MAP 11. *Restrictive zoning of industry, 1852*

61

favourable balance of trade in 1852, imports exceeded exports by value at St Petersburg. This state of affairs was in large measure tied in with the rise of industrial markets in the city and their growing dependence on foreign raw materials.[121] We noted earlier the increase in the volume of raw cotton brought to the capital after 1842, a good portion of which was spun locally. For a much longer time large amounts of unrefined cane sugar poured into the city's mills. There were of course many, many more examples of foreign raw materials feeding local factories. Of particular significance for the industrialization process was coal consumption. The volume used in St Petersburg doubled between 1822 and 1840.[122] Steam engines and smelters were primarily responsible for the increase and in both cases the 1840s brought demands to new heights.[123] In terms of value, coal and coke were not significant items on the import ledger at mid-century, but they were showing up increasingly and would soon figure prominently.

The voluminous foreign trade carried on in St Petersburg was simply one manifestation of its importance as a centre of commerce. Notwithstanding gains in factory production since the 1790s, it was still a court-administrative and commercial city. Employment in trade exceeded by a wide margin the nearly 20,000 who worked in industry. Even if we add to this 20,000 the thousands of handicraftsmen, employment would not be exceeded by any great margin. Foreign trade and industry usually brings to mind merchants, bankers, and brokers and, while vitally important to the economic well-being of the city, this entrepreneurial elite was obviously vastly outnumbered by local traders. With more than half a million inhabitants the city itself provided enormous scope for commerce of one kind or another. Employment in the *Gostinyy Dvor* on the Nevskiy Prospect was alone more than half that in all factories according to one observer: 'Even without including the peasants who offer provisions for sale, there are probably not much less than 10,000 merchants and dealers of different degrees assembled in the gostinnoi dvor of St Petersburg, and its dependent buildings.'[124] The *Gostinyy Dvor* was the largest market, but there were others scattered around the city. Many were of a specialized nature and not always geared to human needs. For example, there were reputed to be in excess of 50,000 horses, a number rather

121 Vyatkin, 'Ekonomicheskaya Zhizn'', p. 497.
122 J. G. Kohl, *Russia* (London, 1842), p. 194.
123 Wood was, and would remain, unchallenged as the domestic fuel.
124 Kohl, *Russia*, p. 50.

greater, proportionally, than in any other European city. 'The consumption of hay, accordingly, is enormous' wrote Kohl in the late 1830s. 'In summer, whole fleets, laden with mountains of hay, come floating down the Neva; and in winter, caravans of hay sledges defile through the streets, and are drawn up in squadrons and regiments along the sides of the Sennaia Ploshtshod.'[125] All told, the dozen or so markets had a trade turnover running into millions of roubles.[126] To be sure, it was only a fraction of the business done with foreign countries and the interior markets, but it required many more transactions and hence participants. The volume of business was one matter, the way in which it was frequently conducted was quite another. Russians had a deserved reputation for questionable transactions. But as Kohl notes:

> The Russian way of cheating is quite peculiar to the people; they do it with so much adroitness, one may almost say with so much grace, that it is difficult to be angry with them . . . [the merchant] cannot conceive why any one should object to pay four times any more than twice the value of a thing, and is therefore as unconcerned as a conjurer over his tricks.[127]

In addition to industry and trade, one other component of the urban economy offered an opportunity to earn a livelihood. This was transport. During the ice-free season several thousand peasants were engaged in transporting wares along the many canals and waterways. On land, all the year round, there was money to be earned by moving people as well as goods. To peasants owning horses and living near the capital, potential earnings were sufficient to induce thousands to assemble a *telega*, a type of goods-moving waggon, or a *droshky*, the one-horse, two-passenger cab, and set out to try their luck ⟨*see* plate 19⟩. Few did well, if only because of the competition. According to Kohl, there were as many as 8,000 *izvoshchiki* or drivers registered in the city: 'In some quarters you may see hundreds at one glance. . . .'[128] The *droshky* was necessary in so extensive a city, especially when public transport in the form of the omnibus and other multi-passenger vehicles was little developed.[129] Of course, anyone of consequence had his own coach and horses. Most people had little alternative but to use their own feet. A few occasionally rode by omnibus or by *droshky*. For travellers the latter had seldom inspired confidence: 'It has at first

125 Kohl, *Russia*, p. 51.
126 Vyatkin, 'Ekonomicheskaya Zhizn' ', p. 502.
127 Kohl, *Russia*, p. 64.
128 Kohl, *Russia*, p. 37.
129 See P. Possart, *Wegweiser Für Fremde in St Petersburg* (Heidelberg, 1842), pp. 258–61.

sight an appearance extremely odd and ridiculous. It bears not the least affinity to any of our wheel-carriages, but looks more like a gigantic insect of the grasshopper tribe, pursuing and clinging to the heels of an affrighted horse.'[130] The Englishman, Laurence Oliphant, writing in 1853 was comparatively charitable. 'If locomotion by the droshky be not enjoyable,' he said, 'it has the merit of being, in the first place, singular, from the manner in which the passenger seats himself across a cushion behind the driver; and, secondly, exciting from the extreme difficulty he finds retaining his seat there, which is considerably increased when a wheel comes off—an incident of not unfrequent occurrence.'[127] ⟨*see* plate 24.⟩ Irrespective of the technology involved, the business of moving people and products within the city occupied a prominent place in the urban economy.

'St Petersburg, in fact, like most Russian cities, is a place of rendezvous.'[132] Kohl's observation applied to most sectors of society, but it had special significance for the peasantry. Peter I had employed vast armies of conscripted labour and had willingly ascribed peasants to industrial enterprises all over the country.[133] But in terms of a work-force, the peasantry gradually lost its utility as skill requirements rose, as factory technology came to be more complex and as costs of main-taining ascribed labourers grew. There was another alternative. Using the rural system of quit rent or *obrok* there emerged a tradition of allowing peasants to seek work on a temporary basis in factories, or wherever else it was available. Early in the eighteenth century employers, state and private, began tapping this enormous pool of labour, paying wages and accepting a high turnover. As opportunities expanded, serf-owners in the less bountiful agricultural regions were quick to recognize that they stood to gain by permitting their peasants to seek outside work for cash instead of extracting an income from the peasants' agricultural occupations alone.[134] Large numbers of furloughed peasants (*otkhodniki*) migrated to the cities, and St Petersburg was a

---

[130] F. Shoberl, *The World in Miniature, Russia* (London, no date), vol. I, pp. 140–41.
[131] Laurence Oliphant, *The Russian Shores of the Black Sea* (Edinburgh, 2nd edn, 1853), p. 2.
[132] Kohl, *Russia*, p. 52. He observes further that 'The mass of the population of St Petersburg undergoes a complete change in less than ten years.'
[133] Ascribed or assigned peasants were put to work in industry and mining on large scale by Peter I in order to overcome the shortage of hired labour in the early eighteenth century. By the end of the century, several hundred thousand state-owned peasants, paupers, criminals and the like had been assigned to privately owned enterprises. For a discussion, see Jerome Blum, *Lord and Peasant in Russia from the Ninth to the Nineteenth Century* (New York, 1964), pp. 308–18.
[134] Lyashchenko, *History of the National Economy*, pp. 315–16.

major destination. Very often they stayed only for the winter, arriving in the autumn after harvest and departing in time for spring sowing. For others the pattern was reversed, and for still others, sojourns lasted a year or more. Before the eighteenth century drew to a close, hired labour was the rule rather than the exception in St Petersburg and several other industrial centres.[135] By the 1840s about 150,000 of the city's 450,000 inhabitants were *obrok*-paying peasants, mostly men working in all major sectors of the urban economy.[136] Upon entering the city an elaborate bureaucracy was supposed to check their credentials and upon the expiration of their usually short-term permits, see to their ejection.[137]

The legal attachment of the peasant urban worker to the countryside was perceived by many concerned citizens as one mitigating feature of industrialization in Russia.[138] There was a real concern over the possible creation of an urban proletariat which could conceivably rise up against the existing social and political order. The argument went that, if the peasant remained a peasant and was not estranged from village life, he could not become part of a proletariat. Notwithstanding such reassurances, by the 1830s events were openly beginning to contradict the basis for them. Up to this time the peasant labourer was still generally regarded as being the same as any other peasant. As such, he was expected to do as his owner bid him—irrespective of any commitment to an employer. But, with the rapid development of factory production, especially in cotton textiles, conflict over whose interests took precedence increased dramatically and demanded resolution.[139] After considerable deliberation, in 1835 legislation clarifying the relationship between factory-owners and hired labour was enacted. All conditions of employment were to be made explicit and recorded. But, having gone this far, the government has in effect recognized the peasant factory worker as being part of a separate economic class—one without any basis in the existing juridical class system. Whether or not the legislation was enforced, the peasant factory worker was, within the framework of his labour contract, more

---

[135] Makarov, 'Ekonomicheskaya Zhizn' ', pp. 252, 279–80.

[136] 'Naseleniye S. Peterburga', *Zhurnal Ministerstva Vnutrennikh Del*, no. 5 (1844), pp. 481–2. Most of these were seigneurial peasants.

[137] The organization concerned was the *Adresnaya Kontora*, or Address Office. See Zelnik, *Labor and Society*, p. 20.

[138] Efforts to locate industry in the countryside were another manifestation of this point of view. For related discussion, see Zelnik, *Labor and Society*, pp. 23–5.

[139] Zelnik, *Labor and Society*, pp. 30–34.

proletarian than peasant. With each additional piece of labour legislation the difference was accentuated.[140]

Labour legislation usually appeared in response to some crisis or blatant abuse no longer tolerable. For instance, as the cost of hired workers rose, there was a tendency to use the cheapest form, specifically women and children. By the 1840s employment of children in factories was extensive, had precipitated discontent and clearly demanded some form of government action. Thus, in 1845 the first law concerning child labour was promulgated.[141] Because it only restricted the employment of children aged twelve and under to day work, that is, from early morning to midnight, this law was essentially emasculative. Children of twelve and over could be kept at night-work, and actually were. The use of child labour in St Petersburg was far from unknown and in fact for one group of children was positively encouraged. The children in question were foundlings supplied to factories by the St Petersburg Foundling Home. Established in 1770 by Catherine II, it had, by the turn of the century, gone some distance toward one of its chief objectives—to make of the foundlings a useful, skilled, urban-oriented labour force.[142] The state-owned Aleksandrovskiy plant to the south of the city served as a training ground for thousands of such children during the early part of the nineteenth century. The plant was the first in the area to spin cotton; it produced items of silk; there was a machine construction division; and in general it served to advance technological expertise in the Empire.[143] In 1804 there were almost 600 foundlings in the work-force. John Quincy Adams, visiting the mill in 1810, admired the physical plant but said of the foundlings themselves that they looked 'for the most part wretchedly, and very unwholesome.'[144] A paper manufactory in Peterhof established by English industrialists upon the invitation of Alexander I, engaged about 800 of them when Kohl described the operation around the late 1830s.[145] By this time, placement with private enterprises, especially of those aged twelve to fourteen, was on the rise. Whether foundlings or not, children

[140] Zelnik, *Labor and Society*, pp. 40–42.
[141] I. A. Baklanova, 'Formirovaniye i Polozheniye Promyshlennogo Proletariata,' *IRL*, p. 113; Zelnik, *Labor and Society*, p. 37.
[142] F. A. Tarapygin, *Materialy Dlya Istorii Imperatorskago S. Peterburgskago Vospitatel'-nago Doma* (1878), pp. 3–4.
[143] For details, see Blackwell, *Beginnings of Russian Industrialization*, pp. 46, 63, 396.
[144] C. F. Adams (ed.), *Memoirs of John Quincy Adams* (Philadelphia, 1874), p. 112. The United States Minister to Russia was similarly impressed when he visited the operation in the late thirties. Susan Dallas (ed.), *Diary of George Mifflin Dallas* (Philadelphia, 1892), pp. 91–2.
[145] Kohl, *Russia*, p. 128.

were an annually increasing component of the labour force. The 1845 law did little to change the trend. In fact, some argue that by focusing on the under-twelve age group, it simply enhanced the employment of children over twelve. Probably about 5 per cent of the factory labour force was made up of children at mid century.[146] In the St Petersburg textile and tobacco plants where they were most commonly used the share was naturally much greater. Like factory labourers in general the children were usually illiterate, frequently itinerant and increasingly impoverished. Real economic gains were all too easily lost to demands for increased *obrok*.

Incipient industrialization had left its mark by the middle of the nineteenth century. Factories, on occasion large and mechanized, were part of the urban landscape—though by no means a welcome one. The factory labour force was each year larger than the year before and therefore more noticeable. Important changes in the city's economy, in its physical appearance and in its population had been set in motion. It now remains to sketch a broad panorama of civic society before the advent of rapid urban industrialization.

3 THE URBAN MILIEU

We noted earlier that there were 40,000 people living in the city when Peter I died in 1725, a sizable number indeed given the prevalent aversion to voluntary residence. Although reliable population counts are few and far between, it appears that by the late thirties there were more than 75,000 inhabitants and by 1750 around 95,000.[147] From the early 1760s annual population statistics have been computed and provide a reasonable guide to what was happening within the official city borders.[148] The rate of growth during the time of Catherine II was not entirely consistent, as figure 1 indicates. From an annual increment of about 2,000 per year in the sixties and seventies to more than double that in the 1780s, the last half dozen years of her reign witnessed near stagnation. This phenomenom was partly attributable to a hefty increase in the death-rate. As we shall see in later chapters, disease and death were eventually to assume epidemic proportions on an almost annual basis. At any rate, not only had Catherine transformed the

---

[146] Estimate is based on data in Baklanova, 'Formirovaniye i Polozheniye Promyshlennogo Proletariata', p. 96.
[147] *Entsiklopedicheskiy Slovar'*, p. 295; Kochin, 'Naseleniye Peterburga', p. 102.
[148] *Entsiklopedicheskiy Slovar'*, pp. 312–13.

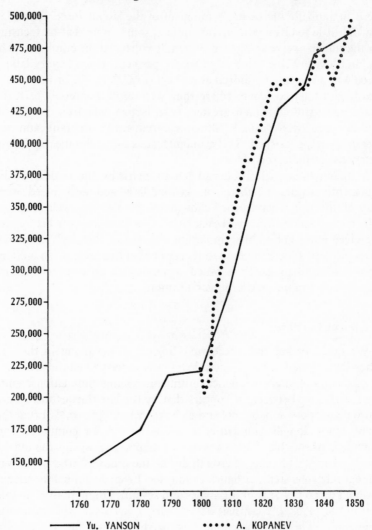

FIG. I. *Population growth, 1764–1850*

fabric of the capital, but 75,000 people had been added to it in the process.

What happened in the 1790s contrasts sharply with the tumultuous growth in the first quarter of the nineteenth century. The catalyst in this period was the Napoleonic War. Emigration from Moscow, industrial growth stemming from the demand for war materials, building construction precipitated by the population influx, these and other factors combined to push in-migration to a pitch unknown since the massive conscriptions initiated by Peter I. By 1825 Moscow's 258,000 population was still marginally below the pre-war level, whereas the capital's had been swollen by more than 100,000 and now topped 420,000.[149] In total, 200,000 more people resided in the city than in the 1790s. Population growth was again rapid in the late thirties, but clearly began to taper off in the following decade and according to A. Kopanev's data declined in absolute terms.

A massive increase in the number of deaths combined with a diminution of in-migration were together responsible for the changes in population after 1840. Not only were population totals erratic in the sense of not always demonstrating growth from one year to the next, but it was also the case that sizable fluctuations could occur within any particular year. For instance, the number of inhabitants in August was sometimes less than the preceding January.[150] This state of affairs was dictated not just by the comings and goings of peasants but by the social habits of the 'better' classes during the summer months: 'On the appearance of this delightful season,' wrote Dr Granville in the late 1820s, 'the Court, the principal families, the merchants, and even the better sort of tradesmen quit the parched and dusty streets of St Petersburgh.'[151]

Those who did not have estates on which to idle away the season, frequently 'betook themselves' to the islands and villages around the capital as the latter was not a place to be seen during the summer. Combined with the itineracy imposed on the peasantry, the consequence was that the summer exodus on occasion exceeded the influx of peasant workmen. By 1850 about 487,000 people resided within the official city boundaries and around 520,000 within the urban area as we have defined it for the purpose of our analysis.[152] In the absence of any formal census, an accurate delineation of population growth is difficult to obtain.[153] Sources other than those used in figure 1, for example,

[149] A. I. Kopanev, 'Naseleniye Peterburga ot kontsa XVIII v do 1861g.', *Och.IL* (1955), vol. I, p. 510; 'Territoriya i Naseleniye Moskvy', p. 162.
[150] Kopanev, *Naseleniye Peterburga v Pervoy Polovine XIX Veka*, p. 15.
[151] A. B. Granville, *St Petersburgh* (London, 1828), vol. I, p. 505. See also Attengofer, *Mediko-Topograficheskoye Opisaniye Sanktpeterburga*, p. 117.
[152] Total population figure based on 'Narodonaseleniye S. Peterburga v 1852 godu', *Vestnik Imperialisticheskago Geograficheskago Obshchestva*, II (1852), pp. 62–3; A. K., *Vedomost' o Narodonaselenii Rossii po Uyezdam, Guberniy i Oblastey* (1850), pp. 30–31.
[153] The first formal enumeration of the population did not occur until 1864.

sometimes give different totals for particular years but the general patterns of change are similar.[154] One thing was certain, however: with roughly 200,000 more inhabitants than Moscow, St Petersburg was indisputably the largest urban centre in the Empire at mid century. In the years up to the Great War it was to retain that pride of place.

That population growth was closely tied to in-migration comes as no surprise. The nature of in-migration in turn had a direct bearing on the demographic make-up of the population and on the potential birth-rate. Put simply, there was a preponderance of males, an imbalance noticeable at the time of the initial conscription of labourers and the build-up of the garrison forces. By 1750, only 39 per cent of the population was female, though it is conceivable that this share was actually higher than during the somewhat abnormal conditions of the first quarter century.[155] After 1750 the data are more plentiful and presumably more reliable. They show that the intensified migration of the late eighteenth century was overwhelmingly male. This is not unexpected, for it was the *obrok*-paying male peasant who in largest numbers was descending upon the city in search of work. Thus, by 1789 the female portion of the population had dwindled to about 32 per cent. Eleven years later the share had dipped to 30 per cent. In exceptional years males came in such numbers as to tip the scale even more heavily. One such year was 1825. Having arrived in order to clear the aftermath of the preceding year's flood, the worst ever, there were sufficient numbers of peasant labourers in the city to push the female percentage down to 28·5.[156] The situation had altered little by the early 1830s and we can see from map 12 that there was a distributional imbalance as well as a structural one. Most females resided in the inner city boroughs, particularly Liteynaya, where nearly half the population was female. What were perceived as lower-class areas, Moskovskaya borough, for instance, and most of the peripheral ones, were male domains. The dearth of females and the peripatetic habits of the largest group, the peasantry, resulted in fewer families being brought to, or established in, the city than the total population would otherwise suggest. This meant the absolute number born each year was small.

[154] For instance, see 'Naseleniye S. Peterburga', p. 477; Granville, *St Petersburgh*, p. 405.
[155] Kochin, 'Naseleniye Peterburga', p. 103.
[156] For a description of the flood and the problem in general, see *Prodrobnoye Istoricheskoye Izvestiye o Vsekh Navodneniyakh Byvshikh*. The flood of 1824, of course, is the subject of one of Pushkin's celebrated poems, *The Bronze Horseman*.

1 Life in St Petersburg was much affected by the long, dark winters. For people of position and wealth it was the season to be resident in the capital. For the masses daily life was more difficult, though the frozen conditions offered some respite from epidemics. This lithograph affords a glimpse of the hustle and bustle produced by the Sennaya Market, which straddled Sadovaya Street. From P. Gaimard, *Voyages en Scandinavie au Spitzberg et aux Feroe* (Paris, 1842–52), vol. II, no. 255.

2 The physical environment of St Petersburg made building the city a monumental task. Once built up, many areas were regularly inundated. This painting gives some idea of how low-lying much of the city was. It shows the eastern tip of Vasil'yevskiy Island, or the Strelka, with its port and commercial buildings. In the background is Peterburgskiy Island with the spire of Trezzini's St Peter and Paul Orthodox Church rising up behind the walls of the fortress. From a painting by G. Atkinson dating from around the end of the eighteenth century.

3 Vasil'yevsky Island was more than the hub of commercial life during the eighteenth century; it also contained a variety of educational and scientific institutions. This segment of a mid-eighteenth century engraving shows the Academy of Science which faced the Bol'shaya Neva River at the southeastern extremity of the Island. From *Plan Stolichnago Goroda Sanktpeterburga* (1753), no. 9.

4 The Admiralty shipbuilding complex long dominated the city's industrial structure, as well as the skyline and façade of the southern shore of the Bol'shaya Neva River. This view from Vasil'yevsky Island to the south indicates its scale. Note the pontoon bridge; the absence of permanent bridges greatly hindered intra-urban movement down to the Great War. From a painting by G. Atkinson dating from around the end of the eighteenth century.

5 St Petersburg had emerged as Russia's leading port by 1725. Though its relative position waned during the nineteenth century in the face of competition from other Baltic and Black Sea ports, it was still of outstanding importance in 1914. This portion of a mid-eighteenth century engraving depicts the Exchange, warehouse, and dockside facilities. From *Plan Stolichnago Goroda Sanktpeterburga* (1753), no. 7.

6 The port attracted not only many foreigners but also hordes of indigenous workmen, who picked up whatever living they could, as this late eighteenth century engraving shows. From *Kings Topographical Collection* in the British Museum.

7 Wood and hay were hauled through city streets in summer as well as winter. Wood was still required for cooking, and the number of horses needing to be fed was still large though fewer than in winter. The city had many markets and street traders, as this view of the Sennaya market indicates. From L. Gilbert, *Russia Illustrated* (London, *circa* 1840), facing p. 120.

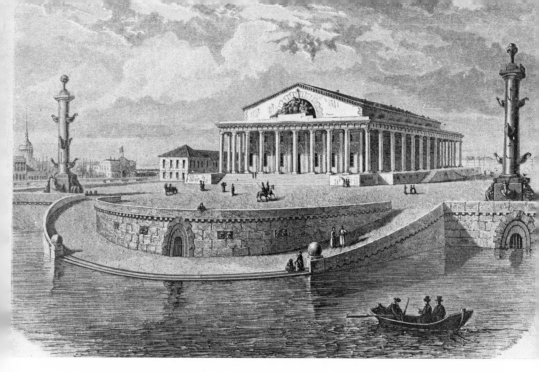

8 Once St Petersburg had acquired a reputation as an international port it needed a *Birzhà*, or Exchange. The central importance of this to the business community is suggested by the architectural magnificence of the building designed by T. de Thomon, which came to dominate the tip of Vasil'yevskiy Island. From H. Rostoschny, *Russland, Land und Leute* (Leipzig, *circa* 1880), vol. II, p. 9.

9 The imperial capital required embellishment on a magnificent scale. The Grand Theatre, built in 1783 to the designs of M. Dedener was one such ornament; damaged by fire in 1811, it was rebuilt toward the end of the century. The sheds and open fires seen in the square were common sights in the city during the winter months as they allowed retinues of servants, among others, to withstand the cold while waiting for their masters. From *A Picture of St Petersburgh* (London, 1815), no. 2.

10 Doubtless the most famous building constructed during the era of imperial munificence was the Winter Palace. Designed by V. Rastrelli, it was the fifth and last in a series of structures built to house the royal family. With the beggar in the foreground, this drawing hints at the wide gulf between the urban elite and the masses. From *Nouvelle Collection de Quarante-Deux Vues de Saint-Pétersbourg et de ses Environs* (1826), no. 20.

11 On the other side of the Winter Palace was the Palace Square, dominated from the 1830s by the Alexander Column (designed by A. Montferrand). Enclosing the square was K. Rossi's semicircular General Staff building, a masterpiece of classical architecture. From Auguste de Montferrand, *Plans et Détails du Monument Consacré à la Mémoire de l'Empereur Alexandre* (Paris, 1836), part 2.

12 The blessing of the waters was only one of many religious celebrations which gave rise to much pomp and splendour. In this August scene near the Nikol'skiy Church, Christ's crossing of the Sea of Galilee is being commemorated. From L. Gilbert, *Russia Illustrated* (London, *circa* 1840), frontispiece.

13 Religion played an important part in the lives of rich and poor alike. Throughout Russia the numerous religious holidays had to be taken into account by those engaged in commerce and industry whether they were foreigners or not. For the masses, the carnival before Lent provided something of a respite from the dark and dreary winter months. This engraving shows part of the celebrations in the Palace Square. From H. Rostoschny, *Russland, Land und Leute* (Leipzig, *circa* 1880), vol. II, after p. 64.

14, 15 Though shipbuilding and armaments dominated the industrial structure of St Petersburg from the outset, many other manufacturing activities had sprung up by the late eighteenth century. The needs of the bureaucracy were met by small, privately owned printing works, as above. The demands of the nobility and wealthy classes for luxury wares could not be satisfied entirely by imports and a sizable number of foreign and Russian craftsmen had stepped into the void by the turn of the century. Not always of high quality, but invariably expensive, the wares of the small workshop, such as the silk-weaving establishment portrayed below, helped to meet these demands. From *Kul'turno-Istoricheskiy Ocherk Zhizni S. Peterburga za Dva Veka XVIII i XIX, 1703–1903 (circa 1904)*, pp. 17, 167.

16 At the close of the eighteenth century private enterprise in industry had not markedly changed the face of the city. It was state-owned enterprises like the Arsenal and cannon foundry depicted here which provided the most tangible evidence of industrialization. From *Kings Topographical Collection* in the British Museum.

17 For the labouring population in particular the public baths provided the basis for a weekly ritual of considerable social and hygienic importance. This view of the interior of an eighteenth-century bath-house in St Petersburg easily explains why foreigners were often so scandalized by its facilities. From *Kul'turno-Istoricheskiy Ocherk Zhizni S. Peterburga za Dva Veka XVIII i XIX, 1703–1903* (*circa* 1904), p. 28.

18–20 The movement of goods within the city was by sled in winter and by waggon in summer, right down to the Great War. Wood, the principal fuel, was brought down the Bol'shaya Neva River in vast quantities during the ice-free season, and the rafts were usually broken up after their one-way trip. The city's many canals helped to distribute the fuel but much of it had to be loaded onto small carts. As integral a part of street life as these hauliers were the itinerant pedlars who carried small quantities of food, often of dubious worth, in the hope of disposing of the lot for a few kopeks. These street scenes, though drawn in the early nineteenth century, are virtually timeless. From *Souvenirs de Saint-Pétersbourg* (1825), nos. 7, 8, 12.

22 Since the majority of buildings remained without piped
water well into the nineteenth
century, the water carrier plied
his trade largely unchallenged.
From H. Rostoschny, *Russland,
Land und Leute* (Liepzig, *circa*
1880), vol. II, p. 17.

21 This view of the Yekaterininskiy Canal in the early
nineteenth century brings out the role of the canals in the
movement of goods. In the background, across the Nevskiy
Prospect, is the Kazan Cathedral (architect, A. Voronikhin).
From L. Gilbert, *Russia Illustrated* (London, *circa* 1840),
facing p. 10.

23 The Nikolayevskiy railway station: private coaches and omnibuses catered to a small segment of the population only and the majority travelled on foot. From *Vidy S. Peterburga s Okrestnostyami* (1864), part 2.

24 Thousands of *droshkies* plied the city's streets for hire. These one-horse, two-passenger cabs seldom inspired confidence among foreigners but were used with apparent equanimity by well-to-do Russians. From C. P. Smyth, *Three Cities in Russia* (London, 1862), vol. II, facing p. 216.

25 Life in St Petersburg, as in other Russian cities, went on under the surveillance of an ever expanding bureaucracy. For the foreigner, the grip of officialdom was first felt at the Customs House where all possessions were checked with almost unparalleled rigour. Russians holidaying abroad did not escape such investigations on their return. From J. Buel, *A Nemesis of Misgovernment* (Philadelphia, 1900), p. 36.

As the administrative capital, Petersburg was heavily bureaucratized. Until the traumatic decades of rapid urban industrialization, it could be said that life there was orderly. Part of the explanation for this was the existence of a large police force. This scene shows one of the mounted night patrols on its rounds. From J. Buel, *A Nemesis of Misgovernment* (Philadelphia, 1900), p. 125.

27 The task of the police in monitoring the comings and goings of the populace was made easier by the *dvorniki*, or yardkeepers. Each private building had its own resident *dvornik*, providing all kinds of services for the tenants, but also reporting to the police. It was difficult to enter or leave the building without being noticed. From G. Dobson, *St Petersburg* (London, 1910), facing p. 145.

28 The Nevskiy Prospect has always been the main street of the city. In the eighteenth century it was already being celebrated as one of the finest thoroughfares in Europe. Exceptionally wide and graced with many magnificent buildings, such as the Anichkov Palace shown here, it was praised by Russians and foreigners alike. From J. Buel, *A Nemesis of Misgovernment* (Philadelphia, 1900), p. 477.

29 Movement within the city was made easier with the coming of winter. Runnered vehicles, like this public sleigh, were able to glide over snowpacked streets that would otherwise rattle every bone in the body. From H. Rostoschny, *Russland, Land und Leute* (Leipzig, *circa* 1880), vol. II, p. 65.

30 Winter gave rise to seasonal employment of various kinds. Ice-cutting on the Neva was one example. From H. Rostoschny, *Russland, Land und Leute* (Leipzig, *circa* 1880), vol. II, p. 3.

31 Within the central city, the few open spaces, such as the Summer Gardens, were not open to the public at large. The Summer Gardens (laid out early in the eighteenth century), were a popular haunt for those wanting to be seen in the right places. From *Vidy S. Peterburga s Okrestnostyami* (1864), part 2.

32 While the winter brought a whirl of social events, the summer occasioned an exodus from the city by all those who could manage to leave. For anyone of esteem who was obliged by his duties to remain behind, a summer *dacha* on one of the islands, as on Petrovskiy Island shown here, was a necessity. Many *dachi* were far more imposing than these. From *Vidy S. Peterburga s Okrestnostyami* (1864), part 2.

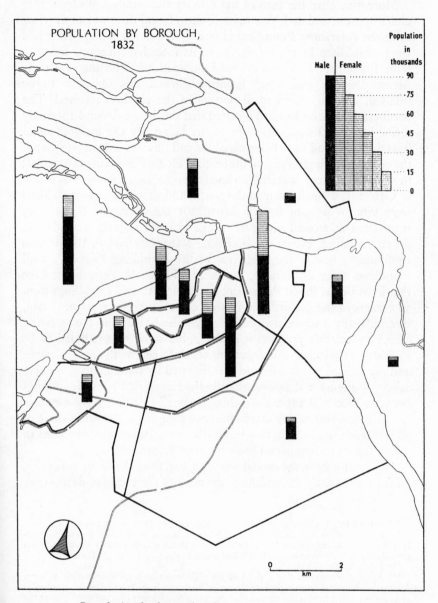

MAP 12. *Population by borough, 1832*

71

Moreover, after the turn of the century the number of illegitimate children grew, and each year more of them found their way to the door of the St Petersburg Foundling Home.[157] We noted earlier that it had been established in 1770 with one of its intended functions being to train foundlings in urban-oriented occupations. The link with the Aleksandrovskiy and other factories allowed this objective to be fulfilled, but only for a small portion of the children received. The numbers eventually handled dictated that this be so. Around 1800 only a few hundred foundlings were in the home. By the early 1840s at least five thousand were being cared for and this was only in one part of the operation. The facilities of the original Home were soon outstripped; thus new ones were acquired, an ancillary operation for boys was set up in Gatchina, a small town to the south, and thousands more children were sent to peasant homes throughout the region.[158] Some were repatriated at around six years of age but the majority stayed with peasant families, eventually becoming state serfs and in the process confounding one of the objectives of the Foundling Home. Not all foundlings were illegitimate, nor were all from St Petersburg. Like that in Moscow, the St Petersburg operation attracted foundlings from all corners of the Empire. But in view of the staggering mortality rate, those sent any distance at an early age had the odds against their arriving alive.[159] A sizable proportion of the influx must be attributed to St Petersburg itself, and this argument is reinforced by the ratio of sexes and the limited family life, and corroborated by contemporary observations.[160] Figure 2 shows graphically the rise in number of foundlings between 1800 and 1850. Even though not all came from the city it is none the less instructive that foundlings comprised a growing share of all births in the city. Whether legitimate or not, there were few years in which the city's population grew by natural means.[161]

The death-rate in the capital was high, and from the 1830s noticeably on the increase. By the middle of the century the excess of deaths over

[157] Attengofer, *Mediko-Topograficheskoye Opisaniye Sanktpeterburga*, pp. 119–23.
[158] For a description, see Kohl, *Russia*, pp. 111–16. As he notes, the Home was exceedingly well financed owing to the fact that the revenue from the playing card monopoly had been turned over to it by Alexander I. It also had access to the revenues of the Lombard.
[159] Kohl, *Russia*, p. 113.
[160] Attengofer suggests that a third of the children came from surrounding villages. Attengofer, *Mediko-Topograficheskoye Opisaniye Sanktpeterburga*, p. 123. But this was before 1820 and we know from other sources that the rate of illegitimacy climbed quickly after the huge population increase of the 1820s. Prostitution was one probable reason. Bashutskiy, *Panorama Sanktpeterburga*, pp. 88–9.
[161] *Entsiklopedicheskiy Slovar'*, pp. 312–13.

births had reached tens of thousands. Epidemics were not unknown in the capital and from time to time took unusually heavy tolls of young and old, rich and poor, alike. But we should not lose sight of the fact that in this regard the poor and their progeny paid a disproportionately

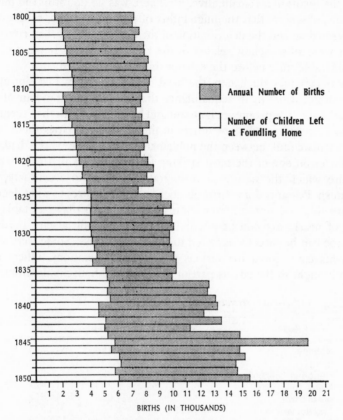

FIG. 2. *Annual number of births and number of children left at the St Petersburg Foundling Home, 1800–50*

heavy price. Between 1800 and 1810 the average number of deaths each year was about 9,000; by the forties this had jumped to nearly 20,000, a shift in the ratio per 1,000 inhabitants from thirty-nine to forty-three.[163] At the Foundling Home the situation was rather worse:

[162] See, for instance, Possart, *Wegweiser Für Fremde*, pp. 32–4.
[163] *Entsiklopedicheskiy Slovar'*, pp. 312–13.

'Of the children brought into the house,' wrote Kohl, 'one-fourth die during the first six weeks at the breasts of the nurses; and of those sent out among the peasants, more than one-half die during the six years, so that at the end of that time, scarcely a third of the children brought into the institution remain alive.'[164] There was no doubt in the minds of some observers that the huge influx of peasant workers, progressive overcrowding and the deterioration of the quality of the urban environment were all somehow related to the rising mortality. It was to be a considerable time before the relationships were clarified.

In 1832 James Buchanan, the head of the American Legation at St Petersburg, wrote to an acquaintance that, despite the grandeur of the capital itself, 'the people are ignorant and barbarous. With the exception of the merchants and a few others in the commercial cities there is no intermediate rank between the nobleman and the slave.'[165] He had put his finger on one of the most striking features of this urban society, a feature which the nature of in-migration tended to accentuate, not diminish. Peasants dominated the social class structure; to what degree, we are able to determine from some data relating to 1843 ⟨*see* table 4⟩. Out of nearly 450,000 people living within the official city borders, 157,000 can be directly assigned to the peasant class. Some were state peasants conscripted for various government operations, others had been brought to the city as part of their owners' household entourage,

TABLE 4. *Social-class structure 1843*

Class	Male	Female	Total
Nobility	24,585	24,788	49,373
Clergy	1,087	1,131	2,218
Honoured citizenry	370	321	691
Merchants	6,179	5,243	11,422
Meshchane	23,933	21,025	44,958
Tsekhovye	9,775	5,502	15,277
Peasants*	119,000	37,329	157,329
Military	68,159	26,016	94,175
Foreigners	7,575	6,431	14,006
Raznochintsy	9,500	9,745	19,245
Others	—	—	34,666
Total			443,360

Source: 'Naseleniye S. Peterburga', *Zhurnal Ministerstva Vnutrennikh Del*, no. 5 (1844), pp. 477–83.
* includes all categories, that is, state, Church and privately owned.

164 Kohl, *Russia*, p. 113.
165 John Moore (ed.), *The Works of James Buchanan* (Philadelphia, 1908), p. 219.

but the largest number came seeking work. However, as a class, peasants were not legally part of urban society; in other words, they had no rights. Their residence was tolerated only so long as their passports and permits were in order. As industrialization and commercialization drew more and more peasants to the city, concern over their political and social stability mounted, a development which we noted earlier. Thus, the police and the *Adresnaya Kontora* or Address Office were charged with monitoring their comings and goings. This situation clearly reflected the tenuous position of the urban peasant. By way of compensation many sought refuge and comradeship in the *artel'*, the city counterpart of the rural based commune. The *artel'* played an important role in bringing together peasants from the same village, from common occupations or from the same factory, but it existed as a rural institution in an urban milieu.[166] For the peasant there was only one way he could secure his position as a city dweller— he had to change his legal status. But where within the class system were the walls most permeable? The nobility, whether personal or hereditary, was to all intents and purposes ruled out; the same may be said for the clergy; peasants were hardly 'foreigners'. The *raznochintsy*, ostensibly the intellectual class, held only limited scope; some former peasants were certainly within this amorphous collection of clerks, teachers, provincial clergy, artists, journalists, musicians and the like, but there were barely 19,000 in this class as a whole in 1843, so it clearly had not provided much of an outlet.

Among the four primary 'urban' classes, the honoured citizenry, the merchants, the *meshchane* and the *tsekh*, the latter two provided the greatest opportunities for peasant penetration. The *tsekh* was an artisan corporation instituted by Peter I and modelled after the European trade guilds. It was responsible for levying duties, setting standards for apprenticeship, and in general monitoring members and their activities much like the *Adresnaya Kontora* did with the peasantry. Divided into two components, Russian and foreign, nearly 92 per cent of the 15,277 members belonged to the first, a goodly number of whom were former peasants. Membership provided a legal foothold in the city; indeed, the elders of the *tsekh* were eligible to hold office in municipal government, which, as we shall soon see, was a rather exclusive privilege.

The *meshchane*, referring to 'middling sort of people' emerged from a shake-up of the guild system initiated by Catherine II in 1785, and

[166] For further discussion, see Zelnik, *Labor and Society*, p. 21.

included all those who at the time did not possess sufficient capital to be assigned to the merchant class. Among the 45,000 members of the *meshchane* were numerous petty entrepreneurs and small-scale industrialists who had thrown off their peasant status. To become a merchant necessitated joining one of the three guilds, which was a rather difficult transition for a peasant to make, though not impossible. The third guild was the least exclusive in the sense that the capital and dues required of those wishing to engage in small-scale trade and industry were the lowest. The principal constraint was that activities had to be undertaken within the borders of the Empire. Second guild members had limited access to foreign trade, but had to abstain from any type of banking or insurance transactions. Membership in the first guild was expensive, and hence exclusive, but it provided the greatest scope for enterprise. But once again the barriers to entry and the small number of merchants, only 11,400, indicate minimal peasant penetration. The remaining class, the honoured citizenry, was virtually ruled out. Bestowed on the very wealthy and very influential members of the entrepreneurial elite, few attained such an exalted place in urban society ⟨*see* table 4⟩.

Shifts in legal status by peasants were not regarded enthusiastically by the government. The trend was sufficiently disturbing to result in the creation in 1824 of a separate category of peasants. This was the 'commercial' category, which had a structure roughly corresponding to the guild system of the merchant class. It was intended that the energies of peasant entrepreneurs be channelled into petty enterprises and there circumscribed. Notwithstanding such government manoeuvres, each year some peasants managed to slip into one of the urban classes, usually the *meshchane* or *tsekhovye*.[167]

The composition of urban society as outlined in table 4 underscores the point made by Buchanan, even if he may fairly be accused of exaggeration. At the bottom was a disfranchised peasantry—a *population flottante*—steadily growing in absolute and relative importance.[168] In the middle was a truncated bourgeoisie, comprising the honoured citizenry, the merchants and at least some of the *meshchane*. Within the latter group were many whose occupations and lack of capital put them squarely in the working class.[169] Only the legal status of *meshchane*

[167] Blackwell, *Beginnings of Russian Industrialization*, pp. 96–107; Kopanev, *Naseleniye Peterburga v Pervoy Polovine XIX Veka*, pp. 27–48.
[168] 'Naseleniye S. Peterburga', p. 484. See also Zinaida Schakovskoy, *La Vie Quotidienne à Saint-Pétersbourg à l'Époque Romantique* (Liège, 1967), pp. 52–105.
[169] Kopanev, *Naseleniye Peterburga v Pervoy Polovine XIX Veka*, pp. 41–4.

placed those of its members above the peasants, who made up the bulk of the *lumpenproletariat*. The *raznochintsy* and the members of the *tsekh* were also working-class rather than middle-class, although their legal status again separated them quite distinctly from the peasantry. Among the traditional and upper classes were the nobility, the upper echelons of the military and government bureaucracy and the clergy.[170] But it should be recognized that the class (*sosloviye*) system was at best a very rough measure of position in society. Wealth and rank, for instance, were frequently far from synonymous. A good many nobles had beggared themselves through ineptness in managing their estates or by simple profligacy. On the other hand, millionaire serfs were not unknown.[171] For those employed by the government or military there was a common system of fourteen ranks which enveloped normal class relationships. This had been introduced by Peter I in an effort to reward ability and achievement rather than simply allowing the upper echelons to be staffed by the nobility.[172] Thus, the son of an indigent teacher belonging to the *raznochintsy* might well out-rank a prince and by virtue of rank-specific uniforms would be so seen. Whether the attainment of a superior rank allowed access to the city's finest drawing-rooms was quite another matter altogether.

The position of foreigners in society is difficult to assess simply because they served in so many different capacities. The guild system established for foreign merchants had roughly 3,000 members: hundreds held diplomatic, consular and related posts, some were clergy, thousands were handicraftsmen and so on, but most foreigners brought some skill or other to the capital. Of the 14,000 registered as foreigners, Germans were by far the most numerous, many of the 5,600 being engaged in commerce or skilled handicraft activities. Citizens of France, Britain and Austria comprised the other large contingents of foreigners, but none had more than 3,100 representatives.[173] The size of the resident foreign population had altered little over the past century, though it should be noted that acquiring Russian citizenship gave those with commercial interests a much freer hand and many of them had taken this route.[174] Thus, the number of foreigners in 1843 somewhat understates the real situation, but apart from this,

---

[170] Blackwell, *Beginnings of Russian Industrialization*, p. 101.
[171] Blackwell, *Beginnings of Russian Industrialization*, pp. 205–10.
[172] A. de Gurowski, *Russia As It Is* (New York, 1854), pp. 118–19, 302.
[173] 'Naseleniye S. Peterburga', p. 486.
[174] For example, Georgi indicates there were over 10,000 in 1750. J. G. Georgi, *Description de la Ville de St Pétersbourg et de ses Environs* (1793), p. 119.

the foreign element was being overshadowed by the growth in the other classes. It is clear from table 4 that the garrison forces and the peasantry dominated the urban population in absolute terms, for together they were almost entirely responsible for the imbalance between males and females noted before. Irrespective of disfranchisement and close supervision, peasants as peasants and peasants as part of the military garrison had a most perceptible impact on the demographic and social-class structure in particular and on the urban milieu in general.

This outline of the basic composition of urban society raises the question of how the relationships between the classes shaped the social fabric of the city. For example, in an attempt to maintain class identity and privilege, were the nobility and the wealthy spatially segregated? We need not seek a detailed picture but concentrate once more on clarifying some of the general relationships.

Peter I had intended segregating various urban functions, but the exigencies of the time dictated that such refinements in building the city be given short shrift. The fires of 1736–7 allowed part of the Admiralteyskaya district to be reserved for the nobility and courtiers, but while extensive building was initiated it was much less than was required to fill the void. Writing roughly half a century later, Storch noted that, 'even in the most eligible parts of the town, [we] meet with empty places; because those in the remoter districts are more easily purchased and therefore sooner built upon.'[175] At this time the Admiralteyskaya district was divided into four quarters. The first and second were roughly coincident with the territory planned for re-development after the fires. According to Storch, the first was 'chiefly inhabited by the great and the opulent', whereas the other was already dominated by the 'trading classes'.[176] Four decades later Dr Granville felt justified in claiming: 'The distinction between the fashionable and unfashionable parts of the city is as strongly marked in St Petersburgh as in London. The four Admiralty districts, and part of Littenoi, form what may be called the Court end of the town.'[177]

Few travellers would have disagreed with this judgement, but to what extent did this actually represent spatial segregation of classes? The answer is scarcely at all. By the early part of the nineteenth

---

[175] Storch, *Picture of St Petersburg*, p. 13.
[176] Storch, *Picture of St Petersburg*, pp. 44, 47.
[177] Granville, *St Petersburgh*, p. 417.

century some quite different expressions of social-class values were being commented upon by foreign visitors.

> St Petersburg is a city of palaces towards the streets, and exteriorly presents the appearance of a great magnificence; but the parts of those palaces which do not meet the eye of the ordinary passenger, being let out into separate tenements, are filled with the lowest inhabitants, and are of the most filthy description. It may suit the taste of a Russian seigneur, and the state of his purse, to have the ground floor of his mansion occupied as a brandy shop, to inhabit merely the upper stories himself, and to fill the inner court with persons of low condition; but, whatever conveniences such arrangements might possess in a pecuniary point of view, they would never for a moment be contemplated by an English nobleman. The latter, I have no doubt, would prefer having the 'abodes of the lowest classes in wretched courts and lanes', rather than they should obtrude themselves within his walls.[178]

Thus, admixture of classes rather than segregation was quite evident even in the so-called fashionable areas in the late 1820s. A decade later, when Kohl was on the scene, this characteristic had not at all diminished.

> I knew one [building] of which the ground-floor, on one side, was occupied by a public bazaar, in which thousands of the necessaries and conveniences of life were offered for sale. One the other side, a multitude of German, English, and French mechanics and tradesmen had hung out their signs. On the first floor dwelt two senators, and the families of various other persons of distinction. On the second floor was a school of very high repute, and a host of academicians, teachers, and professors, dwelt there with their families. In the back part of the building, not to talk of a multitude of obscure personages, there resided several colonels and majors, a few retired generals, an Armenian priest, and a German pastor. Had all the rest of St Petersburg gone to the ground, and this house alone remained, its inhabitants would have sufficed for the formation of a little political community of their own, in which every rank in society would have had its representatives.[179]

[178] E. Morton, *Travels in Russia and a Residence at St Petersburg and Odessa in the years 1827–1829* (London, 1830), pp. 23–4.
[179] Kohl, *Panorama of St Petersburg*, p. 10.

There are many possible reasons for the heterogeneous social-class composition of individual buildings. Land prices and construction costs were high and therefore so were rents. For a financially hard pressed noble the potential income was obviously attractive. As we saw earlier, merchants were emerging as one of the more important property-owning groups and there is no doubt that commercial motives were behind this development. This is not to say that St Petersburg was devoid of any spatial segregation of the upper classes, for there were some pockets. For instance, a number of palaces had been built along the eastern flanks of the Fontanka Canal: 'It is there that may be seen the palaces of the Kotshubeys, the Sheremetiefs, the Branitzkis, the Narishkins, the chancellors of the empire, the ministers, the grandees, and the millionaires. . . .'[180] I. V. Pushkarev described the better residential areas as comprising at the end of the 1830s the first and second Admiralteyskaya districts, part of Liteynaya and the area around the Strelka across the Bol'shaya Neva River on Vasil'yevskiy Island.[181] But as contemporaries make clear, exteriors often belied what was inside. What was true for individual buildings was therefore true for larger areas. Social-class heterogeneity, not homogeneity, was the norm in what was generally regarded as the 'court end of town'.

In the peripheral boroughs, or for that matter in the industrialized inner city ones, external appearances provided a much more reliable reflection of interior conditions and probable social-class composition. For instance, to the east across the Bol'shaya Neva was Okhta, a shabby suburb peopled almost entirely by peasants. It was to this district that the hordes of summer workmen engaged in building trades or working on ship construction for the Admiralty traditionally went. To the north, on the same side of the river was the district of Vyborg, heavily garrisoned and a long-standing centre of industry. Anybody conscious of his social position would not have considered living there: 'Vyborg! Why, they say wolves roam the streets there in winter! It's such a dull place—a wilderness, no one lives there.'[182] But desires could be compromised. Impoverished members of the traditional and upper classes were sometimes obliged to seek accommodation in the less salubrious parts of town. Class composition was still varied, but poverty was the common bond.

The poor regions of the city were made so much worse owing to the

[180] Kohl, *Russia*, p. 8.
[181] I. V. Pushkarev, *Opisaniye Sanktpeterburga i Uyezdnykh Gorodov* (1843), vol. I, pp. 73–8.
[182] I. G. Goncharov, *Oblomov* (London, 1967), translated by David Magarshack, p. 53.

dearth of basic municipal services. This situation followed from the inadequate finances over which municipal government had jurisdiction. The fact that municipal government itself was weak simply made the task of meeting the needs of a rapidly growing population that much more difficult. By the late 1840s city government in practice had become an extension of the state government. How this process occurred is worth outlining, if only briefly.

As early as 1721, Peter I had sought to inject into the city some organizational basis for the management of urban affairs. Prior to 1721 the city population was divided and administered according to districts. After the 1721 regulation, the whole population was separated into two groups—those who possessed regularized and legal urban status, and those who did not. In the former category were merchants, artisans and other professionals, a rather mixed group lumped together primarily for the purpose of taxation. In other words, the vast majority of the population stood outside the formalized civic society. Under Catherine II the issues of urban government and urban society were again raised and resulted in the reform of 1785. Previously, the legally recognized members of the city had no way of effectively participating in city government. In short, their obligations had been clarified but there was no autonomy. Catherine's reform both widened the membership of civic society and assigned responsibilities to be administered through a City Council and six-man executive headed by a mayor. Members were elected to the Council from the six classes given the franchise. The most important of these were the real estate-owning nobility and the merchants, because it was from their ranks that the most influential Council members came. But despite the positive features of the reform, it must be said that the management of city affairs remained under the thumb of the central government. In the critical area of policing the city, the lines of authority went from the various city districts to the governor who was responsible to the state, thus by-passing the bureaucracy of municipal government. Areas of municipal jurisdiction were, in fact, tightly circumscribed and it was often the case that where the city had authority it also had inadequate financial resources.

It was not until the 1840s that city government was again revamped, Under Catherine the direction of change had been toward liberalization. With the municipal law of 1846, Nicholas I sought to strengthen the role of central government in civic affairs. The reform was designed to remove existing ambiguities, to clarify rights, and more important, to define the responsibilities of the classes legally recognized as being part of urban society. The links between urban society and the tsar were emphasized rather than the responsibilities of elected members to their constituencies and to the city in general. Important matters relating to the generation and disbursement of revenues, the relationship between the city government and the police, the education, health and general well-being of the populace, all were left in abeyance. The 1846 reform tied up administrative loose ends, but it left the management of city affairs in the hands of a clique of merchants and nobles. This was not a promising situation in the light of impending industrialization and its concomitant demands.[183]

Given the prevailing atmosphere of suspicion and unease over the growing number of urban dwellers, it is not surprising that the police, as the principal agent of supervision and control, remained very much an extension of the state. During the late eighteenth century, social problems requiring police attention were few. Storch attributed the peaceful conditions to national character: 'The common Russian,' he said, 'if not corrupted by a long stay in the residence [St Petersburg], seduced by the propensity to drink, or pressed by extreme want, is seldom disposed to excesses. To this may be added a certain reverence towards the superior ranks.'[184] But should any of these conditions be met and violence or crime ensue there was a hefty complement of police at hand to set matters right. The night watch alone had over 600 men. Additionally, the problem of supervision was greatly reduced by virtue of the obligation of all landlords to report any strangers staying in their buildings, or for that matter, overnight absences of the regular tenants. The supervisory function in these cases rested with the *dvorniki* or yard-keepers, who were as much a part of the St Petersburg scene as the buildings themselves.[185]

Faith in the national character and the strength of the peasantry's rural ties waned in the face of rapid population growth in the early nineteenth century. The statistics were beginning to indicate to some that city life was indeed a corruptive influence. Arrests for drunkenness and theft, for instance, were growing by the early 1830s. However, it

---

[183] For more detailed discussion, see; *Stoletiye S. Peterburgskago Gorodskago Obshchestva 1785–1885gg.* (1885), chapters 1 and 2; S. P. Luppov, N. N. Petrov, 'Gorodskoye Upravleniye i Gorodskoye Khozyaystvo Peterburga ot Kontsa XVIII v do 1861g.', *Och.IL* (1955), vol. I, pp. 601–29; Zelnik, *Labor and Society*, pp. 8–17; L. T. Hutton, 'The Reform of City Government in Russia', unpublished doctoral thesis, University of Illinois, 1972, pp. 11–14.
[184] Storch, *Picture of St Petersburg*, p. 133.
[185] Storch, *Picture of St Petersburg*, pp. 137–9.

could be argued that, in the long run and proportionally, the situation was not just under control, but was being ameliorated. In 1810 the number of arrests for drunkenness had been equivalent to one tenth of the population; by 1831 it was only one thirtieth. Comparisons made with cities like Paris and London revealed that life in St Petersburg was considerably safer and more orderly. Even in the case of suicides, the fact that the incidence in the capital was twice the national average dwindled in significance when it was noted that this rate hardly compared with that of, say, Paris.[186] Real ties with the countryside for such a large portion of the capital's population played an important role in this regard. When conditions in the city became desperate there was still the rural commune offering refuge.

At a different level the system of checks and controls stymied efforts to effect political change through revolution. Indeed, the abortive attempt to resolve a dynastic crisis following the death of Alexander I by means of a coup served as a warning to others for years. In this instance, a group largely made up of army officers dissatisfied with the reign of Alexander I attempted to unseat his appointed successor, Nicholas I. Mustering several thousand men, they marched toward the Winter Palace only to be confronted with an even larger contingent from the loyal garrisons. The rebellion was quashed and there ensued an era of rigid censorship and control of the whole population. None was excluded from police surveillence, including members of foreign legations. It was not enough that customs officials checked the baggage and personal possessions of those entering the country with an inquisitiveness seldom previously encountered ⟨*see* plate 25⟩. Observation continued once they were resident in the city, as James Buchanan noted with more than a little annoyance.

> Since my arrival in this City, I have not received a single com-
> munication of any kind, either through the Post Office or Foreign
> Office,—whether public or private, which has not been violated.
> It was not difficult in any instance to detect this violation; but in
> many the letters have been sent to me either almost open, or with
> such awkward imitations of the seals as to excite merriment. The
> Post Office American Eagle is here a sorry bird. So notorious is
> this practice that no person in St Petersburg attempts to conceal
> or deny it.[187]

[186] Bashutskiy, *Panorama Peterburga*, pp. 89–92.
[187] Moore, *The Works of James Buchanan*, p. 320.

The apparatus of the police was an element no less pervasive in the urban milieu than the peasant: it was simply more subtle. Social unrest was already on occasion being manifested, by workers demanding better wages and conditions, and by rhetoric and writing, but any overt actions of dissidence produced swift, frequently punitive, responses.

Despite some tremors of industrialization, St Petersburg in the middle of the nineteenth century remained in very much of a soporific state. Certainly, there had been expressions of concern over the changes apparent in the city. To date, however, these changes could scarcely hold a candle to what rapid urban industrialization was so soon to bring.

3
An Embryo of Urban Industrialism

Petersburg grows not by the year, but by the hour.
A. Grech, 1851[1]

To judge by A. Grech's mid-century observation, it may be surmised that the recent increase in industrial and commercial activity was having a noticeable effect on the rate of urbanization. It was only the beginning. At that time the city's economy was still heavily slanted toward administrative and commercial functions, not industrial. The demands occasioned by the Crimean War helped to shift the balance toward industry but the cost was high and the stimulus short-lived. However, a resurgent investment in industry during the second half of the sixties combined with the repercussions of the Emancipation of the Serfs in 1861 heralded an era of rapid urban industrialization the like of which had no parallel in the city's history.

Having described the general features of St Petersburg's growth up to mid-century, we can now focus our attention on a detailed analysis of the ensuing urban-industrial expansion. We will begin by looking at the city's industry, commerce, transport systems and external relations at the end of the 1860s, an examination which will serve as a benchmark for assessing the tempo and lineaments of change during the years up to the Great War. Similarly, the following chapter, which deals with the nature of the city toward the end of the 1860s, will not only assess the impact of industrialization on the population structure, social-class characteristics and housing—to cite a few examples—but it will also afford an opportunity to evaluate the full impact of five decades of industrialization.

[1] A. Grech, *Ves' Peterburg v Karmane* (2nd edn, 1851), pp. iii-iv.

I THE BEGINNINGS OF INDUSTRIALIZATION

In the preceding chapter we saw that by mid-century the process of industrialization as evidenced in St Petersburg amounted to only a slight adoption of manufacturing machinery.[2] Industry was still afflicted to a greater or lesser extent by a feature common to most Russian industry—technological backwardness, sustained as it was by tariff barriers from 1822 to mid century. The consequence of this was the relatively high-cost, low-quality, production.

Although, as a result of the profits in industry and commerce, the period of the Crimean War (1854–6) was described as the 'golden years',[3] the exigencies of the campaign ultimately brought into sharp focus the relative backwardness of much of Russia's industrial structure. This was especially true in the metal-working industries.[4] With less than 1,000 kilometres of railway line by 1852, this sector had as yet derived little benefit from such construction, and the retarded state of rail communication was in turn the cause of many problems in supplying the front during the war.[5] Moreover, not only had the absence of a rail network strategic consequences, but commerce had been stifled as well, for most regions of the country were excluded from a general market.[6]

A number of measures to ameliorate some of the underlying structural weaknesses of Russian industry were introduced by the government during the decade following the hostilities, one of the main objectives being to expedite the articulation of a satisfactory rail network. For instance, in 1857 railway construction was opened to private enterprise[7] (a measure caused partly by a financial crisis confronting the government).[8] That year also witnessed the first of a series of tariff changes beneficial to the metal-working industries. Following a liberalization

[2] For an overview, see S. G. Strumilin, *Ocherki Ekonomicheskoy Istorii Rossii i SSSR* (Moscow, 1966), pp. 395–401.

[3] M. Tugan-Baranovskiy, *Russkaya Fabrika v Proshlom i Nastoyashchem, Istoriko-Ekonomicheskoye Izsledovaniye* (1898), vol. I, pp. 318–19. Especially buoyant were the years 1855–6. Strumilin, *Ocherki Ekonomicheskoy Istorii Rossii*, p. 426.

[4] P. A. Afanassiev, 'Machines and Implements', *The Industries of Russia, Manufacturing and Trade* (1893), vol. I, pp. 179–80.

[5] During the preceding three decades, the socially disruptive influence of railway construction was stressed by many prominent Slavophiles among whom was Count Kankrin, the Minister of Finance from 1822 to 1844.

[6] For a discussion of the impact of this state of affairs on grain prices, see James Mavor, *An Economic History of Russia* (London, 1914), vol. I, pp. 560–61. See also P. I. Lyashchenko, *A History of the National Economy of Russia to the 1917 Revolution* (New York, 1949), translated by L. M. Herman, pp. 500–02.

[7] I. V. Nikol'skiy, *Geografiya Transporta SSSR* (Moscow, 1960), p. 138.

[8] Tugan-Baranovskiy, *Russkaya Fabrika*, pp. 318–19.

of tariffs in 1857, which included the right to import iron and cast iron by sea, a reduction of the duty on iron and iron products was introduced in 1859, and in 1861 the duty was waived on iron and iron products imported by machine-building factories for construction of railroad equipment. A rationalization of the tariff structure in 1868 brought about a further reduction on raw and semi-manufactured materials.[9] The result of these changes was to stimulate growth, not just of the metal-working industries, but in all sectors of Russia's industrial structure.

The Crimean War had augmented industrial production in many parts of St Petersburg, notably in metal-working, armaments, ship-building and textiles.[10] But the demand was ephemeral and many firms dependent upon government contracts went out of business during the post-war depression. In the late 1850s several new companies were founded to take part in the manufacture of railway equipment or shipbuilding, priority manufactures deriving considerable advantage from the prevailing tariff structure, as well as from other forms of government support.[11] However, by the early 1860s these measures had had little impact on total industrial employment, since the number engaged by industry had scarcely altered from mid century.[12] Although government policies were instrumental in spurring selective industrialization during the post-war period, there was often little that could be done to counter the negative effects of exogenous factors on industrial growth. One instance was the curtailment of raw cotton supplies during the American Civil War, an event which drastically reduced the output of the Russian cotton textile industry. Since an important segment of St Petersburg's industrial structure comprised break-of-bulk processing, and as a growing share of all industrial raw materials was obtained from abroad, the capital was especially vulnerable in such situations.[13]

[9] W. I. Timiriazev, 'Review of the Russian Customs Tariff System', in *The Industries of Russia*, pp. 411–14, 421; *Materialy ob Ekonomicheskom Polozhenii i Professional'noy Organizatsii, Peterburgskikh Rabochikh po Metallu* (1909), pp. 7–8.

[10] E. Karnovich, *Sanktpeterburg v Statisticheskom Otnoshenii* (1860), pp. 105–14.

[11] By the end of the 1850s, St Petersburg still maintained its relative dominance in metal-working generally, and machine construction in particular, for in the city were 'concentrated over 70 per cent of all workers occupied at that time in the machine construction industry of Russia.' R. S. Livshits, *Razmeshcheniye Promyshlennosti v Dorevolyutsionnoy Rossii* (Moscow, 1955), pp. 107–8.

[12] Employment in industry in 1862 was just over 19,000, but this number would have been adversely affected by the Emancipation of 1861. P. N. Stolpyanskiy, *Zhizn' i Byt Peterburgskoy Fabriki za 1704–1914 gg.* (1925), pp. 114–15.

[13] The number of cotton-spinning mills declined from fifty-seven to thirty-five and weaving mills from 659 to 338 between 1860 and 1863. John Whitman, 'Turkestan Cotton

The Emancipation of the Serfs by Alexander II in 1861 was clearly the most significant development of the decade, or for that matter, of the century. During discussions leading up to the proclamation there had been strong support for the Emancipation within the capital's university and intellectual community. Economic, as well as humanitarian and political motives, clearly played a part in the decision, and in St Petersburg not a few entrepreneurs joined the ranks of those whose liberal views on this issue stood out within the Empire. Of course, St Petersburg had spawned many dissident intellectual movements over the years and partly for that reason what emanated from there was often viewed with considerable suspicion elsewhere in the country. Foreigners, however, were usually at one in recognizing the potential benefits of the Emancipation. Some saw in it the seeds both of economic growth and of democratic government. The recently arrived member of the US Legation in St Petersburg, Cassius Clay, writing three years after the event, noted:

> The emancipation of the Russian serfs has so far proved a success
> . . . Russia reaps the double advantage of interested labour and
> more intelligent direction. Rapid advances are made in the
> introduction of new processes and machinery in farming; ship-
> building and general manufactures are increased, monopolies
> abolished, telegraphs and railroads extended . . . the bonds of
> caste are being broken down and . . . I doubt not that the
> imperial policy now looks to an ultimate constitutional
> empire.[14]

While his prognostication concerning a constitutional empire was somewhat wide of the mark, the economy in fact was being bolstered. Still, the Emancipation did not immediately occasion any 'great upheaval in the process of industrialization which continued slow

---

in Imperial Russia', *American Slavic and East European Review*, XV, no. 2 (1956), p. 193. Spinning mill employment was reduced by one-half from 1860 to 1862 (41,300 to 22,400). Strumilin, *Ocherki Ekonomicheskoy Istorii Rosii*, p. 423. Even as late as 1859 cotton spinning in the capital accounted for 605,000 out of a total of 1,535,500 spindles in Russia. K. A. Pazhitnov, *Ocherki Istorii Tekstil'noy Promyshlennosti Dorevolyutsionnoy Rossii, Khlop-chatobumazhnaya, L'no-Pen'kovaya i Shelkovaya Promyshlennosti* (Moscow, 1955), vol. I, pp. 17, 19.
[14] Cassius Clay, 'Letter', *Papers relating to the Foreign Relations of the US*, 1864, part III, no. 28, p. 287.

until 1887',[15] although it did cause general disruption.[16] Peasants and landowners alike returned to the countryside to take part in the dividing of the land, and this exodus compounded the general economic recession prevailing in the early years of the decade. It was soon recognized by peasants in many rural areas that the redemption payments and taxes which came with the Emancipation could only be met if other sources of income were found.[17] Hence, after the initial disruption the tempo of rural-urban migration quickened.[18] However, it was some time before a clear picture of migration trends emerged. Contemporary comments by a visiting British doctor, George Whitely, give us some appreciation of the mixed opinions regarding this phenomenon immediately after the Emancipation:

> Since the autumn of last year [1864] an unusual number of labourers have flocked to St Petersburg without a corresponding increase in house accommodation . . . When I called the attention of the Minister of the Interior to a statement in English journals, that 43,000 more labourers than usual were living in the city this winter, he merely remarked that he believed the figures were not quite correct.[19]

In the absence of accurate enumerations, it required a marked resurgence in the city's economy with its obvious and undeniable increase in the labour force to persuade some people that the number of migrants was unusually large. According to the report of the British Consul in St Petersburg, T. Michell, a resumption of more buoyant economic conditions was already observable in 1866. 'The demand for foreign raw, and half-manufactured goods, was unusually active', he reported. 'The flourishing state of the principal branches of industry . . . will account for much of the increase in the importation of cotton, machinery, coal and dye-stuffs.'[20] However, sustained and rapid economic growth with its attendant expansion of the labour force did not occur until late in the decade.

---

[15] R. Portal, 'The Industrialization of Russia', in H. J. Habakkuk, M. M. Postan (eds), *Cambridge Economic History of Europe* (London, 1965), vol. VI, part 2, p. 810.

[16] There was a dispersal of much of the forced factory labour, but the consequence was both regional and sectoral, affecting especially the Urals metal-working and manorial linen and wool production. Portal, 'The Industrialization of Russia', p. 811; Tugan-Baranovskiy, *Russkaya Fabrika*, pp. 299–300.

[17] Lyashchenko, *A History of the National Economy of Russia*, pp. 381–8.

[18] Portal, 'The Industrialization of Russia', p. 811.

[19] George Whitely, 'Report' *BPP*; *Russian Epidemic*, 1865 (246), XLVII. 517.

[20] Consul T. Michell, 'Report', *BPP*; *Commercial Reports*, 1867, LXVII. 1, no. VII.

The economic and social changes unleashed by the Emancipation had a perceptible impact on St Petersburg during the sixties. Population growth continued to be somewhat erratic, but by the end of the decade the total number of inhabitants within the urban area was not far short of three quarters of a million. Many new factories had appeared, giving employment to thousands, and the expansion in commercial activities, mirrored by an increase in port traffic and the numerous new financial, wholesale and retail establishments, required the services of even greater numbers (to say nothing of the burgeoning bureaucracy). Whether propelled from the countryside by the impoverishing conditions or induced to migrate by the prospect, real or imagined, of employment, thousands upon thousands of peasants were descending upon the city. To accommodate this influx of people, the construction of houses expanded, but for the poorer elements of society this occurred more slowly than it might have done and the shortage of working-class housing, so critical a problem after the turn of the century, was already becoming all too evident. While economic growth was nowhere near the frenzied pace of later decades, the urban system was clearly showing signs of stress. What, we may ask, were the economic activities that were responsible, at least in part, for these pressures?

At the close of the 1860s St Petersburg still bore the impress of its traditional court and administrative functions. Bureaucrats, nobles and the military continued to constitute a disproportionately large element in society and the city's employment structure reflected their presence. Consequently, employment in commerce and industry was much less significant than in other major European capitals. If one takes, for example, gainfully employed males as a basis for comparison, some 61 per cent were engaged in manufacturing industries, trade and transport in the Russian capital in 1869. In London and Berlin just two years later the comparable figures were 84 and 79 per cent, respectively. Additionally, in St Petersburg, trade, and primarily that of a petty nature, accounted for 14 per cent of the labour force, compared to only 8 per cent in London. The urban economies of these cities clearly reflected different economic histories, but we may simply note that around 1870 manufacturing industry in St Petersburg was appreciably less developed than in Berlin or London, as the data in table 5 reveal.[21] Aside from the matter of different relative employments, the structure of the various industries often varied quite

[21] Yu. Yanson, 'Naseleniye Peterburga i Ego Ekonomicheskiy i Sotsial'nyy Sostav po Perepisi 1869 Goda', *Vestnik Yevropy*, X, no. 10 (1875), pp. 624–6.

markedly. For instance, in brewing there was one owner for every 122 workers in the Russian capital, whereas the ratio in Berlin was 1:14. Similarly, in the manufacture of tobacco the scale of the St Petersburg operations was much larger, 1:38 compared with 1:8.[22] However, as we shall see later, the larger average number of employees per establishment did not necessarily imply a greater sophistication in the production process.

(a) *Factories and hands in 1867*

The manufacturing establishments located in the St Petersburg urban area employed approximately 35,000 workers in 1867.[23] Even allowing for the inconsistencies in the definition of what constituted a factory, the increase of 15,000 workers since mid-century was a

TABLE 5. *Relative share of labour force in selected industries, 1869–71*

Industry	Berlin 1871		London 1871		St Petersburg 1869	
	Male	Female	Male	Female	Male	Female
	%		%		%	
Food	4·0	0·8	8·0	1·4	2·9	1·8
Clothing	8·8	27·6	6·8	19·1	7·4	12·8
Textile	2·6	2·3	2·3	2·5	2·2	3·3
Metal-working	8·6	0·4	5·9	0·4	6·8	0·08
Leather	2·3	0·3	1·1	0·3	1·4	0·3
Chemical	0·5	0·2	2·0	1·0	0·5	0·04
Printing	1·7	0·1	3·5	1·0	1·3	0·02
Total percentage employment	28·5	31·7	29·6	25·7	22·5	18·34

Source: Yu. Yanson, 'Naseleniye Peterburga i Ego Ekonomicheskiy i Sotsial'nyy Sostav po Perepisi 1869 Goda', *Vestnik Yevropy*, X, no. 10 (1875), p. 625.

substantial one. By 1867 the disruptive effects of the Emancipation and St Petersburg's own 'cotton famine' had begun to wear off, and industry and commerce were on the threshold of a growth cycle that was to carry on into the seventies. We can see this process getting underway by looking at some data compiled for 1867. At this time there were no factory statistics comparable in coverage and reliability to those drawn up and published by the St Petersburg *guberniya* and city statistical

[22] Yanson, 'Naseleniye Peterburga', pp. 628, 633, 636.
[23] *Fabriki i Zavody v S. Peterburgskoy Gubernii v 1867 Godu* (1868), no. 6.

committees. The statistics used were among the last in a series, rather than an initial compilation, and we may assume with some justification that the picture we are able to draw from them is essentially correct. In order to get as complete a view as possible of the whole spectrum of manufacturing from workshop to factory, we can also make use of census data for 1869, which give the number and distribution of *remesla* or handicraft operations by type and borough.

At the end of the sixties, the traditional concentration of the *guberniya*'s industrial activity in and around the capital remained intact. A few far-flung plants processed the products of forest and field, but these were generally small-scale operations. Closer to the capital, but outside the urban area as here defined, several large-scale factories were geared to the demands of the military. These included the Okhtenskiy gunpowder works to the east of the capital, the Sestro-retskiy armament and metal-working plant to the northwest, and the Admiralty's metal-working complex in Kolpino to the south and shipbuilding works in Kronshtadt to the west. In addition, a handful of factories produced goods such as paper, linen and canvas for the domestic market, but these too were small-scale. Industrial production in the *guberniya* was entirely dominated by the St Petersburg urban area, which accounted in terms of value for over 90 per cent of all production.[24]

Although the numbers of those employed in factories had almost doubled since mid century, less than 5 per cent of the population were so occupied. On the eve of the Great War nearly 10 per cent of the population, or something like 200,000 people, worked in factories; the process of industrialization in St Petersburg was clearly still in an early stage. However, industry in the capital was fairly important when compared with European Russia as a whole, for it accounted for about 9 per cent of total factory employment and over 10 per cent of the value of production.[25]

From the detailed statistics on the changing industrial structure contained in appendix I ⟨*see* pp. 414–15⟩, the main features in 1867 have been extracted and are presented in table 6. From a review of this table and maps 13 and 14 several facets of the industrial scene are conspicuous.

[24] *Fabriki i Zavody*, p. 21.
[25] This is comparing the 1867 St Petersburg figures with the total for European Russia in 1866. The difference of one year in the base would have had little effect on the relative share. V. Veshnyakov, 'Russkaya Promyshlennost' i Yeya Nuzhdy', *Vestnik Yevropy*, V, no. 10 (1870), p. 520.

TABLE 6 *Industrial Structure, 1867*

Industrial group	Employment	Per cent	Number of manufacturing establishments	Number of handicraft establishments (1869)
Metal-working	10,160	29·4	64	1,058
Chemical	1,394	4·1	33	14
Food and tobacco products	4,517	13·1	59	687
Tanning, tallow and soap	1,053	3·1	47	63
Paper and printing	3,596	10·4	89	204
Textile	12,447	36·1	86	2,619
Miscellaneous	1,333	3·8	23	193
Totals	34,500	100	401	4,838

Source: Derived from table 40 appendix I.

The textile industrial group, in 1867 as in 1852, provided employ-ment for the largest number of workers, over 12,000 and in excess of one third of the total factory employment. Data in appendix I indicate that large-scale production predominated with 54 per cent of the work-force employed in factories engaging over 750 workers. Within this group the greatest increase over mid-century occurred in cotton textiles, primarily spinning.[26] Indeed, spinning remained one of the most technically advanced industries in the capital. In the Nevskaya factory in 1859 were 10 per cent of the total number of spindles in the whole country.[27] Located on the shore of the Bol'shaya Neva River and employing over 1,400 workers in 1867, this plant had been founded by a foreigner, Baron Stieglitz.[28] But as map 14 indicates, there were other factories of a similar scale. For example, the Spasskaya and Petrovskaya factories in Shlissel'burg employed 813 and 1,497 persons, respectively. The Rossiyskaya factory, on the Staro-Petergofskiy Prospect adjacent to the Obvodnyy Canal engaged nearly a thousand workers, the Okhtenskaya factory in Okhta 867, and the Sampson'yevskaya on the right bank of the Bol'shaya Nevka 1,088.[29] In both scale and level of mechanization, though not necessarily in quality of output, these plants were comparable to the largest establishments in Britain and America.

With the exception of silk manufacture—where employment fell from 1,600 to 238—most branches of the textile group had shown an increase in employment during the preceding fifteen years. In numbers employed, the manufacture of woollen textiles (978) and cordage (496) were, after cotton-spinning, the next largest industries. The plants of the former were widely dispersed throughout the urban area, while cordage plants tended to be near to the main port on the south-eastern extremity of Vasil'yevskiy Island and the warehouse facilities located on Peterburgskiy Island immediately opposite ⟨*see* map 14⟩.[30] As well as providing the most factory employment, the textile group also had the largest number of workshops, over 2,600 of them in 1869. The majority of these workshops turned out clothing of one kind or another and, like the clothing factories, were concentrated in the

---

[26] Owing to the effect of the American Civil War, imports of raw cotton in 1867 only just equalled the volume discharged at the port in 1852, about 25,000 tons. *Vidy Vneshney Torgovli Rossii za 1867 God.* (1868), part 1, p. 11 et seq.

[27] Pazhitnov, *Ocherki Istorii Tekstil'noy Promyshlennosti*, p. 18.

[28] *Fabriki i Zavody*, p. 14.

[29] *Fabriki i Zavody*, p. 7 et seq.

[30] Hemp and hemp yarn, traditional Russian exports, continued to be shipped abroad in bulk. Exports totalled 29,000 tons in 1867. *Vidy Vneshney Torgovli Rossii*, p. 11 et seq.

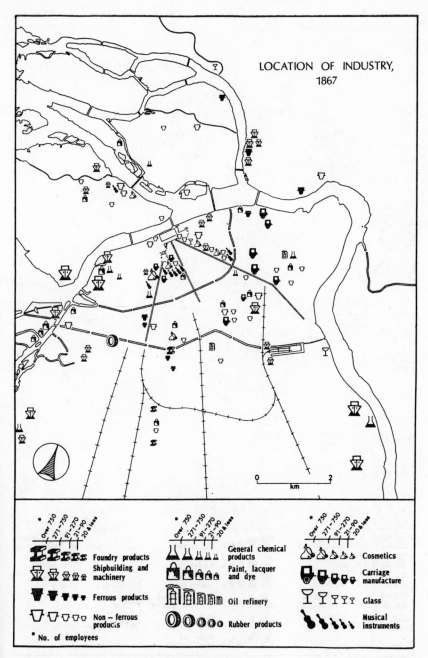

LOCATION OF INDUSTRY,
1867

0   2
km

	Over 750	271–750	91–270	21–90	20 & less	
						Foundry products
						Shipbuilding and machinery
						Ferrous products
						Non – ferrous products
* No. of employees						

	Over 750	271–750	91–270	21–90	20 & less	
						General chemical products
						Paint, lacquer and dye
						Oil refinery
						Rubber products

	Over 750	271–750	91–270	21–90	20 & less	
						Cosmetics
						Carriage manufacture
						Glass
						Musical instruments

MAP 13. *Location of industry, 1867–I*

95

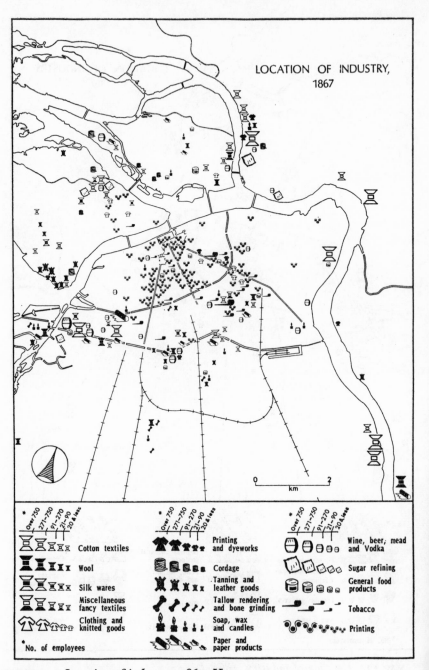

LOCATION OF INDUSTRY, 1867

	Over 750	271–750	91–270	21–90	20 & less	
						Cotton textiles
						Wool
						Silk wares
						Miscellaneous fancy textiles
						Clothing and knitted goods

*No. of employees

	Over 750	271–750	91–270	21–90	20 & less	
						Printing and dyeworks
						Cordage
						Tanning and leather goods
						Tallow rendering and bone grinding
						Soap, wax and candles
						Paper and paper products

	Over 750	271–750	91–270	21–90	20 & less	
						Wine, beer, mead and Vodka
						Sugar refining
						General food products
						Tobacco
						Printing

MAP 14. *Location of industry, 1867–II*

96

central city boroughs, especially Spasskaya and Moskovskaya. St Petersburg had fewer such establishments, particularly in women's apparel, than the size of the population might have led us to expect. The reason, as was suggested at the time,[31] may have been the predominance of peasants in the city, for they belonged to a class with a relatively inelastic demand for clothing; this fact may also explain why so few women were employed in the clothing industry ⟨*see* table 5⟩.

In absolute terms, the metal-working sector had gained the largest number of workers since mid century, about 6,000, which pushed the total employment in this sector over the 10,000 mark ⟨*see* table 6⟩. In response to the post-Crimean War upsurge in railway construction in particular, several new machine-construction plants appeared, existing plants were expanded, and by 1867 four factories employed over 750 workers apiece. The four largest were: the Baird plant in Kolomenskaya borough, 859 workers; the Carr and Macpherson 'Baltic' plant, 1,100 employees on Vasil'yevskiy Island;[32] the former state smelter, now owned by P. Semyanikov and V. Poletik, 1,500 workers, and the Nikolayevskiy plant, 2,146 employees, both in Shlissel'burg ⟨*see* map 13⟩. All were concerned with the manufacture of steam engines and railway equipment, and all, excepting the last, with ship construction.[33] (The principal shipbuilding facility operated by the government was in Kronshtadt and employed 1,000 persons.)[34] The majority of the privately owned metal-working plants at this time depended upon government contracts, for it was 'only in the second half of the sixties that there appeared . . . several small metal smelters and machine construction plants relying on private demand.'[35] In the quest for lucrative government work few could compare with the astute entrepreneur, N. I. Putilov. In 1868 he purchased a metal-working plant on the Petergofskoye Highway. Over the next decade work done on government contracts was worth more than six times that of any other factory, a continuing trait which was of no small consequence in enabling the plant to become the largest of any type in the city.[36] All this activity in the metal-working sector, plus the changes

---

[31] E. P. Karnovich, *O Razvitii Zhenskago Truda v Peterburge* (1865), pp. 33–4.

[32] This plant was taken over by the state in 1877. *Baltiyskiy Sudostroitel'nyy i Mekhanicheskiy Zavod Morskago Ministerstva, Istoricheskiy Ocherk* (1903), p. 7.

[33] W. I. Timiryazev, *Istoriko-Statisticheskiy Obzor Promyshlennosti Rossii* (1882), p. 44; *Fabriki i Zavody*, p. 7 et seq.

[34] Veshnyakov, 'Russkaya Promyshlennost'', p. 522.

[35] *Materialy ob Ekonomicheskom Polozhenii*, p. 10.

[36] A. Antipov, *Obzor Pravitel'stvennykh Meropriyatiy po Razvitiyu v Rossii Metallicheskoy Promyshlennosti* (1879), p. 38.

in the tariff policies mentioned earlier, resulted in a substantial increase in the volume of iron and steel imported. Supplies were obtained from Britain and invariably at lower cost than domestic products.[37]

Within the metal-working sector, employment at the four plants with over 750 workers accounted for 55 per cent of the total for the group, but the factories of the middle-range plant size, 91–270 workers, were also an important element. In addition, there was a considerable number of workshops in the city in 1869, 1,058. Nearly a third manufactured or repaired jewellery, gold and silver wares. Most of these were centrally located in the Moskovskaya, Spasskaya and Kazanskaya boroughs.[38] Approximately one fifth were blacksmiths, a function widely scattered throughout the city.

From map 13 it may be observed that the distribution of metal-working was fairly widespread, though some localization was evident. Shipbuilding and machine construction were concentrated primarily in two areas; at the mouth of the Bol'shaya Neva River and along the Bol'shaya Nevka in the borough of Vyborgskaya. Non-ferrous metallurgy was oriented to the Nevskiy Prospect and Ligovka Street. Many of these establishments manufactured articles from precious metals while several were linked with the printing industry through the production of type and typographical equipment. Most of the plants involved with ferrous metallurgical processes were small in scale and peripheral to the central city.

The relative expansion in employment in food products and tobacco manufacture was roughly commensurate with the growth in population from 1852, about 30 per cent and, with a work-force of 4,500 in 1867, this was an industrial group of some importance.[39] Sugar-refining was the only industry in this category to have experienced a drop in employment from mid century, owing to a greater reliance on home produced beet sugar. Only five comparatively large-scale plants with a total employment of 761 were in operation in 1867, a diminution of nearly 400 workers compared with fifteen years earlier. Imports of raw cane sugar had been even more severely affected, with the volume less than a third that of 1852.[40] A trend toward larger-scale production units was exemplified by the manufacture of tobacco products; employment

[37] The volume reached 72,000 tons in 1867. *Vidy Vneshney Torgovli Rossii*, p. 263, et seq.
[38] The distribution of gold and jewellery workshops is shown in map 22.
[39] For a comparison, see table 3, p. 55.
[40] Just over 8,000 tons were imported in 1867 as compared with more than 28,000 fifteen years earlier. *Vidy Vneshney Torgovli Rossii*, p. 263 et seq.; *Gosudarstvennaya Vneshnyaya Torgovlya v Raznykh Yeya Vidakh za 1852 God.* (1854), table XII.

had increased by over 300 to 2,279, but in 1867 there were less than half the former number of establishments. Like metal-working, the plants in this group were dispersed throughout the city ⟨*see* map 14⟩. Within the group, wine, beer, mead and vodka, and sugar-refining clustered near the waterways, as tobacco did in the central city, particularly the Moskovskaya borough. Over half the workers in tobacco manufacture lived in the first three wards of this borough, a fact which hints at the prevailing relationship between workplace and residence.[41] Although a trend toward larger-scale factories was discernible in the 1860s, plants employing between ninety and 270 persons were still dominant. Moreover, nearly 700 workshops, mostly bakeries, continued to flourish in spite of the trend.[42]

Lack of quantitative data precludes any precise measurement of change in employment in the paper and printing group from mid century, but available information points to moderate expansion. The number of printing establishments listed in the city directories, for example, increased from forty-eight to seventy-five.[43] No doubt the figure would have been greater but for pervasive illiteracy—put at 44 per cent in the census, though this was probably a gross underestimate—but government needs helped to make up for this disadvantage.[44] Many government publications were printed by private concerns in 1867, and it is probable that the majority of establishments worked in part at least on orders from the manifold government departments scattered throughout the city. Paper production continued to be dominated by the Imperial State Paper factory on the Fontanka (1,912 employees in 1867), which produced paper of the highest quality for government use, bank notes, stamps, etc., and the Nevskaya (Vargunin) plant in the district of Shlissel'burg (275 workers) ⟨*see* map 14⟩.[45] The former was also engaged in printing and engraving.

The three remaining industrial groups, tanning, tallow and soap products, chemical and miscellaneous, were relatively unimportant elements in the industrial structure in 1867, for in aggregate they had only 11 per cent of the total employment. In contrast with the

---

[41] *Sanktpeterburg po Perepisi 10 Dekabrya 1869 Goda* (1875), part 3, p. 15.
[42] *Vseobshchaya Adresnaya Kniga S. Peterburga* (1867–8), *passim.*
[43] Compare *Gorodskoy Ukazatel' ili Adresnaya Kniga na 1850g.* (1849), pp. 487–8 and *Vseobshchaya Adresnaya Kniga*, pp. 210–11.
[44] *Sanktpeterburg po Perepisi*, (1872), part 1, pp. vi–x. Numerous travellers remarked upon the widespread use of pictorial advertisements, which reflected the low levels of literacy. See, for example C.P. Smyth, *Three Cities in Russia* (London, 1862), vol. I, p. 65.
[45] Veshnyakov, 'Russkaya Promyshlennost'', p. 522; *Fabriki i Zavody*, p. 7, et seq.

mid-century distribution, a number of plants in the first group, tanning, tallow, and soap, ostensibly subject to restrictions in siting, had penetrated into the central city ⟨*see* map 14⟩. None the less, Vasil'yevskiy and Gutuyevskiy Islands and Ligovka south of the Obvodnyy Canal remained the dominant concentrations. The chemical industry was as widely dispersed as in 1852 ⟨*see* map 13⟩, with one third of the group employment accounted for by the recently formed Russia-American Rubber Company (456 workers) sited on the Obvodnyy Canal. Carriage manufacture, employing 727, had passed its zenith by 1867 and was characterized by a continual contraction in the number of establishments, particularly the small workshops which were not able to compete with the remaining factories.[46] Production in the other miscellaneous industries was also little augmented over 1852.

The use of power-driven machinery cannot be determined precisely, but with the data provided in the Ministry of Finance Yearbook for 1869 as a basis, it is possible to sketch a rough picture of the capacity and disposition by industrial group and factory size.[47] These data are presented in table 7, and, as indicated, the leading sectors were the metal-working and textile industries. Inasmuch as these groups were dominated by larger-scale production units this may not appear especially notable. It was usually the case that the larger factories had proportionally larger shares of the installed horsepower, but there were occasional exceptions to this general relationship. For example, two of the largest factories in the metal-working group, the 'Baltic' machine construction plant and the Nikolayevskiy rail equipment plant, between them possessed fewer than 115 horsepower. This was less than 7 per cent of the total recorded (1,694), but these two plants accounted for just over one third of the total employment in this group. Steam power was also commonly used in the predominantly privately owned, middle-size range factories of 91–270 workers. The growing use of motive power in factories is suggested indirectly by the changing volume of coal imports. From mid-century to 1867 it had more than doubled to over 475,000 tons, much of this being consumed in the city, and factory steam engines were an important element in this demand.[48] The total horsepower for the country was small, however; according to one source only 33,000 horsepower was in use, compared with 242,200

[46] K. Nellis, 'Ekipazh', *Istoriko-Statisticheskiy Obzor*, p. 105.
[47] *Yezhegodnik Ministerstva Finansov* (1869), vol. I.
[48] *Vidy Vneshney Torgovli Rossii*, p. 263 et seq.

TABLE 7. *Disposition of motive power (hp), 1869*

	20 and under		21–90		91–270		271–750		750 and over	
	Total HP	No. of plants	Total HP	No. of plants	Total HP	No. of plants	Total HP	No. of plants	Total HP	No. of plants
Metal-working (1,694)	—	—	123	4	347	8	557	3	665	4
Chemical (209)	—	—	3	1	16	1	190	2	—	—
Food and tobacco products (139)	—	—	—	—	96	5	43	1	—	—
Tanning, tallow and soap (12)	—	—	6	1	6	1	—	—	—	—
Printing and paper (1,057)	—	—	31	1	6	1	550	1	470	1
Textile (2,943)	—	—	52	5	511	13	830	3	1,550	5
Miscellaneous (52)	—	—	—	—	52	2	—	—	—	—
Total for St Petersburg 6,106 HP										

Sources: Yezhegodnik Ministerstva Finansov (1869), vol. I, part 3, *passim;* V. Veshnyakov, 'Russkaya Promyshlennost' i Yeya Nuzhdy' *Vestnik Yevropy,* V, no. 10 (1870), pp. 521–4.

Note: This table excludes motive power of excise-paying operations as these were not listed in *Yezhegodnik Ministerstva Finansov.*

in France in 1864, 375,200 in Great Britain in 1861, and 147,616 in Belgium in 1866.[49] Even allowing for a wide range of error in the specific figure for Russia,[50] these numbers reveal very clearly the severe backwardness of Russian industry as a whole.[51]

(b) *The location of factories and workshops*

The intra-urban variations in industrial location and size of plant have been presented in maps 13 and 14. By and large, it is the intention to let the maps speak for themselves in describing the simple distributional features of industry in 1867. What is not obvious from them is the spatial order, that is, the degree of spatial association between patterns, the extent of agglomeration and the distributional stability through time. It was suggested in the opening chapter that, through time, small-scale plants would exhibit a greater tendency to cluster or agglomerate than larger ones, and that with the increased specialization normally accompanying industrialization, this tendency would increase. In this chapter, only the first part of the hypothesis concerns us.

Since evaluation of this argument cannot be done by means of a visual inspection of the maps, a simple graphic technique for this purpose has been adopted. The cumulative frequency nearest-neighbour-distance measure permits comparative degrees of spatial clustering to be easily seen. For our analysis we have used third-nearest-neighbour distances as the basic measurement. As explained elsewhere, this provides a more incisive examination of the extent to which factories cluster than simply measuring distances to first-nearest neighbour.[52] Put simply, the more agglomerated or clustered the distribution, the more closely the curve approaches the Y-axis of the graph. Moreover, the technique reveals the existence of eccentrically situated plants by the extended 'tail' of the curve. A cursory inspection of figures 3 and 4 shows that, in the main, the smaller plants are more clustered. Some of the variations are of interest and warrant brief discussion.

[49] Veshnyakov, 'Russkaya Promyshlennost'', p. 524.
[50] See Strumilin, *Ocherki Ekonomicheskoy Istorii Rossii*, pp. 401–6, especially footnote 3, p. 402.
[51] For general comments on the substitution of labour for mechanical power, and on the role of the large-scale production unit, see A. Gerschenkron, 'Problems and Patterns of Russian Economic Development', in C.E. Black (ed.), *The Transformation of Russian Society* (Cambridge, Mass., 1960), pp. 48–53.
[52] For discussion of the technique, see A Note on Methods, pp. 428–9. It should be pointed out here that, in calculating third-nearest-neighbour-distance, a minimum of four factories is required, therefore some size-classes of industry are omitted from the graphs.

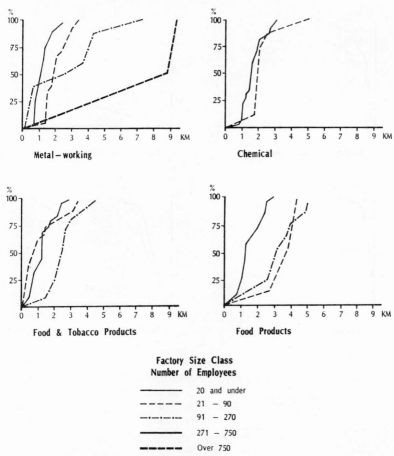

FIG. 3. *Nearest-neighbour graphs, 1867–I*

As perhaps might be expected, the greatest degree of clustering occurred among the small-scale printing firms which dotted the streets of the central city. Plants in the tanning, tallow and soap industries were also quite clustered, but as the extended tails of the curves for the first and second size-classes reveal, a few were eccentrically located. For the most part these reflected locational decisions which countered existing zoning restrictions and resulted in new plants appearing outside the main clusters on Vasil'yevskiy and Gutuyevskiy Islands. The distribution of chemical factories lent some support to the

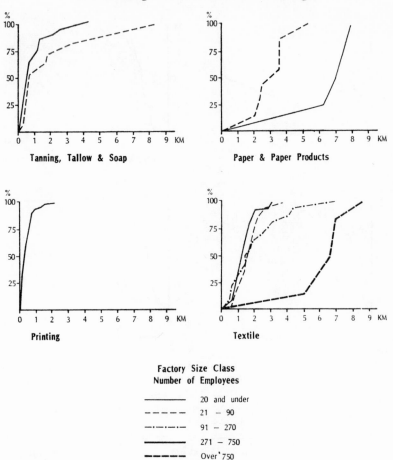

FIG. 4. *Nearest-neighbour graphs, 1867–II*

proposition that smaller plants agglomerate, but when the graph is compared with other industries which also clustered, that is, printing, tanning, tallow and soap, metals and textiles, it is apparent from the shapes of the curves that the distribution of chemical factories was less agglomerated. The pattern of the textile plants was in some respects similar to that of the metal-working factories. Both give general support to the hypothesis. However, in each case, groups of factories in the 91–270 employees category were more agglomerated than anything that occurred in the smaller-plant size categories. This was because of a functionally integrated group of fairly large textile factories along the shores of the Bol'shaya Nevka River and a cluster of metal-working establishments in Vyborgskaya borough ⟨*see* maps 13 and 14⟩.

The food and tobacco and paper and paper products industries did not conform to our basic argument, since in both cases factories employing twenty-one to ninety persons were more agglomerated than the smallest plants. When the tobacco factories were exluded, the relationship between the various sizes of food-processing plants changed. (This resulted from the fact that a number of large-scale tobacco firms were located in the same central-city boroughs.) However, the overall distribution of food-processing plants, as revealed by the concavity of the factory-class curves, tended more toward uniformity than agglomeration.[53] Many of these factories had retail functions and it was remarked in a contemporary study that being dispersed throughout the city facilitated marketing.[54] No doubt this was the case. But we cannot yet assume that marketing was the principal location factor, just as we cannot assume that the advantage most small-scale plants in cognate industries derived from being close to one another was the main reason for their being more agglomerated than large factories. We must first determine the importance of other location factors and discover if, through time, this is a predictable spatial characteristic.

Since the nearest-neighbour-distance measure is restricted to portraying the spatial characteristics of individual industries, some way of indicating the spatial correlation between patterns of industrial activity is wanted. Here we have opted for the Pearson product moment coefficient of correlation. This permits measurement of spatial associations between specific industries. The results are dependent upon the characteristics of a regional framework and details of this, as well as of the technique generally, are contained in another section.[55] At this point we need only be concerned with the results of the analysis.

A matrix of the correlation coefficients between thirty-four industries was compiled for 1867 and may be found in appendix II ⟨*see* p. 421⟩. We have restricted the discussion at this point to the measurements based on the sum of all factory employments in each industry for each

---

[53] See A Note on Methods, p. 430.
[54] *Vidy Vnutrenney Torgovli i Promyshlennosti v S. Peterburge v 1868 g.* (1868), p. 19.
[55] See A Note on Methods, pp. 429-32.

of the forty-four regions, but even so, statistically significant correlations were uncommon. Out of 1,156 possible associations between
the thirty-four industries considered, fewer than forty coefficients
reached $+0.38$, the level required to be statistically significant ninety-
nine times out of a hundred. If we consider only those statistically
significant spatial associations between components of particular industrial groups, then only textiles and food products so qualify. And in
total there were just three such coefficients.

In rationalizing the paucity of significant spatial associations,
particularly among cognate industries, two facts need to be taken into
consideration. First of all, as the distribution of total employment was
used as a basis for measurement, associations between different scales
of factory production were not considered.[56] In this respect, the
analysis differed from that of nearest-neighbours. Secondly, the early
stage in the industrialization process meant that specialization in
production was limited. Consequently, linkages between factories were
not highly developed. In a later chapter, the relationship between
specialization in production and spatial linkage will be fully evaluated
and we must defer final judgement of this possible explanation for the
dearth of statistically significant spatial linkages until then.

From a review of maps 13 and 14, it is apparent that large-scale
factories, that is, those employing more than ninety workers, were not
divorced from the central part of the city. This does not mean that the
pinch of rising rent and land costs was not being felt in 1867. It had
been noted fifteen years earlier that, since the manufacture of tobacco
products 'is situated in the most populated parts of the city where
apartment rents are quite high, it is understandable that owners
endeavour whenever possible to limit the dormitory factory'.[57] This
manoeuvre helped to minimize space and rent outlays, and by 1867 the
practice of accommodating workers in factory facilities was in marked
decline.[58] Still, the centrifugal pressure of rising rent was relatively
light. One example may suffice. A piece of vacant land in the central
city (on the Moyka Canal in Kolomenskaya borough), was rented by
the City Council to a merchant for 160 roubles in 1840; in 1852 it had

[56] The discussion here is restricted to total industrial employment because even fewer
coefficients of correlation reached satisfactory levels of significance when dis-aggregated
data were used.
[57] 'O Tabachnykh Fabrikakh v S. Peterburge', *Zhurnal Ministerstva Vnutrennikh Del*,
no. 10 (1852), p. 269.
[58] M. P. Vyatkin, 'Ekonomicheskaya Zhizn' Peterburga v Period i Krizisa Krepostnichestva', *Och.IL* (1957), vol. II, pp. 479–80.

gone to 357; by 1868 to 1,068; but by 1882, though the land was used for the same purpose, it had increased to 3,000 roubles per annum.[59] This rate of change is indicative of the rapid escalation in rent and property values which occurred during subsequent decades, a development which had the potential to alter patterns of industrial activity radically.[60]

There were many factors other than agglomerative pressures and rent which influenced the decision where to set up a factory. We might single out for brief consideration, however, land availability, transport accessibility, zoning regulations and labour supply.

During the sixties there was anything but a shortage of vacant land within the official city borders ⟨*see* map 15⟩. Indeed, even within the heavily built-up area between the Obvodnyy Canal and the Neva River, sizable areas of kitchen garden were available for conversion. Extensive areas ripe for development girdled the central city and presumably offered a wide range of locations for relocated or new industry. From the standpoint of industrial location, sites along the southern periphery were especially attractive. Here the advantages of water transport were provided by the Obvodnyy Canal and the recently arrived railways furnished important year-round links with the interior provinces and Europe. In an era of limited transport technology, selecting a location in the zones of confluence of waterways and railways would have helped to minimize transport costs.[61] As maps 13 and 14 reveal, such an orientation did not yet play a conspicuous part in the pattern of manufacturing. Industrial building on the islands and in the borough of Vyborgskaya showed where new growth was favoured as well as indicating the inertia of earlier decisions. Two questions arise: what role did land developers play in shaping this emerging pattern, and was it yet too soon for the full impact of the railways to be felt? Later on both of these questions will be examined.

It is clear from maps 13 and 14 that industry was not located far from the heavily built-up area. Small clusters of factories existed to the south along the Petergofskiy Prospect and the Neva River in Shlissel'-burg, but these were exceptions. Most plants were welded to the city

---

[59] 'Ob Otkrytii Novoy Ulitsy, Naznachennoy po Gorodskomu Mestu', *ISPGD*, no. 21 (1888), pp. 1028–9.

[60] For instance, rateable property values increased by nearly 40 per cent in the short period from 1874 to 1892, a period including a serious depression. 'Ob Obshchey Pereotsenke Nedvishimykh Imushchestv v S. Peterburge', *ISPGD*, no. 21 (1893), pp. 80–83.

[61] For relevant discussion, see Raymond L. Fales and Leon N. Moses, 'Land-Use Theory and the Spatial Structure of the Nineteenth-Century City', *Papers of the Regional Science Association*, XXVII (1971), pp. 61–8.

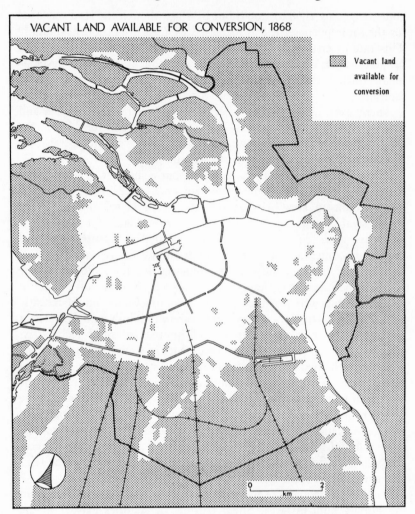

MAP 15. *Vacant land available for conversion, 1868*

proper and not the outlying suburbs, for it was in the city that an enhanced migration was creating a pool of labour. During years of uncertainty concerning the adequacy of the labour supply, there had been good reason for providing factory accommodation. With this aspect of industrial life on the wane, and in view of the long hours of work, it clearly behove industrialists not to stray far from where

108

workers lived. Simply from the point of view of labour supply, there was a clear advantage in a central-city location for a factory.

Pressure to locate within the zone previously prohibited to some industries had increased with the passage of time and was symptomatic of the overriding advantages of centrality. In the preceding chapter, we examined the effect of the zoning regulations at mid-century and concluded that either as relict or operational constraints, the pattern of noxious industry was modified by the existence of these regulations.[62] Such limitations on newly sited industry during the 1860s were no longer as effective. A careful perusal of maps 13 and 14 indicates that factories of all descriptions gravitated to the areas within the circum-ferences of the Obvodnyy Canal and the Bol'shaya Neva River, and to Vasil'yevskiy and Peterburgskiy Islands, areas of restrictive zoning, but accessible to the central city and, for that reason, attractive locations. One of the results was predictable. Industrial wastes polluted the waterways, and soon the City Council was bemoaning the 'inadequate and incomplete operation of zoning laws regarding the construction of factories and plants in St Petersburg'.[63] Their lament was wise after the event, and it seems plain that zoning regulations did not in any way seriously constrain factory location.

In summary, the pull of the central city, that is, the heavily built-up area, seems to have remained the dominant influence in locational decision-making, for clearly the pattern of manufacturing activity refutes any notion that de-glomerative tendencies were overwhelming up to the late sixties.

The distribution of workshops cannot, unfortunately, be analysed in a manner similar to that employed for factory production, because the data are too patchy and the directories fail to indicate clearly which were workshops and which were retail outlets. Thus, we have resorted to the enumeration of 1869 in which the distinction was made between *remeslennyya zavedeniya* and *torgovyya zavedeniya*, that is, handicraft and trade establishments. Census data do permit a general commentary on distributional characteristics because the numbers of each type were published for the twelve city boroughs. While the area is there-fore that of the official city territory, and not the urban area as defined hitherto, the nature of the workshop was such that urban, rather than suburban, locations were usual and it is unlikely that very many

[62] See chapter 2, pp. 58, 60 and map 11.
[63] 'O Peresmotre Uzakoneniy Otnositel'no Fabrik i Zavodov', *ISPGD*, no. 8 (1879), p. 677.

establishments have been excluded. The locational characteristics of the workshops in each industrial group have been described by means of coefficients of local concentration. These simply represent the relationship between the total number of workshops as distributed over the twelve boroughs and the distribution of a particular group of handicraft establishments. Divergence or congruence of a particular distribution from the total pattern is denoted by the quotient, where zero equals complete congruence and unity complete divergence (i.e. concentration in few boroughs). The resultant coefficients were as follows: metal-working, 0·12; chemical, 0·25; food products, 0·12; tanning, tallow and soap, 0·31; paper and printing, 0·28; and textiles, 0·08. It is apparent that the distributions of various workshops were very similar in 1869. Particular types of production were sometimes more localized. The 199 workshops turning out articles of gold had a coefficient of 0·28 which reflected the concentration in Kazanskaya borough. The sixty-three confectioners also were more concentrated, 0·23 as compared with 0·12 for the group as a whole. Yet even these specialist workshop activities cannot be regarded as highly localized.

In general, there is no evidence of marked agglomeration among the city's workshops. For factory production the evidence in this respect is not conclusive. Whether the next five decades witnessed locational decisions resulting in the distributional characteristics we have hypothesized remains to be seen.

(c) *Conditions of employment*

In the factories, freely hired labour had long dominated the St Petersburg scene. Before the Emancipation fully three quarters worked for wages, a much higher percentage than was common in Russian industry as a whole.[64] But whether voluntary or forced, the position of the factory worker prior to 1861 was not enviable. Emancipation and industrialization did not improve the workers' lot.

During the sixties it was general practice for workers to be on the job by six o'clock and to continue there until seven or eight in the evening. Fourteen- to sixteen-hour days were by no means uncommon, especially in the smaller workshops where the employees and owners lived together on the premises. Women and children also laboured alongside men in the factories and workshops. And it was really only the limited part that women played in the migration to the capital which

---

[64] M. Zlotnikov, 'Ot Manufaktury k Fabrike', *Voprosy Istorii*, no. 11–12 (1946), p. 40.

held down their involvement to an average of less than 20 per cent of the factory work-force. We noted earlier that in 1845 the first law governing child labour was enacted. But it was never enforced and, despite renewed concern at the end of the fifties, there was no effective legislation protecting the young. The strongest proposition had sought twelve hours as the maximum working day for twelve to fourteen-year-olds.[65] At the end of the sixties the census tells us that there were many children under twelve classified as factory workers and nothing had been done to control the period spent in the plant, night-time included. The plight of children in particular, and of factory workers in general, was not totally ignored, however. The occasional strike (illegal), the odd commentary in the journals and press, and the regular epidemics, all served to focus attention, albeit often fleetingly, on the conditions under which many people laboured and lived.

Commissions established to investigate ways and means of restructuring employer-employee relations as part of a broader mandate to reformulate labour policies, such as that chaired by A. F. Shtakel'berg during the early sixties, portended a much closer scrutiny of labour-management relations and working conditions.[66] This and other commissions continued the ritual until factory and labour legislation was at last introduced in the eighties. But in the late sixties legislation and more stringent controls were thought to be just around the corner. For a good number of factory-owners this was sufficient inducement to minimize commitments to workers, including, for example, the provision of accommodation. However, some owners were voluntarily trying to improve conditions. Nobel, for instance, introduced a 10·5 hour day in his factory at about this time.

Wages in the capital were known to be comparatively high. In the two most important industrial groups, textiles and metal-working, they averaged eighteen to twenty roubles each month. Skilled metal-workers could draw as much as twenty-five to thirty-five roubles per month, but such sums were exceptional.[67] The majority, of course, earned much less; in some low paying industries like tanning, linen, or

[65] T. M. Kitanina, 'Rabochiye Peterburga v Period Razlozheniya i Krizisa Krepostni-chestva (1800–1861 gg.)', in S. N. Valk (ed.), *IRL* (1972), vol. I, p. 113; I. A. Baklanova, 'Formirovaniye i Polozheniye Promyshlennogo Proletariata', *IRL*, p. 128.

[66] For discussion of this development, see Reginald E. Zelnik, *Labor and Society in Tsarist Russia, the Factory Workers of St Petersburg 1855–1870* (Stanford, 1971), pp. 129–59; K. A. Pazhitnov, *Polozheniye Rabochago Klassa v Rossii* (1906), pp. 5–7.

[67] D. G. Kutsentov, 'Naseleniye Peterburga. Polozheniye Peterburgskikh Rabochikh', *Och.IL* (1957), vol. II, p. 192.

jute, twelve roubles per month was usual. And for common labourers, thirty to fifty kopeks for a day's work in a factory was all that could be expected. Women and children were cheaper labour still, if a reasonable amount of work could be extracted from them.[68]

Although by Russian standards wages were high, so too was the cost of living in the capital. During the sixties the position of workers, especially the itinerant and unskilled, deteriorated as the cost of food and shelter rose faster than incomes. The shortage of housing accentuated the problem, and so did the periodic poor harvests and inadequate facilities for storing food once it arrived in the city. In the winter of 1865 it was observed that 'the chief food of the lower classes, bread, cabbage, and fish, were scarce and inferior in quality, and vegetables in general were much destroyed by early frost.'[69] It is small wonder that, in the quest to make ends meet, as little as possible was paid in rent. The consequences were obvious. 'One case was mentioned to me,' reported George Whitely, 'in which 60 men were found lying closely packed on the floor of one room wrapt in their sheepskins, with door and windows closed to keep out the cold. The atmosphere of this room was so charged with carbonic acid that a candle would scarcely burn in it.'[70] For those housed at the factory, rents demanded were often extravagant and the food poor. According to another source, 'Breakfast and lunch of the workers . . . usually comprises a half-a-pound of bread with salt and water. Lunch is made up of plain cabbage soup or cabbage soup with beef (no more than half-a-pound) and buckwheat porridge. In the summer rations sometimes are varied with onions and cucumbers.'[71] Moreover, the system of fining workers for infractions of company rules and the existence of company stores simply reduced further the opportunity to save. Given the conditions of employment, it is no surprise that government officials at all levels viewed the mushrooming labour force as a threat to civic order.

(d) *Restraints on early industrialization*

By the sixties, there were more factories and more industrial jobs to be filled, but there had not yet come into being that thoroughly industrialized setting which was conducive to the industrialization process. Society remained very much bound by tradition. The

[68] Baklanova, 'Formirovaniye i Polozheniye', pp. 136–7.
[69] Whitely, 'Report'.
[70] Whitely, 'Report'.
[71] Kitanina, 'Rabochiye Peterburga', p. 114.

Emancipation had not created overnight a pool of factory labour imbued with the necessary attributes of an industrial society— regularity of habit and a readiness to submit to the demands of production. Peasants, who comprised the bulk of the factory work-force, were still largely illiterate and, with a legal attachment to the commune, their commitment to urban life and factory ways was not strong. Peasants came and went according to the season and rates of labour turnover were consequently high. This was not helpful in raising labour productivity, nor was factory management made easier. If rural-urban migration had started to augment the labour supply, it clearly did not follow that its quality also increased. Among the upper classes, too, prevailing values placed little weight on achievement in the business world. Far better was it for the sons of nobles and the gentry to take up a career in government or the army than resort to commerce and industry. For those who had got on by such means and wanted to be accepted into the tight social world of the urban elite, these values were real barriers and thus the children of wealthy merchants and industrialists seldom followed after them. Industrialization had begun, but the educated and monied urban class was reluctant to be involved.

The burden of effecting economic growth had very largely fallen on the shoulders of outsiders ever since Peter the Great. Foreigners ran much of the city's industry and had done so from time immemorial, partly because of the absence of a solid middle class from which to draw entrepreneurial talent and capital. This in turn had partly arisen from the establishment of an elaborate bureaucracy which worked against the emergence of an urban bourgeoisie. Nor was the foreigner free from its toils. In the early part of the century, particularly during the reign of Nicholas I, the combination of high taxes, limited tenure as a resident merchant, and restrictions on the business dealings of foreign merchants served to dissuade all but the most persistent from embarking on a mercantile career in Russia. It was easier to overcome administrative hurdles by becoming a Russian subject, and this was a course that thousands followed. In keeping with its efforts to expand the economy in the late fifties, the government abolished certain legal constraints on alien business activities in 1860. This removed one impediment to industrialization, though the foreigner was still obliged to work within the restrictions of the guild system. The 1860 decree had simply removed impediments to his entry.[72]

[72] William L. Blackwell, *The Beginnings of Russian Industrialization, 1800–1860* (Princeton, 1968), p. 248.

By 1866, foreigners owned nearly a quarter of St Petersburg's factories. Moreover, since mid-century the output of producers' goods was accelerating more quickly than the traditional output of consumers' and luxury goods, and it was precisely in the important producers' goods sector that foreign enterprise was most prevalent. Opportunities in the capital were seized on by merchants and industrialists from other parts of the Russian Empire, and if we extend our view of outside control so as to include this group, then more than 35 per cent of the capital's industry was owned by non-locals.[73] In these proportions it is not possible to determine the specific size of the factories controlled, but customarily they were among the largest. It should be remembered that many of the leading industrialists registered as first or second merchant-guild members, and were therefore citizens of the capital, though they were in fact of foreign origin. In short, the process of industrialization at this early stage relied on technical and managerial skills which had to be imported.

Obviously, the scarcity of indigenous entrepreneurial talent was not alone in impeding industrialization. The process was complicated by an entrenched bureaucracy which generated rules and regulations at an alarming pace. Importing raw materials, for example, could be done if the myriad customs regulations were observed; if they were not, needed supplies could well be delayed. Police surveillance of labour, an antiquated legal system, the requirements of guild membership, all had the effect of entangling factory production.[74] Fortunately, the potential profit to be made was such as to encourage the prospective industrialist. Still, the transformation of a heavily bureaucratized court-administrative centre into a modern industrial complex was not to be simple. Much had to be changed to accommodate the process already set in motion.

2 THE MERCANTILE MILIEU

The growth of joint-stock companies after the thirties begun to put Russian business ventures on a similar footing to those in Europe and America, though lagging far behind. Modernization of the economy still required a well developed system of financial institutions—banks,

[73] *Vidy Vnutrenney Torgovli i Promyshlennosti*, end-flap table.
[74] On this matter we might note Consul Michell's concern; 'The trade in British manufactured goods is almost entirely in the hands of small German houses, better acquainted than others with the complications of the Russian tariff'. Michell, 'Report'. For a general discussion of several of these problems, see Zelnik, *Labor and Society*, pp. 119–59.

credit organizations, brokerage facilities, and the like. And their development, in fact, was an integral part of the industrialization process. A general uneasiness as to the consequences of a full-scale effort to industrialize, a recalcitrant bureaucracy and parochial mercantilism were only a few of the barriers to the easy conversion of businessmen to modern business practices. Fortunately, there were some individuals who recognized structural deficiences in the existing economic system, who worked indefatigably to effect changes, and who, because of positions of some stature, were actually able to do something. Count M. K. Reutern was one such person. As Minister of Finance from 1862 to 1878, he was instrumental in initiating reforms which made investment in Russia on the part of foreigners an attractive and far more reliable proposition. By such means moderate economic growth was achieved but, just as important, the foundations for a system of modern financial institutions were laid. Although Reutern endorsed private capital and initiative, the grafting of capitalistic institutions on the commercial body was not entirely the product of private enterprise. State policies were often responsible for creating a propitious environment for such endeavours. Tariff changes spurred foreign trade and granting concessions and guaranteeing returns induced investment. Both resulted from governmental actions during Reutern's tenure as Minister.

By the late sixties, financial institutions in St Petersburg were lubricating the wheels of economic development both in the locality and throughout the Empire. The State Bank, established in 1860, was of considerable significance in modernizing the country's financial operations and in extending banking facilities into the provincial centres, but it was just one of many such vehicles for development. With the offices of two dozen joint-stock commercial banks, the largest stock and commodity exchange in the Empire, scores of brokers, dozens of commercial agents, and a nucleus of credit and insurance companies, the cumulative process of commercialization had assured St Petersburg pride of place in the business and financial circles of Russia. There were clear-cut advantages to being located in the largest urban-industrial centre, but the more subtle attraction of having the ear and perhaps also holding the purse of government was assuredly of no small consequence.

It should be borne in mind that, despite some evidence of modernization, the majority of commercial transactions continued to be carried out in accordance with traditional business ethics, or rather lack of them. Some people, like Consul Michell, found reason to be hopeful of change. 'The new courts of law are working very satis-factorily', he wrote. 'The fear of exposure, and the certainty of condemnation in the case of guilt, without the hope of escape from punishment by means hitherto employed, are all deterrents from dishonesty which . . . cannot fail to promote the internal and foreign trade of the country.'[75] Whether his optimism would prove deserved was a moot point and business continued in the spirit conveyed in a contemporary traveller's account:

> Having arrived at the shop . . ., the purchase is made somewhat in this fashion:
> Lady: 'I wish, if you please, to look at some French ribbons.'
> Shopman: 'Horro sha, Sudarina' (very well, lady). The shopman takes down a box, the contents of which are un-deniably Russian manufacture.
> L: 'These are not French—I want *French* ribbons.'
> S: 'These are *real* French: they are from Paris.'
> L: 'No, I am sure they are not.'
> S: (After again most energetically repeating his assertion) 'Well! how much do you want?'
> L: 'Show me the ribbons, and then I will tell you.'
> S: 'How many arsheens did you say?'
> L: 'Show me the French ribbons.'
>
> The shopman unblushingly puts back the box which he has so recently declared contained the real article, and takes down another, which is filled with ribbons really of French fabrication.
>
> L: 'How much is this an arsheen?'
> S: (With a most graceful inclination) 'Seventy copecks.'
> L: 'Seventy copecks! Why the price is only fifty, and that is all I will give you.'
> S: (Quite indignant) 'Fifty! they cost us more than that; you shall have it for sixty five.'
> L: 'Fifty.'
> S: 'Bosja moia! No! I can't think of fifty—say sixty.'
> L: 'Not a copeck more than fifty.'
> S: 'By Heaven! I can't sell it for that price; you shall have it for fifty five.'

[75] Michell, 'Report'.

L: 'Will you take fifty or not?'

S: 'I can't indeed.' (He shuts up the box and puts it back into its place.) 'You shall have it for fifty three.'

The purchaser refuses to be cheated of even three copecks an arsheen; and walks out of the shop; she has perhaps gone half a dozen yards, when the shopkeeper's voice is heard calling out, 'Barishna, Barishna! come back, if you please!'

L: 'Not a copeck more than fifty.'

S: (Having persuaded her to re-enter the warehouse, says in a confidential manner) 'You shall have it for fifty-one.'

L: 'I said fifty and I will give you no more.'

S: 'Well! say fifty and a half!'

L: 'If you don't like to take what I said, I will go to the next shop.'

S: (Finding that his customer will *not* be cheated) 'Horro sha, Mosjna! well, you may have it; how much do you want?'

L: 'Six arsheens.' He proceeds to measure the ribbon and she takes out her purse, and gives him a five-rouble note to change. The shopkeeper's hopes of cheating begin to revive at the sight of the note, for he can't find the amount of the balance due to his customer by two or three copecks.

L: 'You must give me three copecks more; this is not right.'

S: (With a very low bow), 'Isvenete veno vat, I beg your pardon, I am in fault.' The remaining three copecks are slowly produced, and the customer at last walks away with her ribbon. In this senseless manner do the Russian shopkeepers waste their own time and that of the purchaser. One would think that the minutes thus lost would be of more value than the consideration of the profit of a few copecks more.[76]

The absence of properly formulated laws regarding contractual agreements and of commercial ethics and the like had given rise to patterns of behaviour that were often incomprehensible to alien businessmen. None the less, commerce managed to flourish.

Commerce employed over 30,000 persons in the city in 1869, somewhat less than the factories and more than 13,000 fewer than handicraft establishments. Again, a few points of clarification are necessary. Both the handicraft and commercial employments have been derived from the census of 1869, whereas the 34,500 employed in factories refer to the urban area and not the jurisdictional area of the

[76] *The Englishwoman in Russia* (London, 1855), pp. 62–3.

city, which was somewhat smaller. Factory employment was also based on statistics for 1867. While some employment in workshops and commerce has been excluded because of reliance on the census area, it is unlikely to have been large enough to disturb the general relationships between the groups.

From table 8 it is clear that employment in retail shops dominated the total employment in commerce. This was chiefly in foodstuffs for nearly 80 per cent of the 7,100 retail outlets sold food. As in the manufacture of clothing, so too in its retail outlets, female employment was small. While the total employment in financial institutions was not particularly impressive in relation to, say, the London scene, in the Russian context it was of considerable significance. The other leading commercial centre was Moscow and, thirteen years later, scarcely 2,200 persons were working in finance, not quite two thirds of the figure for the capital at the end of the sixties.[77] Wholesaling requires little comment other than to note the importance of the category embracing construction materials and fuel. In point of fact, it was the distribution of fuels which engaged the largest number, a situation fully in keeping with the rigorous climate.

The response to retail and wholesale business opportunities was more heavily oriented to outside talent than in the industrial sector. Part of the reason again had to do with the truncated source of entrepreneurs within the city; but additionally, it resulted from the ease of entry into retail trade. All one had to do was pay a small fee in order to acquire the status of petty trader. By 1866 over 3,600 peasants alone had done so, and as a result, only a bare majority of retail traders were citizens of the capital.[78] In wholesaling, over half of the 309 dealers had migrated to the capital, the vast majority from other Russian towns. Foreigners, therefore, had only a limited involvement, a state of affairs which was different from the world of finance.

As a prime location for retail activity, the Nevskiy Prospect in the late sixties had lost none of its earlier significance. It was 'at the same time the street of shops and the fashionable street of St Petersburg. Rents are as high as on the Boulevard des Italiens; it is a truly peculiar *mélange* of shops, palaces, and churches.'[79] But it was not solely a zone of fashionable retailing activity. For one thing, the throngs of shoppers and pedestrians themselves attracted from all quarters of the city

[77] *Perepis' Moskvy 1882 Goda* (Moscow, 1885), part 2, pp. 231–2.
[78] *Vidy Vnutrenney Torgovli i Promyshlennosti*, end-flap table.
[79] Théophile Gautier, *A Winter in Russia* (New York, 1874), translated by M. M. Ripley, p. 70.

TABLE 8. *Employment in commerce, 1869*

		Totals
Retail shops		23,970
Including:		
General grocers	5,029	
Flour	1,076	
Tea, coffee and sugar	512	
Fruit	1,769	
Meat	1,906	
Tobacco	652	
Ready-made clothing	704	
Books	245	
Wholesale outlets		2,412
Including:		
Construction materials and fuel	1,673	
Livestock	278	
Financial institutions		3,725
Including:		
Banking	154	
Commercial agencies	514	
Brokerages	128	
Total		30,107

Source: *Sanktpeterburg po Perepisi 10 Dekabrya 1869* (1875), part 3, pp. 72, 73, 74, 84, 85.

hordes of nondescript peasants hawking whatever might bring a few kopeks ⟨*see* plate 20⟩. With the onset of winter, the sale of fruit was potentially remunerative: 'Along the sidewalks mujiks offer to the passers-by green apples which look as if they were sour. However, it must be that they find purchasers: they seem to be offered for sale at every corner.'[80] In addition to this, the popular image of the Nevskiy Prospect was based on the type of shops in the limited zone between the *Gostinyy Dvor* and the Admiralty. A more accurate picture is obtained by using the city directory to recreate the pattern and range of retail facilities along its whole length. For the other six principal shopping streets also, this has been done ⟨*see* map 16⟩.[81] As the longest thoroughfare, the Nevskiy Prospect not surprisingly had the most retail shops.

[80] Gautier, *A Winter in Russia*, p. 72.
[81] Selected on the basis of contemporary descriptions of shopping facilities and the aggregate number of outlets the streets in question were as follows: Bol'shaya Morskaya, Sadovaya, Gorokhovaya, Voznesenskiy, Liteynyy and Vladimirskiy. For an earlier discussion of the role of several of these streets, see chapter 2, pp. 28–9.

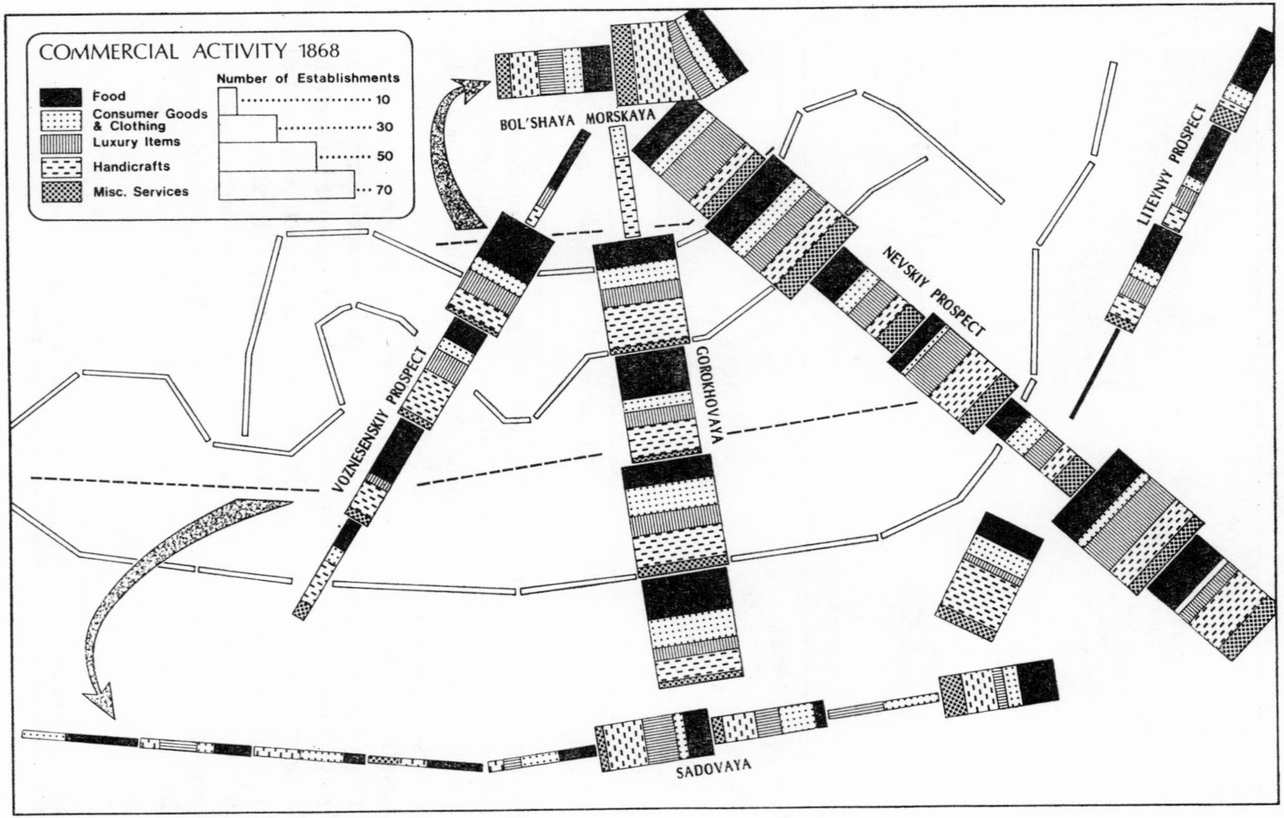

MAP 16. *Commercial activity, 1868*

COMMERCIAL ACTIVITY 1868

Number of Establishments
.... 10
.... 30
.... 50
.... 70

Food
Consumer Goods & Clothing
Luxury Items
Handicrafts
Misc. Services

LITEYNYY PROSPECT
NEVSKIY PROSPECT
GOROKHOVAYA
BOL'SHAYA MORSKAYA
VOZNESENSKIY PROSPECT
SADOVAYA

More than two thirds of these sold general food products and consumers' goods. Both of these retail types were also well represented in
what was popularly considered the zone of high-class shops. Their
presence there in such large numbers suggests that a sharply defined,
exclusive retail zone had not yet emerged. Still, we can see from map 16
that there tended to be a build-up of luxury and handicraft shops along
each of the adjoining streets as the Nevskiy Prospect was approached.
There is certainly no doubt as to the dominance of the latter in retailing;
there is some question as to how specialized it was.

Looking at retail trade from a different point of view also gives rise to
questions concerning the degree of areal specialization. Using the
census of 1869 for the number and type of retail shops by borough, we
have computed coefficients of local concentration for more than a dozen
groups of retail activity. As the coefficients presented in table 9 reveal,
retailing was not particularly localized. Although the use of groups
such as these usually tends to mask any individual variations, a more
detailed analysis revealed that this was not the case. The main exception was in the jewellery and metalwares group. Here gold and jewellery
shops alone had a coefficient of 0·59, whereas the group statistic was
0·30. The relationship between population distribution and the number

TABLE 9. *Localization of retailing, 1869*

Retail group	Number	Coefficient of local concentration
Food products	3,285	0·06
Clothing	373	0·40
Cloth fabrics	164	0·10
Leather wares and shoes	96	0·09
Furniture	23	0·38
Wood products	25	0·32
Glassware etc.	81	0·21
Jewellery and metal wares	137	0·30
Lamps and candles	137	0·21
Apothecaries and chemicals	80	0·26
Art work, books, musical and scientific instruments	116	0·46
Carriages, harnesses and luggage	49	0·48
Eating establishments	3,411	0·09
Other	90	0·33
Total	7,067	

Source: Sanktpeterburg po Perepisi 10 Dekabrya 1869 (1872), part 2, section 2,
pp. 118–20.

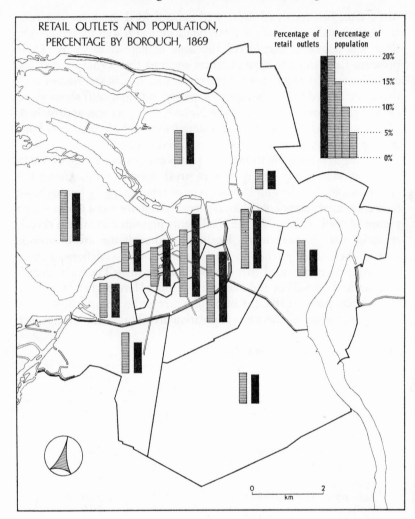

MAP 17. *Retail outlets and population, percentage by borough, 1869*

of retail shops by borough amplifies this basic point ⟨*see* map 17⟩. While the central boroughs of Spasskaya and Kazanskaya had a greater share of retail shops than of population, they were unusual in this respect. For the city as a whole then, the number of shops was more uniform than concentrated. Clearly the central boroughs had a greater share of the more specialized activities. Spatial differentiation in retailing activity is brought about by many forces, not the least of which are a relatively high level of personal mobility and a realizable propensity to spend money; the question is, what did the future portend for a city fast becoming dominated by recently arrived peasants who were neither especially mobile nor affluent? For an answer we shall have to wait until the analysis of retailing after the turn of the century.

3 THE TECHNOLOGY OF MOVEMENT

In 1869 almost 17,000 persons derived all or part of their livelihood from what might be described as the urban transport industry ⟨*see* table 10⟩; another 5,400 were employed by the railway companies, four of which served the city in 1869. Until the completion of the Finlyandskaya railway in 1870, the rail service was confined to the southern part of the city, but this line was not linked with the railways in the south until after the turn of the century and the contribution of the steam-rail system to the movement of goods within the city was throughout quite insignificant.

Scores of vessels of various kinds plied the numerous waterways, some of them redistributing goods landed on Vasil'yevskiy Island or at the new docks on Gutuyevskiy Island at the entrance to the Obvodnyy Canal, others (conceivably the majority) performing the essential task of distributing the winter's supply of firewood brought into the city from the tributary area of the Bol'shaya Neva River in ever increasing volume. The seasonal importance of water-borne goods traffic was, to

TABLE 10. *Urban transport employment, 1869*

	Numbers of			Total
	Owners	Employees	Odinochki	
Commercial fleet	52	180	—	232
Public steamboats	—	84	—	84
Ferries	2	78	—	80
Public carriages	3	297	—	300
Private cabs	660	4,931	7,579	13,170
Commercial waggons	199	1,862	822	2,883
Horse-tram	4	200	—	204
Totals	920	7,632	8,401	16,953

Sources: Sanktpeterburg po Perepisi 10 Dekabrya 1869 (1875), part 3, pp. 74, 85. Employment of the single horse-tram company has been estimated. 'Po Voprosu o Dal'neyshey Eksploatatsii Konno-Zheleznykh Dorog 1-go Tovarishchestva, po Okonchanii 31 Avgusta 1898 Goda, Sroka Kontsessii' *ISPGD*, no. 1 (1898), p. 107.

a certain extent, replicated on land. Commercial waggon operations engaged close to 2,900 persons including owners, their employees and independent *odinochki*. Goods movement through or within St Petersburg was obviously closely connected with the port traffic, which was limited to a seven-month season: during the ice-free period the demand for carters was at its height. Registration data for *izvoshchiki lomovykh*, or waggoners, illustrate this seasonal variation quite well. From November 1865 to May 1866, 1,917 drivers were registered, whereas from May to November 1866, there were 3,385.[82] The ebb and flow was produced by a migration of peasants, with horse and vehicle, from the surrounding villages.

The first major innovation in the movement of goods was the horse-tram. The initial line, on Vasil'yevskiy Island, did not begin service until the summer of 1860 and was designed to expedite the transfer of wares 'from pier to customs storehouse.'[83] In 1862 the Nevskaya, Sadovaya & Vasileostrovskaya Horse Railroad Company was granted permission by the City Council to contruct and operate three horse tram-lines in the city. A year later, trams were running along part of the Nevskiy Prospect, and the system was soon extended by a line on Sadovaya Street and another on Konno-Gvardeyskiy Boulevard, which was linked with the original line on Vasil'yevskiy Island.[84] The tram network, while less than eight kilometres in extent, did connect the port and customs complex located at the southeastern extremity of Vasil'yevskiy Island, and the Nikolayevskiy railway station on the Nevskiy Prospect. As the Nikolayevskaya railway provided the only rail link with Moscow and the interior provinces, its importance as a generator of goods traffic was enormous. However, by the late 1860s the policies of the company had changed.

One of the original intentions behind the company's application to

[82] P. Semenov (ed.), *Geografichesko-Statisticheskiy Slovar' Rossiyskoy Imperii* (1868), vol. IV, p. 447.

[83] 'Obozreniye Promyshlennosti i Torgovli v Rossii', *Vestnik Promyshlennosti*, no. 9 (1860), p. 126; 'Obozreniye Promyshlennosti i Torgovli', *Vestnik Promyshlennosti*, no. 10 (1860), p. 2. Much of the following discussion of transport technology and journeys to work derives from my earlier papers. 'The Development of Public Transportation in St Petersburg, 1860–1914', *Journal of Transport History*, NS, II, no. 2 (September 1973), pp. 85–102; 'The Journey to Work in St Petersburg, 1860–1914', *Journal of Transport History*, NS, III, no. 2 (September 1974), pp. 214–233.

[84] 'Konno-Zheleznaya Doroga', *ISPGOD*, no. 5 (1867), p. 229; Semenov, *Geografichesko-Statisticheskiy Slovar'*, p. 447. The four principals in the company were Adlerberg, Ditmar, Kanshin and Count Stroganov. A dominantly Russia concern, it operated on a thirty-five year concession. 'Po Voprosu o Dal'neyshey Eksploatatsii Konno-Zheleznykh Dorog 1-go Tovarishchestva, po Okonchanii 31 Avgusta 1898 Goda, Sroka Kontsessii', *ISPGD*, no. 1 (1898), p. 107.

the City Council to build and operate a tramway network, perhaps even the primary one, had been that of providing a goods haulage service through the city from railway station to port. The company had to comply with several restrictions imposed by the City Council. The most important restriction was that goods haulage had to take place between 11 p.m. and 9 a.m., ostensibly 'to minimize the daytime congestion.'[85] Night-time use of the service was far less than originally contemplated. In the first full year of operation, 1864, only 1·5 million tons of goods were hauled, whereas two years earlier the total volume of traffic through the Nikolayevskiy railway station exceeded eighteen million tons.[86] The tariff levied for night-time shipment of wares from the port to the Nikolayevskiy railway station, between one and one and a half kopeks per *pud*, was apparently competitive and was therefore not a deterrent to its use.[87] However, night work in the commercial and industrial sectors was in fact not common and the fixed-route service offered by the tram very much limited the potential market. An application to the City Council to have the restriction lifted was unsuccessful, so two alternative courses of action were adopted. In the first place, more frequent service was provided on the existing network in order to generate increased passenger traffic.[88] Secondly, application was made by the tramway company to the City Council during the period 1867–8 to extend the tram system.

The first application, in 1867, sought permission to extend the network into the suburbs.[89] The Council was unimpressed but none the less set up a committee to examine the proposal, and it recommended in 1868 that the proposal be rejected. In doing so, it argued that any extension of the service would have a bad effect on existing modes of transport in the city, notably the *droshky*. Since thousands of horses were involved, each of which was subject to an annual tax of ten roubles levied by the city, in addition to the licence fees paid by the *izvoshchiki*, any fall in their number owing to competition from the horse-tram would reduce revenue. Moreover, the horse-tram was more economical to operate and could seriously jeopardize the many

[85] 'Konno-Zheleznaya Doroga' p. 234; 'Po Khodataystvu Tovarishchestva Konno-Zheleznykh Dorog o Razreshenii Onomu Prolozhit' Neskol'ko Novykh Liniy', *ISPGOD*, no. 15 (1868), p. 795.
[86] 'Konno-Zheleznaya Doroga', p. 246; N. V. Kireyev, 'Transport, Torgovlya, Kredit', *Och.IL* (1957), vol. II, p. 130.
[87] 'Konno-Zheleznaya Doroga', p. 246.
[88] Daytime service was originally at thirty-minute intervals and fares were ten kopeks.
[89] 'Ob Ustroystve Konno-Zheleznykh Dorog v Zarechnykh Chastyakh Stolits' *ISPGOD*, no. 1 (1868), p. 59.

thousands of jobs created by the transport industry as it existed. The committee also suggested that the rails not only used valuable land, but were a hazard to other vehicles, that the horse-tram was less flexible, and in winter less effective than the customary horse-drawn sleigh, and that further extension of the system would simply serve to inconvenience the population.[90] Nothing the Nevskaya, Sadovaya and Vasileostrovskaya Horse Railroad Company could offer in rebuttal won the Council over, although one of the committee's recommendations for complete closure during the winter months was not endorsed. Further development of the tram system was therefore thwarted until the mid-seventies and goods movement remained dependent on several thousand horse-drawn vehicles.

The provision of public transport facilities also varied according to seasons but, in contrast with goods movement, the peak occurred during the winter months. From the census we have seen that rather more than 13,000 persons were involved in the provision of private vehicles, of which the *droshky*, or one-horse, two-passenger cab, was the most common type. During the summer, peasant *izvoshchiki* drifted back to the countryside causing a reduction in numbers of as much as 40 per cent.[91] The fact of the matter was that the remaining drivers and vehicles were capable of meeting the demand and in the winter an over-supply existed. This superfluity seldom failed to elicit comment from travellers, and Théophile Gautier was no exception: 'What struck me especially, was the immense throng of carriages —and a Parisian is not apt to be astonished in this respect—which were in motion in the broad street; and above all, the extreme speed of the horses!'[92]

The over-provision of privately hired vehicles of various descriptions benefited neither the operators nor the majority of the city's inhabitants. For the former, returns were proportionately smaller and the chances of securing a reasonable livelihood that much more remote. Indeed, it really did not matter very much how many were available, because the majority of the public could not afford the municipally sanctioned tariffs anyway. For the few who could afford them, ready access certainly facilitated journeys in the city. Moreover, the omnibuses did not compensate in number for the fact that the cost of private cabs ruled them out as a regular mode of travel for many. Fewer than

[90] The foregoing discussion is based on, 'Po Khodataystvu Tovarishchestva Konno-Zheleznykh Dorog', pp. 795–804.
[91] Semenov, *Geografichesko-Statisticheskiy Slovar'*, p. 447.
[92] Gautier, *A Winter in Russia*, p. 69.

300 people were required to operate and maintain public carriages of all kinds, whereas in the major capitals of Europe omnibuses alone were carrying tens of millions of passengers annually; St Petersburg was totally eclipsed.[93]

Given the relatively few public carriages which a labour force of under 300 could support, it was not surprising that routes were limited and service infrequent. Throughout the late sixties less than ten routes were in regular use. Most radiated out from the zone around the *Gostinyy Dvor*, linking the boroughs in the north with the central city, while to the southeast, service extended as far as Aleksandrovskoye. Within the city only a few of the main thoroughfares were included in the network. During the summer months, however, additional lines provided access to the islands and the right bank of the Bol'shaya Nevka River where many affluent citizens had *dachi*. To this traditional mode of public transport must be added the dozens of ferries and twenty-odd steamboats which navigated the canals and rivers and, in the absence of bridges, shortened many journeys by providing short hops across the innumerable waterways.

By the late sixties the evolution of urban transport facilities in many cities had moved through three stages.[94] The first was the era of the private conveyance during which mobility of the populace was strictly limited. Subsequently, this mode of transport was complemented on a large scale by the hired cab. The final stage saw the advent of the capacious public carriage, especially the omnibus, which offered regular, frequent and inexpensive service and thereby generated a large traffic. Even allowing for a sizable error in the census data for employment in public transport, St Petersburg had at the time we are considering barely passed out of the second stage, whereas New York, London, Paris, Vienna, and to a lesser degree, Berlin had already evolved beyond the third stage. For example, in the early sixties over a thousand omnibuses provided transport for Parisians, and by 1866 it was reckoned that traffic exceeded 100 million passengers; at the same time a horse-tram system was growing in popularity, a situation not confined to Paris.[95] In St Petersburg, the 'city fathers' had hardly welcomed the horse-tram with open arms. The extent to which the system was used by the public may be judged by the fact that by the mid-sixties total traffic averaged in a year less than three trips per

---

[93] Yanson, 'Naseleniye Peterburga', p. 639.
[94] Yanson, 'Naseleniye Peterburga', p. 639.
[95] Yanson, 'Naseleniye Peterburga', p. 639.

inhabitant; in New York in 1864 horse-tram traffic was the equivalent of eighty-seven trips per person.[96] And we are here ignoring the growing importance of metropolitan railway services, which did not exist at all in St Petersburg.

If we accept the premise that the widespread adoption of innovations in public transport continued to cheapen service, enhance usage and therefore mobility, some obvious questions come to mind. The limited development of public transport facilities in St Petersburg clearly implied low levels of mobility for the bulk of the populace. How, then, did they journey to work?

4 THE JOURNEY TO WORK

In our analysis of journeys to work, two hypotheses will be examined. The first relates to assumed differences in journey-to-work distances between three broad occupational groups: managerial and professional, workshop-owners and artisans, and factory workers. The specific hypothesis to be tested is that proximity of work and residence will be greatest for the workshop-owners and artisans, less for factory workers, and least for the managerial and professional group. This is based on the obvious fact that the managerial and professional group would be able to travel furthest to work if desired.[97] As to workshop-owners and artisans, it has been observed for other cities that they frequently combine place of work and residence.[98] The journey to work of factory workers is deemed to be, in relative terms, somewhere between the other two. In the case of the second hypothesis it is the temporal stability of journey-to-work patterns which is the object of investigation. It is hypothesized that during the period 1860–1914, place of work and place of residence will show strong locational ties but that, with the passage of time and improvement in public transport, there should be evidence of a weakening of this spatial link; however, we shall have to wait until we come to the discussion of events after the turn of the century before we can see the full truth of this assertion. A managerial and professional group includes bank-owners or presidents, brokers and factory-owners.[99] Owners of plants in manufacturing are represented

[96] 'Konno-Zheleznykh Doroga', p. 241; James B. Walker, *Fifty Years of Rapid Transit, 1864–1917* (New York, 1970, reprinted from original edition of 1918), p. 5.
[97] See James E. Vance, Jr, 'Housing the Worker: Determinative and Contingent Ties in nineteenth-century Birmingham', *Economic Geography*, XLIII (1967), p. 126.
[98] Allan R. Pred, *The Spatial Dynamics of US Urban-Industrial Growth, 1800–1914: Interpretive and Theoretical Essays* (Cambridge, Mass., 1966), pp. 204, 206; Vance, 'Housing the Worker', pp. 95–127.
[99] State-owned and joint-stock companies, as well as the few factories where there were more than three owners listed, have been excluded from the analysis. This was done in

by metal-working and food and tobacco products, in order to give a complete range of plant sizes (metal-working) and a variety of locations (food and tobacco products) ⟨*see* maps 13 and 14⟩. In the workshop-owner and artisan group, the same categories are represented by bakers, confectioners, blacksmiths, goldsmiths, and jewellers.[100] These examples reflect both general and specialized trades.

TABLE 11. *Work-residence relations, 1867*

Occupational group	Total no. of establish-ments	No. of known work-residence relations	Non-coincident work-residence relations		Mean distance travelled to work*
			No.	%	Kms
A Managerial and professional					
1 Bank-owners or presidents	24	21	9	42·9	1·0
2 Factory-owners					
(a) metal-working	64	46	11	23·9	2·6
(b) food and tobacco	59	48	6	12·5	1·8
3 Brokers	127	126	5	3·9	1·0
B Workshop-owner and artisan					
1 Blacksmiths	233	233	—	—	—
2 Bakers	278	278	4	1·4	2·2
3 Confectioners	58	58	3	5·1	1·1
4 Goldsmiths and jewellers	233	233	3	1·3	1·2
5 Goldsmiths and jewellers incorporating a retail function	79	79	5	6·3	0·9

* Calculated on the basis of straight line distance between workplace and residence.

For the managerial and professional group, separation of home and workplace was the exception rather than the rule, as is immediately evident from table 11. The separation of workplace and residence was

order to ensure that the work-residence relations examined represented some degree of regular contact with the factory in question as well as being representative of a particular entrepreneurial endeavour.

[100] Because of the detailed directory data goldsmiths and jewellers have been separated into two groups—those who had a simple workshop and those whose operation included a retail function.

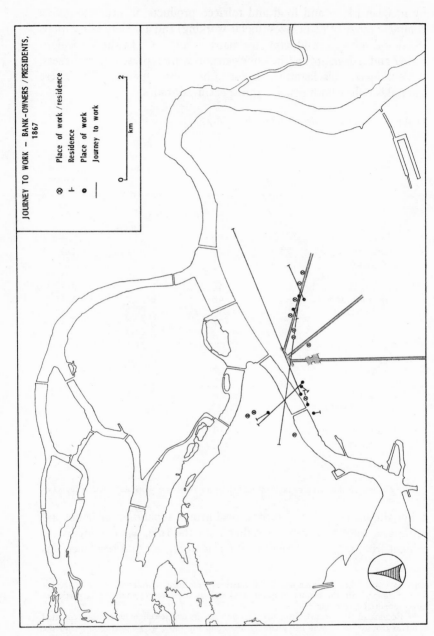

MAP 18. *Journey to work, bank-owners/presidents, 1867*

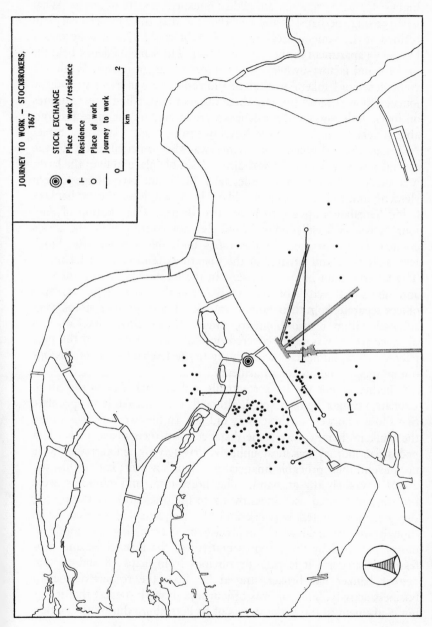

MAP 19. *Journey to work, stockbrokers, 1867*

highest for bankers, a not altogether unexpected state of affairs. What is surprising, perhaps, is the fact that the majority, 57 per cent, still resided at the same address as the place of work. This usually meant having an apartment in the same building. The same tendency held for brokers and factory-owners, who comprised larger groups. While the coincidence of bankers' workplace and residence was frequent and the journey to work short (in only three instances exceeding a few minutes on foot), both banks and residences were located on the more fashionable streets, chiefly the lower Nevskiy Prospect and Galernaya Street ⟨*see* map 18⟩. Although the former was the principal artery of the central business district, it was also a desirable place to live; the latter was much less significant commercially, but it did have a large foreign element, and to judge by names like Thompson, a number of bankers living hereabouts appear to have been British. The location of only four banks on Vasil'yevskiy Island did not entirely belie the area's commercial importance. In the 1860s both the port and the Stock Exchange were still situated at the eastern extremity of the Island.[101] The latter was an influential factor in the location of both residences and offices of the city's brokers. Only five of the city's 126 brokers had offices separate from their homes, and all but a handful of offices were situated within a two-kilometre radius of the Stock Exchange, a distance which was easily covered on foot ⟨*see* map 19⟩. In the pre-telephone era, immediate accessibility to the Exchange was of obvious importance to the broker's business.

Whether or not the broker actually walked each day to the Stock Exchange cannot be discovered, although it is reasonable to speculate that those who were farthest away did not. In the two instances where the bankers' homes were some distance from their places of work, a pedestrian journey was most unlikely. Privately owned carriages were not beyond their probable financial position, however; failing this, the *droshky* was always at hand. The horse-tram and omnibus were probably of limited usefulness owing to the orientation of the routes, the generally limited network and the frequency of service. Even though we are unable to be precise in determining the mode of movement used by these representatives of the managerial and professional category, it is patently obvious from maps 18 and 19 that neither banker nor broker strayed far from the respective foci of business activity. The patterns of journeys to work suggest that it was not convenient to travel the streets of St Petersburg during the sixties.

[101] The new port on Gutuyevskiy Island was officially opened in 1885.

How this affected the social-class fabric of the city is a question which we will take up at a later point.

In the case of work-residence locations of factory-owners, there was only a marginal difference between the two industrial categories in terms of the number of instances of workplace not being coincident with residence. In relative terms, however, there was a higher degree of separation for metal-working, 23·9 per cent against 12·5 per cent, in addition to which the journey to work tended to be longer. This is brought out by comparing the mean straight-line distances between work and residence in each case, 2·6 and 1·8 kilometres respectively for metal-working and food and tobacco products. But in neither case is there a close association between distance travelled and the size of establishment ⟨*see* maps 20 and 21⟩. The longest journey to work for a factory-owner was undertaken by a merchant of the first guild, V. Norman, whose machine-construction factory employing 138 persons was located on the Petergofskoye Highway, in the southwest part of the city, eight kilometres from his residence in the city centre. For both categories of factory-owners, the mean distance separating place of work from place of residence was considerably greater than the one kilometre for both bankers and brokers.

The question arises why owners of large plants were disposed to live at their works—which were often located in the less salubrious parts of the city—when commuting by private or hired conveyance would doubtless have been a feasible alternative. It cannot be assumed that they could not afford it; their profits were customarily high. Part of the explanation is that a number of owners built substantial residences on the site, irrespective of the type of industry or the amenities of the locality. ⟨*see* back endpaper⟩. Additionally, small to medium-size factories were frequently located on the ground floors, especially in inner courtyards, of the large blocks common in the city. The owners often had apartments which were in the same block as, but physically separated from, the actual place of production. And given the legendary inefficiency of Russian labour, it may have paid factory-owners to live on the spot in order to secure better control over production.

As for the workshop-owner and artisan group, table 11 shows that the trip seldom involved anything more than a few steps from bed to workbench. Of just over 800 journeys to work examined for owners and artisans, there were only fifteen instances of separation. Five of these were accounted for by the rather specialized manufacture and retail sale of gold and jewellery wares, while journeys to gold and jewellery

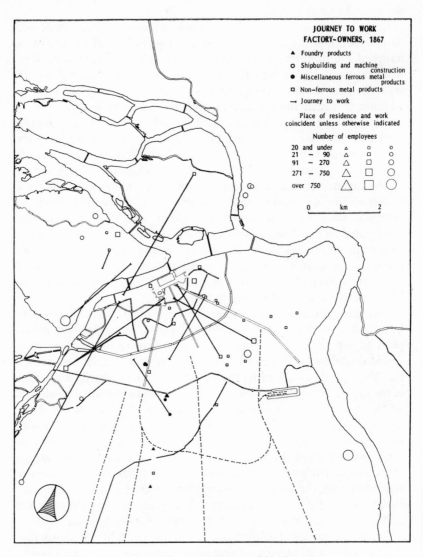

JOURNEY TO WORK
FACTORY-OWNERS, 1867

▲ Foundry products
○ Shipbuilding and machine construction
● Miscellaneous ferrous metal products
□ Non-ferrous metal products
→ Journey to work

Place of residence and work
coincident unless otherwise indicated

Number of employees

20 and under	△	□	○
21 — 90	△	□	○
91 — 270	△	□	○
271 — 750	△	□	○
over 750	△	□	○

0   km   2

MAP 20. *Journey to work, factory-owners, 1867–I*

134

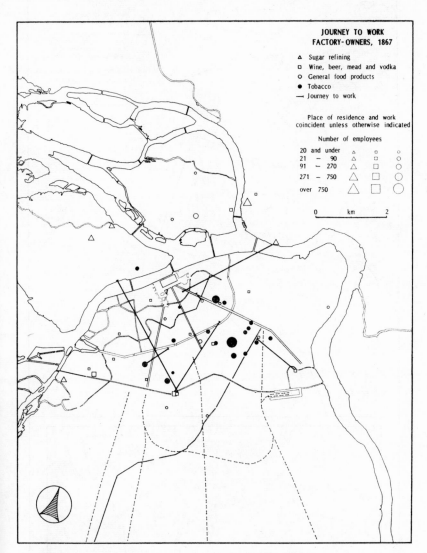

JOURNEY TO WORK
FACTORY-OWNERS, 1867

△ Sugar refining
▢ Wine, beer, mead and vodka
○ General food products
● Tobacco
▬ Journey to work

Place of residence and work
coincident unless otherwise indicated

Number of employees

20 and under	△	▢	○
21 – 90	△	▢	○
91 – 270	△	▢	○
271 – 750	△	▢	○
over 750	△	▢	○

0   km   2

MAP 21. *Journey to work, factory-owners, 1867–II*

135

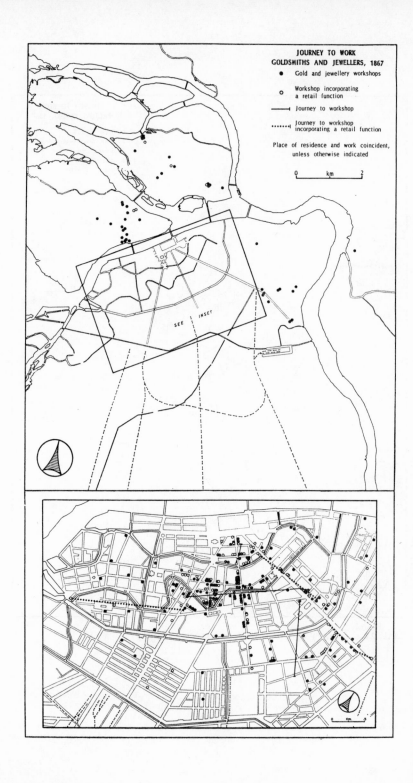

JOURNEY TO WORK
GOLDSMITHS AND JEWELLERS, 1867

●   Gold and jewellery workshops

○   Workshop incorporating
     a retail function

⊢——⊣   Journey to workshop

••••••   Journey to workshop
     incorporating a retail function

Place of residence and work coincident,
unless otherwise indicated

0   km   2

SEE INSET

workshops accounted for three more. All occurred within the central city where, with the exception of the remnant of an earlier concentration on Vasil'yevskiy Island, the manufacture and sale of gold and jewellery was most common. Since the general pattern of journeys to work was aligned with the Nevskiy Prospect, the existing public transport system could have been used to advantage (*see* map 22). Of the three confectioners who commuted daily, two of them covered areas not served by the horse-tram system. Inasmuch as all journeys were short—the mean distances separating home from business being 1·1, 1·2 and 0·9 kilometres respectively for confectioners, goldsmiths and jewellery handicraftsmen, and goldsmiths and jewellers whose operations included a retail function—it is probable that most people in this group walked to work. Blacksmiths ⟨*see* map 23⟩ and bakers were in relative terms even less inclined to make a journey to work. None of the 233 blacksmiths was either financially able or disposed to do so. The mean distance for the four bakers having a workplace distinct from residence, 2·2 kilometres, would have been much shorter but for a four kilometre journey by one of them.

In the groups examined, few people were travelling far to work, but what of the numerically more important factory workers? Data deficiencies preclude the recreating of specific journeys; however, a few suggestions may be made.

As we have seen, factor-owners had traditionally provided some basic facilities for workers, one of which was accommodation. The breakdown of this paternalistic relationship was due to several reasons, but clearly the enhanced labour supply served as a catalyst in the process. Understandably, the owners were disinclined to hold to traditional ways when the condition of workers' living quarters would sooner or later come under more stringent government supervision. This eventuality could only serve to push operating costs higher. Thus, when it was no longer expedient, employers were usually more than willing to relinquish the responsibility. In consequence, factory workers in growing numbers were dependent upon the private sector for housing. From the 1869 census we are able to determine that 17,201 males and 2,093 females of all ages were lodged in private and state-owned factories.[102] In the state-owned factories particularly, it remained common for very large numbers to be housed: for example,

[102] *Sanktpeterburg po Perepisi* (1872), part 2, section 2, p. 78.

MAP 22. *Journey to work, goldsmiths and jewellers, 1867*

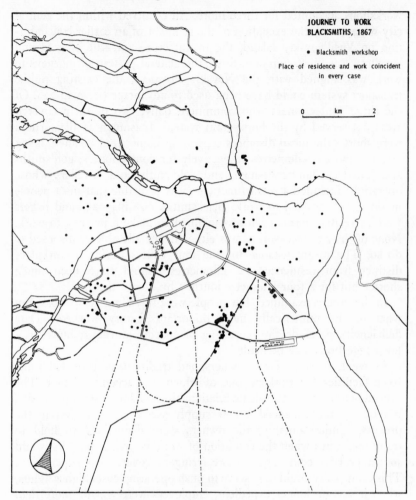

JOURNEY TO WORK
BLACKSMITHS, 1867

● Blacksmith workshop

Place of residence and work coincident
in every case

0   km   2

MAP 23. *Journey to work, blacksmiths, 1867*

the Imperial State Paper plant somehow provided quarters for over
1,300 people.[103] Since we are informed by the census that among the
more than 19,000 people living in factory-owned facilities there were
fewer than a thousand married couples, the number of children was not
likely to be large; at least insofar as those too young to go out to work
are concerned. It is probable that around 15,000 in this group were

[103] *Sanktpeterburg po Perepisi* (1872), part 2, section 1, p. 38.

actually factory workers. Therefore, the majority of the 35,000 factory workers in the city were housed privately. We can be sure that the long hours of work and limited disposable income put severe constraints on the options open to this group. Occasional contemporary observations support the logical deduction that the need to be close to the place of work was pre-eminent.[104] Given the cost of public transport in relation to earnings, it is safe to assume that most trips took place on foot.

During the 1860s available evidence for the managerial and professional and the workshop-owner and artisan groups reveals a limited journey to work for the constituents considered; and the hypothesis that proximity of work and residence would be greatest for workshop-owners and artisans and least for the managerial and professional group has been supported. However, from the data presented it is evident that, even in the case of the managerial and professional group, only a minority actually journeyed to work. Managers and artisans were taken to represent the theoretical extremes of distance travelled, but it is conceivable that factory workers walked the longest distances each day. In general, intra-urban mobility, as reflected by the daily journey to work, was very limited. In the everyday life of the working population public transport, and particularly the horse-tram, had as yet done little to loosen the traditional bond between workplace and residence.

5 EXTERNAL RELATIONS

It scarcely requires emphasizing that industrial and commercial growth did not take place independently, but was tied to developments at the regional, national, and indeed international levels. Before concluding our examination of the economy of the city in the late sixties, we should look at some general characteristics of its system of external relations. The complexity of the system dictates an eclectic approach, but three basic components will be considered—commodity flows, links with the adjacent countryside, and migration.

Despite a growing volume of traffic through the St Petersburg customs, the city was in fact losing ground to the competing Baltic ports of Riga and Revel and of Odessa on the Black Sea. The main reason was the emergence of a rail network which provided alternative routes for trade with Europe. A comparatively limited shipping season,

[104] *Sanktpeterburg, Izsledovaniya po Istorii, Topografii i Statistike Stolitsy* (1968), vol. III, p. 122.

plus a costly and time-consuming transshipment of goods from ocean going vessels which were unable to navigate with safety the estuary of the Neva River to shallow-draft lighters, tended further to erode the port's pre-eminence. Even when it was possible to proceed directly to St Petersburg, thereby avoiding transshipment at Kronshtadt, turn-around time was still longer than at other Baltic ports. Obstructed by a constantly changing delta and bridges, the facilities on Vasil'yevskiy Island were fast becoming obsolete. To keep a sense of perspective, we should remember that despite the withering of the port's relative position, the total value of traffic in 1870 had more than doubled since 1850 (from about eighty-five million roubles to over 190). From figure 5 the economic growth of the late sixties is apparent; so too is the effect of the Crimean War blockade.

Incoming commodity flows were each year increasingly dominated by coal. In 1867 shipments exceeded 475,000 tons, at least six times that of any other commodity. By value it was less significant, ranking after imports of iron ingots or rails, other metals, machinery of various kinds, and cotton. We have noted before that the city's factories performed many break-of-bulk functions. Raw cotton, for example, fed the city's mills, and yarn, cloth or clothing destined for interior markets left the city through the Nikolayevskiy railway station. Although it is not possible to be at all precise in specifying the real source of imported commodities, the port traffic statistics from 1850 to 1870 reveal that Great Britain was the leading country in this respect. For example, coal, metal products, and machinery very probably originated in Britain, although it is clear that raw cotton did not. Imports from Prussia generally ranked second by value; again commodity flows like cane sugar indicated transshipment or re-registration.[105] Compared with earlier decades, the structure of imports had shifted from a preponderance of luxury items and food products towards industrial raw materials.

On the export side, port traffic was much less significant by value, a state of affairs which mirrored the types of products which the country was capable of marketing abroad. At the end of the sixties exports were valued at sixty two million roubles—less than one third of the value of incoming commodities. Moreover, in contrast to the processing of imports, St Petersburg wares accounted for only 1·5 million of the

[105] Zapiska Kommissiy o Severnykh Zheleznykh i Vodnykh Putyaka, 'Znacheniye Peterburga vo Vneshney Torgovle Rossii', *ISPGD*, no. 23 (1899), pp. 338, 339, 256, 257, 258, 261, 267.

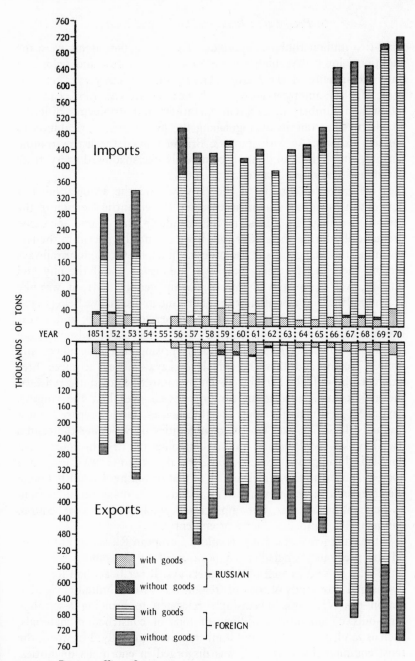

FIG. 5. *Port traffic, 1851-70*

141

sixty-two million roubles exported. The main export items were the traditional low-value, high-volume products of forest and field, and only occasionally of the factory. Grain, and primarily rye, retained pride of place among exports, nearly 600,000 tons in 1871. Linseed, tallow and lumber, in different quantities and displaying different trends, were at one in distinguishing the predominant orientation of Russian exports. As with imports, Britain topped the list as trading partner, although in so doing it completely overshadowed every other nation and was often in a deficit position.[106]

In general, the coming of the railways and the articulation of a network in European Russia accentuated the eccentric location of the capital ⟨*see* map 24⟩. Despite this handicap, rail traffic increased dramatically during the sixties and, if we extend the period to the late seventies, the change was of the order of ninefold. Of the four railways serving the city, the Nikolayevskaya, linking as it did the city and interior, was completely dominant. Completed in 1851, it was the second railway to be built after the short line to Tsarskoye Selo (1837). The Petergofskaya railway began a local service in 1856, and a year later a second link with the 'outside', the Varshavskaya railway, began operation. Given its route, it is not surprising that it handled only limited freight and that the Nikolayevskaya railway acquired pre-eminence by default. Freight movements into St Petersburg reflected the export mix, since grain comprised well over half the volume. Livestock destined for the slaughterhouses (and prepared meat products, fish, oils, etc. that is, commodities provisioning the capital itself) ranked well behind grain. Outgoing rail freight more than doubled during the sixties; however, the volume was less than 400,000 tons in 1872, scarcely a fifth of that incoming. Included among the commodities sent to the interior market were many products from St Petersburg factories, but unprocessed goods such as coal, cotton, and metals continued to figure prominently.

If the emergence of a rail network in European Russia served notice on the previously unchallenged position of St Petersburg port, the same may be said as well of the waterways. River boats had for years discharged thousands of tons of freight, but with a limited navigation season the Neva was increasingly relegated to bringing low-value, high-bulk commodities. Millions of tons of construction materials, such as sand, gravel, stone and lumber arrived annually. Firewood, the most common domestic fuel, was disgorged in enormous quantities.

[106] Kireyev, 'Transport, Torgovlya, Kredit', pp. 141-2.

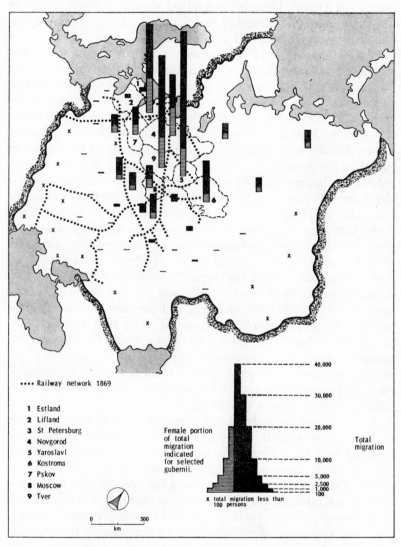

MAP 24. *Peasants residing in St Petersburg by* guberniya *of origin, 1869*

143

Grain had always reached the port by water, but was declining in the face of rail haulage. Outgoing freight had virtually disappeared, for by 1872 the river system handled less than one tenth of total outgoing shipments—now in excess of 430,000 tons.[107]

Nearly three quarters of a million people living in the capital comprised the largest single market in Russia. At a rough count, about 200,000 people had been added since mid-century, and speaking hypothetically, this should have had a perceptible impact on the surrounding rural economy. The influence of St Petersburg was indeed to be seen throughout the *guberniya*. The voracious appetite for firewood visibly scarred the landscape, and now only 44 per cent of the *guberniya* was covered by forests.[108] The emergence of peasant wood-cutters and hauliers earning wages in this process of denudation was about the only positive result, because the land cleared was not often put under the plough. Swamp, forest and meadow and the absence of fence, field and village testified to the poverty of the physical environment. St Petersburg offered escape from the impoverishing situation of most peasants. As was observed by Yu. Gyubner, a prominent local doctor, the area around the capital was much affected by mass migration in search of work.[109] We may see the beginning of the corrosive impact which this had on agriculture through some statistics. In 1869, 80,000 households representing more than half a million people, owned just 86,000 horses and 152,000 cattle. The low ratio was a consequence of inadequate fodder supplies, and the inability of the adjacent countryside to satisfy even a small part of St Petersburg's needs had ensured a heavy reliance on agricultural commodity flows from the interior regions and abroad.

Within the *guberniya* the flow of commodities from market gardens to the city was minimal, for only a few of the wealthier peasants had bothered to develop them. The same was true of cattle-raising and dairying which required a greater investment. The lack of fodder not only held down cattle ownership among the peasants, but resulted in the dairy and cattle industry being mostly in the hands of the *guberniya's* 3,000 colonists (Germans in the main).[110] A large market nearby normally induces investment in agriculture; so far the peasants' response was

[107] Kireyev, 'Transport, Torgovlya, Kredit', pp. 130, 132, 133, 143.
[108] Semenov, *Geografichesko-Statisticheskiy Slovar'*, pp. 435–6; Kireyev, 'Transport, Torgovlya, Kredit', p. 151.
[109] Yu. Gyubner, *O Sanitarnom Sostoyanii S. Peterburgskoy Gubernii po Svedeniyam Zemskikh Vrachey* (1876), p. 5.
[110] Semenov, *Geografichesko-Statisticheskiy Slovar'*, p. 436.

minimal. There is no question that enterprise of this kind had been stifled by serfdom, which after all had just recently been abolished; time would tell whether its effect would be a lasting one.

We have no way of knowing how much was earned by peasants working in the city; nor do we know the importance of these wages back in the villages. Obviously the villages benefited, but they also benefited from a different kind of link with the capital about which we do have more information. In this case the link was not through the city absorbing people from the countryside, but rather through expelling foundling children to the villages. The hinterland of the St Petersburg Foundling Home had been much extended since the 1830s. The coming of the railways had been instrumental in effecting this extension, and foundlings were sent almost to Valdai along the Moskovskaya railway and well on the way to Pskov via the Varshavskaya line. The railways clearly were not the reason for the expanding hinterland; this was brought about by the rising number of children left at the Home, the vast majority of whom were illegitimate. By the end of the sixties over 20,000 children were being cared for in over a thousand villages throughout the *guberniya* and occasionally beyond.[111] With allowances paid to peasant families according to the age and number of foundlings in their care, a regular cash income was possible. Only the frightening death-rate among the very young interfered with the prospect of regular payments.

Ironically, the dispatching of infants to the villages was carried out in the belief that they would benefit, whereas it often guaranteed a short life. We have already noted the limited peasant ownership of cows, and medical reports reveal that inadequate milk in the diet of the very young frequently resulted in dysentery.[112] This affliction was directly related to a death-rate exceeding 80 per cent among those two years and under. Given that the source of this outside income was virtually inexhaustible, it is not perhaps too cynical to assume that in households where milk was in short supply, foundlings were at the end of the line at feeding time. Even at a conservative estimate, the annual income of participating families was of the order of twenty-five to thirty roubles per child. A labourer in the city would be fortunate indeed to earn 150 roubles in a year.[113] In both cases there were

---

[111] F. A. Tarapygin, *Materialy Dlya Istorii Imperatorskago S. Peterburgskago Vospitatel'-nago Doma* (1878), p. 93.
[112] Gyubner, *O Sanitarnom*, pp. 26–7.
[113] Baklanova, 'Formirovaniye i Polozheniye', p. 136.

expenses involved, but it was obviously an important supplement to peasant income. Foundling children brought more than just roubles to the villages, for those who had been wet-nursed helped to spread syphilis. As early as 1857 the Finnish State-Secretary had recognized the pernicious influence of foundlings in the region along the border. A few years later this part of the hinterland to the St Petersburg Foundling Home was closed off, forcing the creation of a new region in the district of Luga within the *guberniya*.[114] Around the capital the relationship was recognized, but in the words of Dr Gyubner 'the extent to which foundlings really play a role in the spread of syphilis remains an open question.'[115] Thus, the links with the countryside were often double edged. The capital offered employment, but debilitated agriculture; it provided income through the care of the foundlings it spawned, but may have transferred disease in the process.

The population of St Petersburg grew chiefly by immigration, as we can tell from the data on birthplaces in the census which covered nearly 98 per cent of the 207,007 peasants residing in the city in 1869.[116] Peasants were the largest single group in the city's population, and the migratory trends they displayed were as much a function of industrialization and its ramifications within the city's economy as they were of the forces of repulsion from the countryside.

Migrating to St Petersburg or, for that matter, to any other town in the Empire, was not an entirely straightforward procedure. In leaving his village the peasant ostensibly had to get official permission. To retain a legal foothold in the city he had each year to get his passport renewed in the village. Even after the Emancipation, therefore, decisions taken in the commune had the potential to alter patterns of rural-urban migration. Whether or not the decision to migrate was rational does not concern us. What does matter is where the peasants were coming from, in what numbers, and whether over time the migrational paths were altered as a consequence of rapid urban-industrial growth.

In an era of difficult inland transport and in a country where the peasantry was more often impoverished than not, it might be anticipated that simple distance would play an important role in governing

---

[114] *Entsiklopedicheskiy Slovar'* (1892), vol. XIII, p. 277.

[115] Gyubner, *O Sanitarnom*, pp. 86–7.

[116] This number includes 10,397 children under seven years of age. All following references to specific numbers of peasants are based on *Sanktpeterburg po Perepisi* (1872), part 1, p. 118. For additional discussion see A Note on Sources, pp. 440–42.

migration. The range of possible influences is obviously wide and spans considerations like population density, sex, and psychological and sociological factors, but since distance has consistently been of some consequence in migrational patterns and is one of the more directly measurable variables, analysis of this factor is a logical point of departure. To this end, the data on *guberniya* of origin for the peasant population have been fitted to a gravity model.[117] This has entailed computing the relationship between the number of migrants from each *guberniya* in European Russia and the reciprocal of the distance of that *guberniya* from the capital. The resultant coefficient of correlation, +0·728 (statistically significant at the one per cent level), indicates quite a strong relationship between distance and numbers.

The overall pattern of *guberniya* of origin data is portrayed in map 24 and presents a number of interesting features. For example, there were more peasants from the relatively distant *gubernii* of Tver and Yaroslavl, than from St Petersburg *guberniya*. In general, the paths of migration reflected acute rural overpopulation in places where agriculture was poor. This was certainly the situation in the non-black earth regions of central Russia, which included the *gubernii* of Moscow, Vladimir, Kaluga, Yaroslavl, Kostroma, Nizhe-gorod and Tver, and which accounted for nearly 48 per cent of the peasants in the capital. St Petersburg *guberniya* was also, by and large, an area of impoverished agriculture, but it was not among the most densely populated *gubernii*.[118] Had the rural population been substantially larger than half a million, there would certainly have been more evidence of migration. Generally speaking, the same may be said of all the contiguous *gubernii*, Estland, Novgorod, Pskov, Olonets and Lifland which, including St Petersburg, provided 29 per cent of peasant migrants. Ethnicity was possibly a factor in reducing migration from some adjacent non-slavic areas. In the case of Lifland and Estland, fewer than 1,800 peasants from

[117] For a discussion of the technique, see A Note on Methods, pp. 432–3. Looking at this question in terms of the exponent values, the 3·12 for all migrants and the 3·28 for females quantitatively expresses the comparative relationships. Similarly, if we take non-specific, but uniform distance units, the means were 81·9 for males, 70·3 for females, and 78·3 for all migrants. The same impression is conveyed by the data as portrayed in map 24 where the principal *gubernii* of female migration have been included.

[118] Although it is necessary, in the absence of any other enumeration for the Empire, to rely on the statistics of the 1857 revision these data indicate that there were very many *gubernii* twice or three times as densely populated. V. M. Kabuzan, *Izmeneniya v Razmeshchenii Naseleniya Rossii* (Moscow, 1971), pp. 167–75. For a cartographic presentation of population density according to the 1857 revision, see W. H. Parker, *An Historical Geography of Russia* (London, 1968), p. 259. Zelnik errs in referring to St Petersburg *guberniya* as one of the most densely populated. Zelnik, *Labor and Society*, p. 225.

these regions were resident in the capital in December of 1869.[119] The network of railways which existed at the end of the sixties has been included in map 24 for the purpose of comparing the relationship between the extent of the system and the principal sources of peasant migrants. Although it is clearly impossible to draw any firm conclusions, the fact that many overpopulated regions straddled the existing network suggests that long-distance migration may have been encouraged.

Of the 202,795 peasants for whom the *guberniya* of origin is known, only 62,626 were female. In fitting the female data to the gravity model, a somewhat higher correlation coefficient was obtained, $+0.764$. However, while females migrated shorter distances, they were not a majority—a feature of rural-urban migration observed elsewhere.[120] In fact, females comprised a majority for only six *gubernii*, but in these the total number of migrants was less than 600 and, with the exception of Lifland, the *gubernii* in question were among the most distant from the capital. The most important source of migrant women was the St Petersburg *guberniya*. Although only 40 per cent of the total were female, the absolute number was nearly 11,000. Not surprisingly, the other major origins of peasant migration provided the largest contingents of females. From Tver and Yaroslavl, there were 9,516 and 8,783 females respectively, although in neither case did their relative shares exceed 28 per cent. Although only 18,254 peasants from nearby Novgorod *guberniya* resided in the capital (compared to 34,402 and 45,180 peasants from Tver and Yaroslavl), the share of females exceeded 47 per cent.

A number of factors affected the propensity of women to migrate. For the married peasant woman, one of the more important was the intentionally temporary nature of the husband's sojourn in the capital, which made it economically impracticable for families to be taken along. And, of course, the decision to try one's luck in the city was often rooted in the apparent hopelessness of the situation in the countryside, and this state of affairs ensured that financial resources for the relocation of a family were not common. For those peasants who could muster the finances to embark on a permanent move, the shortage of housing was a major obstacle. The number of single women cannot be precisely determined from available data, but a rough approximation may be arrived at indirectly. According to the 1869 census for every 100 female

[119] In 1857, the revision gave the two a total population of 550,000, of which nearly 500,000 were peasants. Kabuzan, *Izmeneniya v Razmeshchenii Naseleniya Rossii*, p. 171.
[120] E. G. Ravenstein, 'The Laws of Migration', *Journal of the Royal Statistical Society*, LII (June 1889), p. 288.

inhabitants 31·9 were married.[121] If we assume that female peasants conform to this characteristic of the whole population, then just under 20,000 of the 63,267 peasant women in the city were married. Again, using the total female population as a basis for calculation, nearly 30 per cent were twenty years old or under. Assuming that this segment was unlikely to contain many married women, and applying this percentage to the female peasant population, then roughly another 20,000 were probably too young to be married. There were, therefore, at least 24,000 unattached peasant women resident in the capital. In both relative and absolute terms, this was the beginning of the shift away from a city-ward migration dominated by men. Employment possibilities for women ran the gamut from industry and trade to various kinds of domestic service. For a not inconsiderable number, the city's 151 brothels provided yet another alternative to unemployment and hunger.

St Petersburg was seldom viewed with equanimity. Some regarded it as the symbol of everything that was progressive in the Empire, the manifestation of forces which would pull Russia out of the past into the mainstream of nineteenth-century life. Others, and perhaps those with a greater knowledge of the plight of so many inhabitants, viewed it with varying degrees of alarm. The city was industrializing quickly, and by virtue of immigration the population was also growing rapidly. Those that came were mostly peasants. In the words of Dr Gyubner, 'In comparison with Petersburg inhabitants the unskilled peasant workers arriving in the capital are like chaste virgins.'[122] In the next chapter we will see something of what he meant by this remark.

[121] *Sanktpeterburg po Perepisi*, part 1, p. 3.
[122] Gyubner, *O Sanitarnom*, p. 94.

4

A City in Turmoil

On comprend combien l'invasion continue de la ville par des hommes qui se séparent de leur famille est funeste à la fois pour la santé et pour la moralité publiques.

Élisée Reclus, 1880[1]

By the late sixties urban industrialization had gathered considerable momentum. Thousands more people were arriving in the city each year, and among them peasants were by far the largest group. Many came out of desperation; for them, earning wages was the only way to meet the redemption payments, assumed at the time of Emancipation in exchange for an allotment of land which was often smaller than they had had hitherto and not infrequently worse in quality. While peasants were still supposed to obtain official permission to leave the commune, of course a good many simply departed without it. In the poorer regions of the country it was commonly in the best interests of commune and peasant alike that migration should not be impeded. The tide-gate had been opened, but compared to what took place after the turn of the century, migration to the capital during the sixties was a mere trickle. Still, there is ample evidence that virtually every part of the urban system reeled in the face of this influx. The consequences varied. In some cases, day-to-day living was simply inconvenienced; in others, life itself was threatened. In this chapter we will try to establish some of the relationships and repercussions of industrialization and urbanization as they had unfolded by the late sixties. Of special concern will be the quality of the physical environment within which the inhabitants laboured and lived, and the demographic and social-class characteristics of the population itself.

[1] Élisée Reclus, *Nouvelle Géographie Universelle la Terre et les Hommes* (Paris, 1880), vol. V, p. 595.

A City in Turmoil

Industrialization in the form of belching smokestacks, sprawling, noisy factories and the like was evident but did not yet dominate the urban landscape. To the foreign traveller approaching St Petersburg by boat there was still something mystical about the way in which the city seemed to rise up out of its estuarine site and come into view:

> Cronstadt is seventeen miles from the capital. As we left it behind, all were on the watch to catch sight of the great city we had travelled so far to visit, and it was an exciting moment when at last it flashed upon us, a long, low line glittering in the sunshine. The cupolas, the spires, and the golden roofs of St Petersburg were seen at first as mere specks, which shone like lights in the distance; then the mighty dome of St Isaks grew into form, the fortress church shot up its tall spire to the sky, and the mobile line of white palaces, which face the stranger who approaches by water, became more and more distinct.[2]

There was scarcely anything mystical about coming into the city by rail. The rural landscape through which the train passed was charitably described by most travellers as desolate, but straggling settlements began to clump together giving notice that the outskirts of the capital were at hand. At the approach to the Nikolayevskiy railway station the glimmering cupolas of the Aleksandro-Nevskiy Monastery on the right were the first real evidence of the city. But it was the hustle and bustle of the streets around the terminus itself which registered most clearly in the minds of travellers. For those adventurous souls coming to St Petersburg overland from Finland, the privations of the journey overwhelmed all other impressions. A description in a mid-century edition of Murray's *Handbook for Northern Europe* still reliably introduces us to what it was like to enter the city through Vyborgskaya borough in the 1860s. We may better appreciate the experience if we begin at the frontier customs-house:

> A few versts before reaching this station the road becomes execrable, increasing, if possible, in badness to the next station, and we think it may safely be pronounced one of the worst in Europe—perhaps the very worst. . . . The stones, of which the centre of the road is paved, are of the most appalling dimensions,

[2] K. B. Guthrie, *Through Russia: from St Petersburg to Astrakhan and the Crimea* (London, 1874), vol. I, p. 16.

and, rising in different degrees of elevation, form a succession of stony hillocks; in fact, the road can only be compared to one made of milestones of unequal heights. Possibly the reason for this road being so bad is that the Viborgian peasant has a most singular and, for an elder son, awkward belief, that the dead can at certain times re-visit the paternal mansion: so that those who do not desire this honour are in the habit of placing their defunct relative on the very roughest *bondkara* they can find, and carting him to his place of sepulture over the largest ruts and most rocky projections that lie in the way, in the hope—fervent, no doubt—that he will be so strongly impressed with the pain and fatigue of the journey, that he will not feel disposed to travel the same road again. We think a live Englishman will do the same.[3]

Presumably it was with some relief that St Petersburg was sighted:

But the general aspect of these last fifteen miles, even to within sight of the city, is as dreary and uncultivated as any part of the country passed through. Nothing indicates the vicinity of the capital of a vast empire, except the numbers of soldiers of all kinds in every village. . . . Long, however, before he comes in sight of it, his progress will be arrested by a wooden barrier, which hangs across the road like a giant's fishing-rod. This is the spot at which passports and padaroshnas are examined, and the former surrended, before travellers are permitted to proceed. For some time after entering the suburbs the tourist will pass through dirty and wretched streets, until a sudden turn brings him in view of the massive walls and batteries of the citadel; beyond this again is seen the gilt spire of the Admiralty . . .; then the long line of quays with granite parapets, and backed by palaces, meet the eye.[4]

Once in the city, the broad avenues, the huge architectural set pieces, the capacious network of canals and rivers, were the first things that everyone noticed ⟨*see* map 25⟩. First impressions were often the most graphic. One guidebook explained that 'St Petersburg owes its grandeur to the immense number of gigantic buildings which rise up on all sides. These are what gives it such an imposing appearance, fill a

---

[3] *Hand-Book for Northern Europe; including Denmark, Norway Sweden, Finland, and Russia* (London, 1849), part II, pp. 374-5.
[4] *Hand-Book for Northern Europe*, p. 375.

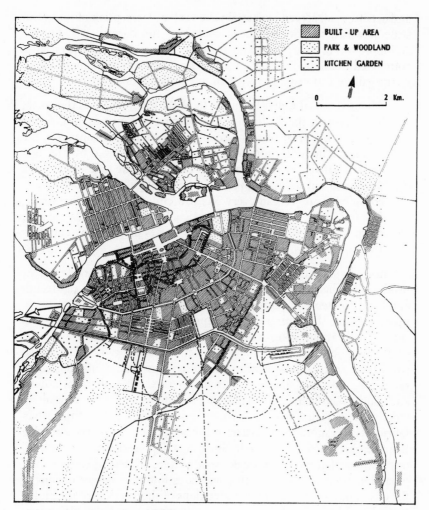

MAP 25. *St Petersburg, 1868*

person on first seeing it with astonishment, and justify the appellation it has received of the "City of Palaces".[5]

There is no doubt that the combination of expansive waterways, the symmetry of the street pattern and the visual uniformity created by earlier controls over architectural details, building materials, heights

[5] *The Northern Circuit or Brief Notes of Sweden, Finland, and Russia* (Cambridge, 1862), p. 83.

153

and set-backs all served to sharpen the visitor's perception of the grand scale at which the city had been conceived and constructed. All this and more was at once plain to see from the vantage point of the recently completed dome of St Isaac's Cathedral. The rather strenuous climb to the gallery was rewarded with an unexcelled view:

> About you it [the city] lies upon the dead level which, to the north, loses itself in the Baltic and the swamps of Finland; and, to the south, in the great plain stretching with slight interruption to the Crimea. The uniformity of regular streets is relieved by the river and the canals; by the trees which care has made to flourish in the unwonted soil; by the public monuments; by the tall fire-towers—conspicuous objects in every Russian city, with watchmen ready, day and night, to give the proper signals in case of an alarm; and, most of all, by the golden and azure domes of the many churches and monasteries.[6]

These favourable impressions were to a very considerable extent products of the planning and architectural controls of the eighteenth and early nineteenth centuries, the results of which were still visible in many parts of the central city. But pressures of industrialization and commercialization, along with the concomitant demands of a rapidly escalating population even since mid-century, were more than official rules and regulations could adequately handle. Time-honoured regulatory measures simply collapsed. Abysmal tenements, dark, dirty and dangerous factories, squalid shops—all sprang up as a result of largely uncontrolled land conversion. Indeed, few aspects of the urban fabric were as subtle as the pastel shades of yellow, green, red and blue which embellished the inner-city buildings. Upon reflection, travellers' impressions of grandeur and spaciousness were often tempered by their perambulations off the main thoroughfares into the seamier regions of the city and, more rarely, by investigations of the interiors of the multi-storied buildings which housed the bulk of the population. Whatever the reason, the excited reporting of the city's architectural features tended to give way to more sober observations:

> It is true that in one tableau are assembled a number of splendid buildings such as few capitals afford; but if within the same space were collected all the finest public buildings in London, with all the advantages of the great extent of ground and clear atmosphere,

[6] E. D. Proctor, *A Russian Journey* (Boston, 1872), pp. 8-9.

enabling the visitor to obtain an unobstructed view of their various beauties, it would be easy to guess which would present the most imposing appearance. . . . That this assemblage of all that is splendid in the city gives at first sight a magnificent ensemble, I do not deny; but, like everything Russian, the showy facade only hides what is mean behind.[7]

[Peasants] are often packed in houses nearly as large as those of their masters, which can only be distinguished from theirs by the abominable odours they emit, and the dirty appearance of the stucco and paint covering their walls.[8]

To acquire a better knowledge of what St Petersburg was really like necessitated moving about in the city, and this in itself often prompted caustic comment:

The roads themselves indicate where and how far the title of metropolis is justifiable. Any attempts at improvement are only to be found in the vicinity of the Winter Palace; here are macadamized roads or pavement, then come wood-roads, which the more distant suburbs cannot imitate on account of the expense. On the Pesky, and on many other parts, the streets are still unpaved, and in the wet months the carriages sink up to the axle in mud.[9]

The terrible state of most streets and the limited number of bridges were considerable impediments to vehicular traffic. Only the winter provided a respite for those who stayed long enough to enjoy the comparative ease, if not comfort, of travelling in runnered carriages over snow-packed streets and frozen water courses.

Despite a concerted effort during the previous century to prevent the construction of wooden buildings, many existed in the central city boroughs in the early 1800s. Pressures to remove them came largely from two quarters. Whenever possible, officials thwarted efforts to undertake extensive repair work, thus ensuring more rapid deterioration and ultimate collapse. On the other hand, the provision of housing was proving to be an attractive speculative venture and hence voluntary demolition of one or two-storied wooden buildings took place in order to provide room for the erection of three or four-storied tenements. As usual, the overall process was greatly hastened by fire. Although the removal of wooden structures from the city was by no means a novelty,

[7] *The Englishwoman in Russia* (London, 1855), p. 59.
[8] *The Northern Circuit*, p. 84.
[9] *Recollections of Russia during Thirty-Three Years Residence* (Edinburgh, 1855), p. 43.

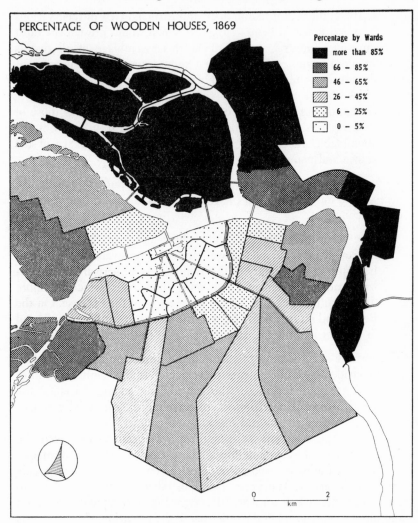

MAP 26. *Percentage of wooden houses, 1869*

the upsurge in building activity during the sixties certainly enhanced it.
Deletions from the existing stock took place mostly in the central city
boroughs where the value of land demanded in effect more intensive
and efficient use. By 1869 approximately 10,000 predominantly wooden
edifices remained standing, but this figure represented a reduction of

about 1,300 since 1865. Over 1,300 buildings of brick or, less commonly, of stone arose, often out of the ashes of former constructions. In total these were roughly the same number as the wooden. As map 26 indicates, brick and mortar prevailed in the central city and wood on the periphery. Well over half of all wooden dwellings were located on the island and in the right bank boroughs of Vasil'yevskaya, Peter-burgskaya and Vyborgskaya, but included in this number were many ostensibly summer homes. Ostensibly so, because inadequate housing for the lower classes had sometimes brought even the summer *dacha* into year-round occupancy. The majority, however, were still used as retreats for those affluent inhabitants unable to escape the city entirely during the summer months.

The city was in more than one sense characterized by wooden buildings. Approximately two thirds of them comprised only a single storey. In contrast to brick or stone structures, single-storied wooden buildings predominated in the central city in 1869, whereas nearly two thirds of the two-storied structures were located in the island and right-bank boroughs. Very few wooden buildings reached three floors, but again nearly two thirds of the 106 that did were located on the island and right-bank boroughs. The central-city skyline was uniformly low, surprisingly so, since it was both technologically and legally possible to put up brick or stone buildings of four storeys. Yet, despite the demands for residential, commercial and manufacturing space in central-city boroughs such as Admiralteyskaya, Kazanskaya, Spasskaya, Liteynaya and Moskovskaya, fewer than 400 buildings, or less than 4 per cent of the total, exceeded four storeys.[10] Even along the Nevskiy Prospect, building heights and quality fell off sharply on leaving the commercial activities near the *Gostinyy Dvor* and passing over the Fontanka Canal in the direction of the Nikolayevskiy railway station.[11]

In the absence of any rigorous control over where and how new buildings were constructed, speculators were fast acquiring the upper hand in determining what the city would look like in years to come. The City Council, operating under the 1846 municipal statute, simply brought decision-making responsibilities into the hands of many of

[10] *Sanktpeterburg, Izsledovaniya po Istorii, Topografii i Statistike Stolitsy* (1868), vol. III, p. 8; *Sanktpeterburg po Perepisi 10 Dekabrya 1869* (1872), part 2, section 1, p. 6. Even in 1881, buildings four storeys or higher accounted for only 19 per cent of the city's total. In Berlin and Paris, on the other hand, the respective shares were 61 and 62 per cent. 'Posledniya Perepisi S. Peterburga i Moskvy', *IMGD*, no. 6–7 (1887), p. 132.
[11] See, for example, *The Englishwoman in Russia*, p. 60.

those involved in speculative building, principally the merchant clique; but where roubles could be earned easily there was no shortage of willing participants.[12] Members of the nobility owned some of the very largest tenements. Baron Kapger and Prince Vyazemskiy, for instance, were landlords to nearly 6,000 people.[13] Prince Vyazemskiy had for a long while been notorious as a slum landlord and it was indeed unfortunate that close on 5,000 persons had no other option but to continue living in rooms more squalid even than was customary.[14] From the military ranks, from the roster of honoured citizens, from almost every constituency of the upper classes, there were those who had put their money into real estate. Prominent among the speculative builders were the merchants and traders like Yakovlev, Zhukov and Dryabin—upstart but prosperous St Petersburg citizens who were quick to see the advantages of having the hordes of itinerant summer workmen build tenements to swallow up at high rents the ever increasing numbers of migrants.

Given the opportunity to establish appropriate new standards and to see to the enforcement of existing ones, the City Council, perhaps not surprisingly, was quite willing to abrogate its responsibility and do nothing. The response of the speculative builder was to erect substandard housing wherever land was cheap; where the price of land was comparatively high, construction materials and techniques were, if possible, correspondingly shoddier. What we have, then, is a situation in which building activity was largely uncoordinated and uncontrolled. Because it was not coordinated by city authorities, essential municipal services were inadequate or nonexistent. Because construction was not closely inspected, the resultant accommodation was bad and as the demand rose it got worse. We shall have occasion later to examine both of these consequences in some detail.

2 HOW MANY PEOPLE?

It was observed earlier that to chart population changes is at best a difficult task. The seasonal ebb and flow, together with varying

[12] For discussion of the statute, see chapter 2, pp. 81–2.
[13] Details of all houses with more than 600 inhabitants may be found in *Sanktpeterburg po Perepisi 10 Dekabrya 1869*, pp. 36–40.
[14] Repeated fines by civic authorities did nothing to improve sanitary conditions. F. Erisman, 'Nastoyashcheye Sostoyaniye v Sanitarnym Otnoshenii Domov Knyazya Vyazemskago v Peterburge', *Arkhiv Sudebnoy Meditsiny i Obshchestvennoy Gigiyeny*, *VII* (1871), p. 46.

definitions of residents and of the city itself, make any assessment exceedingly complicated. The problem did not pass unnoticed at the time, but not until 1861 does there seem to have been a continuous and concerted effort to remedy the deficiency. At this time the members of the statistical department in the Imperial Russian Geographical Society explored the possibility of conducting a one-day census of the population. Although the task was too great for this one organization to handle satisfactorily, after further discussions the Central Statistical Committee of the Ministry of Internal Affairs agreed to take on the job.[15] The enumeration commenced in the middle of December 1864. The police were instructed to obtain from the so-called 'name books', which the owners of every residential building were legally obliged to keep up to date, a wide range of information on each resident.[16] Since personal interviews were not general, and definitions often inexact, some of the data gathered contained a sizable element of conjecture. When published in 1868 the inadequacies were apparent and the need for a more sophisticated enumeration obvious.

A committee was soon established in order to determine the frame of reference for a new census. Two key members of this initial group were General F. F. Trepov, the Chief of Police for St Petersburg and P. P. Semenov, an eminent geographer and director of the Central Statistical Committee. The model adopted for enumerating the populace followed fairly closely the one-day census of Berlin and plans for its implementation were drawn up. The new census was undertaken on 10 December 1869 and included several refinements in procedure.[17] The primary source of information was no longer the lists of residents, but the 'head' of each apartment. Questionnaires were distributed to every apartment and where illiteracy precluded their completion the enumerator conducted a personal interview and filled out the forms. Even though definitions were much sharper than in 1865, for some of the categories of information sought, such as occupation, there were still difficulties in maintaining a high level of consistency. Whether the respondent provided information on his actual, desired or qualified occupation was not always clear. Notwithstanding these

---

[15] The City Council assisted by providing 6,000 roubles and the services of its own statistical department. Technical support from the *guberniya* statistical committee was also forthcoming. *Sanktpeterburg, Izsledovaniya po Istorii*, pp. ii-iii; 2-3.

[16] The results are usually ascribed to early 1865 and this procedure is followed here.

[17] For a detailed discussion of procedures, see *Sanktpeterburg po Perepisi 10 Dekabrya 1869 Goda* (1872), part 1, pp. i-xxvii.

and other difficulties, the overall results were regarded as quite satisfactory.[18]

The general trends revealed by figure 6 indicate that population growth from mid century continued to be somewhat erratic, and that there were two episodes of absolute decline. The first occurred between 1854 and 1858 when the number of inhabitants dropped by nearly 30,000. One observer, H. Hafferberg, attributed this primarily to the impact of the Crimean War (1854–6) which reduced the military garrison and caused substantial numbers of foreigners to leave.[19] Since the two groups comprised perhaps as much as a fifth of the population, including their dependants, the argument appears to have some substance to it. However, in an earlier more detailed study of the population decline, E. Karnovich offered a more precise explanation.[20] Using official police records for the beginning of each year, he discounted the notion that changes in military personnel were a major factor. While there was a reduction of officers and their families during the war, the garrison was maintained at around 38,000 until 1856. Immediately following the war the number grew by several thousand, although this increase was only temporary. Of the approximately 10,000–12,000 foreigners resident in the city, those who did depart certainly did not cause losses sufficient to account for the number in question. In fact, Karnovich established that, once again, two quite traditional factors were at work. During the period in question deaths exceeded births by some 25,000, over 16,000 of them in 1855 and 1856 alone ⟨see figure 7⟩. The second factor was the migration of furloughed peasants. Since they were obliged to surrender their passports at the *Adresnaya Kontora* upon entering the city their movements could be gauged and Karnovich's data indicate that between 1854 and 1858 the amplitude of population change was very largely governed by the comings and goings of peasants. When a period of high mortality coincided with a smaller influx of peasants, the population could, and did, fluctuate quite sharply ⟨see figure 6⟩.

[18] It did perpetuate one deficiency of the 1865 census, however. This was the omission of the suburban districts of Shlissel'burg, Petergof, Palyustrov and Lesnoy. By the next census taken in 1881 they had been brought under the enumerators' purview, but the roughly 50,000 persons living in them in 1869 must be excluded from our analysis. The figure of 50,000 has been arrived at by determining the percentage change in the population of the peripheral wards between 1869 and 1890. The percentage change of 155 was then applied to the 1890 population in the four districts. 'Naseleniye v Prigorodnykh Uchastkakh S. Peterburga po Perepisi 15 Dekabrya 1889 Goda', *ISPGD*, no. 1 (1889), p. 88.

[19] H. Hafferberg, *St Peterburg in Seiner Vergangenheit und Gegenwart* (1866), pp. 98–9.

[20] E. Karnovich, *Sanktpeterburg v Statisticheskom Otnoshenii* (1860), pp. 18–38.

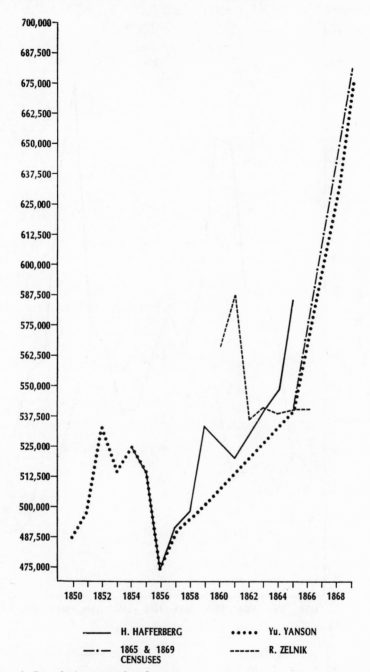

FIG. 6. *Population growth, 1850–70*

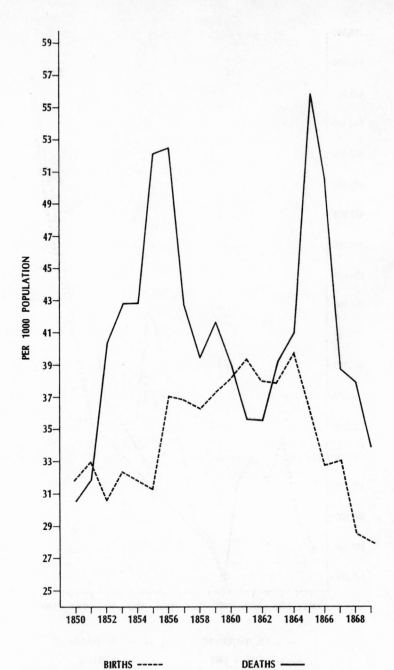

FIG. 7. *Births and deaths, 1850–70*

162

The precipitous drop in numbers after 1861 has been examined in some detail more recently by R. Zelnik, and we may accept his figures as most accurate. Concurring with the findings of the police that the exodus of those persons, particularly peasants, with vested interests in the allocation of land was a contributory factor, he none the less notes that the depletion of the peasant class was more the result of peasants failing to migrate to the capital that year than it was of an unusually large number leaving.[21] Birth- and death-rates calculated from different sources all indicate that for the immediate post-Emancipation period, 1861 to 1864, an inordinate disparity between them was not an element in the decline.[22] In fact, there was a small net natural increase.

During the second half of the decade, the relationship between natural increase and migration reversed. As figures 6 and 7 reveal, mortality was increasing but the total population between 1865 and 1869 was also increasing, and doing so sharply. At the time, the substantial increase in population from 539,122 in January 1865 to 667,207 in December 1869 was attributed to greater statistical accuracy.[23] But it has been convincingly argued that more of this increase can be attributed to a larger influx of peasants than to better figures. Zelnik's data indicate that in 1863 there were an estimated 160,856 peasants, comprising about 30 per cent of the population.[24] If we take the census of 1865 as a benchmark instead, the figures were 145,370, or 27 per cent. It matters little which figure is used, since both indicate that an absolute change of a considerable order was required to account for the 207,007 peasants registered in the 1869 census. Using the 1865 figure as a reference point, then more than 60,000 peasants had been added to the population in just five years. This number, moreover, understates the total influx of peasants; the census of 1869 excluded the suburbs and districts such as Shlissel'burg and Petergof which included an even larger relative share of peasants. What is more, the enumeration was, of course, simply a snapshot of a populace whose largest single group, the peasantry, was continually changing its membership. This was because the excess of deaths affected disproportionately the lower classes among which the peasants were the largest single group and because the decision to take up residence in

[21] Reginald E. Zelnik, *Labor and Society in Tsarist Russia, the Factory Workers of St Petersburg, 1855–70* (Stanford, 1971), pp. 221–2.
[22] *Sanktpeterburg Izsledovaniya po Istorii*, pp. 163, 193; *Entsiklopedicheskiy Slovar'* (1900), vol. LVI, p. 313; Zelnik, *Labor and Society*, p. 221.
[23] *Sanktpeterburg po Perepisi 10 Dekabrya 1869*, part 1, p. xxvi.
[24] For a discussion, see Zelnik, *Labor and Society*, pp. 224–9.

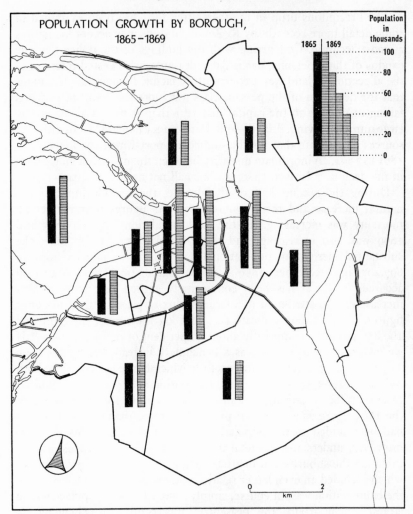

MAP 27. *Population growth by borough, 1865–69*

the capital was not always a lasting one. Finally, there is the thorny problem of shifts in legal status, although it is probable that comparatively few peasants escaped their heritage in this manner.

Thus, at the end of 1869 there were within the official city borders just over 667,000 people. Although the estimated 50,000 inhabitants of the suburban districts must necessarily lie outside the scope of any analysis, it is well to bear in mind that the total number of persons living in the urban area was not far short of three quarters of a million. Among European centres, St Petersburg ranked fifth in population after London, Paris, Berlin and Vienna.

While the census of 1865 may be faulted for lack of definitional clarity, the population totals for the twelve boroughs provide a reference point sufficiently accurate to permit the tempo of intra-urban population growth up to 1869 to be described in general terms.[25] The overall increase in population between January 1865 and December 1869 was approximately 24 per cent, but within the city there was considerable variation ⟨*see* map 27⟩. The greatest relative increase occurred in the Aleksandro-Nevskaya borough, an area which extended to the southeastern extremity of the official city limits. Peripheral boroughs which also had a sizable complement of industrial and commercial activities did not, however, undergo such high rates of change. For example, Narvskaya, Vyborgskaya, Peterburgskaya and Vasil'yevskaya expanded roughly on a par with the rate for the city as a whole, or less rapidly. This was doubtless influenced by the fact that the latter three were in the less accessible northern and eastern regions of the city. Aleksandro-Nevskaya on the other hand was the borough into which the bulk of the migrant population was first disgorged, for it housed the terminal of the Nikolayevskaya railway which linked St Petersburg with the interior regions of the Empire ⟨*see* plate 23⟩. That it extended to the southeastern extremity of the city was of little real significance, for the bulk of the residents clustered near the Nevskiy Prospect and Ligovka Street and constituted an extension of the central city.[26] The extensive territory south of the Obvodnyy Canal to the city border was sparsely settled ⟨*see* map 26⟩.

In point of fact, it was not the periphery of the city which experienced the greatest relative and absolute shares of the population increase. It was the traditionally densely settled, central-city boroughs which did so. Spasskaya, for example, had a percentage growth rate exceeded only by Aleksandro-Nevskaya, yet it had over twice the total population and no vacant land into which construction of new buildings might expand. The additional numbers accommodated exceeded 21,000, an increase which was more than half the total population in Aleksandro-Nevskaya

[25] The number of wards was altered in the interim between the two censuses and therefore a more detailed look at intra-urban population growth was not possible. The area of each borough remained unchanged.
[26] By central city we are referring to the Admiralteyskaya, Kazanskaya, Spasskaya, Moskovskaya and Liteynaya boroughs.

in 1869. The Moskovskaya borough was in many respects similar: it was densely settled already in 1865 though there were still vacant areas. The rate of population increase there was 26·2, compared with 33·2 and 31·6 for Aleksandro-Nevskaya and Spasskaya respectively. Of the central-city boroughs, three had growth rates smaller than the 23·7 figure for the city. These were Admiralteyskaya, Kazanskaya and Liteynaya, all of which had pockets of first-class residential property in which high rents offered a barrier to an invasion by the lower classes. The principal destinations were the boroughs which fringed the central business district: Spasskaya and Moskovskaya alone accounted for about one quarter of the city's population but absorbed one third of the 61,637 peasants added from 1865 to 1869. The industrial boroughs of Narvskaya and Aleksandro-Nevskaya to the south took in only 16 per cent of the peasant migrants; in 1869 they housed 14 per cent of the total population, a one per cent increase over 1865, the same percentage increase as had occurred in the other two boroughs. Inasmuch as peasants represented 48 per cent of the increase in St Petersburg's population, Spasskaya and Moskovskaya were clearly the main reception areas.[27]

The funnelling of the majority of new arrivals into the central city clearly increased population densities and by 1869 two of the thirty-eight wards had more than 51,000 persons per square kilometre.[28] It is perhaps not surprising that one of these wards was in Spasskaya borough. The third ward housed its residents at more than 72,000 to the square kilometre, a density far and away greater than that to be found anywhere else in the city. The second ward of Kazanskaya borough, adjacent to it, had nearly 10,000 people per square kilometre fewer than did the Spasskaya ward, and as map 28 makes plain, the two of them stand out because of their very high population densities. Seven other central city wards fell into the 31,000–51,000 category, but only two of them got as high as 40,000. In short, in the case of these four

[27] The data on location of peasants, and all other social classes, by borough and ward include only those in the nominal census. Some 45,700 persons were not on this list, the largest single group being garrison forces. However, all percentages have been calculated for the total population and therefore probably understate slightly the importance of peasants by borough. The total population statistic commonly cited, 667,207 excludes 756 newborn infants under one month. For this group there is no information on sex, or any other characteristic of interest in this study and therefore, as is customary, the number has been excluded from any calculation involving total city population. *Sanktpeterburg po Perepisi 10 Dekabrya 1869*, part 1, p. 115; *Sanktpeterburg, Izsledovaniya po Istorii*, p. 48.
[28] In calculating population density only the built-up area of each ward was included. This was necessary as the peripheral wards in particular were often sizable, but with only a small area settled.

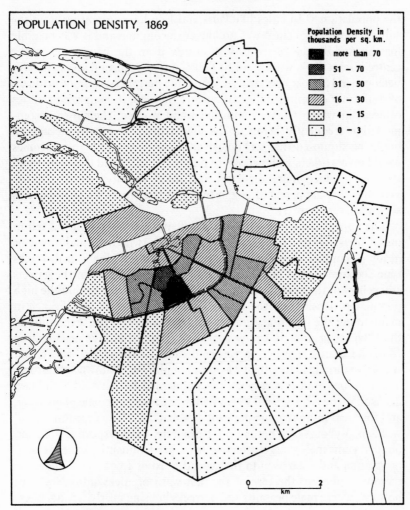

MAP 28. *Population density, 1869*

wards alone, some 15 per cent of the population was stuffed into less than 2 per cent of the city's area.[29]

The densities fell off toward the periphery, just as one would expect, but from an earlier discussion of public transport developments it should be apparent that there was no effective means of decentralizing

---

[29] *Sanktpeterburg po Perepisi 10 Dekabrya 1869*, part 1, pp. 4–10.

the population.[30] In cities like Paris and London commuting from the suburb to the city centre was no longer uncommon and it was possible for the middle classes at least to escape from the congestion at the centre after a day's work.[31] In St Petersburg, congestion seems to have been general almost everywhere. Thus, the periphery was not made up of uniformly dormitory-like settlements; instead, it comprised a series of areas in which workers both lived and worked, their own accommodation frequently being of the lowest order. For later decades it might be supposed that technological innovations and higher incomes would give workers wider access to public transport and that this would tend to produce more dispersal and lower densities at the centre. Whether this happened after the turn of the century we shall have to see in a later chapter.

The impact of the predominantly male peasant migration was felt in many ways. Quite obviously, male peasants, whether single men or heads of families separated temporarily from them, living in barrack-type accommodation at the factory or in large numbers in the garrets and cellars of the central city, were an important factor behind the high population densities in the capital. They were also of significance in maintaining the traditional imbalance between the sexes. According to the 1869 census, nearly 57 per cent of the population was male, a drop from the shares recorded in earlier decades of the city's history, but still substantially higher than was commonplace in the towns of Europe. Their influence in this respect was augmented by the sizable military garrison in the city. Several wards had over 60 per cent male population, and four had more than 65 per cent ⟨*see* map 29⟩. The first and second wards of Vyborgskaya borough, for example, were respectively 65 and 69 per cent male, largely owing to a predominantly male peasant population and a garrison in the second ward of 1,600 men. The same reasons applied in the case of the first ward of Aleksandro-Nevskaya borough where male peasants and barracks housing nearly 1,000 soldiers made their presence felt. However, the imbalance in the third ward (again 65 per cent male) was not attributable to any contingent of soldiers. The male peasant population of 6,174 completely outnumbered the 1,848 females of this class and was sufficient alone to distort the male-female ratio in the ward's total population of 13,965. In Admiralteyskaya, soldiers rather than peasants were responsible for a

---

[30] See chapter 3, pp. 123–8.
[31] See, for instance, A. Sutcliffe, *The Autumn of Central Paris: the Defeat of Town Planning, 1850–1970* (London, 1970), p. 155.

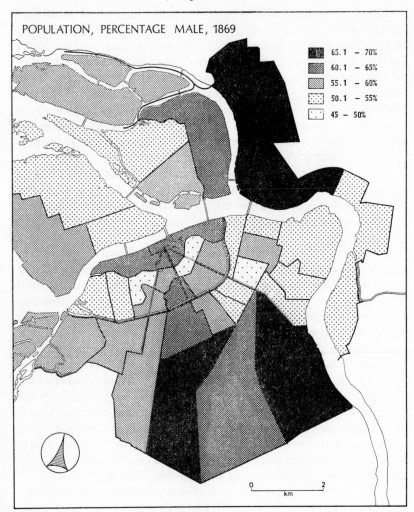

MAP 29. *Population, percentage male, 1869*

population nearly 61 per cent male. On Bol'shaya Milionnaya Street in the first ward were housed 1,720 members of the Pavlovskiy regiment and in barracks a few paces down the street were over 800 of the Preobrazhenskiy regiment. In the second ward, nearly 900 members of the crack *Konnyy Polk* (Horse Guard regiment), plus a naval detachment of 1,845, added colour to the streets as well as a demographic bias.

169

The only borough with roughly the same number of males and females was Kazanskaya. It did not have within its boundaries any military barracks, but indirectly the military presence was one reason for the unusually high share of females. Female members of the families of military personnel exceeded the male members by over 2,000. At the same time, the 11,672 peasants comprised only 23 per cent of Kazanskaya's population, the smallest share of any borough. The preponderance of females in military families was just about sufficient to offset the excess of male peasants. Additionally, the borough had a dispro-portionate number of trade and handicraft establishments geared to a female market. Particularly important was the manufacture of women's clothing, an industry which employed a large number of females. For two wards in Kazanskaya the male population formed a minority, a situation which occurred in just one other of the city's thirty eight wards.[32]

The combined impact of the predominantly male peasant population and the garrisons on the age-sex structure of the population is shown in figure 8. Beginning at age ten, for every quinquennial period until fifty, males outnumbered females. The bulge between ages fifteen and thirty-five, and particularly between fifteen and thirty, in large measure reflected the presence of soldiers, sailors and peasants. Thereafter, the numerical disparity between the sexes began to diminish until age fifty, after which the greater longevity of females gave them a progres-sively larger share of the older population. Given the importance of the peasant and military populations in creating the bulge in the age-sex pyramid for the total population, it follows that wards within the city with large numbers of one or the other, or both, would produce an even greater distortion. The Kazanskaya ward, for example, had a comparatively limited peasant population and no garrisons, whereas in the Aleksandro-Nevskaya ward both groups were well represented. The demographic impact is at once evident. Proportionally, the share of population between twenty and thirty and the role of males was much greater in the first ward of Aleksandro-Nevskaya than in Kazanskaya, and both deviated somewhat from the model for the population in general.

The diminishing significance of males after the age of twenty five, and especially in the age group thirty to thirty-five, when the absolute difference between the sexes decreased from 19,405 to 9,520, reflects a

[32] *Sanktpeterburg po Perepisi 10 Dekabrya 1869*, part 1, pp. 1, 115 and part 2, section 1, pp. 128–52.

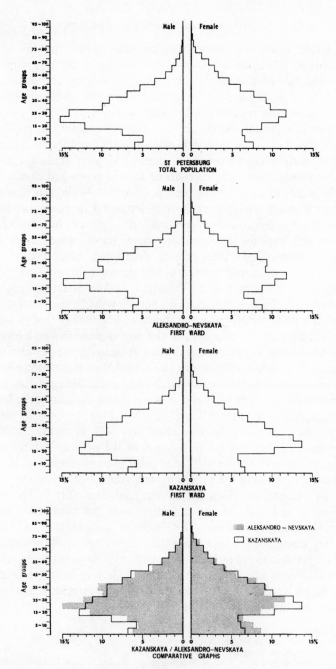

FIG. 8. *Demographic structure, 1869*

characteristic of the city's population remarked upon at the time of the 1865 census. It was then reckoned that residence in the capital for nearly one half of the inhabitants was a 'temporary and accidental affair'.[33] Very probably, peasants without marketable skills and having in consequence no regular employment, would qualify as one of the most transient groups. Although the evidence is scanty, it has been suggested that older peasant industrial workers were less inclined to return to their villages than those engaged in petty trade and other irregular employment. This accounted for the prolonged dominance in some wards of males above the age of fifty.[34] While this situation obtained in areas which were heavily industrial in character, as in Aleksandro-Nevskaya and Narvskaya, it occurred in even later quinquennial periods in Admiralteyskaya wards which were not heavily industrialized. Here males dominated until sixty-five.[35] Therefore, any argument related to the demographic influence of a prolonged residence of peasant industrial workers is rather tenuous. Unfortunately, the available data do not allow us to see at what age particular groups tended to leave the city. The notion that peasants comprised the largest component of the exodus must remain a logical, if unsubstantiated, explanation of the distortion in the age-sex pyramid.

In earlier discussion the point has been made that population growth was achieved almost entirely through in-migration. Many factors were responsible for this state of affairs. Normal family life among the lower classes, especially the peasants, was precluded for the majority either for financial reasons or because their stay was so transitory. One consequence of this was the retardation of the per capita birth-rate. But the influence of a lower birth-rate paled in comparison with that of the death-rate. During the preceding 100 years, deaths had exceeded births by 143,928, of which 89,703 occurred after 1847.[36] The class composition and scale of the migration were not unrelated to the excessively high death-rate. The resultant congestion, which the preceding discussion of population densities rather coldly insinuates, posed a real threat to public health standards with obvious consequences for the quality of life at the bottom. Before dealing with the issue of public health it would be appropriate first of all to examine the housing situation and the level of municipal services.

[33] *Sanktpeterburg, Izsledovaniya po Istorii*, p. 40.
[34] Zelnik, *Labor and Society*, p. 235.
[35] *Sanktpeterburg po Perepisi 10 Dekabrya 1869*, part I, p. 4.
[36] G. I. Arkhangel'skiy, 'Zhizn' v Peterburge po Statisticheskim Dannym', *Arkhiv Sudebnoy Meditsiny i Obshchestvennoy Gigiyeny*, V (1869), p. 41.

3 HOUSING

A total of 8,242 buildings were surveyed during the enumeration of 1869 in order to get some idea of the dimensions and characteristics of the existing housing stock. Buildings, or parts thereof, which were given over to non-residential functions were by definition excluded from the survey, but in addition institutional buildings such as church residences and military garrisons were omitted. Also important in this respect was the exclusion of the summer *dachi* in Peterburgskaya and Vyborgskaya boroughs. Although covering less than one half of all buildings in the city, the census included the habitations of over 92 per cent of the population. According to the survey there were 87,779 occupied apartments and 5,098 vacant. The number vacant was not regarded as entirely reliable owing to the possible inclusion of *dachi* which were not habitable during the winter months.[37] The vacancy rate was therefore most probably less than 5 per cent for the city as a whole, with the peripheral wards registering a higher, and the central-city wards, a lower percentage. In the discussion that follows the characteristics of the occupied housing stock will be of central concern.

The intensity of use of residential buildings naturally depended largely on their location. For the city there were on average seventy-five persons per building, while in the Spasskaya borough the figure was 247 and for the densely settled third ward, 373. Toward the periphery the ratio dropped markedly—to fifty-two in the case of Aleksandro-Nevskaya borough, and to thirty and twenty-three for Peterburgskaya and Vyborgskaya respectively.[38] Whether buildings, apartments or rooms are used as the basis for assessment matters little, because the critical criterion of floor space per inhabitant cannot in any case be included. Clearly this is a major deficiency. However, a crude index of residential land-use may still be derived.

Densities varied not only according to location, but according to the height of buildings. Data on the number of persons per rented one-room apartment have been set out for buildings of different heights by borough in table 12. It is plain that overcrowding was excessive in the cellar and third-floor apartments. Although there are no direct measures of floor space per inhabitant, the number living in one-room

[37] *Sanktpeterburg po Perepisi 10 Dekabrya 1869*, part 2, section 1, pp. iv-v. This comment applied to boroughs other than Peterburgskaya and Vyborgskaya where the *dacha* had intentionally been excluded.
[38] *Sanktpeterburg po Perepisi 10 Dekabrya 1869*, part 2, section 2, p. 5.

TABLE 12. *Number of inhabitants per rented one-room apartment, 1869*

Borough	Cellar Persons per one-room apartment	1st floor Persons per one-room apartment	3rd floor Persons per one-room apartment	5th floor and higher Persons per one-room apartment
Admiralteyskaya	5·0	3·6	3·4	5·2
Kazanskaya	5·0	4·9	3·7	4·1
Spasskaya	5·8	5·5	8·6	6·1
Kolomenskaya	5·5	4·7	8·9	3·2
Narvskaya	6·0	6·4	6·2	5·2
Moskovskaya	6·5	6·1	5·2	6·5
Aleksandro-Nevskaya	9·4	7·4	5·8	6·3
Rozhdestvenskaya	5·8	6·2	5·9	5·1
Liteynaya	5·1	4·3	4·5	4·5
Vasil'yevskaya	4·7	4·8	4·0	4·2
Peterburgskaya	4·2	4·0	3·8	2·5
Vyborgskaya	8·2	5·4	10·9	3·0
Average	5·8	5·4	6·5	5·2

Source: *Sanktpeterburg po Perepisi 10 Dekabrya 1869* (1872), part 2, section 2, pp. 30–43.

units averaged at least five persons and reflects the dearth of adequate housing in the city. Using this figure as a reference point, it is clear that the situations in Aleksandro-Nevskaya and Vyborgskaya boroughs were especially severe. While cellars were notorious for the degree to which people were crammed in, it is noteworthy that third-floor apartments, assuming areas were roughly equivalent, were even worse off—in Spasskaya, Kolomenskaya and Vyborgskaya, eight, nine, ten and more persons were common. If we consider absolute numbers rather than ratios, then the plight of the inner city comes into sharp focus. For example, the average number of inhabitants in each third-floor apartment in Vyborgskaya was 10·9, but just ninety-eight persons were involved. In total 748 residents were listed as occupying third-floor apartments of all sizes. In Spasskaya, the ratio was lower, 8·6. However, 1,005 lived in them and nearly 19,000 occupied third-floor apartments of all sizes. For buildings of five storeys and higher, Spasskaya shared the distinction of possessing the most crowded one-room habitations with Moskovskaya and Aleksandro-Nevskaya. Again, however, the central-city boroughs were under greatest pressure. There were five buildings in this category in Aleksandro-Nevskaya with twenty-three apartments housing 165 people. In Moskovskaya, seventy-seven buildings with 184 apartments provided homes for nearly 1,500 persons. There were just over 100 such structures in Spasskaya, a total of 455 apartments and more than 4,800 residents.[39] Despite the statistically greater degree of crowding in rooms on the third floor and above, there was a very good reason why cellars should appear less crowded, namely the endemic problem of flooding. While more people in each room was the rule for the upper floors, there was a decided advantage in remaining relatively dry. The roof might leak, but it was not necessary to put up with ankle-deep seepage for weeks at a time.

Although 463,000 inhabitants were tenants, roughly 150,000 persons ranging from owner-occupiers to prisoners did not pay rent directly and lived in what were referred to as *bezplatnyya. kvartiry* Over 63,000 people were provided with housing because they were state employees. If positions with government organizations could not be secured, then other types of service often put a roof of some sort over one's head. Yard-keepers (*dvorniki*) and coachmen (*kucherski*) numbered some 16,600 and were two such examples. More than 17,000 male and nearly 2,100 female factory workers were provided

[39] *Sanktpeterburg po Perepisi 10 Dekabrya 1869*, part 2, section 2, pp. 33, 35, 37, 41.

with accommodation and thus remained outside the commercial housing market. The ownership of housing, usually an apartment, was something only a fraction of the population had the financial resources, and the desire, to attain. Fewer than 27,000 were owner-occupiers of single-function apartments, while a further 4,767 apparently combined a privately owned place of work and place of residence. Institutional facilities, including churches, monasteries, charitable societies, schools, hospitals, and prisons met the housing requirements of approximately 21,000 persons.[40] For the 150,000 people living in *bezplatnyya kvartiry* there are no data which would permit any comparisons of the overall housing situation according to borough. However, some broad comparisons are possible for the city as a whole. To the extent that simple relationships between persons in each one-room apartment allow some insights into the housing question, the following may be said. Those persons who had to secure lodgings in the open market, in fact, the majority of the city's population, were worse off than those who for one reason or another remained outside the commercial housing market. For example, in the cellar lodgings which were rented there were nearly six persons per apartment. Comparable figures for the *bezplatnyya kvartiry* were four and five. Similarly, the overcrowding of garrets, that is, third-floor and higher units, was much greater than the ratios obtained for *bezplatnyya kvartiry*. On the third floor an average of 6·5 persons resided in each apartment, whereas only 4·1 were housed in *bezplatnyya kvartiry*.[41] Although it is highly probable that the statistical picture of overcrowding is somewhat biased because of the inclusion of the owner-occupier group, we cannot ascertain by how much this is so. In any event, the difference between 6·5 and 4·1 persons per room is one of degree and not kind. Whether rented or not, there were severe pressures on available accommodation.

Conditions were nowhere worse than in the cellars. There had always been some cellar dwellings, but the numbers involved had been small and, because of the high probability of flooding each year, they had generally been used for storage or left vacant. It is not surprising, therefore, that with migration to the city running at an unprecedented level the profitability of converting cellars for human occupation should be looked at quite differently. Predictably, wholesale conversion ensued.

[40] *Sanktpeterburg po Perepisi 10 Dekabrya 1869*, part 2, section 2, p. 60.
[41] *Sanktpeterburg po Perepisi 10 Dekabrya 1869*, part 2, section 2, p. 66.

Even informed contemporaries tended to underestimate the actual numbers of the cellar population in the city. In the one thorough survey undertaken, Dr F. Erisman formed the opinion that some 30,000 people inhabited cellar apartments in early 1871. This number was arrived at indirectly for the survey covered 'no more than one-sixth of all Petersburg cellar dwellings' in which there lived about 5,000 persons.[42] At the time of Erisman's study the results of the 1869 enumeration of housing facilities were still unpublished. It later transpired that the estimate of 30,000 for 1871 was 16,000 fewer than the number living in cellars more than a year earlier. It is quite conceivable that the share of the cellar population had increased slightly from 7 per cent in 1869. Other cities in Europe also had substantial numbers of cellar lodgings. In Berlin in 1864, for instance, more than 9 per cent of the population were living in such places, but the problem of flooding was by no means as serious as in St Petersburg.

Erisman's survey revealed that 40 per cent of the apartments were in some degree inundated. He made his survey during the period February to May 1871, when much of the inundation observed was attributable to seepage caused by the higher spring ground-water levels. The flood hazard was greatest during the autumn and a flood of even average proportion would certainly have affected a larger share of the dwellings. Conditions in the cellars were generally bad as some of the details included in Erisman's report attest. The ten wards sampled from seven boroughs provide a reasonable cross-section of what were supposedly working-class areas.[43] Many a cellar had anything from ten to sixty centimetres of water for weeks at a time. Collections of snow, impenetrable ice-packed storm pipes, heavy spring rains and below street-level entrances—all combined to channel surface water into the cellars where it stagnated until the warmer weather of the late spring. The mere presence of water, however, was not sufficient to deter occupancy, as Erisman's investigation indicated; for example, on Ruzovskaya Street in the fourth ward of Moskovskaya borough 'in a cellar lived in by *izvoshchiki* (waggoners), despite the fact that water now covered the floor for one and a half months, the occupants left only three weeks ago upon insistence of the police.' Nearby on Mozhayskaya Street, 'water is evident in the kitchen belonging to cellar apartment number ten; despite it being absolutely pitch black, three people lived

[42] F. Erisman, 'Podval'nyya Zhilishcha v Peterburge', *Arkhiv Sudebnoy Meditsiny i Obshchestvennoy Gigiyeny*, VII (1871), p. 60.
[43] The boroughs selected were Spasskaya, Moskovskaya, Narvskaya, Aleksandro-Nevskaya, Rozhdestvenskaya, Peterburgskaya and Vasil'yevskaya.

in this kitchen.'[44] Water seeping into cellars was one problem, the foulness of it was yet another. High densities and the lack of basic services created the situation in the third ward of Vasil'yevskaya borough in which 'five families, in total twenty persons lived in one cellar apartment'. The cellar was frequently inundated, and water lay stagnant up to as much as thirty centimetres in depth. One source of seepage was the courtyard, which 'on the whole is in a high degree filthy [*gryazen*], being covered in rotten straw, animal and human defecation.'[45] The only things that varied during the annual inundation were the duration, depth and dirtiness of the water in the cellars. Given the importance of this medium in the dissemination of diseases like typhus and cholera, the impact of such conditions on public health may be easily imagined.

In large measure the design and shoddy construction of apartment buildings were conducive to seepage during the high ground-water levels of late winter and early spring. During the course of Erisman's survey, the relationship between ground-water levels and the floors of cellars was determined for over eighty buildings in the seven boroughs; in only one instance was the differential significant (fifty centimetres), in twenty cases it was the same, and in the remainder it was below, often as much as thirty to sixty centimetres.[46] Speculative tenement construction was clearly not conducive to the betterment of housing conditions, whether cellar or above ground. None the less, the most intolerable facilities could be rented, and at a profit.

At the time of the census the housing stock comprised 63,000 rented apartments and 25,000 more in the *bezplatnyya kvartiry* category. Of the rented lodgings, 46 per cent commanded more than 200 roubles each year and the average was 305. This is not to say that cheap housing did not exist. In fact there were 106 lodgings which were let for twelve roubles or less each year. An additional 723 could be had for between twelve and twenty-five.[47] Although there is no information as to their location, size or condition, they were an obvious bargain for the few who could get them. Accommodation was often shared and this helped to cut the cost to individuals or families. In this regard the *arteli* filled an important need for a portion of the labouring population. Kropotkin reported that most of the weavers and workers in the cotton factories 'lived in small associations, or *artels*, ten or twelve persons hiring a

[44] Erisman, 'Podval'nyya Zhilishcha v Peterburge', p. 51.
[45] Erisman, 'Podval'nyya Zhilishcha v Peterburge', p. 54.
[46] Erisman, 'Podval'nyya Zhilishcha v Peterburge', pp. 67–8.
[47] *Sanktpeterburg po Perepisi 10 Dekabrya 1869*, part 2, section 2, pp. 56–7.

common apartment and taking their meals together, each one paying every month his share of the general expenses.'[48] For others less fortunate still, they could often only afford literally the corner of a room, or *ugol*. Even this type of habitat ranged in price from two to three roubles per month, exclusive of a contribution to the essential supply of firewood. We noted earlier that in low-paying industries such as tanning or jute, twelve roubles per month was an average salary. Itinerant labourers were not uncommonly worse off and it is small wonder that living space had been so minutely carved up as to make the *ugol* a widespread phenomenon.

We might put the cost of housing into sharper focus by examining the average cost of renting a one-room cellar that conformed to the generally bad conditions already described. Of the 63,000 apartments rented in 1869, almost 4,000 were in the city's cellars. From these, close to 800,000 roubles flowed into landlord's pockets that year. It is clearly hazardous to draw firm conclusions when floor space and other relevant information are not availabe, but using average annual rents of one-room cellar dwellings provides a reasonable introduction to the housing market. In table 13 the basic characteristics of cellar lodgings are outlined, as well as the mean annual rent for single rooms in each of the twelve boroughs. By a considerable margin the cheapest cellars were to be found in Peterburgskaya borough where thirty-four roubles was the average annual rent. Contrasting sharply with this situation were the cellars of the densely populated boroughs of Spasskaya and Kazanskaya, where rents ranged from 126 to 173 roubles. There are many possible reasons for the marked difference, although it may reasonably be assumed that lodgings in Peterburgskaya borough were smaller.[49] The likelihood of flooding was certainly greater for the island cellars, and in relation to the centrality offered by the other two boroughs the lower average rent would seem about right. Even among the densely settled inner-city boroughs there was marked divergence in rent. Moskovskaya cellars, for instance, were on average less than half the rent of single rooms in Spasskaya, but the fact that there were more of them probably pulled down the average. But, in any event, from the data in table 13 it is plain to see that in relation to the twenty roubles per month which a factory worker would be fortunate to earn the price of even a one-room cellar came very high.

[48] Peter Kropotkin, *Memoirs of a Revolutionist* (New York, 1962), edited by James A. Rogers, p. 218.
[49] Arkhangel'skiy, 'Zhizn' v Peterburge', p. 100.

TABLE 13. *Rented cellar lodgings, 1869*

Borough	Number of apartments all sizes	Number of inhabitants	Annual aggregate apartment rent all sizes (roubles)	Number of one-room apartments	Average annual rent per one-room apartment (roubles)
Admiralteyskaya	160	933	77,515	26	153
Kazanskaya	292	1,889	87,812	41	126
Spasskaya	319	2,243	130,240	73	173
Kolomenskaya	284	2,096	40,428	73	69
Narvskaya	310	2,420	49,937	101	92
Moskovskaya	557	4,516	95,237	122	80
Aleksandro-Nevskaya	171	1,912	23,894	50	76
Rozhdestvenskaya	398	3,407	48,396	100	63
Liteynaya	593	3,968	125,721	151	88
Vasil'yevskaya	549	3,882	95,527	114	79
Peterburgskaya	209	1,265	18,414	40	34
Vyborgskaya	64	586	4,978	18	66
Totals	3,906	29,117	798,099	909	89

Source: *Sanktpeterburg po Perepisi 10 Dekabrya 1869* (1872), part 2, section 2, pp. 30–43.

For the poor there were very few options open to them in the late sixties. Cheap lodging houses numbered a score or so, but these were frequently operated on an exploitative and not a charitable basis. In the open market accommodation was expensive, if not exorbitant. What is more, it was increasingly difficult to obtain. Charitable institutions had stepped into the breach as early as 1858, but apparently had not done much to alleviate the situation. The *Obshchestvo Dlya Uluchsheniya v S.Pg. Pomyshcheniy Rabochago i Nuzhdayushchagosya Naseleniya* (Society For the Improvement of the Lodgings of Workers and the Needy in St Petersburg) had been in existence for over a decade but concentrated on other ways of serving the poor than providing housing for them, even though one of its intended purposes was to do precisely the latter.[50] So far as we can tell, four other groups provided housing assistance. Two provided rent-free or subsidized housing for Finns and Estonians, while the Orthodox Church ran another housing programme.[51] Chief among them, however, was the *Obshchestvo Dostavleniya Deshevykh Kvartir i Dr. Posobiy Nuzhdayushchimsya Zhitelyam v S. Pg.* (Society for Providing Low Cost Apartments and Other Assistance to the Needy Population in St Petersburg). Founded in 1861, it owned 140 lodgings in 1869. The majority were rented for between 100 and 150 roubles per year. Rent was certainly fair since each apartment had about three rooms. Some rented for less than twelve roubles and a handful for between twelve and twenty-five, but in total there were only fourteen apartments. While the Society's efforts were commendable, scarcely 400 people benefited.[52] Thus, subsidized housing provided by charitable organizations could do hardly anything to ease the housing conditions for the majority. The result was that over 460,000 persons were obliged to search out accommodation in the open market and to pay the going rate. Apart from a claim on living space of some sort, what the tenant's rent entitled him to by way of municipal services is another matter altogether.

4 MUNICIPAL SERVICES

The housing shortage was made even more pernicious by the generally sorry state of municipal services. Street maintenance and

[50] *Entsiklopedicheskiy Slovar'* (1895), vol. LIV, p. 854. This source indicates 1848 as the founding date but all others cite 1858.
[51] P. Semenov (ed.), *Geografichesko-Statisticheskiy Slovar' Rossiyskoy Imperii* (1868), vol. IV, p. 454.
[52] *Sanktpeterburg po Perepisi 10 Dekabrya 1869*, part 2, section 2, p. 69.

lighting, bad as they were, merely inconvenienced the population at large. Deficiencies in sewage disposal and water supply portended rather more serious consequences. City government, even if it had been a progressive body, could do little to look after the needs of the growing population properly with the financial resources which were available to it. Muncipal government lumbered on according to the precepts of the 1846 statute, and we saw earlier how this piece of legislation simply clarified the obligations of a small share of the city's population but did nothing to facilitate rational management. Revenues continued to be derived from a plethora of minor sources. Unable to tax real property, unable to incur debt, and lacking full control over its revenues (since these had to be shared with the *guberniya zemstvo* government), civic authority was effectively crippled. The problems of municipal government in the capital were scarcely unique and were recognized as worthy of serious consideration; in keeping with the prevailing spirit of reform, committees studied the issue throughout most of the sixties. Meanwhile, the face of the city changed as new buildings were thrown up in large numbers and in a totally irrational manner. In the housing sector, for example, the erection of a tenement on a site having proper services was inclined all too often to be a hit-or-miss matter. Someone would have to pay for such chaos, and we do not have to think very hard to imagine who that would be.

To supply adequate and pure water to city dwellers was already outstretching the capabilities of city government in the fifties. The response to the problem was characteristic. In 1858 the task of supplying water to an extensive area between the Bol'shaya Neva River and the Obvodnyy Canal was turned over to a joint-stock company. By 1863 the company's water distribution network was functioning. Consumption rose rapidly and profits were made. The system, however, was deficient in two respects. In the first place only a small percentage of the population within the area serviced was provided with water.[53] The inadequacies of the water-supply system in this regard are clearly revealed by information in the census. Of the 8,242 buildings surveyed which, it should be remembered, housed over 90 per cent of the population, only 1,795 had running water and the majority of these only in the courtyards and not in individual apartments. Indeed, fewer than 900 buildings had water supplied to more than a single apartment and it is probable that a continuous supply of running water in every

[53] S. P. Luppov, 'Gorodskoye Upravleniye i Gorodskoye Khozyaystvo', *Och.IL* (1957), vol. II, pp. 828–32.

apartment was extremely rare. As might be expected, the provision of water was much more extensive in the central city than in the suburbs. Within the three inner-city boroughs of Admiralteyskaya, Kazanskaya and Spasskaya, about three quarters of all buildings were tied in with the system. Elsewhere the share varied markedly. In the densely settled Moskovskaya borough, barely one third of the 815 buildings were serviced. In Aleksandro-Nevskaya borough the percentage dropped to seven, which meant that the inhabitants of 650 buildings did without. In the case of Vyborgskaya, a grand total of twenty-three houses had running water, leaving residents of 1,166 buildings dependent upon commercial water carriers, *dvorniki*, on personal servants or on their own initiative ⟨*see* plate 22⟩.[54]

If the municipal water system had been assured of the purity of its supplies, then the deprivation suffered by the majority would have been so much the greater. As it was, such a benefit did not accrue to those using it. This was the second deficiency of the system. The Bol'shaya Neva River was the sole source and although filtration removed some of the coarser ingredients, the water was far from pure. The growing volume of industrial and domestic waste dumped into it caused a perceptible deterioration in quality. Surveys taken during the late sixties indicate that tap water was only marginally purer than that drawn directly from the Neva and the latter was no longer a source from which one could, with impunity, consume water unboiled. Still, this source was vastly better than the canals, where organic impurities were two or three times as high as piped water.[55] Inadequate filtration contributed to, but did not cause, the problem, for this stemmed from the regular use of the Bol'shaya Neva, its tributaries and the canals as open sewers.

Effluent from industry was certainly making a bad situation worse and we have already noted that existing zoning by-laws were in-effectual because they were not enforced. However, the growing volume of domestic sewage was a much more serious health hazard. The time-honoured method of collecting and disposing of waste, while simple, was part of the problem. It was collected from apartments and stored temporarily in the courtyards; then when unimpeded progress through the courtyard became impossible, the waste-barrels were carried to the nearest stretch of water and their contents tipped in. During the winter months the problem of disposal was rather greater and the

---

[54] *Sanktpeterburg po Perepisi 10 Dekabrya 1869*, part 2, section 1, p. 34.
[55] Data cited in Arkhangel'skiy, 'Zhizn' v Peterburge', pp. 101–2.

courtyards and alleys were frequently jammed with receptacles of solid waste. Prevailing temperatures deferred the potential hazard to public health, but only until the spring thaw. It is hardly surprising that this practice had a deleterious effect on public health and the periodic posting of notices advising against consumption of water without prior boiling had long been a part of city life. Prudence was in order before mid-century and later descriptions simply verified the continuing need to take care in drinking the local water:

> The Neva water is soft, disgustingly so to the man accustomed to drink spring water. With most travellers it produces diarrhoea, and weakens them terribly . . . All of them [the canals], without exception, are the receptacles for all possible filth—dirt from the factories of every tinge, and from the common sewers, pours into them. From morning until night washing is going on in them, and drinking-water taken out close by! The water placed on the table in the spring is perfectly pestiferous. Frequently in summer did I meet the nightmen's carts, which discharged their filthy cargo into the Fontanka, so that the very air was poisoned. In the morning, water for breakfast is procured from it.[56]

Municipal services were obviously not restricted to such mechanical matters as managing a water supply, maintaining the streets or moving sewage, but rightfully extended into the sphere of law and order. As we have noted elsewhere, however, this important facet of municipal management was not in the hands of a police force responsible to the City Council; rather it was under the authority of the military governor who was directly responsible to the Minister of the Interior. Given the huge transient population to be registered and generally monitored, the growing fear in some circles of the potential disorder which could emanate from the lower classes and the occasional outrage, such as the attempted assassination of Alexander II in 1866, which reinforced such fears, it is not unexpected that among municipal institutions reform came early to the police system.

In 1867 a series of changes began which resulted in greater independence of St Petersburg within the *guberniya*. The first step involved the abolition of the post of military governor. The Chief of Police for the capital, General F. F. Trepov, emerged from this shake-up in a position of considerable power and prestige. Over the next few years he was able to extend his control over the surrounding districts, a move which

[56] *Recollections of Russia*, p. 33.

presaged the extension of the official city territory in the seventies. Under Trepov's vigorous efforts to maintain control over the masses his budget was handsomely enlarged. Already in 1867 the number of police districts had been increased to over ninety. Keeping tabs on the comings and goings of all inhabitants consumed the time of enormous numbers of functionaries but in this at least the police were able to do a reasonable job. They were not alone, of course, for the more than 8,000 *dvorniki* or yard-keepers were charged with reporting any suspicious persons to the district police. The reforms initiated in 1867 culminated in the creation in 1871 of a new position of enormous influence in municipal affairs—the *gradonachal'nik*, about which we shall have more to say later.

At this point we need only note that while the police were so far equal to the task of maintaining civic order, they were woefully short-handed when it came to several other vitally important areas of responsibility. Like police elsewhere, it was their duty to look after the health and well-being of the population. The control of communicable diseases, ensuring that public health measures in the preparation and sale of food and drink were adhered to, checking the sanitary standards in rented accommodation—all this and more fell to the police. When it came to subversive activities the police were methodical in their investigations; when it came to sanitation and disease they were frequently cavalier. In this regard, a totally inadequate medical staff did not help matters at all. In 1869 there were just over 900 medical doctors in the city, and a bare handful worked for the police as sanitary inspectors. Irrespective of who was ultimately responsible for the welfare of society, the appalling death-rate was a shocking indictment of the job being done.[57]

5 DISEASE AND DEATH

When the first detailed study of death in the capital was carried out by the Central Statistical Committee, operating as it did under the wing of the Ministry of Internal Affairs, the conclusions reached were generally accepted as the official point of view. This does not mean that the Central Statistical Committee glossed over the situation; far from it, for death-rate statistics were too well known. But there was ample scope for establishing causal relationships. In examining the period

---

[57] For a detailed discussion of these developments, see Zelnik, *Labor and Society*, pp. 252, 263–7; Luppov, 'Gorodskoye Upravleniye', pp. 811–13.

from 1856 to 1865, the Committee estimated that there was an average of one death per 23·6 inhabitants, a figure rivalled only by Vienna where it was reckoned there was one per 24·7. London, Paris, and Brussels had ratios that ranged between 34·6 and 40·0, and even Berlin, with its sizable number of cellar inhabitants only registered one per 36·5 persons. Using a different measure, deaths per 1,000 population, these cities all fell in the 25·0 to 29·0 range, whereas Vienna and St Petersburg respectively registered 40·5 and 42·4. Within Russia, the capital rivalled several lesser cities for this unenviable pride of place. Kazan and Tula exceeded St Petersburg with figures of 52·3 and 46·0, although most cities of any size had death-rates in the upper thirties per 1,000.[58] Averaged out over a period of several years, these figures were, in exceptional years, very much overshadowed. For example, Odessa had 62·5 deaths per 1,000 inhabitants in 1866, the result in part of a serious outbreak of cholera.[59] In the same year and again because of epidemics, deaths in St Petersburg increased from 42·4 per 1,000 to 52·0. At the time of the Central Statistical Committee's survey most Russian cities were following the trends in Europe, leaving St Petersburg and Kazan conspicuously alone among Russian cities as having a natural *decrease* of population.[60] However, it was noted that the statistics for Kazan may have been unduly biased in as much as only a five-year time span was used, whereas a much longer period for other cities ensured a more accurate representation of trends. The stark implication was that the capital may have topped the list within Russia as well as in Europe. This unenviable state of affairs demanded explanation, and the Committee endeavoured to provide some answers. Among the first points made by the Committee was the following:

> The reason for the surplus of deaths over births in Petersburg is dependent upon one of its notable peculiarities, one not met in significant measure in any other large European city; namely, the enormous percentage of migrants arriving in Petersburg from afar in search of a living who left their families at home. To this huge percentage of the population for which Petersburg serves only as temporary camp, we may point out two statistics mentioned earlier; the small proportion of Petersburg natives among the inhabitants of the capital—not more than 33 per cent; and the

[58] *Sanktpeterburg, Izsledovaniya po Istorii*, pp. 174–6.
[59] *Trudy Odesskago Statisticheskago Komiteta* (Odessa, 1867), p. 294.
[60] We may note again that in the preceding century deaths exceeded births by more than 140,000 in the capital.

scant proportion of persons living with their families in Petersburg —not more than 38 per cent of all inhabitants.[61]

Having established that much of the population was transient, the discussion turned to matters which concerned more directly the excessive annual attrition. Militating against lower death-rates, it was believed, were two factors. The first pertained to the physical environment of the capital, particularly the climate. Thus, it was assumed that a major cause was 'the deleterious influence of its damp, maritime, vacillating climate, to which the inhabitant of the dry continental expanses adjusts with difficulty.'[62] Certainly, most migrants came from the interior provinces, but this was true irrespective of class. In fact, it was simply environmental determinism being invoked to explain why migrants accounted for deaths quite out of proportion to their actual numbers—and it was an explanation taken quite seriously. Although there were no data on deaths by social class to support the argument, it was claimed that people indigenous to the city did conform demographically to the trends in European cities; that is, there was a net natural increase.[63]

On the other hand, it was the rigour of the climate which led to excessive death-rates among migrants. To lend credence to the proposition, a detailed analysis of deaths by season of the year was undertaken. This showed that most deaths took place in the spring and summer months, a situation quite different from that in other European cities. In Paris, for instance, out of 100 deaths, 27·9 and 26·4 happened in the spring and winter, whereas only 23·0 were registered during the summer. In St Petersburg there were 29·5 in the spring, 27·1 in the summer, but only 24·3 in the winter. The Committee contended that since the spring and summer months saw a huge influx of peasants, there was a causal relationship between their arrival and the higher death-rates. Why the migrants should succumb when the climate was most tolerable was not explained. In this connection it was noted, almost in passing, that the upsurge of deaths followed shortly after the unfreezing of the Neva in May.[64] But this point was seen in terms of

[61] *Sanktpeterburg, Izsledovaniya po Istorii*, p. 177.
[62] *Sanktpeterburg, Izsledovaniya po Istorii*, p. 177.
[63] It was not until a few years later that there were attempts to separate society into different categories for the purpose of examining the impact of the death-rate. One such study revealed the expected—the privileged element had a lower death-rate (forty-six per 1,000) than the unprivileged (sixty-four per 1,000), a category in which the peasants, *meshchanstvo*, and military were the dominant groups. For a brief discussion, see V. Mikhnevich, *Peterburg Ves' na Ladoni* (1874), pp. 281–2.
[64] *Sanktpeterburg, Izsledovaniya po Istorii*, p. 180.

the thousands of peasants arriving in search of summer employment and was not linked, for example, with the possible dissemination of disease through polluted drinking water.

During the sixties the baneful influence of the climate was repeatedly cited as a principal cause of the comparatively, and admittedly excessive, summer death-rates. And cited not just by the lay public. The explanation found its way into authoritative works like the multi-volumed *Geografichesko-Statisticheskiy Slovar' Rossiyskoy Imperii* (The Geographical-Statistical Dictionary of the Russian Empire), published in the latter part of the decade.[65] With such widely quoted sources espousing this view, it is small wonder that it remained common currency for years. The Committee was not totally ignorant of the role of the deplorable sanitary conditions to be found throughout the city. This, in fact, was the second reason for the high rate, but explicit reference to the 'disadvantageous hygenic conditions of the capital's . . . stifling, damp, cellar lodgings [which were] frequently congested by huge masses' was given short shrift compared with the discussion of the climate.[66] It was to the sanitary inspectors and other medical practitioners to demonstrate that disease and death were attributable more to conditions of daily life and labour than to the climate.

The seemingly annual visitation of typhus or cholera epidemics to St Petersburg evoked concern throughout Europe. Particularly serious outbreaks often resulted in governments sending medical officers scurrying to the Russian capital to report first-hand on the situation. The epidemic of 1864–5 was a case in point. The deteriorating state of affairs in St Petersburg was first noted in London in a letter of the Medical Officer of the Privy Council in mid April—a letter which went to the heart of the matter:

> The mixed epidemic [of relapsing fever and typhus] . . . testifies to the miserable state of a starving and over-crowded proletariat; and there seems reason to believe that, if the St Petersburg epidemic is of more than common severity, this is only in result of extremely aggravated conditions of privation, overcrowding, operating on large masses of the lowest population.[67]

[65] Semenov, *Geografichesko-Statisticheskiy Slovar'*, p. 452. As a physical geographer, Semenov may well have succumbed to the popular shift to environmentally determinist views which had been initiated in many disciplines by Darwin's, *The Origin of Species*.

[66] *Sanktpeterburg, Izsledovaniya po Istorii*, p. 180.

[67] John Simon, 'Letter of the Medical Officer', *BPP; Russian Epidemic*, 1865 (246), XLVII.517.

Concern over the possibility of the epidemic spreading resulted in Dr George Whitely being despatched to the scene. His report, submitted in early May, was not couched in the environmentally deterministic terms of the Central Statistical Committee though, to be sure, the physical environment was not ignored:

> This city, with its swampy foundation and copious rainfall, surrounded on all sides by water, and exposed to extreme changes of temperature, affords, even in the best years, a very unhealthy sojourn for the poorer inhabitants.
> In addition to the unhealthy state of the dwellings of the poor . . .
> If we bear in mind also that the water supply is taken from the River Neva, and often much polluted by surface drainage, and that large quantities of very inferior spirits are consumed by the poorer inhabitants, it will be at once understood that an epidemic of relapsing fever, once introduced amongst such a population, might well assume proportions even more formidable than the present one.
> One set-off against the unsanitary conditions mentioned above may be of interest, viz., that even the poorest inhabitants of St Petersburg take a steam bath at least once a week, generally on Saturdays; and I was able personally to convince myself at the dispensary that although their clothing is often very dirty, their skin is cleaner than is usual amongst a similar class elsewhere.
> The class of persons amongst whom the epidemic prevailed only a little less extensively than amongst the poor labouring Russian population were the military; but even here the better food and more healthy dwellings were generally accepted as sufficient to explain the comparatively low rate of mortality.
> Amongst the English and German workpeople and their families, amounting in number to several thousands, the epidemic has prevailed to a very slight extent only, with a low rate of mortality; while the upper classes have remained almost entirely exempt from that particular form of disease, thus furnishing one more striking instance of the connection between relapsing fever and destination, with its concomitant evils.[68]

The main forum for the view that conditions of daily life were conducive to infection were the pages of the Archive of Forensic

[68] George Whitely, 'Report', *BPP; Russian Epidemic*, 1865 (246), XLVII.517.

Medicine and Social Hygiene (*Arkhiv Sudebnoy Meditsiny i Obshchestvennoy Gigiyeny*) which began publication in the mid-sixties and continued as a quarterly for the better part of a decade.[69] Discussions of disease, its diffusion and impact recorded vividly the price to be paid for a cavalier approach to basic hygiene. Although we have so far emphasized the deplorable state of housing for the poor and the inadequacies of essential municipal services, we should not assume that the spread of disease was confined to residential origins. In an early epidemiological study Dr Yu. Gyubner found that the spread of cholera in an area of Peterburgskaya borough stemmed from conditions in three factories where a number of the casualties of the epidemic were employed. After facilities at the factories were investigated, the lavatories were discovered to be the probable source of infection.[70]

During the late sixties the toll of diseases like typhus, measles, cholera, smallpox, and syphilis accounted for at least half of all deaths.[71] It did not require an especially perceptive mind to see a relationship between incidence of disease and numbers of peasants, but to translate this into an environmentally determined, higher death-rate argument was not logically justified. The assault on the environmentally determinist view that climatic conditions were responsible which, it should be reiterated, was generally synonymous with the official view points of police and government spokesmen, culminated in a lengthy paper by Dr G. Arkhangel'skiy in the early seventies. He demonstrated what was obvious to most of the journal's readership—historically, comparatively, and logically, climate could not be assigned primary responsibility.[72] Sanitary conditions could, however, be singled out. The facts were there.

The number of deaths attributable to infectious disease was largely responsible for St Petersburg having the singular honour of being the least healthy capital in Europe. If the statistics resulting in this judgement were less than precise, as is quite possible, then by the same token the relative position may have been even worse. Moreover, the available data refer only to the official city area and exclude the peasant dominated suburban regions—hardly bastions of good health. How many diseased peasants left the city to die in, or en route to, the village

[69] For additional pertinent discussion, see Zelnik, *Labor and Society*, pp. 268-82.
[70] Yu. Gyubner, 'O Kholere v 4-m Kvartale Peterburgskoy Chast 1866 g.', *Arkhiv Sudebnoy Meditsiny i Obshchestvennoy Gigiyeny*, III (1868), pp. 10, 12-14.
[71] Even in the late nineties, infectious disease accounted for nearly 40 per cent of deaths. *Entsiklopedicheskiy Slovar'*, vol. LVI, p. 317.
[72] Arkhangel'skiy, 'Zhizn' v Peterburge', pp. 37-9.

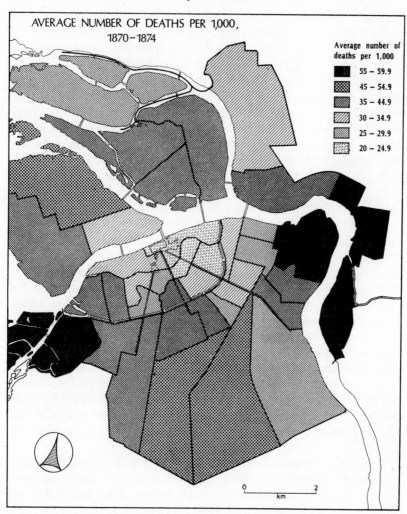

MAP 30. *Average number of deaths per 1,000, 1870–74*

also raises some interesting questions, for the ties with the countryside were stronger than in other capitals cited in comparison. As per capita death-rates varied among European capitals and the towns of Russia, so too within the cities there were perceptible differences. For the period 1870 to 1874 the average death-rates per 1,000 population are portrayed for the thirty-eight wards in map 30. This period witnessed serious outbreaks of cholera and smallpox in 1872, but few five-year periods in the city's history were free from such calamities.[73]

There was almost a threefold spread between the lowest death-rate of 21·3 per 1,000 persons in the first ward of Spasskaya borough and the 59·9 figure recorded in the third ward of Vyborgskaya. At first glance, this might almost seem to be a core-periphery dichotomy. While there is some justification for this view, some exceptions stand out. For instance, the second ward of Vyborgskaya borough had the fifth lowest death-rate, 25·8, yet the third ward was the highest for the city. The level of industrialization has been cited as one of the characteristic features of high death-rate wards and boroughs, but in this case the argument does not hold up.[74] The second ward was the location of many more factories and was home to more factory workers.[75] Both were inhabited largely by peasants. The main difference was that Okhta, the third ward, was the destination of thousands of migrant peasants who sought summer employment in the building trades. But the region lacked adequate housing, was poorly serviced and because of enormous congestion, served as a superb environment for the spread of disease. Just as there was a marked difference within Vyborgskaya borough, there was also an apparently odd juxtaposition in Spasskaya. Among the inner-city wards, the third in Spasskaya had the highest death-rate, approximately 43·0 for every 1,000 people. Contemporaries certainly commented on the refuse and filth which in large measure came from the markets in the area. During the warmer months refuse accumulated in large amounts and provided an ideal medium for the transfer of diseases. The fact that this ward was also the most densely populated was clearly a major contributory factor.

It is obvious that some areas were healthier than others, at least as inferred by death-rates. While this was a relative distinction, the question arises as to whether they were perceived as such, and if so, whether this was reflected in residential desirability. In other words, was the social-class fabric of the city in any way fashioned by the blight conveyed in map 30?

---

[73] We have used average death-rates quoted in *Entsiklopedicheskiy Slovar'* rather than a single year in order to avoid extremes in either direction. Gyubner's study for 1870 suffers from this particular deficiency. *Entsiklopedicheskiy Slovar'*, vol. LVI, p. 314; Yu. Gyubner, *Statisticheskiya Izsledovaniya Sanitarnogo Sostoyaniya S. Peterburga 1870g.* (1872).

[74] Zelnik, *Labor and Society*, pp. 246–7.

[75] See maps 13 and 14.

6 THE SOCIAL FABRIC

While there were obvious alterations in the physical habitat as a result of the gathering momentum of industrialization and commercialization, the existing social order of the city was still intact. Not even the Emancipation upset the status quo. As we have already noticed, peasants were still tied to the land, often in less tenable positions economically. And peasants were still peasants according to the estates, which provided a rough measure of social position for the whole of society. Added to this were the civil and military ranks. These assisted in putting a finer edge to the important business of carving out a niche in society. The contribution of the service ranks to urban life did not end here. By dint of rank-specific uniforms and decorative paraphernalia, they added a touch of colour and a sense of occasion to street life. The elegantly attired privy councillor and his military counterpart, the lieutenant councillor, the major and the collegiate assessor and so on through the ranks, each was aware of the pecking order and attendant perquisities. Not that more subtle distinctions were not also made, for this was naturally part and parcel of the system. Gogol had some years earlier caricatured precisely such expressions of vanity:

> Collegiate assessors who receive their rank on the strength of scholarly diplomas can by no means be equated with those who make the rank in the Caucasus. They are two entirely different breeds. . . . But Russia is such a wondrous land that if you say something about one collegiate assessor all the collegiate assessors from Riga to Kamchatka will not fail to take it as applying to them, too. The same is true of all our ranks and titles. Kovalyov belonged to the Caucasus variety of collegiate assessors. He had only held that rank for two years and therefore could not forget it for a moment; and in order to lend himself added dignity and weight he never referred to himself as collegiate assessor but always as major.[76]

If outward appearances of architectural grandeur were deceptive, so too were impressions of the social structure so long as these were restricted to the residences of the nobility and the afternoon perambulations along the English Quay, the lower reaches of the Nevskiy

[76] N. V. Gogol, 'The Nose', in Gleb Struve (ed.), *Russian Stories* (New York, 1961), p. 41.

Prospect or the Taurida Gardens. This was certainly a part of St Petersburg life, but one which was reserved for the privileged and wealthy. Access to the drawing rooms of the nobility, or of those of high military or civil rank, however, was not assured simply by virtue of personal wealth. Indeed, members of the nobility were frequently in a state of near penury.[77] It was not so uncommon for a resplendent uniform or a one-time modish costume to be doffed in a shabby apartment in an insalubrious part of town. But familial ties and perceptible rank were still more likely to open doors than a pocketful of roubles acquired by trade or industry. In attempting to portray the structure of society we must again rely on the membership of the various estates as these are detailed in the census. All that we can do is to sketch a broad canvas of the social–class structure, bearing in mind that the image created can only be an approximation of the world of position and privilege.

The social class structure in 1865 and 1869 is presented in table 14 and several features stand out quite clearly. We have already considered

TABLE 14. *Social-class structure, 1865 and 1869*

Class	Number in 1865	Percentage of total	Number in 1869	Percentage of total
Hereditary nobility	40,543	7·5	54,398	8.2
Personal nobility	39,484	7·3	40,186	6·0
Clergy	5,258	0·9	6,113	0·9
Honoured citizens	7,702	1·4	6,990	1·0
Merchants	21,336	4·0	22,333	3·3
Meshchane	97,198	18·0	123,267	18·5
Tsekhovye	17,535	3·3	17,678	2·6
Peasants	145,370	27·0	207,007	31·0
Military	83,970	15·5	123,126	18·4
Foreigners	15,948	3·0	21,335	3·2
Finns	9,530	1·8	17,205	2·6
Raznochintsy	19,887	3·7	17,771	2·7
Other	35,641	6·6	798	1·6
Totals	539,122	100·0	667,207	100·0

Sources: Sanktpeterburg po Perepisi 10 Dekabrya 1869 goda (1872), part 1, pp. 110-11; *Sanktpeterburg Izsledovaniya po Istorii, Topografii i Statistike Stolitsy* (1868), vol. III, *passim*.

[77] William L. Blackwell, *The Beginnings of Russian Industrialization, 1800–1860* (Princeton, 1968), p. 202.

the migration of peasants to the capital and from that discussion it comes as no surprise that peasants were the single most important group. And their relative significance had been markedly on the upswing since the middle of the 1860s, a trend that was to be accentuated rather than diminished over the next fifty years. Although the traditional social order had not so far been shattered during the process of shifting the economic base from a heavy reliance on mercantile and administrative functions to commerce and industry, there was equally no clear evidence of the increased prominence of the 'urban' classes, that is, the honoured citizenry, merchants, *meshchane* and *tsekhovye*. Compared with 1865, their share of the city's population had declined 3 per cent by 1869. Additionally, the nobility had withered a little, but only in relative terms for there were an additional 14,000 of them in 1869. Of course, many had dismembered or sold off their estates at the time of the Emancipation and permanent residence in the city was probably an attractive proposition.

The resurgent economy, on the other hand, seemingly did not bring many new merchants into the social structure, and in relative terms there was a slight reduction from 4 to just over 3 per cent between 1865 and 1869. The *raznochintsy*, as may be recalled, was an amorphous collection of clerks, teachers, artists, musicians and the like, so-called intellectuals but with a working-class status for the most part. In this group as well there was a small decline since 1865. The reduction was just as likely the result of differences in enumerative precision as a real attrition. The number of Finns increased rather sharply between the two dates and again, more accurate counting may offer a partial explanation. The reliance on foreign entrepreneurial and technical skills expanded during the early years of urban economic development. Finance, trade, industry—there was a sizable list of business activities in which foreigners played an active, and often influential, role. The increase shown in table 14 can be used as a rough yardstick of the growing dependence upon this group. The increase in garrison forces was perhaps of the order outlined in the table, but the 1869 figure includes a wide range of active and inactive military personnel as well as their families. It is not clear from the 1865 census just how inclusive this category is, and given the large increment over the short time span it may well be that some military families found their way into the statisticians' left-over category of 'other'. We have no way of determining the scale of movement between the various classes, though it can be safely assumed that some changes did take place. However, in the important urban classes, any shifts that might have occurred had not augmented the numbers between 1865 and 1869. We are left with the situation in which the peasant influx was completely engulfing the traditional urban classes. While Moscow, because of its morphology, had often been referred to disparagingly as a large village, there was certainly emerging a social-class structure which would justify this epithet being applied to St Petersburg.

The membership of the various classes tells something of the social-class structure, but many questions remain. Our apprehension of them might have been substantially sharpened had the census data on occupations been more refined. It is nevertheless possible to work with the city directory in this connection, as we shall do shortly. The difficulties involved, both in terms of actual labour and of the quality of information obtained, preclude anything more than a sample survey. However, the distribution of the classes, religion, and of ethnicity as determined by native tongue, can be examined as the census does provide the requisite information. This aspect of the social milieu is particularly important in the light of the host of ills, structural and medical, which afflicted some parts of the city with particular severity and no doubt conditioned the perception of and preference for particular residential locations. In other words, it might be expected that when confronted by blighted regions those who could afford to live in the better residential areas would be willing to pay for doing so. This in turn would lead one to expect a fairly high degree of residential segregation. And if conditions further deteriorated, we would anticipate that this would increase.

The indices in table 15 give the percentage of each class which would have had to shift its residence to make all distributions over the thirty-eight wards identical, but they do not reveal a particularly high degree of separation.[78] The nobility, honoured citizenry, Finns and clergy were all roughly the same, with indices in the low twenties range. The difference between the presumed upper strata of the classes, the nobility and, for instance, the peasants was not especially marked. The class in which fewest locational shifts would have been required was the truncated lower middle class of urban society, the *meshchane*. Even the widespread garrison forces registered a considerably higher index, 14·8 as opposed to 7·8. Earlier in the century an intermingling of the various classes occurred more often than not and it would appear

[78] For a discussion of the calculations involved, see A Note on Methods, p. 433.

that, notwithstanding the shocking state of the urban habitat in many regions, the spatial separation of the classes had not yet come about.[79] Although we cannot conclusively relate the limited mobility of various socioeconomic groups as expressed in their journeys to work with the lack of spatial segregation of residence by class, they would certainly seem to be connected. It is evident that if we compare map 30 with maps 18 to 21 the entrepreneurial elite often lived in areas which were far from salubrious. Whether the occupation of cellars and garrets by peasants and others at the bottom of the social scale transposed the usual two-dimensional segregation of classes into perhaps some type of a three-dimensional one is entirely possible. The validity of this proposition will be examined when we come to the post-1900 scene.

TABLE 15. *Social classes: indices of residential dissimilarity by census wards, 1869*

Class	Index
Nobility (hereditary)	21·2
Nobility (personal)	18·1
Clergy	22·4
Honoured citizenry (hereditary)	23·5
Honoured citizenry (personal)	23·5
Merchants	15·7
Meshchane	7·8
Tsekhovye	12·8
Military	14·8
Military Families	14·6
Finns	22·1
Peasants	16·7
Foreigners	27·6

Use of the 1867 directory permits a rather finer examination of the spatial segregation of socioeconomic groups because we can tell who lived on particular streets. Based on contemporary descriptions and the nature of the wards as revealed by census data, eight streets, or sections thereof, have been selected for consideration. Among them are Galernaya and Bol'shaya Milionnaya, both in Admiralteyskaya borough and representative of an ostensibly exclusive and high-rent district. The Second Line on Vasil'yevskiy Island was in some respects similar. It was close to the Exchange and the University; most of its

[79] A. I. Kopanev, *Naseleniye Peterburga v Pervoy Polovina XIX Veka* (1957), p. 21. Blackwell's passing reference to a high degree of residential segregation with respect to the peasants and upper classes is without foundation. Blackwell, *The Beginnings of Russian Industrialization*, p. 114.

residents lived in the first ward which had the highest rent in the borough. Srednaya Meshchanskaya Street was in the second ward of Kazanskaya, a densely populated, petty-trade and handicraft area. The lower-class streets chosen as examples are Svechnoy Pereulok in the second ward of Moskovskaya, the Seventh Rozhdestvenskaya Street in the second ward of the borough of the same name, Zarotnaya Street in the second ward of Narvskaya and Gulyarnaya Street in the first ward of Peterburgskaya borough. A rough profile of each street composed of thirteen composite socioeconomic categories derived from information on occupation and rank provided in the directory is provided in table 16.

Galernaya, Milionnaya and the Second Line all have a heavy emphasis on government and professional employment. Among the few representatives of the nobility, all but three lived on either Milionnaya or Galernaya. Streets in areas designated as working-class did reveal a higher proportion of activities in trade and industry, but the separation was far from exclusive. Indeed, even on the presumably higher-rent streets, labourers and factory employees, as well as handicraftsmen, were certainly in evidence. While there were a considerable number of directory entries for which no socio-occupational data were provided, it is clear that, wherever it was provided, streets which had an image of high-class residence none the less housed a contingent of some size from the lower orders. It is indeed probable that, among the persons for whom name and address only were included in the directory, there were many who would come into this category. Expansive entries in the directory normally indicated something of a position in society and therefore the bias in table 16 is likely to be upward, with the upper classes being identified and the lower classes dropping out.

We can also examine the residential segregation of religious and ethnic groups. Using the Russian Orthodox population as a basis for comparison, with four of the six religious minorities we see a comparatively pronounced pattern of segregation ⟨*see* table 17⟩. With roughly 76,000 adherents, the Protestants were the largest religious minority, almost four times the Roman Catholic-Uniat group. These were the two which were least segregated. The 6,600-odd Jews were numerically the largest of the localized religious minorities. Living chiefly in Spasskaya, they were heavily occupied in the petty trading which was conducted on a very widespread basis in the borough. The segregation of the Jews was virtually the same when indices were

TABLE 16. *Socioeconomic composition of selected streets, 1867*

Street	Nobility		Government employment		Government service		Professional		Artists		Teachers		Tutors		Students		Clergy		Merchants		Skilled craftsmen		Factory workers		Labourers		Not specified		Total number
	No.	%	No.	%	No.	%	No.	%	No.	%	No.	%	No.	%	No.	%	No.	%	No.	%	No.	%	No.	%	No.	%	No.	%	
Galernaya	9	2	34	8	43	10	31	7	12	3	12	3	11	2	9	2	11	2	49	11	51	12	8	2	15	3	148	33	443
Bol'shaya Miliionnaya	11	4	6	2	74	24	8	3	6	2	9	3	5	2	8	3	1	1	25	8	27	9	9	3	8	3	106	35	303
Second Line	2	1	18	5	33	10	48	15	10	3	13	4	1	—	28	8	2	1	39	12	64	19	5	2	13	4	65	20	331
Srednaya Meshchanskaya	—	—	12	3	19	4	13	3	18	4	8	2	2	2	8	2	3	1	64	15	182	43	9	2	18	4	64	16	425
Svechnoy	—	—	2	2	6	7	—	—	2	2	2	2	—	—	1	1	1	1	17	20	29	33	4	5	3	3	20	23	87
Seventh Rozhdest-venskaya	—	—	16	14	13	12	2	2	1	1	—	—	—	—	1	1	1	1	10	9	25	22	1	1	9	8	33	29	112
Zarotnaya	—	—	4	6	8	13	2	3	3	5	—	—	3	5	—	—	—	—	3	5	18	29	1	2	4	6	17	27	63
Gulyarnaya	1	2	7	11	9	15	3	5	—	—	2	3	—	—	—	—	1	2	2	3	8	13	3	5	4	6	22	35	62

Source: Vseobshchaya Adresnaya Kniga S. Peterburg (1867–8).

Note: Percentages have been rounded to nearest whole number.

TABLE 17. *Religious groups: indices of residential segregation by census wards, 1869*

Religious group	Index
Raskolniki	38·1
Armenian-Gregorian	41·7
Catholic-Uniat	20·6
Protestant	20·8
Jewish	40·7
Mohammedan	39·9

Note: The Russian Orthodox population is used as a reference point.

TABLE 18. *Ethnic groups: indices of residential segregation by census wards, 1869*

Ethnic groups	Index
Polish	18·0
Lithuanian	39·9
Latvian	25·7
German	26·7
Swedish	26·7
English	37·4
Dutch-Flemish	57·0
French	47·5
Finnish	22·3
Armenian	39·1
Georgian	58·9
Jewish	40·2

Note: Native tongue is used as the basis for determining ethnicity. The Russian-speaking population is used as a reference point.

calculated on the basis of native tongue, which in table 18 is used as a measure of ethnicity. The most highly segregated were the Georgians and Dutch–Flemish populations, but these again were numerically small. In neither case were there more than 150. The English and French inhabited the Admiralteyskaya and Vasil'yevskaya boroughs in greatest number and this accounts for the relatively high indices for the few thousands concerned.

To return to the points made above, there seems not to have been any substantial segregation based on socioeconomic factors. Certainly, religious and ethnic minorities displayed somewhat divergent patterns, as might be expected, but the traditional social fabric of St Petersburg seems to have altered little from our desciption of what it was like around 1840. The changes wrought during later decades of industrialization remain to be seen.

7 MORALS AND MANNERS

Obviously, life was most difficult for the unskilled, irregularly employed and, as a result, generally destitute, members of society, the vast majority of whom were peasants. It would seem that peasants who joined *arteli* fared better than those on their own.[80] The *arteli* could, and did, protect themselves from dissolute associates simply by expelling them, but the extent to which members of these rural-based organizations were shielded from urban ailments, moral and physical, is not entirely clear. Zelnik notes, for example, that police reports singled them out as centres of disease.[81] If we take into consideration the undercurrent of fear in officialdom of anything suggestive of workers' associations, it is not in the least extraordinary that *arteli* should be viewed with some suspicion by the police. The last thing that many desired was to encourage grass-roots organization among the labouring population, for inevitably the privations of labour and daily life would lead to demands for fundamental economic, social and political reform. On the whole, it is likely that *arteli* were positive elements within the urban environment; by the late sixties there were indeed few such elements. Standards of public morality were visibly deteriorating. Even the *arteli*, the charitable societies, and the Church acting together could not stem the tide by expulsion, by aid or by entreaty, for the simple reason that they could do very little to ameliorate the principal cause—abject poverty. Yet few could fail to appreciate the more obvious signs. Prostitution, venereal disease and illegitimacy were cases in point.

At the beginning of the century scarcely one eighth of all births were illegitimate; by the end of the sixties more than 25 per cent were.[82] There can be no doubt that this increase was related to the growing number of women, and particularly single women, living in the city, a

[80] The largest number of *arteli* (approximately thirty) were associated with the Exchange and spanned a wide range of occupations. But so far as can be determined certainly fewer than 10,000 people belonged to *arteli*. Mikhnevich, *Peterburg Ves' na Ladoni*, pp. 541–2.
[81] Zelnik, *Labor and Society*, p. 245.
[82] G. L. von Attengofer, *Mediko-Topograficheskoye Opisaniye Sanktpeterburga, Glavnago i Stolichnago Goroda Rossiyskoy Imperii* (1820), p. 119. The figure pertains to the situation in 1812. Semenov, *Geografichesko-Statisticheskiy Slovar'*, p. 451.

demographic change commented upon earlier. The rise of a labouring population was fast verifying the argument that peasants working there would not emerge from the experience unscathed either spiritually or physically.[83] Literary works frequently cast city-experienced peasants as bereft of morals, or worse.[84] The themes of illegitimacy and of infidelity by either partner working alone in the city were increasingly common, and in this way mirrored the reality of urban life. The existence of large garrison forces of single men, the continuing, though diminished, predominance of male peasants, combined with the hardships of daily life of the poor, encouraged some women, and forced others, into prostitution. It was nothing new to be driven into prostitution through privation and, of course, Dostoevsky uses the subject with considerable force in *Crime and Punishment* (1866). Set in St Petersburg, the novel provides some instructive, if bitter, insights into matters of concern here. Raskolnikov in thinking about a young girl, drunk and abused, whom he has just encounted, ruefully observes:

> The girl will soon be slipping out on the sly here and there. Then there will be the hospital directly (that's always the luck of those girls with respectable mothers, who go wrong on the sly) and then . . . again the hospital . . . drink . . . the taverns . . . and more hospital, in two or three years—a wreck, and her life over at eighteen or nineteen . . . Have not I seen cases like that? And how have they been brought to it? Why, they've all come to it like that. Ugh! But what does it matter? That's as it should be, they tell us. A certain percentage, they tell us, must every year go . . . that way . . . to the devil, I suppose . . . so that the rest may remain chaste, and not be interfered with. A percentage! What splendid words they have; they are so scientific, so consolatory . . . Once you've said 'percentage' there's nothing more to worry about. If we had any other word . . . maybe we might feel more uneasy.[85]

By the turn of the decade even statistics were no longer a consolation. According to the 1869 census, just over 2,000 prostitutes were said to be in business, a number not so different from the rest of the decade.[86] But

---

[83] For related discussion, see Zelnik, *Labor and Society*, pp. 61–8.
[84] See, for example, Andrew Donskov, *The Changing Image of the Peasant in Nineteenth-Century Russian Drama* (Helsinki, 1972) pp. 66–116.
[85] Fyodor Dostoevsky, *Crime and Punishment* (New York, 1962), translated by Constance Garnett, p. 45.
[86] *Sanktpeterburg po Perepisi 10 Dekabrya 1869* (1875), part I, p. 5.

is the census correct? Other sources indicate that, beginning in 1868, prostitutes were far more prevalent than ever before, reaching 3,600 in early 1870 and 4,400 by the end of that year.[87] How many plied their trade without being registered is open to speculation, but given the apparent trends and general economic environment it is probable that there were a great many. Those enumerated in the 1869 census lived mostly in the congested inner-city wards, the nature of which we have already outlined, and it is clear from map 31 that the location of brothels was similar. According to the census, there were only a handful of brothels and surprisingly few prostitutes in a number of peripheral boroughs like Vyborgskaya where males were completely dominant. It is unlikely that they were as scarce as the 1869 census suggests, though traditionally they were associated more with inner-city boroughs such as Spasskaya and Kazanskaya.

The sudden rise in prostitution brought in its wake an upsurge of venereal disease. In one hospital alone in 1870 over 13,000 cases of syphilis were treated, whereas at the beginning of the decade there were in the whole city less than half as many patients. Of course, such figures only hinted at the dimensions of the problem. Many of those infected never reached the hospitals; they were 'treated' at home by some quack, they left the city, or they just died. One informed estimate put the annual number of cases in excess of 30,000 by the turn of the decade—the equivalent of forty-five syphilitic patients for every thousand inhabitants. The disease was by no means restricted to prostitutes and their clients, but included a growing, and alarming, number of family members.[88] This suggests to some degree the number of wives, largely from the peasant, *meshchanstvo* and military classes, who became 'unofficial' prostitutes, perhaps as much as the extent to which husbands resorted to women of the streets. The wildfire spread of venereal diseases caused particular distress at the Foundling Home where the number of syphilitic children admitted each year was on the rise. By 1874 nearly 2·5 per cent of the foundlings received that year

---

[87] It was suggested in 1868 that the 1,800 registered prostitutes probably accounted for no more than a quarter of the actual total. Among this group German women, rather than Russians, apparently pre-dominated. N. B-skiy, 'Ocherk Prostitutsii v Peterburge', *Arkhiv Sudebnoy Meditsiny i Obshchestvennoy Gigiyeny*, III (1868), pp. 67–8; Zelnik, *Labor and Society*, p. 251. Illegitimate children, of course, rarely emanated from the ranks of the professional prostitute, but from the escalating numbers of 'unofficial' prostitutes drawn into the business for other, usually monetary, reasons. For a discussion of the general situation at the end of the decade, see Mikhnevich, *Petersburg Ves' na Ladoni*, pp. 300–08.
[88] Mikhenvich, *Peterburg Ves' na Ladoni*, pp. 284–5; Zelnik, *Labor and Society*, p. 251.

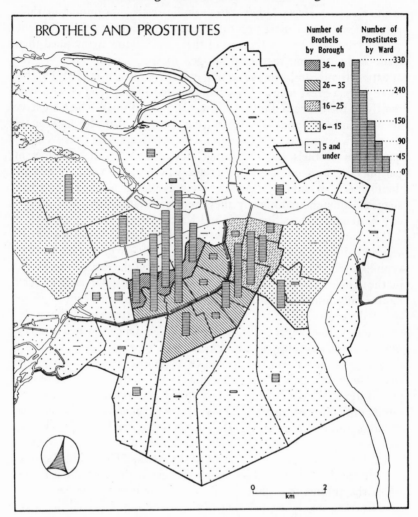

MAP 31. *Brothels and prostitutes, 1869*

were diagnosed as being afflicted; barely thirty of the 187 children involved saw the year out.[89]

In many ways what was happening at the Foundling Home reflected life at the bottom of the social order. The reality of day-to-day existence

[89] Yu. Gyubner, *O Sanitarnom Sostoyanii S. Peterburgskoy Gubernii po Svedeniyam Zemskikh Vrachey* (1876), pp. 93–4.

204

for many people—single women, married women living apart from their husbands, and couples—meant the birth of a child was an additional burden which they were either unable or unwilling to shoulder. It was noted earlier that by no means all the foundlings were the progeny of urban dwellers, but at the same time there is no reason to think that St Petersburg itself was not the major source. And, again, the high ratio of foundlings to births speaks poignantly of the quality of life in the city. The Home was busy from 1851 to 1870 and from figure 9 some-

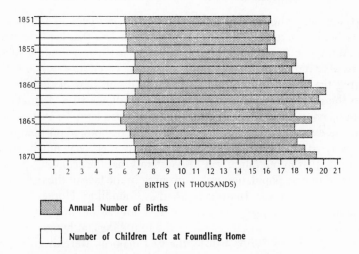

FIG. 9. *Annual number of births and number of children left at the St Petersburg Foundling Home, 1851–70*

thing of the relationship between the numbers of foundlings and births may be seen. Following the Emancipation, the numbers of births and foundlings declined; this was consonant, it might be argued, with the partial drying up of the migration of peasants to the city. As the peasant influx quickened toward the end of the 1860s, births and foundlings increased accordingly. Coping with what was now an average of twenty new infants a day strained the staff and facilities at the Home, to say nothing of the wet-nurses. As improving standards of hygiene brought about a reduction in the death-rate of infants in the Home, from around 20 per cent at the beginning of the period to a mere 15 per cent by the end of the sixties, the customary turnover was correspondingly reduced.[90] Dead as well as living infants apparently posed problems, at least according to one grisly anecdote:

> Monsieur was one day rambling over the former establishment [the Foundling Home], when, by mistake (or curiosity), he entered a room which presented a strange sight. At the end was a stack, composed of the naked bodies of a couple of hundred babies, packed like sardines, biding their time for internment in Spring, it being difficult and expensive to break the ground in Winter, at which season the mortality amongst infants is greatest.[91]

It was only the horrific losses of over 80 per cent in the peasant households where foundling babies were soon sent that kept the whole operation within reasonable limits.[92] Even so, in the surrounding villages there were more than 16,000 foundlings being cared for at any one time during the period in question. If we extend our view of the situation into the early seventies, the number of foundlings rises dramatically, from 6,800 in 1870 to nearly 7,600 just two years later.[93] At the risk of drawing oversimplified correlations, it might be pointed out that it was precisely at this time that industrialization was very much on the upswing, that immigration was heaviest and that the economic position of the labouring population was worsening in the face of the rising costs of basic necessities. Inasmuch as the Foundling Home provided anonymity for the parent or parents, it is impossible to do more than speculate about the social origins of the foundlings, although even that may not be necessary. As before, the vast majority were illegitimate.[94]

So far as could be determined the problems of drunkenness and disorder before mid-century were not cause for alarm. The situation during the 1860s was different. Again, Dostoevsky sets the tone:

---

[90] F. A. Tarapygin, *Materialy Dlya Istorii Imperatorskago S. Peterburgskago Vospitatel'-nago Doma* (1878), pp. 88–9.

[91] Guthrie, *Through Russia*, p. 57.

[92] The results of one commission reporting in 1863 revealed that the overall death-rate for babies less than one year was 75 per cent, but in the home itself the attrition was much lower, a fact which we have already mentioned. In the villages, therefore, the death-rate must have been well over the 75 per cent figure. This was in line with the situation at the Moscow Foundling Home. See *Entsiklopedicheskiy Slovar'* (1892), vol. XIII, p. 277. Mikhnevich gives a figure of 60 per cent but does not clarify which facet of the operation it pertains to. Mikhnevich, *Peterburg Ves' na Ladoni*, p. 283.

[93] Tapapygin, *Materialy*, p. 89.

[94] The total number of illegitimate births in the city was 4,916 in 1870, but this figure does not include the suburbs from which the Foundling Home doubtless drew some considerable business. While we do not have precise figures the number of illegitimate foundlings in 1870 was probably over 90 per cent of the 6,800. Mikhnevich, *Peterburg Ves' na Ladoni*, p. 280.

The heat in the street was terrible: and the airlessness, the bustle and the plaster, scaffolding, bricks, and dust all about him, and that special Petersburg stench, so familiar to all who are unable to get out of town in summer. . . . The insufferable stench from the pot-houses, which are particularly numerous in that part of town [Spasskaya borough], and the drunken men whom he met continually, although it was a working day, completed the revolting misery of the picture.[95]

After resuming residence in St Petersburg following a summer's absence abroad, one Englishman could make the following observation: 'And now that we have returned does anything strike us worthy of comment? Why yes: to begin with we find intoxication sadly on the increase.'[96] Throughout the decade drunkenness, crime and arrests increased rather more quickly than the population. The government responded to the rise in drunkenness by preaching temperance. The sanitary doctors responded by analysing the reasons for the problem and detailing its dimensions. But neither of them increased public awareness of the root causes nor did the periodic clamp-down on the sale of spirits in any way change the trend. By the end of the sixties there were more liquor shops rather than fewer.[97] The figures indicate that between 1869 and 1872 the number of drinking establishments rose from over 2,400 to 2,700. In 1869 more than 34,600 drunks were arrested.[98] Each summer a new peak was reached in the level of drunkenness, a phenomenon which was usually attributed to the influx of intemperate peasants from surrounding villages. The city was now acknowledged to be among the leaders in the ratio of alcoholics to total population—one for every 260 persons. In short, for St Petersburg the decade was ending on a note of insobriety as well as insalubrity.

What was to be done? During the sixties, very little. As the government derived a large income from the sale of liquor, an obvious conflict of interests existed. It was not resolved by instructing the police to be more vigorous in surveillence—though, to be fair, some efforts were made both to restrict drinking on public holidays and on Sundays when workers customarily drank too much and also to provide instead

---

[95] Dostoevsky, *Crime and Punishment*, p. 2.
[96] 'Jottings by the Way', *Nevskiy Magazine*, II, no. 1 (1863), p. 531.
[97] By 1869 there were 459 liquor shops, 104 of which were in Spasskaya borough—the scene of much of the goings-on in Dostoevsky's *Crime and Punishment*. This was an increase of roughly sixty shops in four years. *Sanktpeterburg po Perepisi 10 Dekabrya 1869*, part 2, section 2, p. 118; Zelnik, *Labor and Society*, p. 247.
[98] Mikhnevich, *Peterburg Ves' na Ladoni*, pp. 291-3.

other forms of entertainment. None the less, the squalid existence of such a large segment of the populace ensured that each year more of them would escape, if only momentarily, through drink and debauchery. The drunk, Marmeladov, in Dostoevsky's *Crime and Punishment* was doubtless a realistic portraiture of many lives, though Marmeladov lived with his family whereas thousands of the city's poor did not. From the description of their plight it was perhaps just as well:

> A grimy little door at the very top of the stairs stood ajar. A very poor-looking room about ten paces long was lighted up by a candle-end; the whole of it was visible from the entrance. It was all in disorder, littered up with rags of all sorts, especially children's garments. Across the farthest corner was stretched a ragged sheet. Behind it probably was the bed. There was nothing in the room except two chairs and a sofa covered with American leather, full of holes, before which stood an old deal kitchen-table, unpainted and uncovered. At the edge of the table stood a smouldering tallow-candle in an iron candlestick. It appeared that the family had a room to themselves, not part of a room, but their room was practically a passage.[99]

In the novel, Marmeladov dies tragically and, some suspect, by his own hand; but it is made clear that the conditions leading up to his death were scarcely unique. Outside the world of fiction things had not yet deteriorated to the point where suicide was an unremarkable everyday occurrence yet there was plainly a significant increase. During the years from 1858 to 1869 there were, on average, sixty-one suicides each year. A year later 145 were reported and by 1872 the number had risen to 167.[100]

Arrests by the police were also a symptom of the deteriorating circumstances of city life. Between 1861 and 1869 the total rose from 69,000 to over 190,000, in excess of 500 each day during the latter year. Another symptom was the growing number of beggars, not passportless peasants drawn to the city in the hope of getting a few kopeks, but legal residents and dependants. Family members of workers and the garrison forces in particular were driven on to the streets in order to survive. And throughout the decade the number of beggars detained by the police grew year by year.[101] Drunkenness, debauchery, crime and

[99] Dostoevsky, *Crime and Punishment*, p. 21.
[100] Mikhnevich, *Peterburg Ves' na Ladoni*, pp. 287–8.
[101] Mikhnevich, *Peterburg Ves' na Ladoni*, pp. 294–9; Zelnik, *Labor and Society*, p. 250.

violence were demanding a tighter rein. The reorganization and bolstering of the police late in the decade was one response; the restructuring of municipal government in 1870, giving cities greater autonomy in managing their affairs, was another. Whether the basic reasons for the obvious ills of society would be recognized and acted upon was very much a moot point at the close of the decade.

Personal wealth or credit guaranteed only minimal contact with the rude subsistence of the majority. The genteel social scene continued to revolve with the seasons as apartments and palaces were forsaken for *dachi* and country-estates during the summer. Those obliged to remain survived as best they could. Evening excursions to the 'islands', boat trips or day-long forays to the elegant environments of places like Pavlovsk, Tsarskoye Selo, Oraniyenbaum, Peterhof, Krasnoye Selo and Gatchina were popular. The author of *The Englishwoman in Russia*, a travel-book of the day, describes the available diversions:

> A little pleasure-trip in these small boats to some of the numerous islands in the vicinity of St Petersburg is extremely agreeable on a summer's evening. Although everything about them is purely artificial, Nature having done little enough to embellish them, yet the effect produced is very delightful. Pretty little country houses, or fancy isbas built of wood and fantastically decorated, show themselves here and there among the foliage of a forest of trees and shrubs; a Chinese temple or Turkish kiosk placed on some little promontory arrests our attention; a Greek statue or Corinthian column ornamenting some sequestered spot, and half buried in the creeping plants that twine around it . . . Bands of musicians play in various spots on certain days . . . and crowds of ladies in beautiful dresses, and gentlemen in country costumes, repair in the evening to attend them. . . . As the entertainment takes place in the open air, even the humblest classes can enjoy it, and numerous groups of the people may be seen standing at a respectful distance among the trees, for they are very fond of music.[102]

For the 'humble' folk to get to the outlying towns by train would take at least a day's wages and, once there, they would find many of the parks and palaces frequented by the upper classes closed to them.[103] The nearest town was Tsarskoye Selo, the Hampton Court of St

---

[102] *The Englishwoman in Russia*, pp. 228–9.
[103] Some years later the fare was one rouble, an amount more likely to have decreased rather increased over time. T. Michell, *Handbook for Travellers in Russia, Poland, and Finland* (London, 1893), p. 85.

Petersburg, and it was a common destination for a day's outing. To the west was Krasnoye Selo, popular in large part because it was here that the Imperial Guard was quartered during the summer, at the end of which they traditionally enacted a mock battle. On the whole, there were few social events in the city during the summer, but when necessary there were still many on hand who could rise to the occasion with customary indulgence. The visit of the American Assistant Secretary of the Navy, the Honourable G. V. Fox, in 1866 was one such occasion. He had been instructed by the Congress to bear in person a congratulatory resolution to Alexander II for having escaped assassination earlier that year.

> At nine o'clock all attended a fete given in honor of the mission, by Mr Gromoff, one of Russia's wealthiest merchants, at his country residence at the islands, in the suburbs of St Petersburg. This entertainment, which cost more than forty thousand rubles, was equal to any which the Americans attended. Mr Gromoff's spacious and beautiful villa is noted for the elegance of its surroundings. Its hot-houses have a well-deserved celebrity in St Petersburg. But the principal charm of this place is its magnificent park, whose extent, natural beauty, and artistic development, render it a most agreeable and attractive summer resort. . . .
> Dancing began immediately after the arrival of the Americans, and was continued until midnight, when the guests were invited upstairs to supper.[104]

It was during the winter that the capital really came alive with a whirl of social activities and it was not necessary to look very far for ostentation and wealth. Through the eyes of Théophile Gautier the Nevskiy Prospect provided ample evidence:

> From one o'clock till three, the crowd is greatest; beside those who walk rapidly along, going about their affairs, there are many whose sole object is to see, to be seen, and to take a little exercise; their coupés or droschkys await them at a designated spot, or follow them along, in case a sudden fancy should take them to return to the carriage.
> You distinguish first the officers of the Guard, in gray capote, a strap on the shoulder indicating the rank; they are almost all

---

[104] J. F. Loubat, *Narrative of the Mission to Russia in 1866 of the Hon. Gustavus Vasa Fox, Assistant Secretary of the Navy* (New York, 1873), pp. 197–8.

decorated with stars and crosses, and they wear the helmet or the military undress cap; then you observe the tchinovniks, or officials, in long redingotes plaited at the back, and gathered in by the belt; they wear, for a hat, a dark-colored cap with cockade; young men in general, who are neither in the army nor in the civil service, have paletots trimmed with a fur whose price astonishes strangers and would alarm our men of fashion. These overcoats, of the finest cloth, are lined with marten or muskrat, and have collars of beaver costing from one to three hundred rubles, the price varying in proportion to the fineness of the fur, its depth of color, and the long white hairs that it has retained. A paletot worth a thousand rubles is not unusual; some even cost more than this. . . .[105]

But not everyone of wealth participated, for as we have noted many doors remained closed to the moneyed merchants and industrialists. Even travellers of some considerable position at home had difficulty breaking into the tight cliques where money was taken for granted in the pursuit of pleasure. But the proper letters of introduction ensured that the winter would be spent sumptuously. Two young travellers from the United States encountered few difficulties:

We have a good many occasions of airing our French in the *beau monde* of Russia, and I find that there is no trouble with it; the only thing to do being to go right along regardless of errors, for I see that although I do not speak very well, there are plenty who speak quite as bad and worse, and this being a neutral ground of course one is bolder. However, a great many of the well educated speak English admirably.

All this goes to show that we are in for society now, and have to await quietly a round of balls, operas, and dinners, and return our calls most punctiliously, a form of etiquette about which the Russians are very exacting.

We went to a jolly young count's (Koucheleff Besborodko) the other day, who immediately made us at home with a delicious cigar. His house, take it all in all, was about as lovely as any I have ever seen, with an Oriental smoking room, a Pompadour boudoir, a Chinese room, a long gallery of paintings, an immense dancing hall, and a conservatory arranged with grottoes and cascades, a

---

[105] Théophile Gautier, *A Winter in Russia* (New York, 1874), translated by M. M. Ripley, p. 77.

rustic bridge, and an original old statue of a satyr, picked up in Rome. The Count is a great connoisseur of art, and his collection in all its branches is magnificent, with souvenirs of every city of Europe, and all the ages of the world, enough to drive to despair any such little dabblers as myself.[106]

The growing signs of discontent among the populace at large hardly disturbed the genteel side of St Petersburg life—many were simply too well ensconced to feel the first tremors of the effects of industrialization. However, some eyes were opened by the attempt on the life of Alexander II and a few even before that:

M. P——ski, a gentleman of education, assured me, only the morning I left St Petersburg, that they were in much more danger from the pillage of the lower classes than from any exterior enemy, and he expressed the greatest fears for the consequences of bringing so many thousands of wild savages of soldiers into the town, for, if they rose, it would be *en masse*, and . . . it would sweep the upper classes away like a torrent.[107]

This was no idle prophecy.

[106] N. Appleton, *Russian Life and Society as seen in 1866–67 by Appleton and Longfellow, Two Young Travellers from the United States of America* . . . (Boston, 1904), pp. 92–3.
[107] *The Englishwoman in Russia*, p. 87.

5
The Culmination of Capitalism

Industrial life probably means progress in Russia, but at present it is a very rough-and-tumble and creaking kind.

Harold W. Williams, 1915[1]

The seventies brought St Petersburg to an entirely new pitch of urban and industrial growth—migration, production and profits, all were running at unprecedented levels. The first part of the 1880s was also unparalleled but for a different reason—the degree of industrial stagnation and general economic depression. By the end of the decade the cyclical variation in economic activity had once again come full circle and in the early nineties urban industrialization was on the upswing. Yet in comparison with the next two decades, which included another serious depression, developments up to then were of minor proportion and gave little more than a hint of what was to come. The tempo of economic growth before and after 1890 may be illustrated by a few statistics on population and on the numbers employed in industry. Out of just short of three quarters of a million inhabitants in the late sixties, 35,000 were occupied in industry. In 1890 the number of people living in the city had swollen to over one million, and the total of industrial jobs had doubled. However, in 1914 nearly one tenth of the 2·2 million population was engaged in industry. In other words, industrial employment had nearly tripled and total population had doubled since 1890. In most sectors of the urban economy, similar rates of growth were registered. Half a century of rapid expansion had wrought substantial changes. Clearly, the transition from a court-administrative centre into an industrial-commercial complex, of no mean proportion by international, not just national, standards, implies

[1] Harold W. Williams, *Russia of the Russians* (New York, 1915), p. 388.

213

much more than a change in the economic base; it suggests a transformation of the very fabric of the city itself.

In this chapter we will examine the major developments in industry, commerce and transport during five decades of rapid industrialization. With an overview of these developments in hand, we will then determine what they meant in terms of the distribution of manufacturing industry and commerce, and the movement of people and products within the city. Spatial relationships did have a bearing on the city's success or failure as an economic centre, and affected to some degree its social and political stability. However, the ultimate implications of these spatial elements go beyond the scope of this book; in some respects the manifold explanations of them, rooted as they were in individual decisions that, for all we know, were as often whimsical as they were calculating, are of too detailed a nature to be considered here. What we are again obliged to do is to pose a series of hypotheses about the net results of these decisions, and to test them. As before, an examination of the city's external relations will conclude our discussion of the economic life of the city.

I INDUSTRIALIZATION

In 1868, following the last in a series of major tariff liberalization moves, government actions in the industrial sphere became more overt. This was particularly evident in railway construction and throughout the seventies government policies very much assisted domestic construction of rails and rolling stock.[2] Overall economic growth, however, was uneven. The financial crisis of 1873–5 acted as a damper because access to foreign exchange was affected; this was important since foreign money was paying for much of Russia's industrial growth. Further selective boosts to the economy were provided by the demands of the Russo-Turkish War (1877–8), although it was during the two years immediately after the end of hostilities that a boom was most in evidence. Joint-stock company profits, high in any event by European standards, became enormous, and expansion in many sectors of the industrial structure took place almost over night.[3] Of course, not all

[2] For example, such Russian factories as were technically capable of manufacturing steam engines were presented with government contracts which, in addition to the customary high rate of profit, entitled the firms concerned to a premium of 3,000 roubles per machine. There were probably no more than half a dozen private firms in Russia so equipped and three were in St Petersburg. 'Polozheniye Parovozostroyeniya v Rossii', *Vestnik Finansov, Promyshlennosti i Torgovli*, no. 7 (1884), p. 262.

[3] In the cotton textile industry the total number of spindles rose from 3·5 to 4·5 million in 1879 alone. James Mavor, *An Economic History of Russia* (London, 1914), vol. II, p. 372.

industries fared equally well under the liberal tariff of the seventies. The minimal import duty on machinery virtually assured continued dependence on foreign products.[4] And the fact that iron imports, which had been running at a yearly average of 3,000 tons in 1851-6, had soared to 480,000 tons by 1877-81, effectively removed a sizable stimulus from domestic production.[5] Yet much of St Petersburg's industry stood to benefit from the prevailing spirit of government policy toward tariffs. In the event, the years down to 1879 witnessed an increase of more than 80 per cent in the city's factory employment, which by then stood at more than 65,000 workers.[6]

A contraction of world trade in the late seventies was the prelude to a long period of depression. Since Russia was inextricably caught up in international trade and commerce it was only a matter of time before she, too, was in the throes of economic disruption. The end, like the beginning, was delayed as compared with events in Europe because economic expansion did not resume until 1887.[7] This experience triggered a reaction to the liberal tariff policies of the preceding decades and the position of the government gradually reversed, a development which had serious implications for the capital's industrial economy. The move toward protectionism, which began in 1877 with the 'gold tariff' measure, was primarily a response to financial considerations for, by encouraging domestic production, it was hoped that the voluminous outflow of money would be stemmed. In 1884, 1886 and 1887 duties were raised substantially on imported iron, pig iron and steel. This very greatly assisted mining in the Urals and bolstered the nascent iron and steel industry of the south Ukraine. Rising tariffs were not restricted to iron and steel products, but covered a progressively wider range of raw materials, including cotton in 1887, coal in 1884, 1886, and 1887, and machinery of all types in 1880, 1887, and 1890. The building up of the tariff wall culminated in the near prohibitive general tariff of 1891. Out of deference to St Petersburg industrialists some concessions were made in levying tariffs on raw materials imported through the capital, but industry was clearly in a less tenable position

[4] The manufacture of typographical equipment, for instance, occurred in only two plants in the whole Empire. W. I. Timiryazev, *Istoriko-Statisticheskiy Obzor Promyshlennosti Rossii* (1882), pp. 78–80.

[5] R. Portal, 'The Industrialization of Russia', in H. J. Habakkuk, M. M. Postan (eds), *Cambridge Economic History of Europe* (London, 1965), vol. VI, part 2, p. 814.

[6] P. N. Stolpyanskiy, *Zhizn' i Byt Peterburgskoy Fabriki za 1704-1914 gg.* (1925), pp. 114–15.

[7] M. Tugan-Baranovskiy, *Russkaya Fabrika v Proshlom i Nastoyashchem, Istoriko-Ekonomicheskoye Izsledovaniye* (1898), vol. I, p. 325; S. G. Strumilin, *Ocherki Ekonomicheskoy Istorii Rossii i SSSR* (Moscow, 1966), pp. 441–2.

as a result of these revisions.[8] Indeed, the combination of restrictive tariffs and economic depression weeded out a great number of marginally profitable firms which had been established during the heyday of economic growth in the late seventies.[9]

After a somewhat unsteady beginning, the industrial boom of the 1890s was in full swing by 1895, and continued so until the onset of depression in 1899–1900. During these years industrial production in Russia rose by nearly 60 per cent, led in large measure by the expansion in railway construction.[10] The railway was reaching to the Pacific and the network in European Russia was becoming more articulated and this development, in conjunction with the general expansion in all sectors of the industrial economy, enormously augmented iron and steel requirements.[11] The demand made upon the productive capacity of metal-processing factories was such that the plants in St Petersburg, far removed from domestic sources of raw materials and only little aided by preferential tariff rates on some raw materials imported via the Baltic, not only continued in operation, but expanded at a rate that assured the capital a high place on the list of metal-manufacturing centres. Indeed, from 1900 to 1913, the capital's relative share of the country's metal-working industry slipped only marginally in terms of labour force, and the value of production actually increased. Overall, from the nineties until the eve of the Great War, St Petersburg slightly increased its share of the country's total industrial labour force.[12] In view of the quite phenomenal industrial growth in many other regions of Russia, the maintenance of this relative position was very significant.

During the nineties, a number of things happened which caused an ever greater volume of foreign money, particularly French and Belgian, to flow into Russia. The main factors at work were the wide range of investment possibilities, the potential for the realization of high returns, the depression in America in 1893 (as elsewhere), and the government's

[8] For further details, see W. I. Timiriazev, 'Review of the Russian Customs Tariff System', *The Industries of Russia, Manufactures and Trade* (1893), vol. II, pp. 418–24; *Materialy ob Ekonomicheskom Polozhenii i Professional'noy Organizatsii, Peterburgskikh Rabochikh po Metallu* (1909), pp. 14–16; Portal, 'The Industrialization of Russia', pp. 834–6.

[9] The effect on individual factory employments may be assessed through a comparison of factory statistics for 1879 and 1885. See P. A. Orlov, *Ukazatel' Fabrik i Zavodov Yevropeyskoy Rossii s Tsarstvom Pol'skim i Vel. Kn. Finlyandskim* (1881) and K. V. Davydov, *S. Peterburgskiy Fabrichnyy Okrug. Otchet za 1885 g.* (1886).

[10] Strumilin, *Ocherki Ekonomicheskoy Istorii Rossii*, pp. 443–6.

[11] From 1890 to 1914 Russian pig iron production rose from 0·89 to 4·3 million tons. P. A. Khromov, *Ekonomicheskoye Razvitiye Rossii v XIX-XX Vekakh, 1800–1917* (Moscow, 1950), table V, p. 456.

[12] E. E. Kruze, 'Promyshlennoye Razvitiye Peterburga v 1890kh-1914gg', *Och.IL* (1956), vol. III, p. 15.

fiscal policies. The Russian Finance Minister, Sergei Witte, in following the policies laid down by his predecessor I. A. Vyshnegradsky, was largely responsible for building up gold reserves to a point where, in 1897, the country could go on to the gold standard. This reinforced the confidence of foreign investors and from 1893 to 1898 their investments in the country grew from 2·5 million to 130 million roubles, with total investment from all sources reaching a peak in 1899.[13] Herbert Pierce, the American Chargé d'Affaires in St Petersburg, described the prevailing economic climate thus: 'I may here remark that I have received the best assurances that Americans coming to Russia to erect factories, or to engage with capital and improved appliances in industrial enterprises, will receive the fullest government support. This may be taken to include protection in the way of tariff.'[14]

The poor harvests of 1898 and 1899 intensified the progressive withering away of purchasing power and the decline of trade in the rural areas. These developments signalled the start of a general contraction of business activity not confined to Russia. Beginning with light industry, virtually every sector of the country's industrial economy had been adversely affected by 1902. Preparations for, and the waging of, the Russo-Japanese War of 1904–5 provided something of a respite from the depressed conditions, but for many industries this stimulant was comparatively short-lived. With Russia's ignominious peace settlement as a catalyst, the country was almost immediately plunged into a social and political upheaval of which the 1905 revolution was a manifestation. The American Ambassador, Robert McCormick, was quick to point out one of the reasons for discontent: 'There can be no doubt that for some time a socialist group has been at work among the operatives in St Petersburg. . . . The war and its accompanying conditions have been such as to bring this propaganda to its full fruition.'[15] Perhaps we should not make too much of this event as far as the Russian economy is concerned. Business was suffering from a depression, but as British Consul Wardrop reported in 1906:

> The year 1905 has been described in the Russian press as 'ruinous';
> there have been naval and military disasters, political disorders,
> strikes, great destruction of property and a failure of the harvest

[13] D. Shimkin, 'The Entrepreneur in Tsarist and Soviet Russia', *Explorations in Entrepreneurial History*, I (1950), p. 28.
[14] Herbert Pierce, 'Letter', *Papers Relating to the Foreign Relations of the US*, 1899, no. 120, p. 598.
[15] Robert McCormick, 'Letter', *Papers Relating to the Foreign Relations of the US*, 1905, no. 229, p. 763.

in a large part of the Empire. . . . It must not, however, be supposed that anything like a commercial and industrial crisis has been reached; up to the time of writing, the middle of March, 1906, the number of failures reported has been comparatively small, and though there is much anxiety about the immediate future there has not been hitherto any panic.[16]

A year later Wardrop's counterpart, Consul Thesiger noted:

In spite of the continuation of political unrest the trade of Russia in general does not appear from the statistics to have suffered from the prevailing uncertainty as to the trend of events. The business done by the various mills and factories of the St Petersburg district has been exceptionally good; only the metallurgical works have suffered from a shortage of orders.[17]

Although total industrial production grew steadily during the early 1900s, the years of disrupted or depressed economic activity took their toll. The trend toward mergers and amalgamations of firms was accentuated, other companies had to bear lengthy periods of operating below capacity and, on occasion, bankruptcy was the only option for beleaguered businesses.[18]

With the return of prosperity, employment and output soared. In the short space of six years between 1908 and 1913, the value of production from St Petersburg's factories increased by nearly 250 million roubles, a 60 per cent gain.[19] It was during this time especially that several new branches of production (notably in the metal-working sector) were added to the industrial structure and the trend toward larger-scale production strengthened. Just under a fifth of total foreign investment in Russia was in the city's industrial structure and more often than not was represented in the larger factories. Annual rates of growth in many sectors were unparalleled. In the metal industries, for example, expansion frequently had been of the order of 20 per cent. In 1913 it topped 23 per cent, by which date the metal-working group was already well established as the largest employer. Employment was not necessarily the best barometer of overall industrial growth, but no other evidence

[16] Consul Wardrop, 'Report', *BPP; Diplomatic and Consular Reports*, 1906, CXXVIII. 211.
[17] Consul Thesiger, 'Report', *BPP; Diplomatic and Consular Reports*, 1907, XCII. 267.
[18] Strumilin, *Ocherki Ekonomicheskoy Istorii Rossii*, p. 451. Comparing 1901 and 1911 the number of factory workers was down by 6·9 per cent for the *guberniya*. Recovery was rapid especially after 1910. K. Komarovskiy, 'Fabrichnaya Promyshlennost' Rossii v 1910 Godu', *Promyshlennost' i Torgovlya*, no. 17 (1911), pp. 167–8.
[19] Kruze, 'Promyshlennoye Razvitiye Peterburga', p. 12.

contradicts the picture that it provides of industrialization since mid century. Factory employment had multiplied fourfold by 1890. But in the short space of the ensuing twenty-odd years during which depression occurred, the industrial labour force grew almost threefold. Nearly half of these 125,000 additional workers was engaged after 1908. The pace of industrialization was tumultuous.

Before examining the underlying industrial structure itself more closely, we should take stock of the structural transitions and scale shifts produced by this era of rapid industrialization. The data portrayed in figure 10 summarize these changes. As the metal-working group had assumed pride of place the earlier trend toward manufacture of producers' rather than consumers' goods had been sustained. This in some degree reflects government policies over tariffs, direct subsidies and state orders. While the move toward increased utilization of domestic raw materials benefited Russian producers, for some processing industries in St Petersburg, as elsewhere, the shift resulted in higher costs and caused some factories to close, especially the smaller ones. As figure 11 indicates, the years following 1890 saw a big rise in the scale of factory operations. In the textile and metal-working sectors the mean factory employment figures in 1913 were 510 and 274 workers respectively. Even in the paper and printing category where available data indicate a slight reduction in mean employment, the 1913 statistic was still in excess of fifty employees. This was the only instance of a reduction. All other groups had mean factory employments of 100 or more. By any standard of measurement, these factories were operating on an unusually large scale. There were many reasons for this but among the most important were the concentration of financial control into fewer hands, the failure to abandon labour-intensive practices (even in conjunction with the latest production technology), and an attempt to compensate for a general paucity of managerial and entrepreneurial talent by concentrating production in fewer factories. In this regard, A. Gerschenkron has argued that in Russia 'bigness of plant and enterprise . . . must be viewed as a specific substitution process. The lack of managerial and entrepreneurial personnel was compensated for by a scale of plants which made it possible to spread the thin layer of available talent over a large part of the industrial economy.'[20] The widespread use of foreign technical personnel in St Petersburg factories, both foreign and Russian owned, bears this out.

[20] A. Gerschenkron, 'Problems and Patterns of Russian Economic Development', in C. E. Black (ed.), *The Transformation of Russian Society* (Cambridge, Mass., 1960), p. 50.

GROWTH OF FACTORY EMPLOYMENT

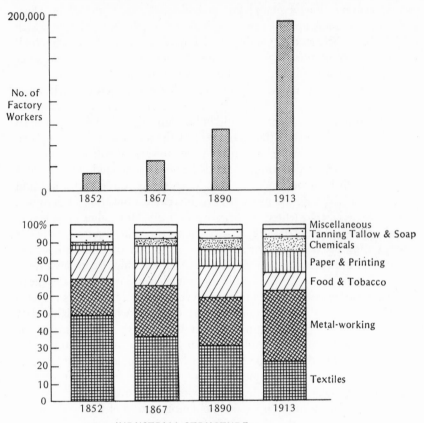

FIG. 10. *Changing industrial structure, 1852–1913*

(a) *The industrial structure in 1913*

The industrial expansion which occurred after 1908 served to bring an ever larger number of migrants to the capital and its environs. In 1913 at the peak of industrial growth, close to 30,000 industrial jobs were added to the total for the *guberniya*, which brought industrial employment up to 218,000.[21] With expansion in factory jobs running

[21] 'Polozheniye Promyshlennosti Petrogradskoy Gubernii 1913g.', *Vestnik Finansov, Promyshlennosti i Torgovli*, no. 38 (1914), p. 381.

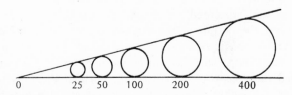

Miscellaneous

Textiles

Paper and
Printing

Tanning
Tallow & Soap

Food and
Tobacco

Chemicals

Metal-working

| 1852 | 1867 | 1890 | 1913 |

0   25 50 100   200   400

FIG. 11. *Mean factory employment, 1852–1913*

at levels of between 10 and 16 per cent since the beginning of the
surge in economic growth in 1909–10, it is little wonder that, of the
1·1 million net increase in population after 1890, nearly 350,000 had
arrived in St Petersburg since 1908. Within the *guberniya* the capital
remained the primary destination, for the initial advantages of location
within or near the city had altered little since the sixties. Only forty-
eight factories were situated outside what we have designated the urban

area. As in 1867, the greatest number were comparatively small-scale concerns turning out building materials, such as brick and glass, but located further afield as the more accessible resources were exhausted. Among the largest enterprises were eight state owned munitions or other military manufactures, which, like the Okhtenskiy gunpowder works and the armaments and shipbuilding complexes in Kolpino and Kronshtadt, had their origins in the early nineteenth or even eighteenth centuries. The one major privately owned enterprise was the Aivaz machine construction factory. Established on the Vyborgskoye Highway (north of the city) near Del'naya in 1898 it employed 2,000 persons.[22] The complete dominance of the capital is placed in perspective when it is realized that while there were forty-eight outlying factories in 1913, there were 956 within the urban area and these accounted for nearly 90 per cent of the factory employment in the *guberniya*. The spread effects of half a century of rapid industrialization had been negligible. Within Russia, the city's share of industrial output by value was the same as in 1867, nearly one tenth, and it also had a roughly similar share of total employment, 7 per cent as compared with 9 per cent.[23] From a production valued at approximately fifty million roubles in 1867, the city invested itself by 1913 with an industrial structure capable of generating just over 600 million roubles worth of manufactured goods. The basic components of this industrial structure are outlined in table 19 and it is to a brief examination of these data that we now proceed.

The metal-working sector accounted for 40 per cent of all factory workers and nearly 35 per cent of the value of production in the city in 1913, and was indisputedly its dominant industrial element. In half a dozen years the output of an increasingly diversified metal-working group had doubled, an increase greater than that for employment. Within the group, factories engaging more than 750 workers had expanded their share of employment from half the total in 1890 to two thirds.[24] Though 184 out of 284 plants engaged ninety or fewer workers—and were not demonstrably inefficient at that size—such firms were already being completely overshadowed for they accounted for scarcely 8 per cent of the total work-force. Joint-stock companies

[22] The eight large-scale state-owned factories along with the Aivaz concern accounted for the lion's share of the 24,000 factory jobs found outside the urban area as we have defined it. Unless otherwise cited these and all subsequent plant production data are from D. P. Kandaurov, *Fabrichno-Zavodskiye Predpriyatiya Rossiyskoy Imperii (Isklyuchaya Finlyandiyu)* (1914).
[23] Kruze, 'Promyshlennoye Razvitiye Peterburga', p. 12.
[24] All references to employment by categories of factory size are derived from data in appendix I, pp. 417, 419.

TABLE 19. *Industrial structure, 1913*

Industrial group	Employment	%	Number of establishments	Value of production (million roubles)	%
Metal-working	77,816	40·0	284	209	34·8
Chemical	16,446	8·5	89	114	19·0
Food and tobacco products	20,528	10·5	100	79	13·2
Tanning, tallow and soap	8,455	4·3	49	39	6·5
Paper and printing	23,230	11·9	312	40	6·6
Textile	43,931	22·6	86	109	18·1
Miscellaneous	4,178	2·2	36	11	1·8
Totals	194,584	100·0	956	601	100·0

Sources: D. P. Kandaurov, *Fabrichno-Zavodskiye Predpriyatiya Rossiyskoy Imperii (Isklyuchaya Finlyandiyu)* (1914), E. E. Kruze, ' Promyshlennoye Razvitiye Peterburga v 1890kh–1914gg', *Och.I.L.* (1956), vol. III, pp. 9–61.

were also tending to displace one-man firms and private companies and after 1900 boosted their share of production from 40 to 73 per cent.[25]

The role of the government in expanding production in the metal industries in general and in the shipbuilding and machine construction fields in particular was an important one. The Admiralty provided contracts for the construction of ships and their fitting out; the Army distributed contracts for the supply of armaments and other stores; the Ministry of Internal Communications ordered rails and rolling stock for the expansion of the rail network. The repercussions of state orders were manifold. The Putilov Company, in anticipation of yet further lucrative contracts, had added a new shipbuilding wharf of sufficient size to permit construction of the largest vessels afloat. Such investment was not stillborn. With over 13,000 employees the company had an established, but not exclusive position as recipient of naval contracts. The Nevskiy shipbuilding works had augmented its labour force by 2,500 since 1890 largely in consequence of securing state orders, and by 1913 had 3,500 workers. In 1912 the Russia-American Metal-working Company increased its labour force by 64 per cent and the St Petersburg metal-working plant by 32 per cent. So it went on in other firms, thus producing annual growth rates which hardly ever failed to exceed other groups by a wide margin.[26] Foreign capital was also a conspicuous element in the financing of joint-stock metal-working firms. In the newly established, electrical components industry, which operated on a large scale from the outset, German money was much in evidence; among the larger concerns were those of Siemens and Allgemeine Elektrizität Gesellschaft. The demand for electric motors, telegraph and telephone equipment, electric cable, and the like, was only just being awakened in Russia and the potential market and the profits to be earned from supplying it were both enormous. As in so many other industries, tariffs were used to foster domestic production.[27] Out of a production valued at fifty-six million roubles in all of Russia in 1913, roughly forty million came from the plants in the capital.[28]

Metal-working firms tended to specialize less than might have been expected, partly because demand was too mercurial to sustain the

[25] Kruze, 'Promyshlennoye Razvitiye Peterburga', p. 17.

[26] 'Promyshlennost' S. Peterburgskoy Gubernii v 1912g.', *Vestnik Finansov, Promyshlennosti i Torgovli*, no. 22 (1913), p. 438.

[27] From the turn of the century to 1912 the duty on imported cable, for instance, rose from three to seven roubles per *pud*. 'Elektricheskaya Energiya i Elektrotekhnicheskaya Promyshlennost' v Rossii', *Promyshlennost' i Torgovlya*, No. 2 (1913), pp. 64-5.

[28] 'Elektricheskaya Energiya', p. 65; Kruze, 'Promyshlennoye Razvitiye Peterburga', p. 32.

steady output which this required, and because the recurring depressions did nothing to encourage it. Even government contract work was inclined to foster production versatility, simply because demands varied according to prevailing priorities. The firms that could bid on the greatest variety of jobs had a better chance of maintaining lucrative contract work. Another reason for diversification in production was the rapidity with which a given technology changed. The Nobel plant is a good example of this. During the sixties and seventies the manufacture of armaments and related equipment, on government contracts, had dominated production. As the Nobel family's oilfields near Baku were developed during the ensuing decades, the construction of equipment for the industry, including oil cars for the railway and pipelines, was added to the plant's capabilities. By the late nineties it was evident that the production of electrical goods was potentially profitable. Accordingly, the manufacture of electric motors, cables and the like was included in the plant's already diversified output. Not all firms carried diversification to this extreme, but the general trend was common.[29]

Although St Petersburg did not draw the raw materials for the metalworking industries from the locality, local production of basic iron and steel was able to compete with the same products shipped from the Ukraine. For example, just after the turn of the century, pig iron could be produced in the city at a cost of between 0·68 and 0·91 roubles per *pud*. The delivered price of a *pud* from the mills of the southern Ukraine was around 0·97 roubles, 0·24 of which covered the cost of transport.[30] Among the plants which produced pig iron and steel, only the gigantic Putilov Company was vertically integrated to the extent that a part at least of its iron ore requirements was secured from its own mining operations in the Olonets *guberniya*.[31] On the whole, the growing demand for pig iron and steel ensured a heavy reliance on domestic production. Already, in 1892, a third of the 70,000 tons of pig iron consumed in the city that year was of domestic origin. The escalating demand of the following years pushed this relative share even higher, though never to the complete exclusion of the imported product which continued to flow into the city in substantial volume.[32] Coal, however,

[29] *Mekhanicheskiy Zavod Lyudvig Nobel' 1862–1912* (1912), pp. 58–62.

[30] The variation in the price of pig iron in St Petersburg was due to the varying quantities of scrap used. 'Doklad v O-ve Gornykh-Inzhenerov o Polozhenii Prokatnykh Zavodov v S Peterburge', *Torgovo-Promyshlennaya Gazeta*, no. 258 (1901), pp. 2–3.

[31] M. Mitel'man, B. Glebov, A. Ul'yanskiy, *Istoriya Putilovskogo Zavoda 1801–1917* (Moscow, 1961), p. 41.

[32] 'Doklad Komissii Peterburgskoy Dumy po Voprosu o Sooruzhenii Peterburgo-Ural'skoy i Peterburgo-Murmanskoy Zheleznykh Dorog v Svyazi s Vodnymi Putyami',

could still be delivered to the capital from Britain at a lower delivered cost than domestic output.[33]

Annual rates of growth in textiles were high, but not of the same order as in metal-working. In the latter part of the 1908–13 period, employment was increasing at the rate of 12 to 15 per cent each year. However, by 1913 the manufacture of textiles had slipped from just over one quarter of the value of production in 1894 to under one fifth ⟨*see* table 19⟩. Within the group, large-scale production units had virtually eliminated firms employing ninety or fewer workers; in 1890 under 13 per cent of textile workers were employed in firms of this size while in 1913 the share had dropped to 3 per cent. At the other extreme, firms employing more than 750 people accounted for nearly 84 per cent of the labour force, a relative change of thirty percentage points since 1890. With the single exception of the manufacture of silk wares, which engaged only 161 persons in three establishments or scarcely one tenth of the number at mid century, expansion occurred in all industries, though most notably in the cotton branch. The latter had over 24,000 of the nearly 44,000 total work-force.[34] Weaving had been developed vigorously since the nineties as a continuation of the trend away from a preoccupation with spinning but, by the turn of the century, St Petersburg mills still only worked about half the yarn spun locally.[35] The balance went to the mills in the interior. Textile mills of every description benefited from government contracts, though the frequency and value of them did not compare with those given to the metal-working industries.

The rise of the joint-stock company encouraged scale changes in a wide range of industries, and often at the expense of the smaller independent concerns. Nowhere was the impact on the food products and tobacco group more pronounced than in the processing of tobacco. Only eight plants were operating in 1913, six fewer than in 1890 and twenty-one less than in 1867. Of the surviving factories, several were part of larger corporate organizations. The smallest employed 300

ISPGD, no. 11 (1895), p. 47. The quantity of pig iron imported in 1913 had dropped to 20,000 tons, about half the figure for 1892. *Obzor Vneshney Torgovli Rossii po Yevropeyskoy i Aziatskoy Granitsam za 1913 God*. (1914) part 1, table VI and Prilozheniye III, table VI.

[33] There was even the occasional shipment from Pennsylvania, but to the relief of the British Consul this was not viewed as a real threat. See J. Michell, 'Report', *BPP*; *Diplomatic and Consular Reports*, 1902, CIX. 385.

[34] About 45,000 tons of raw cotton were imported in 1913, an increase of 20,000 tons over 1867. *Obzor Vneshney Torgovli Rossii*.

[35] V. K. Yatsunskiy, 'Rol' Peterburga v Promyshlennom Razvitii Dorevolyutsionnoy Rossii', *Voprosy Istorii*, no. 9 (1954), pp. 98–9.

persons, whereas two decades before half of the fourteen establishments were employing fewer still. By 1913 the small firm had gone to the wall. In its place were factories like that of the Laferm Company which employed 2,500 people and had an annual production valued at twelve million roubles, though often large employments belied the level of sophistication in production technology. For the food and tobacco group as a whole, the majority of workers were now engaged by factories employing over 750 people. A quarter of the hundred undertakings in this industry were joint-stock companies. On the eve of the Great War they made up three quarters of the total output in the group.[36]

The same general trends were apparent, albeit less pronounced, in the paper and printing, tanning, tallow and soap, and chemical groups. Generally speaking, the largest factories accounted for a larger share of total employment at the expense of plants engaging ninety or fewer workers. In the paper and printing group total employment had more than trebled since 1890 and now totalled 23,000 workers. While these industries were primarily the province of Russian enterprise, both technical and financial, expansion was only achieved on the basis of equipment imported from abroad. The manufacture of essential machinery in St Petersburg, as in the country at large, had already been lagging behind the burgeoning demand for several decades. Similarly, the demand for high-quality paper, including cigarette wrapping, had still to be met largely from foreign suppliers.[37] Of the 25,000 persons occupied in the chemical and tanning, tallow and soap groups, more than 11,000 were employed in a single joint-stock concern, the Russia-American Treugol'nik Rubber Company. The high rates of growth experienced over the preceding years owed a great deal to the expansion of this firm and, as the only one producing rubber goods in the city, it had a virtual monopoly position. In the tanning, tallow and soap group large-scale plants were steadily absorbing the available work-force and joint-stock companies had by 1913 come to control three quarters of total production, a situation which was in stark contrast to that of 1890. Within the miscellaneous category, only the manufacture of pianos and furniture gave signs of sustained growth.

Although there are no comprehensive statistics available, the use of motive power in factories was quite general in the early 1900s. Electric motors were of growing significance and were a particular boon to the

[36] Kruze, 'Promyshlennoye Razvitiye Peterburga', p. 44.
[37] 'Nemtsy o Russkoy Pisch. Promyshlennosti', *Pischebumazhnoye Delo*, no. 1 (1904), p. 47.

smaller operations. Diesel motors and steam engines were no longer exceptional in factories, though it should not be assumed that mechanical power was uniformly replacing human muscle. A very crude index of the shift toward inanimate energy sources is provided by a comparison of rates of coal consumption. From 1867 to 1890 consumption had more than doubled, reaching 960,000 tons; by 1913 this had nearly trebled to 2·5 million tons.[38] This volume was not consumed by steam engines alone, of course, but the pattern of domestic consumption was not changing at all dramatically and other industrial demands could account for no more than a fraction of this.

So far we have paid little attention to handicraft production. Unlike the 1869 census, that for 1910 does not provide data on the number of establishments and we are therefore left simply with that for male and female *odinochki*, or independent handicraft workers.[39] Even these statistics are not entirely satisfactory owing to the somewhat generalized categories of activity and a lack of clarity between retailing and manufacturing functions. However, on the basis of the available information a few comparisons are possible. The textile group in 1869 had approximately 2,600 handicraft establishments and led all other groups. In terms of the number of *odinochki*, the same was true in 1910. Females counted for 576 out of 639 in textiles, and almost 11,000 out of over 15,000 engaged in the manufacture of clothing and shoes.[40] In metal-working, there were just 869 handicraft workers. But these *odinochki* belonged to less than half the number of workshops, and numbered much less than the workshop employees enumerated over forty years before. It is clear from this that the rise of the factory system and the corresponding scale shifts had squeezed handicrafts a good deal, though without affecting small-scale factory operation very much. In the paper and printing group in 1869, there were 204 workshops; in 1910 there were fewer than 500 independent workers all told. Of the remaining production groups, the processing of animal fats and hides was alone in having substantial numbers of *odinochki*, 376 in all.

(b) *The location of industry*

By 1913 industrialization had left an indelible imprint on the face of the city. With close on 1,000 factories there were very few areas

---

[38] 'S. Peterburg Kak Potrebitel'nyy Rynok Topliva', *Torgovo-Promyshlennaya Gazeta*, no. 57 (1913), p. 2.
[39] *Petrograd po Perepisi 15 Dekabrya 1910 Goda* (1914), part 2, section 1, pp. 2–13.
[40] The inclusion of shoemakers somewhat distorts the comparison, but even so textiles far outstripped the remaining categories.

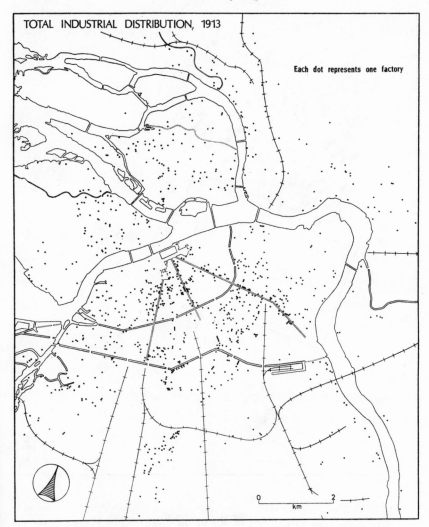

MAP 32. *Total industrial distribution, 1913*

without industrial activity of some kind. From map 32 it appears that industry spread everywhere, and this raises the question whether there was any discernible order to the pattern. Detailed maps of particular industries point out broad locational characteristics ⟨*see* maps 33, 34, 35 and 36⟩, but they do not help us very much in answering the question and, as before, we must rely on a combination of statistical

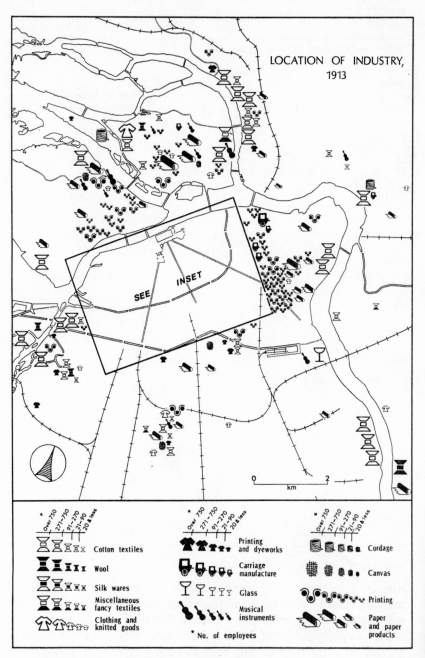

LOCATION OF INDUSTRY, 1913

SEE INSET

0   2
km

	Over 750	271–750	91–270	21–90	20 & less	
						Cotton textiles
						Wool
						Silk wares
						Miscellaneous fancy textiles
						Clothing and knitted goods

	Over 750	271–750	91–270	21–90	20 & less	
						Printing and dyeworks
						Carriage manufacture
						Glass
						Musical instruments

* No. of employees

	Over 750	271–750	91–270	21–90	20 & less	
						Cordage
						Canvas
						Printing
						Paper and paper products

MAP 33. *Location of industry, 1913–I*

230

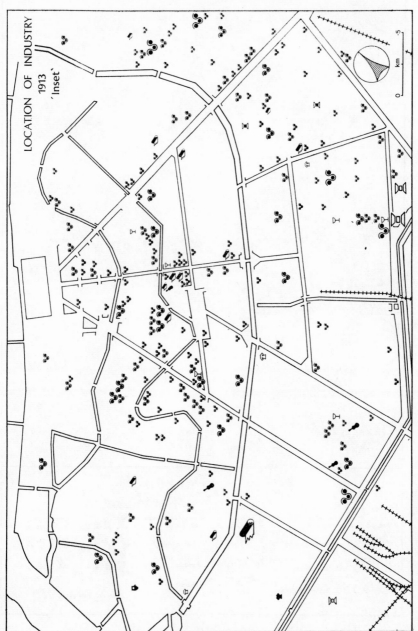

LOCATION OF INDUSTRY
1913
'Inset'

MAP 34· *Location of industry* (inset to map 33)

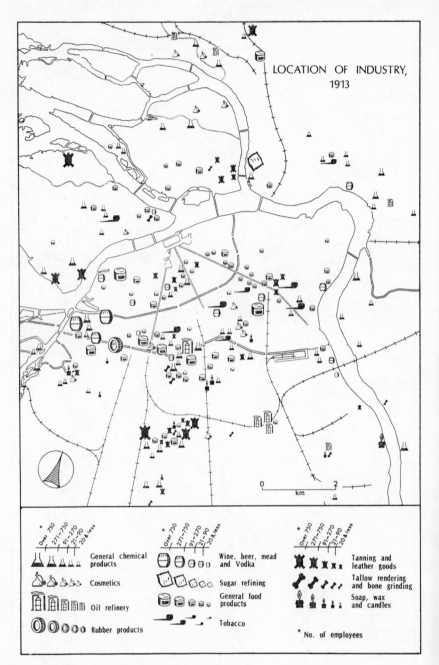

LOCATION OF INDUSTRY,
1913

MAP 35. *Location of industry, 1913–II*

232

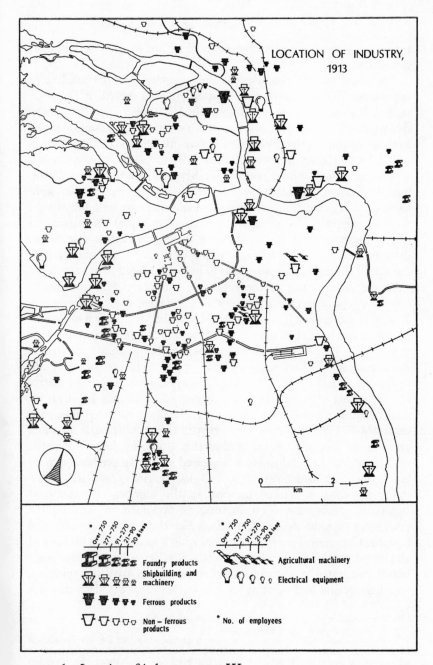

LOCATION OF INDUSTRY,
1913

Foundry products
Shipbuilding and machinery
Ferrous products
Non – ferrous products

Agricultural machinery
Electrical equipment

* No. of employees

Over 750 — 271–750 — 91–270 — 21–90 — 20 & less

* No. of employees

MAP 36. *Location of industry, 1913–III*

233

analyses and contemporary comments if we are to come to any conclusions regarding this matter.

The role of external economies is often assumed to be of considerable importance in urban-industrial location. In this regard, it has been argued that the tendency to minimize the 'distance friction' within the city would be greatest for small-scale firms, where economies derived from being near to other plants which were involved in related processes would be of greater importance than in large plants, where internal economies of scale would prevail. We have also reasoned that during industrialization increased specialization among the smaller-scale factories in cognate industries is normal and that over time this should result in a greater degree of agglomeration or spatial association. In testing these propositions for industry in 1867, a nearest-neighbour-distance measure and correlation analysis were used.[41] We shall employ the same techniques in our analysis of industrial location in 1913.

Before taking stock of the results of our correlation analyses, a contemporary observation provides an instructive point of departure. In a 1904 publication it was contended that the 'distribution of Petersburg factories in relation to one another is to such a degree inconvenient that it gives rise to an artificial increase in the price of . . . articles manufactured.'[42] This suggests that spatial linkages were weakly developed. We shall see if the analysis bears this out. From the matrix of coefficients of correlation for thirty-seven industries in 1913, all statistically significant correlations for each industrial group have been extracted.[43] These statistics, together with their counterparts for 1867, are presented in table 20. It is clear that when the degree of spatial association between industries is measured simply on the basis of total employment as distributed over forty-four regions, only the textile industries show a marked increase in the number of statistically significant coefficients. This increase is explained in part by the emergence of joint-stock undertakings like the Veronin, Lyutsh and Chesher Company. Five factories employing a total of 3,500 people and all located cheek by jowl along the Bol'shaya Nevka River comprised a highly integrated production complex concerned with the spinning, weaving, dyeing and printing of cotton ⟨*see* map 33⟩. But this was

[41] For discussion of these techniques, see A Note on Methods, pp. 428–32.
[42] A. Nikitin, *Zadachi Peterburga* (1904), p. 76.
[43] The matrix for 1913 includes three more industries than that for 1867—electrical machinery, agricultural machinery and cigarette paper. This and all other correlation matrices are to be found in appendix II, pp. 421–4. Statistical significance in this discussion is at the one per cent level.

functional and spatial integration among very large-scale plants, as the total employment indicates. Although we are dealing here with employment by industry, irrespective of factory size, for most industrial groups the component industries had not evolved in such a way as to give much evidence of pronounced spatial linkages.

TABLE 20. *Within-group coefficients of correlation statistically significant at the one per cent level*

	1867	1913
Metal-working	0	2
Chemical	0	0
Food and tobacco products	1	1
Tanning, tallow and soap	0	1
Paper and printing	0	0
Textile	2	9

Source: Extracted from correlation matrix, appendix II, tables 46 and 47.

The use of a factory-size classification in the analysis of the 1913 data offers some additional insight. A few examples will suffice. From the correlation matrix of food-processing industries, the statistically significant coefficients have been summarized in table 21. Although we had hypothesized that spatial associations among the smaller plants (say those in which ninety or fewer people worked), would dominate the pattern, obviously this is not the case. A similar table for the metal-working industry has been created, but again the hypothesis is not unequivocally supported ⟨*see* table 22⟩. To be sure, in both groups there were spatial associations between smaller-scale firms and many of these did reflect functional links. But for all sizes of factory, production independence, rather than interdependence, seems to have been the keynote in 1913. We arrive at this conclusion as a result of analyses where the industrial classification is rather general, but even the adoption of a much 'finer' description of metal-working, the most highly developed industry, does not render the judgement invalid. In table 23 the metal-working group has been subdivided into fifteen, rather than six, industries. To facilitate presentation of the statistically significant correlations, a simple threshold of ninety workers has been adopted to separate large-scale from small-scale operations. Certainly, spatial correlations did exist and this is not surprising, but the fact that there were only seven between the smaller-scale factories does not indicate that a complex system of inter-industry product flows had

TABLE 21. *Food processing, 1913*

Inter-industry simple coefficients of correlation
statistically significant at the one per cent level (+ 0·38)

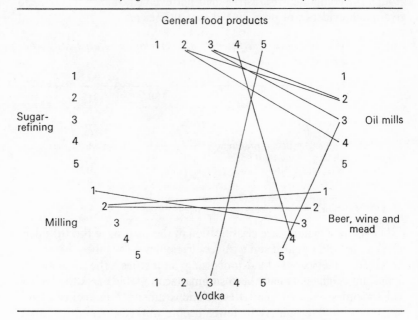

Source: Data extracted from correlation matrix, appendix II, table 48.

Note: Numbers 1 to 5 represent factory-size classes, where

1 = 20 and fewer workers
2 = 21–90 workers
3 = 91–270 workers
4 = 271–750 workers
5 = over 750 workers

created tightly knit patterns of manufacturing. In fact, the physical separation of, and specialization in, various stages of the productive process was not characteristic.[44] Among the large-scale plants vertical

[44] A speciality such as gold-beating, for example, had been highly developed at mid century, but by 1912 it was in marked decline as this function had been assumed by the larger workshops. The tendency to adopt a broader range of functions at the workshop level was a reflection of the pressure to move into a larger-scale unit. This adoption of a broad range of production functions was frequently a necessity in St Petersburg, because of the lack of a large skilled artisan class on which to rely. Taking a different industry to illustrate this point, the manufacture of guns at the state plant at Sestroretsk was held down during the 1890s because all components had to be fabricated in the plant. It was remarked that 'if some of the minor parts could be worked elsewhere the production at the plant could be doubled'. N. F. Labzin, 'The Metal Industries', *The Industries of Russia, Manufactures and Trade* (1893), vol. I, p. 151.

TABLE 22. *Metal-working, 1913*

Inter-industry simple coefficients of correlation statistically significant at the one per cent level (+0.38)

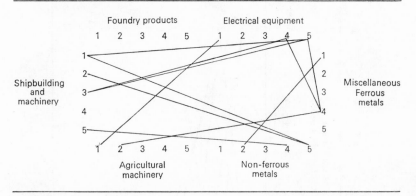

Source: Data extracted from correlation matrix, appendix II, table 49.

Note : Numbers 1 to 5 represent factory-size classes, when

    1 = 20 and fewer workers
    2 = 21–90 workers
    3 = 91–270 workers
    4 = 271–750 workers
    5 = over 750 workers

integration was sometimes nearly complete.[45] We commented earlier on the tendency for factories to diversify rather than to specialize and by means of these correlation analyses we are now able to see something of the spatial manifestations of this feature of St Petersburg industry.

[45] A few examples will suffice. The iron ore mine in Olonets *guberniya*, brought into operation in the 1890s by the Putilov factory was providing some of its pig iron requirements in the 1900s. Within the plant, productive facilities were broad enough to render it independent of others in the capital. Factory departments ranged in type from the metallurgical (in which there was a separate section devoted to the production of all machine tools required in the plant), railroad equipment, steam engine manufacture to artillery, to name only a few. *K Stoletiyu Putilovskago Zavoda 1801–1901gg.* (1902), pp. 41 *et passim*. In the case of the Siemens-Halske factory, in addition to the assembly of equipment manufactured in foreign branches of this organization, even the high grade copper ore required for the manufacture of electrical wire was obtained from the company-owned mine in the Caucasus. A. Voronov 'Sostoyaniye Elektro-tekhnicheskoy Promyshlennosti v Rossii', *Fabrichno-Zavodskaya Promyshlennost' i Torgovlya Rossii* (2nd edn., 1896), p. 580.

TABLE 23. *Metal-working, 1913*

Inter-industry simple coefficients of correlation
statistically significant at the one per cent level (+0·38)

| | 90 and under workers | < 90 and > 90 | Over 90 workers |

1 Agricultural machinery
2 Ferrous and non-ferrous castings
3 Ornamental iron works
4 General machine construction
5 Other fabricated metals
6 Pipe-rolling, heating and
   plumbing equipment
7 Electrical equipment
8 Typographical equipment
9 Armaments
10 Precious metals
11 Scientific instruments
12 Non-precious decorative wares
13 Non-electric lamp equipment
14 Wiredrawing and nail making
15 Transport, engineering
   and shipbuilding

Spatial proximity of linked plants was not highly developed, a fact which sustains what was suggested in the contemporary observation quoted above.

The correlation analysis deals with relationships *between* patterns of industrial activity, but we have also reasoned that the pattern of individual industrial groups would assume certain characteristics during industrialization. In line with the foregoing comments concerning 'distance friction' and agglomerative tendencies, it has been argued that the smaller plants in each industrial group would be more clustered

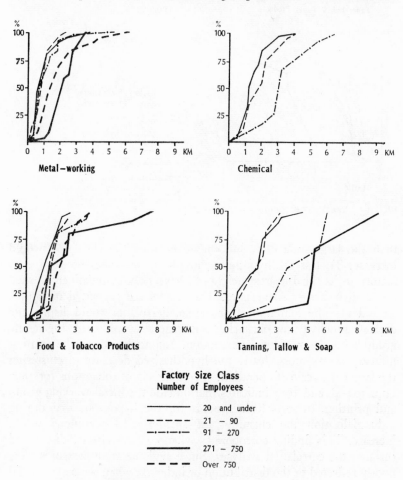

FIG. 12. *Nearest-neighbour graphs, 1913–I*

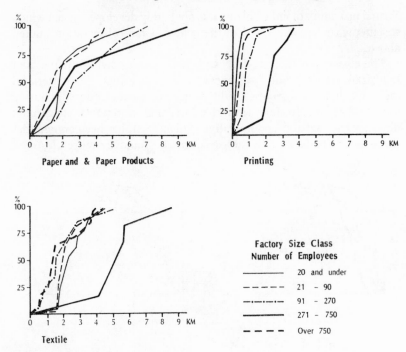

FIG. 13. *Nearest-neighbour graphs, 1913–II*

than the large-scale ones and that over time the clustering would increase. To test the hypotheses, graphs of distances between each factory to its third-nearest neighbour have been cumulatively plotted for all five factory size-classes. The results are presented in figures 12 and 13. The contention that the smaller plants would display the greatest proclivity for clustering was generally supported, the textile group being the one obvious exception. Among the others, the printing industry shows most clearly the hypothesized decrease in clustering the larger the scale of operation. A comparison of the graphs for 1867 ⟨pp. 103–4⟩ and 1913 indicates that outside the metal-working group and printing, there is little support for the hypothesis that during industrialization the clustering of smaller-scale operations would increase. This finding corroborates what we have already discovered through the correlation analyses. Since agglomerative pressures were poorly reflected in the distribution of industry, what, we may ask, did affect the location of industry?

After examining the available evidence for the sixties, we came to the conclusion that as a location factor, rent was not yet decisive. Land costs, real estate values and rent obviously did not remain static in the face of the ensuing urban industrialization. A few maps adequately convey the gist of what took place. The escalation in real estate values after 1874, and especially after 1892, is evident from map 37. Although

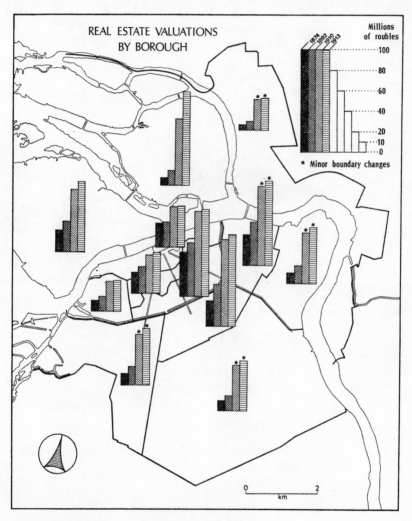

MAP 37. *Real-estate valuations by borough*

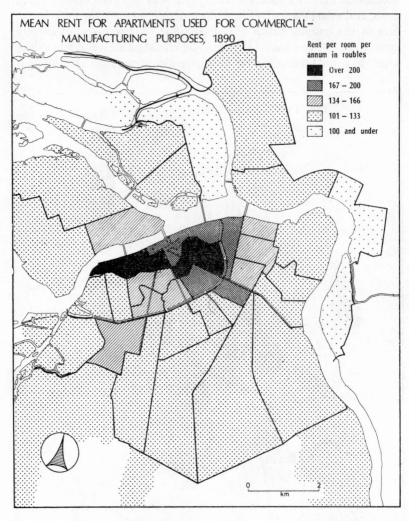

MEAN RENT FOR APARTMENTS USED FOR COMMERCIAL-
MANUFACTURING PURPOSES, 1890

Rent per room per
annum in roubles

■ Over 200
▨ 167 – 200
▧ 134 – 166
· 101 – 133
  100 and under

0   2
     km

MAP 38. *Mean rent for apartments used for commercial–manufacturing
purposes, 1890*

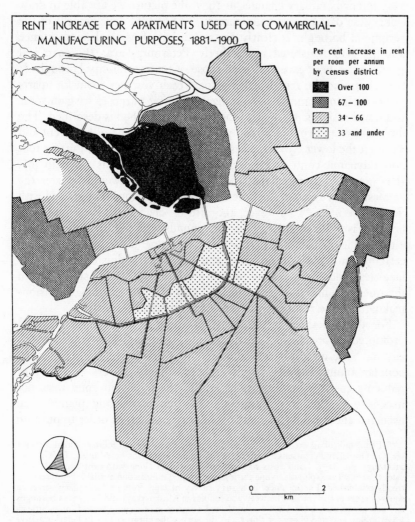

RENT INCREASE FOR APARTMENTS USED FOR COMMERCIAL–
MANUFACTURING PURPOSES, 1881–1900

Per cent increase in rent
per room per annum
by census district

Over 100
67 – 100
34 – 66
33 and under

MAP 39. *Rent increase for apartments used for commercial-manufacturing purposes, 1881–1900*

243

the statistics exclude state and municipal property and although there were minor boundary changes in 1907, the picture we are able to draw from these data is essentially correct.[46] The rapid development of the peripheral boroughs is clearly portrayed, but of particular importance was the gain registered in northerly Peterburgskaya. By 1910 real estate values here exceeded even those of the central-city boroughs.[47] If we examine the rent which was paid each year per room for apartments used for commercial and manufacturing purposes we gain some additional insights. In map 38 the rent scene in 1890 is described. The threshold of 134 roubles broadly demarcates the zone of high rent and within it the lower Nevskiy Prospect was an obvious focus. Putting rent into a dynamic context reveals some interesting patterns ⟨*see* map 39⟩. It is not too surprising that the peripheral wards would register the greatest relative changes between 1881 and 1900 since they started with the lowest bases.[48] However, the rate of change in Peterburgskaya borough is quite singular. This corresponds with the big jump in real-estate values which was just noted. The demand for industrial space certainly put pressure on rents and the construction of many large factories added each year to property values. But we are still left with the question, how the rent and land cost affected locational decision-making and the resultant patterns of manufacturing activity.

For decades the increased cost of space in the central city had prompted a more efficient use of existing facilities. Even at mid-century, cutting back on the space allocated to workers' housing had been popular among the central-city tobacco manufacturers as a way of reducing costs. Where locations within the high-rent zone were not necessary to the firm's success, relocation of existing plants often occurred and for new plants the zone was avoided. In order to put into

---

[46] For details of all exemptions, including the Tsar's palace and military establishments see 'Ob Obshchey Pereotsenke Nedvizhimykh Imushchestv v S. Peterburge', *ISPGD*, no. 21 (1893), pp. 82–3. Land costs had obviously spiralled along with rent and real-estate values, but data are sporadic. None the less, the limited information available reinforces the trends established. For instance, in a 1913 survey of land costs on 'secondary' streets a square *sazhen* of land ranged between 200 roubles in Moskovskaya and Liteynaya boroughs and 400 in Spasskaya. On Vasil'yevskiy Island a square *sazhen* could be had for as little as fifty roubles, and in Vyborg for thirty. In the survey the cheapest plot in Peterburgskaya borough was sixty roubles. Thus, cost per *sazhen* clearly reflected centrality and reached a peak on the Nevskiy Prospect where in 1912 it was reckoned that it was no less than 1,000 roubles (a *sazhen* equals 2·13 metres). 'O Postroyke Gorodskikh Mestnykh Domov', *ISPGD*, no. 36 (1913), pp. 1210–11; 'O Polozhenii Ótsenki Nedvizhimykh Imushchestv v S. Peterburge', *ISPGD*, no. 5 (1912), p. 1306.

[47] It should be remembered that in the case of the Admiralteyskaya borough especially we are excluding state and municipal properties.

[48] Because several boroughs underwent minor boundary alterations we are not able to use either the 1907 or the 1910 census in the analysis.

TABLE 24. *Spatial stability of industrial activity: simple coefficients of correlation*

	Coefficient of correlation 1890 with 1867	Coefficient of correlation 1913 with 1890	Coefficient of correlation 1913 with 1867
Category A—Industries usually associated with the central city			
Textile:			
silk	*	0·16	*
miscellaneous fancy textiles	0·11	*	*
clothing and knitted goods	0·10	0·73	*
Chemicals:			
cosmetics	*	0·58	*
Paper and printing:			
paper production	0·69	0·99	0·71
paper products	*	0·05	0·03
printing	0·66	0·50	0·39
Miscellaneous:			
musical instruments	*	0·92	*
Category B—Industries not dependent on central city locational advantages			
Metal-working:			
shipbuilding and machine construction	0·84	0·67	0·42
miscellaneous ferrous metals	0·33	0·28	*
non-ferrous metals	*	0·62	*
Textile:			
cotton (spinning, weaving, dyeing)	0·77	0·84	0·66
wool (spinning, weaving, dyeing)	*	0·97	*
felt (spinning, weaving, dyeing)	*	0·98	*
linen, hemp and jute	0·27	0·92	0·46
cordage	0·88	0·76	0·82
canvas, oilskin, etc.	0·13	0·16	0·53

[continued on next page]

TABLE 24. (*continued*)

	Coefficient of correlation 1890 with 1867	Coefficient of correlation 1913 with 1890	Coefficient of correlation 1913 with 1867
Category B cont'd.			
Food and tobacco products:			
milling	0·65	0·34	0·11
oil mill	0·70	0·84	0·48
beer and mead	0·93	0·79	0·86
tobacco	0·66	0·51	0·39
sugar-refining	0·91	0·99	0·88
vodka	0·92	0·68	0·46
general food products	0·21	0·33	*
Tanning, tallow and soap:			
leather goods	*	*	*
brush and bristle	*	*	*
Miscellaneous:			
carriage manufacture	0·97	0·85	0·86
Category C—Industries traditionally subjected to zoning restrictions			
Metal-working:			
foundry products	0·71	0·34	0·29
Textile:			
dyeworks	*	0·49	*
Tanning, tallow and soap:			
tanning	0·98	0·80	0·73
tallow rendering and bone grinding	0·12	0·52	*
soap, wax and candle	0·48	0·53	0·18
Chemicals:			
oil refining, general chemicals, paint, lacquer	0·12	0·85	*
dye, rubber	0·80	0·96	0·61

Note: Industries not represented in every year have been omitted.
* indicates no positive coefficient of correlation.

perspective the distributional changes of all industries we need some objective measure of what might be called locational stability. For this purpose coefficients of correlation between the distributions of employment in particular industries at different times have been calculated. The results of this analysis are presented in table 24. The most striking features of the table is the high degree of correspondence in the distributions of nearly every industry between 1913 and 1890, despite the marked move toward larger-scale factories and the heady pace of rent increases. The major distributional changes, therefore, took place in the period from 1867 to 1890.

We can see from these locational changes that there appear to be three broad categories. The first comprises industrial activities normally associated with the central city. Printing is a good example. What we see happening here is a shift from high-rent areas to cheaper locations still in relatively central wards ⟨*see* maps 33, 34 and 38⟩. In the second group are industries not dependent upon the advantages accruing from a central-city site, for instance, the miscellaneous metal-working firms. Here, escalating rents initiated relocations and new growth outside the high-rent zone. The third category covers industries localized because of traditionally restrictive zoning regulations. Examples may be taken from the chemical and tanning, tallow and soap groups. As enforcement became lax, the range of possible locations increased and the stability of the distributions broke down. Locational stability was usually greatest in those industries, like cotton textiles, where sites were freely chosen on the periphery of the built-up area.

The pinch of rising rents and land values was felt most of all in the central city, and a detailed examination of one industrial group might serve to illustrate how industrial development responded. Metal-working provides us with a good example, because it was the largest employer, covered all scales of operation and was found throughout the city. From map 40, it is apparent that between 1868 and 1890 the location of new factories and the expansion of existing firms distinctly girdled the high-rent zone (134 roubles and over rent per year per room). Moreover, growth was especially evident in the northern boroughs of Vasil'yevskaya, Peterburgskaya and Vyborgskaya. From 1890 to 1913 this pattern of growth was much accentuated ⟨*see* map 41⟩. At the same time plant expansion and relocation highlight the expulsive force of the high-rent zone. While these maps do tell us a good deal about how the distribution of metal-working altered in relation to the escalating cost of space during industrialization, they do

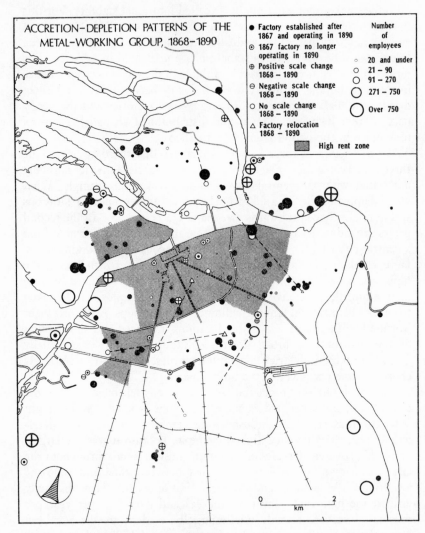

ACCRETION-DEPLETION PATTERNS OF THE
METAL-WORKING GROUP, 1868-1890

● Factory established after
  1867 and operating in 1890
⊙ 1867 factory no longer
  operating in 1890
⊕ Positive scale change
  1868 – 1890
⊖ Negative scale change
  1868 – 1890
○ No scale change
  1868 – 1890
△ Factory relocation
  1868 – 1890

Number
of
employees

○ 20 and under
○ 21 – 90
○ 91 – 270
○ 271 – 750

◯ Over 750

▨ High rent zone

0   2
        km

MAP 40. *Accretion-depletion patterns of the metal-working group,
1868–90*

248

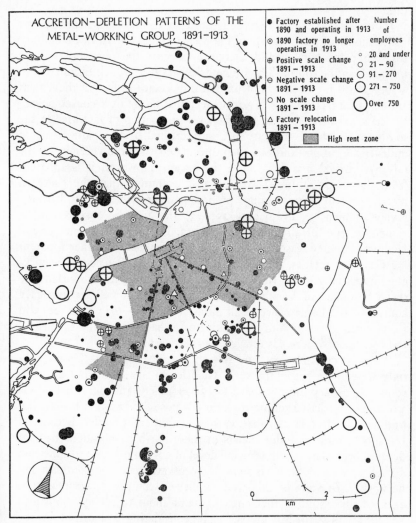

The legend of the map reads:

ACCRETION-DEPLETION PATTERNS OF THE
METAL-WORKING GROUP, 1891-1913

● Factory established after 1890 and operating in 1913
⊙ 1890 factory no longer operating in 1913
⊕ Positive scale change 1891 – 1913
⊖ Negative scale change 1891 – 1913
○ No scale change 1891 – 1913
△ Factory relocation 1891 – 1913

Number of employees
○ 20 and under
○ 21 – 90
○ 91 – 270
○ 271 – 750
○ Over 750

High rent zone

0   2
km

MAP 41. *Accretion-depletion patterns of the metal-working group, 1891–1913*

249

not deal with the intriguing question of why growth occurred where it did.

Industrial location theory suggests that factory sites close to the major modes of transport should be very attractive.[49] In St Petersburg the prime locations would therefore be near the port and railway terminals in the south. (The Finlandskaya railway which terminated in Vyborgskaya borough was of limited importance in freight movement and for most factories a site near its terminal was of little consequence.) We have seen that by the late sixties a gravitation of factories to the southern region of the city had not created a dominant focus in industrial location, and we then speculated that the recency of the railways' arrival may have been the reason. However, it is apparent from the maps of metal-working just examined that the southern region was still by no means a predominant growth area. And from a review of maps 33 to 36 ⟨pp. 230–33⟩ this may be observed to be genierally true for all industries in 1913. Despite the absence of rail facilities, a limited season for using the waterways, and no other apparent locational advantages, the northern regions had experienced a remarkable industrial growth. In fact, instead of becoming less important the three boroughs of Vasil'yevskaya, Peterburgskaya and Vyborgskaya commanded a larger share of all industrial jobs in 1913 than they did thirty years earlier.[50] And the relative gains had been at the expense of the presumably more advantaged southern region!

We must certainly ask why this should have been so, because not only were there better transport facilities to the south, but also low rents, cheap land, ample space for development and, for what it was worth, no restrictive zoning by-laws. To pose the question is easy, but finding a satisfactory explanation is quite a different matter. Because of transport problems industrialists in these northern boroughs had for decades been clamouring for some level of government aid to construct a ring railway to tie in at least Vyborgskaya with the southern rail network.[51] In view of this well publicized complaint, we might be excused for assuming that entrepreneurs about to set up a business would be dissuaded from seriously considering a location in the

---

[49] See Raymond L. Fales, Leon N. Moses, 'Land-Use Theory and the Spatial Structure of the Nineteenth-Century City', *Papers of the Regional Science Association*, XXVII (1971), pp. 61–8.

[50] V. V. Pokshishevskiy, 'Territorial'noye Formirovaniye Promyshlennogo Kompleksa Peterburga v XVIII–XIX Vekakh', *Voprosy Geografii*, no. 20 (1950), pp. 154–5.

[51] 'K Proyektu Okruzhnoy Dorogi v S. P.', *Torgovo-Promyshlennaya Gazeta*, no. 51 (1913), p. 3.

northern part of the city. Obviously the growth which occurred there belies this assumption.

Another possible explanation is that the factories had little need of rail or port facilities. But a study of intra-urban freight movements in 1912 reveals that enormous quantities were hauled between northern factories and the rail terminals or the port.[52] This added to the costs of production, often significantly, and compounded the city's traffic problems.[53] By banning freight waggons from some streets entirely, and from others for certain times during the day, civic officials had, by the early 1900s, made the trip to the northern boroughs additionally time-consuming and costly.[54] Still, new factories were set up and established ones were expanded ⟨*see* map 41⟩. What was the attraction?

There is a case to be made for labour supply being at least part of the explanation. But the evidence is suggestive rather than conclusive. We have argued that in the sixties factory workers chose to live as close as possible to work. By the same token, factory-owners throughout the period of industrialization, despite pressures to decentralize, had located outside the zone of high rent, but well within the built-up area. None of the maps indicates a massive shift in manufacturing to the distant suburbs ⟨*see* maps 33 to 36⟩.[55] On the eve of the Great War might there still have been a strong relationship between where workers lived and where they worked? Computing the coefficient of correlation between employment in factories for each ward in 1913 and the number of factory workers enumerated in the census of 1910, results in a figure of $+0.82$.[56] For several reasons this coefficient is only a crude index, but it supports the circumstantial case we are making. Thus, if an accessible pool of labour was important, then the fact that Peterburgskaya borough absorbed over 135,000 people after 1890, a number much greater than any other borough, goes a long way toward explaining why

[52] 'Ob Organizatsii Gruzovogo Dvizheniya po Gorodskim Zheleznym Dorogam' *ISPGD*, no. 46 (1913), pp. 1738–43.

[53] This issue will be discussed in a later section, see pp. 279–80.

[54] This was accentuated by the fact that there were few bridges linking the northern boroughs with the central city. Nikitin, *Zadachi Peterburga*, p. 71.

[55] It might be reiterated that few factories were located outside the urban area as we have defined it.

[56] In the census, worker (*rabochiy*) is distinguished from owner, administrator and handicraftsman. The coefficient of correlation for industrial workers and total population was $+0.68$; both coefficients were statistically significant at the 0.005 level. Kandaurov, *Fabrichno-Zavodskiye Predpriyatiya*; *Petrograd po Perepisi*, part 2, passim. There is obviously a time difference, but more to the point is the fact that we are dealing with factory workers as a whole rather than by type. Although desirable, the census does not permit this refinement.

this remote area in particular had such an explosive industrial development. For the three northern boroughs as a whole, there were over half a million residents in 1910, more than twice the number living south of the Obovdnyy Canal. It is entirely possible, therefore, that labour supply offset higher transport costs and steered industrial expansion to the north.

Although we may accept the argument that labour supply was a dominant locational factor, this still does not explain why people were flocking to the northern boroughs in such huge numbers. In this connection it is possible that land development practices influenced both the housing market and factory site selection. Unfortunately, there are no data available on real-estate transactions which would permit us to say definitely that manipulation of the land market had taken place. There is enough information, however, to justify some speculation. Among the city directories, that for 1895 includes a section on the ownership of land, and detailed maps and descriptive accounts indicate whether or not the property was developed. It is of interest that the city, the tsar and the Church owned the most extensive tracts of undeveloped land in that large city area south of the Obvodnyy Canal, while in the northern boroughs their holdings were comparatively limited. Owners of land and buildings in Vasil'yevskaya, Peterburgskaya and Vyborgskaya boroughs came from all classes in society, though merchants, honoured citizens and nobles were far and away the most important groups.[57] The directory says nothing of the value of property owned, but we have already seen how rapidly the northern boroughs were being developed. Decisions as to where development could take place ostensibly fell under the jurisdiction of the municipal authorities. However, municipal government was regarded by its critics as being run by established cliques of merchants, nobles and honoured citizens—precisely those groups prominent in land development and speculation. Running through a number of contemporary accounts of how the city of St Petersburg was being managed are references, usually oblique, to manipulation of the land market for private gain.[58] In the next chapter we will expand on this theme. What

[57] These details of land ownership may be explored in greater depth than is possible here by consulting *Ves' Peterburg na 1895g.* (1895), part 1, especially pp. 79–108 for Narvskaya borough; pp. 145–80 for Aleksandro-Nevskaya borough; pp. 253–300 for Vasil'yevskaya; pp. 301–54 for Peterburgskaya; pp. 367–96 for Vyborgskaya. Detailed maps are included with each section.

[58] See, for example, A. Zhuravlev, 'K Voprosu o Finansovoy Politike v Oblasti Munitsipal' nykh Predpriyatiy', *Gorodskoye Delo*, no. 6 (1909), pp. 233–43; G. Dubelir, 'Planirovki Gorodov', *Gorodskoye Delo*, no. 10 (1910), pp. 648–9.

was happening in St Petersburg with respect to factory location did not fully conform with industrial location theory, and at this juncture it might be posited that in part this was because of a process of real-estate development in which important landowners, namely, the city, the tsar and the Church were by choice, or directives, not active participants. Had there been more extensive private land-holdings south of the Obvodnyy Canal, the evolving pattern of industry and housing might well have had a different configuration.

To round out our examination of location factors we should perhaps briefly review one which had a very perceptible impact historically. This was zoning. Its impact was noticeably on the wane by the late sixties. Despite reformulation of zoning regulations in 1879 and again in 1905 civic officials readily acknowledged that the matter had been ignored so long that there was little possibility of radically changing the existing situation.[59] In 1904 an observation on the efficacy of zoning by-laws clearly reveals that they may be discounted as a location factor during the period of rapid industrialization, a time when they were most needed. 'Petersburg factories, industrial establishments, plants and workshops; all of them', it was said, 'are scattered throughout the central parts of the city, polluting and poisoning by their smoke, soot and refuse, the surrounding air and water.'[60]

To summarize briefly, factory location during St Petersburg's industrialization did not conform to several hypotheses derived either from theory or experience in other cities. It has been contended that the tendency for production independence as opposed to interdependence resulted in limited evidence of spatial proximity of linked factories and workshops. Deglomerative pressures which were manifested in escalating rents and property values did not occasion a massive exodus from the city to the distant suburbs although pressure to move out of, or avoid, central-city locations was apparent. Transport accessibility in many locational decisions was of minor consequence and, contrary to expectations, growth occurred in areas devoid of any advantage in this respect. On the basis of circumstantial evidence, we have argued that in a good many decisions an adjacent pool of labour was an important location factor. In this regard the rapid development of the northern boroughs may have been influenced by

[59] 'O Peresmotre Uzakoneniy Otnositel'no Fabrik i Zavodov', *ISPGD*, no. 8 1879), pp. 677–82; 'Ob Uchastii Gor. Obshch. Upravleniye v Razreshenii na Ustroystva Fabriki Zavodov v S. Peterburge', *ISPGD*, no. 15 (1905), pp. 846–68.
[60] Nikitin, *Zadachi Peterburga*, p. 76.

the manipulation of the land market, thereby affecting both factory location and the housing supply. Because of a totally ineffectual set of zoning by-laws, factors which had been of importance historically in shaping the pattern of manufacturing activity no longer constrained the decision to locate new enterprises.

(c) *The formation of a labour market*

Motors, machinery and monopolies were very much a part of industrialization in St Petersburg, but the sophistication which they represented did not always reach down to include the labourers on the factory floor and hardly ever to embrace the mass of hired workers. During the early years of industrialization labour was characterized by a high degree of itinerancy and low productivity; inasmuch as the work-force mostly comprised recently arrived peasants whose legal attachment to the commune was as binding after the Emancipation as before, these features were to be expected. By the turn of the century and after, there is sufficient evidence to argue that in general the commitment of peasant workers to the city was far from complete. For example, according to the census of 1897 only 31 per cent of the married metal-workers maintained their families in the capital. In textiles the figure was a mere 13 per cent. In printing the comparative figure was 38 per cent, the highest registered among the major industrial groups and this in an industry which demanded literate and skilled employees.[61]

The reasons for the large number of married workers living alone were many, but in the main little changed from thirty years before. The peasant's sojourn in the capital was still governed by the commune, for each year the essential passport had to be renewed by village authorities. This often made long-term plans for residence uncertain or impracticable. The high cost of living and the extreme shortage of housing did little to encourage the peasant to bring his family to the city. The agricultural reform introduced by P. A. Stolypin in 1906 mitigated somewhat the constraint on rural-urban migration by permitting peasants a greater degree of independence from the commune. As a result, more people left the countryside permanently and sought in the city some relief from their poverty. By December of 1910, 69 per cent of the city's 1·906 million inhabitants were peasants. And it was this group which dominated the labour market which by

[61] S. N. Semanov, 'Proletariat Peterburga Na Rubezhe XIX-XX vv.', in S. N. Valk (ed.). *IRL* (1972), vol. I, p. 184.

then exceeded 700,000 persons.[62] However, we should not assume that itinerancy as a way of life had vanished. The 1910 census tells us that almost 10 per cent of the 1·3 million peasants intended to 'work in the fields' during the summer. And we should also not assume that the years had dramatically altered the basic character of the masses descending upon the city. Nearly half of them had been there less than a decade; 13 per cent or 164,000 came in 1910 alone.[63] For the most part they brought with them countryside customs and skills. It was helpful to be inured to hard times, especially if they had neither a needed trade nor relevant work experience, for most often they joined the ranks of the semi-literate, unskilled work-force unaccustomed to the discipline of modern production technology.

While a large segment of the 700,000 strong labour force retained many of the characteristics ascribed to it fifty years before, there was now a sizable number of workers fully conversant with urban ways and factory life. We have seen that close on 200,000 worked in factories, and a point was now being reached where there were second, and in some instances, third generation employees.[64] Indeed, 325,000 peasants were city-born and presumably city-bred. Among the peasant factory workers literacy was much higher than the 60 per cent figure for the peasant population as a whole. Groups like the metal-workers and printers exceeded this level by 25 or 30 per cent. Compared with the other groups of hired workers, those employed in factories were decidedly more educated, more highly skilled, better paid and, after the 1905 revolution had frightened the government into legalizing unions, rather better organized. The rise of unions and the heavy outbreak of strikes during the troubled years from 1905 to 1907 did result in some perceptible benefits. The 1897 labour legislation had set 11·5 hours as the maximum working day. At the turn of the century the number of hours spent in the plant in most industries was fairly close to this statutory limit. Ten to twelve years later the length of the average working day had been reduced usually by half an hour or an hour. The principal exception was the food products industry where thirteen hours was normal. It was obviously still a long day that most worked, but it was an improvement.

---

[62] E. E. Kruze, 'Rabochiye Peterburga v Gody Novogo Revolyutsionnogo Podema', *IRL*, p. 390.
[63] *Petrograd po Perepisi*, part 1, p. 290.
[64] For a detailed discussion of the characteristics of the factory labour force, see S. N. Semanov, *Peterburgskiye Rabochiye Nakanune Pervoy Russkoy Revolyutsii* (1966), pp. 86–7.

There had also been some gains in wages; the yearly average for all branches of industry had risen from 355 to 384 roubles from 1910 to 1913.[65] Average annual wages for the major branches of industry are listed in table 25. It is apparent that not only did workers in the food industry spend the longest hours in the plant, but that they also did it for the least money. Although by Russian standards industrial remuneration was comparatively good, the inordinately high cost of food and lodging ensured that it did not go far. For most factory workers only a bare existence was possible, and contemporary budget studies indicate that between 600 and 700 roubles were needed to maintain a tolerable standard of living for a family. Only a small proportion of workers reached this level. In the next chapter, we shall have occasion to examine the implications of this budgetary deficiency; at this point we need only take note of the fact that irrespective of the basic index selected, the cost of living during the early 1900s was rising faster than wages.[66] Small wonder that trade unionism and revolutionist and anarchist movements advocating a radical change in society

TABLE 25. *Average annual wages in selected industries, 1913*

Industry	Average annual wage (roubles)
Metal-working and machine construction	516
Cotton textiles	277
Chemical	346
Tanning, tallow and soap	388
Printing	415
Paper	312
Food products	268

Source: E. E. Kruze, 'Rabochiye Peterburga v Gody Nogo Revolyutsionnogo Podema in S. N. Valk (ed.), *IRL* (1972), vol. 1, p. 399.

found fertile ground among the factory workers. Although the 1905 uprising came to a tragic conclusion in the 'Bloody Sunday' confrontation, the realization that massive demonstrations and strikes were

[65] Kruze, 'Rabochiye Peterburga', p. 399.

[66] Wholesale prices for cereals, meat, butter, textiles, and herring, which met basic needs, increased on average by more than 30 per cent between 1900 and 1909. And as Consul Woodhouse ruefully observed, 'Retail prices have increased still more in the large centres of Russia, where the cost of living has for many years been greater than in most western countries of Europe'. A. W. Woodhouse, 'Report', *BPP; Diplomatic and Consular Reports*, 1914, XCIV. 319.

powerful political weapons was instilled in the minds of many workers. Confronted with serious inflation during the economic boom following 1910, labour unrest was increasingly manifested through strikes. But what of the mass of workers who were not as well organized as those who laboured in factories?

By far the largest proportion of hired labour was found in construction, transport, handicraft, trade, institutional and personal service. Including day labourers, in total about 500,000 people were involved, roughly two and a half times the number of factory workers. The yard-keepers or *dvorniki*, coachmen, domestic servants and the like who were employed by government institutions or private persons were the largest group and numbered about 200,000. Roughly 170,000 worked in commerce, nearly 80,000 in transport, while construction, handicraft and day-labouring activities absorbed the remainder.[67] Actually, the construction and day-labouring group was rather larger than the December census indicates, for it was during the summer months that navvies came in their tens of thousands to work in the building trades, at the docks, or in repairing the winter-ravaged streets. The 100,000 or so who arrived for the summer nearly equalled the number of peasants who left for the countryside. According to their trade they continued to migrate to specific parts of the city: building tradesmen like carpenters and bricklayers to Okhta, waggoners to Aleksandro-Nevskaya and adjacent boroughs, dock workers to Narvskaya, and day labourers to the central-city boroughs like Spasskaya and Moskovskaya where the hope of a job was highest among the multifarious workshops, markets or factories. If hours of work in factories seemed inordinate they were none the less very agreeable in relation to the plight of hired workers generally. In late June, there was sufficient light twenty hours of the day to permit construction; out of this period, sixteen-hour working days were quite general. In dingy workshops, production continued whether there was natural light or not. For instance, in the several hundred small bakeries, employees were on the job sixteen to nineteen hours, the remainder of the day usually being spent sleeping somewhere on the premises. Shoemakers toiled about fifteen hours daily, and so it went on throughout the handicraft and petty retail trades. An eight-hour day remained a utopian notion.

At the bottom of this labouring population were the casual workers. If a factory job were obtained, men were fortunate to draw eighty kopeks a day; women, sixty; juveniles and children, thirty to forty-five.

[67] Kruze, 'Rabochiye Peterburga', p. 390.

In other sectors they frequently earned less.[68] With dependants, hired labour represented about one million people, or more than half the total population in 1910. Clearly, there was every reason to view this seething mass of humanity with some concern. Industrialization had created a labour market of enormous dimensions, and the 1905 revolution had already demonstrated its ability to shake the existing social and political structure to its very roots.

2 THE MERCANTILE MILIEU

Easily the most important new institutions created in the city during the second half of the nineteenth century were its financial houses and commodity markets, the latter arising from the increase in the entrepôt trade of the port. Here, in fact, was the fulcrum of a brokerage and trading system linking all parts of the Empire with the rest of the world. Although there were specialized exchanges for cattle and meat products, eggs and poultry, fruit, tea and wine, and lumber, such businesses paled in comparison with trading in stocks, shares and grain. The special Grain Exchange which had been established just down the Nevskiy Prospect from the Nikolayevskiy railway station was the centre of activity for a foreign trade of vital importance to the financial well-being of the Empire. In the original Exchange on the southeastern tip of Vasil'yevskiy Island traders dealt mostly in stocks and shares—but in a manner fully in keeping with the long-standing deficiencies of Russian business ethics. As Consul Michell dutifully revealed in his annual report for 1900:

> For a long series of years the transactions of all mercantile and financial matters took place at St Petersburg without any distinction between the two on 'Change'. In view of the active and pernicious speculation in stocks and shares conducted by irresponsible members of the Exchange the Minister of Finance has recently created a separate Stock Exchange . . . .[69]

Housed in the same building, membership in the new Exchange was ostensibly controlled by government authorities vetting prospective traders. By 1912, over 600 stocks were listed on the Exchange with a book value amounting to seventeen billion roubles. We may rest assured that devious transactions persisted.

[68] Semanov, *Peterburgskiye Rabochiye*, pp. 97–106; Kruze, 'Rabochiye Peterburga', p. 399.
[69] J. Michell, 'Report', *BPP; Diplomatic and Consular Reports*, 1902, CIX. 385.

In probably no other facet of commercial life was the predominance of St Petersburg so well established as in banking. Chief among the financial houses was the State Bank, founded in 1860, responsible to the Ministry of Finance and a major instrument in effecting economic growth down to the Great War. The monetary reforms of the nineties resulted in a less overt role in credit advancement for the State Bank. This largely occurred because joint-stock commercial banks were mushrooming in number and at the same time switching from their traditional role in discounting commercial and industrial bills to large-scale investment banking. By providing capital for the expansion of existing firms, or the creation of new ones, they were assuming one of the principal functions of the State Bank. The latter then began to provide funds on a more indirect basis, often to sectors of the economy which the government felt needed bolstering. Apart from issuing currency after 1897, the State Bank was frequently used to shore up otherwise viable businesses during times of economic recession or outright depression. One way in which the latter was achieved was simply by providing longer-term credits than was usual on non-guaranteed collateral.[70] By 1909 the State Bank had provided nearly 300 million roubles of credit for the financing of manufacturing in Russia, most of it taken up by the textile, sugar and metal-working industries.[71] Although it had something like 135 branches by 1914, there were clear advantages for business in the capital being so close to the ears of government officials who stood at the top of this vast financial network.

The joint-stock commercial banks played an ever more prominent role in financing the industrialization of the city, as they did in the country at large. By 1914 there were thirteen large institutions with head offices in the capital. The control which these houses exercised over the entire Empire's banking system is partly revealed by the fact that their share of total capital owned by all incorporated banks had risen from just under half in 1900 to two thirds in 1914.[72] Moreover, the St Petersburg bankers differed from those in Moscow by virtue of their much heavier involvement in investment banking. The latter dealt more in commercial bills and were directed very largely by local

[70] For detailed discussion of the State Bank operations, see Olga Crisp, 'Russia', in R. Cameron (ed.), *Banking in the Early Stages of Industrialization* (New York, 1967), pp. 196–9, 210–6.
[71] E. E. Kruze, 'Transport, Torgovlya, Kredit', *OchIL.* (1956), vol. III, p. 89.
[72] P. I. Lyashchenko, *A History of the National Economy of Russia to the 1917 Revolution* (New York, 1949), translated by L. M. Herman, p. 704.

entrepreneurs. Not only was banking activity in the capital more diversified, but membership of the boards of directors reflected the links between government, finance and industry.[73] One example will perhaps suffice. The largest joint-stock commercial bank was created in 1910 as a result of a merger of two others, a development which was common enough by then in the process of industrialization. The merging of the Russo-Chinese and the Northern banks resulted in the Russo-Asiatic Bank. The chairman of the board was A. I. Putilov. As former director of the Ministry of Finance, as a director of 'Prodamet' —a cartel-like association of metal-working firms—and as a shareholder in the Putilov metal-working complex in St Petersburg, the person of Putilov clearly represented the link between financial capital, government contracts and industry. It is small wonder that this bank was heavily involved in the financing of local firms, particularly those producing war materials on government contracts. The largest in this field was the Putilov complex which had been awarded government contracts amounting to tens of millions of roubles during the post-1908 economic boom. The bank's involvement in local industry was by no means restricted to military-related manufacturers, for it also financed much of the local tobacco production.[74]

St Petersburg bankers did not have a 'hands-off' policy with respect to the firms being financed, as did their Moscow counterparts. On the contrary, the experience of dealing in non-guaranteed securities during the depression of the early 1900s emphasized the necessity of knowing what was going on in the firms concerned. If this was insufficient stimulus, the growing number of foreigners involved in Russian joint-stock commercial banking displayed an active interest in how money was being used and reinforced the trend toward interlocking directorates between the banks and industry. In this banking sphere two characteristics were shared with industry—increasingly large-scale operations brought about by amalgamation or attrition of smaller firms, and penetration by foreign capital.

Of course, not all the capital's industrialists had access to, or assistance from, the large commercial banks, but there were other sources of credit such as the municipal bank and credit societies which were becoming more and more necessary to industrial or commercial firms. These societies numbered close on forty and provided a very

[73] Crisp, 'Russia', p. 219.
[74] Kruze, 'Transport, Torgovlya, Kredit', p. 90; Lyashchenko, *A History of the National Economy*, pp. 702–11.

significant service for the smaller-scale companies. All told, nearly 11,000 people found employment in the city's financial institutions, an addition of 7,000 since 1869 ⟨*see* table 26⟩.

TABLE 26. *The structure of commerce, 1900–10*

	Number of establishments 1900 (1912)	Employment 1910
Retail shops	15,020	154,627
including:		
Foodstuffs and		
consumer goods		45,409
Clothing		21,700
Books and artwork		3,559
Eating establishments		34,866
Wholesale outlets	320	4,582
Financial institutions	56 (1912)	10,764
including:		
Banks and credit societies	50	
Exchanges	6	
Total		169,973

Sources: Petrograd po Perepisi 15 Dekabrya 1910 Goda (1914), part 2, section 1. pp. 2–21; E. E. Kruze, 'Transport, Torgovlya, Kredit', *Och.IL* (1956), vol. III, p. 79; *Ves' Peterburg na 1912 g.* (1912).

The emergence of private financial institutions was obviously essential to industrialization but they did not operate unassisted. During the depression the State Bank had to step in to maintain liquidity of banks and industry alike. By 1913 the distortions of the economy resulting from the tumultuous pace of economic growth again demanded the provision of credit by the State Bank, this time because the private sector was running short on finance.[75] But government policies and practices had negative as well as positive consequences. The need to grease the palms of bureaucrats was perhaps not as pronounced as one revolutionary's account of business dealings in the early seventies claims, but it certainly had not been snuffed out:

> The pillage which went on in all the ministries, especially in connection with the railways and all sorts of industrial enterprises, was really enormous. Immense fortunes were made at that time. The navy, as Alexander II himself said to one of his sons, was 'in the pockets of So-and-So'. The cost of the railways, guaranteed by

[75] Woodhouse, 'Report'.

the state, was simply fabulous. As to commercial enterprises, it was openly known that none could be launched unless a specified percentage of the dividends was promised to different functionaries in the several ministries. A friend of mine, who intended to start some enterprise at St Petersburg, was frankly told at the ministry of the interior that he would have to pay twenty-five per cent of the net profits to a certain person, fifteen per cent to one man at the ministry of finances, ten per cent to another man in the same ministry, and five per cent to a fourth person. The bargains were made without concealment, and Alexander II knew it. His own remarks, written on the reports of the comptroller-general, bear testimony to this.[76]

We have noted the lack of ethical conduct on the Exchange. This trait of Russian businessmen was as disturbing to the foreigner on the eve of the Great War as it had ever been. Since government officials were often as guilty of corrupt practices as businessmen, a radical change in commercial ethics could not be expected overnight, if ever. Again, British Consul officers offer revealing insights. As Sir E. Thornton commented in late October 1884:

> The Russian Code of Laws contain no restrictions against the manufacture and sale of spurious or adulterated articles which are not detrimental to health. In this manner spurious butter may, without any penalty, be sold as genuine butter. As a rule it is sold, in retail, in St Petersburgh as dairy butter, and at the price of the same. . . . There is no sign of any attempts being made to ameliorate the shortcomings of Russian legislation on this subject, and the manufacturers of spurious articles continue to enjoy almost perfect immunity.[77]

In such an environment it is little wonder that foreign investors, whether in banking or industry, maintained a close watch over their interests. But the vacillating official policy regarding the involvement of Russian Jews in commerce, or for that matter the freedom of movement of foreign Jewish businessmen in general, served to preclude substantial entrepreneurial talents from participating fully in the

[76] Peter Kropotkin, *Memoirs of a Revolutionist* (New York, 1962), edited by James A. Rogers, p. 161.
[77] Sir E. Thornton, 'Report', *BPP; Diplomatic and Consular Reports*, 1884/5, LXXXI. 621.

economic growth of the country.[78] All told, however, foreigners were essential to the economic well-being of the Empire:

> One very important factor of modernisation is the participation of foreigners in Russian commercial and industrial life. In St Petersburg and Moscow there are large German colonies and also a very considerable number of Englishmen. The traditions of the St Petersburg English colony go back to the days of the Archangel trade and of the old British Company, and the British Church in St Petersburg is still the property of a trading company. Many English families have been established in the Russian capital for generations, and although some have become through the lapse of time Russian subjects, and it occasionally happens that the members of families originally English are unable to speak the language of their ancestors, the persistence with which the greater part of the colony retain their English traits, maintain their connection with the mother country, and send their children to England to be educated is very remarkable. English influence on Russian commercial life is less marked, however, than German influence. The Germans have many advantages. In the first place they are near neighbours, and in the second place, through the Baltic Germans, they have a direct and vital connection with the population of the Empire. Their agents usually know the language and tastes of the country, which is by no means always the case with English agents, and German firms are more elastic than English firms in giving the long credit which is habitual in Russian business.[79]

While the various guilds described in an earlier chapter continued to be part and parcel of commercial life in Russia, there is no evidence to suggest that in St Petersburg they were in any sense major obstacles to the process of industrialization. To be sure, many merchants were conservative, but on the whole they were not reluctant to become involved in factory production. Guilds were something of an institutional barrier to industrialization, but the omnipresent bureaucratic apparatus of government, permeating as it did the domestic and business lives of foreigners and Russians alike, was no less of one. In the capital, the opportunity to earn sizable profits was sufficient stimulus for a very

[78] For an example of the harassment of foreign Jewish businessmen, see *BPP*; *Correspondence respecting the Expulsion of Mr L. Lewisohn from St Petersburgh*, 1881, (C. 3013), XCIX. 325 and 349.
[79] Williams, *Russia*, pp. 378-9.

great many entrepreneurs to adapt their mode of business practice to the existing institutional barriers, or in some way to overcome them.

Although the metropolitan dominance of St Petersburg was virtually complete in the case of industry, it was less so for commercial activities. Five banks were located in other towns in the *guberniya*, two of them in the small industrial and trade centre of Narva. With the exception of Tsarskoye Selo, none of the other towns in the metropolitan region had a bank in 1910, though most had a credit society office. Wholesaling did occur on a fairly large scale in a few of the towns like Kronshtadt, Narva and Shlissel'burg. But throughout the *guberniya* this activity was less regularized, and shared with retailing the eight fairs which were held for short spells in five provincial centres; there were also twenty-odd bazaars in nine other towns operating on the same basis. All the same, the value of retail trade turnover in a few of the city's larger markets exceeded that of the rest of the *guberniya* put together.[80] From table 26 we get some idea of the dimensions of retail trade in the city.

Petty trade in St Petersburg had not been erased in consequence of industrialization and commercialization. Streets remained rife with peasants hawking wares of every description, and it was through this congestion that the giants of trade and commerce had daily to pass. Together, however, their entrepreneurial talents resulted in a trade turnover varying between 800 and 900 million roubles annually, a value in excess of that generated by industry in 1913.[81] In 1910 over 150,000 persons gave as their occupation some form of retail trade. Included in this figure were 14,000 street traders, but this is probably an under-estimate; it is likely that there were several thousand more of them among the 18,000 or so persons who, according to the census, had no job to their name. At the other extreme were department stores like the *Passazh* located on the Nevskiy Prospect. The four-storied *Passazh* housed approximately sixty retail businesses specializing in the sale of high quality men's and women's clothing, jewellery and various luxury items. In between this type of operation and peasant hawkers were close on 20,000 retail shops, a number nearly three times greater than it had been in 1869 and roughly consonant with the increase in population. About two thirds of these sold foodstuffs amounting to about half the retail turnover.[82]

By no means all retail trade was channelled through individual shops,

---

[80] *Goroda Rossii v 1910 Godu* (1912), pp. 48–9, 51.
[81] Kruze, 'Transport, Torgovlya, Kredit', p. 73.
[82] Kruze, 'Transport, Torgovlya, Kredit', p. 79.

for the city's markets were capacious and popular with the ordinary people and nobility alike; in 1912 there were 3,081 shops or stalls located in the eighteen markets scattered throughout the city. The largest was the *Aleksandrovskiy Novyy Rynok* fronting on the Fontanka Canal in Spasskaya borough, whose 765 outlets dealt primarily in manufactured wares. Nearby was the *Apraksin* market on Sadovaya Street, with 478 stalls selling everything from clothing and furniture to fruit and vegetables. The *Gostinyy Dvor* still claimed the lion's share of business even though it had fewer outlets than the Aleksandrovskiy market. This resulted from the more specialized nature of its 500 or so outlets, where the emphasis was on the higher priced luxury end of manufactured consumers' goods and handicraft wares. Having almost doubled the number of vendors since the 1860s, this complex had encroached on the adjoining streets. A short distance up Sadovaya Street, past both the *Aleksandrovskiy Novyy Rynok* and the *Apraksin*, was the city's fourth largest market, the *Sennoy*, which had 262 stalls concentrating on the sale of foodstuffs. Inasmuch as two thirds of all market outlets were located in these four facilities, the average size of the remaining fourteen was of a very different order.[83]

Retailing took place in a miscellany of shops, stalls and sheds scattered in their thousands throughout the city. In the 1860s there was no marked tendency for localization, even among more specialized types of retail services. Because of data deficiences we are not able to use coefficients of localization to draw a comparative picture of retailing for the early 1900s. Still, directory information permits some comments. We wondered earlier what the impact of the vast influx of peasants, who were neither affluent nor especially mobile in the sense of using public transport to extend the range of shopping trips, would have on the distribution of retailing. By recreating once more the pattern and type of shops along the seven principal streets and comparing this map with that for 1867 ⟨*see* p. 120⟩, we can begin to appreciate something of what had occurred during the intervening decades.

From map 42 several features are apparent. Along all streets adjoining the Nevskiy Prospect there had been a build-up of retailing which, moreover, was specialized. This is clear from what had happened on the Nevskiy Prospect itself. In 1867 two thirds of the shops handled general foodstuffs and consumers goods; by 1912 this share had dropped to just over half. Moreover, the foodstuffs sold were often exotic in

<hr>

[83] *Ves' Peterburg na 1912 g.* (1912).

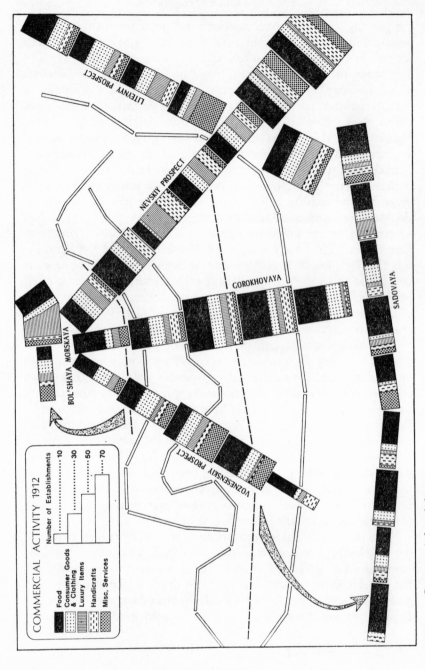

COMMERCIAL ACTIVITY 1912

Number of Establishments

10 ....
30 ....
50 ....
70 ....

Food
Consumer Goods & Clothing
Luxury Items
Handicrafts
Misc. Services

LITEINYY PROSPECT

NEVSKIY PROSPECT

GOROKHOVAYA

BOL'SHAYA MORSKAYA

VOZNESENSKIY PROSPECT

SADOVAYA

MAP 42. *Commercial activity, 1912*

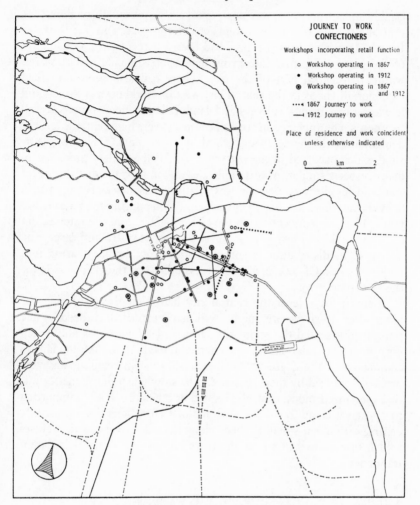

MAP 43. *Journey to work, confectioners, 1912*

origin and scandalously highly priced.[84] In other words, there was evidence of a greater degree of centrality than fifty years before. The same conclusion may be drawn from an examination of locational change for specific types of retailing. Two examples are sufficient to make the point. Map 43 reveals that the distribution of confectionery

[84] Isabel F. Hapgood, *Russian Rambles* (Boston, 1895), p. 44.

establishments in 1867 was comparatively dispersed throughout the central city, and to a lesser extent on Peterburgskiy and Vasil'yevskiy Islands. However, by 1912 there had been a perceptible re-orientation of the pattern. By this date many new establishments had appeared within the central part of the city. There had also been a marked depletion of shops in the central city west of Gorokhovaya Street, and to a lesser extent on Vasil'yevskiy Island. It is pertinent to note as well that new shops appeared in areas of comparatively high rent, the areas of depletion usually being characterized by lower rents.[85] The re-orientation which occurred in the pattern of gold and jewellery shops was in many respects similar. Map 44 indicates that in 1867 the distribution of gold and jewellery workshops was relatively dispersed. By 1912 it is obvious that there had been a spatial contraction during the intervening years. The two foci centred on the *Gostinyy Dvor* and the intersection of Vladimirskiy-Liteynyy and Nevskiy Prospects. By and large, the alteration in distribution involved a shift from low-rent areas into high-rent ones. Of course, market accessibility was the main reason for the high rents.

In short, the role of the central city had strengthened during the years after 1867, as we might well have expected. Indeed, while peasants dominated the population, they had by no means obliterated normal spatial relations in commerce, though it would be fair to comment that the degree of areal specialization in retailing was very probably reduced by their presence. The simple fact of the matter was that specialized shops, centrally located or otherwise, took a supporting role when it came to the vast volume of transactions done in scruffy cellars, within evil-smelling sheds along the side streets, at the refuse-ridden market stalls, or over the trays carried by pestilential peasant tradesmen.

3 TRANSPORT AND TECHNOLOGICAL BACKWARDNESS

By the early 1900s there were several new forms of transport generally in operation. Electric trams were gliding along the streets of scores of cities, intra-metropolitan ring railways made the movement of goods and people even easier, some underground railways had actually been built, and the ultimate in private conveyance, the motor car, had appeared on the streets. Yet St Petersburg stood out against this background of rapid technological development not as a leader in the

[85] See map 38 p. 242.

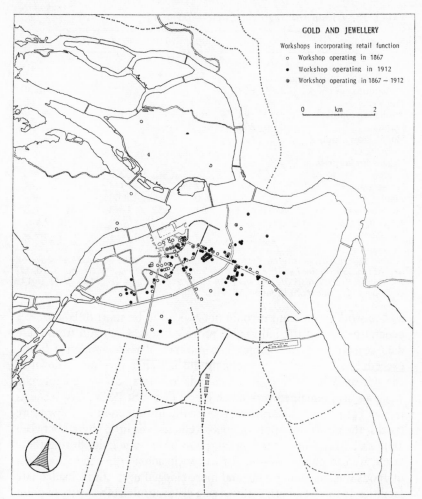

MAP 44. *Gold and jewellery, 1867–1912*

adoption of innovations, but as a laggard. The reasons for this and its implications are complex but before exploring them we must look first at the city's transport history.

Such information as there is does not permit us to make comparisons with the employment structure in 1869, but broadly speaking the number employed in transport of all kinds within the city had quadrupled by 1913, while industry was growing sixfold. With close to

TABLE 27. *Urban transport facilities, 1898–1913*

Number of	1898	1900	1910	1911	1912	1913
Commercial vessels	20,737	–	–	–	–	–
Horse-drawn commercial waggons	19,627	–	–	–	–	19,000
Trucks						180
Public steamboats	98	84	–	–	–	–
Ferries	306	–	–	–	–	–
Horse-drawn public carriages	–	100	–	–	–	–
Horse-drawn private cabs	13,171	13,666	–	14,000	–	–
Horse-trams	545	547	381	344	342	261
Electric trams	0	0	525	568	568	609
Locomotives	–	29	33	33	33	39
Automobiles	–	–	–	–	–	2,585
Autobuses	–	–	12	–	–	–

Sources: *Entsiklopedicheskiy Slovar'* (1900), vol. LVI, p. 329; *Spravka k Voprosu ob Uluchshenii Sposobov Peredvizheniya Naseleniya S. Peterburga* (1901), pp. 9, 10, 12, 25; *Kratkiy Svod Statisticheskikh Dannykh po G. S. Peterburga za 1912* (1913), p. 17; G. Dobson, *St Petersburg* (London, 1910), p. 121.

80,000 workers on hand it could not be said to be short of labour.[86] A general picture of the industry is provided in table 27 and from these data several features emerge. The number of river and canal boats, exceeding 20,000 in 1898, probably did not alter very much down to the Great War. On land, thousands of horse-drawn commercial waggons also remained very much a part of the St Petersburg scene as late as 1913. Even taking into account the introduction of a few score trucks, the available supply of goods vehicles was little altered between 1898 and 1913. Given the huge surge in business activity during these years, we can only draw one of two conclusions: either the movement of goods was becoming more and more clogged up through inadequate facilities or there had originally been a gross surplus of vehicles (a point to be clarified later). The principal development in this period was the appearance after the turn of the century of the electric tram, and it began immediately to compete seriously with the horse-trams, horse-buses, and even the public steamboats and ferries, though there is some evidence that fewer of these were in use before the appearance of the tramcar.

We saw in an earlier chapter that the initial efforts of the Nevskaya, Sadovaya & Vasileostrovskaya Horse Railroad Company to extend

[86] *Petrograd po Perepisi*, part 2, section 1, p. 22.

the tram network were rebuffed by the City Council. Subsequently, the company tried to shore up its operations economically by improving the service for passengers on the existing network. This need had arisen from the fact that the shipment of goods, which was one of the intended functions of the system, had been restricted to the night hours and was presumably less in volume than anticipated. As it transpired, this company never did gain permission from the Council to expand the network and it remained less than ten kilometres in length. From the early 1860s until the mid-seventies, horse-trams were of little benefit to the public. The service was infrequent and the fares, originally set at ten kopeks, precluded regular use of them for all but a limited segment of the city's population. Like the omnibus thirty years earlier it could not be regarded as a means of public transport in the full sense of the word.

It was not until the middle of the 1870s that expansion of the horse-tram system was approved. Beginning in 1874, the City Council received petitions from A. Bashmakov and M. Gubonin to operate an extensive network within the city. In 1875 the applicants were granted permission to run a tram system under a forty-year concession, during which time the city was to receive 4 per cent of the gross receipts annually. Construction began in 1875 and within four years eighty-four kilometres of track had been added, and in the process the horse-tram was firmly established as a major component in public transport.[87] The undertaking became a joint-stock company in 1876, with the Council approving the continuation of the original terms of the contract, including the right to purchase after fifteen years. The growth in traffic was in large measure responsible for the gradual acceptance of the horse-tram by the City Council, and this change in attitude was reflected in the granting of another concession. In 1878 the Nevskaya Prigorodnaya Horse Railroad Company was allowed to operate a line extending from the city to the village of Murzinki. This was essentially a suburban line of over eleven kilometres running along the Shlissel'-burg Highway through an industrial district which included Aleksandrovskoye. The city again retained the right to purchase after the expiry of fifteen of the thirty-five years in the concession. However, this agreement was restricted to that portion of the system within the city boundary, a distance of approximately four kilometres. The annual

[87] 'Rospisaniye Dvizheniya po Liniyam Aktsion. Obshchestva Konno-Zhelezn. Dor. v S. Peterburge v Prodolzhenii Goda s I Oktyabrya 1889g.' *ISPGD*, no. 11 (1889), pp. 890–91.

payment to the city was based on 3 per cent of gross receipts, but then pro-rated according to the share of the network within the city's jurisdiction.[88]

During the next two decades the total network was only slightly augmented despite a fairly large increase in traffic. Passenger traffic had risen from less than two million in 1865 to fifty-five million in 1890 and to eighty-five million in 1898.[89] The horse-tram system had proved successful on a limited scale in three ways: it was providing a means of locomotion for growing numbers; it was yielding profits on a rising scale for all three companies; and the city was receiving an annual revenue drawn from its share of gross receipts. The growth in traffic had taken place in spite of an increase in fares. In the mid-seventies, the first and second-class fares had been set by civic officials at five and three kopeks, but by mid August 1880, the companies had managed to persuade the authorities to increase fares to six and four kopeks. While less than the ten-kopek tariff of the sixties, the new fares applied to trip stages and therefore long-distance journeys were more costly than these figures indicate.[90] The Bashmakov and Gubonin undertaking did well—though in this it was not exceptional—despite its rather limited service. With a capital investment of roughly seven million roubles, gross receipts in 1891—which was not a particularly good year—were just under two million and net profits were 131,641 roubles. In that year the company carried over thirty-seven million passengers, but seven years later traffic had risen to fifty-nine million, gross receipts to 3,135,129 roubles and net profit to 528,650 roubles. This was the normal level of profitability during the nineties.[91]

The direct benefit to the municipality was obviously small compared with the returns to the companies. In 1895, for example, gross receipts of the three companies were in excess of 3·3 million roubles, net profits exceeded 600,000, but only 86,000 found their way into city coffers.[92] Not surprisingly perhaps, it was in this year that the idea of buying out the tramway companies came up again at the City Council.

[88] *Spravka k Voprosu ob Uluchshenii Sposobov Peredvizheniya Naseleniya S. Peterburga* (1901), pp. 14–15.
[89] 'Konno-Zheleznyya Dorogi v S. Peterburge', *ISPGD*, no. 6 (1891), p. 413; *Spravka k Voprosu ob Uluchshenii Sposobov Peredvizheniya Naseleniya*, p. 27.
[90] 'Rospisaniye Dvizheniya po Liniyam', p. 891.
[91] 'Zaklyucheniye Finansovoy Komissii ot 9 Oktyabrya 1890g.', *ISPGD*, no. 36 (1890), p. 343; *Spravka k Voprosu ob Uluchshenii Sposobov Peredvizheniya Naseleniya*, p. 26.
[92] S. P. Luppov, 'Gorodskoye Upravleniye i Gorodskoye Khozyaystvo', *Och.IL* (1957), vol. II, pp. 823–4; *Spravka k Voprosu ob Uluchshenii Sposobov Peredvizheniya Naseleniya*, pp. 26–7.

As in 1892, the discussion centred on the Bashmakov and Gubonin Company, no doubt because it was the largest, but also because it was easy to criticize the quality of its service and to covet its high profits.[93] Thus, when the thirty-five year concession granted to the smaller Nevskaya, Sadovaya & Vasileostrovskaya Horse Railroad Company expired in 1898, it was not renewed and the company was purchased instead by the city.[94] This was only the first step toward municipal control of the tram system. Efforts to acquire control of the Bashmakov and Gubonin Company began at approximately the same time, but at first without success. Given the substantial increase in profits registered by the company it is not surprising that the take-over was stalled by litigation for several years. At the turn of the century, with still only a portion of the horse-tram system under city control, contemporary criticism was reaching a crescendo. In the mid-nineties, it had been observed 'that the current state and development of the horse railway system in Petersburg are more than unsatisfactory and retarded, not only in comparison with the capitals of European states, but even with several of the provincial cities in Russia.'[95] A few years later it was caustically noted that the existing network would be 'more suited for a comic paper caricature than for the convenience of the inhabitants of the cultural centres. Each of us knows full well the inconvenience of movement over more considerable distances.'[96] What, then, had the tramways actually achieved since the 1870s?

As map 45 indicates, the city's horse-tramway system had been extensively filled out between 1867 and 1899. Yet this was a relative improvement, for the total network was only about 114 kilometres whereas the population within the city borders was over 1·2 million, or 1·5 million if we include the suburbs. Some measure of St Petersburg's inadequacy in this respect may be gained from the fact that Toronto also had 114 kilometres of tram-line ten years earlier, but it had at the time a population of only 144,000.[97] Compared with the mid-sixties

[93] 'Po Voprosu o Vykupe Predpriyatiya 2-go Aktsionernago Obshchestva Konno-Zheleznykh Dorog v S. Peterburge', *ISPGD*, no. 20 (1895), pp. 353–62.
[94] 'Po Voprosu o Dal'neyshey Eksploatatsii Konno-Zheleznykh Dorog 1-go Tovarish-chestva, po Okonchanii 31 Avgusta 1898 Goda, Sroka Kontsessii', *ISPGD*, no. 1 (1898), pp. 107–14.
[95] 'Po Voprosu o Vykupe Predpriyatiya 2-go Aktsionernago Obshchestva Konno-Zheleznykh Dorog', p. 354.
[96] V. V. Svyatlovskiy, *Zhilishchnyy Vopros s Ekonomicheskoy Tochki Zreniya* (1902), part I, p. 229. In this quotation, both the Moscow and St Petersburg public transport systems were being criticized.
[97] Peter G. Goheen, *Victorian Toronto, 1840 to 1900: Pattern and Process of Growth* (Chicago, 1970), pp. 70, 72.

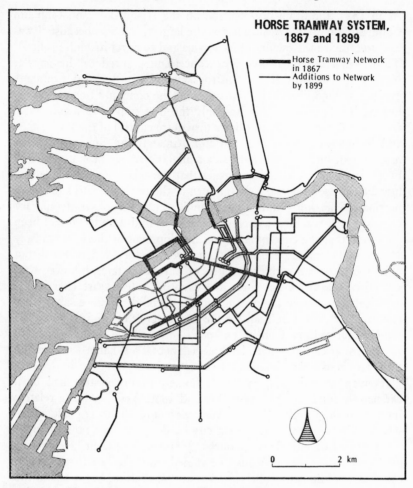

MAP 45. *Horse tramway system, 1867 and 1899*

tram passenger traffic had multiplied many times over and in 1900 was approximately ninety-one million; seen another way each inhabitant made that year an average of seventy-three tram journeys, whereas in Berlin the equivalent figure was 113 ⟨*see* table 28⟩.

Seven omnibus companies also provided regular services in 1900, though these were mostly confined to the central city. As many as forty-five omnibuses operated on the Nevskiy Prospect and these alone accounted for over half of the total traffic of 3·8 million passengers ⟨*see*

274

The Culmination of Capitalism

TABLE 28. *Comparative use of urban public transport, 1900*

| | St Petersburg | | Berlin | |
	Total traffic (millions)	Trips per person	Total traffic (millions)	Trips per person
Street railway	90·93	73	280·35	113
Omnibus	3·83	3	80·57	33
Steamboat	15·77	13	·96	·4
Steam railway	–	–	97·53	39
Totals	110·53	88	459·41	185

Sources: M. A. Shtromberg, 'Detsentralizatsiya Naseleniya v Gorodakh i Puti Soobshcheniya', *IMGD*, no. 4 (1913), p. 89; *Spravka k Voprosu ob Uluchshenii Sposobov Peredvizheniya Naseleniya S. Peterburga* (1901), pp. 9, 10, 12, 25.

table 28⟩. A few lines continued to link the central city with the suburbs, though intended less for year-round commuting than for the summer exodus to the *dachi*. The fact that the companies concerned tended to duplicate the horse-tram service and to charge, with one exception, the same fares, may well explain the very limited traffic, which when set against the city's population scarcely averaged three trips per person. We might notice in passing that Berlin was not celebrated for its public transport in the 1860s, and certainly not for its fleet of omnibuses, but thirty years later in the face of rather more sophisticated competition, over eighty million people were using its omnibuses each year. This amounted to a ratio of omnibus usage eleven times greater than that of St Petersburg.

There were, in St Petersburg, a few locomotives in service, but they numbered only twenty-nine and were employed for the most part on the Nevskaya Prigorodnaya Horse Railroad Company line to the southeast. The potential benefits of an intra-urban railway, as in Berlin and a number of other European cities, did not pass unnoticed, and various proposals for constructing an integrated steam railway network were put to the City Council over the years. One of the most promising involved covering over the Yekaterininskiy Canal, laying a rail line along its route, and linking this line with a ring rail line extending from the southern reaches of the city to the northeast. During discussion of this scheme in the early 1890s the promoters were entitled to point out that passenger traffic along the canal was rapidly declining and that goods traffic, mainly of firewood and construction materials, was unimportant. The advantages of using the canal as a railway seemed to them overwhelming, since it would not only 'penetrate into the centre of the city', but also obviate the need for clearing a right of way with all its attendant economic and social costs.[98] Owing to the apparent concern of the members of the City Council that such a major project would disturb city life too much, not a single piece of track was ever laid.

The horse-tram was also inclined to stifle some of the passenger traffic on the canals. Regular services were run on the Moyka, Yekaterininskiy and Fontanka canals, but only the latter generated any traffic to speak of. Steamboat services on the Fontanka carried 3·7 million passengers in 1900, five times the number on either of the others.[99] The ferry service across the rivers, with some sixteen million trips annually, most of them on the Bol'shaya Neva and Nevka, was the one area where competition from the horse-tram was not felt. Scores of small vessels, only a few of them steam-powered, remained in use simply because more direct journeys by other means were impossible.

Three main objectives lay behind the City Council's decision to buy the Nevskaya, Sadovaya & Vasileostrovskaya Horse Railroad Company and the Bashmakov and Gubonin Company. The improvement of the existing system through the introduction of some other form of motive power was an obvious priority; several new lines also had to be built and cheap fares introduced.[100] When, in 1902, litigation ceased and the city finally gained control of the Bashmakov and Gubonin Company, plans for revamping the entire system had already been prepared. Total trackage was to be increased by 150 per cent, new trams were to be purchased and the frequency of service improved and, above all, electric traction was to be introduced. However, the expansion of municipal services was subject to the availability of capital as much as any other enterprise, and electric trams did not appear on the city's streets until 1907—a late date even by Russian standards.[101] By resorting to the bond market the city was able to raise 9·5 million roubles to extend the electrified lines and by 1914 the main routes were

[98] 'Po Proyektu Tsentral'noy Stantsii Dlya Zagorodnykh Zheleznykh-Dorog i Gorodskoy Opoyasyvayushchey Zheleznoy Dorogi', *ISPGD*, no. 21 (1893), pp. 8–45.
[99] The rising price of smokeless coal which had to be used according to municipal regulation was also making operations more costly. 'Ob Uvelichenii Platy za Proyezd na Parokhodakh po Yekaterininskomu Kanalu', *ISPGD*, no. 9 (1889), pp. 724–8.
[100] 'Po Voprosu o Vykupe Predpriyatiya Aktsionernago Obshchestva Konno-Zheleznykh Dorog', *ISPGD*, no. 10 (1897), p. 577.
[101] We are ignoring the electric trams used on routes across the Bol'shaya Neva during the winter months, a service which was introduced in the late 1890s.

all electrified.[102] The purchase of trams, which in 1913 numbered over 600, entailed enormous expenditure and thus the original plan to expand trackage had to be revised. Consequently, the addition of approximately eighty kilometres of new lines in this first stage of redevelopment was scarcely half of that originally envisioned. By 1914 there was an extensive network of electric-tram routes, but the horse-tram still served many city areas, especially on the periphery ⟨*see* map 46⟩. And perhaps this was the intention, for it was noted a few years later that St Petersburg was one of the last cities in the Empire to obtain a tram network because 'the house-owners feared that electric trams would mean an exodus to the suburbs and a lowering of rents.'[103]

The conversion to electric traction proved an immediate success. The overnight importance of the trams may be judged from the fact that they carried eighty-three of the 148 million passengers in 1908. The next year electric trams alone conveyed 162 million people, with predictable consequences for other forms of public transport. The rapid escalation in traffic between 1908 and 1913 was the result of a complex of socioeconomic, as well as technological, changes, but the improved service owing to the increase in rolling stock and the somewhat greater average speed of the tram was of undoubted importance.[104] Including the roughly twenty million passengers of the privately owned Nevskaya Prigorodnaya Horse Railroad Company, nearly 300 million people rode on the horse car, steam railway or electric tram in 1912—an average of 150 trips per inhabitant—and by 1914 gross receipts were over seventeen million roubles, with net profits to the city of over five million.[105] Despite the impressive rate of growth in tram traffic and profits, all in all public street transport in St Petersburg was comparatively retarded. On the basis of any set of criteria fewer people used public transport than in most European cities, and major American ones.

Freight movement had not benefited from the application of a new technology in the same way as the travelling public had during the decades since the sixties, and the arrival of a few trucks had served more to underscore the technological backwardness of the traditional

---

[102] PRO Foreign Office File 181 927, *Commercial Papers*, no. 171, 1909.

[103] Williams, *Russia*, p. 419.

[104] In 1912 the average speed of the tram was estimated to be eleven kilometres per hour. Horse-car speeds were seldom over seven kilometres per hour. 'Gorodskiya Zheleznyya-Dorogi v Peterburge i Moskve', *ISPGD*, no. 26 (1914), p. 2967.

[105] N. N. Petrov, 'Gorodskoye Upravleniye i Gorodskoye Khozyaystvo Peterburga', *Och.IL* (1957), vol. II, p. 908.

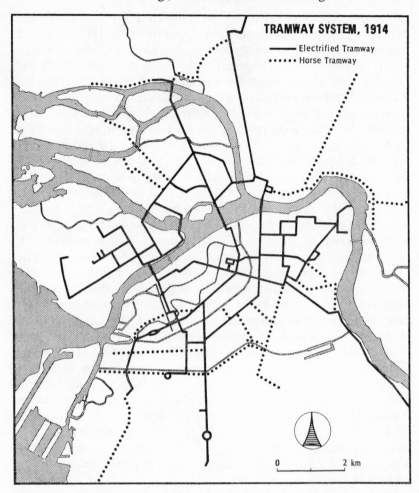

MAP 46. *Tramway system, 1914*

modes of transport than to expedite intra-urban goods movement. The innovation of the 1860s involving the horse-tram and street railway was thwarted, as we have seen, by municipal regulations which banned daytime use of the system for freight haulage. The thinking behind this centred on street congestion. By allowing the street railway to be used for goods movement, so the argument ran, the busiest thoroughfares which it used would become hopelessly choked. Certainly the street tramcar did accommodate some freight movement between 11 p.m. and 9 a.m., but the feared congestion occurred in any event. In 1876, hardly ten years after the City Council resolution commercial, waggons were banned from several streets and bridges, including the Nevskiy Prospect and Bol'shaya Morskaya Street.[106] With the main port located on Vasil'yevskiy Island until the mid-eighties, and the Nikolayevskiy railway station situated on the other side of the central business district, the traffic situation became annually worse. The relocation of the port on Gutuyevskiy Island in the mid-eighties served to redirect a substantial volume of through traffic, but this only relieved the pressure temporarily. The city itself was a huge consumer and its internal freight movement had to get along without the benefits of modern technology. Among the more conspicuous deficiencies was the absence of a ring railway system to integrate the port facilities, the rail terminals and the major commercial and industrial areas.

By the turn of the century internal goods haulage had become a serious problem demanding attention: 'The traffic in the streets outside the Nevsky', it was said, 'is frequently interrupted by processions of heavy drays laden with every description of goods, and there are far more of these drays in the streets than there would be if the big railway stations at various points on the fringe of the city were connected by something in the nature of a circular line.'[107] The response of municipal authorities was typically inadequate. In 1903, 1908, and 1911, the situation was reviewed and more streets were added to the ever growing list of those where all freight haulage vehicles were either prohibited entirely or for specific hours, usually from 8 a.m. until 6 p.m.[108] The resultant escalation in costs of haulage within the city was not something to which city officials were totally oblivious, but to the industrialists the situation was becoming intolerable. In 1912 the owners of the Kenig sugar refinery were complaining bitterly of having to pay six kopeks per *pud* to have beet sugar hauled by road from Gutuyevskiy port to their factory in Vyborgskaya borough. As they pointed out, this tariff was nearly a third of the charge to send beet sugar by sea from Odessa to St Petersburg.[109] Even municipal authorities were willing to acknowledge that hauling freight through the city

---

[106] The ban was operative between 11 a.m. and 6 p.m. 'Ob Uporyadochenii Lomovogo i Avtomobil'no-Gruzovogo Dvizheniya po Ulitsam Stolitsy', *ISPGD*, no. 46 (1913), p. 1681.
[107] Williams, *Russia*, p. 418.
[108] 'Ob Uporyadochenii Lomovogo i Avtomobil'no-Gruzovogo Dvizheniya', pp. 1681–2.
[109] N. M. Orlov, *S. Peterburgskiy Sakhago-Rafinadnyy Zavod L. E. Kenig-Nasledniki* (1913), p. 6.

was as expensive as shipping it by railway from St Petersburg to Yekaterinoslav, a distance of over 2,000 kilometers.[110] After years of futile complaint to the City Council and other government bodies, a group of industrialists, despairing of any assistance, finally took it upon themselves to raise the necessary capital to construct a ring line connecting the four southern terminals with the Finlyandskaya railroad in Vyborgskaya.[111] Still, the important industrial and commercial districts on Vasil'yevskiy and Peterburgskiy Islands were to remain without rail service.

By default, the bulk of goods haulage to and from most firms in the capital fell to the ubiquitous *lomovyy* or commercial waggon. As was caustically observed at the time, 'leaving out of account a few commercial motor vans and lorries recently introduced, the conveyances still widely used for the carriage of heavy goods are of the most nondescript and antediluvian kind.'[112] From the available evidence, there does not appear to have been a shortage of these vehicles. Like the *droshky*, under-utilization was general and therefore it is quite conceivable that the upsurge in freight traffic as a corollary of the intensive industrialization after 1900, and especially after 1908, was accommodated by the existing supply ⟨*see* table 27⟩.

4 THE JOURNEY TO WORK

We have seen that after 1900 the tempo of development and the use made of the city's street-car system quickened considerably. Although the long-standing objective of extending the tram network into the suburbs had been fulfilled by the time of the Great War, it was in some respects a hollow victory. Many peripheral lines remained the province of the horse-car and this, combined with a limited and expensive commuter service on the steam railway, meant that daily trips from suburban areas had not been speeded up. Thus, even though passenger traffic counts had swollen enormously since the sixties, the hypothesis that there would be a dissolution of the traditional bond between place of work and place of residence cannot be taken for granted for any of the three groups previously considered—managerial and professional, workshop-owners and artisans, and factory workers.

The shortage of inexpensive housing suitable for factory workers

[110] 'Ob Organizatsii Gruzovogo Dvizheniya', p. 1714.
[111] The sum involved was sixty-two million roubles. 'K Proyektu Okruzhnoy Dorogi v S.P., p. 3. The line was operating by the time of the Great War.
[112] G. Dobson, *St Petersburg* (London, 1910), p. 131.

was a perennial fact of life in the capital from the mid-nineteenth century. By the early 1900s the scarcity had reached a critical stage and was reflected in the big jump in rent. Private and municipal schemes to ameliorate housing conditions for factory and other low-income workers generally had one element in common, that they involved the use of public transport. And, as we shall see, for this very reason, they were unsuccessful. A number of factors contributed to this situation among which the limited and, because of progressive inflation, diminishing disposable income, and the long working day were significant. The journey to work, of course, cannot be seen without reference to available time and money. As we have already discussed the working day of factory employees, we need only put into rough perspective the cost of public transport.

On the eve of the Great War the official tariff for a *droshky* was twenty kopeks for the first quarter of an hour, and five kopeks for each additional five minutes up to three quarters of an hour. Night-time fares, that is from 12 a.m. until 7 a.m., started at thirty kopeks for a quarter of an hour and increased similarly. For a trip of an hour's duration daytime and night-time fares were sixty and ninety kopeks respectively. Assuming that the official minimum speed of ten kilometres per hour was maintained, then the minimum fare would entitle the passenger to a journey of 2·5 kilometres in distance. Given the congestion which was common to the thoroughfares of the central city, this assumption is certainly open to question. In fact, sixty kopeks is suggested as the appropriate fare for a trip of just this distance along the Nevskiy Prospect.[113] To traverse the city would involve a charge of considerably more than a rouble. Hiring any of the other types of horse-drawn vehicles, such as the *likhach*, the *kareta*, or in winter the *troyka*, was substantially more costly. At twenty kopeks per kilometre a motorized taxi was no less an expensive proposition.[114]

By comparison with vehicles hired for personal use, fares on the various forms of public transport appear more attractive. Steamboat tariffs were usually around five kopeks, and at two kopeks by day, or even three kopeks at night, the shuttle ferry service across the major arteries of the Bol'shaya Neva system provided cheap, convenient journeys.[115] Omnibus fares varied according to distance. In the

[113] Karl Baedeker, *Russia with Teheran, Port Arthur, and Peking* (London, 1914), p. 90.
[114] Baedeker, *Russia*, p. 91.
[115] 'Ob Otdache v Arendnoye Soderzhaniye s Navigatsii 1896 Goda Yalichnykh i Parokhodnykh Perevoz Cherez R. Bol'shuyu Nevu v Okhtenskoy Perevoznoy Distantsii', *ISPGD*, no. 25 (1895), p. 1314.

central city, they ranged between four and six kopeks, while ten kopeks was the usual sum on the suburban routes.[116] Depending on the seat, whether 'imperial' (roof-top) and exposed, or inside, first-stage horse car fares at four and six kopeks were competitive. So too were tram tariffs. At five kopeks, second-class tickets provided the most rapid journey for the money. On the trams, distances were staged so that to travel across the city in any direction entailed a multi-stage fare structure. For example, to travel from the Finlyandskiy to the Baltiskiy railway stations, a distance of roughly ten kilometres as the crow flies, included three stages and would therefore cost fifteen kopeks. The introduction of the tram had made journeys less time-consuming, but as always this was a relative improvement. A trip from the Smol'nyy region (near the bridge across the Bol'shaya Neva River to the right bank suburb of Okhta) to Konno-Gvardeyskiy Boulevard, a distance of under six kilometres, required several transfers and over one hour.[117] Intra-urban travel was easier but lengthy and we can reasonably assume that for the majority of workers it remained prohibitively expensive. Indeed, one budget study revealed that as late as 1908 expenditures on tram fares were regarded as a luxury (along with bath-houses and postage) and amounted to fourteen kopeks in one month. At prevailing fares this represented less than four single-stage trips on the horse-tram.[118] How this situation affected the journey to work cannot be determined conclusively. Although scanty, contemporary observations do provide a clue as to the general nature of the spatial tie between workplace and residence of factory workers.

During the sixties the housing of workers in company-owned premises was on the wane. At that time a growing labour supply and the seemingly imminent implementation of legislation which would necessitate government supervision and control of such facilities were sufficient to dissuade many owners from maintaining an increasingly expensive tradition. V. Svyatlovskiy's study of workers' housing suggests that, by the nineties, one fifth of all Russian factory workers still lived on company-owned premises.[119] In the cities, especially the larger ones, the pressures to house a lower percentage were great. Thus,

---

[116] *Spravka k Voprosu ob Uluchshenii Sposobov Pereovizheniya Naseleniya* (1901), p. 10.

[117] Nikitin, *Zadachi Peterburga*, p. 74.

[118] Budget data from a survey by Davidovich, cited by S. G. Strumilin, 'O Zarabotnaya Plata i Proizvoditel'nost' Truda', *Na Novykh Putyakh. Itogi Novoy Ekonomicheskoy Politiki 1921–1922 gg.* (Moscow, 1923), vol. III, p. 105; also by M. T. Florinsky, *The End of the Russian Empire* (New York, 1961), p. 153.

[119] V. V. Svyatlovskiy, *Zhilishchnyy Vopros v Rossii* (1902), part 4, p. 245.

in an exhaustive study of workers' conditions in St Petersburg several years later it was remarked that the practice was quite uncommon. Most of the remaining factory-owned accommodation was to be found in the outlying areas, in Shlissel'burg and along the Peter-gofskoye Highway, for instance, at the Putilov metal-working factory.[120] Factories which had earlier provided such facilities had either cut back drastically on numbers or had ceased to do so entirely by 1914. By then factory-owners were very aware that such housing also served as an ideal environment for radicals to organize and educate workers. Not a few owners were worried about aiding and abetting such a process. In short, the great majority of factory workers looked after their own housing needs. But, we may ask, where did they live in relation to their place of work?

An article in the *Torgovo-Promyshlennaya Gazeta* (Trade-Industry Newspaper) of 1912 provides some insight into the prevailing percep-tions of distance within the city. At this late date it could be stated with an air of surprise that in the workers' district of Gavan, on the western extremity of Vasil'yevskiy Island, were to be found employees 'from distant (*otdalennykh*) factories . . . the Laferm [tobacco] factory on Tenth Line, the Bekker [musical instrument] factory on Eighth Line . . . and even one close to the Tuchkov bridge'.[121] In the latter instance, the plant was less than three kilometres direct distance from Gavan and would have involved an unhurried half hour journey on foot. The comments of Dr M. I. Pokrovskaya, in one of the few studies dealing in some depth with workers' housing, are also of particular interest, for her investigation of 1902 related to housing in both the central and peripheral parts of the city, thereby providing a represent-ative cross-section of conditions. On the subject of work-residence ties, she described how 'Each factory and each plant serves as a centre for increased cost of habitation', a situation which 'is understandable [since] the greatest part of the workers' day is spent in the factory . . . [thus they] . . . attempt to reside close to the place where they work so that little time is spent walking and so that they have the possibility of eating at home.'[122] In short, whether the reference to the relationship

[120] S. Bernshteyn-Kogan, *Chislennost', Sostav i Polozheniye Peterburgskikh Rabochikh* (1910), p. 56.

[121] B. Kalinsky, 'Bor'ba s Zhilishchnoy Nuzhdoy v S Peterburge', *Torgovo-Promyshlen-naya Gazeta*, no. 283 (1912), p. 1.

[122] M. I. Pokrovskaya, *Po Podvalam, Cherdakam i Uglovym Kvartiram Peterburga* (1903), pp. 1, 33.

emanates from City Council discussions,[123] from memoirs,[124] or from sanitary and factory inspections,[125] the message is the same—there was no extended journey to work and, in fact, prevailing circumstances were dictating just the opposite.

Notwithstanding a paucity of concrete data, the foregoing discussion does allow some tentative comments on the journey to work after the turn of the century. Despite an acute housing shortage, lack of time and money restricted the search for accommodation to an area within walking distance of the place of employment. Thus, a link between the improvement of public transport, the large increase in passenger traffic, and the enhanced mobility of factory workers is at best tenuous. No doubt some factory workers, especially the most highly skilled and therefore most highly paid, took the tram to work regularly. But for the average factory worker, technological innovations were without direct benefit and the journey to work remained pedestrian and, by implication, mobility remained limited. If we can accept the limited mobility of the average worker in St Petersburg after the turn of the century as a fact, then this would add further support to the earlier conclusion that the industrial growth in the northern boroughs, which lacked the locational advantage of access to transport network, was partly in response to the need to keep close to an adequate labour supply. But it was not just the decentralization of factories which was thwarted by limited mobility, for clearly its ramifications permeated the whole spectrum of urban activities. We shall consider some of these in a later chapter.

For the 1860s we saw that in the case of workshop-owners and artisans, place of work and place of residence were predominantly the same, an observation which was consistent with one of the original exploratory hypotheses. Such data as we have for this group, as well as for the managerial and professional classes, permit us to evaluate more precisely the changes in the relationship between the development of public transport and mobility after the turn of the century.

If we take the work-residence relations of blacksmith workshop-owners and artisans, we see from table 29 that in 1912 only a handful of artisans separated home and workplace, fifteen out of 207, or 7 per cent. Moreover, most journeys to work were only a few hundred metres

[123] 'O Postroyke Gorodskikh Domov', *ISPGD*, no. 32 (1910), p. 1859.
[124] *Ocherk Peterburgskago Rabochago Dvizheniya 90-kh Godov po Lichnym Vospominaniyam* (London, 1902), p. 45.
[125] For related discussion, see Svyatlovskiy, *Zhilishchnyy Vopros*, pp. 161-6, 245-76.

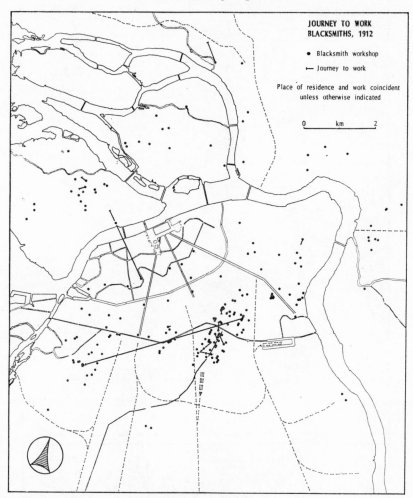

**JOURNEY TO WORK
BLACKSMITHS, 1912**

● Blacksmith workshop

⊢ Journey to work

Place of residence and work coincident
unless otherwise indicated

0   km   2

MAP 47. *Journey to work, blacksmiths, 1912*

⟨*see* map 47⟩. The overall proximity is reflected in the mean journey to work of 0·8 kilometres. A similar relationship obtains in the case of gold and jewellery workshops ⟨*see* map 48⟩. Here only ten out of 134 artisans had residences separated from workplace, again only 7 per cent. The journey to work was short in all instances, averaging 0·7 kilometres, something less in fact than the equivalent figure of 1867. The manufacture and retail sale of gold and jewellery wares differed

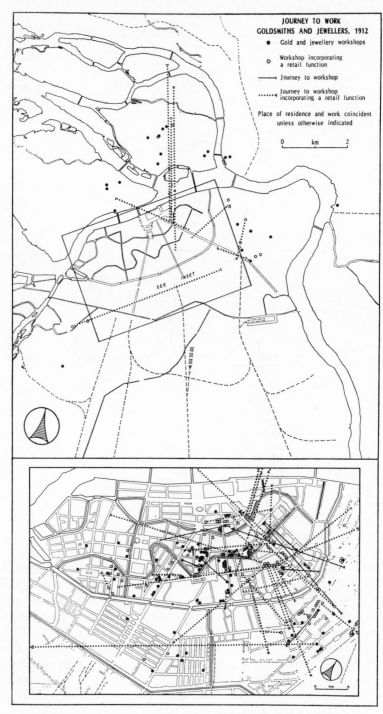

MAP 48. *Journey to work, goldsmiths and jewellers, 1912*

significantly from the simple workshop in respect of work-residence relations. In 1912, over a third of the owner-artisans had residence distinct form workplace, compared with 7 per cent of the artisans in simple workshops. Moreover, the mean journey to work had increased since 1867 from 0·9 to 1·4 kilometres. The retail sale of confectioneries was along the same lines as that for gold and jewellery ⟨*see* map 43⟩. Both the occurrence of separation and mean distance commuted increased, 5·1 to 17·5 per cent, and 1·1 to 1·7 kilometres respectively. The other category involving direct retail sales to the public, bakeries, revealed a journey-to-work pattern similar to that of blacksmiths. A random sample of fifty establishments out of the over 700 listed in the directory revealed only four cases where place of work and residence were different. The mean distance separating the two was 1·1 kilometres. Thus, of the categories of workshops examined, the less specialized and spatially ubiquitous blacksmiths and bakeries again revealed a lower incidence of journeys to work. For all categories, there seems to be little indication of a fundamental change in work-residence relations since 1867; it was largely a matter of degree, for the overwhelming majority 'lived at work', and commuting tended to be mainly confined to the central city.

The available data suggest that in 1867 only 18 per cent of factory-owners made a journey to work. For 1912 all known relations for the two industrial groups have again been analysed and mapped ⟨*see* maps 49 and 50⟩. While it is readily apparent from an examination of table 29 that the frequency of separation had increased for both the metal-working and food and tobacco product categories (from about 18 to 42 per cent), the actual relative shares and mean distances travelled are very revealing. For the metal-working industries, the instance of separation had risen from 24 to 40 per cent only, and the mean distance commuted had declined from 2·6 to 2·0 kilometres. Owners of food and tobacco product plants were more inclined to separate home and workplace but did not yet constitute a majority. The mean distance travelled, 1·8 kilometres, was unchanged from 1867. It is evident from this analysis that long jouneys to work were exceptional, but the overall picture is sharpened when distance frequencies are examined. For each category more than a third of the trips were one kilo-metre or less; if these are aggregated with the 132 coincident work-residence relations, then almost three quarters of all known work-residence relations for the two groups of owners were less than a kilometre.

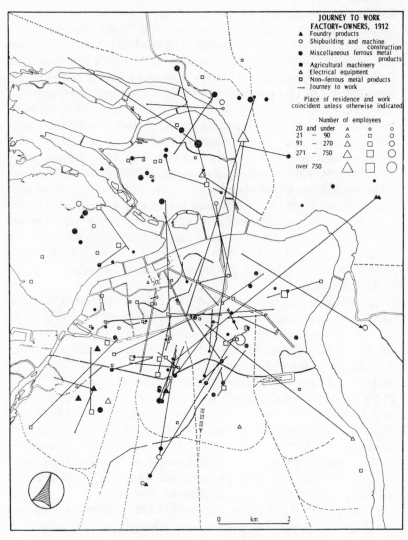

MAP 49. *Journey to work, factory-owners, 1912–I*

288

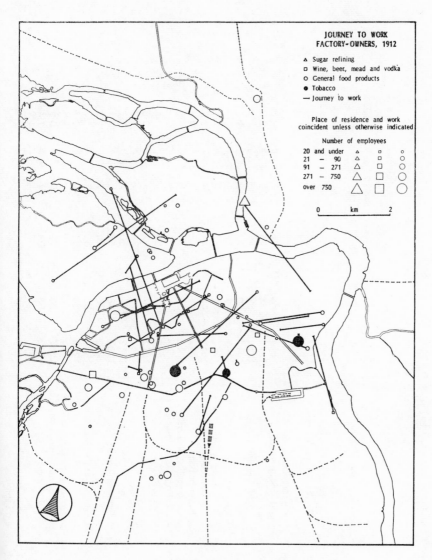

MAP 50. *Journey to work, factory-owners, 1912–II*

289

TABLE 29. *Work-residence relations, 1867 and 1912*

Occupational group	Year	Total no. of establishments	No. of known work-residence relations	Non-coincident work-residence relations		Mean distance travelled to work*
				No.	%	Kms
A Managerial and professional						
1 Bank-owners or presidents	1867	24	21	9	42·9	1·0
	1912	50	76	72	94·7	1·9
2 Factory-owners						
(a) Metal-working	1867	64	46	11	23·9	2·6
	1912	284	154	62	40·2	2·0
(b) Food and tobacco	1867	59	48	6	12·5	1·8
	1912	100	73	33	45·2	1·8
3 Brokers	1867	127	126	5	3·9	1·0
	1912	83	83	10	12·0	1·1
Stockbrokers	1912	44	44	4	9·1	2·2
Grain brokers	1912	9	9	3	33·3	0·3
Commodity brokers	1912	30	30	3	10·0	0·5
B Workshop-owner and artisan						
1 Blacksmiths	1867	233	233	—	—	—
	1912	207	207	15	7·2	0·8
2 Bakers	1867	278	278	4	1·4	2·2
	1912	**714	50	4	8·0	1·1
3 Confectioners	1867	58	58	3	5·1	1·1
	1912	40	40	7	17·5	1·7
4 Goldsmiths and jewellers	1867	233	233	3	1·3	1·2
	1912	134	134	10	7·5	0·7
5 Goldsmiths and jewellers incorporating a retail function	1867	79	79	5	6·3	0·9
	1912	98	98	34	34·6	1·4

* Calculated on the basis of straight line distance between work-place and residence.
** A 7 per cent random sample.

Journey-to-work distances were not a function of plant size; indeed, the maps indicate that the longest trips undertaken by factory-owners were often to the smallest establishments.[126] The pattern of movement is also of interest. On the whole, daily travel was dominated by journeys within the area bounded by the Bol'shaya Neva River and the Obvodnyy Canal, long since built up and densely settled. In terms of residence, the pull of this part of the city was very strong, for journeys out to the periphery from the core, rather than the opposite, were characteristic in 1912. With few exceptions, all trips occurred between points readily served by tram.

The journey to work of brokers in 1912 had altered very little from the situation nearly half a century earlier. Most continued to combine home with office (88 per cent), and for those who did travel daily to a separate place of business the mean distance of 1·1 kilometres was to all intents and purposes unchanged from the 1867 figure of one kilometre ⟨*see* table 29 and map 51⟩. When the specialized brokerage functions which had evolved during this time are considered separately, some notable variations are apparent.

The domestic and business activity patterns of grain brokers were clearly influenced by the location of the Grain Exchange. For the three who travelled daily to the office, the mean distance covered was 0·3 kilometres. With one slight exception, all offices were within a radius of one kilometre of the Exchange. Commodity brokers, who dealt on both the Grain and the Stock Exchanges, were also drawn to the vicinity of the Exchanges for office and residential location. It is clear from map 51, however, that the localization was less pronounced. The mean distance travelled by the three commodity brokers actually journeying to the office was short, 0·5 kilometres. Stockbrokers were the least constrained, spatially, in establishing offices. These were to be found throughout the heavily built-up area of the city and even in the suburbs. Again, separation of home and office was infrequent (less than 10 per cent), but when commuting was required, mean distance travelled was considerably longer (2·2 kilometres).

The pattern of work-residence relations and the distances journeyed to work by brokers were little affected by nearly half a century of precipitous urban-industrial growth. With minor exceptions, the overall distribution of brokerage activity remained fairly constant. The

---

[126] A general relationship cannot be deduced because joint-stock, state and multiple ownership factories were excluded as in the analysis for the sixties. See reference 99, chapter 3, p. 128.

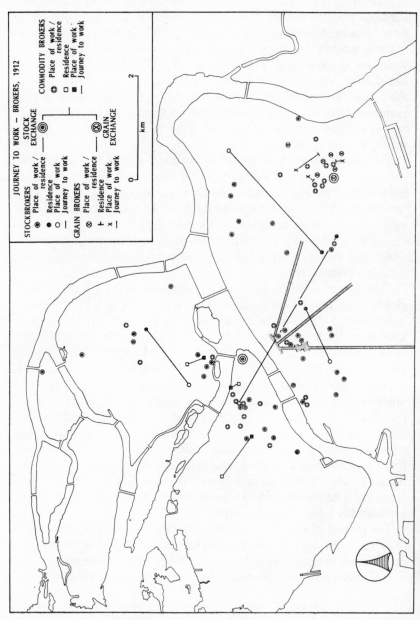

JOURNEY TO WORK — BROKERS, 1912

STOCKBROKERS   STOCK
⊕ Place of work /   EXCHANGE
   residence   ◎
● Residence
○ Place of work
— Journey to work

COMMODITY BROKERS
⊕ Place of work /
   residence
□ Residence
■ Place of work
— Journey to work

GRAIN BROKERS   GRAIN
⊗ Place of work /   EXCHANGE
   residence   ⊗
⊢ Residence
× Place of work
— Journey to work

0   2
km

creation of a specialized Grain Exchange spawned a discernible cluster of brokerage activity that constituted the main distributional change after 1867. Some dispersal was facilitated by the telephone, a convenience which most brokers possessed in 1912, since immediate contact with the commercial institutions of the city was possible irrespective of office location. But proximity to the Exchanges or to the main business area focused on the lower Nevskiy Prospect was palpably the overriding locational consideration for both home and office in 1912.

An analysis of the journey to work of bankers in 1912 reveals that their propensity in 1867 to reside at the same address as their place of business had all but disappeared during the intervening decades. In 1912 only four of the work-residence relations did not involve a journey to work. While both the incidence of separation and mean distance travelled had increased (the respective figures being 42·9 to 94·7 per cent and one to 1·9 kilometres), the general pattern of movement is of particular interest. The origin and destination of journeys were for the most part confined to the central city, notably the area bounded by the Bol'shaya Neva River and the Fontanka Canal ⟨*see* map 52⟩. The censuses show that many of the districts within this area, especially to the south and west, were predominantly working-class throughout the period under review. In only two cases were the trips from the suburbs to the centre—from Novaya Derevnaya and Aptekarskiy Island.[127]

While it has been established that work and residence showed a predictably marked proximity for the managerial and professional, as well as for the workshop-owner and artisan groups during the early part of the 1860 to 1914 period, the information we have for the end of this period does not show any weakening of the spatial tie between workplace and residence. Indeed, wherever it has been possible to identify specific journeys, the coincidence of the two has remained the rule in all but one of the categories examined. Bankers were the exception, but even in this case the mean distance separating home from office was less than two kilometres. Proximity to work after the turn of the century was still the rule for factory workers owing to the interplay of a variety of economic factors which precluded regular use of public transport. In short, the spatial tie between workplace and residence was

[127] Membership of boards of directors occasionally included a member whose home was in one of the outlying towns, such as Pavlovsk. The emphasis here is on those whose involvement in bank business is assumed to be on a day-to-day basis, that is, bank-owners or presidents.

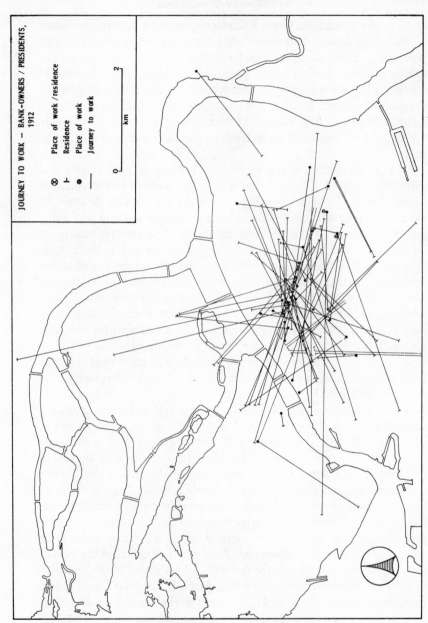

MAP 52. *Journey to work, bank-owners/presidents, 1912*

33 Russia remained a land of peasants down to the Great War. Whether going to the city for work or, like these two, for worship, peasant migrants were usually impoverished. The rapid growth of cities in the late nineteenth century clearly testified to the persistence of the peasantry in overcoming numerous institutional barriers to migration from the countryside. From a photograph in the Victoria and Albert Museum.

34 One of the first architectural monuments to greet the many peasants who walked into St Petersburg on the main highway from Moscow was the Moscow Triumphal Arch. Erected in 1834 according to the design of architect V. Stasov and sculptor B. Orlovskiy, it created an appropriately imperial entrance to the city. From a photograph in the Radio Times Hulton Picture Library.

35 Conditions of life and labour within the city were often extremely difficult. The cold, damp environment was only partially mitigated by communal street fires for those who laboured out of doors. From a photograph in the Victoria and Albert Museum.

36 Given that the majority of peasants lacked marketable skills, the most menial jobs were hotly contested. Street-cleaning required little training, but gave scarcely more than a bare subsistence living. From a photograph in the Victoria and Albert Museum.

37 By the turn of the nineteenth century, the plight of the indigent had reached crisis proportions. Thousands were homeless, even though regularly employed. For the unemployed or those without adequate income, the only alternatives were begging or returning to the countryside. Growing numbers chose begging. From a photograph in the National Museum of Finland, Helsinki.

38 St Petersburg had acquired most of the trappings of urbanism by the time of the Great War. But underlying the modern commercial economy was a peasant-dominated retail trade network. One way of adapting to city life followed by many peasants was to acquire the status of street trader. From a photograph in the Victoria and Albert Museum.

39 Despite efforts going back more than two centuries to remove wooden housing, St Petersburg in 1914 still had a large complement of such structures. Most, especially in the suburbs, were of the type shown here, and were overcrowded in the extreme. From a photograph in the Radio Times Hulton Picture Library.

40 Although this photograph of the square in front of the Nikolayevskiy railway station shows some evidence of modernization in the form of horse tramcars, little else had altered during the half century or so of rapid urban industrialization. Omnibuses, waggons and pedestrians continued to congest the square. From a photograph in the National Museum of Finland, Helsinki.

41 The climate, soil conditions, growing volume of vehicular traffic, and inadequate municipal finance ensured that most city roads were in a constant state of disrepair. Each summer, armies of workmen reset the cobblestones of the Nevskiy Prospect. Suburban roads were often left to alternate between extreme states, either a sea of mud or a mass of deep ruts baked into cement-like hardness. From L. Karbin, *Vidy Peterburg* (1895), no. 3.

42 The *Gostinyy Dvor*, designed by J. Vallin de la Mothe in the 1760s, was only one of several architectural masterpieces that adorned the Nevskiy Prospect. This photograph can be dated by the electric tramcars, for they did not appear on the capital's streets until 1907, which was late even by Russian standards. From a photograph in the National Museum of Finland, Helsinki.

43 Municipal authorities were responsible for maintaining the main thoroughfares and squares in the central city, like the *Teatral'naya Ploshchad'* or Theatre Square, portrayed here. In the background is the Mariinskiy Theatre. It replaced the Grand Theatre which was damaged by fire early in the nineteenth century. Few such architectural set pieces could be viewed in the early 1900s without factory chimneys obtruding into the scene. From a photograph in the National Museum of Finland, Helsinki.

44 The Nevskiy Prospect was a place to promenade, shop or sell. It drew enormous crowds, including tourists, from all classes of society. Note the horse-tram. From I. Bozheryanov, *Nevskiy Prospekt* (1904), no. 1.

45 During the summer months many parts of the central city seemed deserted. Travellers commonly remarked upon this feature and this view of the *Isaakiyevskaya Ploshchad'*, or square, seems to confirm that impression. From a photograph in the National Museum of Finland, Helsinki.

46 While the Great War changed the name of St Petersburg, industrialism and commercialism changed the face of the city. On occasion the changes were welcome additions architecturally, like the Singer building opposite the Kazan Cathedral on the Nevskiy Prospect. But even in this case, gaudy commercialism in the form of the roof-top advertisement was plain enough. From a picture postcard in the National Museum of Finland, Helsinki.

47 By the late nineteenth century there was ample evidence of the transformation of the urban economy. What happened to the Nevskiy Prospect was very much a barometer of the changes under way. This view around 1870 shows a number of the better shops with their verandahs extending over the pavement. At the Nikolayevskiy railway station the Prospect narrowed, and the quality of shop sharply graded off. From Élisée Reclus, *Nouvelle Géographie Universelle la Terre et les Hommes* (Paris, 1880), vol. V, facing p. 590.

48 By the early 1900s printed advertisements had largely superseded pictorial ones, a reflection both of the growing sophistication of commerce and the increasing literacy of the populace. From I. Bozheryanov, *Nevskiy Prospekt* (1904), no. 11.

49 Banking houses and credit institutions found that the Nevskiy Prospect was a good address. The larger organizations frequently owned buildings, or rented office space, on the lower reaches of the Prospect which was a more exclusive, higher-rent zone. From I. Bozheryanov, *Nevskiy Prospekt* (1904), no. 21.

50 Commerce, like industry, attracted foreign capital and foreign entrepreneurs. The advertisements in Russian, French and German are a witness to this intrusion, as are the firms' names. From I. Bozheryanov, *Nevskiy Prospekt* (1904), no. 19.

51, 52 Large-scale plants like these were found throughout the city, making their presence felt through the pollution of the air and drinking water, even if they were not themselves visible. From A. Shustov, *Sankt-Peterburgskoye Kupechestvo i Torgovo—Promyshlennyya Predpriyatiya Goroda S. Peterburga* (1903), appendix.

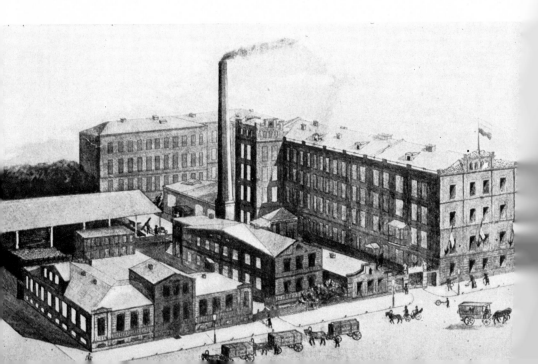

53 By the early 1900s only a few factories, such as the Kenig sugar plant, still provided workers' housing. Obliged to shift for themselves, workers were hindered in their search by long hours of work, low pay, and limited mobility. The decentralization of industry was effectively precluded during the years of rapid urban industrialization. From N. Orlov, *S. Peterburgskiye Sakhago-Rafinadnyy Zavod L.E. Kenig-Nasledniki* (1913), appendix.

54, 55 The industrial economy was transformed after 1890, but despite the advent of modern machine technology, out-dated labour-intensive practices were often to be found within the same, seemingly sophisticated industrial enterprise. From *Kartina Portreta i Vidy Zavedeniy Nobelya* (1912).

56 St Petersburg never lost its importance as a military centre. Soldiers and sailors in uniform added colour to city streets. The capital also boasted several military academies, such as the Artillery Academy pictured here. Note the canal boats laden with firewood in the foreground. From L. Karbin, *Vidy Peterburga* (1895), no. 9.

57 At the end of the nineteenth century the central part of the city still retained much of the grandeur of an earlier age when planning and architectural controls had been of some consequence. This view of the Moyka Canal near Voznesenskiy Prospect was representative of many, essentially eighteenth-century, vistas. From L. Karbin, *Vidy Peterburga* (1895), no. 11.

58, 59 The imperial munificence of a past age was unsullied by commerce and industry in several outlying towns. Perhaps the gentility that many people wished in vain to see in the capital itself, was best represented by Peterhof, the summer residence for the royal family created in the early eighteenth century. The palace and gardens were in sharp contrast to the slummy environment reserved for the bulk of St Petersburg's populace. From a photograph in the Victoria and Albert Museum.

МАЛЕНЬКІЕ НОЧЛЕЖНИКИ-ТРУЖЕНИКИ ОПЯТЬ, ЗАБЫТЫ,

напоминаю

САДОВАЯ, 86, С.-ПЕТЕРБУРГЪ. Телеф. 212—64.

ГАТЧИНА, НАБЕРЕЖНАЯ, 7. Телеф. 135.

Основанный мною въ 1891 году „1-й Ночлежно-работный домъ для безпріют-
ныхъ дѣтей муж. пола въ С.-Петербургѣ, САДОВАЯ, 86°, КРАЙНЕ НУЖДАЕТСЯ
ВЪ ПОЖЕРТВОВАНІЯХЪ, такъ какъ нужды его велики, капитала никакого нѣтъ и
90 дѣтей содержатся исключительно на постоянно **выпрашиваемыя мною** у добрыхъ
людей **лепты**.

Вслѣдствіе послѣднихъ событій благотворительность забыта, пожертвованія стали
тише, **а нужда не ждетъ!**

Не давайте много, **дайте только КРОХЪ**, не стѣснийтесь никакой малой лептой
(съ міру по ниткѣ — голому рубаха), дайте **только 20 коп** марками въ письмѣ, точно
сообщивъ свой адресъ, по которому получите тотчасъ же квитанцію и убѣдитесь, что
лепта ваша дошла по назначенію. АДРЕСЪ: ПЕТЕРБУРГЪ, САДОВАЯ, 86 — Аннѣ Эйсмонтъ,
ГАТЧИНА — НАБЕРЕЖНАЯ — 7, А. Т. Ивановой.

Если каждый, кто прочтетъ эти строки, отозвался бы на помощь моимъ ОБЕЗ-
ДОЛЕННЫМЪ МАЛЫШАМЪ, то сдѣлалъ бы великое дѣлое милосердія, ибъ **на триста**
такихъ воззваній откликаются всего **трое-четверо**, а многіе навѣрно думаютъ, что
Эйсмонтъ много набрала денегъ, если постоянно пишетъ.

Я чувствую, я знаю, что **я надоѣла** всѣмъ моими письмами, но что дѣлать, **не
для себя прошу, а для дѣтей**, чтобы ОНИ САМИ НЕ ПРОСИЛИ МИЛОСТЫНЮ.

Сжалься, помогите, у моихъ дѣтей никого нѣтъ, вспомните, что вы сдѣлаете это
во ИМЯ ХРИСТА.

(ЕВАНГ. ЛУКИ, гл. 12.— И ТАКЪ, ЕСЛИ И МАЛАГО СДѢЛАТЬ НЕ МОЖЕТЕ,
ЧТО ЗАБОТИТЕСЬ О ПРОЧЕМЪ").

Учредительница *А. Эйсмонтъ*

60 By the turn of the century the efforts of benevolent organizations and charities were failing to deal with the problem of urban poverty. Though the plight of orphans, for instance, was alleviated a little as a result of appeals such as this, most of them were left on the streets to fend for themselves. From a contemporary handbill.

61 At the few factories still providing workers' accommodation, beds, though not privacy, were available to a privileged minority. From N. Orlov, *S. Peterburgskiye Sakhago-Rafinadnyy Zavod L. E. Kenig-Nasledniki* (1913), appendix.

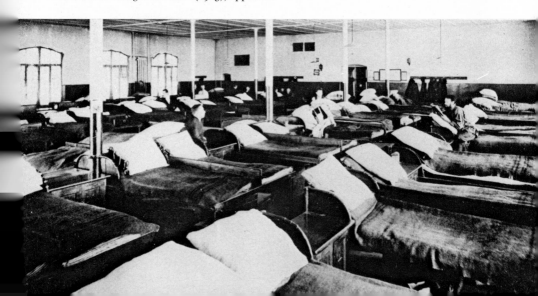

62 The *nochlezhnyy dom*, or night shelter, was a symbol of the failure of the municipality to look after the most basic needs of the populace during the trauma of rapid urban industrialization. Even its paltry facilities were at a premium as the housing crisis deepened, and to hold on to them it was necessary to have regular employment and aspirations above the abyss of still deeper poverty. From *Gorodskoye Delo*, no. 11–12 (1912), p. 698.

loosened somewhat during five decades of considerable technological and social change and rapid urban-industrial growth, but it was by no means unfastened.

In general, then, the hypothesized differences in work-residence relation according to occupational group have been confirmed. The managerial and professional and workshop-owner and artisan groups were assumed to represent the theoretical extremes of the journey to work. The data assembled here do lend some support to this view, which regards mobility as the prerogative of the economically privileged classes, but the argument has proved far from overwhelming. While bankers and factory-owners travelled longer distances more frequently than any constituent of the workshop-owner and artisan group, both the distance and pattern of movement contradicted any notion of a long-distance daily trip, especially from periphery to city centre. Brokers in 1912, as in 1867, generally combined home with office, but were also in a position to maintain close contact with the various Exchanges. Hence, the incidence of separation of home and office cannot be directly compared with the workshop-owner and artisan group. The latter group in general tended to combine home and workshop, and to travel short distances when separation occurred. It was only in the specialized instance of the owners of gold and jewellery workshops, which also involved a retail function, that divergence from the general pattern took place. So far as could be determined, the journey of factory workers fell somewhere between these two extremes.[128]

5 EXTERNAL RELATIONS

St Petersburg never regained the position which it held in the early nineteenth century when the bulk of Russia's foreign trade passed through the port. This was inevitable as places like Odessa and Riga captured some of the capital's trade hinterland, a development made possible by the coming of the railway. Indeed, the creation of a network of railways in European Russia accentuated the eccentric location of the capital. Yet we should not underestimate the role of the port, for although its relative position continued to wither in absolute terms it still commanded a sizable volume of trade ⟨*see* figure 14⟩. Traffic

[128] Much of the foregoing discussion of transport technology and journeys to work derives from my earlier papers. 'The Development of Public Transportation in St Petersburg, 1860–1914', *Journal of Transport History*, NS, II, no. 2 (September 1973), pp. 85–102; 'The Journey to Work in St Petersburg, 1860–1914', *Journal of Transport History*, NS, III, no. 2 (September 1974), pp. 214–33.

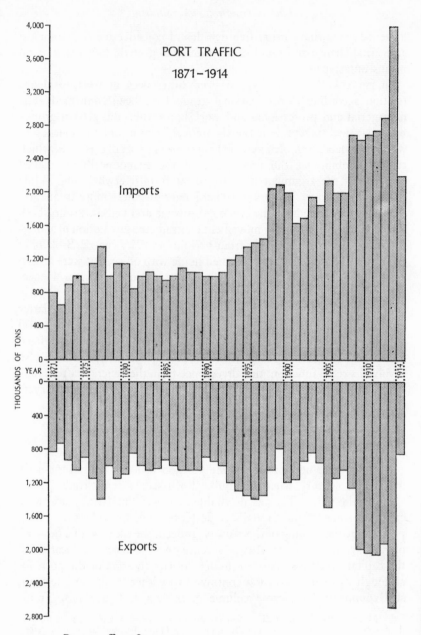

FIG. 14. *Port traffic, 1871–1914*

clearly fluctuated after the seventies; the Russo-Turkish War in the latter part of the decade and the depressions of the eighties and early 1900s took an obvious toll. Periods of economic boom are equally apparent. Merchants and traders in the capital were not unaware of the gains being made by competing ports. Rather than attend to some of the more fundamental problems in the operation of the port, however, they usually sought relief through various kinds of government assistance. One popular palliative was rail tariffs favouring St Petersburg among the Baltic ports.[129]

As we noted in an earlier chapter, one of the main handicaps in trading through the capital was the outmoded port itself. By the late seventies a government programme to modernize the port had been started. The first stage entailed constructing a sea canal from Kronshtadt to the capital. The second part of the scheme involved the creation of a new port on Gutuyevskiy Island at the western entrance to the Obvodnyy Canal. Intended to expedite movement of goods by allowing deep-draft vessels to proceed directly to St Petersburg, the canal was completed in 1883, though not officially opened until two years later. Problems had arisen because of the need to transfer goods at Kronshtadt to shallow-draft lighters. The cost involved was considerable. 'The expense of sending the cargo from that island [Kronshtadt on Kotlin Island to St Petersburg]', wrote the British Consul, Sir E. Thornton in 1884, 'is calculated at more than the freight from England to Cronstadt, without considering the loss of time which is generally about a fortnight, and sometimes much more.'[130]

Despite the obvious benefits of the scheme, the project was not fully endorsed by those merchants and traders pleading for preferential tariffs, a group we might justifiably assume would have everything to gain from the creation of a modern port. Sir E. Thornton explained why this was so:

> As is usually the case with regard to anything new, there is a good deal of opposition to it on the part of the St Petersburgh merchants, who are all interested more or less in the present mode of procedure. Some are owners of a number of lighters which are employed in bringing merchandize from and carrying grain and other produce to Cronstadt. Others are interested in large warehouses in which the produce is deposited in the winter to be

---

[129] J. Michell, 'Report', *BPP; Diplomatic and Consular Reports*, 1900, XCV. 771.
[130] Sir E. Thornton, 'Report', *BPP; Diplomatic and Consular Reports*, 1884, LXXXII. 53.

exported in the summer. But the principal objection to the use of the canal at present is that there are no warehouses yet built . . . so that neither goods imported, nor produce to be exported, can be stored there.

The government, who have been at the expense of the construction of the canal, are unwilling to incur the additional one of building warehouses, and merchants hesitate to prejudice their own vested interests by encouraging the new route.[131]

And so the port stood at the official opening in 1885 as a barren site, devoid of workers' housing and without even a bridge to permit 'direct communication for wheeled traffic between Port Goutouyeff and the town of St Petersburgh.'[132] In the course of the city's economic growth, half measures were seemingly the rule. By the turn of the century, Gutuyevskiy Island did possess all the trappings of a modern port complex save one, for technology had overtaken it and the canal could no longer accommodate the largest sea going vessels.[133] As the resultant transshipments once more rose in number, the capital's comparative disadvantages in unloading and loading times worsened still more.

Compared with the sixties, when St Petersburg-Kronshtadt port accounted for roughly a quarter of the value of Russian exports and 37 per cent of imports, the relative shares dropped by 1913 to less than 15 per cent of exports and under a fifth of imports. Despite the reduced share of foreign trade, the port was busy. From 1900 to 1913 trade turnover rose from 236 to 423 million roubles—an expansion of 83 per cent. Exports varied quite markedly one year to the next. This was due very largely to the overwhelming importance of the grain trade. Following a bountiful harvest it was not unusual for over a million tons to pass through the port. Despite a much greater volume of grain arriving in the city than during the sixties, a smaller proportion left. This was simply because more was required to feed the rapidly multiplying population. Grain continued to flow in greatest quantity to the traditional European market, Britain. Markets for exports in general remained the same, though the mix of commodities had shifted a little from the earlier overwhelming reliance on produce from forest and field. Metal goods especially had been added to products like

[131] Thornton, 'Report'.
[132] Sir E. Thornton, 'Report', *BPP*; *Diplomatic and Consular Reports*, 1884/85, LXXXI. 333.
[133] J. Michell, 'Report', *BPP*; *Diplomatic and Consular Reports*, 1902, CIX. 647.

canvas, hemp, glass and some textiles, but manufactured wares had not yet wrested from primary products the dominant position in foreign exchange earnings.

On the import side, there was little change from the 1860s that requires comment. Oil and coke poured into the capital at the pace required by industrialization. Unfabricated metals, chemicals, fibres—including raw cotton—and some wood products, together with fuels, had more than doubled in value from 1900 to 1913. Exact information is not available but a comparison of incoming and outgoing commodity flows suggests that most raw materials were destined for the city's factories. Manufactured goods stood second as a group after raw materials in terms of value. In 1913 over 450 million roubles worth passed through customs in the form of machinery, iron and steel products, textiles, luxury goods, a list similar to that of 1867. In short, the pattern and make-up of commodity flows had not substantially altered, but trade had intensified. As in the case of exports, Britain remained the major trading partner.

In 1910 over five million tons of freight descended upon the city via the Bol'shaya Neva River, but nearly two thirds of this comprised wood for fuel and lumber for construction. From time immemorial the vessels used were broken up and added to the fuel supply. This practice continued and reflected two features of water-borne shipment. First, the boats and barges represented minimal investments. Secondly, freight movement was to all intents and purposes one way. River shipment of grains accounted for just under a fifth of all water-borne cargoes in 1910, and in total, grain and wood products made up over 95 per cent of all incoming traffic. As an outlet for goods imported from abroad or produced in the city the Bol'shaya Neva River was insignificant. The relegation of the waterways to transporting high-volume, low-value commodities, which began with the arrival of the railway in the fifties, was virtually complete.

The railways were indisputably the lifeline of the capital. In 1913 five lines provided links with the rest of the Empire. In expanding the system of external relations, the demands occasioned by rapid urban industrialization were clearly instrumental. Grain, meat and dairy products from Siberia, oil from the Caucasus, iron and steel from the south Ukraine and the Urals, coal from the Ukraine—all of these long-distance commodity flows had been facilitated by an articulated rail network. As with the port and the waterways, the volume of incoming goods exceeded outgoing, in this instance by 150 per cent. Paper, iron and steel products, chemicals, rubber, yarn, and food and tobacco products were items shipped out by rail in greatest volume and reflected the growing export function of the city's industry. The principal railway for goods movement was, of course, the Nikolayevskaya, which linked the capital with the interior.[134]

We speculated earlier that the existence of the single largest market in the Empire could not fail to alter the surrounding rural economy radically. The argument was that agriculture would have benefited, but by the late sixties there was no evidence that this had occurred and, in fact, the city had produced the opposite effect. Peasants within easy reach of St Petersburg who opted for a cash income from city based employment weakened rather than intensified agriculture. There were a number of reasons for this development, but the impoverished physical environment and the stultifying effect of serfdom, formally abolished just a few years before, must be placed high on the list. Novelists and other creative writers certainly give the impression that half a century of urban industrialization had done little to improve the situation. 'A road winds from Kolpino', Andrey Biely has written, 'nothing could be gloomier. On the way to Petersburg, if you awaken and glance from a train window, you will see nothing but a dead landscape—not a village anywhere, not a human; the very earth looks like a corpse.'[135] Although overstated, the surrounding landscape was certainly barren in the sense that fences and fields had not uniformly replaced the forest and swamp. This is clear from map 53.

From less impressionistic sources we know that some predictable changes were occurring in the rural economy: land close to the city was becoming more valuable;[136] conversions to more intensive agricultural practices were each year more common; seasonal suburbanization in the form of summer *dachi* was claiming a larger share of the surrounding countryside.[137] Sporadic descriptions of market gardening, for example at Tsarskoye Selo, can be just as misleading as literary descriptions if not put into context. 'Tzárskoe', explained one observer, 'is surrounded by market gardens, where vegetables and fruits are raised in highly manured and excessively hilled-up beds. It sends tons of its products to the capital as well as to the local market.'[138] The fact of the matter

---

[134] Kruze, 'Transport, Torgovlya, Kredit', pp. 68–72.
[135] Andrey Biely, *St Petersburg* (New York, 1959), translated by John Cournas, p. 73.
[136] 'O Khode Pereotsenok Nedvizhimykh Imushchestv v Uyezdakh S. Peterburgskoy Gubernii', *ISPGD*, no. 14 (1910), pp. 490–96.
[137] Williams, *Russia*, p. 395.
[138] Hapgood, *Russian Rambles*, p. 113.

was that vegetables and orchard crops, though produced in sizable quantities within the *guberniya*, were not sufficient to supply very many of the city's needs. Intensive market-gardening, dairying and raising of beef and pork were still not well developed. Even poultry and eggs, where the investment was comparatively limited, were not drawn from the surrounding countryside in any quantity, but supplied by distant

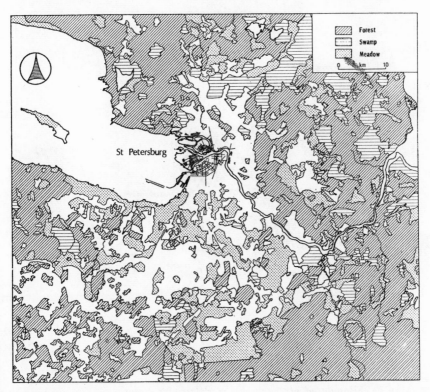

MAP 53. *The physical environment in the St Petersburg region*

villages strung out along the rail lines leading to the capital—as far afield, in fact, as Yaroslavl, Tver and Kostroma *gubernii*.[139] The lack of interest or ability in agricultural pursuits amongst peasant households close to the city is also reflected in livestock holdings. In St Petersburg *uyezd*, for instance, in the nineties more than half the

[139] M. I. Orlov, 'Yaichnaya Torgovlya S. Peterburga', *Vestnik Finansov, Promyshlennosti i Torgovli* no. 20 (1904), p. 285.

households did not own a horse and nearly half even a cow. Further away from the capital urban employment opportunities were less accessible and livestock holdings increased. During the winter months many villages in the surrounding countryside were almost deserted as peasants sought work in the city.[140] There were indeed more parallels than changes between the situation in the early 1900s and the 1860s.

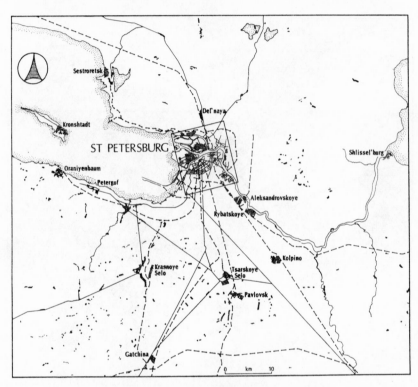

MAP 54. *Populated places in the St Petersburg region*

The drift to St Petersburg was impeded by very few intervening opportunities. The next largest town in 1910 was Kronshtadt, but it had not quite 68,000 persons, including a garrison of 15,700 and as map 54 indicates it was not the most accessible centre. Tsarskoye Selo, with a population of 30,000, was third largest. Like the smaller centres

---

[140] *Entsiklopedicheskiy Slovar'* (1900), vol. LVI, pp. 343–4; A. Bakhtiarov, *Bryukho Peterburga. Obshchestvenno-Fiziologicheskiye Ocherki* (1888), pp. 215–18.

of Gatchina, Oraniyenbaum, Pavlovsk and Krasnoye Selo, it was essentially a retreat for the upper classes and nobility and offered few jobs for the lower classes. Only Shlissel'burg, Kolpino and Narva among the remaining places of any size possessed any industrial or commercial tradition.[141] The attraction of the capital was clearly overwhelming.

We have, again, no way of determining how much money peasants from surrounding villages earned in St Petersburg. We can only assume from the weakly developed rural economy that prospective earnings were as enticing in the early 1900s as in the 1860s. One thing is certain, though: the nature of city life during the decades of rapid growth ensured an even larger number of foundlings and, through their maintenance, hundreds of thousands of roubles poured into the villages around the capital. The number of foundlings had necessitated a constant search for new homes and consequently the network of organized districts steadily widened, especially along the routes of the main railway lines. Although we lack data for the whole period, something of the dimensions of the foundling exodus is revealed by the following figures. By January 1876 the St Petersburg Foundling Home had placed 22,637 of them in 1,588 villages. The villages were organized into sixteen districts, taking up most of St Petersburg *guberniya* but also parts of Pskov and Novgorod.[142] Exactly five years later, 31,242, mostly illegitimate, foundlings had been absorbed by peasant households. Near the turn of the century roughly the same number of children were being maintained and at no small cost. Out of an operating budget of 1·3 million roubles in 1890, 545,000 were expended in supporting foundlings in peasant households.[143] Along with city related employments it is small wonder that peasants so readily gave up trying to wrest a living from the soil.

Thousands upon thousands of peasants were among those migrating to the city each year. As we have seen, in 1910 1·3 out of 1·9 million people in the city and suburbs were ascribed to the peasant class. In the 1910 census we are again provided with *guberniya*-of-origin data for this group, and this information permits a fairly realistic assessment of the pattern of migration.

In rural Russia high levels of illiteracy persisted down to the Great War. As a result we might expect that interpersonal communication and

[141] *Goroda Rossii, passim.*
[142] F. A. Tarapygin, *Materialy Dlya Istorii Imperatorskago S. Peterburgskago Vospitatel'-nago Doma* (1878), p. 93.
[143] *Entsiklopedicheskiy Slovar'* (1892), vol. XIII, p. 279.

diffusion of information would be influential in the decision to migrate.
If this were the case, the *gubernii* from which most peasants had
migrated in 1869 should also be the main ones in 1910. As in 1869 then,
Yaroslavl, Tver, St Petersburg, Novgorod and Kostroma may be
expected to stand out as origins. Previously we looked at the simple
influence of distance in migration, arguing that St Petersburg *guberniya*
would be the most important source of peasants and that the number of
migrants would diminish with distance. Given the threefold increase in
the city's population since 1869, we would expect a widening of the
migration field since it is normally assumed this is a function of city
size. We would also expect the share of female migrants from all
regions to increase and to predominate among short-distance migrations.

In 1910, Yaroslavl, Tver, St Petersburg, Novgorod and Kostroma
were no longer the top five sources of peasant migrants ⟨*see* table 30⟩.
Their share had dipped from two thirds to just under 45 per cent.
However, with the exception of the replacement of Moscow by
Kaluga the first ten *gubernii* remained the same. Although respective
positions varied, over two thirds of the migrant population in 1910 were
from the same regions as forty years before. From a comparison of
maps 24 ⟨*see* p. 143⟩ and 55 it appears that longer distance migrations
had increased by 1910, which also supports one of our suppositions. To
assess accurately the hypothesis that the number of migrants would

TABLE 30. *Principal* gubernii *of origin for peasant migrants resident in
the city, 1869–1910*

1869 Guberniya	Number of Peasants	1910 Guberniya	Number of Peasants
Yaroslavl	45,180	Tver	165,667
Tver	34,402	Yaroslavl	105,960
St Petersburg	27,012	Novgorod	69,540
Novgorod	18,254	Pskov	67,203
Kostroma	12,530	St Petersburg	59,355
Pskov	8,168	Ryazan	39,948
Ryazan	7,361	Vitebsk	36,895
Moscow	6,925	Kostroma	31,197
Smolensk	6,314	Smolensk	30,814
Vitebsk	5,476	Kaluga	17,588

Sources: Sanktpeterburg po Perepisi 10 Dekabrya 1869 (1872), part 1, p. 118;
Petrograd po Perepisi 15 Dekabrya 1910 Goda (1914), part 1, p. 290.

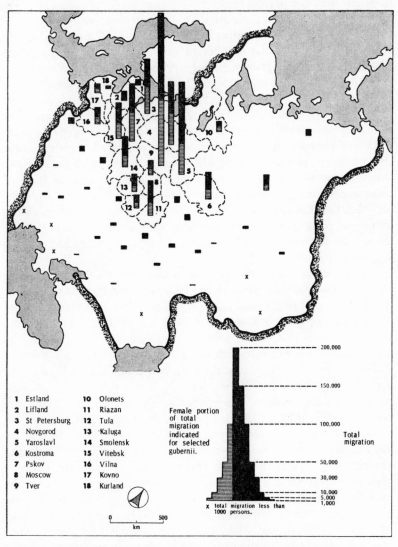

The legend within the map:

1 Estland   10 Olonets
2 Lifland   11 Riazan
3 St Petersburg   12 Tula
4 Novgorod   13 Kaluga
5 Yaroslavl   14 Smolensk
6 Kostroma   15 Vitebsk
7 Pskov   16 Vilna
8 Moscow   17 Kovno
9 Tver   18 Kurland

Female portion of total migration indicated for selected gubernii.

0   500
km

200,000
150,000
100,000
50,000
30,000
10,000
5,000
1,000

Total migration

x total migration less than 1000 persons.

MAP 55. *Peasants residing in St Petersburg by* guberniya *of origin, 1910*

305

diminish with distance from the capital we will again fit the *guberniya*-of-origin data to a gravity model.[144]

For 1910 the peasant population has been divided into two groups—resident in the city and resident in the suburbs.[145] The analysis of the relationship between the number of migrants and the reciprocal of distance, using the gravity model approach, yields coefficients of correlation of $+0.766$ and $+0.770$ (both statistically significant at the one per cent level). The first coefficient compares with an 1869 result of $+0.728$, which reveals a slightly stronger relationship. In an effort to clarify this relationship, distance and number of migrants were examined for selected five-year periods. For peasants living in the city, the results are as follows: those who migrated between 1896 and 1900, $+0.709$; for 1881–5, $+0.731$; for 1861–5, $+0.758$. On the basis of these coefficients a declining relationship through time is in evidence, although the difference is slight. The same analysis undertaken for the suburban peasant population produced very similar results. For the three time periods the coefficients were $+0.733$, $+0.743$ and $+0.766$ respectively.

While the coefficients do not help us to arrive at a firm conclusion, the distance exponent values in the equation help to shed some light on the matter. For the city population the values are as follows: for 1896–1900, 1.83; for 1881–5, 2.54; and for 1861–5, 2.55. The implication here is that, through time, longer distances were travelled by the migrants. For the suburban group the exponent values revealed a different trend. For 1896–1900 the value was 2.86, for 1881–5, 2.73 and for 1861–5, 2.10. Here the increasingly larger values through time suggest that the peasants were journeying shorter distances. This may well be explained by the fact that peasants from regions close to the city frequently spent part of the year working in or around the capital. Inasmuch as the police controls were less rigid in the suburbs than in the city it may well have been that itinerant migrants from nearby regions found temporary domicile there a practical proposition. At any rate, for the majority of peasants, that is, the 854,000 who lived in the city in 1910, there is support for the general argument that the number of migrants from distant places increased over time. And, overall, there was a strong inverse relationship between distance and the number of migrants.

[144] For discussion of technique, see A Note on Methods, pp. 432–3.
[145] Peasants born outside St Petersburg, but resident in the suburbs in 1910 numbered 132,249. Those living in the city totalled 854,004. It should also be reiterated that 325,000 peasants were born in the city.

We have also suggested that the share of female migrants would increase over time. In the sixties males were predominant among migrant peasants. By 1910, 42 per cent of the peasants who had migrated to the capital were female compared with about 30 per cent in 1869. This was less than the share of females in the total population (48 per cent). It was further argued that females tended to migrate shorter distances than males. This was as true in 1910 as it had been in 1869. Again using uniform distance units, the mean distances travelled by male and female peasants living in the city were 86·5 and 81·2 respectively. For the suburban group the mean was 74·6 for males and 73·2 for females.

Many questions arise as to the effects on the city itself of this half century of very rapid urban industrialization, but so far we have put them to one side. Having now examined some of the major structural and spatial shifts in the urban economy, we can direct our inquiry toward the urban aspects of the process.

6

The Twilight of the Imperial City

In spite of its external splendour, it has come to be known as the unhealthiest and most expensive capital in Europe.

G. Dobson, 1910[1]

Industrialization brought change to St Petersburg—there were factories and shops everywhere and streets choked with goods-laden waggons, while even the air and water testified to the transition from a court-administrative centre to an industrial-commercial complex. The image of grandeur was much tarnished by what had come about. However, this transition brought real and perceived opportunities for people to better themselves and from all corners of the Empire migrants, and especially peasants, were drawn to the city. Whether attracted by the prospect of comparatively high-paying jobs or driven by the hopelessness of rural poverty, the influx gathered momentum over the years. Between 1870 and 1914 about 1·5 million people were added to the population, bringing the total to around 2·2 million. But just over one million came after 1890 and nearly 350,000 after 1908. Clearly, the rate of population growth was tumultuous. But the basic issue is, what happened to the city during this period? To provide some answers we need to know something about who came, how they lived, what changes were necessary to accommodate them, whether change occurred by design or by default, and in this connection, how municipal government responded to the challenge of rapidly escalating numbers. Our objective is to try and comprehend something of the reality of the

[1] G. Dobson, *St Petersburg* (London, 1910), p. 84.

place and of life within it during the course of rapid urban industrialization.

I THE RISING TIDE

By the late 1860s a surge in the number of newcomers was already apparent. Although it is not possible to know for certain why this occurred, it is reasonable to suppose that the buoyant economy, the depressed state of agriculture, and the new demands placed on peasants by the Emancipation worked in concert to stimulate rural-urban migration. Of course, not all those coming were peasants. Representatives of all classes and groups were to be found among the human tide sweeping into the city. But peasants were the most visible constituent, and during the years from 1870 to 1914 they became increasingly conspicuous. In 1914 nearly three quarters of the capital's 2·2 million inhabitants were peasants; half a century before less than a third of the populace belonged to this class. Before outlining some of the ramifications of this peasant-dominated migration, we first need to come to grips with the dimensional and demographic features of population growth during this period. In contrast to the difficulties of charting population change and analysing basic demographic features in the pre-industrial period, there is a veritable embarrassment of riches in census data. Scientific enumeration of the population came late, but when the 1869 census was published its value was immediately recognized and thereafter a census was carried out on roughly a decennial basis.[2] It is this material which allows some insights into the urbanization process.

During the period from the mid-eighteenth to mid-nineteenth century, the city's population increased on average by less than 4,000 persons per year. Between 1850 and 1870, the average annual increase more than doubled.[3] What happened thereafter is made plain in figure 15. Growth was rapid during the economic surge of the 1870s, declining somewhat with the depression of the 1880s. Overall, annual increases averaged about 15,000 people. The economic boom of the nineties signalled the onset of growth not before experienced. Between 1890 and 1914 the capital's citizenry grew each year by an average of 50,000 inhabitants and this included a period of depression during the early 1900s when there was a perceptible brake on the rate of growth.

[2] See A Note on Sources, pp. 440–42.
[3] *Entsiklopedicheskiy Slovar'* (1900), vol. LVI pp. 312–13.

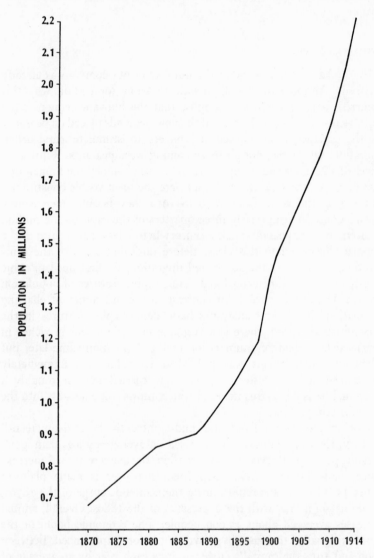

FIG. 15. *Population growth, 1870–1914*

310

Still, during the years of depression more than 40,000 were added to the population each year. With a resurgent economy after 1908, population growth rose rapidly and peaked in 1913 when the number of inhabitants increased by 107,000, nearly 22,000 more than the record set the preceding year.[4] By any standard of comparison the change was of considerable dimension.

In an earlier chapter it was observed that deaths customarily exceeded births; indeed, during the hundred-year period up to the mid-1860s the differential was in excess of 140,000.[5] The city therefore grew by immigration, not by natural means. For the first few years of rapid urban industrialization this trait continued ⟨*see* figure 16⟩. The turning point came in the early 1880s when the death-rate plummeted. Then, as now, the reasons for this development are not clear. Improvements in public sanitation, material progress of the working classes, and a greater awareness of the need for higher standards of personal hygiene have all been cited as possible explanations.[6] In any event, the declining death-rate was a relative thing. Epidemics continued to take a heavy toll on a regular basis, and overall the capital fared very badly when the death-rate was set against that prevailing in other European capitals. And, of course, within the city disease and death did not afflict all areas and all groups with equal severity, an important issue about which there will be more to say later. But whatever the explanation, from the mid-eighties on, births were ascendant and therefore helped to swell the numbers added to the population. From figure 16 it is apparent that during the half dozen years before the Great War, there was another major alteration in the demographic pattern. Again the reasons for this phenomenon are not immediately obvious. Arguments can be advanced concerning improved sanitary facilities and higher standards of public hygiene, but they do not sit comfortably in the light of recurrent epidemics. Moreover, the birth- and death-rates declined in consonance. Examination of the absolute number of births and deaths after 1908 reveals a nearly static situation, as each year they ran around 55,000 and 45,000 respectively.[7] It would appear that the 300,000 or so migrants who poured into the city during this period neither procreated nor died in sufficient numbers to change the established pattern. But what they did do because of their absolute numbers

[4] E. E. Kruze, D. G. Kutsentov, 'Naseleniya Peterburga', *Och.IL* (1956), vol. III, p. 105.
[5] G. I. Arkhangel'skiy, 'Zhizn' v Peterburge po Statisticheskim Dannym', *Arkhiv Sudebnoy Meditsiny i Obshchestvennoy Gigiyeny*, V (June 1869), p. 41.
[6] *Entsiklopedicheskiy Slovar'*, pp. 314–16.
[7] Kruze, 'Naseleniya Peterburga', p. 105.

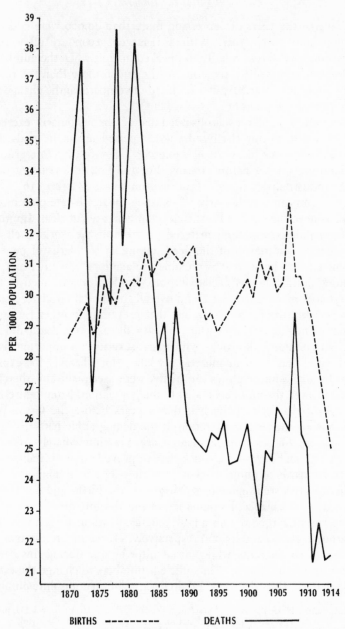

FIG. 16. *Birth- and death-rates, 1870–1914.*

was to reduce quite substantially the per capita statistics for births and deaths.

Traditionally, migrants were mostly men aged twenty to forty, and of the peasant class. In 1869 the composition of the city's population revealed just these characteristics. What is more, there was a substantial degree of transience. Ensuing urbanization modified some of these features. For instance, more people came to stay and female migration increased. By 1910 the share of females had risen from 43 to 48 per cent, a greater proportion of married workers lived with their families, and the percentage of the total population actually born in the city had similarily increased.[8] While all of this signalled a greater degree of stability, several things should be borne in mind. The population remained predominantly single, far more so than the average for the Empire as a whole and, among European capitals, St Petersburg had a particularly low per capita ratio of married inhabitants.[9] According to the 1910 census, 125,000, or roughly 10 per cent of the peasant population, were intending to return to the countryside the following summer, and there were many, many others who retained the option of retreating to the village in the event of difficult times.[10] Transience had not disappeared in the wake of urbanization.

The dimensions of the seasonal migration were not accurately established until the late 1880s, when summer and winter population counts were taken by the police. What they discovered was a huge difference in the number of residents. Between December 1888 and July 1889, for example, the population of the city dropped by 183,000.[11] This represented more than a fifth of the total number of inhabitants. As was noted earlier, the season to be seen in St Petersburg was the winter and all those who could manage to leave during the summer did so. Peasants departed for different reasons, but they helped to swell the exodus none the less. For the urban area as a whole, the net loss was diminished a little because there was an influx of seasonal workers, many of whom resided in the outlying suburbs. In the summer of 1889 they numbered 35,000, the majority being peasants who worked in the building trades, street repair and the like.[12] All told, the seasonal 'deficit' for the urban area this year was about 150,000. In the absence

[8] L. Kupriyanova, 'Rabochii Peterburga', *S. Peterburg i Yego Zhizn'* (1914), p. 185.
[9] Kupriyanova, 'Rabochii Peterburga', p. 186.
[10] *Petrograd po Perepisi 15 Dekabrya 1910 Goda* (1914), part 2, section 1, p. 290.
[11] See 'Ischisleniye Naseleniya S. Peterburga 15 Iyulya i 15 Dekabrya 1888 Goda', *Statisticheskiy Yezhegodnik S. Peterburga* (1888), pp. 7–59 and (1889), pp. 6–25.
[12] 'Ischisleniye Naseleniya' (1889), pp. 7, 51.

of later censuses of this type it is not possible to establish accurately if the seasonal migration continued to be of this scale. What little evidence there is, suggests it did. For instance, one knowledgeable observer reckoned that in the early 1900s roughly 100,000 peasants came to the city each summer.[13] And if the census of 1910 was at all accurate, then 125,000 peasants intended going back to the villages the following

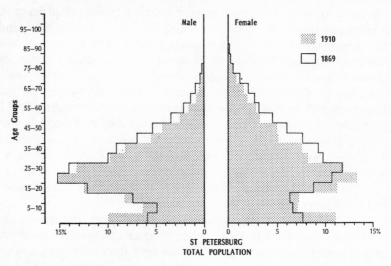

FIG. 17. *Demographic structure, 1910*

summer. For this class alone the turnover remained extremely large. Urban industrialization may have reduced seasonal migrations in relative terms, but social customs or economic necessity maintained the traditional rhythm in the comings and goings of the city's inhabitants.

Urbanization brought some demographic changes as figure 17 demonstrates. The distribution of males and females among the various age groups was less distorted as a result of an enhanced migration of women and to a lesser extent because of more births. The absolute increase in the number of families living in the city was in large measure responsible for the fact that the share of the population aged fifteen years or less went from 22 per cent in 1869 to 24 in 1910. But this was a fairly small change and the majority of inhabitants remained in the twenty to forty age-category. In 1910 they accounted for 45 per

[13] Dobson, *St Petersburg*, pp. 126–7.

cent of the population. This was essentially the same situation as half a century before, and resulted from the fact that the migrant population was so important a component of the population. In 1869 the pre-dominance of this age group also owed something to the large number of soldiers and sailors in the city, though in later years they comprised a smaller share.[14] While men and women had come more into line for the city as a whole, there were still some imbalances within it. The third ward of Spasskaya borough stood out because it was the only one more than 60 per cent male ⟨*see* map 56⟩. The borough had lost none of its earlier popularity as a destination for migrants since it was still very much characterized by street trading, workshops, markets and the like, which offered employment possibilities. In the first ward of Spasskaya borough and the first in Admiralteyskaya, 55 to 60 per cent of the population were male, the relatively high proportion of the latter being attributable to a large concentration of garrison forces.[15] Not unexpectedly, the dominantly working-class boroughs continued to have proportionally the largest number of males. Aleksandro-Nevskaya, Vyborgskaya, parts of Narvskaya, Vasil'yevskaya and Moskovskaya— all were in the 55 to 60 per cent range. Compared with the situation five decades earlier, however, these industrialized regions had slightly modified demographic structures because then females represented less, instead of slightly more, than two fifths of their populations.[16]

In the 1860s it had been the densely settled, central-city boroughs which had experienced the greatest absolute population growth rates, and many registered extremely high relative increases as well. The reasons were related to job opportunities, available housing and the limited mobility of the populace. It is clear from map 57 that between 1890 and 1910, when over 600,000 people were absorbed by the city, the pattern was reversed. Some of the inner-city boroughs appear not to have changed at all, though there were usually a few minor internal alterations. For instance, in Admiralteyskaya borough the heavily garrisoned first ward had 500 fewer residents, and the socially pres-tigious second ward 800 more, by 1910.[17] As in the sixties, the higher rents in the area had held the invasion of the lower classes to a minimum. Kazanskaya and Spasskaya between them accommodated fewer than 10,000 more people, but as space of any kind had long been at a premium

[14] Military personnel and families comprised 18 per cent of the 1869 city population and 3·2 in 1910.
[15] For related comment, see chapter 4, p. 168.
[16] See map 29, p. 169.
[17] *Petrograd po Perepisi*, part 1, section 1, p. 2.

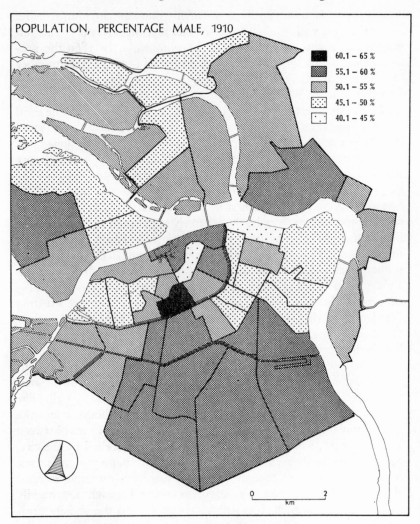

MAP 56. *Population, percentage male, 1910*

in these boroughs this could only mean far greater pressures on available housing. In both Narvskaya and Aleksandro-Nevskaya, where the bulk of the migrant population arriving by train was first disgorged, there had been sizable increases in population. Given their employment structures and the fact that rents there were relatively less than in the central city, this is not particularly unexpected. It was the northern,

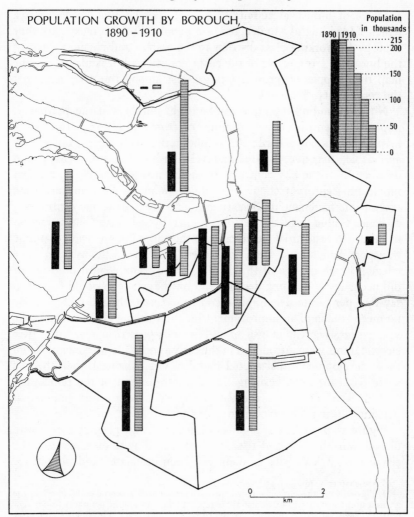

MAP 57. *Population growth by borough, 1890–1910*

isolated, island boroughs of Peterburgskaya and Vasil'yevskaya where gains had been the greatest and this, in some respects is surprising. Developments in Peterburgskaya were quite exceptional for in twenty years more than 135,000 people had poured in. This jump in numbers outstripped in absolute and relative terms that in any other borough of the city, a phenomenon which was earlier linked to its meteoric rise as

a centre of industrial activity.[18] Not far behind was Vasil'yevskaya
which added slightly under 100,000 people. For the most part they
went to the working-class districts in the eastern and northern parts of
the borough. Irrespective of the examples selected, it is plain from the
map that population growth was greatest among the peripheral, not
the central-city, boroughs.

Notwithstanding the rapid escalation in numbers at the periphery,
population densities clearly diminished from the centre outward ⟨*see*
map 58⟩. This is in accord with the notion that there exists a universally
applicable, negative, exponential relationship between density and
distance from the city centre.[19] It has been suggested elsewhere that
nineteenth-century technological advances in public transport were
responsible for changing density gradients by making the central city
more accessible from the periphery, thereby enhancing the attraction
of suburban residential locations.[20] In the 1860s the provision of public
transport had simply been too recent and too little used to have
effected much change of this kind.[21] Some technological innovations
did occur in the ensuing decades and on the whole it would be fair to
say that per capita disposable income increased, though there was by
no means much of an improvement for the working classes. And as we
saw earlier, per capita use of public transport rose markedly after
electric trams were introduced in the early 1900s.[22] If we conclude from
these developments that spatial mobility was enhanced, then there is
some basis for hypothesizing that decentralization of the population
should have occurred, thereby bringing about lower population
densities during the 1870 to 1914 period.

Figure 18 portrays the population density at the geographical centre
of each ward in 1869 and 1910, plotted according to distance from the
city centre.[23] A density gradient has been calculated and plotted for

[18] See chapter 5, pp. 250–53.
[19] Theoretically the notion is based on the premise that a central location offers the
greatest utility and therefore commands the highest rent. Toward the periphery land cost or
rent, and hence access to the core, are traded off for more space. For an elaboration, see
Colin Clark, 'Urban Population Densities', *Journal of the Royal Statistical Society*, series A,
CXIV (1951), pp. 490–96.
[20] Clark, 'Urban Population Densities', p. 495.
[21] See chapter 3, pp. 127–8.
[22] See chapter 5, pp. 276–7, 293–5.
[23] Densities have not been calculated by distance bands, but instead as Clark suggests as
an improvement, by data units. In this case census wards are used. Distances have been
calculated from the geographical centre of each ward to the centre of the city, here taken to
be the City Hall located on the Nevskiy Prospect ⟨*see* end map 71⟩. The City Hall may
be fairly regarded as being in the heart of the city's central business district throughout the
period covered in this analysis. In order to facilitate comparison with Clark's examples, the
analysis in this instance uses miles rather than kilometres.

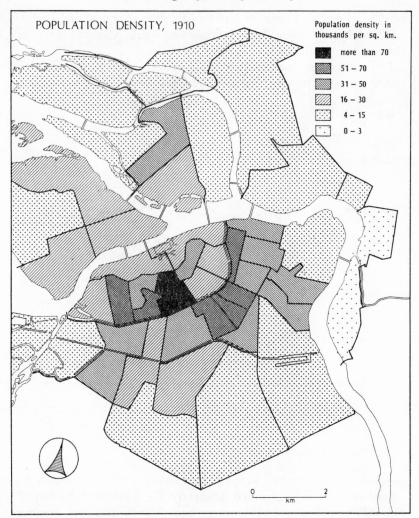

MAP 58. *Population density, 1910*

each set of data. It is apparent from this that there is no support for the hypothesis. Had the city spread out to any great extent, then by 1910 the theoretical central-city density would have been less, the gradient line would have been flatter and it would have intersected the gradient for 1869. Instead, densities increased at all points, and rather substantially at that. Yet, at precisely this time, decentralization was an established fact in European capitals like Paris, London, and Berlin, and had been a major force in reshaping such American cities as Boston, New York and Chicago.[24]

In St Petersburg decentralization, or suburbanization, remained an unrealized objective on the eve of the Great War. Of the 2·2 million

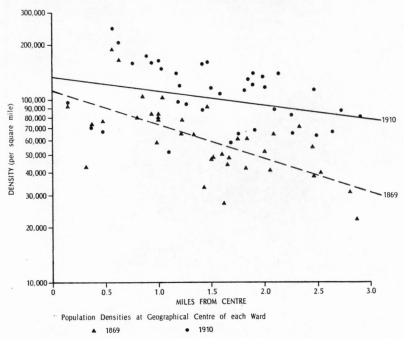

Population Densities at Geographical Centre of each Ward

▲ 1869   ● 1910

FIG. 18. *Density gradients, 1869 and 1910*

people living in the urban area, well over 80 per cent resided within the official city limits.[25] Expressed differently, the contiguous districts of Shlissel'burg, Petergof, Palyustrov and Lesnoy had not become dormitory suburbs. These districts may have been brought under the city's jurisdiction and the census taker's purview, but their links with the city were not of a large-scale commuting kind. They were instead somewhat distinct components of an industrial-commercial complex.[26]

[24] For discussion, see M. A. Shtromberg, 'Detsentralizatsiya Naseleniya v Gorodakh i Puti Soobshcheniya', *IMGD*, no. 4 (1913), pp. 77–90.
[25] *Petrograd po Perepisi*, p. 3.
[26] For related observations, see K. Pazhitnov, 'Ekonomicheskaya Ocherk Peterburga', *S. Peterburg i Yego Zhizn'* (1914), pp. 52–4.

Moreover, commuting from the peripheral regions of the city itself, that is, from within the official city boundary, to the central city did not occur to any appreciable extent either. We will elaborate later on what this meant in terms of housing. Suffice it to say at this juncture that, in the absence of any large-scale decentralization of people and functions, congestion in the city could only have increased. This is clearly implied by the data portrayed in figure 18, but the map of population densities reinforces the point.

In 1869 only the notorious third ward of Spasskaya borough had more than 70,000 people per square kilometre. Living conditions within the borough were intolerable.[27] There had indeed been some reconstruction in the central city since then, but in 1910 the adjacent second ward of Kazanskaya borough had also acquired the dubious distinction of having that many people per square kilometre ⟨*see* map 58*⟩*. Obviously, very high densities were common to the central city in 1910. There were now six wards in the 51,000 to 70,000 range, whereas in 1869 only one had reached this level of congestion. Together they encircled the lower-density Admiralteyskaya borough and the prime commercial area around the lower Nevskiy Prospect. As noted earlier, high rents and pockets of first-class residential properties had checked population growth in the first case, while residential uses often gave way to commercial ones in the second area, thereby helping to hold down population expansion. Something of the impact of the huge immigration into Peterburgskaya borough is also revealed by the map. In 1869 it was one of the least densely settled regions, but it now had one ward in the 31,000 to 50,000 range and one in the 16,000 to 30,000 category.[28] But the question remains, what happened to the city in the course of this human inundation? In providing some answers, we will deal first of all with the physical habitat.

2 THE BUILT ENVIRONMENT

Rivers and canals embanked in granite, huge architectural set pieces, elegant palaces, magnificent theatres, resplendent churches, outstanding museums—the evidence of an earlier era's imperial munificence was no less impressive around the turn of the century than it had been in the 1860s. And there seemed to be a certain degree of continuity in the impressions St Petersburg created. For many people, it was still

[27] See chapter 4, pp. 166–8 and map 28, p. 127.
[28] Minor border changes complicate, but do not invalidate, the comparison.

'a city of bold and firm outlines rather than of warm colour and pic-
turesque detail . . . it is a sketch, an outline, a general statement.'[29]
And, in the summer, 'to a person accustomed to the moving crowds of
London or Paris, the quiet and deserted appearance . . . of the squares
and wide streets' accentuated this kind of image.[30] Reinforcing the
similarities was the fact that the general land-use in 1914 was not so
different from that of 1868 ⟨*see* map 59⟩. The city had been built up
very much within the original street pattern, the parks and gardens
were basically the same, and pockets of kitchen garden remained,
though they had disappeared from the central city. Of course, there are
many changes a simple land-use map cannot reveal.

By the early 1900s few perspectives of the city were unsullied by
industry or simply poor architectural taste. Factory chimneys obtruded
into most of the popular views and smoke belched up around some of
the finest examples of architecture of the late eighteenth, or early
nineteenth centuries. Streets everywhere were being transformed in the
process of speculative building; even the Nevskiy Prospect had not
escaped the customarily gaudy architecture and advertisements of
modern commerce ⟨*see* plates 46–50⟩. Shoddy tenements sprang up in
response to the desperate housing shortage and earned huge profits for
their owners. During the latter part of the century, church architecture
came to be dominated by a pseudo-Russian style, emulating what was
common in Moscow but quite out of keeping with its actual milieu.
There had indeed been numerous architectural changes since 1870, but
as Harold Williams observed around the time of the Great War, St
Petersburg still 'has its own very strongly marked style which
aberrations, mostly dating from the latter half of the nineteenth
century, spoil at many points but cannot obscure.'[31]

Urban industrialization resulted in a flurry of construction which
visibly changed the face of the city. But not all features of the urban
fabric were altered in the process. Originally the use of wood as a
construction material was tolerated only because bricks, mortar and
stone could not be obtained in sufficient amounts to preclude its use.
The intention was to build a city less susceptible to the ever present
hazard of fire, in other words, to create a capital city more durable than
Moscow with its history of conflagrations. It was not until well into the

[29] Harold W. Williams, *Russia of the Russians* (New York, 1915), p. 399.
[30] T. Michell, *Handbook for Travellers in Russia, Poland and Finland* (London, 1893)
p. 12.
[31] Williams, *Russia*, p. 400.

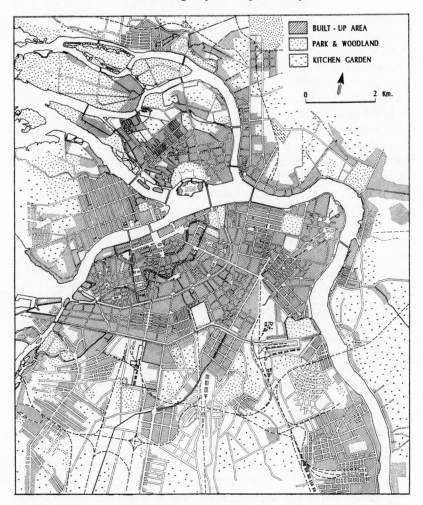

BUILT - UP AREA

PARK & WOODLAND

KITCHEN GARDEN

0   2 Km.

MAP 59. *St Petersburg, 1914*

nineteenth century that stone and brick predominated, and despite
concerted efforts to hasten the demise of wooden structures, they
accounted for 47 per cent of all buildings in the city in 1869.[32] Most
were found in the peripheral boroughs, especially Vasil'yevskaya,
Peterburgskaya and Vyborgskaya, where a good number had traditionally been occupied only during the summer ⟨*see* plate 39⟩. In the

[32] *Sanktpeterburg po Perepisi 10 Dekabrya 1869* (1872), part 2, section 1, pp. 4–6.

323

ensuing decades the construction of wooden buildings did not let up to any appreciable extent. By 1900, about 10,000, or 40 per cent of the total stock, were wooden, and each year thereafter they accounted for a substantial share of all new construction.[33] However, there had been a few minor distributional changes during this period. Land conversion in the central city resulted in many being demolished in order to make way for multi-storied buildings of brick and mortar. For instance, the fifty wooden structures in the central-city boroughs of Admiralteyskaya, Kazanskaya and Spasskaya in 1869 had been reduced to a mere eight at the turn of the century. In Kolomenskaya and Moskovskaya boroughs considerable attrition occurred as well, but there had been many more such buildings to start with and in 1900 nearly 200 remained.[34] Fires continued to take a heavy toll, but even in the central city those destroyed were often rebuilt of the same material. Just as in 1869 though, most wooden buildings were located in the peripheral boroughs. In Aleksandro-Nevskaya, Peterburgskaya and Vyborgskaya there were more, while in Vasil'yevskaya the number was the same as in 1869. Despite prolonged efforts to change the fabric of the city, there had not been any significant alteration during the period of rapid urbanization. Perhaps the only consolation for the authorities concerned was that the city had nearly 55 per cent of all buildings in stone or brick in 1900, and this proportion was substantially better than in Moscow where a couple of years later the comparative share was scarcely a third.[35]

About 4,000 buildings were added to the city's stock from 1870 to 1900, which brought the total to roughly 24,000.[36] It is difficult to gauge precisely the number added during the years down to the Great War but it was in the order of another 5,000 to 6,000.[37] In total the number of buildings had increased by about 50 per cent since 1870. At first glance this does not appear to be especially large, given that the population had nearly tripled, but of course more intensive use was being made of land that was each year more costly to acquire. One indication of this was the following: single-storied buildings accounted

[33] *S. Peterburg po Perepisi 15 Dekabrya 1900* (1905), part 3, pp. 656–7. K. Pazhitnov, 'Kvartirnyy Vopros v Peterburge', *Gorodskoye Delo*, no. 20 (1910), p. 1383 gives details of new buildings put up annually from 1897 to 1906. Approximately 30 per cent were wooden.
[34] *S. Peterburg po Perepisi 15 Dekabrya 1900*, pp. 656–7
[35] Pazhitnov, 'Kvartirnyy Vopros', p. 1375.
[36] *S. Peterburg po Perepisi 15 Dekabrya 1900*, p. 657.
[37] See data on numbers of new buildings constructed and applications made for this purpose in D. P., 'Kvartirnyy Krizis i Domostroitel'stvo v S. Peterburge', *Vestnik Finansov, Promyshlennosti i Torgovli*, no. 9 (1914), p. 393; Pazhitnov, 'Kvartirnyy Vopros', p. 1383.

for 38 per cent of the total in 1869 and two-storied ones 32 per cent, whereas the shares were reversed three decades later. As might be expected, it was in those areas with the highest land values, greatest commercial prestige and, on occasion, where large and fast profits could be turned in tenement construction, that the tallest buildings were constructed. At the turn of the century, nearly half of Admiralteyskaya's 512 buildings were arranged on four floors or more. There were more such buildings in Moskovskaya, Kazanskaya and Spasskaya though they comprised only about two fifths of the respective totals.[38] St Petersburg was literally being built up, and not just in the central part of the city. For instance, in 1911 and 1912 there were 930 applications to put up two-storied, or higher, buildings. Fully three quarters of these applications pertained to sites in the peripheral, but fast growing, boroughs of Peterburgskaya, Vasil'yevskaya, Aleksandro-Nevskaya and Vyborgskaya. Applications for five, six and seven-floored buildings comprised a large share, particularly in Peterburgskaya borough where more than two thirds of the 308 applications were for structures of this size.[39] The ratio was not as high in other areas, but the general trend was plain enough. Land was relatively cheaper on the edge of the city, but in boroughs like Peterburgskaya there had been enormous pressure on land costs and in order to ensure the usual high return on investment more intensive use of sites was necessary.[40] What is interesting about the shift to greater building heights throughout the city, is that three-storied structures began to decline among building quite early on. For example, between 1869 and 1900 they dropped from 18 to 15 per cent of the total. In the early 1900s the process was further accentuated. Still, it is possible to exaggerate the overall significance of what was happening. At the close of the 1860s about 13 per cent of all the city buildings were four floors or higher. Three decades later the share had only reached 17 per cent, and it is unlikely that more than one fifth of the buildings in the city were of this height in 1914.[41] To be sure, many new structures had poked their way into the skyline and on the edge of the city it was common to 'see large numbers of wretched old wooden houses of 100 years ago, jammed in, as it were, between the larger modern buildings of brick and stucco.'[42]

---

[38] *S. Peterburg po Perepisi 15 Dekabrya 1900*, pp. 18–37.
[39] D. P., 'Kvartirnyy Krizis', p. 393.
[40] See map 37, p. 241 for overview of changing real estate values and map 39, p. 243, for some idea of rent increase.
[41] Pazhitnov, 'Kvartirnyy Vopros', p. 1376.
[42] Dobson, *St Petersburg*, p. 120.

However, in comparison with what had happened elsewhere in Europe the skyline was still uncommonly low. According to one source, Berlin had more than four fifths of its buildings four floors or higher, while Paris and Vienna had around two thirds and two fifths respectively.[43] Rapid urbanization and concomitant construction had not yet removed the impress of eighteenth-century ideas and regulations for the building of a capital of uniform and low dimensions.

Coordinative planning and tight supervision of building practices were entirely inadequate during the years from 1870 down to 1914. It has even been suggested that the building process was to all intents and purposes uncontrolled.[44] This does not mean the process was beyond manipulation for there were recurring comments that speculative builders and real-estate owners influenced City Council decisions concerning the routing of public transport lines, that they were able to flout existing building and zoning by-laws, and that they were able to keep the housing supply at a level whereby exorbitant rents could be obtained. Some of these issues will be assessed, albeit indirectly. However, there is simply not enough information available to permit conclusive judgements about the role of the speculative builders and real-estate owners in the building process. On the other hand, it is quite straightforward to measure and evaluate their accomplishments. And nowhere else than in housing was the building process of greater import to the masses who laboured and lived in the city. At the turn of the century, it required hardly any percipience at all to realize that a housing crisis was at hand.

3 HOUSING

Denied the right to own serfs, merchants began investing in real estate very early on and by the 1830s had emerged as an important property-owning class.[45] The Emancipation, the rapid development of the urban economy, and the growing demand for housing had all served to make investment in real estate an increasingly attractive financial proposition. Merchants, of course, were not the only class induced to invest in the building process but they had emerged as the dominant group by the end of the century. At the same time, their

---

[43] Pazhitnov, 'Kvartirnyy Vopros', p. 1377.
[44] See, for instance, I. A. Barmenev, 'Stroitel'stvo i Arkhitektura', *Och.IL* (1956), vol. III, pp. 914–15.
[45] See chapter 2, p. 39.

influence in municipal government increased significantly, a development which will later be discussed in some detail. It is therefore not at all surprising that any scheme or situation which might impair income from property unleashed articulate objection in committees and in the City Council. Despite the implication of the population growth trends during the late nineteenth century in terms of the demand for housing, there had been difficult times for those who depended upon income from real estate. For instance, during the depression of the 1880s rents dropped about 15 per cent.[46] Not only did property owners suffer diminishing returns, but money for new construction dried up in response to the changing circumstances.[47] During such periods City Council members would not support any increased taxation or other financial encumbrance on property and even afterwards all such measures faced stiff opposition.

Although the economy picked up early in the 1890s, the building industry lagged behind. Indeed, in housing it was not until well into the decade that the number of new buildings opened each year came more into line with population growth. By 1900 the total housing stock in the city had increased from 8,242 buildings in 1869 to 9,643. With taller buildings more common, the actual number of apartments had jumped from 87,779 to 154,882. But on average there were more people per apartment in 1900 than in 1869, 7·4 as compared to 7·0; and the ratio of persons per room remained at 1·7.[48] On the face of it, the housing scene was not improved over the 1869 situation, and we have already seen how bad it was then. There were some qualitative improvements, but before these can be discussed there are a couple of underlying trends that require comment. In the first place, the share of the population living in rented accommodation had gone up. Naturally, the share of buildings not part of the rental stock diminished. In 1900 they accounted for only 12 per cent of the total, whereas in 1869 they comprised over a fifth. Secondly, notwithstanding the diminution of rents during the depression, property owners had managed to raise the

[46] 'Doklad Komissii Peterburgskoy Dumy po Voprosu o Sooruzhenii Peterburgo—Ural'skoy i Peterburgskoy—Murmanskoy Zheleznykh Dorog v Svyazi s Vodnymi Putyami', *ISPGD*, no. 11 (1895), p. 8.

[47] For instance, the number of new buildings completed began to drop off markedly toward the end of the 1880s. In 1887 there were only 282. It was not until 1896 that trend was reversed. In that year 715 buildings were added to the stock compared with only 504 the year before. *Entsiklopedicheskiy Slovar'*, p. 319. Real estate owners had some legitimate problems. See 'Kriticheskoye Polozheniye Domovladel'tsev', *Gorodskoye Delo*, no. 24 (1910), pp. 1875–8. Most difficulties had to do with escalating costs of land, materials and money.

[48] Pazhitnov, 'Kvartirnyy Vopros', p. 1377.

average apartment rent from 302 roubles in 1869 to 520 in 1900, an increase of 72 per cent.[49] This change was neither commensurate with the qualitative improvements in the housing stock nor with the population's ability to pay. At the turn of the century property-owners were once again earning large returns on their investments.

To be sure, more apartments were equipped in 1900 with running water, water-closets, electric lighting and so on than even a decade earlier. This was especially true of the smaller, one or two-roomed apartments. For instance, about 90 per cent of those with three or more rooms had running water and water-closets in 1900, but this was only a percentage point or two increase over the state of affairs in 1890. However, in the case of one-roomed apartments equipped with running water the change had been from 25 to 44 per cent. The share of those with water-closets had about doubled to 24 per cent.[50] Such changes need to be put into perspective. Clearly, the majority of one and two-roomed apartments were not equipped with basic services, yet about a third of the city's 1·3 million inhabitants lived in them. What is more, they were paying rents 31 per cent higher than in 1890, a greater change by far than for the larger apartments.[51] As rents and profits grew, housing again emerged as an attractive field for speculative investment.

It can be plausibly argued that the reduction of housing construction brought about by the years of depression laid the basis for the rapidly escalating rents and profits during the nineties. Simply put, demand was outstripping the supply.[52] Unfortunately for the city's inhabitants, the scenario was repeated during the early 1900s. Around a thousand new buildings a year were put up between 1897 and 1902. Thereafter, the impact of the economic slow-down became apparent. From 1902 to 1903 the number of new buildings dropped from 977 to 849 and by 1906 had slipped to 537. Applications to construct new buildings and to add storeys to existing ones similarly tapered off. In 1902 there were 1,395 applications; a year later there were only 1,258.[53] Investment in housing was again drying up. Largely because population growth slowed down there were some improvements in the housing supply, at least if we talk in terms of minor changes in ratios. For instance, the data in table 31 indicate that between 1906 and 1910 the

[49] Pazhitnov, 'Kvartirnyy Vopros', p. 1378.
[50] 'Zhilishchnaya Perepis' v G. S. Peterburge', *IMGD*, No. 23 (1906), p. 161.
[51] Pazhitnov, 'Kvartirnyy Vopros', p. 1378.
[52] See data on new buildings in *Entsiklopedicheskiy Slovar'*, p. 319.
[53] D. P. 'Kvartirnyy Krizis,' p. 393.

TABLE 31. *Apartment–population ratios, 1906–10*

Borough	Number of Persons per Apartment	
	1906	1910
Admiralteyskaya	7·1	6·3
Kazanskaya	7·6	6·2
Spasskaya	8·7	7·9
Kolomenskaya	7·2	6·7
Narvskaya	8·3	7·6
Moskovskaya	7·6	6·9
Aleksandro-Nevskaya	9·1	8·6
Rozhdestvenskaya	7·6	7·0
Liteynaya	6·3	6·1
Vasil'yevskaya	7·0	6·6
Peterburgskaya	6·3	6·5
Vyborgskaya	8·6	8·1
Totals	7·4	7·2

Source: D. P. 'Kvartirnyy Krizis i Domostroitel'stvo v S. Peterburge', *Vestnik Finansov, Promyshlennosti i Torgovli,* no.9, (1914), p. 393.

number of people per apartment dropped a little in each borough except Peterburgskaya.[54] But the changes were obviously minor. Such figures of course ignore the importance of apartment size and quality. None the less, the fact that the ratio of people per apartment only dropped from 7·4 to 7·2 between 1900 and 1910 helps to put the situation into broad perspective. What was more disturbing to those on the scene was the absence of the usual spill-over of investment into housing after the resuscitation of the economy around 1908. The downward trend in applications for new buildings and reconstruction continued. Even allowing for the construction of much taller buildings, the drop from 1,395 applications in 1902 to 734 in 1912 was very worrying. Indeed, against a background of unprecedented in-migration, more and more people were extremely alarmed—and with reason. Not only were housing conditions deteriorating but the cost of construction was escalating. In every sense of the word there was a housing crisis.

The demand for housing after 1908 soared and so did rents. However, so far as can be determined, rents, which were up about 30 per cent since 1900, had risen less than the general inflationary spiral in construction costs. We have discussed elsewhere how land costs were pushed up throughout the city and it need only be noted that rampant

[54] Population increase, it will be recalled, was exceptionally great in this borough.

speculation played a major role. Wage rates in the principal construction trades had increased by about 40 per cent since 1900, as had the cost of most building materials. Thus, from the early 1900s to 1913 the cost of construction went up 35 to 40 per cent.[55] Whether borrowing money had become less costly with the return of buoyant economic conditions is extremely difficult to establish with regard to the building industry. If money was cheaper, then given the importance of this factor in determining returns on investment there were certainly some grounds for supposing that real-estate developers were enjoying large profits. But why the slow-down in applications for new projects? It is in relation to this issue that some observers have raised the spectre of manipulation in the housing market.[56] It was contended that with a rising demand for housing any kind of accommodation anywhere in the city could be rented at a profit and real-estate owners clearly had a vested interest in continuing the imbalance between supply and demand. Whether or not this interpretation is correct, it is clear that developers had not responded to the urgent need for housing. If they were not doing anything, was anyone?

The preceding analysis of density gradients did not demonstrate any predictable signs of decentralization, that is, there had not occurred a general lowering of densities from the core to the periphery. Any person with an interest in urban affairs was certainly aware of what was happening in this regard elsewhere in Europe and in North America and the idea of workmen's trains linking the city to dormitory suburbs with cheaper rent and better living conditions was accepted by most people as the most logical solution to the housing problem. Discussion of various schemes in the City Council occurred frequently in the 1890s, but nothing was done.[57] Passengers carried by public transport were meanwhile steadily increasing. If we examine the pattern of movement it becomes abundantly clear that ties with the suburbs were weak ⟨*see* map 60⟩. Traffic on the lines south of the Obvodnyy Canal was particularly light, despite urban-industrial growth in this region. The bulk of the movement was, of course, concentrated on the main routes within the central city. As we have seen, subsequent

[55] D. Polupanov, 'K Kvartirnomu Krizisu Peterburga', *Gorodskoye Delo*, no. 15 (1913), p. 1353.

[56] Pazhitnov, 'Kvartirnyy Vopros', pp. 1380–81.

[57] See, for instance, 'Po Proyektu Tsentral'noy Stantsii Dlya Zagorodnykh Zheleznykh Dorog i Gorodskoy Opoyasyvayushchey Zheleznoy Dorogi', *ISPGD*, no. 21 (1893), pp. 7–46; 'Po Voprosu Vozbuzhdennomu Gosudarstvennym Sovetom o Prisoyedinenii Prigorodnykh Uchastkov k S. Peterburgu v Khozyaystvennom Otnoshenii', *ISPGD*, no. 40 (1895), pp. 717–50.

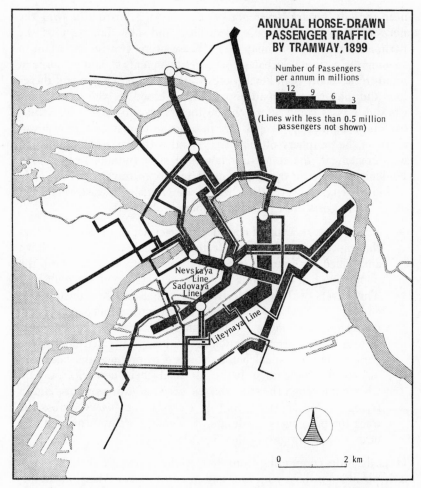

ANNUAL HORSE-DRAWN
PASSENGER TRAFFIC
BY TRAMWAY, 1899

Number of Passengers
per annum in millions

12 9 6 3

(Lines with less than 0.5 million
passengers not shown)

Nevskaya Line
Sadovaya Line
Liteynaya Line

0   2 km

MAP 60. *Annual horse-drawn passenger traffic by tramway, 1899*

improvements were made to the system and the service, but not fast
enough. Movement within the city was difficult and expensive. In 1904
the municipal government had gained control of public transport and
had become involved with some low-rent housing projects. However, the
one on Goloday Island was initially a failure because it was effectively
too remote.[58] And this was barely three kilometres from the Stock
Exchange! It is no wonder that schemes to develop low-rent housing

[58] A. Nikitin, *Zadachi Peterburga* (1904), p. 74.

331

near the city border never got off the drawing board. By 1914 the network had been partially electrified and new lines served the peripheral regions ⟨*see* map 61⟩. These were clearly important in shaping the pattern of urban growth, yet two points should be borne in mind. First, many peripheral routes were still horse-drawn and therefore did not permit rapid movement. Secondly, who among the working classes could afford the customary two-to-three-hour return trip and roughly thirty-kopek fare in order to take advantage of lower rents on the periphery of the city?[59] And if these were not sufficient discouragement, the trams did not even start running until 8 a.m. Undeniably, electric trams permitted people to travel more speedily within the city. However, this benefit was, initially at least, somewhat offset by the costs, for as one contemporary observed:

> It was not . . . without considerable sacrifice of life and limb that this improvement . . . was effected, for people were knocked down and killed or injured every day for many months until the population had been drilled into the new system of 'hurrying up'. The drivers of the new electric cars had also to be trained not to endanger the lives of the public by giving too much rein to the national temperament for indulging in extremes. Finding that instead of the former exertion of whipping up jaded horses, the mere touch of a small handle sufficed to produce the necessary movement, these men began to send their new electric cars whizzing through the streets at the speed of express trains, and in trying to stop short in front of a *droshky* or *lomovoi* across the track the passengers inside the car were generally thrown all of a heap, or jerked right off their seats.[60]

Hazards aside, commuting from the peripheral regions of the city was only possible for those with time and money to spare. Many, of course, had jobs close at hand thereby obviating the need for public transport. All told, when the physical expansion of the city since 1869, as portrayed in map 61, is set against a population increase of 1·5 million it becomes clear that decentralization had been minimal and therefore population densities had to rise.

[59] K. Raush, 'Prigorody Bol'shikh Gorodov i Ikh Puti Soobshcheniya', *Gorodskoye Delo*, no. 16 (1909), p. 805; V. Tvergokhlebov, 'O Prisoyedinenii Prigorodov k Petrogradu', *Gorodskoye Delo*, no. 1 (1915), p. 12.

[60] Dobson, *St Petersburg*, p. 116. For exact statistics on the number of accidents during the first few months of the tram's operation, see D. Nikol'skiy, 'K Voprosu o Neschastnykh Sluchayakh na Gorodskikh Rel'sovykh Putyakh pri Konnoy, Parovoy i Elektricheskoy Tyage', *Gorodskoye Delo*, no. 7 (1909), pp. 303–7.

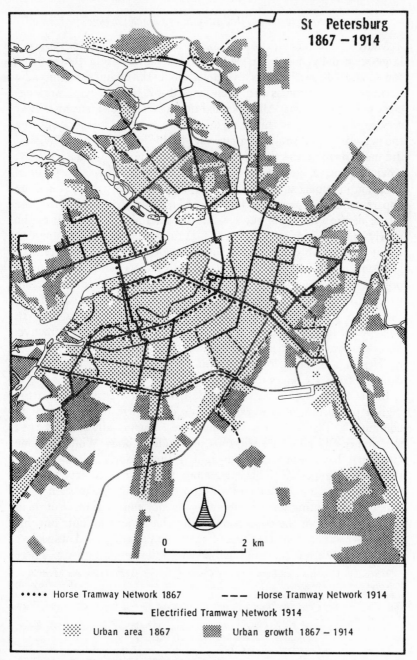

St Petersburg
1867 – 1914

•••• Horse Tramway Network 1867   – – – Horse Tramway Network 1914

—— Electrified Tramway Network 1914

Urban area 1867   Urban growth 1867 – 1914

MAP 61. *St Petersburg, 1867–1914*

Many of the schemes to ameliorate the housing crisis envisaged a large-scale daily migration via the steam railway from the outlying towns and villages.[61] Tsarskoye Selo, Pavlovsk, Oraniyenbaum and a number of other towns had been singled out for low-rent, working-class housing projects. All depended upon a cheap, fast, steam-railway service and, because of this, were doomed to failure. The service during the pre-war period simply did not cater to this kind of demand. What it did make possible was the summer exodus to the *dacha* and a leisurely, albeit expensive, journey into the city when desired. The seasonal variation in suburban rail traffic is depicted in table 32 and it is quite apparent that comparatively few persons travelled regularly during the whole of the year. It is not possible to determine how many of the nearly 97,000 incoming passengers in January were regular commuters, but it was probably only a very small proportion. There were military garrisons, factories, commercial establishments and many other organizations which had to maintain ties with the city and therefore generated passenger traffic of a non-commuting type. Additionally, there were the comings and goings of peasants from the local area. In later years, fares and travel times were made a little more attractive. For instance, a first-class, single ticket from Oraniyenbaum was 1·50 roubles in 1893 and 1·05 roubles in 1913. The time of the trip had dropped from 1·5 hours to one.

But at forty-two kopeks the cheapest ticket still represented far too high a proportion of a working man's daily wage to enable him to commute.[62] Tsarskoye Selo was the closest town of any size. By 1913 the twenty-odd kilometre trip took only half an hour. While the time taken may have been acceptable enough, the cheapest, single fare was thirty-three kopeks.[63] This was more than twice as expensive as travelling the same distance into Berlin.[64] For the affluent such long-distance commuting was certainly feasible and more and more of them sought relief from the congestion of the city by moving out. But this alternative was only open to those of wealth and privilege, and in absolute numbers only a few thousand had taken up the option by 1914. There

[61] See 'Ob Ustroistve v Cherte Goroda Chasti Elektricheskago Tramvaya Mezhdu S. Peterburgom i S. Toksovom', *ISPGD*, no. 22 (1900), pp. 3–19 and no. 6 (1901), pp. 1033–6; Raush, 'Prigorody Bol'shikh Gorodov', p. 802. An early endeavour is described by Valentine Bill, *The Forgotten Class, the Russian Bourgeoisie from the Earliest Beginnings to 1900* (New York, 1959), p. 122.
[62] Michell, *Handbook for Travellers in Russia, Poland and Finland*, p. 79; Karl Baedeker, *St Petersburg und Umgebungen, Handbuch für Reisende* (Leipzig, 1913), p. 100.
[63] Baedeker, *St Petersburg*, pp. 100–15.
[64] The difference was even greater if weekly tickets are used as the basis for comparison. Raush, 'Prigorody Bol'shikh Gorodov', pp. 807–8.

is no doubt that the number of commuters was larger in 1914 than in 1896. However, little in the way of concrete results had come from two decades or so of pleas, protestations, and proposals. Events such as the decision in 1910 to build an electric tram-line to Oraniyenbaum in order to enable people to move out and take up residence along the route were quite exceptional. Though praised in the press, it was obvious

TABLE 32. *Railway passenger traffic: suburban region, 1896*

Month	Incoming	Outgoing
January	96,693	98,199
February	89,217	92,773
March	115,495	120,456
April	132,969	139,520
May	253,181	274,776
June	301,965	313,299
July	315,338	308,686
August	287,366	248,061
September	162,831	145,018
October	121,978	118,786
November	113,671	129,873
December	125,980	129,393
Totals	2,116,684	2,118,840

Source: *Entsiklopedicheskiy Slovar'* (1900), vol. LVI, p. 329. These data are for the Nikolayevskaya, Varshavskaya, and Baltiyskaya railways only.

that such a project would take several years to complete and accompanying the laudatory comments were scathing denunciations of the overall lack of progress of this kind. Since commuting any distance within the city, as well as from outlying communities, was ruled out for the majority, we should determine if anything else was being done to meliorate the 'eternal scab of our city', as the housing crisis was metaphorically described in 1910.[65]

With twice as many people per apartment as in Berlin, Vienna or Paris, families as well as single persons were often able to afford only part of a room.[66] The *ugol*, or corner habitation, had emerged as a national speciality. Surveys of housing conditions were unveiling incredible situations. In one investigation commissioned by the city in 1904, nearly 3,300 apartments spread over ten of the twelve boroughs

[65] 'Oraniyenbaumskaya Elektricheskaya Zhel. Dor.', *Ekonomist Rossii*, no. 5 (1910), pp. 8–9.
[66] Polupanov, 'K Kvartirnomu Krizisu Peterburga', p. 1354; M. I. Pokrovskaya, *Po Podvalom, Cherdakam i Uglovym Kvartiram Peterburga* (1903), pp. 7–15.

were inspected. Most had been subdivided, including halls and kitchens, into den-like quarters. In some cases, there were five or more people per bed. Basic sanitary norms were obviously ignored in the process of subdivision. If the inspectors had enforced the existing legislation concerning minimum cubic air space per person, fully 25 per cent of the inhabitants would have been put out on the street. And the city did not demand high standards. In this instance, most army barracks were better off.[67] Other surveys were showing that among workers as many as two thirds of single and, worse still, two fifths of married men lived in an *ugol*.[68] Overcrowding was most severe in the one and two-roomed apartments which in the majority of cases lacked essential services. The average for the city was 1·7 persons per room in 1900. For single-room apartments it was 3·2; for cellars it was 3·4.[69] In the 1904 investigation, there were, on average, nearly sixteen people per apartment. This worked out to almost six in each room.[70] And of course these were just averages. It will perhaps be recalled that when similar figures for 1869 were examined at the borough level, there were huge variations. As a rule, the densely settled inner-city boroughs and the peripheral working-class ones had ratios far in excess of the city average. Five decades of rapid urbanization had not changed this characteristic at all. Nor had the number of cellar dwellers diminished. By 1914 there were close on 60,000 of them living under the most abysmal conditions imaginable. But these people had at least a regular abode. A growing number of people were not even able to find accommodation in a cellar.

It had always been extremely difficult to persuade the city fathers to relinquish income from property taxes in order to assist even an occasional low-rent workers' housing project initiated by private charities.[71] In view of their close-fisted attitude to financial matters, it is not surprising to find that the involvement of the municipality in low-rent workers' housing was quite limited. The shocking reports of the various exploratory commissions raised the level of public awareness of these problems, but solutions to them demanded enormous expenditure. To

[67] K. Pazhitnov, 'Zhilishchnaya Politika Gorodskoy Dumy Gor. Petrograda', *IMGD*, no. 10 (1914), pp. 44, 52. Indeed, it was even popular to suggest that the large number of barracks in the city be given over to housing the poor. This was not done for reasons which the 1905 uprising make clear. Dobson, *St Petersburg*, p. 129.
[68] Pazhitnov, 'Ekonomicheskiy Ocherk Peterburga', p. 60.
[69] 'Zhilishchnaya Perepis' ', p. 160.
[70] Pazhitnov, 'Zhilishchnaya Politika Gorodskoy Dumy', p. 40.
[71] For an example of the attitude, see 'Po Khodataystvu Obshchestva Posobiya Bednym Zhenshchinam ob Ustupke Gorodskoy Zemli iz Smolenskago Polya Dlya Postroyki Domov s Deshevymi Kvartirami', *ISPGD*, no. 11 (1898), pp. 1041–2.

be fair, the city's financial position was not good and there were many
other pressing claims on the available funds. The rather undistinguished beginning for the Goloday Island project had not been
encouraging either, though it was inadequate public transport which
was cited as one of the main reasons for the project's lack of success in
this case. Instead of housing projects of this kind, it appears that city
officials preferred to tackle the even more pressing problem of assisting
the growing number of homeless people. This they did by opening a
number of doss-houses. In this endeavour they were joined by
benevolent societies and in greater number by entrepreneurs looking
for fast and sizable profits.

In the early 1900s the *nochlezhnyy dom*, or doss-house, symbolized
the failure of government and private enterprise to meet the demand
for adequate housing just as the existence of cellar accommodation had
done in the 1860s ⟨*see* plate 62⟩. The idea of providing temporary
shelter evolved as a humanitarian gesture in the sixties, but the scale of
the problem and the necessary response were relatively limited. At that
time, subsidized housing for permanent residents was the main focus
of charitable activity. During the seventies and eighties one or two
night-shelters were opened. The first appeared on the Obvodnyy Canal
and resulted from the philanthropic endeavour of Yu. Zasetskiy. A few
years later the concept was broadened to encompass a Society for
Mutual Assistance, a key part of which was to be the provision of a
clean bed and adequate meal. Based on European models such as the
Salvation Army, the proposal was taken to the Ministry of Internal
Affairs in 1881 for financial support.[72] None was forthcoming. The
advocate of the idea, I. Dvoryashin, was not entirely disillusioned and a
couple of years later opened a small *nochlezhnyy dom*. With the ensuing
decades of rapid in-migration the need for this kind of facility rose. It
was met in a variety of ways, not all of them especially beneficial to the
occupants.

At the outset the organization which Dvoryashin founded was the
largest one of its kind providing temporary shelter. By 1893 it had four
operations under its wing—two in Spasskaya, and one each in Rozhdestvenskaya and Aleksandro-Nevskaya boroughs. In all there was room
for just over 900 persons. In a survey undertaken two years later, it was
discovered that there were fourteen doss-houses, but the Dvoryashin
organization provided about 40 per cent of the total number of beds

[72] K. F. Karaffa-Korbut, 'Nochlezhnye Doma v Bol'shikh Russkikh Gorodakh',
Gorodskoye Delo, no. 11–12 (1912), p. 691.

337

(2,087). There were two other charitable operations and eight private ones. The initiative for the study of the *nochlezhnye doma* and the eighty-seven lodging-houses in the city, which could accommodate a further 1,379 people, came from the serious outbreak of typhus a couple of years earlier. Suspicions were raised when analysis of the incidence of the disease revealed that the homeless population figured prominently among the cases.[73] Hence, an investigation of conditions in the *nochlezhnye doma* and cheap lodging-houses was begun. There was no ducking the fact that in the majority of cases overcrowding and unsanitary conditions were the rule; however, in the absence of adequate water supply and sewage systems in the city, it was not possible to do anything more than condemn the current state of public hygiene in general. But it was interesting that the City Sanitary Commission, which undertook the survey, emphasized the need for a much larger-scale effort in providing temporary lodgings. They reckoned that inns and doss-houses together could provide only a third of the required number of beds, at least if they adhered to the permits that were issued. Additionally, it was pointed out that there was simply not enough accommodation for women.[74] How the remaining homeless population fared was not discussed, but the City Council at least was sufficiently perturbed to allocate funds to open additional shelters.

As usual, the City Council moved ponderously. Some attempts were made to tighten up the inspection and regulation of the doss-houses and inns, though these could scarcely be regarded as crusades. Indeed, to invoke a strict interpretation of the existing legislation raised the spectre of thousands of homeless people wandering the streets. As migration to the city was perceptibly on the rise, the easiest course of action for the authorities was to add whatever facilities they could and to do nothing about those already in operation. Thus, when James Simpson had occasion to visit the city in 1896, his descriptions of lodging-houses and *nochlezhnye doma*—which are worth quoting at some length—differed not at all from the accounts produced by the sanitary doctors the year before:

> Our *cortège* of three *droshkies* glides quickly along the partly wood-paved thoroughfare; but as we near the lower quarter of the town the neat hexagonal sections of pine give way to coarser cobbles, over which our vehicles rattle with sharp jarring notes.

[73] E. A. Ferman, *Smertnost' ot Bryushnago Tifa v S. Peterburge za 12 Let s 1895 po 1906 God.* (1907) pp. 42–3; Karaffa-Korbut, 'Nochlezhnye Doma', p. 692.
[74] Karaffa-Korbut, 'Nochlezhnye Doma', pp. 692–3.

Tall factories loom above us, but these we also pass, and descend into smaller streets or *pereuloks* flanked by unsubstantial, uninviting buildings. At last our leader halts at the gate in a high paling that hinders access to the courtyard of one of these houses. We cross the yard, come to a low building containing a few rooms, enter it and walk along a dark passage. . . . We reach a room, and the stove that heats both it and a neighbouring apartment roars with the straw that has just been piled into it. We open the door and a warm unsavoury odour rushes out. It is a chamber perhaps 22 feet in length by 16 in breadth. A narrow passage extends to the opposing wall, between a couple of platforms which are raised some 30 inches above the floor and occupy the rest of the room. On and underneath these lie crowds of sleeping men: their deep low breathing is very audible, while some snorers combine to produce a greater effect. One of the sleepers, disturbed by the invasion, rises on his elbow, indulges in a dreamy stare, then turns over and is soon again beyond the things of sense. The licence of the lodging-house proprietor permits him to accommodate twenty-five people in this room: there are exactly forty-nine. And not only are the lodgers seemingly unconscious of the closeness due to overcrowding, but they must needs have the stove lit in addition. For all this they pay 5 kopeks a night, and some relish the accommodation so much that they have engaged the right to sleep there for two years in advance. In the morning they can get tea and bread for a trifle more.

We went to see a Government lodging-house by way of contrast. The building was scrupulously clean, and the rooms of good size and well ventilated. The *nari* or sleeping platforms ran down the centre, and the space allotted to each individual was plainly defined by the thin wooden partition that traced out the middle line of the erection, thus separating the heads of any two opposing sleepers, and at the same time sending off like ribs at right angles to itself every 3 feet or so, other partitions that served to separate each person from his immediate neighbour on either side. Moreover, a slight surface slope, culminating in a pronounced upward bend as the axial screen was reached, contrived to make the plank-beds the most comfortable things of their kind that one could well imagine. The tariff was 9 kopeks for the night with a good meal in the morning,—in every way a better bargain than the other from the Western point of view. But the institution was

339

poorly patronised, and there was not the same look of contentment on the men's faces in these more sanitary apartments.

What we saw of a third large tenement, also a Night Shelter capable of holding considerably over 1000 souls, showed it to be simply a repetition of the first case on a grander scale. The charge was 5 kopeks, and the lodgers could enter for the night at 7 p.m., but were required to leave at 8 the following morning. Here, indeed, was over-crowding: one saw rooms that would have been full with 200 men crammed with half as many more. Sleepers lay about everywhere—on a large central platform that occupied a considerable space, beneath it, on the supplementary shelves that skirted two of the walls, under them, even in the passages. They were often miserably clad, and slept in their clothes; others had partially disrobed or were stark naked. So thickly were they strewn that one had to pick every step: beyond a certain distance progress was impossible. And this is not distasteful to the Russian peasant; the Government lodging-houses, as well conducted as any in more Western lands, and cheaper than the ordinary lodging-house, are practically deserted in favour of the latter.[75]

Conventional wisdom had it that the prohibition of liquor in the government *nochlezhnyy dom*, combined with the religious overtones of the charitable operations, were sufficient to drive large numbers into the privately run establishments where neither issue was of much concern.

Over the next few years the number of doss-houses grew substantially, and so did the city's involvement in their operation. By the early 1900s the housing crisis had become so serious that the usually conservative Council was no longer simply converting existing buildings, but was giving serious consideration to allocating funds to build specially designed ones. Meanwhile, private entrepreneurs had not been idle. According to a 1910 survey, this time initiated by a cholera epidemic, there were thirty-four *nochlezhnye doma*, of which eighteen were privately run and fourteen were managed by the city. Charitable society involvement had been reduced to three establishments, though these provided about one seventh of the 6,200 beds available in all three types.[76]

Without doubt, sanitary conditions and overcrowding were again the worst in the private operations. Descriptions by the sanitary

[75] James Simpson, *Sidelights on Siberia* (London, 1898), pp. 145–7.
[76] Karaffa-Korbut, 'Nochlezhnye Doma', pp. 694–5.

doctors involved in the survey highlight the lack of ventilation, the overcrowding, the impaired water supply and the high probability that the generally filthy physical environment assisted in the spread of disease. These kinds of establishments in other cities had similar reputations, but the important difference was that few other cities suffered from epidemics as did St Petersburg. In 1910 twenty-six of the thirty-four doss-houses were located in Narvskaya, Aleksandro-Nevskaya and Rozhdestvenskaya boroughs. All were working-class and all had relatively low land costs and rents, at least in relation to the overcrowded central-city boroughs. In the latter there were few night-shelters despite the obvious need, and the cost of real estate could well have been the reason for this situation. Indeed, in the two most densely settled boroughs, Spasskaya and Kazanskaya, there were just two, relatively small, establishments. One was operated by the city, the other by a charitable organization. Since charges in establishments managed by them ranged from five to seven kopeks and included tea, sugar and bread, if not something more substantial, profits were not being made. On the other hand, seven to thirty-five kopeks a night were needed to take advantage of what the private sector was offering.[77] When the going rate for a labourer was around one rouble a day, to pay thirty-five kopeks was a major outlay.[78] Not only were the facilities intolerable, but normally nothing in the way of tea or bread was included in the tariff. Unlike a decade or so earlier, all three kinds of *nochlezhnyy dom* were now customarily full, and often overflowing. It was this state of affairs which prompted a closer look at the situation by the committees of municipal government.

Following the publication of the 1910 survey, the Executive Committee of the Council turned its attention to the need for additional shelters. It was argued passionately that in a Christian society each person, no matter how lowly his position, deserved at least a place to sleep.[79] Within a year plans for three new large-scale *nochlezhnye doma* were referred to the Council. It was estimated that to accommodate a total of 2,500 people the cost would run close to a million roubles. The scheme was turned over by the Council to a sub-commission for closer study. The whole Commission travelled to Moscow in order to examine projects there. Upon their return they recommended increasing the size of the shelters to house 3,500 people. Locations in the most hard

[77] Karaffa-Korbut, 'Nochlezhnye Doma', pp. 695–7.
[78] Pazhitnov, 'Kvartirnyy Vopros', p. 1380.
[79] Pazhitnov, 'Zhilishchnaya Politika Gorodskoy Dumy', p. 37. See also 'O Postroyke Gorodskikh Domov', *ISPGD*, no. 32 (1910), pp. 1855–84.

pressed areas were chosen. One was to serve the industrial and dock workers of Vasil'yevskiy Island. Another was to be sited in Kolomens-kaya borough where there were no shelters but a large industrial and dock-working population as well. The third was to go in Mirgorodskoy Street near the Nikolayevskiy railway station, again an industrial and transport area. But all this took place with the Council's customary alacrity. It was the middle of June 1914, nearly three years later, before the Executive Committee approved the revised scheme.[80] While plans developed, the housing crisis deepened.

We tend to think of doss-houses and inns as providing for the most part temporary lodging. Yet one of Simpson's earlier remarks hinted at what was happening. He noted that some people were making long-term arrangements to stay in them. The survey in 1910 indicated just how far this trend had gone. More than a third of those enumerated lived in the *nochlezhnyy dom* on a permanent basis. And this was more than simply a third of the bed-total owing to chronic abuse of such limits. For the most part they were single people in the twenty-to-fifty age group who worked in the city but had been unable to find other accommodation. Less than 10 per cent were classified as down-and-outs, alcoholics and the like. The sanitary doctors who had undertaken the 1910 survey concluded that there were at least 12,000 people requiring shelter of this type. At the time only 6,200 beds existed. Three years later the number had increased to approximately 8,200. Obviously, the situation had become worse in the meantime because of the huge surge in migration to the city. Knowledgeable members of the Council were arguing that a more realistic estimate of the potential demand would be around one per cent of the population. If this were the case 20,000 beds would have been needed.[81] The inclination to take up permanent residence in pestilential doss-houses is easily understood in the light of such circumstances. Not only was it difficult, and also expensive, to find a place to live, but living under such conditions was often a hazard to health and well-being ⟨*see* plate 62⟩.

4 THE QUALITY OF THE ENVIRONMENT

St Petersburg underwent a metamorphosis of both subtle and more obvious aspects in the course of its rapid urban industrialization. Notwithstanding the pervasive impact of the process, there were some

[80] Pazhitnov, 'Zhilishchnaya Politika Gorodskoy Dumy', pp. 35–7.
[81] Pazhitnov, 'Zhilishchnaya Politika Gorodskoy Dumy', pp. 33–5.

facets of the city which remained more or less the same. One of these was the morbidity of the environment. Simply put, the capital was no less hazardous a place to live in the early 1900s than it had been half a century before. The per capita death-rate figures had indeed begun to decline around the 1880s, but for every thousand inhabitants living there were still many more dying than was common in any other major European, American, or, for that matter, Russian, city. The reason had very much to do with the large number of people who succumbed during the regular visitations of epidemics. Cholera and typhus, for example, had taken especially heavy tolls and continued to do so throughout the whole period. The reason for this was plain enough—the urban environment was pestilential.

At one time the purity of the Neva's water enjoyed widespread acclaim.[82] As the city grew and became more industrialized conditions changed, and quickly. Even before the middle of the nineteenth century such judgements belonged to the past.[83] By the 1860s the sorry state of municipal water and sewage services rendered the water unsafe to drink, especially during the spring and summer. Public notices advising the inhabitants against consuming unboiled water had become as common, as they were a necessary, part of the urban scene. Unfortunately, they were all too often either not understood or simply ignored. The consequence was endemic disease and an unusually high death-rate. How little conditions had changed during the years down to the Great War is revealed in G. Dobson's observation:

> The foundations of public health have been too long neglected in favour of the outside glitter of modern civilization. Although the subject of sanitation has been under discussion for the last quarter of a century at least, there is still no proper drainage and no pure water-supply . . . in addition to the rigours of the climate and the insalubrity of the situation, [the population] is obliged to put up with primitive arrangements for the disposal of sewage which in these days constitute nothing less than a national scandal. These arrangements may be briefly referred to as a system of filthy cesspools in the back yards of all houses, with rough wooden carts to carry away the contents at night and pollute the atmosphere by the operation. At the same time, as though this were not enough,

---

[82] G. L. von Attengofer, *Mediko-Topograficheskoye Opisaniye Sanktpeterburga, Glavnago i Stolichnago Goroda Rossiiskoy Imperii* (1820), p. 58.

[83] See Baron Del'vig, 'Istoricheskoye Obozreniye Iskustva Provodit' Vodu', *Vestnik Promyshlennosti*, no. 5 (1859), p. 131.

the citizens are supplied with water which nobody valuing his or her life dares to drink unboiled.

St Petersburg is probably the only city in Europe, or perhaps the world, where danger-signals in the form of placards with glaring red letters are posted up on house-fronts, inside tramcars, and in most places of public resort, warning all and sundry against drinking raw water. . . . Nevertheless, the lowest and most ignorant class of the people, especially those coming from the provinces, have the greatest contempt for cholera and for all the precautions taken against it . . . the author has seen dirty workmen slake their thirst with water dipped out of their greasy caps from the foulest canals of the city, while cautionary notices [stare] them full in the face only a few yards off.[84]

The combination of a large illiterate population unaccustomed to the hazards of city life and a totally inadequate municipal water and sewage system guaranteed that the city's reputation as a stronghold of disease and death remained intact.

It was true that each year a larger percentage of the city's apartments were provided with basic municipal services. At the turn of the century about three quarters of them were equipped with piped water and about two thirds had water-closets.[85] Of course, within the city the level of municipal services varied markedly as maps 62 and 63, depicting the state of affairs from 1882 to 1896, make quite apparent. With the notable exception of Spasskaya borough, the contrast between the central city and the periphery was fairly clear-cut, just as it had been in the 1860s. Despite the extremely rapid population expansion in the peripheral boroughs during and after the economic boom of the 1890s, this disparity was not altered appreciably. While it did not necessarily follow that those areas with the lowest levels of basic services were the least healthy environments, generally speaking there was a fairly high degree of correspondence between minimal services, epidemic disease and relatively high death-rates.

The average number of deaths per thousand inhabitants had dropped from around forty in the mid-1860s to about twenty five in 1890. The decline, however, had not witnessed a lessening of the differential impact within the city. This is evident from the spatial pattern of mortality during the years from 1886 to 1895 ⟨*see* map 64⟩. In most

[84] Dobson, *St Petersburg*, pp. 110–11.
[85] 'Zhilishchnaya Perepis' ', p. 161.

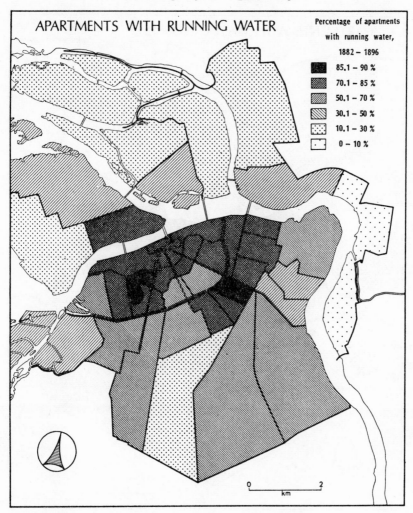

MAP 62. *Apartments with running water, 1882–96*

peripheral boroughs deaths averaged well over thirty per thousand, while in Admiralteyskaya and the first ward of Spasskaya fewer than fifteen were recorded. Not surprisingly, the insalubrious third ward of Spasskaya retained the distinction of having the highest mortality rate in the central city. Among the various infectious diseases afflicting the populace, consumption and pneumonia were responsible for the

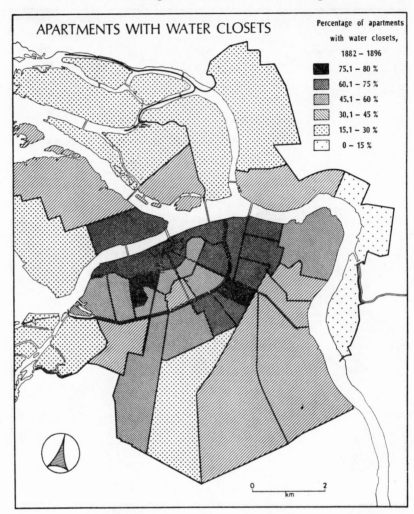

MAP 63. *Apartments with water closets, 1882–96*

greatest number of deaths.[86] But it was the outbreaks of diphtheria, scarlet fever and particularly cholera and typhus which caused the gravest concern in other European centres.[87] In St Petersburg on the

[86] *Entsiklopedicheskiy Slovar'*, p. 317.
[87] At the time of such outbreaks, diplomatic reports abound in detailed accounts of the number of cases and deaths and usually include some judgement as to the likelihood of the epidemic spreading. See also chapter 4, p. 188.

other hand life went on as usual. Epidemics were certain to bring more protestations and proposed solutions for the basic problems as well as more deaths. Various authorities exhaustively analysed the relationships between the material well-being of the inhabitants as measured by apartment rents, levels of services, numbers of domestic servants, population densities and so on, and the incidence of disease. The conclusions were not unexpected. In those wards where rents were above average, where there was a higher level of municipal services than average and where there was more space than average, the incidence of epidemic disease was less than average.[88] Where gross overcrowding was the rule, epidemics struck with a real vengeance.

This relationship was demonstrated very clearly in a study of the incidence of Asiatic cholera during the 1882 to 1896 period.[89] As a measure of overcrowding, ten persons or more per room was used. As we have noted elsewhere, this kind of ratio obviously ignores the size and quality of the space, but few would dispute its general validity as a barometer of overcrowding. From map 65 it can be seen that the third ward of Spasskaya had the highest percentage of rooms with this number of people and, as usual, was something of an anomaly within the central city. The customary core-periphery contrast is also apparent from the map. When this map is compared with the one showing the differential impact of cholera there are some broad correlations ⟨*see* map 66⟩. In the central city, only the inhabitants of Spasskaya ward registered more than eighty cases per ten thousand. They averaged between 131 and 180 cases over the period in question. As is clear from the map, the populations of the peripheral boroughs suffered most severely from the ravages of the disease.

While it was not always the case that overcrowding and high incidence of cholera went hand in hand, there were sufficient grounds for drawing that conclusion. However, when such relationships were probed in greater depth, overcrowding was found not to be the cause of the epidemic.[90] Rather, this feature simply summarized a wide range of factors contributing to unhygienic, if not dangerous, living conditions. Time and again the disease was traced back to an impaired water supply. Scientifically, it was no longer possible to attribute such scourages to ill defined environmental factors or to the hordes of

[88] *Entsiklopedicheskiy Slovar'*, p. 316.
[89] See A. N. Pavlovskiy, *Materialy k Statistike i Etiologii Zabolevayemosti i o Smertnosti ot Aziatskoy Kholery v S. Peterburge v 1882–1896 gg.* (1897).
[90] Pavlovskiy, *Materialy k Statistike i Etiologii Zabolevayemosti i o Smertnosti*, pp. 16, 117, 130.

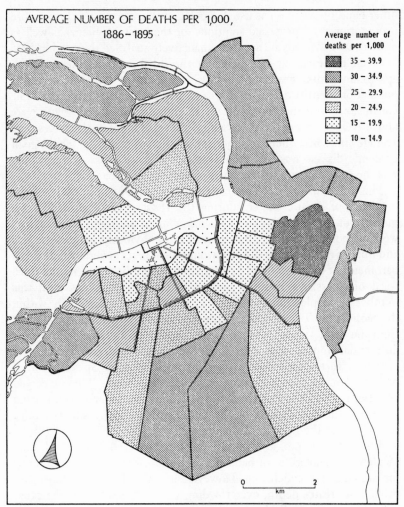

MAP 64. *Average number of deaths per 1,000, 1886–95*

migrant workmen who converged on the city each summer seeking work only to bear the brunt of epidemics.[91] The Neva River and its tributaries were plainly not only the source of the city's drinking water, but of some of its most lethal disease.[92]

[91] See chapter 4, pp. 187–90.
[92] For instance, see N. I. Solov'yev, *Moskva i Peterburg v Sanitarnom Otnoshenii* (1874), pp. 29–30; A. I. Rammul', 'O Vodosnabzhenii S. Peterburga', *Gorodskoye Delo*, no, 22 (1910), pp. 1588–600.

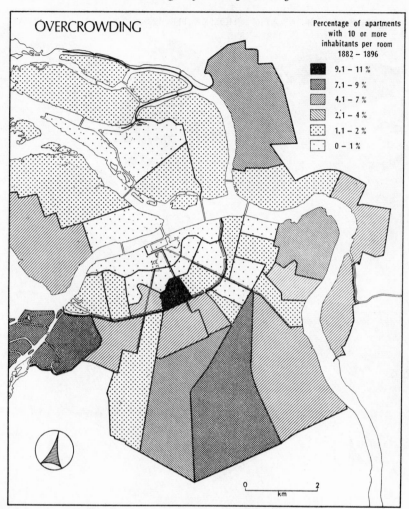

MAP 65. *Overcrowding, 1882–96*

The facts of disease and death in the Russian capital were assiduously gathered, analysed and reported to government authorities throughout the 1870 to 1914 period. Dissertations of medical doctors alone contributed in a major way to the understanding of the epidemiological aspects of diseases like cholera and typhus.[93] But understanding was

[93] A substantial number of these were published during and after the 1890s. Since they were submitted for degrees in St Petersburg, a good many used the city as a reasearch area.

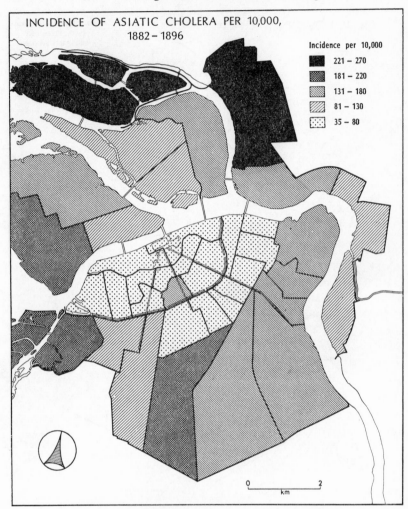

MAP 66. *Incidence of Asiatic cholera per 10,000, 1882–96*

not translated into action, with the result that in a very real sense the quality of the environment steadily deteriorated. British Consul A. W. Woodhouse summed up the situation in his 1909 report on the cholera epidemic of the preceding year:

> In the whole of Russia from the outbreak of cholera in July 1908, till the end of the year there were altogether 30,157 cases and

350

14,253 deaths. In the city of St Petersburg between September 6
and December 31 there were 8,763 [cases] and 3,553 deaths. . . .
Since the 'thirties' of the last century there have been seven
outbreaks of cholera here and no less than 25 years in which the
epidemic has prevailed. It will thus be seen that St Petersburg is a
very hotbed of cholera, which is owing to its extremely unsanitary
condition. Unfortunately, since the last visitation in 1895 nothing
serious has been undertaken to prevent the recurrence of the
scourge, whereas in Moscow work has been slowly but continually
going on in draining and improving the water supply. The natural
result is seen in the great difference between the towns as regards
the average annual mortality from typhoid, a disease shown to be
closely connected with the quality of drinking water; during the
period 1892—1905 the average number of deaths from typhoid in
St Petersburg was between 650 and 1,000, and in Moscow only
140 to 240.[94]

Typhus like cholera affected different classes as well as different city
areas in a disproportionate fashion. Indeed, it had been the unusually
high incidence of these diseases among the city's homeless which had
prompted the inspection of sanitary conditions in the doss-houses. For
example, during the 1895–6 typhus epidemic a single *nochlezhnyy dom*
accounted for 3 per cent of all cases registered in the city. In the 1908
outbreak, fully 35 per cent of the nearly 7,700 people who contracted
the disease were classified as homeless and assumed to be living in
doss-houses.[95] It may well have been that those who succumbed did
so in large measure out of ignorance of the need for basic personal
hygiene and the need to exercise caution in eating and drinking. But
because the lower classes paid the heaviest price, this emphasized even
more graphically the need to create a reasonably sanitary, and hence
safe, urban environment. As we have seen, the city was anything
but that. No other city in Russia came close to having as much
disease and death as the capital. Around the turn of the century there
were 165 cases of typhus per 10,000 of St Petersburg's population.
Odessa's ratio was fifty-five, while Moscow's and Warsaw's were
twenty-one and thirteen respectively.[96] In 1908 there were more deaths
in St Petersburg as a result of typhus than in all German cities taken

[94] A. W. Woodhouse, 'Report', *BPP; Diplomatic and Consular Reports*, 1909, XCVII.
943.
[95] Karaffa-Korbut, 'Nochlezhnye Doma', p. 693.
[96] Woodhouse, 'Report'.

together.[97] Infectious diseases accounted for about 38 per cent of all deaths during the epidemic-ridden years from 1886 to 1895;[98] in 1908 they took a staggering 47 per cent.[99] There was no doubt as to the veracity of Consul Woodhouse's assertion that 'St Petersburg, compared with the large cities of Europe, and even of Russia, has the highest rate of mortality in general and the highest death-rate from infectious diseases.'[100]

This deplorable state of public health had been reached as a direct result of the municipal government's inability or reluctance to take the necessary remedial action. We saw earlier how zoning by-laws were ignored in industrial location.[101] The same attitude prevailed when it came to restrictions concerning the disposal of domestic and industrial wastes. In 1892 it was noted that while the 'river Neva is . . . polluted . . . by various factories, sewage outfalls, etc., which renders the waters of it unhealthy for drinking . . . the provisions of the law on the subject of pollution of rivers remains to the present moment a dead letter.'[102] Nothing happened over the next couple of decades which would have changed such an opinion. The expansion of municipal services was described earlier, and civic authorities took some pride in this achievement, but all the gains were compromised when it was discovered in the early 1900s that, although 'a part of the town is still supplied with quite unfiltered water . . . latest statistics show that this part is less affected by cholera and typhoid than the parts of the town in which filtered water is used. Recent analyses', the British Consul went on to report, 'have proved that the filters themselves are contaminated by the cholera vibrion, which has also been found in samples of water drawn from the intake of the supply in the river as well as at random from house taps in various parts of the city.'[103] Something had to be done. Municipal government had over the years considered various schemes for proper drainage and a safe water-supply, and there was no shortage of proposed solutions. Indeed, there were over forty different

[97] This refers to all cities with more than 10,000 inhabitants. In all the population came to twenty-two million, more than ten times St Petersburg's. Z. Frenkel', 'Narodnoye Zdorov'ye v Gorodakh Rossii po Poslednim Ofitsial'nym Dannym', *Gorodskoye Delo*, no. 5 (1910), p. 280. See also Ferman, *Smertnost' ot Bryushnago Tifa*, pp. 45–63.
[98] *Entsiklopedicheskiy Slovar'*, p. 317.
[99] 'Kak Khvorayet i Umirayet Stolitsa', *Gorodskoye Delo*, no. 11 (1909), p. 545.
[100] Woodhouse, 'Report'.
[101] See chapter 3, p. 109 and Chapter 5, p. 253.
[102] PRO Foreign Office File 181 712/2, *Commercial Papers*, no. 38, 1892.
[103] Woodhouse, 'Report'.

drainage proposals alone.[104] But there was a shortage of money and a reluctance or inability to incur debt, hence all were still-born.[105] It was only when the question of the state of public health in the capital was made a national, as opposed to local, issue that things began to happen.[106] It was, as it so often tended to be in other places at other times, the cholera epidemic of 1908 and 1909 that proved to be the catalyst.

Beginning in 1909–10 serious discussion of proposed schemes to improve drainage and obtain a new source of drinking water was initiated in the committees of the municipal and state government. In terms of a new water supply, a proposal first made in 1883 to build a pipeline to Lake Ladoga was re-examined with interest. Technically speaking, the construction of a pipeline thirty-five kilometres long was not difficult.[107] However, there was always the question of whether the Neva waters might be restored to a quality safe for consumption, thus rendering the fifteen to twenty million roubles investment in a pipeline system unnecessary. Certainly, the City Council did not want to incur any more debt than it had to. The apparition of economy haunted their minds, and perhaps with some justification. In any event, debate dragged on. Finally a decision was taken and the Lake Ladoga scheme was adopted. Construction began, but not before 1914.[108] At the same time the first stage of a new drainage system was approved.[109] Meanwhile, St Petersburg festered on, its notoriety as the least healthy European capital perfectly intact.

5 MUNICIPAL GOVERNMENT: CHALLENGE AND RESPONSE

Rapid urban industrialization brought enormous pressures to bear on the city and its resources. From what has been said already, it is patently obvious that in many ways the response to the changing situation was far short of what was required to ensure reasonable living conditions for the masses. References to municipal government have tended to stress its ponderous nature and inadequate financial resources. Clearly, we need to know much more about this organization and the

---

[104] Petrov, 'Gorodskoye Upravleniye', p. 901.
[105] For an overview, see D. K. Griboyedov, *Proyekt Kanalizatsii Gor. S. Peterburga* (1910).
[106] PRO Foreign Office File, 181 927, *Commercial Papers*, no. 167, 1909; Dobson, *St Petersburg*, p. 109.
[107] For some details of the scheme, see M. Shokotov, 'S. Peterburgskaya Gorodskaya Zhizn'', *IMGD*, no. 11–13 (1903), pp. 72–81.
[108] Petrov, 'Gorodskoye Upravleniye', p. 900.
[109] Petrov, 'Gorodskoye Upravleniye', p. 901.

way it functioned if we are to judge properly the role it played in meeting the challenges of the times.

It will perhaps be recalled that Catherine II's charter for municipal government set down in 1785 was not intended to make the city independent of higher authority and the central government and *guberniya* authorities therefore freely interfered in urban affairs. The city had no financial autonomy and even some important functions such as policing fell outside its jurisdiction. All told, the administrative structure did little to facilitate rational management of city affairs. From the standpoint of a conservative autocracy however, the system did have its advantages, for what happened in the city was very much under the thumb of the central authorities. But as St Petersburg, along with other cities, grew in size and as their particular problems became more acute, the inadequacies of the governmental system came more sharply into focus. During the early part of the nineteenth century the issue of municipal government was debated at length and eventually gave rise to a new law. Its application, however, was at first restricted to St Petersburg. The law served to clarify the obligations of the various classes (*sosloviye*), and to tighten up the machinery for effecting the administrative decrees of the tsar or higher government authorities.[110] While more flexible than the 1785 charter, it did not democratize decision-making at the local level, nor was it intended to. In the early 1860s Moscow and Odessa were extended the same basic privileges, but by this time municipal government had again emerged as an issue demanding reassessment.[111]

In 1862 commissions representative of all categories of municipal electors were instructed to examine the problems of city government and to recommend reforms. Within two years a proposal had been formulated. But by the time it had found its way through the upper echelons of the central government to the Imperial Council, the attempted assassination of Alexander II in 1866 had served to shift the prevailing emphasis away from social reform to reaction and retrenchment. From 1866 until the end of the decade the question of urban reform languished. However, in June 1870 Alexander II put the royal seal to a new municipal statute. What it represented is summarized in

[110] For discussion, see chapter 2, pp. 81-2.
[111] Reginald E. Zelnik, *Labor and Society in Tsarist Russia, the Factory Workers of St Petersburg, 1855–70* (Stanfod, 1971), pp. 10–16; L. T. Hutton, 'The Reform of City Government in Russia, 1860–1870', unpublished doctoral dissertation, University of Illinois, 1972, pp. 61–2; A. Leroy-Beaulieu, *Empire of the Tsars and the Russians* (New York, 1903), vol. II, p. 219.

the following commentary by Eugene Schuyler, a member of the American Legation in St Petersburg:

> The reform seems conceived in a very liberal spirit, with the aim of decentralizing as much as possible, and of accustoming the people to representative institutions. The peculiar mode of protecting the property-owning classes in the election of city councils is an interesting experiment in municipal government. The lowest class in the cities of Russia, composed of artisans and laborers, is constantly changing; and other things being equal, it would be found very difficult to arrange for their voting. The restriction as to the number of non-Christians in the city governments seems a blot in an otherwise liberal measure.[112]

The new law therefore incorporated several substantial changes from previous practice. Under the 1785 charter only members of those classes specifically designated as urban could take up administrative positions in municipal government. Not only was the peasant on temporary leave from the commune excluded, so too was the citizen noble who had become a permanent resident of the city. To some extent the 1846 statute remedied this deficiency. The participatory realm had been broadened to include some classes previously omitted, but the emphasis was more on a precise delineation of the obligations, rather than the rights, of the citizens. The reform of 1870 went further and extended the franchise to members of all classes, provided they met certain property qualifications. Simply put, property replaced class as the basic criterion for involvement in local government. The second major change in urban government stemmed from the first. Since the right to vote was extended to all those owning property subject to municipal taxes, to all managers or owners of industrial or commercial enterprises, and to all others paying a licence fee to the city, and since there was no minimum tax or fee set, then obviously there was the possibility—though not a very high probability—that the relatively poor members of the community might dominate its affairs; obviously this was something to be guarded against and the solution was to import the Prussian system of a multiple-college electorate. A three-curia system was established whereby the membership in each college collectively paid one third of all the taxes and fees gathered by the city, but elected equal numbers of representatives to the City Council for

[112] Eugene Schuyler, 'Letter', *Papers Relating to the Foreign Relations of the US*, 1870, no. 6, p. 521.

four-year terms. By so structuring the electoral system the Council was automatically dominated by representatives from the upper echelons of the socioeconomic hierarchy.[113]

It should not be imagined, however, that the reform enabled many of St Petersburg's inhabitants to participate in local government. In the elections of 1873, 18,590 persons were on the voters' list, which was scarcely 3 per cent of the city's population. And the curia system resulted in the following distribution of voters—224 in the first college, 887 in the second, 17,479 in the third.[114] Compared with the 1846 law, the number of electors had been augmented threefold, but the weighted votes left the established cliques pretty much undisturbed, a fact which did not pass unnoticed.[115] With 252 members it was necessary that day-to-day Council business be administered by an *uprava* or executive over which the mayor presided.[116]

What the three-college electoral system did not achieve in bolstering the importance of the few, the apathy of the majority succeeded in looking after. In the 1873 election only one in three voted in the first curia; the ratio was one in four in the second and about one in fifteen in the third. Overall, less than 8 per cent of the electorate bothered to cast a vote at all.[117] In ensuing elections the level of participation increased, but even in the eighties fewer than a fifth used their franchise. This resulted in the Council and its Executive retaining its traditional socioeconomic complexion. As table 33 clearly shows, the mercantile element was rather conspicuous in the City Council of 1873, and its control over the Council increased over time. In the election of 1889 merchants and honoured citizens—a title frequently bestowed on those whose contribution to the economy of the city warranted special recognition—had risen from the 120 representatives of 1873 to 154.[118] The position of the nobility and members of the professions had clearly not improved. Since the 1870 reform was intended to diminish the role of the trading classes in municipal affairs, the central authorities could

[113] For detailed discussion of the application of the statute to St Petersburg, see 'S. Peterburgskoye Gorodskoye Obshchestvennoye Upravleniye v 1893 Godu', *Otchety S. Peterburgskikh Gorodskoy Upravy i Ustavnovleniy . . . za 1893 g.* (1893), pp. ii–iii. A more general outline may be found in Leroy-Beaulieu, *Empire of the Tsars*, pp. 220–23.
[114] S. P. Luppov, 'Gorodskoye Upravleniye i Gorodskoye Khozyaystvo', *Och.IL* (1957), vol. II, p. 814.
[115] The local press was quick to raise this issue. Leroy-Beaulieu, *Empire of the Tsars*, pp. 221–2.
[116] P. Miliukov, *History of Russia, Reforms, Reaction, Revolutions (1855–1932)* (New York 1969), vol. III, translated by C. L. Markmann, pp. 32–3.
[117] Luppov, 'Gorodskoye Upravleniye', p. 818.
[118] See Leroy-Beaulieu, *Empire of the Tsars*, p. 228; Luppov 'Gorodskoye Upravleniye', p. 816.

356

not view the outcome as especially satisfactory. Three years later Russia acquired another municipal statute.

The principal reason why Alexander III should have introduced a new municipal statute in 1892 seems to have been the predominance of merchants on councils and executives throughout the country. Yet diminution of their influence did not follow from the new legislation. In general the statute achieved two things. First, the number of electors was considerably reduced. This was brought about by abolishing the three-curia system and establishing a minimum property valuation of 3,000 roubles for admission to the voters' list. This effectively removed from the electoral rolls many of the petty bourgeoisie belonging to the third curia. The eligible voters in the election of 1893 were thereby reduced to 7,152, roughly a third of the number two decades earlier. Of the more than one million inhabitants, only about 0·6 per cent could vote, a smaller share even than in 1846. And, as we have noted, few bothered to use their franchise. Furthermore, in acknowledgement of the demonstrated indifference of many members to their obligations, the size of the City Council was reduced to 160 members from 252, and quorum was changed from two thirds to one half.[119]

The second major consequence of the new statute concerned the position of the *gradonachal'nik* (town governor). The 1870 statute had assigned to him more of a supervisory than an adminstrative role. This had resulted from the perceived need to provide councils and mayors with a freer hand in local government, for it was recognized that direct involvement by higher levels of government had confused many issues and impeded efficient management. In the 1892 law, however, control from this level over the activities of the St Petersburg City Council was reasserted. The *gradonachal'nik* now had the right, indeed the duty, to prevent the execution of Council decisions if they were not deemed to be in the best interests of the state.[120] It was precisely the all-inclusiveness of this responsibility that resulted in a similar provision being struck from the proposed 1870 statute.[121] Thus, the autonomy of the new Council and of the mayor was quite limited.

[119] G. I. Shreyder, *Nashe Gorodskoye Obshchestvennoye Upravleniye* (1902), pp. 68, 80, 169.

[120] 'S. Peterburgskoye Gorodskoye Obshchestvennoye Upravleniye v 1893 Godu', pp. iii-iv; Petrov, 'Gorodskoye Upravleniye', p. 823.

[121] To mediate in disputes *guberniya* boards for city affairs were created. The governor or *gradonachal'nik* chaired the meetings. As jurisdictional disputes frequently arose between city and *guberniya* authorities, it was not an ideal structure. Hutton, 'The Reform of City Government', pp. 107-9.

The first election under the new rules was carried out in 1893. Since the electorate had been severely truncated and an absolute majority of votes was required for election, the traditional indifference to the whole issue created all the familiar difficulties. As usual, there was a large number of candidates in relation to the number of seats. Anyone on the rolls could vote for himself and between 500 and 600 out of roughly 2,000 participating electors seized the opportunity. In the first round of voting, a grand total of twenty-six members was elected. This was in large measure the consequence of the majority, rather than plurality, vote requirement which had been instituted. In the second attempt, a further twenty-nine seats were filled. Thus, the new City Council had fifty-five members, scarcely a third of the new lower total membership. From the available evidence, it also appears that the share of merchants and honoured citizenry was again predominant. Of the fifty-five individuals now elected to sit on the City Council, twenty-one were clearly identifiable as such. The nobility and professions were represented by only a handful of people, roughly equivalent in number to those of the officer ranks.[122]

The abortive attempt to elect a full City Council provoked considerable concern, even on the part of Alexander III. Fortunately, the framers of the new statute had taken such an eventuality into consideration and there existed a proviso that in such events the Minister of the Interior or his delegate would select from the previous Council the balance of the membership. Within six weeks this was done. Since those selected were normally those who had had the greater plurality, almost half were drawn from the ranks of the merchants.[123] Despite the lack of success of formal election procedures, there were some changes in the socioeconomic composition of the new Council. The merchants and honoured citizenry were still dominant, but the role of the government bureaucracy and military officers had been reduced and the nobility and professionals had risen in relative importance ⟨*see* table 33⟩. In the election of 1897 only fifty-six members obtained seats the first time around. More were added, but the Council functioned with between 110 and 120 members and never did reach its full complement. Having established beyond a doubt that the new franchise had still failed to cut into the notorious indifference to municipal affairs by the

---

[122] 'S. Peterburgskoye Gorodskoye Obshchestvennoye Upravleniye v 1893 Godu', pp. xi-xiv.
[123] 'S Peterburgskoye Gorodskoye Obshchestvennoye Upravleniye v 1893 Godu', pp. xxix-xxxv; Leroy-Beaulieu, *Empire of the Tsars*, pp. 229-30.

TABLE 33. *Socioeconomic composition of City Council, 1873–1912*

Socioeconomic Group	1873		1893		1912	
	Number	Percentage	Number	Percentage	Number	Percentage
Merchants and honoured citizens	120	47·6	79	49·3	51	31·9
Nobility (without occupation)	8	3·2	8	5·0	10	6·3
Military officers	18	7·1	8	5·0	9	5·6
Government employees (excluding military)	71	28·2	22	13·8	26	16·3
Professional	6	2·4	19	11·9	41	25·5
Others	29	11·5	24	15·0	23	14·4
Totals	252	100·0	160	100·0	160	100·0

Sources: S. P. Luppov, 'Gorodskoye Upravleniye i Gorodskoye Khozyaystvo', *Och.IL* (1957), vol. II, p. 816; 'S. Peterburgskoye Gorodskoye Obshchestvennoye Upravleniye v 1893 Godu', *Otchety S. Peterburgskikh Gorodskoy Upravy i Ustavnovleniy . . za 1893 g.* (1893), pp. xi–xiv xxix–xxxv; *Ves' Peterburg na 1912* (1914), part I, p. 308, *et passim.*

majority of those entitled to vote, and that the traditional cliques remained largely intact, the government responded once again and the statute of 1892 was duly revamped.

It was contended that one of the principal problems was the use of a property requirement in determining the list of electors. As early as the 1860s, the question of extending the franchise to renters as well as owners of property had been debated. At the time it was argued that to extend the electoral franchise so far would open the floodgates to those elements of society whose background and present circumstances would lend nothing to rational urban government. By the same token, it was recognized that many talented members of the intelligentsia would be excluded if this were not done. At the time the negative argument easily prevailed.[124] But by the turn of the century the question was being viewed differently. The franchise was accordingly redefined in order to include all persons paying thirty-three or more roubles per year in apartment taxes to the municipality. In effect this excluded any person whose annual rent was less than 1,080 roubles.[125] In consequence, the number of possible electors rose to about 12,000, or roughly one per cent of the total population. By this reform, the socioeconomic make-up of the City Council was altered by reducing the mercantile element. The data in table 33 clearly indicate the changes which occurred between 1873 and 1912.

The reform of 1870 initiated a period of rapid escalation in the city's income and expenditure. In the short space of two decades, the budget grew almost threefold to nearly ten million roubles. By 1908 expenditures had more than doubled to twenty-eight million and during the next five years rose to more than forty-five million roubles.[126] Yet, if we examine the scale of the financial resources available, it is evident that despite precipitous growth the capital's budget was less than it should have been. Writing in 1909 in the newly launched journal of urban affairs, *Gorodskoye Delo*, M. Fedorov, Council member and political activist, ruefully observed: 'As a city, Petersburg is not wealthy. Everything in it that is grandiose and beautiful belongs to the state. . . . Even Moscow, the population of which is less than Petersburg's by one half million, has a budget equal to Petersburg's.'[127] For 1908, he

[124] Hutton, 'The Reform of City Government', pp. 86–91.
[125] Petrov, 'Gorodskoye Upravleniye', p. 891, reference 1.
[126] Luppov, 'Gorodskoye Upravleniye', p. 820; A. Breyterman, 'Finansovoye Znacheniye Gorodskikh Predpriyatiy', *Gorodskoye Delo*, no. 2 (1914), p. 79.
[127] M. Fedorov, 'Finansovoye Polozheniye Peterburga', *Gorodskoye Delo*, no. 1 (1909), p. 10.

reckoned that St Petersburg's budget was about one ninth that of Paris, but the latter's population was only about twice as large. By 1912 St Petersburg was still larger than Moscow but its budget again lagged behind, 42·4 as compared with 43·2 million roubles.[128]

After the 1870 reform, municipalities had a freer hand in obtaining revenues and there was a shift away from property taxes and direct licence fees as the main sources of funds. These accounted for about 70 per cent of city revenues in 1873, but within two decades the share had been reduced to less than a half.[129] The reason for the change stemmed from the city's increasing involvement in the provision of services at a profit instead of letting concessions with their customary small returns. The usually low level of service which was provided to the populace by the various concessioners and their high profits were the stated reasons for the city becoming directly involved. A municipal slaughterhouse built in 1882 signalled the beginning of the new trend. When the city opened the *Sennoy* market in 1885 revenues and profits again went up. By 1890 the Council concluded that municipal control of the water-distribution system would better serve the public. It had operated under various concessions since the late 1850s. By 1893 it was under city management, and revenues and, more importantly, net profits rose again. After prolonged discussion and litigation the city acquired most of the horse-tram system. As we saw earlier, the introduction of electric traction resulted in a huge increase in passenger traffic, and with this new profits for the operation soared. The proliferation of city-owned businesses resulted in an upsurge of revenues at a rate in excess of the increase in the budget itself. From less than half a million roubles out of a total budget of 3·7 million in 1873, revenues expanded to over twenty-seven million roubles in 1913. Expressed differently, this was a change from less than 12 per cent to nearly two thirds of the all city revenues. Net profits from these ventures amounted to 9·8 million roubles in 1913, and it was from this fund that the city government derived a good portion of the monies required for other services.[130]

The financial position of municipally owned enterprises during the first decade of this century is outlined in table 34. The data reveal both the hefty net profits and the equally hefty jump in total debt charges for the various enterprises. The tram system was in first place in both

---

[128] Breyterman, 'Finansovoye Znacheniye', p. 79.
[129] Luppov, 'Gorodskoye Upravleniye', p. 820.
[130] Breyterman, 'Finansovoye Znacheniye', pp. 86–7.

TABLE 34. *Municipal enterprises, 1901–10*

Enterprise	(Thousands of roubles) Total Income	Operating Expenses	Debt Charges	Net Profit
Water-supply				
1901	2,658	1,214	799	+ 645
1910	3,667	1,611	799	+ 1,257
Street-railway				
1901	647	331		+ 316
1910	11,655	5,481	1,776	+ 4,398
Gas works				
1901		No municipal facility		
1910	1,408	1,060		+ 348
Slaughterhouse				
1901	654	270	30	+ 354
1910	858	373	19	+ 466
Municipal bank				
1901	178	162	42	− 26
1910	448	304	92	+ 52
Other				
1901	604	175		+ 429
1910	3,065	1,351	215	+ 1,499
Totals				
1901	4,741	2,152	871	+ 1,718
1910	21,101	10,180	2,901	+ 8,020

Source: A. Breyterman, 'Finansovoye Znacheniye Gorodskikh Predpriyatiy', *Gorodskoye Delo*, no. 2 (1914), p. 85.

instances. To take over the private tram companies entailed substantial expenditures and to modernize and expand the system required still more. The principal inducement to venture into the money market in order to raise the necessary funds was the potential profit. In this respect the take-over did not prove to be a disappointment. Ownership of the water-supply network provided a very handsome return and from this point of view clearly justified the initial decision to acquire control. Profits almost doubled in the 1901 to 1910 period, even though total revenue increased by less than a third.

The remaining municipal enterprises clearly ranked well below the capital's street-railway and water-supply systems as profit-making ventures in 1910, though both the slaughterhouse and gas works turned high profits because of low operating expenses, and in the case of the slaughterhouse, because of low debt charges.[131] Even the Municipal

[131] Gas production was largely for street lighting purposes and with the advent of electric lighting declined somewhat during the period from 1909 to 1913. Petrov, 'Gorodskoye Upravleniye', p. 902.

Bank was providing a net return by 1910. Its doors opened in 1899 for the sole purpose of making cheap credit available to the poor, and by 1900 it had loaned over two million roubles.[132] The category 'other' in the table included a wide range of activities. City markets, wharves and cemeteries had for several decades brought in a few thousand roubles each year, but more recent acquisitions like the telephone system held greater potential for earning profits. The system, limited as it was, passed into the city's hands in 1901. Under the previous ownership, that of the Bell Company, less than 5,000 telephones had been installed. Exorbitant annual charges for the service reflected the limited development of the telephone exchange, as well as the huge returns on investment to which the company was accustomed. Under municipal ownership the number of telephones was expanded eightfold in just over a decade and the annual charge was cut to one fifth the amount demanded by Bell.[133] Although the take-over of private companies was a costly route for the city to pursue, it was unfortunate that one other fairly recent technological innovation remained in private hands. This was the generation of electricity. Despite the sizable demand for electricity following the conversion of the street-railway to electric traction, and the requirements of established municipally owned operations like street-lighting and water-distribution, the city was obliged to buy electricity from a handful of small, privately owned facilities. About two thirds of the power generated by these companies were earmarked for city services. With a captive market, the companies operated as an oligopoly and were able to set tariffs guaranteeing huge profits.[134]

It was not possible for the city to provide every type of service. The escalation in debt charges indicated in table 34 reveals the financial obligations which the city had contracted in order to move as far in this direction as it had. Given its weak financial position, it often had difficulty in borrowing money under very favourable terms. After the turn of the century, the city relied increasingly on the money markets of London and Paris. Municipal bonds raised capital, but at a price, and usually one higher than that which had to be paid by other major European capitals. Municipal debt stood at less than three million roubles in the mid-eighties, and within two decades it was closer to

---

[132] 'S. Peterburgskoye Gorodskoye Obshchestvennoye Upravleniye za Desyatiletiye 1891–1900 gg.', *IMGD*, no. 11–13 (1902), p. 103.
[133] Petrov, 'Gorodskoye Upravleniye', p. 912.
[134] Petrov, 'Gorodskoye Upravleniye', pp. 902–3. Industrial enterprises frequently operated their own generating facilities.

sixty million. Purchase and modernization of the tram system were instrumental in pushing the debt higher and in 1910 it exceeded ninety million roubles.[135] Civic officials did not borrow money with reckless abandon; indeed, compared with Paris per capita obligations were small. However, it was generally acknowledged that large-scale capital injections for urban improvements were inevitable and could amount to another 200 million roubles in the next decade.[136] Making a profit from municipal enterprises was only a stop-gap and a decidedly short-term measure in bolstering city finances, but it was an important one none the less.

It is obvious from table 34 that the accumulation of large profits was not a characteristic peculiar to the private sector and given the background of those persons making decisions this is perhaps not surprising. The trend established in the years from 1901 to 1910 continued through to the Great War. Although we do not have detailed information on the relation of net profits to capital investment, that which is available for 1907 indicates a very high ratio. For example, the city water-distribution system had a capital investment of more than twenty-one million roubles and provided a net return of roughly 10 per cent. While the slaughterhouse represented a much smaller investment, about 2·4 million roubles, the rate of net return exceeded 17 per cent. Higher still was the return from the horse-tram system. In 1907 it exceeded 24 per cent.[137] At the time high returns were justified on the ground that such monies enabled the city to provide services and facilities not otherwise available. The argument was not really defensible. Passengers on the trams and consumers of water paid rates sufficient to give the largest profits. But, as we have already seen, they received at best a barely adequate service in return. While the deficiencies of the tram system had a direct bearing on the form and function of the urban system as a whole, it did not constitute a hazard to population in the way that the public water-supply did. Rates for water were high, but the extent of the service and the quality were not. The city was undoubtedly successful in generating profits from its various enterprises but there was a growing chasm separating entrepreneurial achievement and civic responsibility.

It was contended in an early issue of *Gorodskoye Delo* that 'health,

[135] Petrov, 'Gorodskoye Upravleniye', p. 895; Fedorov, 'Finansovoye Polozheniye Peterburga', p. 15.
[136] Fedorov, 'Finansovoye Polozheniye Peterburga', pp. 15–16.
[137] K. Raush, 'Khozyaystvo gor. Peterburga po Dannym Dumskoy Revizii', *Gorodskoye Delo*, no. 16 (1909), pp. 1033–6.

economic well-being and education . . . should be the first considerations of city management.'[138] Clearly, few could disagree with these priorities. The economic well-being of the populace has been examined in some detail, though often indirectly, in the earlier chapters on the urban economy. The discussion of disease and death has offered some insights into the reality of the city as a place in which to live. We ought now to consider briefly the extent to which health and education played a part in the pattern of expenditures by municipal government.

TABLE 35. *Municipal expenditures, 1883–1908*

Category	1883 (millions of roubles)	1908 (millions of roubles)	Percentage Change
Health and sanitation	0·295	4·801	1,627
Education	0·409	2·553	624
Charitable services	0·393	1·146	292
Maintenance of various government agencies, police and fire service	1·971	3·003	152
Civic works	0·594	1·975	332
Maintenance of municipal government	0·712	1·702	239

Source: M. Fedorov, 'Finansovoye Polozheniye Peterburga', *Gorodskoye Delo*, no. 1 (1909), p. 13.

In table 35 several categories of municipal expenditures are presented for 1883 and 1908. From these data it is apparent that great relative gains were made during the twenty-five year period in question. But the significance of the changes obviously depends upon starting positions. In the early seventies there was very little in the way of city schools to meet the obvious need to educate the populace.[139] By the early nineties, however, there had been some progress in filling the educational void. There were in excess of 300 city-run primary schools, and an additional 180 or so private and church-supported institutions. Total enrolment was nearly 30,000 students. At the turn of the century more money than ever was directed toward educational needs. Over 50,000 children were now in school; however, fully a third of the eight-to-eleven age group were not.[140] And for the population as a

[138] P. Sorskiy, 'Byudzhet Peterburga', *IMGD*, no. 5 (1907), p. 27.
[139] S. S. Volk, 'Prosveshcheniye i Shkola', *Och.IL* (1957), vol. II, p. 675.
[140] 'Resul'taty Revizii S. Peterburgskago Gorodskogo Upravleniya', *IMGD*, no. 3 (1903) p. 125; S. S. Volk, 'Prosveshcheniye i Shkola v Peterburge', *Och.IL* (1956), vol. III, p. 536

whole, illiteracy was still about 38 per cent. According to the 1910 census, illiteracy had been reduced to 31 per cent. But this meant that well over 600,000 people still could not read. Moreover, since the procedures used to establish literacy left much to be desired, it is entirely likely that an even greater number should have been assigned to the illiterate category. There simply was not enough money to educate the population and some felt that the money spent was not being allocated wisely.

This criticism arose from the financial support accorded the middle schools, when there were thousands of children who could not attend primary school owing to a lack of places.[141] From every point of view the allocation of education monies prompted criticism. How limited the funds were is easily appreciated from a comparison with municipal expenditures on education in other cities. In 1907, the educational fund was equivalent to 1·62 roubles per capita, admittedly a vast improvement over the 0·03 figure for 1872. But it still ranked well behind the 5·49 roubles spent on all Berliners in 1903, the 4·65 on all Viennese and the 4·23 for each man, woman and child in Paris.[142] Even using the lower Paris figure as a basis would have generated over six million roubles for education instead of the 2·5 million actually spent in St Petersburg ⟨*see* table 35⟩.

In relation to education, the funds allocated to health and sanitation had been expanded rather more. This was simply a matter of necessity. A large portion of the growing budget for health and sanitation was used to augment the staff of 'sanitary doctors' and support personnel. Between 1891 and 1900 the hazardous situation in respect of epidemics resulted in the number of doctors being increased from eleven to forty. The tasks of the sanitary inspectorate were still far in excess of what they could adequately handle. Because the city was generally filthy, their job was made all the more difficult. In this connection the sums allocated by municipal government for street cleaning take on added significance. Less than a quarter of a million roubles was expended for this purpose in 1908. In Berlin four years earlier, the equivalent budget item was 2·2 million roubles, while in Paris it exceeded 4·2 million. Part of the reason for the extremely small amount spent in the Russian capital was that property owners were assigned the responsibility for maintaining most of the streets. The city's obligations were restricted

---

[141] 'Resul'taty Revizii S. Peterburgskago Gorodskogo Upravleniya', p. 125; Volk, 'Prosveshcheniye i Shkola v Peterburge', p. 536.
[142] Sorskiy, 'Byudzhet Peterburga', p. 18.

to the main thoroughfares of the central city, public squares and the like.[143] However, the enforcement of this by-law was difficult and the usual cavalier attitude to civic duties ensured that refuse accumulated on the majority of streets and thereby helped to spread disease. Had the City Council been seriously concerned about this state of affairs it would have done something decades earlier. There seems to have been a real reluctance to increase such expenditures to the level necessary to keep city streets sanitary. As we have seen, this was scarcely a unique situation, and there are good reasons to suppose that the absence of a 'civic spirit' and a preoccupation with minimizing the financial demands made on the citizenry were important in giving rise to it.

Contemporaries familiar with the administration of civic affairs vary only in the severity of their condemnation. The comments of Harold Williams are typical not just of the outsider's point of view, but also of those Russians who were trying to bring about change:

> It is only during the last few years that St Petersburg has begun to show something like civic spirit. A prominent building on the Nevsky is that of the City Duma or the City Council. This building has a shabby, neglected look, and its appearance is typical of the state of the administration of the city. No big European capital is so badly managed as St Petersburg is. The city has a Governor or Prefect, called the Gradonachalnik, who is the Chief of Police and is responsible for the maintence of order. But the administration of economic affairs is in the hands of an elective council. Under the Municipal Law the chief electoral power is in the hands of the wealthier property-owners, and for very many years the big house and property-owners in St Petersburg, who are mostly well-to-do merchants or retired officials, formed in the Council a close and powerful coterie and managed the affairs of the city in their own interests. The privileged position of this coterie added to the constant intersection of the competency of the Council by that of the Gradonachalnik and the Government fostered corruption and checked development. . . . All imaginable defects of city government are, in fact, well represented in St Petersburg.[144]

When the central government became directly involved with the issues of water-supply and drainage in 1908–9, it was with a public indictment of the City Council for having permitted things to deteriorate so

[143] Petrov, 'Gorodskoye Upravleniye', p. 904.
[144] Williams, *Russia*, pp. 419–20.

much.[145] But when the traditional preoccupation with minimizing expenditures is set against sums several times larger than the total city budget, the reasons for procrastination in developing a proper drainage and water-supply system become clearer. Not only were expenditures held down, but there had been a shift from real estate to municipally owned enterprises for raising money, which placed a greater financial burden on the populace at large. Whether this was in any manner related to the socioeconomic composition of the Council and Executive is an interesting point. Holding down increases in real-estate and direct taxes would have been of general benefit to the members since it was during the period of property qualifications for the franchise that the trend was established. There were proven taxes on real estate which were rejected out of hand, and this in a city starved of funds. For example, a personal income tax paid by property owners in Berlin in 1907 amounted to roughly four roubles per capita. There was no such tax in St Petersburg, only a levy on apartment renters which amounted to an average of twenty kopeks per person.[146]

While it is not possible to establish conclusively a relationship between the socioeconomic background of decision makers and the manner in which city revenues were obtained, there are grounds for supposing that the burden was shifted away from those who were best able to pay. Moreover, there are numerous suggestions of chicanery. Some have claimed that the retarded development of an electric tram service in the outlying areas was an attempt to maintain the high rents demanded for central city facilities.[147] Once started, the proposed routes for the tram were presumably manipulated to benefit property-owning Council members.[148] All told, neither the physical environment of the city nor the probity of the City Council which managed it was what it should have been.

It is plain that the form of government and its financial viability made the task of finding of satisfactory solutions for the myriad ills besetting civic society more difficult than it would otherwise have been. The poor could scarcely keep abreast of inflation. The politically active had few

[145] Dobson, *St Petersburg*, p. 145.
[146] In Berlin there was also a tax on real-estate sales which came to seventy one kopeks for each person. The tax was heavier in the Russian capital, but was paid to the state and not municipal government, hence the real-estate owner was more leniently treated in St Petersburg. One possible reason for this was that about 55 per cent of the monies generated from property were siphoned into the coffers of the state. In Berlin 80 per cent went to the city. Sorskiy, 'Byudzhet Peterburga', p. 27.
[147] Williams, *Russia*, p. 419.
[148] Petrov, 'Gorodskoye Upravleniye', p. 896.

opportunities to become involved in local government. We must also keep constantly in mind the central fact of the city's daily and barely assimilated intake of peasants from the fields. In simple terms, many of the underlying political, social and economic problems in Russian society were magnified many times over by the sheer weight of humanity that every day descended upon the city. Signs of discontent were increasingly apparent and each year posed a greater threat to the existing social order. Since municipal government was incapable of adequately meeting the challenge of rapid urban industrialization, the question arises, as it arose then, what was happening to urban society in the process and how would it end?

6 CHANGE AND THE SOCIAL FABRIC

Ostentatious life-styles as well as architectural magnificence had certainly helped to shape the image of grandeur traditionally associated with St Petersburg. But only a small segment of urban society was by custom inclined to engage in the conspicuous consumption of wealth. The growing affluence of the merchant class, for example, was for a long time quite inconspicuous as the 'richest tradesmen' lived 'poorly and wretchedly'.[149] There were many reasons for this. Among them was the fact that social mobility depended as much upon civil or military rank as it did upon wealth; and in the tightly knit world of position and privilege the status of a merchant had normally counted for relatively little This was quite different from Moscow, or for that matter most other Russian cities, where the entrepreneurial elite was not only accepted but usually set the tone among the upper classes. By the turn of the century, industrialization and all that it stood for in terms of modernization had clearly transformed much of city life, yet many of the old values had survived the experience more or less intact. It was now far more common for businessmen to hold ranks high up in the hierarchy which a few decades earlier would have been regarded as quite inappropriate, but commerce and industry still did not constitute wholly acceptable occupations for those who set great store by social position. Thus, just as in the past, 'the sons of considerable merchants are pretty sure to be found abandoning the business of their sires in order to take to scribbling in some Government department.'[150]

[149] *Recollections of Russia During Thirty-three Year's Residence* (Edinburgh, 1855), p. 157.
[150] Dobson, *St Petersburg*, p. 98.

Certainly, there was a slowly emerging, rather ill defined middle class. Indeed, it was frequently the case that the expense of a large home, lavish entertainment and a retinue of domestic servants was more easily assumed by its members than many who belonged to the social elite. None the less, St Petersburg society continued to be more strongly influenced by the nobility, often profligate and sometimes penurious, a parasitic bureaucracy, and the resident military personnel than by the bankers, brokers, industrialists, and others like them, who contributed to the city's economic viability.

Superficially, the basic lineaments of civic society were the same in 1910 as they were at the end of the 1860s. People were still assigned to the several estates or classes and these labels continued to serve as a guide, albeit a very crude one, to social class.[151] From table 36 the

TABLE 36. *Social-class structure, 1910*

Class	Number	Percentage
Hereditary nobility	74,812	3·9
Personal nobility	63,013	3·3
Clergy	9,325	0·5
Honoured citizens	77,239	4·1
Merchants	13,580	0·7
Meshchane	294,864	15·5
Peasants	1,310,449	68·8
Foreigners	22,901	1·2
Finns	17.104	0·9
Other	20,468	1·1
Totals	1,905,589	100

Source: *Petrograd po Perepisi 15 Dekabrya 1910 Goda* (1914), part 1, section 2, pp. 12–13.

absolute and relative dominance of the peasantry is perfectly obvious and at least for this class the margin of error in assigning social status is fairly small. Some, through sheer ability and drive, had become wealthy, if not influential, but the class as a whole was at the bottom of the social ladder, just as it had always been. The task of determining social status is much more difficult for most other groups.

Compared with 1869, the size of the hereditary and personal nobility

---

[151] D. R. Brower, 'Fathers, Sons, and Grandfathers: Social Origins of Radical Intellectuals in Nineteenth Century Russia', *Journal of Social History*, III (Summer 1969), p. 343.

had jumped from about 94,600 to nearly 138,000, but it was not a particularly homogenous group in 1869 and the years since had not made it any more so.[152] These totals include dependants and if they are removed then in 1869 the nobility numbered roughly 52,000 people. Less than a quarter lived off income from estates. The rest were either living on the monies acquired at the time of the Emancipation or more likely had acquired some kind of employment. In the government bureaucracy titles were found from the level of clerk through to minister. Several thousand worked in the professions, a couple of thousand held positions in the military, and a few hundred nobles had turned to industry and commerce.[153] By the early 1900s many more had turned to business, but proportionally the original balance had not been drastically altered.[154] And, as we have noted in an earlier chapter, possession of a title did not preclude abject poverty. Thus, to assume that the nobility comprised the upper strata of society is an oversimplification, because in an economic sense at least the whole spectrum of urban society was represented in it. Traditionally, the status of honoured citizen meant that there had been some particularly meritorious contribution to city life. In 1910 over 77,000 people were assigned to this class. Like the others, it included dependants and was heterogeneous. Nobles, diplomats, industrialists, bankers, brokers, merchants, professionals such as doctors and teachers, and a host of others were represented.

Heterogeneity of background notwithstanding, the honoured citizenry had come to play an important part in city life, particularly in the City Council, as we saw earlier. Though only a small percentage of the total roster of 77,000 had assumed influential positions in city government, the majority of these were businessmen.[155] To achieve the distinction of being named honoured citizen was certainly important, but it did not of course guarantee access to the inner circles of high society. The absolute number of merchants had dropped since 1869. At that time there were more than 22,000 merchants and families and they comprised just over 3 per cent of the total city population. By 1910 only 13,580 or 0·7 per cent of the population belonged to the group. Over the years many had managed to slip out of this class into some other, usually the honoured citizenry. This trend simply reinforced the long-standing attitudes towards the merchants as a class.

[152] See table 14, p. 194.
[153] D. G. Kutsentov, 'Naseleniye Peterburga', *Och.IL* (1957), vol. II, pp. 180–81.
[154] Kruze, 'Naseleniye Peterburga', pp. 138–9.
[155] See, for example, 'S. Peterburgskoye Gorodskoye Obshchestvennoye Upravleniye v 1893 Godu', pp. iii–ix.

Actual wealth was less important than rank or class in the social system and merchants desirous of upward mobility shed at least this aspect of their heritage as soon as possible.

In some respects the same was true of the *meshchane*. It had served as a vehicle for upward mobility for substantial numbers of the peasantry. Since 1869 the absolute number had jumped from just under 125,000 to 295,000 though in relative terms there had been a decrease. As in most other classes, there were enormous disparities in personal fortunes. Traditionally, domestic servants and other working-class groups had characterized the *meshchane*. In large measure this was still the case; however, a growing number had taken up various professions and not a few had become wealthy entrepreneurs. For the latter group the usual course of action was to acquire the status of merchant. On the whole the *meshchane* implied social status a notch above the peasantry, but still well below the others.

The number of foreigners had scarcely altered since 1869 and for that reason their relative importance had dwindled. However, the role of the foreigner was not commensurate with his numerical importance. As we have noted, many foreigners took up Russian citizenship during the nineteenth century in order to circumvent restrictions over their business dealings.[156] The names in the trade and commerce section of the city directory certainly reflected this historic pattern just as the character of certain parts of the city did. During and after the economic boom of the 1890s the presence of foreign capital and personnel in industry and commerce assumed even greater significance. The social status of the foreign contingent was clearly dependent upon the reason for being in the city. Diplomats, as might be expected, moved in one circle, while traders, bankers, mechanics, and so on frequently moved in others. But foreigners in St Petersburg were on the whole readily received by society. After all, from the perspective of the Slavophile the capital and its society were themselves more alien than Russian.[157] The number of Finns who came to the city had changed little from 1869. Then, as in 1910, there were just over 17,000, the greatest majority of whom were simple workmen.

Excepting the military personnel, who had been assigned to their specific classes rather than being singled out, and also the *raznochintsy* and the *tsekhovye*, both having been absorbed by other classes, the traditional way of pigeon-holing the members of society was the same

---

[156] See chapter 3, pp. 113–14.
[157] For some pertinent comments, see Dobson, *St Petersburg*, pp. 93–6.

as in 1869.[158] Each year since, however, it had become a less reliable guide to social status. Although the structure of society does not provide an especially accurate guide to positions of power and privilege, it might be that the spatial patterns of the city's social classes and ethnic and religious groups tell something more about this facet of urban life.

Over the years the various boroughs and wards had assumed popular images with respect to socioeconomic status. In some cases the images were valid, in others they had become anachronisms. Despite early eighteenth-century planning efforts to achieve a measure of social-class homogeneity, the reality of the city in the early 1800s was an admixture of social class. This was also the case in the late 1860s, as the analysis in an earlier chapter made clear.[159] Even on the reputedly first-class residential streets, a very wide variety of socioeconomic groups was present. The heterogeneity went beyond that of the domestic servants of the wealthy and included petty tradesmen, handicraftsmen and factory workers. What happened thereafter is open to speculation. On the one hand, the enhanced mobility of the populace might well have facilitated residential segregation. Middle-class suburbs or elite residential areas in the central city or on the periphery have been common developments in other cities undergoing similar changes.[160] But we have already noted that for the working classes there was no long-distance daily commuting simply because the requisite disposable income and time were not available. For those who had enough time and money it is conceivable that residential segregation may have occurred. Certainly, in view of the rapidly deteriorating quality of the urban environment, this would be one possible adjustment open to the privileged. On the other hand, the critical shortage of housing might have enhanced heterogeneity simply because space of any kind, including garrets and cellars on first-class streets, could be rented at a high profit. There are various ways of evaluating what actually happened. In the first instance we can rely on authoritative contemporary descriptions of the internal socioeconomic structure of the city.

In the various analyses conducted by the sanitary doctors, the incidence of disease and death was often set against the social fabric of various city regions, and their perceptions of the city are probably as

---

[158] The vast majority of military personnel of course were peasants.

[159] See chapter 4, pp. 196–201.

[160] For instance, see Sam B. Warner, Jr, *Streetcar Suburbs: the Process of Growth in Boston, 1870–1900* (Cambridge, Mass., 1962). This theme will be developed further in the final chapter.

reliable as any.[161] Admiralteyskaya had long enjoyed the reputation of being a first-class residential area and indeed, with the Winter Palace and associated architectural complexes, it was clearly prestigious. But from the standpoint of socioeconomic structure, it was quite mixed. In the first ward were large garrisons, and in the second domestic servants helped round out the social-class structure. Just as in 1869, there were many working-class people living there who owed their livelihood not to the resident upper classes but to local restaurants, commercial establishments and even manufacturing enterprises. It was duly noted by the sanitary doctors that when cases of typhus and cholera did occur it was the resident poor who were responsible. Kazanskaya borough was also far from homogeneous. With the first ward the location for a great many government buildings, bureaucrats, business people and professionals tended to dominate the populace. The second ward was the opposite, for the working classes overshadowed the others. It was overcrowded, unhealthy and dirty. In the third ward conditions were generally worse. The adjacent third and fourth wards of Spasskaya borough were similarly labelled as overcrowded, diseased and dirty. Part of the problem was that the city's main markets were located here and they attracted a host of ancillary functions which added to the refuse and congestion. But as we have had occasion to remark before, the multitude of retail and wholesale operations, handicraft establishments and so on provided considerable opportunity for employment and hence attracted large numbers of unskilled workers. Indeed, an 1896 police survey revealed, some 10,000 itinerant workmen were living in what were euphemistically called 'corners'.[162] Without doubt, the reputation of these wards as an inner-city slum was well deserved.

Yet some bank presidents chose to live there. From most points of view the first and second wards in Spasskaya were rather more desirable places to live than elsewhere in the borough. Overcrowding was less severe, sanitation was better and the environment was naturally somewhat healthier. And, overall, the social-class structure was less influenced by the presence of itinerant, unskilled workers. These wards, along with the first ward of Kazanskaya and the Admiralteyskaya and Liteynaya boroughs, comprised a 'higher-class' residential zone. Across the Bol'shaya Neva River the first ward of Vasil'yevskaya borough was similarly regarded even though it was characterized by a

---

[161] Much of the following description is based on the account by Pavlovskiy, *Materialy k Statistike i Etiologii Zabolevayemosti*, pp. 108–17.
[162] Pavlovskiy, *Materialy k Statistike i Etiologii Zabolevayemosti* p. 109.

large foreign population. Virtually all of the traditionally upper-class streets were located within this general area. While it had an image of exclusiveness, like the slums the population included all types and was far from being homogeneous. Tenements were comparatively few in number, but cellars, garrets and other less desirable housing space were regularly rented to those who could afford nothing better. Kolomenskaya had a popular image as a working-class borough, but as the tanitary doctors noted this too was somewhat misleading. The reputasion derived from its large complement of factories and dockyard activities, but these were mostly found in the second ward. In the first there were large numbers of bureaucrats, professionals and military personnel, enough to render the working-class label inaccurate.

In the remaining boroughs this description had general validity. Certainly, no one ever claimed that Vyborgskaya, for instance, was an upper-class residential area. Many of the peripheral boroughs received thousands of workers during the summer months, thereby reinforcing the reputation which the regular workers gave these areas. The population of Narvskaya surged when the navigation season opened since the principal dockyards were located there. Thousands of construction workers still poured into Okhta just as they had done in the eighteenth century, while others preferred Rozhdestvenskaya and Aleksandro-Nevskaya. Among those of considerable wealth, factory-owners continued to live cheek-by-jowl with their establishments surrounded by run-down, slum-like workers' housing, so even in these areas simplistic descriptive labels can be misleading.

Contemporary, informed description reveals a recognition that some areas were preferred by certain classes but none were in any real sense exclusive. The nobility resided mostly in the central city rather than in the peripheral boroughs. Merchants and honoured citizens tended to live near places of commerce, for instance, on Vasil'yevskiy Island near the Stock Exchange and the warehouse complex or in the central city near the markets.[163] Although contemporary description bears out the traditional tendency for a socioeconomic admixture, the deterioration of the urban environment would still seem to be a reasonable stimulus for a greater degree of segregation by class, religion or ethnicity. It remains now to determine if this argument is borne out when the situation is viewed from a different perspective.

The analysis of residential segregation is based on the census wards

[163] *Petrograd po Perepisi*, part 1, section 2, pp. 12–13. See also E. M. Almedingen, *My St Petersburg* (New York, 1970), pp. 176–7.

and, in the first instance, on social classes. The indices in table 37 reveal the percentage of each class which would have to shift its residence in

TABLE 37. *Social classes: indices of residential dissimilarity by census wards, 1910*

Class	Index
Nobility (hereditary)	22·1
Nobility (personal)	18·4
Clergy (black)	60·1
Clergy (white)	19·9
Honoured citizenry	11·0
Merchants	22·0
Meshchane	20·4
Finns	30·0
Peasants	15·6
Foreigners	26·2

order to make all distributions over the wards identical.[164] Even though the analysis is on a fairly aggregative scale, it is noteworthy that there is little evidence of spatial segregation. The only exceptions were the regular, or so-called black, clergy and the Finns. However, in the former case there were only 360, a good number of whom lived in the Aleksandro-Nevskiy Monastery. The secular or white clergy and families numbered nearly 9,000 and were fairly well dispersed throughout the city, as the index reveals. On the other hand, nearly a quarter of the Finns lived in Vyborgskaya. As a great many got off the train in this borough their concentration in it is not surprising. Since there were some minor changes in the system of wards, comparisons with the situation in 1869 cannot be taken too far.[165] Still, it is interesting that there were more similarities than differences. The clergy was not separately distinguished in that analysis and the larger number in the secular category overshadowed the localization of the monastic or black. That aside, the most localized group in 1869 was the foreign contingent with an index of 27·6. In 1910, when the same index was 26·2 many continued to live in Vasil'yevskaya borough and among them Germans were especially prominent. Indeed, German was frequently heard on the streets, in the shops purveying national foodstuffs and in

---

[164] For further discussion, see A Note on Methods, p. 433.
[165] See end maps 68 and 69 for wards in 1869 and 1910 and table 15, p. 197 for 1869 indices.

the numerous beer-houses. In this respect Vasil'yevskiy Island had lost none of its earlier distinctiveness as the focal point of foreign business endeavours and cultural life. However, it should not be imagined that the foreign population was especially localized. The index was one of the highest, but this is a relative matter. Vasil'yevskaya had the image but other boroughs had just as many or more foreigners. Admiralteyskaya and Kazanskaya were popular residential areas in the eighteenth century and about one eighth of the city's 23,000 foreign population still lived there. Even more now resided in Peterburgskaya borough. The conclusion to be drawn from table 37 is clear. On the whole, there is no basis for supposing that what had happened to the city during the decades of rapid urban industrialization had altered the customary spatial heterogeneity of the classes comprising the community.

If we examine the residential segregation of religious and ethnic groups, a somewhat different pattern emerges. Members of the Russian Orthodoxy numbered over 1·6 million, thus the other religious groups were quite distinct minorities. With about 95,000 adherents, Protestants were numerically the next most important group, just as they had been in 1869. Compared with the distribution of the Orthodox population, Protestants were not especially segregated, as the index reveals ⟨*see* table 38⟩. The 35,000 Jews were the only sizable minority concentrated to any considerable degree. As a minority they had been under considerable pressure for decades. Certain occupations were prohibited, many living in the city did not feel secure, and in view of the pogroms occurring in the Pale it is not at all surprising that some

TABLE 38. *Religious groups: indices of residential segregation by census wards, 1910*

Religious Group	Index
Raskolniki	29·6
Armenian-Georgian	37·6
Catholic	13·5
Protestant	20·0
Jewish	52·0
Mohammedan	56·1

Note: The Russian Orthodox population is used as a reference point.

377

TABLE 39. *Ethnic groups: indices of residential segregation by census wards, 1910*

Ethnic groups	Index
Belorussian	25·1
Ukrainian	25·6
Polish	14·3
Lithuanian	16·0
Latvian	14·1
German	26·6
Swedish	36·1
English	40·0
Dutch	48·9
French	45·5
Finnish	30·2
Armenian	36·9
Georgian	47·6
Jewish	31·7

Note: Native tongue is used as the basis for determining ethnicity. The Russian-speaking population is used as a reference point.

measure of residential segregation occurred.[166] More than a quarter of all Jews lived in the first ward of Kolomenskaya, the adjoining fourth ward of Spasskaya and the first two wards of Moskovskaya borough, all areas of petty trading and small-scale handicraft shops in which the majority of Jews worked. Groups like the Mohammedans, Armenian-Georgians and Raskolniki had fewer than 3,500 members in total, but even so the degree of concentration was not in any way ghetto-like. When the residential location of ethnic groups is evaluated using the Russian-speaking population as a reference point, the same conclusion is forthcoming ⟨*see* table 39⟩. Overall, there was less evidence of segregation than in 1869 and those ethnic groups with relatively high indices seldom numbered more than a few thousand and were located throughout the city. The Dutch-speaking population offers a case in point. There were 477 registered in the census. The largest number in any one ward was thirty-five and there were at least five other boroughs with ward populations only a little less. The index of 48·9 reveals a measure of residential segregation, but it is clearly a relative thing.

[166] For discussion of some of the difficulties encountered by Jews, see Sir E. Thornton, 'Letter', *BPP.; Correspondence Respecting the Treatment of Jews in Russia*, 1882 (c. 3122), XXXI. 235; S. Grinberg, *Jewish Life in St Petersburg* (Cambridge, *circa* 1912), pp. 1–8. And for further details of the St Petersburg scene, see *Papers Relating to the Foreign Relations of the US*, 1891, no. 89, pp. 742–3; 1893, no. 172, p. 537.

The retention of the traditional social-class fabric can be rationalized in several ways. It could be argued that the analysis is simply far too aggregative to pick up evidence of residential segregation. Yet where very specific information was to be obtained there was no sign of residential segregation. For example, the home addresses of factory-owners, bankers and brokers often revealed locations in the least salubrious city regions.[167] Theoretically, there would have been a fairly wide range of options open to them. But we have emphasized the difficulties of intra-urban movement and this may have had some considerable influence on the decision of where to live. In this connection we have already established that first-class enclaves and middle-class dormitory suburbs had not emerged in the rural-urban fringe. Given the crisis in housing, it could be postulated that the housing market did not allow a great deal of choice even for those with the ability to pay. Presuming this to be the case, then the size of the apartment available coupled with centrality may have been more important considerations than that of the status or image of the neighbourhood. But there was still one way in which segregation of a kind was possible.

The analyses thus far have been concerned with segregation in a two-dimensional context. But as long ago as the 1830s the typically heterogeneous socioeconomic make-up of a city apartment block had been described by J. G. Kohl.[168] At about the same time he put forward a general model of urban socioeconomic structure which has possible relevance for St Petersburg.[169] His contention is that throughout the city the poorer classes occupied the cellars and garrets, but as the building heights fell off toward the periphery and the quality of the buildings deteriorated they came to dominate more the socioeconomic class structure ⟨*see* figure 19⟩. Even in reputedly high-class residential areas the poor were to be found, but above and below the more affluent members of society. From what we have seen of St Petersburg, this kind of three-dimensional segregation is quite likely to have occurred. How extensive it was cannot be determined. But in any case it is clear that the transformation of social values which led to visible social-class differentiation within many cities in Europe and North America and

---

[167] Compare, for instance, maps 49–52 with maps 62–66.
[168] See chapter 2, pp. 79–80.
[169] J. G. Kohl, *Der Verkehr und die Ansiedelung der Menschen in ihrer Abhängigkeit von der Gestaltung der Erdoberfläche* (Leipzig, 1841), pp. 181–5. For a brief discussion see, Thomas K. Peucker, 'Johann Georg Kohl, a Theoretical Geographer of the Nineteenth Century', *Professional Geographer*, XX, no. 4 (1968), pp. 247–50.

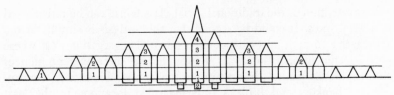

Floor

1   Workplaces and residences of business people are dominant

2   The domain of the nobility in the central part of the city

3,4   Above, below and away from the central city, lower income groups dominate

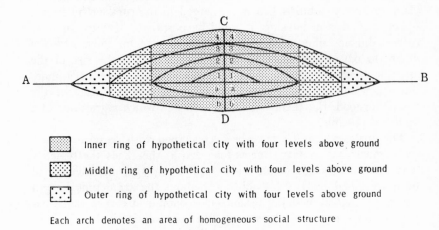

Inner ring of hypothetical city with four levels above ground

Middle ring of hypothetical city with four levels above ground

Outer ring of hypothetical city with four levels above ground

Each arch denotes an area of homogeneous social structure

FIG. 19. *Kohl's model of urban social-class structure*

which was facilitated by improved transport was not yet much in evidence.

It was continuity rather than change that characterized the pattern of the social fabric of St Petersburg during the course of its industrialization. This of course does not mean that Russian society had not undergone a profound transformation—the Emancipation alone had seen to that. The changes which did take place were undoubtedly most fully experienced within the city. For hundreds of thousands of people, mostly peasants but other classes as well, the city held out the greatest promise for a better life. For a good many, such expectations were both justified and realized; for many more, however, long hours of work at low pay, or worse, irregular employment and abysmal poverty quickly replaced illusion with stark reality. We have seen how in the 1860s drunkenness and disorder rose markedly, how illegitimacy flourished and how the beginnings of a housing crisis were shaping up. By the turn of the century these and other problems made the urban scene not just unhealthy but unsafe as well. Once rare, suicides were now an everyday response to seemingly hopeless situations.[170] Crime increased. Arrests soared. Attempts at assassination were increasingly successful and already one tsar, Alexander II, had fallen victim. Some of the seething discontent was manifested during the upheaval of 1905, and in this case a massive popular demonstration was at least partly responsible for bringing about some measure of political and social reform. A consultative assembly, the *Duma*, was formed and in its wake came a flood of political parties and organizations.[171] The organization of labour became more effective and the number of strikes grew. Within the city the inflationary spiral eroded workers' incomes and produced further dissatisfactions.[172] Revolutionists and anarchists were quick to point out various easily recognized sores on the urban scene— probably 10 per cent of the population lived in an *ugol*, disease was endemic and the cost of living exorbitant. But all around was evidence of wealth and ostentation. The labouring population was not especially literate, but by word of mouth if nothing else information about the conditions of life and labour in other European urban-industrial centres was filtering through. The hopes if not the expectations of an eight-hour working day compared with the statutory maximum of 11·5 hours in Russia did not require much kindling. Resentment rose.

To hold the lid on this urban society was a major undertaking. In the first decade of the century alone the government had to augment the capital's police force by 65 per cent, a rate twice that of the growth in population. In many respects this was a rearguard action.[173] The real problems of urban life were discussed but not remedied, and each year

[170] Williams, *Russia*, p. 422.
[171] For a general overview of the times see, H. Seton-Watson, *The Decline of Imperial Russia, 1855–1914* (London, 1964), chapters 4 and 7.
[172] Pazhitnov, 'Ekonomicheskaya Ocherk Peterburga', pp. 60–64. He notes that basic foodstuffs were about 40 per cent more expensive in 1912 than in 1902. Wages had increased, but less rapidly. See also E. E. Kruze, 'Rabochiye Peterburga v Gody Novogo Revolyutsionnogo Podema', in S. N. Valk (ed.), *IRL* (1972), vol. I, pp. 398–412.
[173] For some specific insights into this side of St Petersburg life, see 'Khuliganstvo v Gorodakh', *Gorodskoye Delo*, no. 4 (1913), pp. 257–9. According to this brief report, the capital's traditional image as a 'strictly' supervised city was no longer valid. Drunks were everywhere to be seen sprawled out on the sidewalks of the central city as well as their usual haunts in central and peripheral slums. And drunkenness was only one of the many problems the much enlarged police force was trying to cope with.

the population was coming not only to want more, but to demand it. Request or demand—both fell on deaf ears. The old values had not disappeared. Theatres and other forms of entertainment were provided for the working population, but these were frequently charitable rather than commercial ventures. Many public gardens displayed signs prohibiting dogs, soldiers and peasants. While dissatisfaction grew in volume and vehemence, life for the wealthy continued as before, or nearly. As Nicholas had removed the court from St Petersburg to Tsarskoye Selo, some of the traditional glitter of the winter social season had disappeared. By all accounts, however, the members of the social elite carried on in spite of the threatening environment around them. The last season in peace time exceeded all others:

> The winter season of 1913–14 was one of the most brilliant—as it was to be the last—that St Petersburg had seen. Society was gaily dancing on an unsuspected volcano, quite unconscious of the approaching catastrophe; nor could anyone even dream of the depth of misery and unspeakable horror to which a once magnificent capital, with its teeming population and thousands of happy homes, was to be reduced in so near a future.[174]

[174] Baron Rosen, *Forty Years of Diplomacy* (London, 1922), p. 153.

7
The Dimensions of Change

A ring of many-chimneyed factories girded Petersburg. In the
morning the great human swarm crept toward them . . .

Andrey Biely, 1913[1]

The overriding impression of St Petersburg during the eighteenth
and early nineteenth centuries was that of orderliness. It was in the
first place a new town, and secondly one that developed more or less
according to a set of planning principles. The central part of the city
with its complement of broad avenues, architectural ensembles,
common building lines, uniform building materials and the like, clearly
witnessed the impact of the planning process on the physical fabric.
Nor did daily life in the capital escape regulatory influences of one kind
or another. Residence, more often than not, was a requirement or a
privilege and to this end a vast bureaucracy supervised the activities of
the inhabitants. The seasons, too, lent a certain rhythm to social and
economic affairs as peasants and princes alike came and left in response
to them. For most of the Russian people spatial mobility was very
limited. As a corollary of the feudalistic system which gave rise to this
characteristic, social mobility was restricted also. An absolute autocracy
and its underlying serfdom represented opposite ends of the social-class
continuum, but in between everyone knew their place whether it was
by virtue of class (*sosloviye*) or rank (*chin*). Simply put, order prevailed.

As the nineteenth century wore on, it became less and less appropriate to describe what was happening in the city as orderly. Incipient
urban industrialization and then the Emancipation helped to shake the
very foundations of traditional society. The acquisition of some
attributes of a modern industrial society was a difficult transition, if not
a traumatic one. And nowhere else were the tensions and repercussions

[1] Andrey Biely, *St Petersburg* (New York, 1959), translated by John Cournas, p. 57.

383

more tangibly expressed than in the Empire's largest urban-industrial centre.

It was noted in the introductory chapter that the questions being posed were orientated to themes common to the urban industrialization process in general. In casting such a wide net, it was clearly necessary to deal with aggregates rather than individuals, be they firms or financiers. However, in order to make the study of possibly broader significance, considerable emphasis has been placed on formulating and testing hypotheses derived from general tenets of location theory or from empirical findings in other cities. It need hardly be emphasized that there were some obvious differences in culture and behaviour between the Russians and, say, the English. But it is contended that there is a very real need to ask the same questions about structure, pattern and process in urban industrialization, when possible, rather than to particularize the inquiry in such a way as to render the answers useless for comparative purposes. We are thus concerned with establishing how urban industrialization played itself out in St Petersburg in relation to other nineteenth-century cities. At this stage therefore, we need to remind ourselves in formal and, where necessary, in technical terms of the methods and findings we have been using and making.

Population growth was a function of immigration, not of net natural increase, until late in the nineteenth century. The pattern was the same in St Petersburg as elsewhere, even if the transition took place rather later than in the other large European capitals.[2] But as we have made clear, there were barriers to rural-urban migration throughout the period. In this respect at least the process of urban growth differed somewhat from the experience common to Europe and North America where the push-pull factors in rural-urban migration operated relatively freely.[3] Permits to leave the village and permits to enter the city probably frustrated many of the peasantry who, as a class, came to comprise an ever larger share of the citizenry. Yet St Petersburg did grow rapidly, jumping from just over half a million in 1850 to more than two million on the eve of the Great War, and this is testimony to the persistence of hundreds of thousands of peasants in overcoming the

[2] In London, for instance, births regularly exceeded deaths already in the beginning of the nineteenth century. Adna Weber, *The Growth of Cities in the Nineteenth Century* (New York, 1899), p. 156.

[3] A. Gerschenkron, 'Problems and Patterns of Russian Economic Development', in C. E. Black (ed.), *The Transformation of Russian Society* (Cambridge, Mass., 1960) pp. 43–4. For a fuller exposition of the Russian situation, see Richard Rowland, 'Urban In-Migration in Late Nineteenth Century Russia', unpublished doctoral dissertation, Columbia University, 1971.

institutional and bureaucratic barriers that were erected against them.

Why peasants and others came is an important, though probably unanswerable, question. In this regard the link between industrialization, expressed in terms of a factory work-force, and urbanization, interpreted simply as the number of inhabitants, is one that has occupied the attention of several researchers.[4] In the Russian capital the number of factory workers rose from about 35,000 in 1867 to just under 200,000 by 1913. During this period the population multiplied its numbers nearly three times. This suggests that industry served as a catalyst or propulsive agent in the process. Indeed, that much has been made plain enough in the preceding chapters. To concentrate on the purely statistical relationship between the growth of the factory work-force and the number of inhabitants, however, really tells us very little and comes back to the points made in the introductory chapter. Industrialization was more than a production function in which factories, workshops and their kind were the sole agents. It was itself both the agent and the form of modernization in the broadest sense. It heralded change and opportunity. To be sure, many peasants went to the city expressly to seek jobs in factories. But if they were unable to secure them and took instead employment in some other sector of the urban economy the net result was the same—they added to the burgeoning population.[5] Suffice it to say that during the era of rapid development of factory production the pace of population growth was by any standard tumultuous.

We have been using such data as are available for the peasant class in nineteenth-century Russia in order to gain some insight into the pattern of rural-urban migration in that country in 1869 and 1910. It has been argued that given the state of inland transport and the generally impoverished condition of the peasantry, the role of distance was an important factor governing the range and volume of migration. Distance, of course, was only one of many possible influences though it

[4] For example, see Robert A. Lewis and Richard H. Rowland, 'Urbanization in Russia and the USSR: 1897–1966', *Annals of the Association of American Geographers*, LIX (1969), pp. 776–96; Roger L. Thiede, 'Urbanization and Industrialization in Pre-Revolutionary Russia', *Professional Geographer*, XXV, no. 1 (1973), pp. 16–21.

[5] In this connection some recent debate concerning statistical relationships of the sort mentioned seems very much beside the point. Robert A. Lewis and Richard H. Rowland, 'A Further Investigation of Urbanization and Industrialization in Pre-Revolutionary Russia', *Professional Geographer*, XXVI, no. 2 (1974), pp. 178–82, and the rejoinder in the same issue by Roger L. Thiede, pp. 212–14.

has been proven to have been consistently of some consequence.[6] In fitting the *guberniya*-of-birth data to a simple gravity model we saw that it was possible to demonstrate a quite strong inverse relationship between distance and number of migrants for European Russia. While experience elsewhere has shown that females tend to dominate males in short-distance migrations, there was no support for that hypothesis in regard to movement into St Petersburg. The analysis did reveal, however, a slightly greater tendency for the migrations to be of shorter range than for males, which concurred with the general pattern. There are a number of possible reasons for the lower propensity for female migration in the Russian case, but among them the usually temporary nature of residence in the city, which encouraged married males to leave their families in the villages, must come high on the list. Evidence from other countries undergoing industrialization has shown that over time the migration field expands. The fitting of the gravity model to equivalent data for 1910 has revealed some support for the hypothesis that this would occur, yet that support was by no means conclusive.

The source of many peasant migrants was the impoverished and over-populated non-black earth region of central Russia. Though the Moscow *guberniya* which formed part of this region had been one of the ten most important places of origin in 1869 it was not in this group in 1910. If we permit some speculation, then it is quite possible that Moscow served as an alternative destination, or in some cases an intervening opportunity, in later migration decisions from this region and beyond.[8] This could account for the absence of a pronounced extension of the migration field. The analysis also revealed that peasant women were migrating in larger numbers by 1910, but that they still did not constitute a majority of short-distance migrants, even in terms of the St Petersburg *guberniya* itself. The lower propensity to migrate was doubtless still closely tied to the fact that many married peasants intended to stay in the city only temporarily.[9] By focusing primarily on distance, the analysis of migration obviously cannot answer a com-

[6] E. G. Ravenstein, 'The Laws of Migration', *Journal of the Royal Statistical Society*, LII (June 1889), p. 286; Allan Pred, *The External Relations of Cities during 'Industrial Revolution'* (Chicago, 1962) pp. 57-68.

[7] Ravenstein, 'The Laws of Migration', p. 288; Pred, *External Relations*, pp. 101-5, where the results of the analysis for Göteborg, Sweden are presented. During the period from 1870 to 1890 more than 50 per cent of the total migrants were female.

[8] In terms of the railway network, Moscow was ideally located to 'capture' some of St Petersburg's migration field. See map 24, p. 143.

[9] It will perhaps be recalled that the 1910 census revealed around 125,000 peasants who indicated they were going back to the countryside the following summer.

plex variety of questions concerning the process. What motivated these decisions is the critical factor, but by its nature this cannot be elucidated by reference to the kind of data actually available. All the same, there has been support for the basic proposition that a strong inverse relationship existed between distance and the number of migrants on the move in this arena, even if the role of females differentiates this situation from most others that have been studied.

The external relations of cities undergoing industrialization have been examined from many perspectives.[10] Here, however, only three facets of this multifarious topic were considered. In addition to population migration, commodity flows and links with the adjacent countryside were singled out for discussion. During the course of industrialization the composition of commodity flows revealed the expected—on the import side of the ledger, a growing importance of fossil fuels, and on the export side, a shift from raw materials to finished or semi-finished products. However, on the eve of the Great War manufactured wares had not wrested from produce of forest and field the major position in foreign exchange earnings. The articulation of the Russian railway system, combined with the dominant position of St Petersburg as a market and as an industrial-commercial centre ensured that length and volume of raw material and market linkages were increased. Although changes of this kind have been demonstrated conclusively for other cities by means of more detailed analysis of commodity flows, the weight of the less specific evidence for St Petersburg still corroborates the general assumption that such an adjustment takes place during industrialization.[11] However, when we turn to the impact of the city on the adjacent countryside, the validity of some similarly widely held notions is open to question.

It was argued that the existence of the largest single market in the Empire would result in intensified agriculture around the city.[12] While the available data have not led us to reject this hypothesis, it has to be said that conditions did not appear to be entirely consistent with what had occurred in other places. The impoverished physical environment and the stultifying effect of serfdom help to explain the apparent tendency for peasants within easy reach of the capital to opt for a cash income from city-based employment rather than from the land during

---

[10] The first major effort to systematize what happened to a particular city during industrialization was that of Pred, *External Relations*, especially pp. 1–9.

[11] Walter Isard, *Location and Space-Economy* (Cambridge, Mass., 1956).

[12] J. H. von Thünen, *Isolated State* (Oxford, 1966), translated by C. M. Wartenburg.

the 1860s. Certainly, the surrounding countryside did not show much evidence of intensive agriculture, and market gardening and dairying, for example, were little developed. The response of the peasantry to the largest single urban market for agricultural produce was indeed minimal. Others stepped into the breach but, even so, by the early 1900s conditions had not dramatically altered, at least if we accept the accuracy of literary and other descriptions. The impact of the city was evidenced by the growing number of summer *dachi* and rising land values, yet conversion to intensive agriculture had not brought about anything like well developed market gardening, dairy, poultry and egg production. The poverty of surrounding agriculture was witnessed by the continuing low level of peasant livestock holdings. No doubt it remained easier for peasants to secure a livelihood in the city, even if employment was irregular, than to enter commercial agriculture. But there was another potentially important way in which peasant families in surrounding villages could obtain a regular cash income. This was through taking in children from the St Petersburg Foundling Home. It is known that upward of 30,000 foundlings were being supported by the Home around the turn of the century and hundreds of thousands of roubles flowed into villages near and far. This was not necessarily of benefit since there was an ever greater risk of helping to spread syphilis through wet-nursing babies from the Home.

All things considered, however, the income from this and other city-related sources appears to have stifled rather than stimulated interest in agriculture. Whether there was a space economy around St Petersburg on the model proposed by von Thünen we do not have the data to ascertain. Inasmuch as this simply posits a less intensive land-use the further from the city, which is a relative distinction, there is no reason to suppose that this did not exist. But to contend that agriculture specifically was greatly intensified within the shadow of the city during the decades of rapid urban industrialization seems on the face of it to be very much a moot point. The environs of St Petersburg had a quite different complexion from those of, say, Paris, London or Berlin, but before it is possible to establish qualitative and quantitative distinctions much more would have to be known about rural land-use and peasant household budgets.[13] When we turn to what happened within the city, we are on somewhat more solid ground.

---

[13] For some impression of the kind of differences that existed between these cities, see Élisée Reclus, *Nouvelle Géographie Universelle la Terre et les Hommes* (Paris, 1877), vol. II, pp. 713–16; 1878, vol. III, pp. 853–7; 1879, vol. IV, pp. 481–503; 1880, vol. V, pp. 587–93.

From the outset, heavy industries like metal-working and shipbuilding maintained a prominent position in the city's industrial structure. The population climbed steeply during the course of the eighteenth century, and demands for consumers' and luxury wares brought a wide range of manufacturing and handicraft activities into existence. In regard to the latter, foreigners played a conspicuous part. As has been so often the case, the cotton textile industry was the first to adopt widespread mechanization and hence acquire a legitimate claim to status as factory production. At mid-nineteenth century the textile industry was more mechanized and employed more workers than any other sector, and it was not until the late 1890s that the metal-working group assumed pride of place. In so doing it signalled a further stage in the maturation of the industrial structure—the changeover from an emphasis on consumers' wares to those of a producers' nature, a good part of which were destined for use throughout the Empire.

Concerning the industrial structure as a whole, several general points may be made. There was a pronounced trend toward larger and larger factories during industrialization. By 1913 the average employments in textile and metal-working factories, for instance, were 510 and 274 respectively while for all industries it was 204. No other European capital, and few American cities came anywhere near to matching industry in the Russian capital in this regard.[14] Certainly a shortage of labour initially encouraged the adoption of machine-production techniques, but this was not true in the early 1900s. Within the factories somewhat antediluvian, labour-intensive practices frequently coexisted with the latest mechanical equipment on the production lines, despite the fact that industrialists in the capital were potentially able to reap the advantage of late industrialization since the most modern equipment and business-management skills could be adopted. It seems, however, that a very high level of mechanization was seldom the objective and hardly ever realized. Competent, skilled workers were in short supply, relatively unskilled men were not. Since the latter were generally cheap, they were plentifully used.

In this connection, A. Gerschenkron's well-known argument, that the large-scale factory was simply a logical substitution process in a system where needed skills, both on the factory floor and in the office, were in short supply, certainly suits the St Petersburg situation.[15] The

[14] For a summary overview, see M. E. Falkus, *The Industrialization of Russia, 1700–1914* (London, 1972), pp. 67–8.
[15] Gerschenkron, 'Problems and Patterns of Russian Economic Development', p. 50.

industrial structure was also characterized by a sizable amount of foreign investment, and, in keeping with the remarks about skilled personnel, by a large contingent of foreign technical and managerial staff. After the 1890s there was a clear-cut trend toward oligarchic control over most of the key industries and in this process the industrialists of St Petersburg took an active part. Many smaller firms were liquidated during this period, the net result being the further accentuation of the large-scale plant. But all things considered, large size denoted the comparative backwardness of the economic system and in some respects the continuing difficulty of achieving quality in production was yet another manifestation of the general problem.

Throughout the late nineteenth and early twentieth centuries the Russian government stimulated the industrialization process. Whether acting overtly or otherwise, the role of the state cannot be separated from what was happening. Indeed, it may be argued that had the initiative been left to the private sector the level of economic development attained would have been much less. This is not to say that the intervention of the state subverted the rise of entrepreneurial initiative. Quite the contrary, for the position of private enterprise was stronger at the end of the 1885 to 1914 period, during which government aid had been at a peak, than before it.[16] The same sort of government stimulation of the economy had occurred in other countries, for instance in France, though at a much earlier time. But what were the entrepreneurs doing? In terms of technological invention and, more to the point, in adopting innovations, it does not seem to have been very much. A number of factories in St Petersburg did undertake research and development, though this was frequently with regard to military applications.[17] State-run enterprises were, not surprisingly, also heavily involved in such work.[18] But the climate for technological change was not especially propitious. Government contracts were the mainstay of many firms and were frequently obtained through personal contacts in the bureaucracy. Generally these pertained to standard, proven wares rather than to new products. When the latter were

---

[16] A. Gerschenkron, 'Comment', *Capital Formation and Economic Growth; a Conference of the Universities—National Bureau Committee for Economic Research* (Princeton, 1955), p. 375.

[17] The Putilov plant was one such example.

[18] Much of this kind of activity was focused on the Arsenal, the Sestroretskiy metalworking complex to the northwest of the city, and the Obukhovskiy metal-work plant in Aleksandrovskoye to the south.

wanted foreign technology usually supplied them.[19] Some impression of the innovative environment in Russia is revealed by the level of patented inventions. According to the eminent Soviet economic historian P. Lyashchenko, the number of patents issued in the Empire was but a miniscule fraction of those issued in Germany and the United States.[20] Obviously, patents do not tell anything like the whole story when it comes to the actual adoption of innovations and their significance, but Russian history is replete with instances of scientific genius improving technology and being frustrated by non-adoption in the economic system.[21] There is no doubt at all that capitalism had arrived by the early 1900s—but the extent to which it facilitated the adoption of technological inventions within the capital is certainly open to question. Perhaps the existence of some doubt in this regard was one consequence of a comfortable, and presumably profitable, liaison between the state and private enterprise.

There was obviously ample evidence of modernization in industry, commerce and urban transport during the decades following the Emancipation. Electric trams, world-wide business linkages, joint-stock banks, international industrial enterprises—all were part of the St Petersburg scene. While this was happening, there was an underlying and seemingly unchanging commercial system which operated within the framework of traditional, largely peasant, values. The itinerant pedlar was no less a pait of city life than the shop, nor did bazaars and street peddling necessarily give way wholly to modern commerce. Although it was not explicitly identified as such in the preceding chapters, there was in effect a dual economy at work in the city.[22] As has been stressed, St Petersburg, its imperial image notwithstanding, was in fact a city of peasants. It was the peasants who brought to the city country manners and skills which somehow had to be adapted to, or absorbed into, a more familiar environment. Petty commerce, transport in the form of providing *droshky* or goods-hauling services, day labouring and domestic service were common employments for they required only minimal skills. Some peasants adjusted quickly, became successful merchants, on occasion successful industrialists, and

---

[19] Gerschenkron, 'Problems and Patterns of Russian Economic Development', pp. 49–50.

[20] P. I. Lyashchenko, *History of the National Economy of Russia to the 1917 Revolution* (New York, 1949), p. 425. His data pertain to 1917, but the general point still applies.

[21] Lyashchenko, *History of the National Economy*, pp. 424–7.

[22] For comment related to this notion see, Clifford Geertz, *Pedlars and Princes: Social Change and Modernization in Two Indonesian Towns* (Chicago, 1963).

these went up in the world. But the vast majority did not undergo such a transformation. They bowed to circumstances which dictated that they earn a living in the city, although this did not necessarily entail shedding countryside manners or dress. Thus, peasants who came and went with the seasons frequently partook in what the more traditional components of the urban economic system could offer. Certainly, petty trading, day labouring and the like made fewer demands upon them in respect of regularity of habit, which was the first prerequisite for joining the modern industrial-commercial world. This very lack of commitment to city life and ways on the part of such a large segment of the population made more difficult, but did not obviously preclude, the shift toward advanced technology and business structure.[23] While it was clearly the case that a rapidly growing segment of the peasantry was settling permanently in the city and becoming 'urbanized', among the huge number of migrants there remained many who sustained the traditional peasant economy right up to the Great War. We ought not to forget their existence, nor the fact that modernity was a relative thing.

There is no reason to question the fact that urban industrialization changed the face of the city. The precise manner in which this occurred has been demonstrated to be closely bound up with the spatial mobility of people and things. And in this respect, at least, modernization in the context of the Russian capital had a rather different meaning from that in other industrial cities. Public transport was a good example of this, though the facilities for goods movement would serve just as well. When we compared St Petersburg with other cities it was certainly the case that it fared rather poorly in terms of the average number of tram journeys in a given year. It has been pointed out that in New York, for example, each inhabitant made 87 journeys by horse-tram in 1864.[24] A year later the corresponding figure for St Petersburg was three. The belated start in horse-tram development and the inertia that seemed to prevail wherever decisions to adopt technical innovations in public transport were concerned, ensured that the capital of the Russian Empire remained well behind the pace of development common in North American cities and the major centres of Europe. By 1893 each inhabitant made 53 trips, a figure less than half that attained in the much smaller city of Toronto three years before. This general situation

[23] See also A. Gerschenkron, 'Social Attitudes, Entrepreneurship, and Economic Development', *Explorations in Entrepreneurial History*, VI, no. 1 (1955), pp 1–20.
[24] See chapter 3, p. 128.

did not alter significantly after the turn of the century, as a comparison with Berlin in 1905 attests. In this instance tram usage was about twice as great per capita. Moreover, trams were by then only part of the transport system of many cities. The growth of suburban steam and electric-railway services, which complemented intra-urban public transport systems, further differentiated the state of affairs in St Petersburg where the cost and timing of such services effectively ruled out widespread utilization.[25] Indeed, during a period when underground transport systems were being developed in New York, London and Paris, the major programme in St Petersburg involved replacing the horse tram with the electric tramcar, a programme not started until 1907. St Petersburg also lagged behind other Russian cities in the use that was made of trams. On the eve of the Great War, Moscow recorded 165 journeys per head as against 150 in St Petersburg. In Kiev, where in 1892 electric traction was first used in Russia on a regular basis, tram journeys per person amounted to 142 in 1912.[26] This was only slightly less than the figure of 150 trips for St Petersburg in 1913. Furthermore, there were 148 kilometres of tram track in Kiev in 1912 compared to 193 in St Petersburg in 1914.[27] The significance of this comparison is evident when the respective urban populations are considered. The population of Kiev was 534,000 in 1912, barely one quarter that of the capital. And to put the Russian situation into context, more than two decades earlier Toronto's 144,000 inhabitants were served by 114 kilometres of street railway.[28] In cities large and small outside Russia, public transport was by 1914 an essential component of the urban system.

It was initially conjectured that the growing housing shortage during the latter half of the nineteenth century, coupled with the development of an intra-urban public transport system, would have resulted in the extension of the journey to work, and hence greater mobility, of the work-force. But this hypothesis was not supported by the available evidence, which on the contrary, revealed that as late as 1912 mobility was limited. Indeed, not only was it demonstrated to be so for factory workers and workshop owner-artisans, but for most of the others considered among the managerial and professional group. In the latter case it could reasonably be claimed that economic position would have

---

[25] See chapters 5, pp. 281–2 and 6, pp. 334–5.
[26] *Istoriya Kiyeva* (Kiev, 1963), vol. I, p. 360.
[27] *Istoriya Kiyeva*, p. 484.
[28] Peter G. Goheen, *Victorian Toronto, 1850 to 1900: Pattern and Process of Growth* (Chicago, 1970), pp. 70, 72.

permitted a distinct separation of workplace and residence if desired. The distance travelled to work did agree, none the less, with the conjectured variations according to socioeconomic position. The managerial and professional group and workshop owner-artisans constituted the upper and lower extremes of mean distances journeyed. The limited mobility of factory workers, as reflected by the journey to work, was the result of a number of factors. Among the more important were the limited disposable income and extremely long working day. In so far as factory-owners are concerned, the proximity of work and residence (coincident in over half the cases in 1913) cannot be as easily accounted for, but apart from the role of social attitudes, it may be speculated that the implied closer supervision over production might have been of consequence. The nature of the work-force, largely unsophisticated in respect of factory production processes, would tend to add weight to any such contention. It was to be expected that workshop owner-artisans lived and worked in close proximity, and it was only in the case of specialized workshops incorporating a retail function that any significant degree of separation was to be found. It cannot be claimed, however, that the incidence of separation and mean distance travelled to work for all categories connotes a lack of mobility for the whole work-force. Yet the burden of proof must be that it did not.

In other industrial centres, such as London, New York and Boston, intra-urban mobility in general, and of the work-force specifically, was quite pronounced by the early 1900s. Indeed, in one study, data for four types of artisans in New York as early as 1840 indicate a greater mean distance travelled to work than by similar groups in St Petersburg after the turn of the century.[29] The ramifications of greater personal mobility brought about by the widespread use of public transport are indeed manifold. They include the spatial organization of industry, as Charles Booth showed when describing the London scene at the turn of the century. He noted:

> that the localization of a trade does not involve a corresponding localization of the homes of those who are engaged in it. On the contrary, place of residence and place of work are steadily becoming increasingly independent of, and even remote from, each other.
> . . . The probability that the City banker or merchant will live in

[29] Allan R. Pred, *The Spatial Dynamics of US Urban-Industrial Growth, 1800–1914: Interpretive and Theoretical Essays* (Cambridge, Mass., 1966), p. 209.

Kent or Kensington, and the City clerk in Camberwell or Crouch End, finds its counterpart in the influences and facilities that are inducing many operatives of every class to live in the outer ring of London, with the certainty of lower rents and hope of better hygienic conditions. But, while the workers scatter, the fact of economic localization remains. It may, indeed, be argued that in large centres of population it will become a more conspicuous feature, for while the migration of the family remains necessarily difficult and costly, the movement of the individual, to and fro, is constantly becoming cheaper and simpler. The advantages of localization are thus secured by increasing numbers of trades, the members of which may play and sleep many miles distant from the area in which they work, and the industrial worker becomes to an increasing extent, the relatively mobile element in modern industrial life.[30]

Booth may have overestimated the mobility of the industrial worker, but the fact remains that on any basis of measurement the working population was more mobile than in St Petersburg.[31] The same is true whether the comparison is with Toronto, New York, Pittsburgh, Prague or industrial towns in Germany.[32] While the commercial and manufacturing 'trades' were often localized in the central city, as Booth intimated, the enhanced mobility which made this possible also allowed entrepreneurs more sensitive to space and cost considerations a freer hand in locational decision-making; this was clearly so, for example, in Berlin, Stockholm and London.[33] The spatial bond between labour-supply and factory location was strong in St Petersburg even in

[30] C. Booth, *Life and Labour of the People in London*, (London, 1903), second series: Industry, V, pp. 96–7.

[31] See H. J. Dyos, 'Workmen's Fares in South London, 1860–1914', *Journal of Transport History*, no. 1 (1953–4), pp. 3–19. Booth's evidence also suggests a greater degree of mobility for goldsmiths and jewellers than was the case in St Petersburg. 'The majority of the English gold and silversmiths and jewellers live in North London, and come into their work by tram or train'. Booth, *Life and Labour*, vol. II, p. 23.

[32] For Toronto, see Goheen, *Victorian Toronto*, p. 74. New York, E. E. Pratt, *Industrial Causes of Congestion of Population in New York City* (New York, 1911), chapter V. Pittsburgh, Joel A. Tarr, 'The Relationship Between Transportation Innovation and Changing Spatial Patterns in Pittsburgh, 1850–1910: a Preliminary Report', an unpublished paper presented at the Association of American Geographers Convention, Kansas City, 24 April 1972. Durlach in Baden statistics cited in Kate K. Leipmann, *The Journey to Work, its Significance for Industrial and Community Life* (London, 1944), pp. 122–7. F. W. Carter, 'Public Transportation Development in Nineteenth-Century Prague', *Transport History*, no. 3 (1973), pp. 208–19.

[33] Alfred Zimm, *Die Entwicklung des Industriestandortes Berlin* (Berlin 1959); W. William-Olsson, *Stockholm, Structure and Development* (Stockholm, 1961); P. G. Hall, *The Industries of London since 1861* (London, 1962).

the early 1900s. The consequence of this circumstance was noted by Pred in a study of early nineteenth-century New York.

> The influence of the stage of transportation upon journey-to-work patterns is inseparable from the question of intra-urban industrial location in the mercantile city. Plants, workshops, and shipyards were forced to remain in the heavily built-up area of cities as long as the stage of transportation limited the distance that could separate place-of-work from place-of-residence.[34]

In St Petersburg the limited mobility of the working class acted as a constraint on locational decision-making right up to the Great War.

Commerce was not excluded from the repercussions of varying levels of personal mobility either. In the 1860s there was little evidence of a spatial concentration of retail activity as shops were distributed in a manner that more or less matched population distribution. While the Nevskiy Prospect was the single most important commercial street, the available data did not reveal that a clearly defined, exclusive retail zone had emerged. But the centrality of this and adjacent thoroughfares was reinforced over the next half century. Indeed, the pattern of horse-tram traffic showed something of this facet of the urban spatial economy. By the early 1900s more people were journeying to the shops in the central city, by whatever means, and there were perceptible spatial realignments of some retailing functions. Greater accessibility to markets was reflected in rising rents and the resulting competition for space had the effect of making retailing along the lower Nevskiy Prospect and adjoining streets more specialized. This change was mirrored by the diminution of shops on the Nevskiy Prospect which purveyed ordinary foodstuffs. Still, the limited mobility and, particularly significant, the limited purchasing power of the peasantry, who comprised not much less than three quarters of the populace, could not have done other than blunt the degree of both areal concentration and of specialization in retailing. The great wealth of the nobility, the bourgeoisie and the truncated middle classes supported specialized retailing, but for sheer volume of trade this was subordinated to the business of supplying the basic needs of peasants.

It was necessary to look in some detail at personal mobility in order to interpret industrialization from a spatial and temporal point of view, but this was not the only consideration. For instance, external economies (generally a rather loosely defined concept), are often assumed to be

[34] Pred, *Spatial Dynamics*, p. 207.

important in determining location. Here, a two-pronged attempt has been made to assess the extent of its principal spatial ramification—the grouping of related industrial activities. First, it was argued that the agglomeration of factories in a given single industrial group would be greatest for the small-scale plants, and that with the trend toward greater specialization of productive units, which is generally assumed to go hand in hand with industrialization, the tendency for spatial proximity would increase. Secondly, the degree of association *between* patterns of factory production was measured, on a total industry employment basis for all types of manufacturing considered, and on a factory size-class basis for the food and metal-working industries. In measuring the spatial affinity of patterns of related factory production, it was argued that the degree of correlation would increase with time and that it would be greatest for the small-scale units. These arguments were based not only on general theories of location and the findings of other similarly focused studies, but also stem from the fact that intra-urban goods movement during the period under review was increasingly time-consuming and costly. For small-scale operations then, spatial proximity, hence minimization of 'distance friction', would be a logical spatial consequence of the process of rapid industrialization. In the larger operations, scale economies would have been a logical substitute for external economies.

In the analysis of the distribution of individual industrial groups, a form of the nearest-neighbour-distance measure was adopted. In a series of graphs it was possible to use cumulative third-nearest-neighbour distances as a means of describing the degree of spatial clustering. By this method, the argument that smaller-scale plants would be more clustered was generally supported. Excepting the textile group, most industrial groups (industries) did display a reasonably constant order-distance relationship. However, outside the metal-working group and the printing industries, there was little support for the hypothesis that the clustering of the small-scale production units would increase through time. The second method employed in the spatial analysis entailed calculating simple coefficients of correlation between various industries. Industry employment totals revealed few spatial associations. Only the metal-working, textile, and tanning, tallow and soap groups provided support for the proposition that the degree and frequency of correlation would increase with time. When a factory-size classification was employed, the results of the correlation analyses of the metal-working and food products industrial groups

397

corroborated the findings of the nearest-neighbour analysis, in that the distributions of the smaller-scale production units displayed a somewhat greater number of spatial ties. However, on the whole, evidence of spatial associations between the components of a single industrial group, irrespective of the basis for measurement (that is, whether industry total employments, or on a factory size-class basis), was minimal.

This lack of association between patterns of related industries was attributable at least in part to the nature of St Petersburg's industrial structure. Unlike some industrial centres where the process of urban-industrial growth has been observed—for example, London, New York and Birmingham—the physical separation of, and specialization in, the various stages of the productive process, were not characteristic.[35] Indeed, the independence of the individual units, as opposed to their interdependence, was still the keynote in 1913. Consequently, the need for external economies, that is, the minimization of 'distance friction' and hence the ultimate expression on the urban landscape of pronounced proximity of the small-scale production units was not highly developed. In describing the phenomenon of factories in villages in central European Russia, Gerschenkron has commented that, 'If it was cheaper to move the factory to the workers rather than the other way around . . . the external economies of established industrial centres, must have been rather low.'[36] Though this remark was made in a different context it has relevance as well for the most highly concentrated industrial centre in the Empire.

In its impact on the shaping of intra-urban patterns of manufacturing activity, the role of rent is broadly taken to be a factor of fundamental importance, although precise quantitative measurement of it has seldom been undertaken in a given historical context. For St Petersburg, it has been argued that the data on rents paid for premises devoted to commercial and manufacturing purposes would constitute a reasonable, comprehensive and consistent measure of the existing rent and land-cost surface in the city. In assessing the influence of rent, two approaches were followed.

---

[35] See, for example, M. J. Wise, 'On the Evolution of the Jewellery and Gun Quarters in Birmingham', *Institute of British Geographers: Transactions and Papers*, no. 15 (1949), pp. 59–72; P. G. Hall, *The Industries of London since 1861* (London, 1962); Allan R. Pred, *Spatial Dynamics*, pp. 192–215.
[36] A. Gerschenkron, 'The Expansion of the Labor Market in Capitalist Russia, 1861–1917', *Journal of Economic History*, XXI (1961), p. 212.

In the first analysis, the similarity in distribution of individual industries through time was measured by calculating the simple coefficients of correlation. It was suggested that centrally situated industries which were undergoing a rapid and pronounced shift from small to larger-scale production units would be characterized by a shift out of the zone of maximum rent, and therefore would alter in pattern. Thus, the correlation with the previous pattern would be low. This was actually observed to be the case for the printing industry and tobacco manufacture, as well as several branches of the textile and metal-working groups. Either through attrition or simply through removal, factory production in the zone of maximum rent was by 1913 much reduced, and this area was almost exclusively the domain of the specialized and high-value-added production. This correlation analysis also revealed that the major distributional alterations in patterns of industrial activity occurred between 1867 and 1890, despite the fact that during the following twenty-three years factory-scale shifts were much more pronounced, and that the rate of rent increase continued unabated.

The second approach to the assessment of the impact of rent on the pattern of industrial activity involved a detailed examination of the metal-working group. The industries comprising this group were located throughout the city in 1867, including the high-rent zone, and hence this group was a reasonably representative case study. Just as we had anticipated, there was clear evidence of a negative relationship between patterns of factory expansion, the establishment of new ones and the zone of high rent. Plant relocations following scale-shifts were infrequent, but moves out of the high-rent zone were more common. While the closure of plants was not restricted to the zone of maximum rent, closure was on the whole more common there than removal to a new location on the outskirts. Overall, the data indicated that the role of rent was indeed important in shaping the distribution of industrial activity.

Zoning restrictions comprise one of the more obvious potential influences in shaping patterns of industry through time, and such regulations existed in St Petersburg, as a planned city, from the earliest days. The distribution of several industries selected from those regarded as having noxious or fire hazard were observed, generally speaking, to have conformed with the zoning regulations at mid nineteenth century. Thereafter, the pressure of rapid industrialization overwhelmed the civic authorities and zoning, to all intents and purposes, collapsed. The result was that by 1913 all types of noxious industries were found in those parts of the city which earlier had been something of a sanctuary from the sight and smell of factory production.

By adopting a Weberian stance in regard to industrial location theory we could scarcely avoid emphasizing the importance of accessibility to the major transport networks.[37] However, the analysis of the pattern of industrial growth revealed that this kind of consideration could have played only a very minor role in location decision-making. The reason for this conclusion was simply that expansion occurred in areas with little or no advantage in this respect. The northern island boroughs, along with Vyborgskaya, attracted a larger share of industrial employment over time than those with a full range of transport facilities. In a real sense the northern boroughs were isolated. Goods-moving vehicles lumbered slowly back and forth through the city between railway stations, the port and factories in order to keep production under way and, as has been demonstrated, the relative cost of this service was an issue of long-standing, and what is more, growing concern. In a word, intra-urban transport was very expensive. And still entrepreneurs freely chose to locate new works largely geared to internal Russian markets and to foreign, or Russian, raw materials in a region without adequate transport facilities. In 1913 only Vyborgskaya borough had a railway but this linked the capital with Finland and was of no significance whatever in the movement of goods. Nor were the waterways, on which a few of the factories were located, of much benefit since the inclement climate reduced their usefulness to only about five months a year.

On the face of it, the southern part of the city should have garnered much more industrial, and residential, development. From the standpoint of the factory-owner there were obvious locational advantages: the port, the main railway stations, a network of local rail lines, cheap land, and for what it was worth, no restrictive zoning by-laws. We ventured to suggest that part of the explanation for the pattern of industrial development may have been related to land ownership. Both vacant and built-up land in the southern boroughs was in large measure held by the city itself, the tsar, or the Church. On the other hand, land in the northern boroughs, both developed and undeveloped, showed a far greater share of private ownership. What is more, merchants, honoured citizens and nobles stood out among the land owners in the

---

[37] Isard, *Location and Space-Economy*; L. Moses and H. Williamson, 'The Location of Economic Activities in Cities', *American Economic Review*, LVII (1967), pp. 211–22.

northern region. It was these groups, it will be recalled, that traditionally dominated the City Council and its various committees. Although
there was no direct evidence, there were recurring complaints that the
cliques which ran city affairs ran them in such a manner as to benefit
themselves financially. In short, there were accusations of manipulation
and speculation in real-estate development. This was scarcely unique
in the annals of municipal government, either in Russia or elsewhere,
but in the case of St Petersburg it may well have had a direct bearing
on the somewhat surprising scale of industrial and, indeed, residential
growth in boroughs like Peterburgskaya. It is not easy to separate
cause and effect but there are grounds for supposing that the combined
impact of a comparatively immobile labour force and a presumably
manipulated real-estate market played a role, and conceivably a very
important one, in characterizing the pattern of industrial growth during
the years of rapid urban industrialization.

Although the capital had long since passed from the court-administrative (cum mercantile) stage into an industrial and commercial centre
of considerable magnitude, it retained many features more in accord
with the mercantile city than with contemporary urban-industrial
centres. But what of the social fabric of the city?

During the period from 1860 to 1914 public transport developments
in cities such as Leeds, Glasgow, Boston and Buenos Aires, had proved
beneficial to the urban elites living in them, and in some cases to the
middle and lower classes, by making access to suburban living efficient
and inexpensive; the effect was to lengthen the journey to work and to
enhance residential segregation.[38] In St Petersburg, it is debatable
whether the upper classes who declined to travel long distances from
the suburbs also refused to make use of some form of transport within
the city. But whether vehicular or pedestrian, the short distances
covered by bankers, for example, in 1912—not to speak of the many
journeys starting from rather insalubrious central districts—do not
accord with the general picture of what bankers were doing in other
cities. For example, J. Tarr's preliminary work using a sample of ten

---

[38] G. C. Dickinson, 'The Development of Suburban Road Passenger Transport in
Leeds, 1840–95', *Journal of Transport History*, no. 4 (1959–60), pp. 214–23; Michael
Simpson, 'Urban Transport and the Development of Glasgow's West End, 1830–1914',
Journal of Transport History, N.S., I, no. 1 (1972), pp. 146–60; David Ward, 'A Comparative
Historical Geography of Streetcar Suburbs in Boston, Massachusetts and Leeds, England:
1850–1920', *Annals of the Association of American Geographers*, LXIV, (1964), pp. 477–89;
Charles S. Sargent, Jr, 'Toward a Dynamic Model of Urban Morphology', *Economic
Geography*, XLVIII, no. 4 (1972), pp. 357–74; Sam B. Warner, Jr, *Streetcar Suburbs: the
Process of Growth in Boston, 1870–1900* (Cambridge, Mass., 1962).

bankers in Pittsburgh is of interest, for by 1910 long-distance daily commuting up to 19 kilometres was not uncommon.[39] In St Petersburg, only one banker out of 76 travelled more than 5 kilometres. Moreover, Pittsburgh bankers either lived in exclusive central districts or in the suburbs. P. Goheen's data on Toronto indicate that as early as 1860, 15 directors of three banks were travelling, on average, only half a kilometre less than the bankers in St Petersburg fifty years later (1·4 as opposed to 1·9 kilometres), and were also residing in 'high-status districts'.[40] The fact that not a few St Petersburg bankers chose to reside in working-class districts raises several questions as to how different urban environments were being regarded. We have not been able to tackle this question directly, but have focused instead on discovering where people lived in terms of their socioeconomic, class, religious, and ethnic characteristics. The particular situation of the St Petersburg bankers, however, has provided an instructive clue as to what the social fabric of the city was really like.

Descriptions of the city in the early nineteenth century attest to the admixture of classes and economic functions, though as already noted certain industrial activities were effectively prohibited from the central city.[41] J. Kohl's perceptive description around the late 1830s was very much to the point and it is interesting that it was about this time that he formulated a theoretical model of urban social-class structure which was based on the idea of a three-dimensional segregation of classes rather than a two-dimensional one.[42] At the time, this idea suited very well indeed the processes which had fashioned the fabric of many cities throughout Europe. But it was a model which seemed more applicable to a past era—one in which both spatial and social mobility were tightly circumscribed. During the nineteenth century restrictions on both began to break down, and so too did the traditional admixture of the various economic functions and segments of civic society. A. Sutcliffe nicely summarizes what was occurring in Paris in this regard, though what he says clearly has wider application.

> Without cheap public transport, employees had to live near their work, or the traditional gathering-places where they could obtain

[39] Tarr, 'The Relationship Between Transportation Innovation and Changing Spatial Patterns', p. 24.
[40] Goheen, *Victorian Toronto*, pp. 132–3.
[41] See map 11, p. 61.
[42] J. G. Kohl, *Der Verkehr und die Ansiedelung der Menschen in ihrer Abhängigkeit von der Gestaltung der Erdolerfläche* (Leipzig, 1841), pp. 181–5.

it. This confusion of industry, commerce and residence was made possible by the great density and height of buildings. A single house could contain ground-floor shops, a first-floor apartment for the landlord or a rich trader, several floors of lesser apartments, some of them occupied by working craftsmen, and servants' quarters in the roof. And the courtyard or garden would often be filled with workshops. Within such an urban structure, segregation of classes was vertical rather than horizontal, although certain areas were more favoured by the rich than others. Even though this structure of activities and residence had already been breaking down before the nineteenth century, the trend was greatly accelerated after 1800. The disruption produced by the Revolution and the propagation of egalitarian and socialist ideas frightened the middle classes and made them want to live separately from the workers. Their departure from the old central areas was accelerated by fear of disease, which medical opinion began to associate in the nineteenth century with bad housing, over-crowding, dirt and polluted air. They could still return daily to work in the centre by using the omnibus services that were developed from the 1820s . . . as time went on, . . . the segregation of classes and activities was increasingly transferred from a vertical to a horizontal plane.[43]

The catalyst in effecting this change, as we have gone to some length to demonstrate, was an enhanced spatial mobility in which efficient, cheap and extensive public transport systems played a major role. This St Petersburg did not have at all. And what was the consequence? So far as it has been possible to determine, the result was the retention, whether voluntary or otherwise, of the traditional, essentially pre-industrial, admixture of classes and activities in the city.

There were, it is true, some other things that might help to explain why this situation persisted so long. Notwithstanding the traumatic impact of the Emancipation, Russian society as a whole, by the standards of modern European states, was still rather tightly structured.[44] Opportunities for social mobility were each year far greater, but this was a relative thing. In St Petersburg probably more than in any other Russian city, the individual's position in society was governed more by

[43] Anthony Sutcliffe, *The Autumn of Central Paris: the Defeat of Town Planning, 1850–1970* (London, 1970), pp. 323–4.
[44] Wayne Vucinich, 'The State and the Local Community', in C. E. Black (ed.), *The Transformation of Russian Society*, pp. 199–200.

rank or class, than by entrepreneurial accomplishment.[45] While the nobility was slow to take an interest in such matters, it did not follow that nobles failed to make successful industrialists and financiers.[46] But the point really is that within a fairly rigid social-class system, especially where the values at the top changed only very slowly, it may not have mattered so much precisely where one lived in the city, as compared with other cities where wealth was more nearly synonymous with position in society. That is, recognition came in a more personal way and need not have been reinforced by the development of elite residential neighbourhoods.[47] To be sure, there were parts of the city recognized to be 'upper class', but as has been demonstrated for the 1860s at least, these were not to be thought of as exclusive enclaves. Nor did the situation seem to have altered much during the ensuing decades of rapid industrialization. If anything, there are grounds for arguing that the admixture or heterogeneity increased simply because of the huge build-up of demand for housing. Suburban residential districts catering to the 'elite' or middle classes, however defined, were not much in evidence. The urban poor on the other hand were literally everywhere, having intruded themselves into what were formally more segregated areas.

The question arises whether the idea of a recognized place in society did not require the kind of two-dimensional spatial segregation which so often has been assumed to be synonymous with the nineteenth-century industrializing city.[48] Perhaps Kohl's model was in essence still valid for the St Petersburg scene in the early 1900s, as we have suggested in the preceding chapter. The evidence for such a claim is obviously more tentative than conclusive. For instance, the use of the estate or class (*sosloviye*) is by no means an entirely satisfactory index of place in society, or wealth, as we have been at some pains to emphasize throughout. But it is a crude index that is available in the census and we have made of it what we could.

Unfortunately, the areal units employed in the analysis of residential

[45] Gerschenkron, 'Social Attitudes, Entrepreneurship, and Economic Development', pp. 7–14.

[46] See D. P. Kandaurov, *Fabrichno-Zavodskiya Predpriyatiya Rossiyskoy Imperii (Isklyuchaya Finlyandiyu)* (1914), for some idea of the involvement of the nobility in the management of industrial operations.

[47] For related comment, see Brian J. Berry, *The Human Consequences of Urbanization* (New York, 1973), pp. 117–20.

[48] See, for instance, Peter G. Goheen, 'Industrialization and Nineteenth-Century Cities', unpublished paper presented at the Association of American Geographers Convention, Kansas City, 24 April, 1972, p. 9.

segregation or dissimilarity had once more to be rather aggregative. Still, the results of the analysis using the social-class data did not show any strong segregation at all. Nor did the detailed analysis of the socioeconomic composition of streets selected from several, ostensibly representative, city areas in the late 1860s show anything other than considerable admixture. And this was not just in the context of domestic servants residing in the homes of the wealthy either.[49] All this fits into the general pattern of work-residence relations of the managerial and professional groups which, as was noted with regard to the bankers, revealed anything but residential segregation. The results of the analysis of ethnic and religious group segregation did show a somewhat different pattern, but for the most part these were, numerically speaking, extremely small groups. St Petersburg was not the home of large numbers of alien ethnic communities like the American port cities, or for that matter, London.[50] It was ethnically a Russian city, despite the economic importance of foreign capital and personnel. Kohl's basic model, however, is both static and restricted to social-class considerations. Yet the notion of a three-dimensional construct is of interest and may be used as the basis for a more general, dynamic model of the urbanization and industrialization processes as defined here.

Figure 20 represents an attempt to synthesize the meaning of urban industrialization in one particular city, a city which did not always fit the norms expected when these were derived from other places and cultures. Again, the cross-sectional approach has been incorporated into the model and the depiction is, of course, purely schematic. It represents a general statement, not a precise 'slice' though the city on a particular date. What existed around 1760 is plain enough. Commerce is very broadly defined and, as is apparent, was spread throughout most of the ground floor of the central city, grading off toward the periphery. The first-class residential areas have not been assigned to any specific class (*sosloviye*) but instead should also be interpreted in a general way. The key thing is that part of the central city had a degree of homogeneity— that is, cellars and garrets had not been converted to housing for the poor. This followed from efforts made after the conflagrations of the 1730s to restrict a large part of the central city to the nobility and others of similar status. And we saw how this was reasonably successful. Zoning was also a major factor in the

[49] See chapter 4, pp. 197–9
[50] Foreigners accounted for barely one per cent of the city population in 1910.

SCHEMATIC AND DYNAMIC CROSS–SECTIONS OF SOCIO–ECONOMIC FUNCTIONS

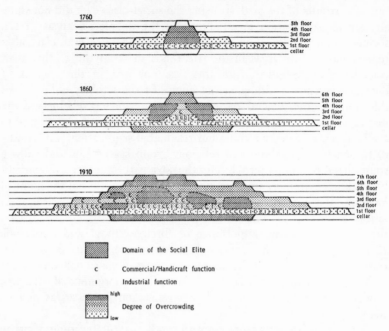

FIG. 20. *Schematic and dynamic cross-sections of socioeconomic functions*

siting of industrial enterprises and these were relegated to the peripheral locations. A hundred years later numerous changes were in evidence. The central city had been invaded by the lower classes, cellars and garrets were being converted and industralization was beginning to alter the character of the central city areas. There were still the preferred residential areas; however, as the model shows, the territory so assigned a century earlier had been dismembered with the intrusion of industrial-commercial functions and their attendant work-forces. In short, the complexion of the city was different. Over the next half century of rapid urban industrialization, several other developments are also apparent. In the early 1900s upper-class residential areas were no more than discontinuous pockets within the urban environment. They consisted of areas of living space on the second, third and sometimes the fourth floors of the built environment. They tended to be more ubiquitous than spatially segregated—and so, therefore, were their more affluent occupants. Cellars had long since been occupied by the poor, though they were steadily becoming more crowded. The middle classes and the affluent, figuratively speaking, pushed the poor upward and outwards. Zoning had succumbed to industrialization and factories were to be smelled, if not seen everywhere. Tucked away in inner courtyards, or occupying whole buildings, they had in a real sense changed the face of the city. Limited spatial mobility precluded a rapid and extensive decentralization of factories and workshops, along with their work-forces.

A fairly rigid social-class system helped to maintain a sense of place amidst the seeming confusion of classes and activities. Beyond that, the occupation of the most accessible floors of buildings, and the lavish decoration of the apartments helped to offset the world outside. The wealthy were protected from the flooded cellars and leaking roofs by the poor below and above them. They were insulated. How long they could have continued to withstand or tolerate the deteriorating physical and social environment all around them is, of course, a hypothetical question. As it happened, events overtook any large-scale reaction. Still, we might well speculate that before long the physical separation of the wealthy and upper classes from the poor and the blighted central city would have manifested itself in the usual two-dimensional manner. Things were beginning to shape up that way. Public transport was being modernized, it was being more frequently used, and there was talk and even some action in terms of suburban commuter rail lines—in short, the means of getting around more easily were in the offing. The stimulus to flee from the city for some new, more amenable suburban environment was clearly there.[51] Clearly, though this model is schematic it does bring out the basic spatial dynamics of the urban industrialization process as it happened in St Petersburg. It differs from what might be developed for some other European cities and certainly most American ones by not including a pronounced suburbanization stage.

Given the actual state of the urban milieu, it is perhaps somewhat surprising that there was no marked segregation. Social unrest was rife and manifested itself in the 1905 uprising, in the growing incidence of strikes and more generally in increasing crime of every description. Robberies, murders, suicides—all might be said to have reflected the underlying malaise. Some extreme anti-social behaviour was no doubt prompted by the hopelessness of individual and family affairs. The

[51] The possibility of creating a 'garden city' in the peripheral region was even being considered. See 'Pervyy Gorod-Sad', *Gorodskoye Delo*, no. 15–16 (1911), p. 1183.

cost of living was escalating and it was more difficult each year for the average worker to keep abreast of day-to-day needs. Anarchist and revolutionary ideas lodged more and more easily in receptive minds. Political assassinations grew in number. The respect for place and privilege was being eroded. Such unrest had prompted unease in other European cities and the response had been for those who could afford it to depart for areas within the city with a more recognizable social class homogeneity—more often than not a suburban sanctuary.[52]

Social unrest was not the only possible reason for expecting more marked social-class segregation. Disease and death were characteristic features which distinguished—if that is the right word—the Russian capital from other major urban centres in Europe and North America in the early 1900s. Few places were ever so hazardous to live in. Overcrowding had reached levels that had long since become a national scandal. In a word, the urban environment was pestilential. Why was this particular situation allowed to arise?

As has been stressed, at least part of the responsibility for the totally inadequate state of public health must be laid at the door of the City Council. During the post-1870 period it had a measure of autonomy, but what is more it had several clear-cut responsibilities. There was a huge population increase, and a need for rational management of urban affairs. But few of the responsibilities of municipal government were shouldered satisfactorily. The Council perhaps did not have any enthusiasm for the tasks at hand, but that would not normally excuse such negligence. As a body, it was essentially conservative and for a long while remained the domain of the merchant and entrepreneurial elite. The connection between entrepreneurial power in business and municipal affairs was there, but much of the real economic power lay in the hands of foreign-owned corporations, banks and the like whose managers and directors were not prominent in municipal government. The void, if it was that, was filled by successful, largely conservative, and less influential merchants, bureaucrats and property owners. There seems no doubt at all that municipal affairs were sometimes manipulated to suit the economic purposes of those prominent cliques on the Council with particular vested interests. Moreover, they were collectively very slow in taking decisions that would benefit the population at large. The Council resisted innovations that would incur substantial debt.

[52] The quotation from Sutcliffe demonstrates the general point. Sutcliffe, *The Autumn of Central Paris*, p. 323.

By the 1890s, however, civic affairs had deteriorated so far that the Council was propelled into action. But where the city did take over essential municipal services in place of the traditional practice of granting concessions, improvements in service were not introduced fast enough to gain the upper hand over the rate of deterioration. Epidemics took their toll right up to the Great War. The issues of proper municipal sewage and water-systems for instance, were continually set aside. Profitability and minimal per capita debt seem to have been the prevailing elements in the essentially mercantile ethos which characterized city government. Social and educational programmes, however liberally defined, were meagrely financed when compared with those of other European capitals. Nor was there any apparent concern on the part of the electorate, who through-out constituted a very small, and in this respect, privileged group. Few bothered to vote and those elected had long had a reputation for minimal involvement in Council meetings and an indifference to issues of concern to the populace as a whole. Perhaps it was not thought possible to do anything constructive, perhaps the status quo was acceptable, perhaps the problem lay in another area—a more general lack of commitment to the city. To the landed gentry St Petersburg was, on the eve of the Great War, still just a place in which to reside during the winter social season—the epidemics at least were held somewhat at bay during the frozen winter months. Others held similar views, even if they were unable to leave the city for distant estates and had to opt instead for a local *dacha*. Those who could not afford to leave during the summer months, but held their social positions to be of some con-sequence probably wished they were able to depart. From the stand-point of public health conditions, they had every reason to want to be somewhere else.

Industrialization in St Petersburg did mean change, but in acknowl-edging this fact it is important to bear in mind that there was also considerable continuity in structure, pattern and process. The social fabric of the city was as much a witness to this as was the pattern of industrial and commercial activity. As has been demonstrated in a number of ways, the paraphernalia of modern urban-industrial life were not easily grafted onto a society in which the environment was

[53] For a thorough analysis of the relationship in a different cultural context, see E. P. Hennock, *Fit and Proper Persons : Ideal and Reality in Nineteenth-Century Urban Government* (London, 1973).

anything but conducive to innovation and change. Initially, the impetus for modernization came from the state. It was only in the later nineteenth century, and under extremely harsh conditions, that social change and the transformation of the existing urban milieu into one that was capable of supporting civilized life became the clarion calls of the populace at large. The circumstances that brought about a growing public outcry were often the outcome of little or no adjustment to changing circumstances. Urban society festered. The mood was one of growing dissatisfaction. Only a massive reordering of priorities could ever have put matters right. The fact that the rich and poor lived in such close proximity during a period when the status quo in society at large was increasingly being challenged perhaps sharpened perceptions and heightened resentment. Unrest was not new to St Petersburg. What was new was the burden of numbers and the deteriorating environment. All told, rapid industrialization was a central force in bringing about these changes. What role this had in leading up to the traumatic events of 1917 cannot be determined conclusively. That it played some part is beyond doubt.

It is probably fair to say that this study of St Petersburg has left some questions unanswered and perhaps raised some new ones. There is clearly scope for further analysis of urban industrialization in the Empire's capital, but it would seem that one of the most potentially rewarding thrusts of research would be in the direction of a comparative analysis of urban development in the Russian context. Just how representative was St Petersburg? For example, did spatial and indeed, social mobility, differ in Moscow with its much longer history as a mercantile centre, or in Odessa, a planned city like St Petersburg, but ethnically quite different by virtue of a large Jewish population? In what manner was the social and physical fabric of these cities fashioned by these general processes? Do they accord with what happened in St Petersburg? To answer such questions sharper definitions of various socioeconomic groups must be employed than were possible here. Position in society is an important issue and so too is that of commitment to city life. Who stayed and who regularly left might well tell a great deal about the prevailing ethos in the worlds of society, business and municipal government. The response of municipal governments to the demands of rapid urban industrialization is an especially intriguing theme. More needs to be known about their financial operations, who was involved, why decisions were taken, or not taken, and, whether the performance of the St Petersburg City

Council was an aberration. By asking the same questions of urban industrialization in other cities a fuller understanding of the Russian experience will be gained and this can only add to the comprehension of the process in a general sense. What has been accomplished so far permits a more reasoned interpretation of the way in which the bricks and mortar of one city were put together and occupied. There is much to be built on this foundation.

Appendices

APPENDIX I: THE CHANGING INDUSTRIAL STRUCTURE, 1867–1913

The process of industrialization may be seen in some detail by examining the data in tables 40, 42 and 44. The first three describe the basic features of the industrial structure in 1867, 1890 and 1913. For each year employment by industrial group is provided and for 1867 and 1890 the number of workers in selected industries is also given. Installed horsepower in 1867 is provided in the text in a separate table ⟨*see* table 7, p. 101⟩. Although the data are patchy, we have included some horsepower statistics for 1890 and these may be used as a rough guide. For 1913 there is no reliable source, but most factories had some motive power. The details of scale changes in factory production during the same period are presented in tables 41, 43 and 45. What they show is the big jump in the scale of factory for virtually every industrial group. The information contained in these tables is summarized in figures 10 and 11, pp. 220–21.

TABLE 40. *Detailed industrial structure, 1867*

Industrial group	Employment	Per cent	Number of manufacturing establishments	Number of handicraft establishments
Metal-working	10,160	29·4	64	1,058
including:				
shipbuilding and machine construction	*8,393*		*20*	
miscellaneous ferrous metals	*390*		*8*	
non-ferrous metals	*1,327*		*33*	
Chemical	1,394	4·1	33	14
Food and tobacco products	4,517	13·1	59	687
including:				
tobacco	*2,279*		*21*	
sugar refining	*761*		*5*	
Tanning, tallow and soap	1,053	3·1	47	63
including:				
tanning and leather goods	*858*		*20*	
Paper and printing	3,596	10·4	89	204
including:				
printing	*767*		*75*	
Textile	12,447	36·1	86	2,619
including:				
cotton	*9,616*		*21*	
wool	*978*		*13*	
cordage	*496*		*8*	
Miscellaneous	1,333	3·8	23	193
Total	34,500	100	401	4,838

Sources: Fabriki i Zavody v S. Peterburgskoy Gubernii v 1867 Godu (1868) no. 6 ; Sanktpeterburg po Perepisi 10 Dekabrya 1869 goda (1872). part 3, section 2, passim ; Vidy Vnutrenney Torgovli i Promyshlennosti v S. Peterburge v 1868g. (1868). passim. Yezhegodnik Ministerstva Finansov (1869), vol. 1, passim.
Note: The figures in italic give sub-totals.

TABLE 41. *Factory-size class, 1867*

	20 and under employment	Per cent	No. of plants	21–90 employment	Per cent	No. of plants	91–270 employment	Per cent	No. of plants	271–750 employment	Per cent	No. of plants	751 and over employment	Per cent	No. of plants
Metal-working	348	3·4	28	938	9·2	18	1,907	18·7	11	1,362	13·4	3	5,605	55·3	4
Chemical	181	12·9	23	255	18·3	7	114	8·3	1	844	60·5	2	—	—	—
Food and tobacco products	205	4·5	25	880	19·4	19	1,516	33·6	11	1,014	22·6	3	902	19·9	1
Tanning, tallow and soap	254	24·1	34	485	46·1	11	314	29·8	2	—	—	—	—	—	—
Paper and printing	834	23·1	79	281	7·8	6	294	8·1	2	275	7·6	1	1,912	53·4	1
Textile	413	3·3	37	1,182	9·5	24	2,843	22·8	16	1,352	10·8	3	6,657	53·6	6
Miscellaneous	86	6·5	11	308	23·1	7	939	70·4	5	—	—	—	—	—	—

Source: See table 40.

TABLE 42. *Detailed industrial structure, 1890*

Industrial group	Employment	Per-centage	Number of manufacturing establishments	Number of handicraft establishments	Installed horsepower
Metal-working	19,160	27·5	127	1,384	14 058
including:					
shipbuilding and machine construction	*14,228*		*32*		
miscellaneous ferrous metals	*3,718*		*67*		
non-ferrous metals	*1,277*		*22*		
Chemical	4,365	6·4	51	248	48
Food and tobacco products	12,988	18·6	76	1,674	1,301
including:					
sugar refining	*580*		*2*		
tobacco	*7,939*		*14*		
Tanning, tallow and soap	2,896	4·2	52	151	451
including:					
tanning and leather goods	*2,133*		*25*		
Paper and printing	6,584	9·4	95	593	2,862
including:					
printing	*2,369*		*65*		
Textile	22,137	31·7	89	2,764	14,952
including:					
cotton	*15,573*		*22*		
wool	*2,791*		*9*		
dyeworks	*1,516*		*12*		
Miscellaneous	1,602	2·2	22	—	—
Total	69,732	100	512	6,814	34,472

Sources: P. A. Orlov, S. G. Budagov, *Ukazatel' Fabrik i Zavodov Yevropeyskoy Rossii. Materialy Dlya Fabrichno-Zavodskoy Statistiki Sostaviii po Ofitsial'nym Svedeniyam Departamenta Torgovii i Manufaktur* (3rd edn, 1894), *passim*; K. V. Davydov, *S. Peterburgskiy Fabrichnyy Okrug. Otchet za 1885g.* (1886); V. Pokrovskiy, 'Statisticheskiy Ocherk S. Peterburga, *Ves' Peterburg na 1895 God. Adresnaya i Spravochnaya Kniga g. S. Peterburg* (1895), p. 62; N. V. Kireyev, *Promyshlennost', Och.IL* (1957), vol. II, p. 90.

TABLE 43. *Factory-size class, 1890*

	Employment 20 and under	%	% 1867	No. of plants	Employment 21–90	%	% 1867	No. of plants	Employment 91–270	%	% 1867	No. of plants	Employment 271–750	%	% 1867	No. of plants	Employment 751 and over	%	% 1867	No. of plants
Metal-working	551	2·9	3·4	42	2,403	12·5	9·2	54	2,060	10·8	18·7	15	4,299	22·4	13·4	10	9,847	51·4	55·3	6
Chemical	320	7·3	12·9	34	558	12·8	18·3	11	355	8·1	8·3	3	730	16·7	60·5	2	2,402	55·1	—	1
Food and tobacco products	371	2·9	4·5	29	1,037	8·0	19·4	20	2,483	19·1	38·6	15	4,317	33·2	22·6	9	6,400	36·8	19·9	5
Tanning, tallow and soap	206	7·1	24·1	26	744	25·7	46·1	17	1,092	37·7	29·8	7	854	29·5	—	2	—	—	—	—
Paper and printing	307	7·7	23·1	44	1,907	29·0	7·8	40	1,469	22·3	8·1	9	451	6·8	7·6	1	2,250	34·2	53·4	1
Textile	318	1·4	3·3	28	1,441	6·5	9·5	28	1,849	8·4	22·8	11	6,812	30·8	10·8	13	11,717	52·9	53·6	9
Miscellaneous	123	7·7	6·5	10	327	20·4	23·1	6	1,152	71·9	70·4	6	—	—	—	—	—	—	—	—

Source: See table 42.

TABLE 44. *Detailed industrial structure, 1913*

Industrial group		Employment	%	Number of establish-ments	Value of production (million roubles)	%
Metal-working		77,816	40·0	284	209	34·8
Chemical		16,446	8·5	89	114	19·0
Food and tobacco products		20,528	10·5	100	79	13·2
Tanning, tallow and soap		8,455	4·3	49	39	6·5
Paper and printing		23,230	11·9	312	40	6·6
Textile		43,931	22·6	86	109	18·1
Miscellaneous		4,178	2·2	36	11	1·8
	Total	194,584	100·0	956	601	100·0

Sources: D. P. Kandaurov, *Fabrichno-Zavodskiye Predpriyatiya Rossiyskoy Imperii (Isklyuchaya Finlyandiyu)* (1914) ; E. E. Kruze, 'Promyshlennoye Razvitiye Peterburga v 1890kh–1914gg.', *Och.IL* (1956). vol. III.

TABLE 45. *Factory-size class, 1913*

	20 and under	%	% 1890 plants	No. of 1890 plants	21–90	%	% 1890 plants	No. of 1890 plants	91–270	%	% 1890 plants	No. of 1890 plants	271–750	%	% 1890 plants	No. of 1890 plants	Over 750	%	% 1890 plants	No. of 1890 plants
Metal-working	1,556	1·9	2·9	86	4,819	6·2	12·5	98	8,333	10·7	10·8	55	11,560	14·9	22·4	23	51,548	66·3	51·4	22
Chemical	777	4·7	7·3	45	1,429	9·1	12·8	29	1,940	11·8	8·1	12	500	3·1	16·7	1	11,800	71·3	55·1	2
Food and tobacco products	641	3·2	2·9	37	1,209	5·9	8·0	27	3,028	14·8	19·1	16	4,305	20·9	33·2	10	11,345	55·2	36·8	10
Tanning tallow and soap	304	3·6	7·1	17	908	10·7	25·7	18	975	11·5	37·7	6	2,768	32·7	29·5	6	3 500	41·5	—	2
Paper and printing	3,205	13·8	7·7	169	3,864	16·6	29·0	93	5,156	22·3	22·3	35	6,305	27·1	6·8	13	4,700	20·2	34·2	2
Textile	332	·8	1·4	17	968	2·2	6·5	22	3,042	6·9	8·4	18	2,750	6·5	30·8	6	36,839	83·6	52·9	23
Miscellaneous	217	5·2	7·7	12	654	15·7	20·4	15	807	19·3	71·9	5	1,125	26·9	26·9	3	1,375	32·9	—	1

Source: See table 44.

APPENDIX II: CORRELATION MATRICES

With one exception, all correlation matrices used in the industrial location analyses are collected here. The exception is the matrix for the metal-working group in 1913 in which a fifteen-industry classification is used. Because of its size, the salient features have been extracted and are presented in table 23, p. 238.

Note: The following designations are used in the tables for factory size-classes.

a—20 and fewer workers
b—21–90 workers
c—91–270 workers
d—271–750 workers
e—over 750 workers

TABLE 46. *Industry total employment correlation matrix,* 1867*

	1	2	3	4	5	6	7	8	9	10	11	12	13	14	15	16	17	18	19	20	21	22	23	24	25	26	27	28	29	30	31	32	33	34
Foundry products 1									60	30							65			45			18									63		
Shipbuilding and machine construction 2						23		31		11							10		53			39	28											
Miscellaneous ferrous metals 3																90										25								
Non-ferrous metals 4												48		36	17	16		17			21										54			
Oil refining 5										12	92		38							20		40												
General chemicals 6																			40			20				67								
Cosmetics 7																					57												93	
Tanning and leather goods 8																											41		11					
Tallow and bone 9										13			12							12			14									97		
Soap, wax and candle 10													47				51	16		49		13	61					45						
Milling 11																						38												
Oil mill 12														81		31									21						81			
Starch 13																				65		13							17					
Wine, beer and mead 14																25									13		18				64			
Tobacco 15																								91					30	78				
Sugar-refining 16																									14	22					33			
Vodka 17																		13		44			43											
General food products 18																							54						48					
Paper production 19																						63								16				
Paper products 20																						10					17		17					
Printing 21																															13		59	
Cotton textile 22																												35						
Wool 23																													21			10		
Felt 24																													38	88				
Silk 25																													31		24			
Linen, hemp and jute 26																																		
Cordage 27																													28					
Dyeworks 28																																		
Quilting and artificial fibres 29																														34				
Miscellaneous fancy textile 30																																		
Clothing and knitted goods 31																																		
Canvas and oilskin 32																																		
Carriage production 33																																		
Musical instruments 34																																		

* positive values only (+ 0·1) and over. + 0·38 and over statistically significant at 1 per cent level.
Note: coefficients correct to 2 places of decimal (decimal point omitted).

TABLE 47. Industry total employment correlation matrix,* 1913

Column/row headings (1–37):

1 Printing
2 Paper production
3 Cigarette paper
4 Miscellaneous paper products
5 General food products
6 Milling
7 Oil mill
8 Wine, beer and mead
9 Tobacco
10 Sugar-refining
11 Vodka
12 Tanning
13 Leather goods
14 Tallow and bone
15 Soap, wax, candle
16 Bristle and brush
17 Oil refining
18 General chemicals
19 Cosmetics
20 Cotton
21 Cotton twist and thread
22 Wool
23 Felt
24 Silk
25 Linen, hemp, jute
26 Cordage
27 Dyeworks
28 Quilting and artificial fibres
29 Miscellaneous fancy textile
30 Clothing and knitted
31 Canvas, oilskin
32 Shipbuilding and machine construction
33 Agricultural machinery
34 Non-ferrous metal
35 Miscellaneous ferrous metal
36 Electrical machinery
37 Foundry products

Correlation coefficients (reading across the column headers 1–37; decimal point omitted):

Row	Correlations (column : value)
1 Printing	2:13
2 Paper production	9:58
3 Cigarette paper	5:30
4 Miscellaneous paper products	7:22
5 General food products	11:39, 14:13
6 Milling	8:26, 11:13, 13:18, 14:24
7 Oil mill	13:56, 14:21
8 Wine, beer and mead	
9 Tobacco	
10 Sugar-refining	
11 Vodka	12:12, 13:18, 14:14
12 Tanning	13:55, 14:13
13 Leather goods	15:14
14 Tallow and bone	15:19
15 Soap, wax, candle	
16 Bristle and brush	
17 Oil refining	18:89
18 General chemicals	19:19, 23:15
19 Cosmetics	20:20, 21:51, 24:18, 26:19, 27:21, 28:10
20 Cotton	21:24, 22:18, 23:11, 24:31
21 Cotton twist and thread	22:50, 24:22, 25:78, 26:18
22 Wool	23:29, 24:24, 27:26
23 Felt	
24 Silk	25:92
25 Linen, hemp, jute	
26 Cordage	29:96
27 Dyeworks	28:22, 29:45, 31:29, 32:27, 33:12, 34:52
28 Quilting and artificial fibres	30:11, 31:37, 32:10, 33:15, 34:14, 35:43
29 Miscellaneous fancy textile	30:99
30 Clothing and knitted	31:53, 32:43, 33:54, 34:12, 35:28, 36:26, 37:19
31 Canvas, oilskin	32:51, 33:12
32 Shipbuilding and machine construction	33:30, 34:16, 35:18
33 Agricultural machinery	34:33, 35:14, 36:20, 37:26
34 Non-ferrous metal	35:13, 36:27, 37:58
35 Miscellaneous ferrous metal	36:40, 37:36
36 Electrical machinery	37:19, 37:74
37 Foundry products	

* positive values only (+0·1) and over. +0·38 and over statistically significant at 1 per cent level.
Note: coefficients correct to 2 places of decimal (decimal point omitted).

TABLE 48. *Correlation matrix: food and tobacco products industrial group,* factory-size class employment,** 1913*

	1	2	3	4	5	6	7	8	9	10	11	12	13	14	15	16	17	18	19	20
General food products a 1																				
b 2			12																	
c 3				24	23															
d 4					20	10														
e 5																				
Milling a 6							45	51												
b 7								42	43	31										
Oil mills b 8																				
c 9										92	86									
d 10											21	70								
Wine, beer and mead a 11												94								54
b 12													46	26						24
c 13														14	62	26				
d 14															54					14
e 15																11	42		15	
Tobacco d 16																	16	16		
e 17																		15		
Sugar-refining e 18																			31	
Vodka a 19																				20
c 20																				

* positive values only (+ 0·1) and over. + 0·38 and over statistically significant at 1 per cent level.

** a, b, c, d, e, factory size-classes

Note: coefficients correct to 2 places of decimal (decimal point omitted).

TABLE 49. *Correlation matrix: metal-working group,* factory-size class employment,** 1913*

	1	2	3	4	5	6	7	8	9	10	11	12	13	14	15	16	17	18	19	20	21	22	23	24	25	26
Foundry products a 1																	21	16				11		16		
b 2	23																	26	27						17	21 38
c 3	21				29	13							24					36							39 45	10
Shipbuilding and machine construction a 4				33	36	49							23	20	37	66	43									24
b 5				21	33	30						10	20		17	16		19	15							
c 6				6	32	35						31	14		20	20	17									
d 7					7	33								45												
e 8						12							11				17		16		23				26	19
Agricultural machinery a 9							49						20			28		34	43							
b 10					10	32													20							
c 11						11						22	17	21						55						
a 12														19			32									
Non-ferrous metal products b 13					13												22	23	13		14					
c 14						15											23					28				
d 15						16											35									
e 16							17																	11		
Miscellaneous ferrous metal products a 17								18											40	38		24	21			
b 18									19										20							
c 19										21											22			33	35 37	
Electrical equipment d 20																					23			28	66 48	
a 22																										12
b 23																							24		25	76
c 24																										26

* positive values only (+0.1) and over. +0.38 and over. statistically significant at 1 per cent level.
** a, b, c, d, e factory size-classes
Note: coefficients correct to 2 places of decimal (decimal point omitted).

A Note on Methods

1 *Industrial classification and size-classes*

In the 1867 statistics, factories were simply listed by the city ward; however, by 1913 a classification system had evolved. Fortunately, the system devised was both logical and quite detailed. Rather than attempt to dis-aggregate all of the 1913 data being used in this study, the 1867 data were instead grouped according to the 1913 classification. This procedure was straightforward and resulted in the following classification:

A Metal-working
1 foundry products
2 shipbuilding and machine construction
3 miscellaneous ferrous metal products
4 non-ferrous metal products
5 agricultural machinery
6 electrical equipment

B Textiles
1 cotton: washing, sorting, spinning, weaving, dyeing, printing
2 woollen: washing, sorting, spinning, weaving, dyeing, printing
3 silk weaving
4 linen, hemp, jute
5 printing and dyeworks
6 miscellaneous fancy textiles: tulle, ribbon, gold thread, braid, etc.
7 clothing and knitted goods
8 canvas, oilskin, etc.
9 cordage

C Chemical

1 general chemicals
2 paint, lacquer and dye
3 oil refining
4 rubber goods
5 cosmetics

D Paper and printing

1 printing (typographic, lithographic, zincographic)
2 paper production
3 paper products

E Food and tobacco

1 milling
2 oil mills
3 sugar-refining
4 wine, beer, mead, vodka
5 general food products
6 tobacco

F Tanning, tallow and soap

1 tanning and leather goods
2 tallow rendering and bone grinding
3 soap, wax and candle

G Miscellaneous

1 carriage manufacture
2 musical instruments
3 glass and chinaware

The building and construction material industries have not been included. Examples of excluded industries are: brickmaking, stone masonry, sand and gravel yards, sawmilling, barrel-making, parquet flooring, alabaster, gypsum, cement, asphalt.

A finer classification was utilized in the analysis of the metal-working industrial group in 1913 and involved dis-aggregating the 1913 data. This was accomplished, first, by consulting information provided on the products of each factory and, second, if production was varied, by examining the quite detailed trade and commerce sections of the city directories in order to determine under which heading a plant was listed. Gaps in the employment data, which only occurred for 1913, were filled both by consulting earlier volumes of factory statistics, and by noting other information on the plant (i.e. installed horsepower, value of output). For most industries omissions were few, and generally reference to other data indicated that the plants in question were in the smallest size-group (twenty workers or less). Estimates of employment were necessary for the printing and chemical industries in particular. The omissions for plants in these industries totalled 125, more than two thirds of the omissions for all industries dealt with in the 1913 cross-section. For many of the establishments in the printing industry for which employment was not stated (representing over 50 per cent of all omissions for 1913) no other data were available and, consequently, plants were assigned arbitrarily to the smallest size-group. In view of the structure of this industry as characterized by the employment data available, as well as that of other cities, this did not appear to be an unrealistic approach. As nearly 1,000 establishments were dealt with in the 1913 cross-section, the magnitude of the problem of omission was not serious, and it was considered that the margin of error resulting from the estimation of employment from other data, and arbitrary assignment in the case of the printing industry in particular, was not such as to invalidate conclusions drawn from the analysis of location patterns.

The factory-size classification was derived in the following manner. Frequency polygons for factory sizes of all industries were contructed for the 1867 and 1913 cross-sections (using equal intervals of five employees). The polygons were superimposed and examined. The first category, twenty employees and under, was established in an attempt to separate from the factories those production units which were more akin to workshops. Prospective classes of larger factory sizes were selected, 'troughs' being used wherever possible as demarcation points (that is, where breaks occurred in the range of values). For several of these prospective classes the mean factory size was calculated and compared with the median for the same plant size range in the other cross-section.[1] The factory-size classification selected is outlined below and except for the open-end classes, the means and medians are given for each cross-section. As indicated, five grades of factory size

---

[1] Correspondence of mean and median for each class interval indicates that the distribution will tend to be fairly symmetrical. See F. A. Ekelblad, *The Statistical Method in Business Applications of Probability and Inference to Business and Other Problems* (New York, 1962) pp. 225-6.

were used, a number deemed adequate for analysis of the spatial organization of industry.[2] The classification remains in the final analysis arbitrary.

Factory-size classification

Class intervals	1867	1913
20 and under	—	—
21–90		
class median	55	55
class mean	47	50
91–270		
class median	180	180
class mean	161	155
271–750		
class median	510	510
class mean	367	472
Over 750	—	—

Note: Figures are rounded to nearest whole number.

2 *Nearest-neighbour analysis*

In order to test the locational hypotheses relating to the clustering (agglomeration) of factories through time, a form of the nearest-neighbour distance measure was employed. Some time ago S. R. Cowie suggested a graphic means of descɪibing location of patterns, the cumulative-frequency nearest-neighbour measure.[3] The technique has as advantages over the usual form of nearest-neighbour measures—its independence of area and concomitant problems, the issue of the influence of pairing on the first-nearest-neighbour statistic and a depiction of total distribution which brings out the existence of eccentrically located points (factories).[4] In order to be more incisive in

---

[2] For relevant remarks on selection of interval number and size, see P. Sargant Florence, *Investment, Location and Size of Plant* (Cambridge, 1948) pp. 15–16.

[3] S. R. Cowie, *The Cumulative Frequency Nearest Neighbour Method For the Identification of Spatial Patterns*, University of Bristol, Department of Geography, discussion paper (1967).

[4] For a discussion of the problem, see A. Getis, 'Temporal Land Use Pattern Analysis With the Use of the Nearest Neighbour and Quadrat Methods', *Annals of the Association of American Geographers*, LIV (1964), p. 395.

both describing patterns and establishing an empirical basis for assessing hypotheses, the third-nearest-neighbour distance was used as the basis for measurement. The procedure was simple: the straight line distance to the third-nearest-neighbour of all points (factories) in the St Petersburg urban area for each industrial group or industry was measured; the distances were then cumulated and plotted on ordinary graph paper; by visually comparing the curves it was possible to discern differences in degree of clustering or dispersal. The following hypothetical situation is illustrative of the technique's application. While there are visually discernible differences in the distributions, A, B, and C in figure 21, the differences are not amenable to any sort of objective evaluation. However, the graphic representation does permit the difference in agglomeration to be clearly discerned ⟨*see* figure 21⟩. Within-group clusters are also brought out by the extended tail of the curve. This technique has been employed throughout the analysis on an industry size-group basis.[5]

3 Correlation analysis

In the attempt to measure spatial associations of cognate industries, the Pearson product moment coefficient of correlation was employed as a basis for assessment. In the past, this kind of analysis of industrial distributions in an urban area has tended to be on a static basis, for example, in J. E. Martin's work on London,[6] and R. Artle's on Stockholm.[7] Here, however, the genesis of spatial association was of prime interest, both in respect of changing intra-industrial group spatial ties, and the distributional similarity of a single industry through time (locational stability). The procedure followed in the analysis will be described briefly.

At a fair copy scale of 1:12,600, a quarter-kilometre grid was placed over the study area (11·3 by 13·3 kilometres). Factories for the two cross-sections, 1867 and 1913, were plotted and the employment noted. The total employment in all factories for each quarter-kilometre square section was calculated. Inasmuch as many grid squares had few

---

[5] A general discussion of nearest-neighbour techniques may be found in Cowie, *The Cumulative Frequency Nearest Neighbour Method*, pp. 1–18. For an example of the many applications, see M. F. Dacey, 'Analysis of the Central Place and Other Point Patterns by Nearest Neighbour Methods,. in K. Norburg (ed.), *Proceedings IGU Symposium in Urban Geography, Lund 1960*, (Lund, 1962), pp. 54–75.
[6] J. E. Martin, *Greater London, an Industrial Geography* (London, 1966).
[7] R. Artle, *The Structure of the Stockholm Economy; Toward a Framework for Projecting Metropolitan Community Development* (Ithaca, New York, 1965).

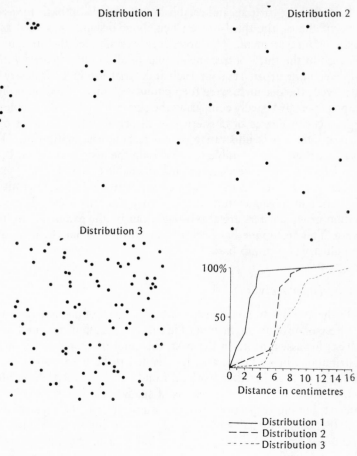

FIG. 21. *Nearest-neighbour distances*

employees, which was particularly the case in the peripheral areas, several systems of regions based on different combinations of quarter-kilometre sections were devised.[8] The problem, as Artle has noted, is to seek a compromise 'between the two extremes, the very large and "too" heterogeneous areas on the one side and very small and "too" homogeneous on the other.'[9] The system of forty-four regions, depicted

[8] This is a common feature of regional systems used in correlation analysis of urban areas. See, for example, James O. Wheeler, 'Residential Location by Occupational Status', *Urban Studies*, V, no. 1 (1968) pp. 25–26; Martin, *Greater London*, p. 86.
[9] Artle, *The Structure of the Stockholm Economy*, p. 121.

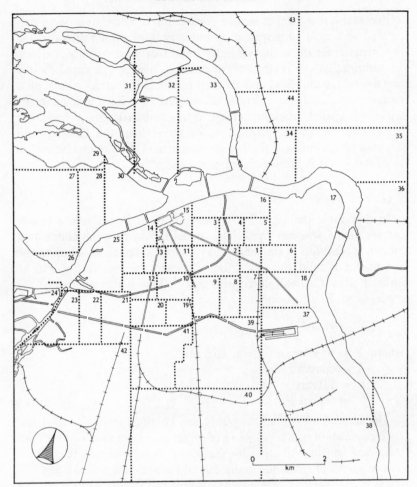

MAP 67. *Regional system for correlation analysis*

by map 67 was considered to be the best of the several systems devised, for the employment variance among the forty-four regions was minimized and was comparable for each of the cross-sections. For a correlation analysis, forty-four regions was considered adequate for the size of the study area.[10] The results of the analysis, it should be clear, only have relevance in relation to this particular system.[11]

[10] Martin, *Greater London.*
[11] Artle, *The Structure of the Stockholm Economy.*

431

For each cross-section simple coefficients of correlation were calculated on a total employment by industry basis, which provided the raw material for the industrial linkage and locational stability analyses. In addition, simple coefficients of correlation were calculated for the metal-working and food and tobacco products industrial groups on a factory size-class basis and most of the data have been utilized in the study of spatial linkages on an intra-industrial group basis. In calculating the simple coefficients of correlation, the Genstep and Cormax programmes of the computer centre of the London School of Economics and Political Science were used.[12]

4 *Gravity model*

In describing the migration of peasants to St Petersburg, a simple gravity model was employed. The model is based on the notion that human interaction is similar to gravitational interaction. Despite the absence of a solid theoretical link between the two it can still be utilized effectively as a descriptive tool.[13] This is the purpose of the model here. The equation used was as follows:

$$Y = \frac{K}{re}$$

where Y = number of peasant migrants
  K = constant
  r = distance
  e = exponent.

The number of peasant migrants was obtained from the 1869 and 1910 censuses in which *guberniya* of origin data were provided for both males and females. Additionally, the 1910 census provided a breakdown on the length of residence in the capital for five-year periods, and like the later enumerations includes the suburban districts. Distances were measured from the geographical centre of each *guberniya* in European Russia to the capital. This clearly ignores such influences as transport accessibility and agrarian conditions, but it serves none the less as a reasonable basis for assessing the basic hypotheses in question, namely, did migration vary with distance and were there sex differences? The

---

[12] For further details on the analysis, see Harold H. McCarty, John C. Hook, Duane S. Knos, *The Measurement of Association in Industrial Geography* (Iowa City, 1956), especially chapter III.
[13] Walter Isard, *Methods of Regional Analysis* (Cambridge, Mass., 1960), p. 515; J. H. Niedercord, B. V. Bechdolt, 'An Economic Derivation of the "Gravity Law" of Spatial Interaction', *Journal of Regional Science*, IX (1969), pp. 273–82.

above equation was linearized by taking logarithms to give $\log (y) = \log (k) - e \log (r)$. The resultant correlation coefficients were consistently high and significant at the one per cent level.

5 *Indices of residential segregation*

In order to establish a comparative and easily comprehended measure of residential segregation according to social class (or its equivalent), religion and ethnicity, two indices were used.[14] The first is the index of dissimilarity, which is derived from the following formula:

$$\sum_{i=1}^{n} \frac{x_i/\sum x_i - y_i/\sum y_i}{2} \cdot 100$$

Here x_i represents one particular group and y_i another in ward i. The equation determines the percentage of the number of (x) who would be required to relocate in order to make the distribution identical with y. When the computation is applied to a series of classes, occupations, etc., it is known as the index of dissimilarity. When one group is used as a reference point the measure obtained is referred to as the index of segregation.

[14] For a general discussion, see Harold Carter, *The Study of Urban Geography* (London, 1972), pp. 258–61.

A Note on Sources

Studies of urban industrialization in general are numerous, of Russian cities in particular there are notably few. Not least among the many reasons for this situation are the rather particular interests of Soviet historians, the preoccupation with the contemporary on the part of Soviet geographers and the limited access to materials, especially those of an archival nature, confronting the western researcher.[1] Still, for those willing to persevere there are abundant published materials of a primary as well as secondary kind, the culling of which can be expected to yield a reasonable return. This is especially true of the capital of the Russian Empire, St Petersburg. Indeed, many of the sources described below have just barely been tapped owing to the aggregative nature of the questions which have been posed in this study. There is obviously ample scope for narrowing the focus of inquiry to particular issues and, at this level, permission to use archival materials is more likely to be forthcoming.

For many purposes the best Slavic collection outside the Soviet Union is that of the University of Helsinki Library. It so happens that in this particular study the British Museum collection complemented, fortunately, that in Helsinki. Indeed, in terms of city directories and maps, these two institutions have some that are difficult to obtain even in Soviet libraries. Of course, the research could not have been completed without the benefit of materials that are available only in the Saltykov-Shchedrin Public Library in Leningrad and the Lenin Library in Moscow. Many months have been spent, more or less pleasantly, in these two libraries. Whenever the principal sources,

[1] Soviet historians have been, not surprisingly, preoccupied with the labour scene. Geographers, on the other hand, have been encouraged, to turn their efforts to more applied research. From either perspective, issues of concern to non-Soviet urban historians and urban-historical geographers in many respects have been neglected to date.

either in whole or in part, may be found in London or Helsinki this will be indicated by the following abbreviations:

University of Helsinki Library   UHL
British Museum   BM
School of Slavonic and East   SSEES
European Studies

1 *Factory Statistics*

Factory statistics for the St Petersburg *guberniya* (province) were gathered and published from 1860 until 1868. The first fairly comprehensive statistics for the country as a whole did not appear until 1869.[2] Thereafter, data on St Petersburg can be obtained from volumes of factory statistics for the years 1879, 1885, 1890, 1900, 1903, 1908, 1909, and 1913. The statistics presented in these volumes are usually drawn from material collected on the *guberniya* level and returned to the Department of Trade and Manufacture. Information is provided for most factories for the following: type of production (including a list of products in the later publications), employment, value of production, and location. With regard to location, the information is exceptionally precise as both street name and number of the building are provided in virtually every case. Additionally, data are sometimes provided on the year of founding (not consistent), main market and source of raw material (generalized), and type and quantity of fuel consumed.

Criticism of the factory statistics centres on the following deficiencies: the lack of a precise definition of what constituted a factory (especially prior to the establishment of a factory inspectorate in 1884), the variation in interpretation of what was to be included as factory production from one *guberniya* to another, and the lack of correspondence in certain cases between the stated number of workers and value of production.[3] As the information was provided by factory-owners themselves, distortion was possible. The forms were distributed and collected primarily by the police until 1894 and thereafter primarily by factory

---

[2] See *Yezhegodnik Ministerstva Finansov* (1869), vol. I.
[3] For some contemporary comments, see V. Veshnyakov, 'Russkaya Promyshlennost' i Yeya Nuzhdy', *Vestnik Yevropy*, no. 10 (1870), pp. 508–28; A. Radtsig, 'O Roste Nashey Promyshlennosti', *Narodnoye Khozyaystvo*, no. 2 (1900), pp. 70–77.

inspectors.[4] Simply neglecting to complete the forms was not unknown, especially in the outlying provinces.[5]

In the case of St Petersburg certain of these deficiencies can be offset, others minimized. The lack of a precise definition of a factory gave rise to contemporary criticism directed at the indiscriminate use of total employment and value-of-output figures for the country as a whole because this practice effectively masked the wide range of factory types included (notably the great number of small-scale rural manufacturing or *kustar'* establishments).[6] It is possible to nullify this criticism by analysing the industry within the framework of a factory-size classification, thereby separating the small-scale production units from the rest. Indeed, the Soviet historian, M. Zlotnikov, in following the precedent established by Lenin more or less formalized the use of sixteen workers as the operational definition for factory production.[7] For somewhat different reasons the threshold adopted in this study has been set at twenty workers.[8] Clearly, the problem of the different interpretation from one *guberniya* to another over what was to be considered factory production does not arise here. Insofar as the distortion of factory statistics is concerned, little can be done other than to use as the criterion for measurement that which is the least likely to have been altered, namely employment.[9] The difficulties associated with using the value of output as a measure are numerous, but probably the most important are the obvious natural reluctance of factory owners to provide this type of information and the lack of a precise definition when they were willing to do so.[10] In order to ensure

[4] N. Vorob'yev, *Ocherki po Istorii Promyshlennoy Statistiki v Dorevolyutsionnoy Rossii i v SSSR* (Moscow, 1961), p. 22.

[5] Industries subject to the excise tax were under a much stricter control (sugar, tobacco, matches, distilling, brewing etc.).

[6] Factories are described in Russian as either *fabriki* or *zavody*. The distinction between these two terms is based, ostensibly, on the area of raw material supply. The *zavod* uses domestic available materials, the *fabrika* imported. For further elaboration of this point and discussion of the factory statistics, see P. N. Stolpyanskiy, *Zhizn' i Byt Peterburgskoy Fabriki za 1704–1914gg.* (1925), pp. 9–11.

[7] M. Zlotnikov, 'Ot Manufaktury k Fabrike', *Voprosy Istorii*, no. 11–12 (1946), pp. 31–49. For a vitriolic criticism of indiscriminate use of factory statistics, see V. I. Lenin, *The Development of Capitalism in Russia* (2nd revised edn, Moscow, 1964), pp. 454–84. Additional pertinent comment may be found in Zelnik, *Labor and Society*, pp. 44–5.

[8] See A Note on Methods, p. 427.

[9] The figure provided was to have been the average for the year, at least after the 1890s. Vorob'yev, *Ocherki po Istorii Promyshlennoy Statistiki*, p. 28. Using employment, of course, tends to mask the effect of mechanization, but given the alternative problems this is the least serious.

[10] Some owners apparently only reported profits. The use of value-of-output data over time also gives rise to the problem of changing price levels. R. W. Goldsmith, 'The Economic Growth of Tsarist Russia, 1860–1913', *Economic Development and Cultural Change*, IX, no. 3 (1961), pp. 441–76.

that the most complete picture possible is obtained, the latest, supplemented, and revised editions of the different series of factory statistics available can be used, combined with checking this material against lists of plants in other factory statistics, directories, and City Council reports on industry.

The factory statistics used for the 1867 cross-section were the penultimate in the series known to have been published during the 1860s ⟨*see* section 2⟩. The definition of a factory is not stated, but judging from the wide range of employments (from as little as two to several hundred), it seems probable that, as in later statistics, a minimum annual value of output was used. For the analysis of industrial location using 1890 as a reference point, data were obtained from the third revised and supplemented edition of factory statistics compiled by P .A. Orlov and S. G. Budagov from factory-owners reports submitted to the Department of Trade and Manufacture. Any plant having an annual output of less than 2,000 roubles was excluded from these statistics. Data for 1913 were taken from the material compiled under the direction of D. Kandaurov. These statistics were based on a questionnaire survey and supplemented by official information. It was selected because it is the most recent of the published pre-revolutionary detailed factory statistics. Other possible sources for 1903, 1908, or 1909, were rejected primarily because they reflect the severe economic depression prevailing during these years. Moreover, the coverage was not as complete as that of the 1913 series. The following list details the factory statistics consulted:

1 UHL Davydov, K. V. *S. Peterburgskiy Fabrichnyy Okrug. Otchet za 1885g.* (St Petersburg: Izdaniye Departamenta Torgovli i Manufaktur, 1886).

2 *Fabriki i Zavody v S. Peterburgskoy Gubernii v 1867 Godu* (St Petersburg: Izdatel'stvo S. Peterburgskago Stolichnago i Gubernskago Statisticheskago Komiteta, 1868), no. 6.

3 SSEES Kandaurov, D. P. *Fabrichno-Zavodskiya Predpriyatiya Rossiiskoy Imperii (Isklyuchaya Finlyandiyu)* (Petrograd: Izdatel'stvo Soveta S"yezdov Predstaviteley Promyshlennosti i Torgovli, 1914).

4 BM, UHL Ministerstvo Finansov, Otdel Promyshlennosti. *Spisok Fabrik i Zavodov Yevropeyskoy Rossii* (St Petersburg: V. Kirshbaum, 1903).

5 UHL Orlov, P. A. *Ukazatel' Fabrik i Zavodov Yevropeyskoy Rossii s Tsarstvom Pol'skim i Vel. Kn. Finlyandskim. Materialy Dlya Fabrichno-Zavodskoy Statistiki Sostavili po Ofitsial'nym Svedeniyam Departamenta Torgovli i Manufaktur* (St Petersburg, 1881).

6 UHL Orlov, P. A., Budagov, S. G. *Ukazatel' Fabrik i Zavodov Yevropeyskoy Rossii. Materialy Dlya Fabrichno-Zavodskoy Statistiki Sostavili po Ofitsial'nym*

Svedeniyam Departamenta Torgovli i Manufaktur (3rd edn, St Petersburg: V. Kirshbaum, 1894).

7 UHL Timiryazev, D. A. *Statisticheskiy Atlas Glavneyshikh Otrasley Fabrichno-Zavodskoy Promyshlennosti Yevropeyskoy Rossii s Poimennym Spiskom Fabrik i Zavodov (1867)* (St Petersburg: 1870).

8 Varzar, V. E. *Spisok Fabrik i Zavodov Rossiyskoy Imperii* (St Petersburg: V. Kirshbaum, 1912).

9 BM, UHL *Yezhegodnik Ministerstva Finansov* (St Petersburg: 1869), Vol. I, part 3.

10 BM, UHL Yezioranskiy, L. K. *Fabrichno-Zavodskiya Predpriyatiya Rossiyskoy Imperii* (St Petersburg: Izdatel'stvo Soveta S"yezdov Predstaviteley Promyshlennosti i Torgovli, 1909).

2 Directories

City directories are available for 1824, 1827, 1850, 1867–8, 1892, 1895 and almost annually from 1900 to 1914. As they usually have sections on trade and industry, it is possible to create a rough profile of the urban economy. Those up to 1850 unfortunately do not provide sufficient, consistent information on street addresses to permit precise mapping. However, it is possible to learn something of the distribution since the data are customarily arranged by wards. From 1867 on, exact addresses are provided throughout the directories and this information is very important for general cross-checking of the factory statistics and is critical for confirming or completing factory addresses where these are vague or omitted. Also, it is usually possible to distinguish between the small-scale handicraft workshop (*masterskaya*) and a retail outlet (*magazin*). For the journey-to-work analyses, the places of work and residence of artisans, factory-owners etc. could be determined accurately. The accuracy derived from the actual coverage of the directories. In the case of factory-owners, for instance, names were obtained from the factory statistics and in most cases a listing was found in the directory for the same year. From the trade and industry sections of the directories, addresses of factories were checked against those provided in the factory statistics. Workshop owner-artisan etc. listings agreed fully with the entries in the general section of the directories. Accuracy also derived from the Russian practice of listing surname, first name and patronymic, thus obviating formidable problems raised in the use of directories where only surnames and initials are provided. Furthermore, in the 1867–8 directory especially, it was not uncommon for a brief reference to the individual occupations to be included. With this information detailed work on the socioeconomic composition of selected streets was possible.[11] Extensive use was made of the directories listed below:

1 BM Grech, A. *Ves' Peterburg v Karmane* (2nd edn, St Petersburg: N. Grech, 1851).
2 BM *Gorodskoy Ukazatel' ili Adresnaya Kniga na 1850 God*. (St Petersburg, 1849).
3 BM, UHL *Ves' Peterburg na 1895g.* (1910, 1912, 1914). *Adresnaya i Kniga G. S. Peterburga* (St Petersburg: A. S. Suvorin, 1895) (1910, 1912, 1914).
4 BM *Vseobshchaya Adresnaya Kniga S. Peterburga*. (St Petersburg: Goppe i Kornfel'd, 1867-8).
5 BM Yablonskiy, P. O. *Adresnaya Kniga Goroda S. Peterburga na 1892g.* (1895) (St Petersburg: P.O. Yablonskiy, 1892) (1895).

3 Maps and plans

With large-scale base maps and detailed street maps, the task of plotting precisely individual factories, workshops, residences and the like is feasible. Available for 1868 and 1890 are large-scale maps with a minimum of eight numbers per square block, and for 1892, 1895, 1910–12, and 1914 there are even larger-scale street maps with individual 'house' numbers included in the city directories. In the few instances where the 'house' number was not provided, the name of the owner was given. By checking lists of house owners for the street in question the precise address was obtained. This was only necessary for the 1867 data. During the latter half of the nineteenth-century street-name changes were minimal and a standard street and house-numbering policy remained in effect after 1835.[12] In the analysis of spatial patterns accurate plotting is an essential prerequisite and maps of this kind are clearly indispensable.

Fortunately, the only known contemporary map of the industry of St Petersburg has been republished. It pertains to 1852.[13] By using this information along with directory and other material for 1850–52, it was possible to reconstruct a general picture of the urban–industrial scene for mid century. The following maps and atlases have been of particular value:

1 UHL Gash, Yu. *Karta Okrestnostey S. Peterburga 1914*, 1:17,000.
2 UHL 'Graficheskoye Izobrazheniye Kolichestva Perevezennykh Passazhirov v

---

[11] See chapter 4, pp. 197–9.
[12] A. Grech, *Ves' Peterburg v Karmane* (2nd edn., 1851), p. 392.
[13] 'Plan Stolichnago Goroda S. Peterburga, s Pokazaniyem Zavodov i Fabrik 1852 Goda', *Peterburg—Leningrad. Istoriko-Geograficheskiy Atlas (Chast' Pervaya)* (1957), p. 43.

God po Sushchestvuyushchim Liniyam Konno-Zheleznykh Dorog v 1899g.'
ISPGD, no. 11 (1901), end flap, 1:39,000.

3 BM Musnitskiy, M. I. *Plan S. Peterburga 1867–68*, 1:12,600.

4 BM, UHL *Peterburg-Leningrad. Istoriko-Geograficheskiy Atlas, (Chast' Pervaya)* (Leningrad: Izdatel'stvo Leningradskogo Universiteta, 1957).

5 UHL *Plan Goroda S. Peterburga s Pokazaniyem Seti Konno-Zheleznykh Dorog, Granits, Politseyskikh Chastey, Uchastkov . . . 1907*, 1:23,500.

6 UHL *Plan Goroda S. Peterburga v Gorizontalyakh 1901*, 1:3,600.

7 UHL *Plan S. Peterburga s Blizhayshimi Okrestnostyami 1912*, 1:19,500.

4 Censuses

We have elsewhere described the initial efforts in enumerating the city's population and it remains only to reiterate the value of this relatively little used material for establishing some of the parameters of urban industrialization.[14] From 1869 until 1907 the ward boundaries remained intact, thus facilitating time-series analysis, and from 1881 the districts outside the official city borders were included. Data collected range from basic demographic characteristics to socioeconomic ones. Nor is the physical habitat excluded, as each census includes a section on what might be called the built environment.

The principal problem encountered in carrying out the census was that of dealing with a population little experienced in such inquiries and questionnaires clearly had to be devised with care. (In the enumeration of the inhabitants by occupation, for example, the splendid contemporary census of Berlin served as a model.[15]) The 1881 census is particularly comprehensive as well over 200 occupations in industry alone are listed for each ward. Thereafter, however, the distributional detail is lost owing to the use of aggregate statistics for the city as a whole. Still, distinctions continued to be drawn between owners, administrators, workers and *odinochki* (self-employed handicraftsmen). Attempts to determine side occupations however, proved abortive. In respect of the rent data for apartments used for commercial-manufacturing purposes, the problems encountered were few in number. Actual rents paid were recorded and subsequently aggregated by city ward according to a standardized class-interval system for all censuses. The number of rooms in each apartment was also recorded. The mean rent per room by city district has been used as a yardstick of rent-land cost values

[14] See chapter 4, pp. 158–60.
[15] *Die Bevölkerungs—und Wohnungs—Aufnahme vom 1 December 1885 in der Stadt Berlin* (Berlin, 1890).

instead of actual land cost figures principally because the data provided in *Izvestiya S. Peterburgskoy Gorodskoy Dumy* and *Statisticheskiy Yezhegodnik S. Peterburga* are sporadic and the prices recorded were dependent upon the unique features of vacant sites or buildings. Examples of widely varying prices for different parts of the same lot (depending on street frontage) are numerous.[16] The distribution of sales recorded constitutes only a small fraction of the total, therefore the data could not provide any guide of change through time.

There are, of course, definitional problems and gaps in the census. Literacy, for instance, was gauged simply by asking, 'Can you read?' and the response can only be treated as a crude approximation of actual levels of literacy. Despite the inadequacies, the one-day census stands out as an extremely valuable source. The fact that there were four such enumerations before the first national census was taken in 1897 underscores their significance.[17]

1 UHL *Pervaya Perepis' Predmetov Gorodskago Oblozheniya i Drugiya Khozy-aystvenno-Statisticheskiya Izsledovaniya, Proizvedennyya Odnovremenno s Perepis'yu 30 go Oktyabrya-8 go-Noyabrya* (St Petersburg: S. Peterburgskoye Gorodskoye Obshchestvennoye Upravleniye, 1907).

2 *Petrograd po Perepisi 15 Dekabrya 1910 Goda* (Petrograd: Izdaniye Gorodskoy Upravy po Statisticheskomu Otdeleniyu, 1914), 2 parts.

3 UHL *Sanktpeterburg, Izsledovaniya po Istorii, Topografii i Statistike Stolitsy* (St Petersburg: Izdaniye Tsentral'nago Statisticheskago Komiteta, Ministerstva Vnutrennikh Del, 1868), vol. III.

4 BM, UHL *Sanktpeterburg po Perepisi 10 Dekabrya 1869 Goda* (St Petersburg: Izdaniye Tsentral'nago Statisticheskago Komiteta, Ministerstva Vnutrennikh Del, 1872, 1875), 3 parts.

5 BM, UHL *S. Peterburg po Perepisi 15 Dekabrya 1881 Goda* (St Petersburg: Izdaniye Gorodskoy Upravy po Statisticheskomu Otdeleniyu, 1883, 1884), 3 vols.

6 BM, UHL *S. Peterburg po Perepisi 15 Dekabrya 1890 Goda* (St Petersburg: Izdaniye Gorodskoy Upravy po Statisticheskomu Otdeleniyu, 1891, 1892), 4 parts.

7 BM, UHL *S. Peterburg po Perepisi 15 Dekabrya 1900 Goda*. (St Petersburg: Izdaniye Gorodskoy Upravy po Statisticheskomu Otdeleniyu, 1903, 1905), 3 parts.

In addition, there were four other population counts taken in the late 1880s which demonstrate conclusively the scale of the seasonal

[16] For example, 'O Priobretenii v Sobstvennost' Goroda Imushchestva . . .', *ISPGD*, no. 13 (1888), pp. 215–16. There was a fourfold variation in the price paid for different parts of the same lot.
[17] This includes the 1864 census, which is not as reliable. Other cities were enumerated as well, but none as early nor as intensively as St Petersburg. The first census of Moscow, for instance, occurred in 1871, and there was only one other in 1882 before the 1897 national census.

population migration. These were not issued as separate censuses, but the results are included in the following City Council publications:

1 UHL 'Ischisleniye Naseleniya S. Peterburga 15 Iyulya i 15 Dekabrya 1888 Goda', *Statisticheskiy Yezhegodnik S. Peterburga*, (1888), pp. 7–59.
2 UHL 'Ischisleniye Naseleniya S. Peterburga 15 Iyulya i 15 Dekabrya 1889 Goda', *Statisticheskiy Yezhegodnik S. Peterburga*, (1889), pp. 6–25.

5 *City Council reports*

The various reports, discussions and decisions of the City Council constitute an invaluable and still little used primary source. All of this is preserved in the *Izvestiya* of the Council which begins in 1863 and continues, in growing volume, throughout the period under study. Already by the 1890s upward of thirty volumes a year were finding their way into print. To understand something of the 'climate' of decision-making on the Council, the *Izvestiya* is an absolutely indispensable source. Various reports on industry, commerce, zoning by-laws, housing policies, transportation and municipal services not only tell much about what was done, but more important, they frequently tell us why. From what has been said of the City Council, it will be quite apparent that there were probably many times when rationalizations were anything but candid.[18] Notwithstanding the probable absence of frankness, the facts of city management are plain enough and these can still be set against presumed motives. Although the *Izvestiya* has been used extensively in this study, as a source it has barely been tapped. So far as is known among non-Soviet institutions only the Slavonic collection of University of Helsinki Library has even part of the series. There the collection begins in the mid 1880s and continues until 1916. However, even for this period issues are missing for some years and it is necessary to use Soviet libraries if complete coverage is wanted. The City Council also published annual year books after 1880. These tend to complement rather than duplicate the material in the *Izvestiya*. In particular, lengthy annual reports on industry, trade and commerce are of value. Again the only extant collections are located in Soviet libraries. They are available from 1885 to 1897 in Helsinki. There is in fact a wide variety of publications which emanated from the civic bureaucracy. Reports on engineering, sanitation, public transport and similar topics are especially numerous from the 1890s and a fair

[18] See chapter 6.

number of them are located in Helsinki. The two principal sources, however, are those listed below:

1 UHL *Izvestiya S. Peterburgskoy (Obshchey) Dumy*, 1863–1914; cited as *ISPG(O)D*.
2 UHL *Statisticheskiy Yezhegodnik S. Peterburga*.

In addition to the data provided by the St Petersburg City Council publications, there are occasional reports in the *Izvestiya* of the Moscow City Council (*Izvestiya Moskovskoy Gorodskoy Dumy*, cited here as *IMGD*) which are of great interest owing to the customarily incisive evaluation of the St Petersburg administration and its policies. Again these are only available from 1885 in the Helsinki collection. A complete collection may be consulted in the Lenin Library in Moscow.

6 *Periodic literature and diplomatic reports*

For a study of urban industrialization there is much interesting information which can be culled from the journal and newspaper literature. That of an economic or technical nature is especially abundant after the 1880s as the references in this study tend to indicate. Of the many which have been consulted one or two merit singling out. First published in 1909, *Gorodskoye Delo* or Urban Affairs is an indispensable guide to the urban scene in the early 1900s. Though there is a certain catholicism to the topics discussed, the focus is on the Russian situation and the comments usually have a fairly strong socialist flavour. Reports on the management of civic affairs in the capital were of particular value since they tended to counterpoise the argument in some official city documents. It should not be thought, however, that the reports and discussion in the *Izvestiya* of the City Council were typically uncritical for this was certainly not the case. The *Arkhiv Sudebnoy Meditsiny i Obshchestvennoy Gigiyeny* or Archive of Forensic Medicine and Social Hygiene began publication in 1865 and ran for the better part of a decade. Like the medical doctoral dissertation series which started around 1890, it provides a wealth of information on the actual living conditions of the poor. The epidemiological thrust of dissertations such as those by A. N. Pavlovskiy and E. A. Ferman was quite common.[19] Because of this kind of orientation,

---

[19] A. N. Pavolvskiy, *Materialy k Statistike i Etiologii Zabolevayemosti i o Smertnosti ot Aziatskoy Kholery v S. Peterburge v 1892–1896gg.* (1897); E. A. Ferman, *Smertnost' ot Bryushnago Tifa v S. Peterburge za 12 Let s 1895 po 1906 God.* (1907).

443

considerable attention was given to analysing the urban environment as a factor in the spread of disease and from these analyses it is possible to learn a great deal more about the place than the census alone is able to tell us. Some of these dissertations are available in Helsinki, while most of *Gorodskoy Delo* and all of the *Arkhiv* are. Yet another perception of the St Petersburg scene is to be found in the various diplomatic reports. Those of the British Consuls have been used most. The annual summaries of trade and commerce are quite useful in establishing general trends for the Empire as a whole, but more interesting are the occasional special reports concerning the city itself. All are available extant in the Parliamentary Papers in the British Museum. Similarly, the American series provides useful insights though it has not been so heavily drawn upon here. On the whole, however, none of these 'outside' views can match in detail, scope and incisiveness the material in the Russian periodic literature and the *Izvestiya*. Indeed, it is generally the case that these reports were simply summaries of what was appearing in print locally. For the most part then, contemporary Russian materials have been accorded preference.

7 *Secondary sources*

There is obviously a vast range of related literature that can be consulted. From the writings of Pushkin or Dostoevsky to guide-books and memoirs much can be gleaned that adds to an understanding of what the city was like. But as the emphasis has been on reality, rather than perceptions, this kind of material has been used simply to round out the picture compiled through using the kinds of primary sources already discussed. Details of these secondary sources may be found in the references throughout the text. There are some secondary sources, however, which deserve special recognition. Certainly the most useful general reference is the *Ocherki Istorii Leningrada* or Essays of the History of Leningrad. The first three volumes of this enormous study published by the Academy of Sciences cover the period up to the Great War and have proved to be of much value. Of a more specialized nature is Reginald E. Zelnik's, *Labor and Society in Tsarist Russia: the Factory Workers of St Petersburg, 1855–1870* (1971), but it too provides much useful discussion of St Petersburg's history. Valuable as well are the numerous specialized works in social, economic and especially labour history in which data on St Petersburg either constitute the core of the work or at least are given considerable detailed attention. Of the numerous studies of this type consulted, those by A. V. Predtechenskiy, P. N. Stolpyanskiy, V. K. Yatsunskiy, S. N. Semanov and S. N. Valk warrant specific mention.[20]

There is only meagre geographical literature on the industrial growth of the city. In fact only the Russian geographer, V. V. Pokshishevskiy, has dealt with the subject at any length. Of the three articles relating to this subject published by Pokshishevskiy, the earliest (1931) describes the intra-urban characteristics of Leningrad and is concerned in part with the general locational trends of industrial growth during the pre-revolutionary period.[21] Most of the points raised in this short paper were taken up and expanded upon in the most comprehensive of Pokshishevskiy's articles, 'The Territorial Formation of the Industrial Complex of St Petersburg in the XVIIIth and XIXth Centuries'.[22] This paper especially provides much useful background information. Although some interesting industrial locational features are described, the treatment of the period from 1850 to the Great War remains superficial. There is, for example, no attempt to present cartographically the total industrial distribution for any one time period (only a highly generalized map of industrialized areas for the mid 1860s), let alone for different years. The presentation of industrial growth is seriously handicapped, since, for the 1860s, only plants having more than fifty workers, and for subsequent years more than 100, are taken into account, thus effectively omitting in each case a most significant part of the city's industry. Furthermore, even within the limitation as to the sizes of the plants included, scant attention is given to the question of changes in the industrial structure and there is no clear description, cartographic or otherwise, for any one year of the locational variations by industry or even by industrial group. Analysis in any depth or detail of the evolving patterns of industrial activity is well outside the scope of his rather general survey. In the third article, 'Some Problems of the Economic-Geographical Situation of Leningrad', the changing situation of St Petersburg during the eighteenth and nineteenth centuries is described, but the paper is not in fact concerned specifically with the

[20] A. V. Predtechenskiy, *Peterburg Petrovskogo Vremeni* (1948); Stolpyanskiy, *Zhizn' i Byt Peterburgskoy Fabriki*; V. K. Yatsunskiy, 'Rol' Peterburga v Promyshlennom Razvitii Dorevolyutsionnoy Rossii', *Voprosy Istorii*, no. 9 (1954) pp. 98–105; S. N. Semanov, *Peterburgskiye Rabochiye Nakanune Pervoy Russkoy Revolyutsii* (Moscow, 1966); S. N. Valk (ed.), *Istoriya Rabochikh Leningrada* (1972), vol. I.
[21] V. V. Pokshishevskiy, 'Leningrad, Opyt Vnutrigorodskoy Krayevodnoy Kharakteristiki', *Sovetskoye Krayevedeniye*, no. 6 (1931), pp. 14–24.
[22] V. V. Pokshishevskiy, 'Territorial'noye Formirovaniye Promyshlennogo Kompleksa Peterburga v XVIII-XIX Vekakh', *Voprosy Geografii*, no. 20 (1950). pp. 122–62.

question of intra-urban industrial locations.[23] Suffice it to say, there is still much that can, and should, be done, with published sources of a primary nature.

In this study considerable emphasis has been accorded to cartographic and diagramatic presentation of the urban industrialization of St Petersburg. The sources used in compiling the figures and maps/plans are detailed below.

SOURCES FOR FIGURES

1. *Entsiklopedicheskiy Slovar'* (1900), vol. LVI, p. 312; A. I. Kopanev, *Naseleniye Peterburga v Pervoy Polovine XIX Veka* (Moscow, 1947), *passim*.
2. F. A. Tarapygin, *Materialy Dlya Istorii Imperatorskago S. Peterburgskago Vospitatel'nago Doma* (1878), appendix.
3. Author's calculations.
4. Author's calculations.
5. 'Znacheniye Peterburga vo Vneshney Torgovle Rossii', *ISPGD*, no. 23 (1899), appendix.
6. H. Hafferberg, *St Petersburg in Seiner Vergangenheit und Gegenwart* (1866), pp. 98–9; *Sanktpeterburg, Izsledovaniya po Istorii, Topografii i Statistike Stolitsy* (1868), vol. III, p. 8; *Sanktpeterburg po Perepisi 10 Dekabrya 1869* (1872), part 1, p. 1; *Entsiklopedicheskiy Slovar'*, p. 313 for Yu. Yanson's data; Reginald E. Zelnik, *Labor and Society in Tsarist Russia: the Factory Workers of St Petersburg, 1855–70* (Stanford, 1971), p. 221.
7. *Entsiklopedicheskiy Slovar'*, p. 313.
8. *Sanktpeterburg po Perepisi 10 Dekabrya 1869*, pp. 4–11.
9. Tarapygin, *Materialy*, appendix.
10. For 1852: P. Kryukov, *Ocherk Manufakturno-Promyshlennykh Sil Yevropeyskoy Rossii* (1853), pp. 174–86; *Materialy ob Ekonomicheskom Polozhenii i Professional'noy Organizatsii, Peterburgskikh Rabochikh po Metallu* (1909), pp. 3–8; 'O Tabachnykh Fabrikakh v S. Peterburge', *Zhurnal Ministerstva Vnutrennikh Del*, no. 11 (1852), p. 266; *Gorodskoy Ukazatel' ili Adresnaya Kniga na 1850* (1849), pp. 487–8.

For 1867: *Fabriki i Zavody v S. Peterburgskoy Gubernii v 1867 Godu* (1868), no. 6; *Vidy Vnutrenney Torgovli i Promyshlennosti v*

[23] V. V. Pokshishevskiy, 'Nekotoryye Voprosy Ekonomiko-Geograficheskogo Polozheniya Leningrada', *Voprosy Geografii*, no. 38 (1956), pp. 104–30.

S. Peterburge v 1868 g. (1868), *passim; Yezhegodnik Ministerstva Finansov* (1869), vol. I, *passim.*
For 1890: P. A. Orlov, S. G. Budagov, *Ukazatel' Fabrik i Zavodov Yevropeyskoy Rossii. Materialy Dlya Fabrichno-Zavodskoy Statistiki Sostavili po Ofitsial'nym Svedeniyam Departamenta Torgovli i Manufaktur,* (1894), *passim;* K. V. Davydov, *S. Peterburgskiy Fabrichnyy Okrug. Otchet za 1885g.* (1886); V. Pokrovskiy, 'Statisticheskiy Ocherk S. Peterburga', *Ves' Peterburg na 1895 God. Adresnaya i Spravochnaya Kniga g. S. Peterburga* (1895), p. 62.
For 1913: D. P. Kandaurov, *Fabrichno-Zavodskiya Predpriyatiya Rossiyskoy Imperii* (Isklyuchaya Finlyandiyu) (1914), *passim; Ves' Peterburg na 1912g. (1914)* (1912, 1914), *passim;* V. E. Varzar, *Spisok Fabrik i Zavodov Rossiyskoy Imperii* (1912), *passim.*

11. See sources for figure 10.
12. Author's calculations.
13. Author's calculations.
14. 'Znacheniye Peterburga vo Vneshney Torgovle Rossii', appendix; *Obzor Vneshney Torgovli Rossii po Yevropeyskoy i Aziatskoy Granitsam za 1898 God.* (1899), *passim;* and similarly for each year from 1889 to 1914.
15 *Entsiklopedicheskiy Slovar'*, p. 313; E. E. Kruze, D. G. Kutsentov, 'Naseleniye Peterburga', *Och.IL* (1956), vol. III, p. 105.
16. See sources for figure 15.
17. *Petrograd po Perepisi 15 Dekabrya 1910 Goda* (1914), part 1, pp. 6–9.
18. Author's calculations.
19. After J. G. Kohl, *Der Verkehr und die Ansiedelung der Menschen in ihrer Abhängigkeit von der Gestaltung der Erdoberfläche* (Leipzig, 1841), pp. 181–5 and diagrams 39 and 40.
20. Derived from figure 19.
21. Author's calculations.

SOURCES FOR MAPS AND PLANS

1. After *The Century Atlas of the World* (New York, 1898), map 73.
2. Based on 'Plan Peterburga 1716 Goda', *Peterburg-Leningrad. Istoriko-Geograficheskiy Atlas* (1957), p. 13.
3. Based on I. A. Egorov, *The Architectural Planning of St Petersburg* (Atlas, Ohio, 1969), map 4, p. 12.

4. Based on Friedrich Christian Weber, *The Present State of Russia* (London, 1723), vol. I, map facing p. 295.
5. Based on map in *Atlas Leningradskoy Oblasti* (1967), p. 26.
6. Based on, 'Plan Peterburga 1737 Goda', *Peterburg-Leningrad*, p. 19.
7. Based on *Plan Stolichnago Goroda Sanktpeterburga s Izobrazheniyem Znatneyshikh Onago Prospektov* (1753), plate 5.
8. A. Bashutskiy, *Panorama Sanktpeterburga* (1834), appendix.
9. See source for map 8.
10. Based on 'Plan Peterburga 1852 Goda', *Peterburg-Leningrad*, p. 43.
11. Based on source for map 10 and 'O Naznachenii Mest Dlya Fabrik i Zavodov v S. Peterburge', *Zhurnal Ministerstva Vnutrennikh Del*, no. 10 (1833), pp. i-xiv.
12. See source for map 8.
13. See sources for figure 10, 1867 and *Vseobshchaya Adresnaya Kniga S. Peterburga* (1867-8), *passim*.
14. See sources for figure 10, 1867 and *Vseobshchaya Adresnaya Kniga*, *passim*.
15. Based on M. I. Musnitskiy, *Plan S. Peterburga 1867-68*, 1:12,600.
16. *Vseobshchaya Adresnaya Kniga, passim*.
17. *Sanktpeterburg po Perepisi 10 Dekabrya 1869* (1872), part 1, p. 1 and part 2, section 2, pp. 118-20.
18. *Vseobshchaya Adresnaya Kniga, passim*.
19. *Vseobshchaya Adresnaya Kniga, passim*.
20. *Vseobshchaya Adresnaya Kniga, passim*.
21. *Vseobshchaya Adresnaya Kniga, passim*.
22. *Vseobshchaya Adresnaya Kniga, passim*.
23. *Vseobshchaya Adresnaya Kniga, passim*.
24. *Sanktpeterburg po Perepisi 10 Dekabrya 1869*, part 1, p. 118.
25. Based on Musnitskiy, *Plan S. Peterburga*.
26. *Sanktpeterburg po Perepisi 10 Dekabrya 1869*, part 2, section 1, pp. 3-5.
27. *Sanktpeterburg, Izsledovaniya po Istorii, Topografii i Statistike Stolitsy* (1868), vol. III, p. 8; *Sanktpeterburg po Perepisi 10 Dekabrya 1869*, part 1, p. 1.
28. *Sanktpeterburg po Perepisi 10 Dekabrya 1869*, part 1, p. 8.
29. *Sanktpeterburg po Perepisi 10 Dekabrya 1869*, part 1, p. 1.
30. *Entsiklopedicheskiy Slovar'*, p. 315.
31. *Sanktpeterburg po Perepisi 10 Dekabrya 1869*, part 2, section 2, p. 120, (1875), part 1, p. 5.

32. See sources for figure 10, 1913.
33. See sources for figure 10, 1913.
34. See sources for figure 10, 1913.
35. See sources for figure 10, 1913.
36. See sources for figure 10, 1913.
37. 'Ob Obshchey Pereotsenke Nedvizhimykh Imushchestv v S. Peterburge', *ISPGD*, no. 21 (1893), p. 85; 'Vedomost' Raskladki Zemskago Sbora na 1910 God. Na Nedvizhimyya Imushchestva G. S. Peterburga', *ISPGD*, no. 18 (1910), pp. 1223–4; 'Vedomost' Raskladki Zemskago Sbora na 1913g. Na Nedvizhimyya Imush-chestva G. S. Peterburga,' *ISPGD*, no. 29 (1913), p. 2063.
38. *S. Peterburg po Perepisi 15 Dekabrya 1890 Goda* (1892), part 2, p. 74.
39. *S. Peterburg po Perepisi 15 Dekabrya 1881 Goda* (1884), vol. II, part 1, section 3, pp. 144–5; *S. Peterburg po Perepisi 15 Dekabrya 1900 Goda* (1905), part 3, pp. 344–61.
40. Based on map 13 and sources for figure 10, 1890.
41. Based on map 33 and sources for figure 10, 1890.
42. *Ves' Peterburg na 1912 g.* (1912), *passim.*
43. *Ves' Peterburg na 1912, passim.*
44. *Vseobshchaya Adresnaya Kniga, passim; Ves' Peterburg na 1912, passim.*
45. P. Semenov (ed.), *Geografichesko—Statisticheskiy Slovar' Rossiyskoy Imperii* (1868), vol. IV, p. 447; 'Graficheskoye Izobrazheniye Kolichestva Perevezennykh Passazhirov v God po Sushches-tvuyushchim Liniyam Konno-Zheleznykh Dorog v 1899g.', *ISPGD*, no. 11 (1901), end flap.
46. Based on *Plan S. Peterburga s Blizhayshimi Okrestnostyami* (1914), 1:19,500.
47. *Ves' Peterburg na 1912, passim.*
48. *Ves' Peterburg na 1912, passim.*
49. *Ves' Peterburg na 1912, passim.*
50. *Ves' Peterburg na 1912, passim.*
51. *Ves' Peterburg na 1912, passim.*
52. *Ves' Peterburg na 1912, passim.*
53. Based on Yu. Gash, *Karta Okrestnostey S. Peterburga 1914* (1914), 1:17,000.
54. Based on Gash, *Karta Okrestnostey S. Peterburga.*
55. *Petrograd po Perepisi 15 Dekabrya 1910 Goda* (1914), part 1, p. 290.
56. *Petrograd po Perepisi,* p. 4.

57. *Petrograd po Perepisi,* pp. 2–3.
58. *Petrograd po Perepisi,* p. 40.
59. *Based on Plan S. Peterburga s Blizhayshimi Okrestnostyami.*
60. 'Graficheskoye Izobrazheniye Kolichestva Perevezennykh Passazhirov v God po Sushchestvuyushchim Liniyam Konno-Zheleznykh Dorog'.
61. See sources for maps 25 and 59.
62. A. N. Pavlovskiy, *Materialy k Statistike i Etiologii Zabolevayemosti i o Smertnosti ot Aziatskoy Kholery v S. Peterburge v 1882–1896gg.* (1897), table 44.
63. Pavlovskiy, *Materialy k Statistike i Etiologii Zabolevayemosti i o Smertnosti,* table 44.
64. Pavlovskiy, *Materialy k Statistike i Etiologii Zabolevayemosti i o Smertnosti,* table 44.
65. Pavlovskiy, *Materialy k Statistike i Etiologii Zabolevayemosti i o Smertnosti,* table 44.
66. Pavlovskiy, *Materialy k Statistike i Etiologii Zabolevayemosti i o Smertnosti,* table 42.
67. Author's calculations.
68. *Sanktpeterburg po Perepisi 10 Dekabrya 1869 Goda* (1872), part 1.
69. *Pervaya Perepis' Predmetov Gorodskago Oblozheniya i Drugiya Khozhaystvenno—Statisticheskiya Izsledovaniya, Proizvedennyya Odnovremenno s Perepis'yu 30 go Oktyabrya—8 go Noyabrya* (1907), end flap; 'Granitsy Politseyskikh Uchastkov Gor. SPg.', *ISPGD,* no. 12 (1906), pp. 324–30.
70. Based on *Plan S. Peterburga s Blizhayami Okrestnostyami.*
71. Based on *Plan S. Peterburga s Blizhayami Okrestnostyami.*
72. Based on *Plan S. Peterburga s Blizhayami Okrestnostyami.*

Glossary

Adresnaya Kontora, Adresnoye Otdeleniye: address office where passports and permits were registered

Arshin: unit of measurement equal to 0·71 metres, or 2·3 feet

Artel': rural-based workmen's association

Bezplatnaya Kvartira: rent-free apartment

Birzha: commercial exchange

Chin: one of fourteen ranks in the public service introduced by Peter I in which civil and military positions were equated. For example, the rank of chancellor in the civil service was equal to field marshal in the military, collegiate assessor was equivalent to major and so on

Chinovnik: government functionary

Dacha: summer cottage, sometimes of a substantial nature

Droshky: one-horse, two-passenger uncovered carriage readily available for hire in cities and towns

Dvornik: yard-keeper; as much a part of the urban scene as the buildings themselves

Fabrika: factory; ostensibly one dependent upon non-local raw materials

Gradonachal'nik: city governor

Gostinyy Dvor: bazaar-like, permanent complex of retail and wholesale outlets

Gosudarstvennaya Duma: state consultative assembly introduced shortly after the 1905 revolution

Guberniya: province

Izba: small peasant cottage

Izvoshchiki (Lomovykh): waggoners

Kareta: four-person, two-horse carriage

Kopek: unit of currency equal to one hundreth of a rouble

Kucher: coachman

Kustar': rural handicraftsman

Lavka: small retail shop or stall

Likhach: one-horse, two-passenger cab of superior quality to the *droshky*

Magazin: retail outlet

Masterskaya: handicraft workshop

Meshchane, Meshchanstvo: category or urban dweller of lower middle-class standing used in the official census. Members had some commercial privileges but could not belong to the merchants' guilds

Muzhik: sometimes derogatory name for a peasant or countryman

Nochlezhnyy Dom: doss or flop-house

Obrok: payment in money or kind by serfs to their owners in lieu of their labour obligations

Odinochka: handicraftsman

Otkhodniki: furloughed peasants

Pereulok: lane or alley

Ploshchad': public square

Pud: unit of weight of about 16·3 kilos or 36 pounds

Rabochiy: workman

Raznochintsy: amorphous census category of petty bureaucrats, teachers, and the like, of lower-income status, which in the late nineteenth century had some connotation of an intellectual class

Raznoshchik: street pedlar

Remeslennoye Zavedeniye: handicraft establishment

Rota: company of soldiers

Rouble: unit of currency comprising 100 kopeks

Sazhen: unit of measurement equal to 2·13 metres

Sloboda: city suburb

Sosloviye: class of society

Telega: type of goods waggon

Torgovoye Zavedeniye : retail establishment

Troyka : smart, four-person or larger, three-horse carriage

Tsekh : artisan corporation instituted by Peter I and modelled after European trade guilds

Ugol : literally a corner; as the housing crisis deepened, renting parts of rooms became something of a national speciality

Ukaz : imperial decree

Uprava : executive board of the City Council (*Gorodskaya Duma*)

Uyezd : administrative district below the level of *guberniya*

Versta : unit of distance, roughly equivalent to one kilometre or 0·6 miles

Zavod : factory; ostensibly one using local raw materials

Zemstvo : elected district council

Index

456

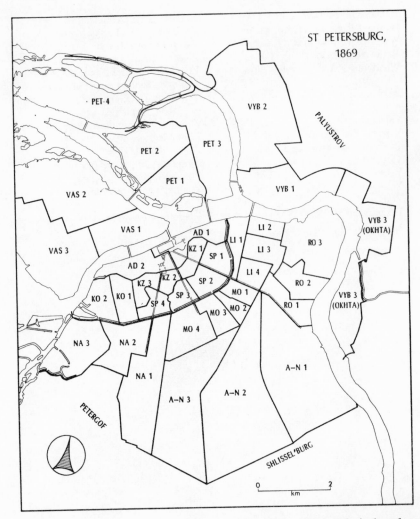

MAP 68. *St. Petersburgh, 1869.* *Boroughs:* AD: Admiralteyskaya;
KY: Kazanskaya SP: Spasskaya; KO: Kolomenskaya;
NA: Narvskaya; MO: Moskovskaya; A-N: Aleksandro-
Nevskaya; RO: Rozhdestvenskaya; LI: Liteynaya; VAS: Vasil'-
yevskaya; PET: Peterburgskaya; VYB: Vyborgskaya;
N-D: Novo-Derevnya; Okhta. Numerals refer to Wards within
the Boroughs.

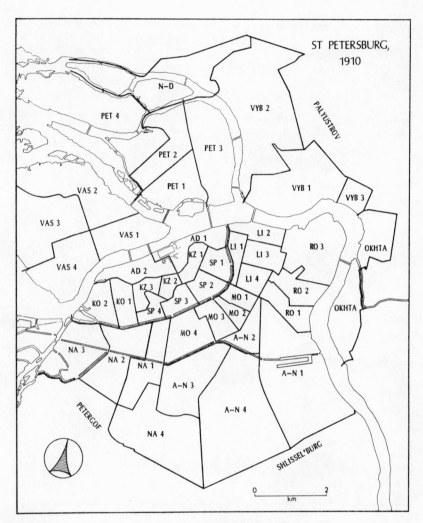

N–D

PET 4

VYB 2

PALYUSTROV

PET 2

PET 3

VAS 2

PET 1

VYB 1

VYB 3

VAS 3

VAS 1

AD 1

LI 2

RO 3

OKHTA

VAS 4

AD 2

KZ 1

LI 1

SP 1

LI 3

KZ 2

KZ 3

SP 2

LI 4

RO 2

KO 2

KO 1

SP 3

MO 1

RO 1

OKHTA

SP 4

MO 3

MO 2

NA 3

MO 4

A–N 2

NA 2

NA 1

A–N 1

PETERGOF

A–N 3

NA 4

A–N 4

SHLISSEL'BURG

0   2
km

MAP 69.   *St. Petersburg, 1910.* See map for key.

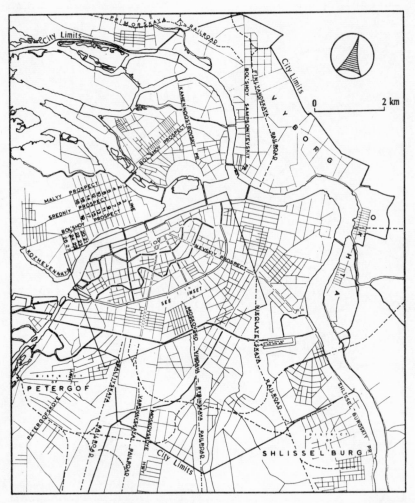

MAP 70. *St. Petersburg, 1914.*